To Edwin
Christmas 1943

The Wake of the Prairie Schooner

THE MACMILLAN COMPANY
NEW YORK · BOSTON · CHICAGO
DALLAS · ATLANTA · SAN FRANCISCO

MACMILLAN AND CO., LIMITED
LONDON · BOMBAY · CALCUTTA
MADRAS · MELBOURNE

THE MACMILLAN COMPANY
OF CANADA, LIMITED
TORONTO

The Wake of the Prairie Schooner

BY

IRENE D. PADEN

WITH PEN AND INK DRAWINGS
BY THE AUTHOR

NEW YORK

THE MACMILLAN COMPANY

1943

PRINTED IN THE UNITED STATES OF AMERICA
AMERICAN BOOK—STRATFORD PRESS, INC., NEW YORK

To My Husband

whose life's avocation and contribution to the sum of human knowledge has been the retracing and mapping of historic trails, I dedicate this unexpected result of the nine years of field work now ending

Acknowledgments

I COULD NOT, with any sense of completeness, publish this volume without a few words to express the pleasant burden of gratitude I bear to our friends and to those various chance acquaintances along the trail who so materially aided our efforts. Among the many I express specific thanks to the staffs of the Bancroft Library and of the California State Library for years of helpful cooperation; to Mrs. Alex. C. McMillan for many hours spent in constructive criticism; to Mrs. Jane C. Lanktree for a haven in which to work; to Mr. George E. Russell for his generous help in cartography; to Dr. Herbert E. Bolton for advice and guidance in my research activities; and, above and beyond all, to my father, Wilbur J. Dakin, without whose encouragement and tireless assistance over a period of years, it could never have been completed.

Preface

OTHER BOOKS HAVE BEEN WRITTEN about the overland trails from the Mississippi Valley to Oregon and California. But this one is different. As no other book on the subject has done, it makes the past come alive. Persons who read it will be eager to be on their way to see what the Padens have seen and to do some of the things which the Padens have done.

Of all the great pioneer routes of travel in North America, none surpassed in importance those leading from the Missouri River to Oregon and California: by the former went trappers, missionaries, and settlers from the east to the great northwestern wilderness and transformed it into an American commonwealth; over the latter beaver hunters, gold seekers, adventurers, and settlers found their way to California in the days before the transcontinental railroad.

These pioneers came on foot, on horseback, pushing handcarts, or in conveyances drawn by oxen, horses, and mules, in various combinations. The earliest woman overland migrant to Oregon came as a bride in a gig, fashioned by the groom from two wheels of a wagon, the major portion of which had to be left behind on the trail.

"The Wake of the Prairie Schooner" is not only interesting but thoroughly sound. Every page bubbles with human emotion evoked by the author's sympathetic interpretation of old documents and her examination of surviving vestiges left by wayfarers along the trail. The Padens—for it has been a family enterprise—have spent years of eager research in preparation for their work, unearthing scores of overland diaries hitherto in hiding. They have supplemented this indoor study by many exciting summers of exploration in order to relive the experiences of the pioneer wayfarers on these historic travel routes. They are veterans in outdoor life and have a pioneer's instinct for "sign," as I know from having been with them on other trails.

Retracing the overland routes segment by segment, the Padens have reconstructed them with an accuracy never previously achieved. There were not only main trails but also many cutoffs. All these have been identified, retraced, and put on the excellent maps with which the book is equipped. Through their thorough research and their minute reconnoissances, they have made many corrections and additions to all former maps of these overland routes.

Mrs. Paden has given these old trails the breath of life recalled. The reader is witness of an Indian massacre, a buffalo stampede, a flood, a breakdown, or a sandstorm. There are births, courtships, weddings, deaths, burials, a sermon, a Mass. One hears the songs the pioneers sang to keep up their courage. The vicarious traveler watches for the accustomed springs, camp sites, and river fords; the quicksands, canyons, sloughs, hostile Indians, and other hazards to be avoided by the emigrant or encountered by him to his sorrow.

The trails are still strewn with relics of the great trek—scars on the land, carvings on the rocks, abandoned ox yokes, wagon tires, cookstoves, sometimes discarded to lighten the load for the faltering beasts—sometimes lying beside the skeletons of the unfortunates who failed to "get through."

The book is sincere and meticulously authentic. The reader will be as much interested in the experiences of the Padens on the trail as in those of the "Oregonians" or the Forty-niners.

Not least in merit are the excellent and appropriate pen-and-ink sketches made by the author herself.

HERBERT E. BOLTON

Contents

Introduction

CONTRARY TO WHAT I should imagine to be the custom of authors, these introductory words of explanation are being written last, in a state of perplexed astonishment that there should be any need to write them at all. It is true that my family and I have traveled many thousand miles on the old prairie schooner trails, but it was certainly far from my mind that it would fall to me to prepare our field data for printing.

There are four of us: my husband; our son Bill who was plunged unenthusiastically into the project at the age of ten and, at nineteen, still goes along from habit; Dr. Clarence W. Neff, an orthodontist from San Diego, California, and myself.

Every summer for nine years we consumed weeks driving, riding, and walking along the fast-disappearing ruts of the Oregon-California Trail until members of the faculties of our neighboring universities commenced to list us among the unpopular people who collect and hoard book material and never use it. It slipped lightly from my husband's conscience. He was interested solely in the geography of the trail—in fact had almost completed a detailed set of Oregon-California Trail maps—and had no time to write. As a result I commenced to arrange the field notes and, at last, started the first chapter—a step that resulted in five years of steady six-hours-a-day work, most of it research.

That phase of the American picture which gave birth to the overland trails, caused them to be in more or less constant use for half a century, and then let them sink into oblivion can be summarized in a few pages.

It was the most natural thing in the world for Americans of the early nineteenth century to keep moving. The very thought of unclaimed homesteads to the west was a constant challenge. Using the rivers as highways in their restless search for new and uncleared farm lands, they gradually won their way through the matted wilderness of trees lying east of the Missouri River and, by the 1820's, had established a frontier on its bank.

Here the familiar forests came to an abrupt end and undulating prairies stretched, boundless as the sea, toward the west. Strangely enough, these questing farmers did not think of the open land as cornfields already cleared for the planting, but, because it bore no trees, called it the Great American Desert and left it to the Indians.

Meanwhile, beginning in the second decade of the century, a hardy breed, called "mountain men," ranged through the unmapped regions between the Missouri and the Pacific Coast in search of the highly prized beaver pelts. They began by following the Missouri to its sources but soon filtered here and there along the watercourses of the lonely West, concentrating finally upon the waters of the Great Platte which they followed to the Rocky Mountains, and braving hunger, thirst, and the uncertain red man in their relentless pursuit of marketable furs. When in the territory of a friendly tribe they used the Indian trails or, being lost between rivers, followed buffalo paths to water. Both provided the best and shortest possible route between any two given points but, as the buffalo trails tended to pursue a north-and-south course and usually ran straight out from the river toward the open prairie where the great beasts fed, they were used but seldom in comparison with the Indians' trails, which often paralleled the watercourses.

The topography of the Great American Desert made for a new type of travel. East of the Missouri River the tree-bristled earth had been resentful of roads, but the waterways were deep and dependable. West of it the rivers were unnavigable and could be used only as life lines and guides, but the bare solid prairies lay open to the horseman. Even so the "mountain man," or trapper, traveled light and produced no trails discernible from those left through the centuries by the Indian; but, by reason of the trapper and his needs, a transcontinental roadway was born.

Once a year, in midsummer when the accommodating beaver was shedding and therefore valueless, the trappers gradually circled in from all points of the compass toward a rendezvous determined during the previous year, usually near the Rocky Mountains in what is now Wyoming. Ponies and patient Indian wives were burdened with bales of dressed beaver pelts taken through the season and destined for the great fur-trading center at the frontier city of St. Louis. On the trails and at the rendezvous they met tribes of friendly Indians likewise bringing furs taken during a year's hunting. Several hundred souls might gather at the appointed spot to meet the supply caravan sent out by the fur company, and to gamble, drink, and revel away the proceeds of a whole season's labor. It was the trail pounded out by the supply trains (growing deeper and more unmistakable as each succeeding caravan traveled along the faint trace left by its predecessor) that eventually became the first half of the overland route to the west.

At first the traders' trains were composed simply of pack mules; but in 1822 wagons were taken over the trail to Santa Fe, then in old Mexico. The first wheel marks on the road to the rendezvous were probably made ten years later, in 1832, and are credited to the exploring and trapping expedition of Captain Bonneville, that debonair soldier of fortune on leave from the United States Army. Common sense and the experiences of the Santa Fe traders told him that wagons would require fewer animals, would make a good fort in an emergency, and would eliminate the daily packing and unpacking. The physical practicability of getting them over prairies, rivers, and mountains he chanced. The Rocky Mountain traders were quick to see the advantages presented by wagon trains and, by the thirties, a recognizable road had been beaten as far as the Green River in Wyoming.

The rich coast of Oregon was peopled much earlier. Following the return, in 1806, of the government-sponsored expedition of Lewis and Clark, a fur-trading post was founded at the mouth of the Columbia where the expedition had wintered. The post was established in 1811 by the men of the farseeing John Jacob Astor, some of whom went by sea and some overland at the cost of excessive hardships. In the summer of 1812 it became necessary to send a party back to the States with dispatches for Mr. Astor and, in seeking a better route, they left the first footprints known to have been made by white men along the length of what was later the Oregon Trail. Only while crossing Bear River Divide and the Rockies was their road essentially different from that used by the emigrants of later years. The War of 1812 threw Astoria into English hands; but upon cessation of hostilities it was restored by treaty, and the United States agent was taken to the fort by a British ship which politely saluted the newly unfurled American flag before retiring.

England then concentrated her attention at the confluence of the Willamette River with the Columbia, some hundred miles inland. Fort Vancouver was established thereabouts, and the Hudson's Bay Company (old and exceedingly wise in the ways of the red man) soon had a prosperous headquarters for its other outflung posts and a firm grip on the Indian trade. The paths of her trappers, extending east, gradually connected with those of the Rocky Mountain and Green River trappers. It was now possible to travel from the Missouri River to the rendezvous with the fur traders' caravan, to hire an Indian or mountain man as a guide, and to proceed northwest to any of the several Hudson's Bay Company's forts. It was by this method, in the 1830's, that the Protestant missionaries reached the Oregon country.

Word came back to the States of the forested coastal valleys of the Pacific—such country as the American farmer knew and loved. Word came also of the need for American settlers due to the rivalry, dignified but vital, between two sovereign nations for the land drained by the lower Columbia. The rights of Spain and Russia were eliminated by purchase and treaty. Only England and the United States remained as claimants, and England was in possession.

For two decades the factors of Hudson's Bay Company held benevolent sway. According to their custom they did not bring out families from the homeland nor attempt to strike down roots into the new country. They never thrust English standards or ways of life upon the Indians but, taking wives from among the natives, made for themselves a few tight little centers of English habits, customs, and even culture at the various fort headquarters and let the Indian lead his own life unmolested.

All this was eminently satisfactory to the red man, who had no wish to be disturbed from his fish-eating summers and starvation winters. He could trade his furs for knives, implements, clothing, and gewgaws (the Company did not permit him to have liquor) and be the happier for the presence of men who produced such treasures, even though these same men were exploiting one country to enrich another.

Meanwhile, responding patriotically to the need for American settlers and heeding their own inbred urge toward pioneering, many venturesome souls broke away from the Missouri frontier and started across the treeless prairies to the lush valleys of Oregon, two thousand miles away. In the main the overland trail kept along the Platte River, and after crossing the Rockies picked up the course of the Snake. Its travelers used wagons adapted from those proved practical by the traders. They encountered everything from cholera and hostile Indians to storms, starvation, and stampedes. Some died, but more survived to reach the Pacific. A few, but not many, turned aside from the beaten Oregon Trail, lured by the romance of Mexican California. The steady, ever increasing trek to the west coast of America—the greatest migration in the known history of the world—had begun.

The incoming American settlers were of a different caliber from the officers of the Hudson's Bay Company. It could not be said that they were more honorable, more likable, or even more energetic, but they were actuated by different motives. They brought their own women. They took up land and built homes in which they fully intended to grow old and eventually die. They raised white families in the American tradition. They were a suitable nucleus for a new state.

The year 1843 brought the "Great Migration" of some thousand souls to the Oregon country. A small but decisive majority of American over English settlers established an efficient government within a twelvemonth.

For another six years Time strode on, kicking into the light of history events of such importance that they were not—could not be—appreciated at the moment. The dislike of the Indians for the Americans who took their lands and scorned their women flamed into the Cayuse uprising. Marcus and Narcissa Whitman, Protestant missionaries, with eleven others then at the mission, were killed. A message sent to Washington for help resulted in territorial status for Oregon. The United States now stretched from ocean to ocean.

Meanwhile the reports of Frémont's exploring expeditions roused much enthusiasm for the flower-strewn, game-covered valleys of Mexican-owned California. Various parties left the Oregon-bound emigrant trains and, after some experimenting, selected the Humboldt River as the best life line available to sustain them through the sage deserts that must be traversed east of the Sierras. Bad water, hot sand, and implacable Indians made any route a deadly one. Trails through the deserts and over the mountains continually changed in the search for a more practical road, without marked success in any instance. And then Time, in his rough-shod progress, arraigned the governments of Mexico and of the United States one against the other. War was declared and won by the States, and the storybook land of California was a prize.

Still another westward movement marked those eventful six years between '43 and '49. The Mormon people, unable to live in amity with their neighbors along the frontier, began their trek to the valley of the Great Salt Lake. In a final gesture, partly of patriotism and partly of expediency, five hundred of their young men formed what was known as the Mormon Battalion and set off for the war in Mexico. They saw practically nothing in the way of combat and, after a march that has gone down in history, turned up in California at the close of the war and were disbanded. While they were tarrying another winter on the Pacific Coast in order that there might be fewer mouths to feed in the newly established Mormon colony at Salt Lake City, a group of them in company with James Marshall obtained work from Captain John Sutter and began to erect a mill in the foothills of the Sierras. It was here that Time, in his unheeding march, struck gold from the ancient river beds of the California mountains—and these men were there to see.

Down the Sacramento River to the port of San Francisco streamed the news of gold, and out from San Francisco to the world at large. The rush of adventurous humanity toward the lure of easy riches pounded roads through the scorched wastes of the Great Basin; and, although the vanguard suffered and died and left the deserts piled with the bones of their cattle and marked with the sinking sands of shallow graves, the survivors plodded on by the accepted routes and came at last to California.

And so we note that the American movement to the west, including the Mormon migration into Utah, tended to follow the Platte River—using both the north and the south bank. The emigrants then struck across the Rockies and overland until they reached the Snake River, which the Oregonians followed almost to the Columbia. The Californians broke away to follow the Humboldt River into the shadow of the Sierras. These main stems, with their tributary feeders, supplementary short cuts and split termini, carried the wagons, cattle, and personnel of the greatest of all human migrations. With the aid of maps—old and new—and material gathered from many journals written by emigrants while actually on the trail, I have tried to portray where and why and how the migration began, swelled to a mighty concourse, and finally dwindled away in favor of the stagecoach and the railroad—the story of the Great Overland Road to the Pacific.

The summer when we drove from our home in California to Independence, Missouri, in order to start at the eastern end of the overland trail and return "across the plains" on its indistinct ruts, was the culmination of years of study and planning on my husband's part. It was the achievement, as a man, of a boyhood ambition. While waiting for the day when we might spend the necessary time and money to do this thing, we had traced many miles of historic trails in the west—old Spanish trails, Frémont's routes, the Anza trail, the Bidwell trail and others; but, through it all, we looked forward to following the Oregon-California Trail as the great adventure.

We made nine long trips with uncounted short jaunts in between. They did not deal consecutively with continuous stretches of trail. They were made in several cars of different size and horsepower, and in all kinds of weather. They included a son who grew from a small boy to a junior in college. Meanwhile I browsed in the available historical libraries and compiled notes from journals kept by emigrants while traveling the trail and other contemporary writings. So many, in fact, that I could substantiate every statement by quoting anywhere from one to a hundred authorities —many of them eyewitnesses. From these notes and from the field data of our careful trail tracings I have assembled this unusual travelogue, only altering the exact sequence of our trips to form a consecutive journey from east to west on the greatest emigrant trail of all history.

The Wake of the Prairie Schooner

As It Was in the Beginning

WE PASSED A ROAD SIGN.

" 'Independence—Five miles,' " the four of us pronounced in unison. I giggled as a dependable expedient in moments of stress, and then shivered from pure excitement.

Five miles!—no, four now—and we should be at the long dreamed-of spot which we had come two thousand miles to find, the beginning of the Oregon Trail.

"What will it be like?" asked Bill absently, then added with sudden glowing interest: "Will it be big enough to have a real good garage? The car needs a grease job."

"How should I know what it's like?" retorted his father. "I've never been there; but I'm told that it's a good-sized city. You can get two grease jobs if you want them."

We rode on.

"Looks just like any other place to me," said Bill presently as we turned into the service station. "You can leave me with the car to remind them to grease the fittings underneath. Are you going, Doc?" he finished a little anxiously, for Dr. Neff (actually a bachelor cousin but for all practical purposes a pal) is a big circumstance in his life.

"No, I guess not. Let your mother and dad get through with the Chamber of Commerce and Public Library end of it first. They can pick us up when there's something to see."

So it was settled to every one's perfect satisfaction, and my husband and I walked out into the hustle and bustle of Independence, Missouri.

It seemed a normal and prosperous little city, spread out on all sides, hot and extremely busy under the summer sky. Not one person looked historic. Expectation of a romantic setting for the start of our adventure was like a toy balloon with the string loose—more drooping with each passing moment; and yet, from these few acres of ground sprang the beginnings of two great roads, the Santa Fe and the California-Oregon trails. And either of these two would have been sufficient to alter and give new trends to the whole course of American history.

The first, of course, was the Santa Fe. It had been a known route for years; but with the breaking of Spanish power in Mexico the frontier was thrown open to American trade and the "old Taos Trail" immediately became of commercial importance. For a short period it reechoed to the pounding hoofs of pack animals routed by way of Raton Pass. William Becknell's train was the first to pioneer the road leaving Missouri on September 1, 1821. In the spring of 1822, he set out again, this time taking two or three wagons and going by way of the dangerous Cimarron Desert to avoid the pass; and to him belongs the honor of leaving the first wheel ruts on the famous old trade route. From then on, huge and creaking freight wagons drawn by wiry Spanish mules made fortunes for their owners by hauling selected cargoes from the Missouri steamboats across eight hundred miles of hostile Indian country to Taos and Santa Fe, returning loaded down with buffalo hides and silver. Later the California-Oregon Trail branched off from this known thoroughfare and carried the horde of emigrants and gold seekers that colonized the West.

Choice of a river port where the cargo might be transferred from boat to wagon was limited by the geography of the country and of the river itself. The mighty Missouri, sweeping swiftly down from the north, turns abruptly where Kansas City now stands and makes a giant swing to the east. The point of contact must be near that bend. Every mile either up or down the river was a mile wasted to wagons traveling from old Mexico, far to the southwest.

Independence was not ideal, but it was on the spot—or nearly so. Actually it was about five miles from the river and slightly east of the bend, having been first explored by Daniel, son of Daniel Boone, and first settled by a man named Weston. It was hand-picked in 1827 for the seat of government of Jackson County and built up around a fine spring to take care of the water supply. On the river was a landing to serve its needs. In fact there were several through the years, for the temperamental Missouri had a disconcerting habit of removing anything that interfered with its changing ideas of direction.

The town soon adapted itself to the necessities of the Santa Fe trade. There were provisions for handling the heavy freight, a bank for the moneys involved, wheelwright and blacksmith shops to turn out the wagons, and all the ingredients of a thoroughgoing spree for the bull-whackers. This included the milky "undistilled whisky" peculiar to Missouri and a fearsome combination of the same with molasses, known as skull varnish. There were also mule markets of such capacity as to be famed throughout the nation. For the Santa Fe trade it was sufficient that a mule be wiry and tough and provided with the requisite number of legs. It was not to be imagined that any one should break him to drive. The immense wagons themselves were heartbreaking guarantees that he would not run far after being harnessed. Leaping, kicking, plunging, falling, braying its wrongs to the wincing heavens, often with a broken leg or neck, after a while, the team went on, pulling those of its number who, from death or accident or just plain mulishness, did not at the moment wish to run.

This Wild West show took place, as a matter of course, anywhere in town that happened to be handiest. Most of the excitement occurred around the old square, centered first with a sturdy log courthouse, later with a quaint spired edifice and rimmed with a wide, deep-rutted road that was bottomless mire in the spring months. "Such were the crowded condition of the streets of Independence by long traines of Ox teams mule teams," wrote Captain Pritchard, "men there with stock for sale and men there to purchase stock that it was all most impossible to pass a long." Freighters blocked the street until loaded, and then lurched and creaked and jangled their way out of the settlement toward the west; settling down to the eight-hundred-mile grind into Taos and Santa Fe, the northerly outposts of old Mexico. Every single mile of the trek carried its own particular discomfort or danger, but these nonchalant sons of the West loved the trail for its own sake, and tasted danger as the spice that made the wine of life worth quaffing.

When, in the thirties, the westward urge lured the first intrepid souls to brave the longer and practically unknown route to Oregon, what could be more natural than to come straight to Independence, the spot where outfitting a wagon train was an old story? What more natural than to take the Santa Fe road and stay with it as long as possible, postponing the inevitable time when the Kansas River must be crossed and the journey undertaken alone into uncharted distances?

As the spring of each successive year arrived, Independence teemed with the life and color of the fur-trading expeditions and the small western migrations, until at last the news of gold in California flung itself around the globe, and the spring of '49 found the city submerged under tossing wagon tops and tents.

From then on through the early fifties, Independence was not a place for the timid soul. Day and night, during the spring and summer—night and day of incessant noise and of a swarming confusion, bewildering, yet purposeful. At the mule market, the milling of hoofs, the squeals and the cursing in your ears, the mule hair and the smell of ammonia constantly in your nostrils. At the river landing, the thud of baled merchandise, snort of whistle-blast and smell of sweat and tar. In the town, the clang of hammer on metal, stentorian shouts of "Whoa, stand over," with the accompanying odor of burned hair and hoofs. In the streets, the plop and suck of the countless feet of animals in and out of countless mudholes, the creak of lumbering wagons and jangle of chain harness, as the giant wheels rolled into casual miry sinks and out again, to the obbligato of a continual volley of oaths. Gambling ran riot, and the acrid smell of powder vied all too often with the other characteristic odors of the town. The noise of gunshots was simply part of the general hubbub during the spring outfitting season.

In fact a close second to the excitement caused by the unbroken animals was the menace of deadly weapons in the hands of the hundreds of novices who were bound for California. The amount of death and mutilation caused by the sudden arming of men totally unaccustomed to guns was estimated by some to be more than the carnage of all the Indian attacks put together. A point, of course, entirely incapable of proof.

One young wife, Lucy Cooke, wrote to her sister: "Our men are all well armed. William carries a brace of pistols and a bowie knife. Ain't that blood-curdling? Hope he won't hurt himself." No regular he-man but carried a "shooting iron" on this dangerous enterprise, all unconcerned that he possibly increased the danger by so doing. The weapons ranged from the tiny derringer of the professional gambler and the "scatter gun" of the daily meat hunters, to the rifle of the trained frontiersman. The sharp crack of the latter, the whine and the twisting motion of the ball, were considered by the Indians as too close to the supernatural to be healthy.

With one or more of these death-dealing instruments dangling on his person, the regular, run-of-the-mill emigrant went sight-seeing in Independence.

A great many of the men, whose diaries have been preserved to tell the tale, finding themselves uncomfortable in this whirlpool of sweating and shouting humanity, allowed themselves to be eddied out instead of sucked in, and camped some miles from town, usually making pathetically frequent trips for the mail that so seldom came. Among the milling thousands were occasional newlyweds. Happy men with girl brides who had chosen a hasty wedding and hardship rather than a long separation. We have found mention of several marriages occurring in the river towns or at the camps before the great day came for departure. The charivari which followed was fully as barbaric as anything the Indians could contrive, and rivaled for excitement the howlings of a well conducted aborigine funeral. It usually ended by pulling the wagon of the happy couple over a few carefully prepared piles of oxyokes.

They had time to be married, to be born, or to die while they waited in camp for the grass to sprout upon the prairie. This was absolutely vital, for, until it was high enough to provide feed for the animals, only those horse and mule teams carrying grain dared to start the journey. Oxen, not having been provided by nature with the dental equipment necessary to cope with short grass, were forced to wait longer, and the trains depending on them often put in several anxious weeks. Settling the starting date was a delicate decision that caused many a quarrel and split many a party. For, weighed against present inconvenience, was future disaster. The grass of the western sage and desert country was very limited and late comers had a bad time of it which was incomparably worse than anything endured by those who jumped the gun at the eastern end.

Little as they liked the delay, it was sometimes a good thing. For, unless the emigrant was the provident type who had brought his own teams, he must get them from among the contumacious animals presented for his inspection at the markets of Independence; and, in nine cases out of ten, both he and the newly acquired livestock were in for trouble.

Half-broken or, in many instances, totally wild steers and mules were calmly sold to men who might never in their lives have driven anything more dangerous than a buggy mare. The hazards of necessary contact with these young furies who pawed and cut with murderous front feet;

bit hunks out of shoulders and faces; and kicked like the recoil of a cannon, were quite deadly. They didn't even like *each other*. John E. Brown wrote that, after he had found pairs that would not start a fight on sight, it was next to impossible to get four that would tolerate each other. In which case the leaders (having the advantage of position) kicked the wheelers clear out of the harness.

Steers were little better, but they usually ran when frightened; which trait, with good luck, could be utilized; with bad luck it resulted in splintered wagons and disabled men. Nor were the horses behindhand in contributing their bit. A Scottish sea captain with two sailor sons had difficulty with his ox team and a lead mare who was supposed to be hitched in front, but who had thrown herself around until the terrified oxen had reversed positions and she was hopelessly tangled in their chains. An amused bystander heard one of the sons shout to his father that the "larboard ox was on the starboard side—the starboard ox on the larboard side—the mare foul in the rigging and all going to hell together."

It is hard to visualize now, in the midst of a busy modern city, the old square and its surrounding melee of all too intermingled men and teams. We decided to take our points of interest one at a time, and forthwith went back to the garage to get our rejuvenated automobile and the rest of the family.

I must say that the grease job was far more visible on Bill than on the car, but they were both running smoothly and without undue friction so that I resisted the temptation to comment and we drove peacefully out into the bright, hot streets.

"Where are we going now?" he asked his father as we turned the first corner.

"Down to Main and Kansas streets first, I guess." My husband glanced at a rough sketch in his hand. "The original log courthouse has been moved there."

The buzz and clack denoting the office of some government project greeted us through the open windows as we crossed the porch, and we were met and shown through the rooms by a gentleman who either was there for the purpose, or else made it his business. For (you must understand) the town is proud of this sturdy, stubby log building which has seen one century through and bravely started another. The back portion is now unused, but the smoke-blackened, hewn-timbered ceiling sheltered in its day many youthful and protesting historians. It was the first school of the city.

Many of the Argonauts of '49 got their initial idea of Independence from the ugly little steamboat dock on the river called Wayne City or Independence Landing. Sunk deep below its own bluffs, and so crooked that it was said a flock of geese could not fly across it, the great Missouri apathetically allowed the river steamers to struggle up against its steady current, and dock at this point. Here they unloaded thousands of bales of freight, hundreds of braying, bellowing, and squealing animals, and myriads of passengers.

Steamboat on the Missouri River.

It is to be presumed that the majority of those booked for Independence Landing arrived safely at their destination; but some did not. It was nothing extraordinary for a river steamer in '49 and the early fifties to tie up by night to a lonely shore while anywhere from one to ten or twenty cholera victims were buried in one grave.

Some of the water craft drafted into use by the increasing pressure of travel were old and flimsy, and chugging along upstream, were all too easily sprung open by the great snags, or sawyers, in the river—trees whose heavy butts lay sunk in mud, and whose jagged tops swung down with the current. "Whole trees are drifting and rolling over in the stream," wrote an apprehensive European heading west for gold. "They dive away out of sight and then shoot up into the air, throwing out their arms like strange monsters. Many of the trees are caught along the shores and some sink to the bottom of the river. Steamboats are often snagged by them and cut in two or otherwise wrecked." River craft, especially if of value, were usually tied up at night—sawyers and the ever shifting sand bars were bad enough to encounter in daylight. In dry seasons, it was no uncommon thing to see all the passengers footing it along the bank while the steamer was jacked over a slightly submerged bar by means of ingeniously arranged poles and cables. Then, too, very few credentials were required of their engineers, and the neglected boilers were so thin that sometimes very little but a layer of rust stood between a full head of steam and the outside world.

Certainly they blew up—quite often. And why not? One woman remarked that the explosions occurred most often within sight of the landing places, and that she thought it was caused by the passengers crowding en masse to the side of the boat in order to see better.

On April 27, 1852, Lodisa Frizzell was on a river boat steaming upstream to St. Joseph. As she was passing the landings that served Independence she noted the wreck of the steamer *Saluda* which had exploded on April 9th, killing two hundred people. She wrote that men were still busily digging graves and hanging on a long line muddy clothing taken from the bodies. The dangers of the journey had commenced even before civilization was left behind.

To get to the site of old Independence Landing we went slantingly down the steep bluffs, and became horizontal again on a shelf of land that paralleled the river immediately above the water line. Railroad tracks, coerced by the windings of the current, lie like a dingy striped ribbon along the skimpy strip of usable ground, and the big buildings of a cement company sprawl over a large segment of the remainder.

Under a glaring sky the great road of the river winds like a giant highway—smooth, lead-gray, and refracting a deadly heat. In the center, rocky Rabbit Island splits the tolerant current with the calm disregard of a safety zone.

Cement bumpers along the bank long ago took the place of the old wooden ones, but even these are no longer visited by steamers. Disuse has fallen like a blight upon the place—not that it was ever rosy, even in its heyday. In the spring of 1850, E. A. Tompkins stepped hopefully from a river boat onto the bank, where we now sat, and took a look around. "We landed at Wayne City," he confided to his journal that night, "the most miserable of all wretched collections of log huts that were ever inhabited by pickpockets, grog venders and vagabonds of every shade, name and nature."

It is apparent that the old landing place, upon which Nature bestowed dignity and beauty, has never received much for which to be grateful from the efforts of man; yet, as we sat at the brimming edge of the river and looked through the leafy branches, the uncompromising outlines of railroad and cement highway were lost, and just the hazy thread of the old ox road swung west and up the hill before our eyes. The same historic pathway where, in years gone by, toiled a mass of humanity and livestock pulling tons of foodstuffs and camp necessities that soon would be swept into the maelstrom that was Independence; emerging after a time to attach themselves to some convenient nucleus which, in a few days or weeks, would grow into the proportions of a caravan.

It is hard to say what different elements entered into the coming together and fusing of a wagon train. Most families, or companies of men, had from one to eight or ten wagons. Yet, by the time they rolled out onto the prairies, they would be enrolled in a train of fifty to a hundred. This was true until '49 and '50, when the prairie was so covered with wagons that the matter of traveling in large caravans for protection from Indians was submerged by the weightier question of where and how to get grass for the stock. Then, after the gold frenzy died out and the spring migrations became smaller and smaller, the trains grew increasingly larger until, in 1865, a train of 214 wagons took the road.

Some of the men who, in the gold-rush years, made their way from Independence Landing up the old ox road, were keeping definite appointments to join organized parties. Others were simply "going west"— all details to be settled as the need arose. These latter, if well armed and mounted, would have little difficulty in being accepted into a train in return for their services with the stock and on guard duty.

There were also many men of character and determination who, having sold everything they had and prepared an outfit with great care and forethought, had brought their families and practically all their assets to effect a passage of the wilderness and found a new home. Some of these were of restless pioneer stock. Others came only because they foresaw that, one by one, their sons would be swept away and they would be left alone.

On the other hand, jostled about in this rude, turbulent human river, were farm boys—brothers or neighbors—pushed out of the home nest early, as they were in those days of large families. To such as these the lure of the excited throng moving west was irresistible. Their simple equipment was probably one wagon, several pair of oxen or mules, and the neighborhood blessing. Possibly they had the proper food, tools, and courage to meet the hardships which were most assuredly waiting for them. More likely not. There were boys who had actually been sold to companies for a few dollars and a promise to see that they got some schooling.

Bearded frontiersmen swelled the crowd, and wild, loose young ne'er-do-wells, keen for new experiences; adventurers grubstaked by timid stay-at-homes, gamblers, Mexicans, the fur traders to whom all this commotion was merely a hindrance, invalids desperately grasping at the chance for health, discharged soldiers, riffraff, thieves wanted by the police of many countries, and hard, reckless women for whom life in the newly awakening West might be better since it could not well be worse.

Then, most pathetic of all, hardest to refuse but surest to be a dangerous drag if admitted to a train, was the unsuccessful man: one who, having failed in life, was hoping to get a fresh start in Oregon or to strike it rich in the mines of the west. Poorly equipped with cheap wagons and inferior stock, undersupplied with food and necessaries for his usually overabundant family, his lot was hard from the beginning. He was not a welcome addition to any train, and unless some one, actuated by pity, "took him on" as a burden he gravitated naturally into a group of similar undesirable outfits. From then on, a prey to everything from Indians and cholera to exposure and hunger, these weaker brethren made trail history what it is.

In later years the oxen at Wayne City were supplemented by a small, mule-drawn train which ran (believe it or not) on steel-faced wooden rails, and plied between the landing and the town; but the picture, as most emigrants remembered it, was glimpses of the straining ox teams seen between clouds of dust.

We entered the city again by way of the old residential section. It is lovely in a staid, dignified way, with large dark houses that could only belong to sterling citizens and leafy streets like unceiled tunnels; but we did not linger, for we had promised ourselves to pay our respects to the spring whose existence was the main reason for the selection of the site of Independence.

It still flows undaunted in one of the dingier back streets. With the laudable intention of improving its flow and keeping it clean, some one has piped it into a cement vault. No doubt a very desirable and healthful proceeding; but as we parked our car in the sun and looked across the street at the blistering affair, which could not boast so much as one spear of grass to soften its uncompromising concrete, it occurred to me that even such a chemically pure arrangement was an anticlimax to the life of a fine old spring.

A flight of steps led down to the water, and my grievance faded as a cool breath dared come halfway up to meet us freighted with a steady pleasant murmur as honeybees flew in and out again. At the bottom, walled into dark seclusion, flowed the ageless spring. Beside it a dog lay spraddled widely on a moist patch to cool his stomach, and blinked at us without lifting his flattened nose before rolling his eyes back toward the noisy little jet of water.

We drank where so many westward-facing travelers had stopped to fill their water casks—to the success of our novel venture. Then Bill produced with a flourish our almost-latest-model thermal jug with a chained cork stuck firmly in a wart on one side and filled it with the utmost sanitation at the old Independence spring. We bade the dog goodbye and, feeling that we had made the most appropriate preparation possible, started westward on the trail.

2

The Raveled Ends of the Cord

RUNNING SOUTH FROM INDEPENDENCE toward the little village of Raytown is a ridge—nothing spectacular in a mountainous way, but higher than its surroundings. On a certain July noon, we approached this modest geographical bulge, drove our car to the summit, and proceeded along the hogback. It was healthily green, rather wooded on the sides, with the broken foamy white of some blossoming weed on top, like the crest of a wave.

"What's the idea of riding up here in the sun?" I asked. "Where are we going?"

"This place is Blue Ridge," my husband informed me. "The old emigrant road went from Independence to the prairies along this rise. We are whooshing along on it because, very fortunately, somebody built a highway on top of the old ruts."

"Oh," I said comprehendingly. Then, with another inspiration, "The gentleman at the courthouse told you all about it yesterday, didn't he?"

"Uh-huh, while you were digging into something we won't need until next week."

"Well, you always get all the necessary things," I replied speciously. "So I just go in for unnecessary items—rather well, too, if I do say so."

Getting no reply to this, after sufficient time, I tried again.

"Is this the only way they went?"

"No, there was a later road north of here going to Westport and from there to the prairies. We'll take that tomorrow, but this was the original Emigrant Road."

At this point Dr. Neff looked up from the messy hand-drawn map he had been trying to interpret, and inserted himself into the conversation. "We're pretty close to the old Camp Cemetery," he informed us. "It's near the intersection of Blue Ridge Road—that's the one we're on—and

Highway 40. Say! They didn't even wait to get started before they died, did they?"

"From what I heard yesterday, they must have buried 'em here in bunches in cholera years," said Bill. "Pretty tough, too, when you stop to think they had just started."

According to Bill, a few wolves and Indians in the first stretches would have amply compensated for a lot of cholera to follow; but many a poor fellow never got a chance to stand lonesome night watches in Indian country, or to get homesick and goosefleshy listening to the wailing howl of the wolves. And the old Camp Cemetery marked the finish of many a high hope as the grisly harvest of victims disappeared into its insatiable maw with grim finality. Their forgotten graves uneasily suggested that this business of traversing the two thousand miles of the old Emigrant Trail was not to be entirely a pleasure jaunt.

From our elevation the view was unbroken on either side, for Blue Ridge separates the watersheds of the Big and Little Blue rivers, tributaries of the Missouri. They must not be confused with the Big and Little Blues whose waters run into the Kansas River much farther west. They flow slightly east of north and lose themselves in the mighty Missouri without causing a ripple in the great unheeding current which lies sunk between its own bluffs, and was at the moment out of our range of vision.

Little by little our ridge became flatter and less distinct. Little by little it showed more signs of care and cultivation until, at last, we were traveling between small farms. On the high, shady porch of a ranch house a little old lady stood and watched us pass. We turned back to question her.

Yes, she remembered well, she said, when the pasture across the road yonder had many a night stood full of wagons, and campfires had blazed up everywhere. A little creek had headed there and provided water. Then, too, she remembered, it was just a nice short journey out from Independence, and made a good trial camp. If (as usually happened) they had forgotten something, a horseman could ride back to town. Pain-killer, soda, laudanum, sheets of enameled or rubberized cloth—they forgot so many things.

This was the south road where she lived, but there was another one north of here that was always called the Westport Road. She remembered

Westport when it had been only a little settlement. Nowadays, she bragged delicately, it was getting to be quite a place. (Reverting in our minds to the mighty sky line of Kansas City, so lately seen, we mentally agreed.) There used to be just the two roads, she went on, because the Big Blue was a cantankerous, crotchety stream. When it was up, there was no doing anything about it—the teams just waited. When it was down, it was so sort of oozy that they had to go miles for a solid bottom ford. The Westport Road crossed it at one solid place and the south road at another. The south crossing was just ahead of us, and we would see a red bridge there. It was a new bridge, she informed us with tremulous pride, but the old weatherboard bridge used by emigrants of later years had been red too, with a lovely slanted, shake roof. The wagon trains had forded just downstream from it, and in those days the place was called the Ford; but since the days of the first bridge it always has been known as Red Bridge Crossing.

And so—to Red Bridge Crossing we went, by the way of the wagons, crossing Bannister Road, and paralleling it west through Holmes Park. From there the trail cuts southwest through the fields, but we rode sedately around them to our destination.

The bridge was only new by comparison; but it was red all right and, at the moment, smelled vilely of defunct catfish discarded by some careless fisherman. With my historical ardor almost as oozy as the Big Blue itself, I braved it, and, stooping under the wire fence, followed the men down to the bank of the stream.

Immediately below the bridge was the west end of the ford. It had crossed on a slant coming upstream so that the rushing water would not strike the wagons and animals broadside. This was customary in small rivers. In a larger stream the slant would have been down with the current. Beyond lay an open meadow, where the pale gilt of the grasses caught and reflected the blazing sun above, haloing the slim silhouettes of its scattering trees with a hazy gold border. Beneath their shadow fat and prosperous cattle stood motionless, and formed unfavorable opinions of our intrusion.

The abutments of the original red bridge still remain and show that it spanned the river just below the one now in use, bisecting the slant of the old ford.

As we were returning to the car Bill was struck with an idea. "Do you know, I never thought about a river without a bridge before? What did they do when they wanted to cross?"

"That's a question," his father answered, "that bothered the emigrants a lot more than it does you. A bridge isn't what you'd call an unfailing appendage to a river, and there are some pretty big streams farther west."

To many of the Oregon Trail emigrants, as to Bill, the Big Blue of Missouri caused the first awakening to the very uncomfortable truth that, from then on to the Pacific coast, they would take their rivers in an unadorned state of nature. If a whimsical spring freshet had been induced by one of the frequent prairie storms, they might camp here a week or more while the river ran bank-full across their path.

The camps at the Blue were straggling; the wagon trains were in the formative period and, as a rule, were still unorganized without definite membership or leaders. Often a captain would not be voted in until after a week of travel, thus giving the voters a chance to form some idea of what manner of man they were choosing. Until that time the camps were composed of carelessly clustered wagons, each owner taking complete charge of his own cattle and chores.

Living conditions on the California-Oregon Trail varied almost as widely as they do in any town. The mansion and the shanty were both represented—the one having its counterpart in the specially built, outsized wagons, the other in the wheelbarrows and pushcarts with which many started their journey west to mend their fortunes.

The most efficient outfit consisted of a short wagon, well made of seasoned hardwoods, minus all excess baggage, and drawn by sturdy animals. Three yoke of medium-sized oxen could haul twenty-five hundred pounds, the customary allowance for four men. It was, however, foolish in the last degree to travel without extra animals to take the place of those which would inevitably fall by the wayside.

The various advantages of horses, mules, and oxen were disputed so often that almost every man and woman who kept a diary of trail happenings had his or her opinion. After weighing many of these opinions we have concluded that a mixed outfit of horses and mules was best for the experienced frontiersman—the horses for saddle animals and the sturdier mules to do the heavy hauling. They were much harder to care for than oxen and needed better forage, but the experienced westerner knew where to leave the trail in order to find good pasturage for them.

Moreover such an outfit was fast-moving, and could cover twenty-five, thirty, and even forty miles daily in flat country. For the inexperienced emigrant, oxen gave better service on the wagons although, of course, a few saddle horses were indispensable. The ox traveled only twelve to fifteen miles each day but thrived on food which a horse would not touch; and, for the traveler who must cling to the beaten path, he was immeasurably easier to keep in condition. Then, too, the Indian to whom horses meant wealth had no use at all for oxen except as food. They were quite exempt from attack until after the buffalo country was passed; and even then a hungry Nevada Digger-Injun would just as soon eat horse and found them much easier to run off in the night. If an ox was accidentally lamed he could be killed by his owner and the meat jerked, and so was not a dead loss. Moreover—and this was often the deciding item— he was much cheaper than a horse.

A yoke of milch cows was often included in the ox team, led behind the wagon, or driven loose with the extra stock. There are records of favorite cows which gave milk clear to Oregon or to the Humboldt Sink in western Nevada. The cows were milked morning and night. The morning's supply was placed in a covered bucket and swung behind the wagon. At night, with no further ado, it was removed in the shape of sweet buttermilk and butter. The night's milking was used for the evening meal.

Many of the wagons, grouped carelessly here and there on the banks of the Blue, were huge prairie schooners covered with the cylindrical white tops of cotton material so familiar in pictures. The inside surface of these tops was a maze of patch pockets, storage for small articles of everyday use. The heavy guns hung suspended from the hickory bows which arched above the driver's head.

A few tents might be seen, polka-dotted sparingly in the bold pattern made by white wagon tops against the dark green background of the rolling valley. There were not so many used as one might, at first thought, imagine; and we have record that, in at least one of the river outfitting towns, there were none for sale and the tent-minded emigrant had to buy material and make his own. Weather conditions had a good deal to do with the situation. An energetic prairie storm could cover fairly high ground "shoelatch-deep" with running water, and low land promptly assumed the aspect of a storm-tossed lake. In fact, as one man wrote, "theare was not much chance to sleep without you could fancy wet blankets and a torrent of water running under you." What chance had a tent, anyway, with tornadolike winds above and either the rich wet loam of Kansas or the sand of the Platte Valley below—none of them a respecter either of persons or of tent pegs? Those who owned wagons slept in them, and those who did not rolled their blankets underneath as a slight precaution against being stepped on if a stampede should start.

Everywhere among the wagons smoke columns poured defiantly from short lengths of stovepipe. It were well if the sentimental traveler, gazing about him at the camp on the Blue, would now shed a tear for the stoves which here smoked in unison for the last time. Practically every one brought them, for a shortage of wood was unthinkable to natives of the limitless eastern forests; but the next twenty-five miles would open a new world to their eyes—a world of clearings not made by man and of rolling plains over which the eye could not carry—a world where there was no timber, nor even a bush big enough to furnish a riding whip.

The two great staples of ordinary diet were "sowbelly" and "biscuit"—which, being translated, meant bacon and hot bread baked in a Dutch oven. In a camp exclusively masculine this was not varied much. Sometimes they had beans or "slam-johns" (the current slang for flapjacks) with occasional game and a pickle now and then as a precaution against scurvy. The whole was washed down by gallons of coffee, the universal drink of the plains. Women, on the other hand, were invariably prejudiced in favor of a better variety of food. They carried potatoes and squash, eggs safely packed in corn meal which could be used up as the eggs vanished, rice, preserves, pickles, and other imperishable commodities. Breadstuffs were often carried in barrels which could be utilized when empty as water containers on the western deserts. Beginning in the middle fifties, we find a few references to tinned goods; but the supreme luxury was dried fruits, with which the women made a most delectable pie, rolling the dough out on the leather wagon seat and baking it in a Dutch oven.

Strangely enough, the greatest service which the women were able to render the migration was brought about by their constitutional inability to relish water containing "wiggle-tails." They would not drink it unless it had been made into tea or coffee as a sort of camouflage, in which process it was quite incidentally boiled. This feminine whimsy saved untold lives. The overpowering majority of the migration was, however, deprived of the ministrations of the daintier sex and drank its infant wiggle-tails raw.

Surrounding this more or less experimental camp on the Blue grazed the half-wild stock—unbroken oxen which shied away and bellowed at every approach, and mules which we are told on good authority managed to go back to the Missouri River every night for a week until their new and all-too-trusting owners learned to cable them to the wagon wheels.

Leaving the Red Bridge Crossing, the emigrants suddenly, and for the most part unexpectedly, left the friendly forests of small leafy trees which grew so evenly over the country east of the Missouri as to be almost like a nap on earth's green carpet. In a few miles—long before they camped again—the wavering lines of wagons would have left the forests behind and be creeping, like long gray caterpillars, between an empty earth and a still more empty sky.

Reluctantly we salvaged our car from a swarming sea of gnats and set our faces toward the open prairie. Near Dallas, and almost on the Missouri-Kansas state line, stands the settlement known in trail days as Little Santa Fe. The dragging bull trains returning from the summer trade in Mexico reached it a full day before arriving at Independence; and the thirsty packers sought relief without too much regard as to whether they drank real liquor or the pink-elephant mixture of new whisky and molasses known as skull varnish. In like manner this first-and-last-chance town stood ready to supply the final liquid opportunity for the westbound travelers. Later, a third type of customer invaded the ill-smelling dives, as a military road running south from Fort Leavenworth along the state line brought marching soldiers this way.

The community, slightly glossed over with the title New Santa Fe, is now a prosaic and pleasant place to live; but it looks back to a hell-roaring past.

The south road, from Independence, across Red Bridge, through Little Santa Fe to modern Gardner, Kansas, is one of the two main stems of the Santa Fe Trail. The other, farther north, started from Westport, now included in modern Kansas City. Along both these stems went the pioneer travelers who intended to leave the Santa Fe in about forty miles and turn northwest on the fur traders' route toward Oregon and Cali-

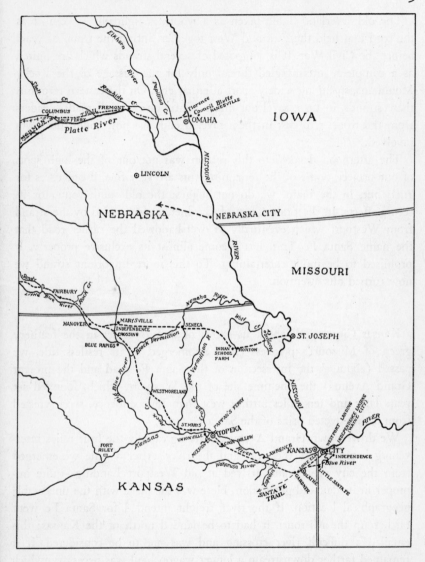

fornia. This last-named road we hoped to be able to trace through to the Pacific coast. It is best known as the Oregon Trail even though thousands more followed its erratic course to California than ever reached Oregon by its means, but the older maps also call the stretch through Kansas and Nebraska the California Road.

The old Overland Trail, taken as a whole, is rightfully spoken of as the cord that held the East and West together during the troubled years before the Civil War. It is composed of several strands which are united as a complete, intermingled thread only for the passage of the Rocky Mountains, springing widely apart at either end. On the eastern terminus these strands, in turn, ravel out into a confusion of small roads—feeders from the frontier towns. In these raveled ends we now found ourselves involved.

The afternoon devoted to this section was not one of the high spots of our project. Some of the remaining ruts are very fine, if one cares for ruts; but, in the main, we do not suggest the old south route for its scenic effects. In the prairie, east of Gardner, it was joined by the strand from Westport which eventually so overshadowed the earlier road that the name Santa Fe Trail has become almost its exclusive property. It promised to be more entertaining. To this more important strand we now turned our attention.

*   *   *

Kansas City lay all about us—acres of dun roofs set in the feathery green of Missouri's priceless trees. Submerged in its restless tide, we passed (about at the intersection of the Santa Fe road and the present Grand Avenue) the one-time site of old Westport, which, founded six years later and ten miles farther west than Independence, soon wrested from it the coveted prize of the Santa Fe trade.

We drove down Grand Avenue, covering rapidly the four miles intervening between old Westport and the river. After a time we emerged from the city proper and arrived at old Westport Landing—quite improper in its day and generation. Here was the place with the unbeatable geographical location. If the river freight intended for Santa Fe went farther up the Missouri, it had to be landed north of the Kansas; this entailed a difficult river crossing and was not to be considered. If it remained farther downstream a longer wagon haul was necessary, which took time and was costly. It was impossible to ignore Westport Landing.

Close by this settlement, but antedating it, were two others. The first in point of time was the headquarters of a French fur trader known simply as Chouteau's. The foundation of the second was laid in 1832 when a group of French Canadians with their Indian wives set up housekeeping in the timber of the west bottoms near the confluence of the Missouri and Kansas rivers. In early days the latter was more commonly called the Kaw, and the cluster of tiny cabins was called indiscriminately either Kansasmouth or Kawsmouth. The two French settlements were located, without fuss about mosquitoes or controversy over pure water, by simply arriving at the most convenient spot for trading purposes and remaining there. They, with their later neighbor Westport Landing, formed the nuclei of Kansas City. In April of the year 1839, Dr. Wislizenus, an early-day traveler, left St. Louis by boat for Chouteau's Landing—a six-day trip. He wrote: "The border village, Westport, is six miles distant from Chouteau's Landing. There I intended to await the departure of this year's annual caravan. The village has perhaps thirty or forty houses, and is only a mile from the western border of the State of Missouri. It is the usual rendezvous for travelers to the Rocky Mountains, as is Independence, twelve miles distant, for those journeying to Santa Fe."

David Cosad arrived at Kansasmouth on April 11, 1849. He called it Kansas and described it as a steamboat landing a short distance below the mouth of the Kansas River, and said it "bid fair to be a smart place for business."

Two miles beyond the "frontier of the State of Missouri" the westbound travelers came to a mission. This was undoubtedly the Shawnee Mission—still in existence and well worth a visit. Trees and little rolling hills shut it away from the houses and hubbub of Kansas City which actually surround it on all sides. It was a notable landmark and the missionaries were making a real attempt to mitigate the evils caused by the juxtaposition of negroes, unscrupulous whites, and border Indians who were "thick as toads on a mill pond" and all too often drunk. Here, according to Mr. Cosad, were found "half bloods, quarter-bloods and all mixtures of Indians negroes and Wites. It seems," he moralized, "if they have tried to enlighten them . . . they have not neglected to lighten the skin at the same time."

It was a breath-catching moment for the pioneers when the large, brick Mission building disappeared from view, for this was one of the last outposts of the border towns. Leaving it behind was a distinct wrench such as an uncertain swimmer feels when he gets beyond the end of the wharf.

It seemed distinctly irritating that we should still have to negotiate the miles of scattering outskirts which surround Kansas City; but we did so and soon began to encounter large and self-conscious signs informing us that, if we wished to travel in the footsteps of the pioneers, we should take the paved highway modernly entitled the Santa Fe Trail. Here was a pretty how-do-you-do.

"Why should we travel a highway?" I demanded. "Certainly we didn't come clear back here to find a strip of pavement, and I don't believe they put a highway right on top of an old ungraded road."

"It looks silly to me," said Bill. "If they went this way, they must have driven those heavy wagons on top of all the hottest hills. It just doesn't make sense."

"You'd better take your trail where you find it; and, if it's easy for a while, you're that much to the good. It'll be tough enough later on," advised Dr. Neff practically.

But I had expected rough sod and the great outdoors. This was a mere highway—quite a good highway, no doubt, but mere. What I wanted was prairie.

There was a sufficiency of the latter in sight, so they humored me, and we spent several hours bumping around on it while conversation ceased and amiability waned. Finally, as the day wore on toward an almost unbelievably hot midafternoon, I began to think that possibly something was wrong with me instead of with the road signs. While I was in this open-minded condition, we saw a man in a shady farmyard with his feet in a pan of water.

"There's the most sensible person I've seen today," exclaimed my husband as he punctiliously parked the car with its nose to the hitching rack. "Let's go talk to him."

We didn't discommode him in the least. In fact we didn't even cause a splash in the pan when we leaned over his fence in an earnest, questioning row and listened to his laconic statements.

The old Santa Fe trace lay yonder. Our eyes followed sweepings of his brown, leathery hand and shirt-sleeved arm toward the scorned highway. It rode the swell of land that divides the waters of the Wakarusa from those of the Kaw, and only made short, circling detours northward into the lower land when there was a large creek to cross. In this way they avoided the steep short canyons which would have entailed doubling the teams and cost them precious hours in the long run.

The trail rode the swell to keep above the storm-sodden prairies and also because in Indian country the emigrants avoided the low land—in spite of its nearness to water and the easier pulling. They stayed with the ridges (if any) or at least kept on top of whatever protuberance lay handy at the moment. Thus the wagon trains were not exposed to unseen attack; and even though the Indians of eastern Kansas happened to be friendly it was just as well to be cautious.

With this new light on the case, we looked again at the country in which we had played hide-and-seek for the last few hours and shuddered. Interminable small steep rolling hills of blackish earth lay along the river, tree-grown in the hollows to the last inch.

"I guess a traveler in those days wouldn't have been found dead here, would he?" Bill ventured.

"No, kid," said our informant, "not dead probably, because the Kansas Indians didn't do much killing; but if he happened to meet a bunch of young Pawnee braves out on the prowl, he would sure as fate be left afoot, and mebbe naked, to get back as best he could. That was their idea of a joke."

But it wasn't exactly a joke even to the Indians. Oh, of course, they enjoyed it as an entertaining and profitable incident, but it was really a matter of business. And that, I have since found out, was why a small party of young braves was more dangerous to encounter than a much larger party under an older chief.

They were trying to establish themselves, both financially and in the matter of prestige. A young Indian had nothing to start with. Emphatically he had to bring home his own bacon in order to give suitable presents to his bride's father and to set up housekeeping. The regular proceeding was to take it away from some other tribe, but a few lone white men were a bonanza. They had better horses, so that it took fewer animals to make a suitable exchange for a nice young squaw. The warpath, for a young Indian, was almost in the nature of a business venture.

Shadows were dusky among the trees and were flung long and sharp across our road as we said goodbye to our philosophic friend and started back to the highway we should have taken in the first place, leaving him competently killing flies.

Our way led over a succession of grassy swells spaced at intervals with breezeless hollows. What a country to have traveled before the day of the graded road and the planted tree! Driving an ox team over these endless, rolling hillocks was a task from which the very imagination recoiled. However—this was July and the emigrants went through, each year, in May.

They started in good weather, of course. The sun shone upon a "grand and beautiful prairie which can be compared to nothing but the mighty

Schooner on rolling prairie.

ocean." A succession of rich, shining green swells was star-dusted with small frail blossoms and splashed with the hardier varieties like great spillings of calcimine powders. Here a patch of mountain pink, here spiderwort—while, ahead, a spreading of purple over a sunny slope proved, on closer acquaintance, to be larkspur. Bobolinks sang where currant bushes lined the meandering watercouses, and the line of white wagon tops stretched like a shining ribbon across the curving velvet breast of the prairie.

On such a heavenly spring day nothing could be more breath-catching than to top a verdant, grassy swell and to feel the soft breeze curling past—to pause there full-throated and inspired by the sheer loveliness of earth and sky before sweeping down the next rolling dip.

Many early travelers, both men and women, have described it so even in the first grief of parting from home and friends.

But spring is uncertain. Quite as readily the sullen, implacable prairie storms would blot out any inspiration; and the weary marchers, plodding heavily against an icy wind, chattered and shook as they looked in vain for some spot more sheltered than the rest; blew on half-frozen fingers as they dug trenches around the tents; wakening in the morning, if they had been fortunate enough to sleep, to a dreary desolation of gummy mud and no fire for breakfast.

Comfort and even life itself, on the trail, was horribly and helplessly dependent on the vagaries of elements completely out of any one's control. If the sun shone and the grass grew, they crossed the prairies happily. If the scourge of cholera and the ungoverned winds held aloof, they might write rapturously of the mysterious gray beauty of the Platte Valley splashed with its vivid wildflowers. If a light rain and a cool night fell as a blessing from heaven itself, they might cross almost any of the deserts and write only of the solemn stillness of the all-night trek and of a weary arrival at water the next morning. But who could guess or avoid his fate! If the storm came in the Platte Valley and the scorching blast of a hot wind on the desert, none could avoid great hardship; and only the few were equipped to keep their families from unendurable misery and the likelihood of a newly filled grave wept over and abandoned within the day.

Why then should we complain, even though the whole Middle West was in the throes of a prodigious heat wave which had struck an all-time peak, and the country was as hot as a boiled egg and had its apparent faculty of never cooling off? The highway we had scorned was at no great distance and, with our egos considerably deflated, we decided to take it and follow the Santa Fe Trail signs into Olathe. We wanted to see the old survey maps of Johnson County, and Olathe is the county seat.

After quite a session at the courthouse, we emerged importantly with tracings of the trail clear through the county, a proceeding that we duplicated at each county seat until we reached Nebraska. The highway proved not to be entirely coincidental with the trail, but it is close enough for practical purposes and is the best base of operations in studying it.

About a third of the way from Olathe to Gardner, or thirty-four miles from Independence, we passed near the site of the famous old Lone Elm where many camped on the first night out from Westport. Being very definite as to location, it was often used as a rendezvous. It was on the headwaters of Cedar Creek, and the solitary elm, three feet in thickness, was credited with being the only tree on the prairie within sight of the road. It was mentioned by nearly all the early travelers, but it disappeared during the gold rush. "This old tree will never put forth its leaves again," wrote D. Jaggers on the evening of May 18, 1849. "The hunters have long since robbed it of nearly all its branches and the numerous parties who have encamped here this year have nearly stripped it of its bark also, and the lone tree of the prairie will soon form a landmark no more."

We were still traveling southwest on the slight elevation called, by courtesy, a ridge and now approached the point where the Westport road met the southern route from Independence.

My husband studied the tracings with keen interest. "Evidently there was only a mile or two where all the wagons used one road," he said, and pointed to the spot on the map. "Almost as soon as the Independence and Westport roads got together, the wagons for Oregon and California turned off and left the Santa Fe freighters lumbering along by themselves. Do you know," he went on, "that for two days I have asked every man with a visible gray hair, and not a soul can tell me where that split came!"

"Niles Searls said the junction was on Cow Creek," I proffered, "and that in '49 a semibarbarian named Rogers lived there with an Indian wife."

"Well, the best I could gather out of a dozen or so modern books was rather fuzzy," said Dr. Neff. " 'Near Gardner, Kansas,' is about as definite as any one gets."

"Look at this, and improve your average." My husband shoved the tracing at him. "The old survey shows that the original split was on the E. C. Cochran ranch, and it's two miles west of Gardner."

A subsequent visit confirmed this, but at the moment we were entering Gardner itself and the subject changed abruptly.

"What we need now is an old-timer," announced the head of the house as he parked with a flourish. "I'll go get one," he finished optimistically.

He was better than his word; and Mr. Bigelow, who was born in Gardner more than seventy years ago, gave us the simple story of the parting of the ways as Gardner people know it. In the first few years of its use (so he told us), the fork was definite and occurred on the Cochran Ranch. Later, as the compact wagon trains of the early emigrants gave way to the tremendous traffic of '49 and the fifties, the exact spot became lost in a bewildering maze of turnouts. The country is more or less flat, and the temptation to jayhawk a little across the corner was too much. Especially was this true if a fast-moving mule outfit happened to be pulling up behind an ox train at the critical point. These short-cut roads gradually pushed farther and farther back from the original fork until at last the most popular turning was in Gardner, about a short city block from the monument in the school yard.

The trail became very wide, as was only natural with all outdoors in which to spread. Later, as land began to have value, limits were set. It was pushed back within certain confines, and on that definite course the wagons must travel. No longer did they jaunt merrily around a boghole in the road. When they could no longer go through it, somebody had to fill it in, and they went over it. This was "the law of the trail."

Mr. Bigelow also recalled when, seventy years ago, he played as a boy in the wagon ruts. At that time, standing at the first fork of the road, near where the schoolhouse is today, was a simple sign which read, THE ROAD TO OREGON. Four words which changed the course of life itself for those who took that turning.

Beginning at this place, the two intermingled streams of humanity, which had traveled the forty-odd miles from Independence in an indistinguishable tangle, sifted out—each to his own kind. The contrast was marked even to the eye. Southward to old Mexico went the battered, tough old wagons with the weather-beaten tops. They were accompanied by men—tough also and weather-beaten—to whom this tiresome, dangerous journey was a chosen means of livelihood, just routine, with dangerous dirty routine duties, spiced with the stimuli of Indian attacks, to which they were only too well accustomed.

In startling contrast, the white-topped wagons that turned slowly toward the north were new—their tops as yet unsullied by storms and dust and snagging branches, their hickory wheels unscarred by granite-strewn mountain sides and river gorges—untried prairie ships, each on its maiden voyage, turning from the charted course and with an anxious captain and an inexperienced crew, setting sail for an unknown shore and a fabulous reward. The voyage of the Argonauts!

3

Paging Mr. Blue Jacket

To the chronically thirsty emigrant the most important landmarks were the creeks. Hills and dusty plains, they took in their daily march and forgot if they could. But a creek was a different matter whose delights were only partly counterbalanced by the tragic fact that the barrel containing the luster tea set had got loose during the crossing and Heaven only knew how much was broken, and that the wall-eyed mule had stepped into the Dutch oven with disastrous results to everything concerned. Indeed fatal accidents often occurred from less contributing causes than that, and very frequently they happened at the crossings. No—they never forgot the creeks.

For this reason we noted historic Kill Creek and Captain Creek with interest and set our faces for the short journey to the Wakarusa.

We were now traveling on the highway, and making short detours over to the trail, which we sometimes explored on foot, but, more often in this open country, carried with the eye to the next point of contact. The Wakarusa proved to be an ill favored stream. In spite of the belief among the emigrants that its Indian name meant to walk around, or surround, it is said to indicate "thigh-deep," and it appeared to be all of that or more as it lay some twenty feet below us at the bottom of precipitous banks. "It would be a physical impossibility to get a wagon across this groove," I remarked, being sincerely puzzled by the problem. "It must flatten out toward the mounds."

"Well, the ford's there, so evidently it was the flattest place the emigrants could find," my son agreed impatiently.

"We'll soon find out," said my husband easily. "We may as well go see the old Blue Jacket's crossing before lunch. Blue Jacket was a smart Indian, they tell me, with an eye out for profit. He kept a roadhouse at the ford. It won't take an hour."

We had no misgivings as we turned south and drove down the narrow, dusty little lane.

The heavy, golden wheat fields of Kansas hemmed us in on all sides, broken here and there by patches of green waste land. Now and then we crossed small, unpleasant-looking watercourses lying in murky, currentless pools of unguessable depth. These lay far down in deep-gutted ravines below spidery old bridges.

A ranch house loomed ahead, surrounded by pasture instead of wheat land. A rounded elevation rose on either side, the larger one darkly timbered and for that reason known as Blue Mound. The fields were full of cattle. Entering the farmyard, we saw no one but a friendly dog who escorted my husband to the house and back again wagging his tail deprecatingly. His very actions said that there was no one home; so on we went. In fact we went on and on.

I have always wondered why it is that all information extant on any given historic spot is always somewhere else and the immediate neighborhood is in complete and blissful ignorance. This occasion was no exception. All the rest of the morning and most of the afternoon we went in and out of ranches inquiring stubbornly for the erstwhile residence of Mr. Blue Jacket. The replies varied from the indignant disclaimer of the woman who thought we had lost a sweater to the bewilderment of the man who gathered that we were hunting a variety of dry fly for fishing purposes.

The sun swung noon-high and began its downward journey while we snatched a hasty lunch and started out again to circle the country in the approved manner of the man in the old problem who was hunting a baseball in a round field. About three o'clock we were near the center of our imaginary circle at a point between the two mounds. My husband remained firmly intrenched in the well grounded Paden belief that we can overcome almost any type of ill-adventure simply by outlasting it. Our prospects were good for continuing to page Mr. Blue Jacket far into the night. It was really very trying, and my thin layer of patience peeled off and left me frankly exasperated.

"This is what I call downright inefficiency," I grumbled. "You'd think we were trying to get to the stratosphere."

"Now just sit tight," he advised. "Here's the house where we stopped first this morning. Remember? There wasn't any one at home then."

"That was about five hours and three gallons of gas back," I remarked acrimoniously, and breathed firmly through my nose.

He got out and the familiar dog came to meet him, capering this time with enthusiasm at our recurrence on his horizon, and led the way to the front door with confidence.

"The family's home this time all right," said Dr. Neff, "and the dog knows it."

The door opened wide with a friendly air, and a man appeared in its framing rectangle. He made hospitable gestures but, after a dialogue unheard by us, he joined my husband and they both walked out to the car.

This, it seemed, was the Smith Ranch and had been in the family since 1854. We were at the moment standing on the Emigrant Road or rather on the branch that went between the mounds. The old road had split for a few miles right along here, and this section was less used than the other; but Mr. Smith could remember when numbers of the great prairie schooners came down this very road every day of the late spring and early summer, lumbering along the peculiar swale between the mounds.

But, he said, even though many wagons came this way, by far the greater number took the other branch which went north of Blue Mound and used Blue Jacket's ford.

At the mere mention of the name we became eloquent and told our troubles at length.

"The old-timers here—the ones who could have set you right—usually go into Lawrence to shop on Saturday morning, and this is Saturday. The others, who shop any day, might be home, but they wouldn't know. You see—it's simple—really."

Well, something was simple all right but there was no time to go into the matter now. We took his adequate directions and started out again.

Five minutes later Blue Jacket's roadhouse loomed ahead of us. Would my husband select this occasion to flaunt his superior tenacity of purpose? I waited. Nobly he did not, and I softened somewhat, unslung the camera, and got ready to enjoy myself.

The old two-story house was a miracle of unattractiveness and stood outlined starkly against a protesting sky. We have often wondered why the frame houses of the fifties are as devastatingly ugly as the simple log cabins are picturesque. A group of people sat on the porch. A man among them got up and came over to see what he could do for us. As we might have expected, there was no one present who knew the history of the place. Blue Jacket's had encountered hard times and had fallen, at last, into the hands of an insurance company for which the man who had greeted us was the agent in charge. He looked at the paintless old building with extreme disfavor. "It's useless the way it is now," he said reasonably enough, "but probably it can be remodeled."

"Oh—" I began hastily, and stopped.

He looked receptively at me and waited for my contribution, but I reconsidered. What earthly reason could one give to an insurance company for preserving intact the forgotten roadhouse of a defunct Indian? Just the same I was glad that we had arrived today—Saturday marketing notwithstanding—rather than six months later.

"Is it all right for us to go down to the ford?" Dr. Neff asked.

"Didn't know there was one. Good Lord, man, you'd need a parachute to get off the bank! Anyway, help yourself. You're welcome to go any place."

Ahead of us, across a wide field, lay the ribbon of thick dull greenery that, of late years since the Indians have ceased to burn off the prairies, is the telltale evidence of every watercourse. Within a hundred yards, we found the wagon ruts and followed them. They were grass-grown and old—so old that a large tree grew midway of the sunken marks. They were deep to start with and grew deeper as the slope increased. Here the drivers had locked their wheels.

This proceeding was not a simple matter of stepping on a brake. As late as 1855, Helen Carpenter wrote that brakes were newfangled inventions of which there was but one in her entire company. The emigrants kept the heavy wagons under control when descending slopes or creek banks by first coming to a full stop and chaining the rear wheels. This worked well enough if the necessity could be foreseen but left much to be desired in the case of a runaway. And runaways were the chief excitement of the first few weeks. Even when engaged in the everyday practice of starting and stopping the cumbersome vehicles rolled and lurched, throwing the unwary occupants completely off balance and sometimes to the ground. Then Heaven help them if not thrown clear, for those Juggernaut wheels could not be halted.

Gilbert L. Cole told of a shocking incident that happened on the prairie not far from where we now stood. His wagon company had been forced to cross a slough: an ordinary slough, no doubt—they crossed lots of them, planless ditches holding unambitious water. They were miserable things to ford, having no dependable bottom and offering most of the difficulties of a creek with none of its luxury.

The animals were badly in need of a breathing spell after the struggle up and out. Mr. Cole, who was driving on that particular day, pulled his wagon abreast of another, standing motionless with its team sagged back out of their collars and chains dragging. The unknown wagon was of the type with a flap door in its canvas side and in the door stood a beautiful baby girl about four years old. She smiled coyly at him—a lovely picture for a home-starved man—and he snapped his fingers to amuse her. Suddenly her father, on the driver's seat, cracked his whip, probably in sudden worry at the time lost or in fear of losing his precious place in line. The animals took up the slack in the chains with terrific suddenness. The wagon gave a lurch, and the little girl was on the ground.

The great iron tire went over her at the waist line, wrote Mr. Cole, with her "pretty head and hands reaching up on on one side of the wheel." The mother threw herself after the child but unavailingly. "Such excruciating sobs of agony I hope never to hear again," he wrote. "But why say it in that way when I can hear them still?" In another instance a baby was thrown from the seat followed by the mother who had frantically reached too far. The father, walking by the rear wheel, saw them in a horrible, nightmare flash and flung his wife aside. He couldn't save the baby. The first death in the Great Migration of '43 was six-year-old Joel Hembree, killed by a wagon. Available journals mention dozens of instances. Usually the victim died.

Most of the wagons came this way. Maybe, I thought, those soon-to-be-bereaved mothers carried their babies down this very hill not knowing how little time was left to love and to enjoy them. But they didn't bathe any babies in the Wakarusa, I decided, for it lay below us in a sequence of murky, brown pools whose opaqueness defeated the eye and had a slimy glisten as of water snakes and leeches.

We separated. Dr. Neff went upstream, and Bill down, to locate the confluence of the Little Wakarusa which our map showed arriving at this point in a sky-blue wavering line. My husband and I remained to investigate the ford. It was some fifteen or twenty feet below us, and the approach was the next thing to perpendicular. We scrambled, slid, and then dropped to the dry, rocky bed between the pools where it was plain that the channel carried a great deal of water in the spring floods. On the near side, which happened also to be the deep side, the emigrant wagons had been let down with ropes—plunging in, head on. They were rescued from this unprofitable status by men and teams on the opposite bank who commenced, at the critical moment, to pull lustily at long ropes attached to the front axle. What happened here to the walnut whatnots and the eggshell china, with which many of the emigrants started (and very few finished), is best left to the imagination.

On the far side the banks were lower and allowed some freedom of action. The problem of pulling out had not been as difficult as the descent.

Meanwhile Dr. Neff had found the Little Wakarusa, which, far from being a sky-blue streamlet, looked like the incarnation of a dark brown taste and was slowly adding its daily dozen dirty drops to the collection of nearly motionless pools which was the Wakarusa.

Blue Mound is visible a long way in all directions. In fact Frémont, starting his expedition of 1843, placed a prearranged signal on its summit to summon his Indian hunters. One of them, a good-natured old redskin, had that deep loyalty to the "Great White Father" at Washington so often found in the Indians along the Emigrant Trail. He was unusual solely in the number of his sons, and these, his only creative work, he had dedicated to the cause of patriotism by unctuously naming them for a convenient number of the Presidents. On the occasion mentioned, he was accompanied only by Thomas Jefferson, a shy young Indian with very little English. It is interesting that on the day the hunters arrived, Marcus Whitman, missionary to the Oregon country, was the guest of the Frémont party. The "Great Migration" was just ahead, and he was hurrying to overtake them. It was in the vicinity of Blue Mound that the meeting took place between these two men, each of whom carved for himself such a prominent niche in history.

The city of Lawrence lies a few miles away on the banks of the Kansas River, but the early trail passed it by. Later a ferry was established there—

one of five which, we were told, flourished on the Kansas between the Missouri River and modern Topeka.

For miles we remained with the trail on top of the watershed south of the Kansas River. On all sides stretched an appalling number of low knolls, curling away to the horizon in never-ending waves and rolls. In all other years when we have passed this way the world has been a lovely study in green and gold—green in tall waving spears of tasseled corn, and gold in bending breeze-swept wheat fields—for the valley of the

The trail shows even through cultivated fields.

Kaw is one of the storehouses of the world. This particular season, 1936, was hot, and the earth was toasted quite brown under the broiling grid of the heavens.

At Kanwaka we turned to the right. Notched out of a hill curve was "the old gouge" winding its unheeding way through pasture and cultivated ground alike, northwestward toward the river. It was most often on the knoll tops that we saw the wheel marks, for Kansas, fertile prairie state that she is, covers her surface too well to show many scars except where the top of a sudden swell, drier and less productive than the rest, shows against the light.

As the days went by and we talked with some of Kansas' historians, and many of her farmers, we found unexpected ways of quickly noting the presence of the almost forgotten road, even through cultivated fields. It seems that the prairie grass, decaying through innumerable years, has formed a top layer of mulch more than a foot deep. The heavy wagon wheels bit so deeply into its moist richness that great clods were pulled out and scattered aside. In time the path of the wagons lost its fertile top coating and a red clay remained which was comparatively poor.

To this long thread of depleted ground various things have happened, but it is never quite the same as its surroundings. Sometimes, in the midst of a healthy green hill slope, its ill nourished grasses show sparse and yellow. Sometimes it has filled with cockleburs—easy-going weeds with few requirements, which live long after the rest of the field has dried. To the searching eye this appears as a long blurred ribbon of soft green through the indefinite golds and tans of the summer turf.

Sometimes the old trace appears merely as an otherwise unexplained lightness of crop through a certain stretch. Quite often it is a definite, elongated swale, a senseless rounded groove showing even through crops on fields long cultivated.

In the sage desert country, far to the west, we later found the evidence to be entirely different, for there the slowly moving caravan gave to the earth more than it took away and a strip of rank-growing sage, three times the height of that surrounding it, marks the fertilized path of thousands of driven cattle.

These signs show the way of the grinding wheels and pounding hoofs.

By one token and another it was usually possible to locate the road accurately enough to carry its line with the eye from one point of contact to the next. This we did, day in and day out, gathering a bewildering mass of details which would be of such monotonous similarity that there is no need to recount them here.

We soon came to and passed Coon Hollow Camp—or Big Spring, as it is sometimes called. It was a favorite camping spot of the fifties. Here the trail split. The later-used fork went, in plainly visible gouges, up the hill toward Tecumseh and on to Topeka where a Frenchman named Papin ran a famous ferry. The older fork wound prosaically across the fields to the left, continuing south of the river to the ford at old Unionville, opposite modern Rossville.

The day wore on in direct proportion as we wore out. The last few miles through the hot evening were long ones, but eventually we arrived at Topeka and the Kansas River. The air had a smothering quality, as of feather beds, that made sleep unthinkable. On the streets, under great flares of light, crowds of languid people wandered in and out of stores, apparently willing to do anything within reason except to go home. Their strolling figures, weirdly haloed in the white glare, matched their constant purposeless movement with the ceaseless activity above as millions of downy, soft night-flying things circled and beat in futile and aimless bursts of speed.

We drove on in search of a cooler breath and came at last to the Kansas River at the site of Papin's ferry where in later trail days thousands of emigrants crossed in comparative safety.

A little warm breeze puffed along the water and sent it glinting and shimmering under the lights until the lady river seemed to have put on a sequin garment for the evening.

The bridge arched its back over its own reflection, blurry and distorted, as the bright-edged ripples sliced it through and through; and on it, sad to say, my scientifically accurate notebook leaves us hesitating (in common with the rest of the city) as to whether it would be more fatiguing to sit up all night or to undertake the exertion of going to bed.

4

Hazards of the Prairies

IT WAS TEN O'CLOCK the next morning before we were ready to start. There are so many historic spots in and around the city of Topeka, and so few of its busy population who know where to find them, that we decided to go straight to headquarters for our information. With that purpose in mind we invaded the offices of Mr. George Root of the Kansas State Historical Society, to whom we are indebted for more than one boost over the difficult spots in our self-imposed journey. We came out armed with a rough outline of our next two days' journey.

Papin's ferry (sometimes spelled Pappan's) came rather late, he told us, into the history of the Oregon Trail. So also did its small attendant village of Kansasville, whose scattering log houses formed the beginnings of Topeka. The first crossing used by fur traders, hunters, travelers, and the earliest emigrants was just south of what is now Rossville. Instead of turning toward the Kansas River at Coon Hollow these early wayfarers remained south of the river, keeping well out of the timber that lined its course and fording Otter and Mission creeks.

Near the latter they found a Baptist Mission with a farm maintained for the benefit of the surrounding tribes. It was a heavy stone structure and is now incorporated in a dairy barn on the Prairie Dell Farm five or six miles west of Topeka. It was along the river that Niles Searls met a solemn Indian on a pony. Slung to one side of his mount was a live fawn while, balancing it on the other, was a whopping-big turtle craning its neck around as it hung by the tail. No spoiled meat for him. He brought them back alive.

We crossed the Kansas (or the Kaw—just as one elects to call it) near Rossville and were told by old settlers that the bridge is located at the site of the earliest crossing. The attendant settlement was situated on a hill some three-quarters of a mile south of the ford and was called Union Village. In '49 it consisted of a few log buildings and an encircling Indian encampment. At the end of a dry season the ford offered no insurmountable problem as the bottom was gravelly and the current evenly spread and wide; but the emigrants arrived in the spring when fording was not practical. Those who could afford it used the ferry, belonging to two Indians, which consisted of a couple of fairly substantial scows. The others went boating on the snow-swollen stream in their wagon-beds, calked for the occasion. The unfortunate livestock swam. Take it all in all, one season with another, the Kansas crossing was a reasonable and gentle introduction to the adventures in store for the travelers on the capricious bosoms of the western rivers.

It was traditional to elect company captains, and sometimes secretaries and other officers, at the Kansas crossing. The early Oregon-bound wagon trains held formal meetings for the purpose, and many later companies held to the custom. One amusing election was decided by starting the candidates out at a brisk walk. Their respective supporters fell in behind and were soon hanging to one another's coat tails in a long line. The one who circled back with the most impressive appendage of voters won the honor. From that moment the captain—or "wagon boss," as he was later called—wielded no mean powers, and his subordinates were highly respected.

Good leadership and a tight organization were beginning to be essential. The very early emigrants found conditions vastly different after leaving the broad well marked Santa Fe Road, for the faint trace leading to the Rocky Mountains and Oregon was at times almost imperceptible and the wagons were simply driven in the general direction indicated.

On the north bank, a mile and a half beyond the crossing of the Kansas at Union Village, was the toll bridge over Cross Creek held by the Pottawatomies and some ten miles up the river from Papin's ferry at Kansasville (and therefore between the two crossings on the north bank) were two of the Kanza villages and the Methodist Mission with its farm and a sawmill. Now the Indians so far had been "civilized" to a degree—which, to the emigrant ladies, meant that they wore pants. Somewhat to their disquietude they found conditions north of the Kaw quite different. The Kanzas were a piquant item of the emigrants' experience. The government had made a determined effort to make these difficult foster children self-supporting. It supplied cattle and pigs and built fences. But the scheme of life of a Kanza was devastatingly forthright. When winter came he tore down the fence and used it to cook the pig. Three villages are mentioned, looking (so travelers said) like a collection of giant molehills and detected more easily by the nose than by the eye. They were permanent residences, however, and a definite step ahead of the other plains Indians, whose huts were only small affairs of brush and mud.

The Kanza women were ungarnished, in a sort of leather overshirt and loose drawers, with virgin and untrammeled mops of hair. The men, on the contrary, were gluttons for punishment when it came to style. This, in fact, was the rule rather than the exception among Indian braves, who stopped as a matter of course to make up their faces and arrange their accessories before entering a village or showing themselves in any position of dignity. The Kanza braves shaved their skulls (a distinct asset from the emigrant's point of view) and left only a thick strip of hair running from front to back and roached into an upstanding comb, forming a handy gadget in which to fasten feathers. They favored vermilion face paint applied in lurid rings around the eyes. They wore an apron about the loins but protruded starkly above and below. Occasionally they wrapped themselves in blankets. When the white man camped near them the amiable aborigines arrived early and stayed late. The travelers could have borne up better under these social calls if their red brothers had not been extremely filthy and crawling with vermin.

Now we hold no brief either for or against the Indians of the trail. We simply are familiar with the unbiased accounts of dozens of emigrants who encountered them. Their natures ran the gamut of human characteristics, from the arrogant Sioux to the animal-like root digger of Nevada. The conflicting opinions penned by the travelers who kept diaries mirror to a great extent their own different viewpoints and degree of tolerance or nervousness. Sometimes they recorded reactions displayed by the Indians which were directly attributable to the amount of common sense they had themselves shown. One woman wrote that, unless the Indians were already wrought up over some incident, one could go a long way on the Golden Rule.

The thoughts, ideals, and desires of the normal plains Indian of that era were what they had always been—tuned to nomadic living and frequent bloody raids on tribes whose possessions they happened to need. Those enthusiasts who feel that modern civilization encroached upon and ruined an idyl of unspoiled and untrammeled children of nature might feel differently had they been required to live with them. Without going into the rights and wrongs of the case, and granting that the period of adjustment has been difficult in the extreme and is not yet over; still the prosperous, educated, and still dignified Indian of today is a far cry from the constantly warring tribes (either terrorized or predatory as their strength permitted) who stole one another's wives and property, tortured and were tortured, starved in the winter and deserted their helpless old people. The "half-civilized" Kanzas were no exception. John Bidwell, a member of the first American party to reach California overland, wrote in 1841: "Several Kanzas Indians came to our camp; they were well armed with bows and arrows, and some had guns, they were daily expecting an attack by the Pawnees, whom they but a short time ago had made inroads upon, and had massacred at one of their villages a large number of old men, women and children, while the warriors were hunting buffalo." When Frémont passed that way the next year, 1842, the Pawnees had unpleasantly retaliated by demolishing the most accessible Kanzan village (that at the mouth of the Red Vermillion River) and scalping a few representative specimens. This shoved up the Pawnee morale considerably, and the undamaged Kanza survivors accepted calmly the uselessness of doing anything about it until such time as they could catch the Pawnee squaws and children at home alone again.

Although the hard-working missionaries did what they could, they had not overcome the evil effects of the unscrupulous men who went out to get rich at the Indians' expense by unfair trading and who had permanently warped many of them into a few extracurricular bad habits of which they previously had been unaware. The white man's whisky, for which they had an inordinate appetite, had brought many to complete ruin; and the white man's diseases, against which they had built up no resistance, practically wiped out whole tribes and left them at the mercy of their enemies.

Until well into the fifties, the Indians east of the Rockies made little organized opposition to the migrations; and the emigrant was looked upon variously as anything from an unwelcome intruder who was running off the indispensable buffalo, to a generally harmless source of bright mirrors, calico, little tin horns, and stolen horses. The tribes just west of the frontier, who received more attention from the government and who did less hunting, had nothing to lose by the advent of the prairie schooner and soon came to regard the yearly migration as more or less in the nature of a meal ticket. The Indians farther west, such as the Sioux, the Crow, and the Cheyenne, were friendly or hostile at various times in accordance with the current policy of their chieftains. The Shoshone, or Snakes, were almost affectionate. Up to and including the first few years of the gold rush, no successful attempt had been made to Christianize or civilize the Indians found along the California trail anywhere west of Kansas, and the Oregonians traveled fifteen hundred miles before reaching the circle of influence emanating from the northwestern missionaries. The last nucleus of Christian ministry was the Catholic outpost at St. Mary's some twenty-odd miles northwest of the "Frenchman's ferry."

A Catholic college now occupies the site where, from the year 1848, stood the mission to the Pottawatomies. A kindly old priest let me examine and sketch the framed picture of the original building which hangs inconspicuously at the end of a long dark hall. The drawing shows a little L-shaped log structure with a sharply pointed cupola containing a bell at the east end. The wigwams of its parishioners often clustered about it, and the whole ensemble was adjacent to the old overland road where the creaking wagon columns filed past.

The main problem now presented for the company leaders to worry about was the deeply cut prairie creeks. In 1849 the emigrants struggled with them as a matter of course. By June of 1850 the canny Pottawatomies had bridged three that we know about and charged toll. Adding this outlay to the Kansas ferry fare, which was in the neighborhood of five dollars a wagon, it was plain that the spare stock of cash was dribbling away at what was to many an alarming rate. In some ways the pioneers would be relieved to be among Indians who were not quite so civilized.

On the second day after leaving the Kansas bottoms, the wagons brought up short on the perpendicular bank of the Red Vermillion just above the confluence of its tributary, Rock Creek. Why it should have such a cheerful name is beyond my comprehension—it being a perfect serpent of a river, narrow, dark, and opaque at the bottom of its deep-gouged ravine. This stream flows into the Kansas and should not be confused with the Black, or Big Vermillion—a tributary of the Big Blue, which the wagons negotiated within the next day or two.

A noticeable rift in my otherwise sweet disposition is due entirely to the maddening habit of using the same name again and again, so characteristic of early travelers. Three Big Blue rivers in three different states confuse the issue for would-be students of trail geography—practically any number of Sandy rivers and uncounted Rock springs. Apparently they went on the premise that if a name had given uniform satisfaction before, it would again.

At any rate, there were two Vermillions and the emigrants had now arrived at the first one, marking a very definite stage in their progress. It was the generally acknowledged boundary between the Pottawatomies and the Pawnees. The former were a known quantity—the Pawnees, never!

Guard duty at night was now a necessity. No one liked it, and very few were efficient, but nevertheless the hours were divided into watches and each able-bodied man took his turn. This was never an idle precaution. Even when the Pawnees were friendliest, they manifested a guileless interest in their white brothers' horseflesh resulting in an occasional nocturnal raid. At one of these crises the safety of the entire wagon train rested with the guard who was watching the horses, and he— poor man—was only too apt to be a peaceful soul who had never been used to firearms. As uneasy night followed weary day, each unwilling watcher with the grazing horses found himself the only waking soul within speaking distance. Except during gold-rush years he was practically alone in the limitless prairie night. "A few glimmering fires around the camps of distant emigrants, and the almost incessant howl of wolves, were the only things which showed aught living upon the ocean of grass." The bolder spirits among the wolves crowded close—their eyes showing like coals in the sooty shadows—and, probably in indignation at finding no doorstep, snarled and snapped so that the impact of their teeth could be plainly heard.

Besides having a doubtful charm, this serenade kept the weary animals restless; and their constant milling and stamping blurred the fancied sounds for which the watcher listened with his scalp prickling. Not that he ever really heard it! When the Pawnees came they made no noise. But how was he to judge? He had never met a stalking Pawnee outside a nightmare. The grass rustled! A twig cracked! In a frozen agony of fright and indecision he fired at a nonexistent Indian and probably killed a blaze-faced steer.

Instantly the camp was in an uproar. But very few laughed at such seriocomic incidents. It was all too certain that on some future watch (and each man fancied that it might be his own) something would stir in the shadows: a menace, the more terrifying because unseen, that would turn the inside of his throat hot and his hands cold; until finally naked bodies, like slipping shadows, would materialize from out the darkness— painted faces that would be no nightmare figment of his imagination, but stark reality—and the dreaded moment would have come. Struggling in a smother of uncertainty he would shoot and quite possibly *be* shot.

Night guards.

Almost all trail diaries recount some such incident—if not in their own party, then in another which they met. If the guard shot in time the Indians slipped away; but if the foremost Pawnee reached the horses and unloosed them the story was different. It was seldom that the emigrants got them all back, and the attempt was very dangerous.

The pioneers now found the novelty of living in wagons wearing thin. Their store of delicacies from home was gone, and they were on unadulterated prairie rations. It was at this stage of the journey that one willing but inexperienced cook prepared rice for his particular "mess" (probably six to ten men) and provided fifty with that welcome change in diet, utilizing the washboiler for the overflow. The unaccustomed traveler was thoroughly tired but not yet inured to hardship, and many were developing colds, rheumatism, and fevers from continued dampness. On the 28th of May in 1844, Clyman wrote: "Billitts of wood oxyokes Saddles and all kinds of matter now Became in requisition to raise our bodies above the water and we spent a verry uncomfortable night in all the forms of moisture short of swiming."

Edwin Bryant, crossing in '46, complained that it rained until the dough was batter and the fire put out. Evidently he wasn't sufficiently persevering, because one of the women in Clyman's party proved that she could cook under any and all conditions. This item appears in Clyman's journal: "here let me say there was one young lady which showed herself worthy of the bravest undaunted poieneer of the west for after having kneaded her dough she watched and nursed the fire and held an umbrella over the fire and her skillit with the greatest composure for near 2 hours and baked bread enough to give us a verry plentifull supper and to her I offer my thanks of gratitude for our last nights repast."

Prairie storms were dangerous as well as uncomfortable. Besides the rain, which fell all at once like a solid thing, there was hail variously described as anywhere from the size of a hen's egg to that of a lemon or peach, occasional bizarre items such as cyclones or waterspouts, and (most dreaded of all) the lightning. Edwin Bryant wrote, semihumorously, that it seemed as if a man couldn't lie down without being drowned, nor stand up for fear of lightning.

Unless the mud which followed was too deep for easy progress, the prairie schooner families had some reason to be grateful for damp ground. It conserved the grass supply. On the occasions when the blossoming prairies basked under a week of continued sunshine, the Pawnee rose to the possibilities of the situation and set fire to last year's grass which rose dry and dead above the pricking green of the new growth. The danger was inconsiderable and could be defeated by well managed backfiring, but it was a definite blow to the fuel supply. With the long dry grass gone there was nothing to burn in the stoves. One at a time they were left behind; the men parting from theirs as good riddance, the women regretfully—if, indeed, they could bear to let them go. Surely somewhere in a journey of two thousand miles, they thought wishfully, they would find wood again. Meanwhile the cooks dug trenches for tiny fires made of anything they had collected during the day. Trees were soon stripped from the stream banks near the crossings and it was necessary to go far afield for anything at all to burn. Branches of trees and small logs were dragged to the road and slung beneath the wagons to be used very sparingly. These precious windfalls, scarce even in '49, were soon gone, and the ravaged creeks left stark and bare.

A few hours' drive beyond the Red Vermillion, the wagons arrived at the valley of the Black, or Big, Vermillion. E. A. Tompkins wrote that, when they entered its confines on May 30, 1850, they unknowingly drove directly between the invading forces of the Pottawatomies to the south and the resisting Pawnee braves to the north. A war had broken out, but how could the travelers be expected to know where it would be encountered? As ignorant of the danger as children, they blundered calmly along. Suddenly some one found a scalped Pawnee in a ravine beside the road. He was quite dreadfully dead. The bloody tonsure and slit throat gave them cause for thought but there was no guarantee that it would be any safer to turn back, so they scurried anxiously along, following the fresh tracks of the wagons ahead. A detachment of Pottawatomies stalked speechlessly through their line of march. They had a Pawnee prisoner draped about the shoulders with a wolfskin and wearing nothing else but a rawhide knife girdle. No doubt he envied his former comrade whose life blood was soaking so peacefully into the bottom of the dark ravine.

In half an hour the real war began, and the crack of rifles, whine of bullets, and whir of arrows filled the air. Still no one paid the slightest attention to the emigrant families who scuttled along on the thin edge of the battle. Afterward they heard that the Pottawatomies were victorious.

Father De Smet held that the tribes of the Kaw region were better fighters than the Pawnee, and he was probably right, as Henry Stine, who was traveling very close to Mr. Tompkins, wrote that five mounted Pottawatomies chased eight Pawnee right through their line of wagons at top speed and killed one just beyond.

Never a dull moment! And yet Henry, who was very young and traveling alone, wished mightily that he had stayed at home.

Fighting with the victors was a number of young Americans who had been relieved of some extra horses by the Pawnee, and who wished to recover them. It was quite excusable but nevertheless *not* conducive to a perfect understanding with the Pawnee Nation, and probably the next white party, to whom it could give adequate attention, suffered accordingly.

At the Black Vermillion, or rather just before arriving at its precipitous banks, the Forty-niners and those who came after them had a choice of routes. The early travelers, including such famous companies as Frémont's, Jesse Applegate's "Cow Column," and the Donner Party, turned left, went roughly north for five or six miles and then angled off to the northwest, crossed Mosquito Creek and forded the Big Blue River (the famous one) near the confluence of Alcove Spring Creek. This ford was called the Independence Crossing, in all likelihood to distinguish it from the crossing at Marysville, Kansas, used by those who did *not* come from Independence. The latter was necessitated by the great crowds coming across the prairies from St. Joseph, a favorite river port of the gold seekers. In '49 a new trail was blazed from the Black Vermillion up the east side of the Big Blue to Marysville so that the travelers from Independence might, if they chose, short-cut to the St. Jo road and use its crossing.

We found the second Vermillion to be of the same general type as the first, oozy and odorous, lying incredibly far below its ancient, one-way bridge.

We leaned over the railing and caught the reek of the steaming eddies. "They needed an elevator here instead of a boat," I said.

"It wouldn't be half so far down in spring flood time," Dr. Neff gave as his opinion. "But what an impossible thing to get a wagon across! A raft would be of no use at all. It's like a big crack with water in the bottom instead of a river."

"At that, it's a fair example of the prairie streams," my husband reminded him. "They were the worst hazard the emigrants had to face until they encountered the Pawnee."

We started for the Independence Crossing. Information was almost impossible to get. No one was outdoors who could find a cool cellar to sit in. According to the evening newspapers, the mercury soared to 118 that afternoon, an all-time peak for the locality, and the world had retired to the privacy of the nearest bathtub.

In Blue Rapids we sighted a crew of surveyors who had laid off from work and invaded the courthouse lawn. It was a big piece of luck, because it is doubtful if ten people in town could have given the directions which they mapped out for us as a matter of course.

About six miles out of Blue Rapids we looked for and found the ranch of Mr. Arthur McNew and thankfully took refuge in his living room. All that we asked was permission to go to the ford and to Alcove Spring Creek; but when our hostess found that we had come so very far to see these places, and that time did not permit us to find a shady spot and droop for the rest of the afternoon, she commenced very efficiently to plan. It was finally decided that Mr. McNew should go with us to be sure that we made no mistake.

We got into the car and turned into a struggling wood lane that traversed a hilly field. Where the gradually thickening growth finally engulfed our road, we left the car and walked. The muggy smell of hot, wilting leaves and scarcely dried mud filtered through the undergrowth as we picked our way down a shady incline toward the bottom of a swale.

Part way down the slope, under a tree whose trunk and wide spread of limb were ragged with age, our guide stopped.

"What does this place look like to you?" he inquired of all concerned.

I'll confess it didn't look like anything in particular to me, but my husband had already stopped to run an exploring finger around the base of a rather ordinary rock at the foot of the tree.

"A grave!" he replied with conviction. And there really was little doubt that the rough, tablet-shaped rock, so deep-set in the earth, had been put there with a pick and shovel. Smaller rocks some five feet distant seemed to mark the foot of the grave; and its situation on a slope under an old tree, near a well known emigrant camp, also bore out the theory.

"There must be any number of people buried around here," Dr. Neff said. "Lots of the emigrants who came this way camped before they crossed the river."

"I wonder if this could be Grandma Keyes' grave," I hazarded. "Edwin Bryant was in her party, and he wrote quite a bit about the funeral. It must have been just about here."

"Who was *she?*" asked Bill. "I thought you said everybody was young on the trail. Well, of course, not everybody—but most of them."

"That was true of the gold rush," his father corrected. "This happened in '46. Mrs. Keyes was the mother-in-law of James Reed, one of the leaders of the Donner Party. Do you remember how they marked her grave?" he asked.

As it happened, I didn't; but we looked it up later and discovered that they had "graved" an inscription on the headstone and also on a large oak which overhung it. Our oak was old enough but was guiltless of any "graving." It was called to our attention the next day that John Ellenbecker of Marysville has located her grave beyond much doubt, and that it lies in the open.

Those who are familiar with the tragic story of the Donner Party remember that this brave little lady of seventy, being told that she had only a few months to live, decided to spend them prodigally and insisted on starting west with her daughter. A specially constructed wagon with a door in the side was obtained for her; she was comfortably installed with her rocking chair and set forth as bravely as the rest. Much later in our field work—in Utah, to be exact—we encountered portions of this wagon.

The Big Blue was in flood when the Donner Party reached it, and they camped to build a clumsy catamaran raft of two cottonwood logs, grooved to hold the wagon wheels; thus gentle Grandma Keyes was enabled to die quietly, as she would have wished, without delaying the caravan.

The river carries a heavy current when it floods, and Mr. McNew said that there had been a spell of high water recently, during which even Alcove Spring Creek had run ten feet deep.

"We're too high up on the slope to see the effects yet," he said. "They put the graves high on purpose. That's why the emigrants who kept to the trail never saw a tenth of them. There are several other rocks up here that look like markers, but none I could swear to. This rock is rough," he continued, stooping and laying his hand on a rough fragment, "but I'm sure it was meant for a headstone. It was the best they could find, probably."

Yes, everything connected with a funeral on the Emigrant Road was makeshift—just the best they could do; and yet, standing at this particular grave of the Unknown Emigrant lying alone near the banks of the Big Blue, we felt that it did not need clipped lawns and decorations of briefly beautiful flowers to compel respectful attention. Shafts of light where the sun struck down through the greenery above and festooned its rude and inscriptionless headstone with wreaths of living sunshine were memorial tokens from the heavens themselves unchanged by passing years.

A secretive little path led down from the graves, ducking under broken and crackling shrubbery but politely skirting the great swaggering nettles. At the foot of the slope, we came to the recently dried bed of Alcove Spring Creek, steamy and unpleasantly suggestive of sink drains. We turned into it and followed its windings upstream. I picked my way gingerly, with a wary eye out for snakes or other discomforts, and soon came to the head of a tiny box canyon which ended in the peculiar formation known as the "alcove."

It looks like an old-fashioned seashell bandstand, being a structure of rotten sandstone of which each successive stratum overhangs a few inches out and beyond its supporting neighbor. The upper lip, over which the creek descends in an abrupt fall, is level with the field that surrounds the little gully. It was plain that in flood time quite a volume of water descended. This was emphasized by the great fragments of broken rock which had been torn loose and were cluttered in the dried mud of the stream bed below the alcove.

To the right, just above where the big bass drum used to be in the bandstand, was a clean-cut opening in the rock from which trickled a stream of clear water.

"There's Alcove Spring," said Mr. McNew and stepped briskly toward it.

Of course we sampled the water. It was cool and good. Then, obeying Mr. McNew's directions, we climbed up the side of the gully, or tiny box canyon, and walked out on the lip of the fall.

Edwin Bryant wrote: "We named this the 'Alcove Spring': and future travelers will find the name graven on the rocks." He was right. We found it carved deeply and well in letters around eight inches high just above the brink of the fall.

"Whoever did that job certainly got ahead of the bunch that called every hole in the ground 'Emigrant Springs,'" said Bill, recalling the titles that clutter maps of the western states. "When he named anything, it stayed named. I wonder who did it?"

At the time no one could answer; but we later found, among the manuscript diaries at the Bancroft Library in Berkeley, California, a small notebook. It had been handwritten in 1846 by George M. McKinstry. The notation for Saturday May 30, read in part: "About a half mile from camp up the spring branch on the right hand fork is a most beautiful

Carvings at Alcove Spring.

spring and a fall of water 12 feet. Mr. Bryant of our party has named it the 'Alcove Spring.' . . . I this day cut the name of the spring in the rock on table at the top of the falls."

"There's a story that George Donner carved his name somewhere around here," said Mr. McNew, "but, although I've looked carefully, I can't find it. Here's something interesting though. Look here."

A rock as large as the top of our car lay in the stream bed. It had plainly been part of the visor of the alcove but had fallen out in some long-gone winter and had been buried under a coating of mud and, presumably, other fragments. Sometime in the last few years, a heavy flood had cleaned it off. Firmly carved, large letters showed upon its surface, "J. F. Reed—26 May—1846."

"There's Reed's name, just as he carved it," Mr. McNew said. "That's what I wanted you to see."

After a while we walked down to the Independence Crossing of the Big Blue, using for a pathway the bed of Alcove Spring Creek. We walked in dense and comforting shadow, for the belt of timber that lines the Big Blue is really extraordinary for the prairies. Sycamores, elms and hackberries were there, and oaks too, with notched leaves as long as my arm from wrist to elbow.

Except under abnormal conditions the camp site under these old trees was an oasis, comfortable and even luxurious with fresh-water clams from the river, berries from the woods and even wild honey from an occasional bee tree. Given the added fillip of a pretty girl or two, it became a treasured memory to the "army of boys" who traveled west. It may well be stressed, just here, that the bulk of the gold migration was young—splendidly, adventurously, pitifully young, the average age being estimated as less than twenty-five years; and nothing short of a comprehensive avalanche could have prevented a certain amount of love-making.

Here at the Big Blue where the evening camps smelled pungently of wood smoke; where the declining sun distilled the nostalgic fragrance of wild grape, renewing memories and fostering hope; where the prying moon rose two hours high before it got so much as a peep at the camps within the perfumed woods—here romance flourished. Many and many a lifelong comradeship was blossoming by the time the river was crossed at last and the wagons moved on into the shimmering distances ahead.

5

The Road from Old St. Jo

OUR FIRST IMPRESSION on entering Marysville was of a motley assortment of red brick buildings erupting into a perfect rash of outdoor stairways. A low brick wall broken by a lion-guarded gate crouched at one side of the street while, ahead of us, the clock in front of the funeral parlor was suitably dead. There was no need for time today. No one was keeping appointments.

Marysville was the direct result of a route surveyed from Fort Leavenworth to Salt Lake City in 1849 by Lieutenant Stansbury. At this point he was concerned mainly with locating an easy ford across the Big Blue. The town sprang up unbidden; its small board shacks mushroomed amongst the hurly-burly of wagons camped at the crossing, and its first citizens lived by the traffic of the trail.

Our routine visit to the courthouse ended in disappointment. The original surveys had been removed. So far they had been available at each county seat, and we had come to depend on them. This time we assembled instead a topographic map, a modern county map and an ancient affair in a massive frame which hung immovably on the wall, but the most intense and persevering scrutiny failed to give us any inkling of tomorrow's route. I must say that the people in the county offices delved quite passionately into the problem of finding something for us to do farther down the road, but exactly where to do it remained unsolved. Finally some one suggested Mr. J. G. Ellenbecker as the possible answer to our unusual needs, and we set out for his ranch just beyond the town. We had heard of him before, in fact had read a book or two of his authorship on trail subjects, so that we felt the utmost confidence in his ability to put us on the right track. In the end we left his house equipped with the data necessary to locate the important landmarks for many miles ahead and very detailed information as to the whereabouts of the junction of the Independence Road with the road from St. Joseph, Missouri.

It seems to me that the time has come to deal firmly with the just-mentioned "St. Jo Road," as its importance to the emigrants of '49 and the fifties can hardly be overestimated. It began in the city of that name and ended just west of Marysville at the much-described junction.

In the beginning St. Joseph was the pet project of Joseph Robidoux, one of the six Robidoux brothers of pioneer and fur-trading fame. He commissioned two men to submit plans for the city. One of them presented a drawing which he had titled St. Joseph after the patron saint of his employer. Both plan and name appealed to Robidoux—and St. Joseph it became. It was only natural that it should be a favorite take-off for the overland trail, for it lay a full two-day steamer journey from Independence, up the Missouri toward the mouth of the Platte, every mile of which was an advantage. In addition it was considered to be seventy miles farther west—or about four days' steady travel by ox team.

The emigrant camps at St. Joseph during the gold rush were fully as congested and as picturesque as those already described at Independence. In spite of this emigrants often sent their womenfolk as far as the river ports by steamer, mistakenly imagining that they would be more comfortable on the boat than trekking overland with the wagons. And so, in the spring of 1852, we find two young wives traveling up the Missouri some three days apart. Both of them were interesting women and will be frequently mentioned and quoted. The first, Lucy Rutledge Cooke, with her baby, began her voyage on the steamer *Pontiac;* but it inconsiderately sank, luggage and all, and she, with the other passengers, spent a day on the bank in the wet woods until a passing boat picked them up. At the nearest landing it turned back and they were put ashore again. The next steamer accepted them, or rather graciously allowed them to remain in its company; but, as it was very full, the men had to keep pace with it along the bank. By this time Lucy's baby was sick, and she was allowed the doubtful privilege of remaining aboard. Lodisa Frizzell got along better on her steamer but, upon arrival at St. Joseph, found that she had out-arrived. She could find no lodgings and was forced to cross on the ferry and camp on the west bank of the river, herded in with hundreds of distanced her husband and would be alone in the town until his company brusque and uninterested strangers—just a small, uneasy unit of the tremendous migration. Unless she became ill she would come to no actual harm, but difficulties—big ones—would have to be faced alone.

The first annoyance came promptly as some two hundred Indians, Pottawatomies and Winnebagos, came down the river. They had thirty or forty small ponies almost invisible under enormous loads to which were added excrescences composed of chickens, papooses, dogs, puppies, and infirm Indians. They were in a hurry, and the ferry could take only a few at a time, whereupon the old squaws retaliated by bestowing freely upon the ferrymen epithets of the most staggering frankness, which a trapper, who happened to be near by, interpreted for the delectation of the crowd. A fat puppy, struggling on top of a load, howled. An Indian calmly shot it with a blunt arrow and threw it into the river. It was a coarse and callous atmosphere for a lonely woman. Night was but little better. One of the braves died; the mourning Indians howled until daylight, as was their custom, and there was little sleep for any one.

In a few days she got lodgings at a private home, and put a letter in the post office for her husband to claim when he should arrive, telling where she might be found. The letter was nailed on the door, and each successive day more letters were nailed on top of it. When Mr. Frizzell finally arrived in St. Joseph there was no one at the post office who knew anything about the mail, and he hunted distractedly through the town, almost from house to house, without any word of his wife. The next morning in desperation he went to the post office again, saw the collection of epistles nailed to the door, and tore every one off until he came to hers. Within the hour she was established in the wagon train.

There was also (in the late fifties) a steam train into the town. The line was the Hannibal & St. Joseph Railroad, and the emigrants sometimes apprehensively entrusted it with their livestock—hastily opening the cars immediately upon arrival to see if the animals had survived. So far we have found no evidence that they ever submitted their wives to its tender mercies.

St. Joseph was not, during the peak of the western migration, quite as well established as Independence. The home from which Lodisa was so gladly rescued was doubtless a typical frontier establishment. W. W. Wixom wrote: "The inhabitance of the state of Missouria They generaly have small farms two or three negroes one or two wenches a half dozen mules and one or two saddle hosses for the females. . . . the buildings are generaly log one & two small ones for the negroes situated just behind the masters."

There were many sights and sounds in St. Joseph which were novel to the emigrants. Some had never before seen slaves. Some had never slept in rooms topped with calico ceilings which bellied in each puff of breeze. Some had never thought to see women brazenly attired in bloomers. Some had never seen Indians naked—or nearly so. "Their uniforms were neat but not gaudy," wrote Lydia Waters, "a breech-clout and moccasins. They did not approve of water—used instead the entrails of some small fat animal, a skunk or raccoon, which looked as if it were dried in the smoke. They were dirty and took the greatest comfort lying in the sun rubbing themselves with these greasy insides, I don't know where they kept them except in the breech-clout."

And so the emigrants waited at St. Joseph just as at any other river port, buying, selling, sightseeing, writing, gambling, marveling, anticipating, dreading—each according to his nature—until at last they were organized and ready to start. And here they came upon a factor that did not have to be faced at Independence. They must get their wagons across the Missouri.

By repeated inquiries we found the site of the old ferry landing at the foot of Francis Street. St. Joseph was decidedly overmodest and had apparently given no thought to the possibility that some one might find its eventful past interesting. We were most courteously received, but neither the Chamber of Commerce nor the Public Library was equipped to give us any help. We located most of the places of historical interest with the aid of information already in our possession. Where Francis Street ended we left the car, crossed the railroad tracks on foot, and brought up on the river bank under a frowzy and discouraged tree.

"I'd hate to cross here with the river full of logs and big chunks of ice," remarked Dr. Neff, recalling its occasional unworthy conduct in early spring.

"Well, you can count me out any time—especially now," I told him. (I'm not fond of water in bulk, and the Missouri impressed me as needlessly large.)

"It does look quite a bit like a young ocean," my husband agreed absent-mindedly. "Just imagine making your favorite horse try to swim it—or a good old milch cow."

A moment passed while I seemed to see tiny, bobbing heads far away, struggling against the remorseless current.

"The ferry must have landed about here," continued my husband thoughtfully, "and, right where we are standing, the driver who held the next number to be called waited his turn."

"Ezra Meeker wrote," I educated them relentlessly from my notes, "that the collection of wagons waiting for the ferry looked like a great white flatiron with its point to the river."

"Yes, and what did the ferry look like?"

" 'A small flat-boat,' " I read, " 'made of hewn timbers and powered by huge sweeps.' Thought I wouldn't have it, didn't you? What are sweeps?"

"Immense oars. A man stood up and used both hands and all his muscle on just one of them. Take a few minutes, and see whether they ever ferried the cattle, will you?"

The river refracted the noon sun and hurt my eyes. I moved to shade them, sat down, and commenced hunting through the notes which had been brought along—a typical medley compressed into a fat loose-leafed binder in which no one else can ever find anything, and I have to be very lucky to turn up what I want. Bill calls it the Paden Encyclopedia.

"It doesn't seem as if they did," I remarked midway of my search. "Here's the diary of a man who says that they tried twice to swim the cattle in the middle of the day, and the glare confused them so that they swam in a circle for hours and at length came back to the east side again. Finally they guessed what was the matter, and the next time started them in the early evening when they could see the opposite shore. They tied an active young steer to a boat and towed him across. The others followed without any trouble."

"Say," interrupted Bill, "did you know that Robidoux named all the streets in St. Joseph after his kids? The officer up there says so."

"He must have had plenty of children," Dr. Neff said dryly.

"Well, the officer says so, anyway, and this is Francis Street. I guess he named them that way as long as the supply lasted." Irresistibly Bill was moved to rejoin the informative officer of the law.

"Large families must have been fashionable," my husband volunteered. "One of the mountain men that the emigrants encountered in St. Joseph bragged that he had over a hundred half-breed children between the Missouri River and the Rockies."

I ignored him and found another item: "Here's a woman who writes that the men stripped the wheels off their wagons and fitted the beds on a raft. They piled the wheels in next to the wagons, and she and the other women sat on the floor, wherever they could squeeze in, and prayed that a floating log wouldn't hit them. These people had seventy wagons, and each time they went across they towed a bunch of cattle behind the raft. She says here," I went on, "that the men watched like hawks in order to cut the cattle loose if they got tangled up in anything. It was better to lose them than to tip the raft. They couldn't cross in a high wind either, and sometimes that held them up for days."

At the bottom of the page I found the incident I had been looking for. "Here you are," I called to my husband who, having succeeded in getting me to work, had withdrawn slightly, the better to enjoy himself. "Here's a case where they definitely had stock on the ferry. Not that it worked out very well," I added to myself as my eye glanced on to the end of the paragraph. "It's from Ezra Meeker's book, 'Ox-Team Days on the Oregon Trail': 'I saw a third victim go under the drift of a small island within sight of his shrieking wife. The stock had rushed to one side of the boat, submerging the gunwale, and had precipitated the whole load into the dangerous river.'"

"There's your answer," Dr. Neff said. "No wonder they swam them."

I got up and looked across the majestic sweep of mighty waters. A flatboat of a size to carry a wagon, or even two, would look in comparison with its vastness, like an overgrown graham cracker; and it seemed to me that before I exposed my person, of which I am rather careful, to such an experience, I should have another try at getting along in my home town.

The St. Jo road actually commenced on the west bank of the Missouri at Ellwood, and, utilizing what was later known as the old creek road, proceeded to Mosquito Creek, where the wagons often nooned. It was on this stretch of road that Lodisa Frizzell saw a grave topped with a pathetic feather bed for the two small children of the dead couple who now slept under a cold blanket of earth. As no one wished to return with the two small incumberers of the earth, they were entrusted to an old Indian chief to take back to St. Joseph. In all likelihood he performed his obligation, for most tribes were notoriously fond of children and spoiled their own greasy offspring prodigiously.

After Mosquito Creek the toiling caravans passed, in staging days, an important home station called at first Kickapoo Agency and later Kenne-kuk Station in honor of chief Kennekuk of the Kickapoo. The military road from Fort Leavenworth to Fort Kearney joined the Oregon Trail at Kennekuk, and all travelers proceeded together to Wolf Creek where they camped. They found here a rude log bridge floored with poles guarded by the Sac and Fox Indians, and toll was collected by friendly but firm braves who looked (so one woman wrote) ten feet high. The very moderate price was twenty-five cents. Every one used the bridge and begrudged the money verbosely in his or her diary. Near by was the old stone mission to the Kickapoo, which could be seen for miles in all directions and was surrounded by cultivated farm lands. Many of the emigrants blamed their vanished coin on the business acumen of the white missionaries; but others, watching the imperturbable Sac and Fox playing cards in the intervals of collecting two-bit pieces, figured that they were quite capable of thinking it up for themselves.

The wagons, starting early after an uneasy night, passed the mission and kept the divide between Wolf and Walnut creeks to the north and Cedar Creek to the south, moving on toward the crossing of the Nemaha. They reckoned this as fifty-seven miles from the toll bridge, a three-day trip. On this stretch they crossed small muddy gullies on brush fills, breasted continuous wind of almost hurricane proportions, cooked in their small stoves with wild-pea grass and killed an unbelievable number of rattlesnakes. From the Nemaha, which was steep-banked but not hard to ford unless in flood, it was nearly forty miles through Pawnee territory to the Big Blue.

It is astonishing that the people of the Pawnee Nation were not more openly hostile, for they had been real sufferers from the approach of civilization. Smallpox had so decimated them that they were left easy victims to the Sioux, and they sadly missed the old abundance of buffalo. They were thieves, though, and tried to make up in emigrant biscuit and bacon what they lacked in big game. One of their most upsetting activities was the habit of arriving without warning. When least expected the river greenery would erupt Pawnees to an indefinite extent. A band of two hundred is oftenest mentioned, but the writer of one journal saw (or thought he saw) two thousand. Sometimes a chieftain made definite demands in return for unmolested passage through his country. The small trains paid. The larger caravans sometimes displayed their weapons to good advantage—guns, pistols, knives, each man wearing ostentatiously all that he had—and marched straight through. They were not stopped but probably paid "through the nose" later in loss of stock.

Sometimes a blanketed Pawnee arrived bearing a note which he proudly displayed as a guarantee of good character. As often as not the treasured note read in effect: "Look out for him. He is a thief and a liar." Almost invariably he had come to beg. Food and tobacco were the wants to which he gave voice, although guns, whisky, and horses were to the Pawnee, as to all the tribes, the ultimate desire. Certain policies and rules of behavior toward the Indians gradually became understood. It was considered expedient to feed them and to furnish them with medicine and trinkets, but never under any circumstances to give them liquor or firearms. In regard to horses there was an unfortunate laxity. All Indians were particularly proud to be seen on an American horse, the bigger the better, and would readily exchange two ponies for one. The stringy toughness of their ponies made this offer rather tempting to travelers whose more pampered horseflesh was beginning to give out, and some horses were traded. The practice was always more or less frowned upon, however, as it was highly desirable that a white man should be better mounted than an Indian. His life often depended on the fact that in a chase the Indian could not catch him.

With all this in mind the emigrants eyed the visiting Pawnee, and the Pawnee eyed the guns and horses. Meanwhile food and "tobac" was produced, and the red men settled down to remain as long as the white men stayed in that particular camp. Sometimes, if it suited their convenience, the tribe refused to leave, and traveled with them a day, or even several. The braves, who of course had nothing whatsoever to do, dismounted and settled themselves about the emigrants' fires as soon as they were built. The squaws came, in chattering groups, whenever they could find time. The vocabulary of all trail Indians was simple and to the point, being chosen from words of which they had the greatest need or had heard pronounced with most vigor: tobac, whisky, woman, swap, how-do, and a variety of profanity. One well intentioned old Indian managed to convey through a medley of sign language and broken English that there was good grass ahead for the whoa-haws but no clean water where the God-damns could camp.

Pawnees, both men and women, had abysmal appetites, and the store blankets in which they were wont to wrap themselves had an amazing capacity for stolen articles. They ate with great earnestness and simplicity when food was proffered, cleaning up such comestibles as rancid bacon and sour beans, and, if refused further supplies, helped themselves with calm deliberation. It was a temptation to let them have their loot and save possible trouble; but in this the emigrants had to consider their public. The saving of face was of the utmost importance. The Indians carried on a sort of contemptuous horseplay which ceased if it must, but got worse by the minute if allowed. They had to be strongly and continuously resisted. They must never be allowed to consider themselves masters of the situation, even though they knew, and the white man knew, that he couldn't get rid of them. It was a sort of game, and those trains fared better which were under the guidance of mountaineers or frontiersmen adept at playing it.

The trail Indians as a rule did not resent being handled forcefully. A man might safely wrench his gun from a pilfering young Indian's hands and whack him over the head with it. In fact the tribe had nothing but contempt for an emigrant who failed to do so; young braves drawing their bows as an impudent gesture were disarmed with impunity and a ten-foot ox whip, but woe betide the man who unexpectedly injured the dignity of a warrior with a reputation to uphold.

We have never been students of Indian customs and are only giving the point of view of the trail journalists; but there seems to have been a wide gulf between the headstrong young fry, who presumably had no dignity to injure, and the wise men, elders, and chieftains. These latter might demand tribute in person, but they are not commonly recorded as coming to beg. They often, it is said, counseled good conduct and moderation in dealing with the Americans, and less often enforced it, and a tribe traveling under the personal supervision of its chief was always, in peacetime, much safer to meet than scattered bands of young braves.

A chief saved an emigrant boy who had furiously followed his stolen horse into the Pawnee village—and even returned the horse; while a group of women and children casually called on the squaws once during the absence of both sets of husbands. The red husbands were, it seems, just ahead of the paler ones and were accompanied by most of the latter's horses, but the squaws were hospitable. Great kettles of savory meat were stewing and those ladies less allergic to dirt than others accepted chunks.

What the pale (very pale) husbands said when they got back is no part of this sober history.

So much for the Pawnee Nation, contradictory, unpredictable—in whose domain the emigrants were to spend the next two or three weeks.

Forty miles west of the Nemaha the rolling caravans found shade at last in the dense line of forest that edged the east bank of the Big Blue. Here was a large city of tents, dancing each evening, and preaching on Sunday. It was seldom that the same tent remained two nights or that the listening trees vibrated twice to the notes of the same violin. Only when the river flooded did the buzzing, busy emigrants have time to get acquainted. During a normal stop there was so much in the way of accumulated work, washing, mending, and baking for the women, harness repairing, animal doctoring, and wagon mending for the men, that if they got an extra minute they were glad to throw themselves down and rest. Only the young people and the men who were responsible for the well-being of the train moved about among the wagons. The young folks in the age-old search of youth for youth—the wagon bosses, or captains, to exchange opinions and anxieties with men of other trains.

And here in the crowded camp, among the other activities of camp duties, love-making, cholera, etc., Fate threw in for good measure a few vigorous cases of measles. Measles on damp ground, buffeted by a cold wind, dieted on bacon and beans, minus medicine and minus proper nursing, led almost inevitably to a sad conclusion.

Those unknown men, dead of measles, whose forgotten graves are somewhere in Marysville, under cottage, busy street, or in the corner of some one's garden, those poor fellows paid a high price for a few weeks' adventure. They must have thought with regret of the security of home and the comfort of loving care, realizing with a quick shuddering panic that, in the tremendous surge of moving humanity, one death made little difference.

*   *   *

Here at Marysville the travelers from St. Joseph merged with that part of the traffic from Independence, Missouri, which had continued up the east bank of the Big Blue. They all forded at one place in an indistinguishable mass and went on six miles to the next point of interest, the junction of the St. Jo Road with the one which came swinging up from the Independence Crossing.

We left the historic stream lying in uncommunicative silence among its yesterdays, and started west for the first time since crossing the Kansas.

How in the world were we to locate any road at all—let alone a junction—in the midst of the interminable grain fields which lay west of the river? No track seemed possible to follow in this modern, cultivated section.

I have always maintained that it would be helpful if some one could paint the country to match the maps. It sounded businesslike to be on our way to the northwest corner of Section 19 of Logan Township, but it was a little difficult to accomplish in a district planted so heavily to grain.

The sky above us was luminous and milky, crinkled with skimmings of vapor. A hawk wheeled, black against its eye-stinging luster. In the west great piles of sullen clouds still held promise of a storm before evening, and catapulting grasshoppers clattered against the body of the car with the irrational urgency of popping corn.

For fifteen minutes we counted miles, and then came to the designated crossroad where we turned north. In one-half mile we bisected the old trail from Independence Crossing which was running northwest. In another mile we crossed the St. Jo Road going due west to meet it. The famous intersection occurs in a field within a hundred yards of the county line. It is probably not more than six miles in an air line from Marysville.

We crossed a spread of recently cut stubble which had evidently been storing up heat all day for the generous purpose of letting us have it now. The marks of great wheels were plainly visible through the short-cut stalks. Even when the crops are high, Mr. Ellenbecker had told us, the path of the wagons may be faintly discerned because of the different color and density of the wheat.

Straight west to this point came the caravans from St. Joseph. Converging to meet them, the drivers could see the crowds from Independence— a melee of flapping canvas, bobbing horsemen, and gleaming steel moving northwest over the curling prairie horizon. Horace Greeley wrote: ". . . the white coverings of the many emigrant and transport wagons dotted the landscape, giving the trail the appearance of a river running through great meadows with many ships sailing in its bosom." From here the two roads were one, stretching endlessly over the shallow swells and swales, high under the Kansas sky to where the declining sun, apparently loath to grant any surcease of discomfort to the expectant earth, seemed to be exploding into great fiery clouds. And there, ahead of us on the slowly darkening prairie, lay tomorrow's problem, in the vast sunsoaked expanse of Nebraska.

6

The Valley of the Little Blue

EARLY IN THE MORNING, near the town of Hanover, we had our first glimpse of the Little Blue—a small and gentle river, always to be remembered fondly by the westbound families who, except during Indian uprisings, looked forward with happy anticipation to the days in its rolling valley. Wood, water, and grass were plentiful and, best of all, the headwaters lay to the west so that for almost a week's journey the caravans camped cozily side by side on its shady bank. Here, if anywhere, the "Oh, Susannah" quality of the journey across the plains flourished at its inspiriting best.

The presence of a girl or two always noticeably increased the tempo of any gathering, but at the camp sites along the Little Blue it seemed to draw music from the very air. A fiddle, banjo, or possibly a jew's-harp materialized accommodatingly from some near-by camp; a space for dancing apparently cleared itself, and the young men drew in from all directions like bees around a honeypot, for it sometimes happened, during the frenzied rush to California, that, for a thousand miles, a company of men would not set eyes on a white woman. To meet the need of dancing partners handkerchiefs were tied upon the heads of stalwart and protesting teamsters, distinguishing them as "ladies."

Some few trains, graced by one or more girls, had music or dancing whenever they were not too tired to keep awake, and the overland journey to their new home progressed romantically, like a novel by Stewart Edward White. But the sad truth remains that most companies lacked girls and, without that inspiration, were too tired at night to do anything but roll in, leaving the prairie quiet broken only by the stamping and munching of the staked horses and the croaking of a million frogs.

At dawn they shivered out of their blankets, snatched a hasty breakfast, "ketched up" the animals, and the great schooners rolled majestically into line. Each wagon kept a permanent place in the caravan. The one whose turn it was to leave camp first remained in the lead all day, crawling steadily at its tortoise pace over the sunny rolling knolls with the Little Blue purling along at the left. On the following morning it would be relegated to the rear, to work its way forward day by day to the lead position again. Once in motion on the daily trek, the entire wagon train was also supposed to keep its place in the general line-up, pausing if necessary to allow camped trains to cut in. But this unwritten law of the overland road was not always followed; now and then in a favorable spot, a horse or mule train would manage to get by an ox-drawn caval-cade—a proceeding somewhat comparable in difficulty to one auto cara-van of, say, fifty cars passing another of similar size on an extremely bad detour. In addition, the train wishing to pass was hampered by what would now be considered a slow pick-up and the fact that the ox caravan was not obligated by either custom or courtesy to make room for it. Early in the day, although the ox drivers certainly would not aid the process by turning out, they might do nothing to hinder; but, just before camping time or when approaching a ferry, any efforts to pass sent their blood pressure up like a thermometer. The air grew brittle with profanity and the pistol-like crack of the bull-whips, and they would sometimes even lock wheels with their rivals in superb disregard of consequences.

About the last week in May, along the valley of the Little Blue, early-day pioneers were thrilled to the core by encountering the cortege of the returning fur traders. Not, of course, those from the famous yearly ren-dezvous on Green River—*they* would not return until late in the sum-mer. These wagons were from the North Platte country and carried buf-falo hides. They were often found to be the "Robidoux outfit"; and one of the famous brothers sometimes accompanied them, riding comfortably in a special equipage like a potentate. The rest of the concourse consisted of a long line of clumsy, ox-drawn carts piled with stiffened hides. These top-heavy cargoes of greasy wealth had high rounded contours that re-sembled marching elephants—and smelled worse. The piratical aspect of the attendant drivers was not reassuring; but they were generally helpful and willingly gave reports on road conditions, camp grounds, and Indian eccentricities. They also accepted letters (for a stipend) to carry back to the States and the nearest post office—and sometimes mailed them.

The monthly mail wagon to Fort Laramie also interested the home-hungry travelers. The mail wagon itself—slow, solitary, and defenseless—

was gradually replaced by fast Abbot, Downing stagecoaches, convoyed in later years of Indian trouble by eight or ten cavalrymen. The sight of these swaggering vehicles, so lately from civilization, fairly electrified the emigrants as they tore past the plodding teams. The guard, or "messenger," sat on top with the driver and would accept mail if it were tightly wrapped and handed to him by a horseman riding at a gallop—nothing was allowed to slow the stages.

After a regular stage line with relay stations had been established from the Missouri River to the Pacific Coast, the Little Blue Valley was considered by crew and passengers to be the cream of the whole trip. The road was good; the scenery, pleasant and quite diversified in comparison with the monotonous prairie which lay behind them; the stations, comparatively well outfitted; the horses, the best of the line, matched in color and size and spectacular as to speed. Records for fast traveling were continually made and broken along this favorable stretch. The record accepted as unbeatable was fourteen miles in fifty-two minutes, made by a coach and four, carrying twelve passengers and one-half ton of express and mail—a fraction over sixteen miles an hour.

The horses were changed at "line" stations, placed at varying distances according to the difficulty of the road. "Home" stations were reached at noon and night. They served meals and lodged travelers if desired (generally on the floor or dining-room table). Every one slept in his or her clothes, and women seldom were able to obtain any more privacy than the men. In spite (or perhaps because) of these accommodations, it was quite customary for the passengers to travel day and night on the coach, waking in the morning, after a rough night, to find themselves pretty well intermingled. The women, with a limit of thirty pounds of free baggage, usually wore all their clothes; and six or eight petticoats plus a jacket or two came in handy in lieu of a mattress. But one wonders how the lady managed who was discovered to have five flatirons under her crinoline.

The home stations along the Little Blue were especially blessed with farm products—eggs, cream, butter, cheese, and vegetables. Nowhere else along the emigrant road, except at Salt Lake City, were these commodities found. The charm of home-grown viands was somewhat marred for the curious soul who, in wandering about behind the house, saw the chickens roosting for the night on the butchered pig destined to be his morning pork-chops. But hunger was a potent sauce. No doubt he ate the chops and washed them down with coffee, abundant and hot—the unchallenged beverage of the plains.

When, in the spring of '60, the Pony Express was ready to begin operations, the stations had been increased to approximately one every ten or twelve miles; and the very finest of saddle stock was posted along the route. Two thousand miles in two hundred forty hours! What speed! The flying express riders were watched for eagerly, and cheered as they passed. They were described as "of slight build—thinly clad, with hat often hanging down their backs; with bright colored handkerchiefs tied around their foreheads; belts around their waists, and their packages of letters fastened to the saddle tree behind. As they came upon you like a flash, with a yell or cheery laugh, passing you at full speed, one could not help admiring them."

In the summer of '60, the Indians were uneasy. Rumors reached the East and, as a result, the stages (running almost empty of passengers) were accompanied by a "whipper" who rode at a full gallop beside the straining team and plied a blacksnake. Sometimes they were even guarded by soldiers; but the daring express boys, each astride a magnificent horse that the Indians would readily kill ten men to get, rode alone.

For years Marysville, Kansas, marked the end of the truly settled country; but the Little Blue Valley, so charming and so fertile, sheltered a sort of border zone of ranches lying beyond the pale of civilization. It began to be inhabited in the fifties and became more populous as the staging industry formed a life line to hold it to the Missouri, but it paid a dreadful price in '64 when the Indians rose against the white settlers in one terrific onslaught, hoping to drive them out forever. The farms were burned; the families murdered and most fantastically and unprintably mutilated. The historic valley was the center of attention for the whole nation— outraged and aghast.

But, with all their war paint and horrors, the redmen could not stay the inexorable westward drift. The stages were scarcely delayed a week. The dead at the stage stations were buried and replaced by grim-faced newcomers. The destroyed shacks were rebuilt—this time very often of sod which could not burn.

And, through it all, the marching thousands trod the trail—frightened women and desperate men, like a column of ants, never halting or turning aside but blindly facing danger in one of its most terrible forms. Those who perished were buried where they died. The rest, pushing along in companies and possessed by an energy seemingly outside themselves, went on to their ultimate destination through the valley of the Little Blue.

*   *   *

The overland road entered Nebraska at the dividing line between Gage and Jefferson counties, one-time land of the Otoes, self-styled "brothers of the whites." We kept about two miles north of the river, stopping now and then to explore some exceptionally deep wheel ruts, and, when some two miles northeast of Endicott, came to Rock Creek and the site of the old Rock Creek Station.

Here we took referee's time out for consideration of a famous quarrel and to look curiously at the setting of the historic gun fight between David McCanles, owner of the log station building leased to the stage company, and handsome Wild Bill Hickok. The latter was entered on the pay roll of the company under his rightful name, James Butler Hickok, as a stock tender. In the year 1861 Horace Wellman, the station keeper, with his wife and a second stock tender, constituted the rest of the personnel.

The immediate cause of the shooting (on which no two accounts agree) was the arrival of McCanles at the station building, liquored up and belligerent. Encountering Mrs. Wellman at the door, he roughly demanded to see her husband. It would seem that he desired to inform Wellman that the stage company was behindhand in lease payments due him, and that if the company didn't do something about it pretty quick, he would take his indignation out on Wellman. It was not a quiet argument. Hickok stepped to the door to interfere, and two of McCanles' men came running from the barn. It was a perfect setup for the quick gunplay of the day, and when the smoke cleared McCanles and his two men were dead while Hickok still stood in the door. Hickok was tried for murder, acquitted, and spent the remainder of his short and colorful span of life entirely on the side of law and order, first as a Federal spy in the Civil War, then as one of Custer's scouts, and still later, as marshal of Abilene, Kansas, the intractable terminus of the Texas cattle trail, and of other wild and woolly towns of the still impolite west. McCanles, on the other hand, bore a very unenviable reputation.

Fortunately for our own peace of mind we were not, at this late date, trying to prove anything about the case but simply, in the course of the day's work, to see where it all happened. We found a ranch at the site of Rock Creek Station and advanced circumspectly, peering ahead to see if the family were up yet. Of course the dog barked—any self-respecting dog would at the sight of four pussyfooting strangers—and a small boy walked out of the barn to investigate.

He was a newcomer but was already steeped in sanguinary lore and could tell us about each corpse with considerable precision. He had also, with ghoulish small-boy curiosity, asked questions until he had located the former position of the station and the barn with the purpose, I believe, of knowing exactly where the blood had flowed. He walked with us, chattering excitedly, to the edge of the higher land where the corrals had been; and we looked across to a line of heavy, round-topped trees showing the course of Rock Creek. They grew in the very bottom of the watercourse, and only their upper halves appeared above the steep bank like a row of inverted green bowls of assorted sizes. The old road showed plainly as it neared the water, while beyond the crossing the persevering ruts continued westward.

At last, having circled back to the buildings again, we came to a large boulder bedded in weeds and partially shaded by a ragged tree. It loomed harsh and foreign to the ordinary domestic appearance of the farmyard.

The boy waved his hand toward it with an instinctive sense of the dramatic. "And there's McCanles' grave," he said.

There are others buried in these quiet acres, victims of Indian massacre and of thirty years of trail disaster. No doubt spilled blood fertilized the trees under which we stood. The history of Rock Creek is not amusing; its enmities were deadly; its tragedies, profound. I felt the repercussion of their horror as I stood at the grave of the leader of the "McCanles gang" and helped the boy to get his killings straight.

"I wonder if he is historically minded," I whispered to my husband as the youngster turned to speak to Dr. Neff. "Or does all his interest center in the shooting?"

"Oh, he's just the bloodthirsty age. But, at that," my husband summed up, "give me a small boy for a guide any time. They never miss a trick."

*   *   *

On the bank of a microscopic streamlet, about a mile from the grave of

David McCanles, rises a rocky cliff. At the top is a high, iron-spiked fence guarding a short section of the face of the cliff. We had come here to see the most illustrious names which are carved anywhere in the two thousand miles of trail, and the protecting fence at once focused our search on the rock behind it. Steadying ourselves by occasionally holding to the iron pickets, we spread out along its short length and scanned the marred surface of the sandstone. Bill, who had moved to the extreme left, saw the carvings first and set up a racket that demobilized the army of blackbirds and brought us all on the double-quick.

"Here they are," he called. "John Frémont and Kit Carson—1842."

"Sure enough," his father agreed. "There they are. Say!" he added with slow emphasis. "That's funny—or is it, just possibly, phony?"

"What's phony?" I demanded with more interest than I had yet shown.

"Look at the carving of those two names in comparison with the rest, and you'll see."

Other signatures, partially obliterated, and other dates, old enough to be noteworthy in themselves, crowded the rock. A slight discrepancy was certainly noticeable. The names of later date were much more worn and illegible than the two we had come to find.

"Maybe somebody deepened the carving in good faith for fear that it would weather away," Dr. Neff contributed sensibly. "But, if so, we'll never know." And we left it at that.

* * *

From Quivera Park, the trail crossed the road and drifted in the hot summer haze through the fields to the right; dipping into a swale and then climbing into the pale, shining gilt of the next grain field; continuing, through meadows strong and sweet with ripening grass, into Fairbury. It was a little before one o'clock when we arrived in this city, our first county seat in Nebraska, and we went directly to the courthouse.

The hallway was quiet and empty, the general exodus to lunch having taken place some time before, and a series of grimly fastened doors confronted us. The very walls were reticent. However, it was cool. We sat down on the stairs and relaxed.

Presently a large man arrived, and almost in a moment the passageways were filled with replete lunchers. The first comer claimed us by right of discovery, and we asked him the usual questions. Here we struck our first real snag. A county engineer, did we say? Why, Nebraska is too full of counties to need an engineer for each. Why spend the money? Well, of course the competent gentleman could see that, from our point of view, a surveying crew in each county would undoubtedly be desirable, but still he didn't consider the reason adequate. It boiled down, didn't we think, to why, after all, Nebraska should spend the money?

It began to look as if we might be going to spend a little money ourselves while going through this lovely but so economical state. An adequate supply of modern county maps was to be had only at the State Capitol. Certainly the competent gentleman sympathized, but what could he do?

What, indeed, could any one do? We had to have them; and, on this particular trip, time was so essential that a separate excursion to Lincoln was out of the question. The mapping project through Nebraska would have to wait for another year. As a matter of fact my husband later made a trip to Washington, D.C., for them but, at the moment, our thoughts, prospecting possibilities in company with the competent gentleman's, had not wandered so far afield. The disappointment was of such proportions that we postponed considering it.

Meanwhile we were propelled toward a department where, we were told, was a lady whom we should meet. The suspicion which I at first entertained, that the competent gentleman was shoving a troublesome issue onto a defenseless woman, was erased when he proceeded to stay sociably around to see if she would prove an adequate substitute for the surveying crew.

The lady soon proved her worth. She produced a book entitled "Pioneer Tales of the Oregon Trail and of Jefferson County," that saved us days of work. It was published in 1912 by Charles Dawson, then a resident of the county for forty years, who had traced the old road on foot and had mapped it very carefully by sections. Among other items found in this interesting book is a list of the names carved on the rock at Quivera Park. Many of them have become illegible in the quarter-century that has elapsed since he copied them. Mr. Dawson was taking steps to prevent this (so he wrote) in the case of John Frémont and "Chris" Carson by slightly deepening the carving. And so our puzzle was solved before the day was over.

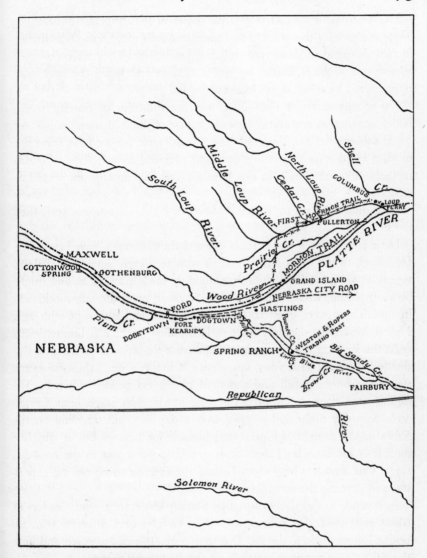

In the old days Whisky Run Station sheltered its quota of the famous stage horses at a spot some two miles northeast of Fairbury. Beyond it we came to a split-off from the original trail, called the Virginia Cutoff, that avoided five small creeks. I mention it merely to get rid of the subject of alternate routes. There is no object in detailing all the changes brought about by the years. The immense number of them encountered in two thousand miles of trail makes it prohibitive. They were no small part of our problem, being, by virtue of their later date, the only ones remembered by most of the local patriarchs.

An equally effective time-killer was the difficulty of finding roads, paths, or wheelbarrow tracks near the course of the trail, along which we could squeeze the car. Finding these "roads" took (so we have since figured) a third of our traveling time and provided a perfect field for differences of opinion both in our family group and among our would-be advisers.

Most difficulties we overcame by hook or crook—if not one year, then the next.

Little Sandy Creek was entirely dry and the country billowed from one fat hillock to the next. Each knoll in turn seemingly supported a cloud which, as we neared the summit, obligingly made way for us and might be seen, plump, white, and glistening, reposing upon the hummock next in line. There were giant cottonwoods, ragged and unkempt with age. Naked windmills, sketchily built of laths, idled in the soft breeze.

At the Big Sandy old wheel scars still mar the sloping banks. The Big Sandy Station, in its heyday, saw plenty of life, raw and otherwise as the stages ran bursting full and the tired passengers bedded down on the dining-room floor. A minister, traveling overland by stage, once arrived on a Saturday night and stopped over a day to avoid traveling on the Sabbath. On Monday he presented himself for passage but it was five days later on Saturday before he was able to get a seat in the crowded stage. One wonders how often he had the courage to repeat the experiment in crossing the continent.

In contrast to this delay caused by Sunday observance, many leaders of trains gave credit for prompt arrival in Oregon or California, with no undue loss of stock, to the fact that they rested one day in seven and kept the Sabbath, as nearly as possible, in the customary manner.

Before leaving the land of the Pawnee—and we were now approaching what might be termed border-line country—I want to repeat an incident which is the only confirmation we can remember of the persistent rumor of Masonry among some of the dignitaries of the plains Indians. It came to our attention in manuscript form, a letter from Nathan Aldrich to his

wife, mailed on May 27, 1852, at Fort Laramie where he found himself
with the vanguard of that year's emigration. "Some companies," he wrote,
"have had trouble with the Pawnias [Pawnee] Indians having their provisions taken away and in some cases their cows shot full of arrows so they
would have to be left, and two white men wounded by them, one thought
to be mortally, but we got along through them remarkably well on the
account of the chief being a Mason and Mr. Brown gave him the sign
which was answered by the chief and there was a small boy that could
talk English and Mr. Brown told him we had not more provisions than
would do us on our journey and if they would let us pass we would give
them a sack of corn and a ham, which they took and we passed along.
That was before we got in company with Pierson and there was but four
wagons of us together at the time and there was about two hundred of
the Indians placed upon both sides of the road with their bows and
arrows."

The band of two hundred is so often mentioned by emigrants that it
seems either to have been exceptionally active on its own account, or to
have been deputized by the Pawnee Nation as a reception committee.

Near Kiowa Station the nature of the terrain changed. The hitherto
smooth slopes broke into rain-gutted saddles and deep-washed gullies.
The wagons had steered a dizzy course like a line of ants disturbed. A
few big dollops of rain fell—great drops that plunked through the pow-
dery surface of the tiny hay road we followed and sent up plumes of dust.
On either side the fields were heaped with heavy sheaves of grain. The
old wagon ruts, climbing to a near horizon where metal-bright corn thrust
its gleaming lances into the sky, dropped from the eternally new miracle
of a summer's growth to the age-old trees at Oak Grove Ranch where we
came to a monument commemorating the victims of the Indian massacre
of '64.

Oak Grove Ranch once boasted a stage station where, because of its
situation in the no man's land between Sioux and Pawnee, the family in
residence was sometimes treated to a little gratuitous excitement.

On one occasion the arriving stage found the doorstep graced by a
Sioux war party garnished with everything from buffalo horns worn over
the ears to halolike hatbrims bristling with buzzard feathers. They were
demoniacally painted in black and red and were waiting (quietly
enough) for the stage driver to arrive and tell them the whereabouts of

their hereditary enemy, the Pawnee. To the discreetly invisible station master and his family it was evident that these self-contained individuals were "warriors" with scalps to their credit as distinguished from "braves" who were merely on the preferred list with laurels yet to be won. Needless to say the warriors were much safer to have around.

According to our maps, "the Narrows" was the next place of interest. It is mainly notable because, at this point on the Little Blue, the emigrants seemed to forget all their hard-learned rules of Indian strategy and crowded their wagons into a bottleneck between the river and encroaching bluffs. Progress at this juncture was never monotonous. One of the most hair-raising incidents recorded was Bob Emory's wild drive from the Narrows to the next station east, while a Sioux brave who had procured a really fine horse literally rode circles around the stage and, at each lap, sent a volley of arrows toward the windows. If he had shot the plunging animals matters would have been over quickly. He may have wanted to take them alive but it is quite likely that he was simply enjoying the pleasures of the chase. The enigmatic red man had a peculiar slant on what constituted sport; and simple, direct amusement such as this was always acceptable. Crouched on the seat, fully exposed to the whizzing arrows, Bob Emory drove like a madman, and succeeded in reaching the next station with his passenger list intact. Just one instance among many of the almost superhuman endurance and daring of the stage drivers.

* * *

A storm caught us in the valley of the Little Blue. It was a welcome change, for we had entered on a period of the hot days and cold nights quite common to the eastern slope of the Rockies, which so astonished the emigrants that the fact is almost invariably mentioned in trail journals.

When the highway turned, we timorously deserted it and trusted ourselves to the good graces of a small road so serpentine that it seemed to have stiffened while wriggling to avoid the mudholes. Thence our soggy progress was punctuated gloomily enough with small, muddy towns. First settlers moved heavily like flies on a frosty morning and expectorated more or less successfully as they watched us seesaw through slick black mud where the storm had washed the road out and the overhanging banks in.

Finally my husband spun the wheel, slid the car broadside onto an island of solid gravel, and we stepped gingerly out to reconnoiter. "What do you think about going on?" he asked me.

I looked at the car. It resembled a wet swallow's nest more than anything else. The road ahead was no worse than that behind us, and it happened that a small patch of blue sky lay to the west. "Let's chance it," I decided. And we plunged along after the old wheel gouges through semi-fluid fields.

My blue sky was a true prophet. The storm had been local and, after we had worked our way slowly through ten more miles of mud, things became more normal. Along little roadways with reassuringly solid bases we really enjoyed the refreshing, pungent odor of earth freshly drenched and strung with puddles. The sun reflected pleasantly from the white knoll at the site of old Liberty Farm Station and struck diamond points of light from the rain-soaked masses of trees behind it. This station did not survive the terrible massacre in 1864 but was replaced by one known as Pawnee Station located at a more favorable site.

About the middle of the morning, we began to watch for the place where the old military road from Fort Riley to Fort Kearney crossed the trail of the prairie schooners. We had obtained the necessary data after some research and a good deal of difficulty, so that it was a letdown to find a marker fairly exuding information on the subject.

We crossed Pawnee Creek just above the trestle. A few hundred yards downstream, at its confluence with the Little Blue, stood in the old days Weston and Roper's trading post. From there we went to Spring Ranch, which developed years ago into a village—now hoary and gray. On the outskirts of town an ancient blacksmith shop raised its impressive two-story false front while opposite stood the quaintest old church imaginable.

We continued to move along in the angle between Pawnee Creek and the Little Blue on a road dotted with Nebraska's numerous trail markers. In time our course climbed slightly to a flat upland covered with grain. This was evidently Nine Mile Ridge, where in staging days stood Lone Tree Station. The solitary tree for which the station was named used to be visible for a long distance in each direction and helped to break the monotony of the bare, rolling prairie hills. It was hard to imagine such a condition faced, as we were, with ranches and roadsides planted thick with shrubs and shade trees.

Next the westbound travelers encountered the windings of Thirty-two Mile Creek, a main tributary of the Little Blue. The wagons cut straight through its loops, crossing three times and getting their supply of water at the fords. On this portion of the road they passed the long and low log cabin which served as Thirty-two Mile Station.

And now, with the passing of this tenuous stream, the watershed of the Kansas was left behind and we, together with the pioneers of old, were cast adrift to cross the waterless divide that separates it from the Valley of the Platte.

7

The Schooners Sight the "Coast of Nebraska"

THE TRAIL LAY TO OUR LEFT, easily accessible at all times; and on it, near the summit of the rise, the old stages found the last stop before the long waterless drive over to the Platte River. Here stood Summit Station. Perhaps "stood" is not the best word, for the building was only three feet above ground and extended four feet below. Near it, in the year '59, a wagon company camped. They carried water some distance from the tiny seasonal tributary of the Platte which served the station, picketed their riding horses, and turned the rest loose to graze.

The company had been much interested during the day by the passing of several wagons full of returning, disgusted Pikes Peakers. Their attempt at quick wealth in the mines of Colorado had been (to them) a complete failure. That they and others like them had played a very valuable part in the settlement of the state never occurred to them, and would have been no comfort if it had. The same wagons, which had been so gayly inscribed with big black letters, "PIKES PEAK OR BUST," now had an added scrawl, "BUSTED WIDE OPEN," and one inquired blackly, "OH WHY DID I LEAVE MOLLY AND THE BABY?" The California-bound company, encamped near the station, were still discussing the inscriptions and getting a certain amount of amusement out of the situation when the cry went up that all the loose stock had disappeared.

The incident that followed epitomizes the rough and callous aspect of the emigration.

The young men of the company took the picketed saddle horses and searched for several days until they discovered some of the missing ponies tied in a sheltered spot which could not be overlooked from the road, and where the station keeper had assured them there were no animals but his own. They were indignant and promptly hanged the station keeper until he was nearly dead. Then they cut him down, wiped the bloody froth from his lips, nursed him back to consciousness, and asked him what he had done with the rest of their horses.

He insisted that he hadn't done anything, and they regretfully hanged him again, this time for so long that it seemed as if they might possibly have overdone the matter. As soon as they were sure he would live they trooped out, "feeling that if the man was innocent he had had very harsh and unfair treatment . . . and on the other hand if he were guilty he was certainly grit to the core."

Seven miles beyond this station were the famous (or rather infamous) buffalo-wallow water holes. Theodore Talbot, who was with Frémont in 1843, minced no words in his description of them. "These ponds or wallows," he wrote, "are formed by the buffalo wallowing, an amusement they are very fond of. When any rain falls it is collected in these places and here the buffalo come to drink and stand during the heat of the day, adding their own excrements to the already putrescent waters. This compound warmed for weeks in a blazing sun and alive with animalcules makes a drink palatable to one suffering from intense thirst. Oh! that some over dainty connoisseur might taste of it!" Emigrants of later years, warned by the numerous guidebooks that flooded the market, carried water for emergencies from the last creek. But very early Oregon-bound travelers, delayed by one accident and another on this, the longest waterless stretch they had to cross, were sometimes forced by the intensity of their need to use this nauseating substitute for water.

It was here that the travelers were astonished at great circles of rank grass mixed with mushrooms and a heavy growth of pigweed. These pixy rings grew at random on the prairie and were thought to be caused by groups of buffalo cows who bedded at night in circles inclosing the calves and who shook from their heavy manes the seeds in which they had rolled all day.

And now the emigrants (and we after them) looked forward only a few miles to the first view of the great Platte River. Some say it was first known as Nebrathka, an Otoe word for weeping water, because of the sad tones of its current rushing swiftly among the sandy islands. Later it was called Platte by the French trappers on account of its gray flatness. Swiftly the miles passed, and a slightly higher row of knolls confronted us. We plowed up a sandy hill to the very top and stopped. The downslope on the far side broke into bluffs and dunes, and continued to flat sand—white as a beach. Beyond this shorelike stretch extended, as far as the eye could see, the green bottoms of the Platte. From this very ridge the schooners sighted the "Coast of Nebraska."

Somewhere among the labyrinth of dunes we hoped to find what is locally known as the Lone Grave. We had gathered its pathetic story piecemeal, during the last half-day. A young bride, journeying west with her husband, died with stunning suddenness. The story told to us gave "poisoned spring" water as the cause of her death, but I think it more likely that she drank contaminated water from one of the shallow wells which had been dug at so many of the camp sites, and which were a generally acknowledged source of Asiatic cholera.

The unmarked grave among the monotonous, rolling sand hills filled the husband with horror lest he forget the exact spot where he had buried her. He set up a temporary sign and turned back to St. Joseph for a marker. He hadn't money enough left for a wagon of his own, and he found that a gravestone was a most unwelcome bit of luggage in any stranger's outfit. At last, so the story goes, he bought a wheelbarrow and trundled it before him throughout the long hard journey to the Platte. He accomplished his purpose—immortalized her resting place and disappeared from history.

The road to the grave, when found, proved to be the trail itself with deep sandy ruts and a high center of heavy grass reaching above the front bumper. In sharp relief against wind-riffled clouds was a grassy hilltop, and here, overlooking the great valley of the Platte, Susan Hail lies beneath a stone with her name upon it, in one of the comparatively few known graves among the tens of thousands who lie unhonored and unsung along the great Pioneer Road.

For some miles we kept on the trail itself which, at this point, is quite practical although heavily grass-grown. The Lone Grave is close to the Adams-Kearney county line. We crossed it and found ourselves traveling among the Kearney County wheat fields. Drainage ditches had been dug around most of them, and in the ditches stood waist-high grass, lush and green, giving the big square golden fields the look of plush mats edged with narrow green borders.

Not many miles ahead of us the old road from Nebraska City joined the one from St. Joseph and Independence on which we were now bouncing along at considerable risk to our springs. The infant Nebraska City (a drab affair but useful) suddenly mushroomed on the bank of the Missouri River in the year 1854. It was about forty miles below Council Bluffs and was a favorable location from which to pursue an easy route to the south bank of the Platte. Like Independence, Nebraska City lay on the west bank of the river, and most of the emigrants were safely landed there by river steamer before they commenced to pack their belongings into wagons so that, after the companies were organized, they did not have the disrupting experience of ferrying across the churning, sediment-filled Missouri.

None of the pioneer routes leading to the Platte Valley could compare, for ease and comfort, with the Nebraska City Road. It kept well up on the divide between the watersheds of the Little Nemaha and Salt Creek, and it crossed no large stream until the Big Blue was reached—high up toward its source. This was readily forded immediately above its confluence with the West Fork. The wagons then remained for a day's journey on the northern bank of West Fork and encountered Beaver Creek, which flows into it from the north. This they forded almost at the junction, and proceeded along its south bank. Near the old Millspaw Ranch they finally left the headwaters of the little stream behind them and picked up the course of an uncertain sloughlike creek which provided them with water for the stock until they reached the Platte, and turned to follow its south bank.

This favored route came too late for thousands of the westbound colonists; and even in its heyday, owing to its position about midway of the starting points on the river, it did not readily catch the travel from the north or south.

As soon as possible we abandoned the ruts of the trail and turned back toward the junction of the two roads now surrounded by very respectable groves of trees. These modern arboreal specimens are quite foreign to the pioneer traveler's picture of the spot, for in the old days the Platte Valley was treeless except for the willows and the cottonwood on the islands. The supposed fertility of the islands in contrast to the banks puzzled many a traveler, but the answer was simple. Every year the Indians burned the prairies to facilitate the hunting of rabbits and other game and no tree survived unless surrounded by water.

In trail days there was a utilitarian, if ugly, settlement at the junction, bearing the vulgar title Dogtown. As late as 1865, it was the first town west of Marysville, Kansas, a journey of nearly a hundred fifty miles. It is likely that the name originated in the "town" or "village" of prairie dogs near by. There were several prairie-dog settlements along the Platte, each of some acres in extent, looking, so the emigrants fancied, like an immense field of sweet potato hills. The dumpy little creatures barked hysterically at the first wagons of each season, but grew more philosophical as the steady procession flowed by them.

The Platte, in trail days, was tremendously wide and shallow. It was of a temperament entirely different from the tossing flood of the Missouri, the deep and steady Kansas, or the beautiful, benevolent Blue. The Platte itself made excellent going but, beyond the unalterable fact that it was wet, seldom helped any one else on his way. It furnished no shade. Its water was poor to taste and too dirty to wash in. Its bed was quicksand—not violent in action, but of an insidious sucking variety that tugged at the boots of those who dared to wade, pulled at the lunging horses and slowly dragged down any wagon unfortunate enough to stall in mid-current. Its silvery, shallow waters flowed with deceptive swiftness along the hardly noticeable declivity of its course, spreading over an incredible breadth of territory. Some of the emigrants credited it with a width of two miles as it neared the Missouri. One, who saw it in extreme flood, believed it to be three. It existed for and with itself. The stage drivers said that it didn't even overflow, to enrich the valley, but merely saturated its quicksand banks so that they rose with the rise of the current and retained the flood waters within its channel. Emigrants who saw its "mad, majestic course" in flood said it looked higher than the road.

It could not be ferried for lack of depth. It was difficult to bridge beyond any means available to the emigrants, and it was dangerous to ford. Its shining waters carried such a burden of suspended earth and debris that the disgusted travelers accused it of flowing bottom-side up, and a child, once swallowed in its swift and turgid flood, was lost to sight even though the water might be shallow enough for rescue.

At Dogtown, we were still some eight or nine miles from old Fort Kearney, toward which the trail continued up the flat river bottoms. On the south (which was now to our left, and was to remain there for many miles) were the low, hummocky, green bluffs which we had just quitted, and which inclose the bottoms.

Of the five historic trail "forts"—Kearney, Laramie, Hall, Boise and

Bridger—we were now approaching the first in point of geography, last in point of time. It was established in 1848 as a curb on the exuberant habits of the Indians and was the only one of the five actually to be built for the accommodation of soldiers (the other four were originally trading posts and were established much earlier). It was first called Fort Child in honor of Brigadier General Child of the United States Army. Later, by order of the government, it was changed to Fort Kearney, honoring Colonel Stephen Watts Kearny. The error in spelling was due to some mistake in the Post Office or War Department. In accordance with the casual habit of the day, the name was a duplication of an older and already abandoned fort on the Missouri River just below Table Creek.

In '49, a year after its establishment, Fort Kearney was said to consist of several huts of sod, one store, one smithy and "a few drunken, lazy soldiers" who ignominiously rotted with scurvy and complained passionately to passing gold-seekers that the place was a living death and they would rather be anywhere else. In this at least some of the emigrants heartily concurred, feeling that the place with its far from ornamental soldiers was discreditable.

Spring supplies of dried fruits, pickles, and vinegar soon vanquished the winter's scurvy, as the hordes of gold-seekers banished the deadly monotony. By summer of '49, the post teemed with activity; and by '50, it was well equipped to organize the tremendous migration as it flowed past. Small groups of wagons were advised to join with larger companies. Soldiers were sent out to settle intertribal difficulties and in later years, as Indian troubles grew in importance, accompanied the caravans through the dangerous sections. Well qualified guides were available for sums approximating four dollars a day, and one guide would handle a train of a hundred fifty wagons. Jim Bridger and W. F. Drannan (who was Kit Carson's "adopted nephew") spent several summers in this work.

Drannan was a hard-bitten scout if one ever lived, but even his cast-iron nerve was shaken by an incident that happened near the fort in the spring of 1850. As he told the story, a train of thirty wagons from southeastern Missouri had approached within ten miles of the fort when one of their number deliberately shot and killed a squaw who was sitting peaceably nursing her baby on the edge of an Indian village. He had bragged that he would kill the first redskin he could get a bead on. No one, of course, had dreamed of believing him; but he was an unnatural miscreant, sadistic, and no doubt drunk. The members of his train were horrified by the senseless brutality of the act, and his closest associates shrank from him.

The Indians arrived at once and demanded the murderer. There was nothing to do but yield. Indeed the company realized that they were lucky, for it would have been quite within the bounds of native etiquette to shoot a few white women at random and square the account.

The elders of the village received the culprit in dour triumph, carried him away a little distance and skinned him alive—quite publicly. His former comrades, utterly unable to do anything about it, moved on to the fort, sickened and unnerved.

The gruesome retribution inflicted by the red men is told today as the reason for the naming of Rawhide Creek near Fremont, Nebraska. Nor can we criticize too much from an angle of superiority, remembering that Captain Bonneville's men, while temporarily away from his leadership, burned an Indian alive for horse stealing—in full view of his friends.

There were a few nonmilitary buildings at Fort Kearney, erected outside the quadrangle. The post office was probably of most interest to the pioneers of the gold rush. Letters could be mailed here for a small fee, and it was the intention of the Government that letters should also be received. The disgust and disappointment of homesick travelers, who almost invariably failed to connect with their mail, fills pages.

The sod post-office building also, in later years, housed the telegraph office, which was for some time the most westerly point at which a telegram could be received. From here the message was rushed to the Pacific coast by horse and man power. Stage station and stables flanked the post office some forty rods west of the barracks, and there is mention in a '49 diary of a boarding house run by Mormons.

From '49 on, supplies could be purchased at Fort Kearney by those emigrants who had not planned on the enormous prairie appetites so unexpectedly acquired, and Indians often brought such commodities as they had to sell or trade. On a melting day in 1856, a brawny brave arrived at the camp of Mrs. Helen Carpenter to sell some buffalo meat. She questioned him as to its freshness and amount, and he proudly delivered himself of an extra-large chunk which he had carried on his chest under a heavy blanket and over which rivulets of perspiration were wending their tortuous way. She declined the delicacy and went up to the store to buy some cheese instead. One taste took the skin off the end of her tongue, and she wrote that the military officers should have mustered it out long since, as it was too old to be in service. However, she did manage to buy some canned peaches and blackberries—the earliest purchase of canned goods we have so far noted.

The ceaseless, buzzing activity of the fort began in April of each year with the coming of the Platte River fur wagons and the first emigrants. It lasted through the summer until the last California-bound stragglers had driven through, worried and desperately hurrying. In the fall the dirty wagons of the fur traders came back from the Green River rendezvous loaded with cargoes worth a fortune. Afterward the fort settled down to a lonely, desolate winter broken only, in later years, by the regular arrivals of the stage.

The first thing we saw as we neared the site of the fort was the flag. It still flies at the center of the parade ground though the buildings have disappeared and only an indefinite line of dirt mounds is left to guard it.

Dr. Neff dragged out a copy of Root and Connelley's "Overland Stage to California" and found a sketch of the fort drawn in 1864, at the height of its usefulness.

We all peered over his shoulder.

A large rectangle of parade ground, centered by the high flagpole, was contained within a raised earthwork barricade. Outside the low mound-like wall, the barracks and officers' homes faced inward, their windows like eyes peering across at one another. Young shade trees lined the inside edge of the wall, and on the south side were alternated with small but energetic-looking cannon.

"I'm glad I didn't live in the barracks," Bill volunteered. "The cannon point straight in at the windows."

"Maybe," I suggested, "we'd better allow the sketcher a little artistic license. After all, he had to point the cannon somewhere, and the houses seem to go all the way around. To look at it now you would never dream this had been a busy place, would you? Even the trees are gone."

"Maybe the artist took a little license with them too," contributed Bill.

"No," I said, "they grew all right. Mr. Root wrote that they were immense by the turn of the century."

"I wouldn't be surprised if that grove of old trees to the west is where the post office and stage station used to stand," Dr. Neff said. He put the book away and got out of the car. "There's a man there cutting wood. I'm going over to ask him."

Slantwise through the fort we strung along in single file. There was nothing at all to halt progress. I could have pushed a perambulator up and over the old wall. There was a break in the rectangular mounds showing where the large gateway had been, but we made no effort to use it and kept on an air line straight for the wood-chopper.

On closer examination the man proved to be cutting posts. They were, so he informed us, intended for a fence around the old fort site.

"Good work," my husband responded. "Our historic spots should be protected. There's little enough left of them as it is."

Our informant regarded him with a twinkle. "In this case," he said reflectively, "there's too much left for safety. That's why there's some talk about a fence. You see the young folks like to drive their cars back and forth across what's left of the walls—sort of scenic railway effect— and, unless we can manage to discourage 'em somehow, sure as you're a foot high somebody's going to get hurt!"

8

A Few Mental Detours

THE FOURTH OF JULY FELL, this year, on a Sunday, and we left Fort Kearney just as the neighboring farmers were starting for church. Two miles to the west we arrived at the spot where once flourished the hamlet called Dobeytown, a squalid settlement of 'dobe huts whose very mention was next door to an indelicacy. It was the ordinary type of hell-hole that clung to the fringes of any military reservation and, owing to the fact that Fort Kearney was far toward the western edge of its reserve, the group of mud buildings was within a mile or two of the barracks.

We found Leo Nickels' Ranch on the spot where many a foolish traveler lost his last cent—if not his life. The casual tourist may recognize it by a row of evergreens along the fence line instead of the more common cottonwoods whose silky fluff everywhere fills the air.

In staging days a large reserve stable for work stock was erected at Dobeytown, and the name Kearney City was arbitrarily selected in a vain attempt to throw a veil of respectability over the community. The name never "took" with those who knew the place, but it looked well in print and was reassuring to the more gregarious of the emigration. I have seen one small, leather-bound diary where a woman's delicate handwriting announced that they were to camp in the "suburbs" of Kearney City; and doubtless after arrival she stayed right in the "suburbs" and let the city take care of itself, for the women of the migration seldom found it advisable to invade the trail settlements.

The permanent population was about two dozen inhabitants, mainly gamblers, saloonkeepers, and loafers who made a good living by running off the emigrants' stock at night, laying it to the Pawnee, and hiring out to find it the next day. Only the most cast-iron type of hard liquor was available at Dobeytown (as beer and wines were considered an unpardonable waste of hauling space), and the thirsty drivers and crews of the great bull-drawn freight wagons were frequently drugged and robbed.

"There was no law in Dobeytown, or at least none that could be enforced." The place was a grisly combination of delirium tremens, stale humanity, and dirt.

In contrast to the ugliness of this festering product of civilization, the natural beauty of the Platte Valley in spring provoked many a wordy rhapsody. Banks of vivid wildflowers extended parklike for a hundred miles, and it is not unusual to find a specimen pressed in a manuscript diary. Blossoming cacti in exquisite shades of rose, cream, and citron yellow delighted the eye and lamed both the cattle and the barefoot children. And it is impossible to omit mention of the wild onion, which had turned up in time to flavor the buffalo meat and was more popular with the men than the wildflowers.

Acres of prairie-dog villages were frequent along the watershed of the Great Platte. A few of the emigrants ate them and claimed that they were very tender and good; but mainly the "pups" were taboo for table purposes. One woman grieved Spencerianly in her diary at the touching sight of several (cannibalistic) prairie dogs "trying to carry home the body of a wounded comrade"—a choice bit of misinformation. As a matter of fact the number of false statements which the emigrants entrusted to their journals in perfect good faith gave us several years of mental exercise; and their efforts to do justice to new words and experiences is nothing short of paralyzing. David Cosad, for instance, never tired of expressing his amazement and interest in the phenomena of the trail. Thus Mr. Cosad: "saw heads of buffaloes which is as big as a man can carry saw buffalo tracks hundreds of perrari dogs holes & some a barking heard coiata a yelling all night while standing gard."

Wooded green islands—dozens of them—provided grass and a limited supply of fuel. Along the roadway, for the entire length of the river, were strewn towels, gowns, hairpins, playing cards, and the forgotten impedimenta of camping thousands; and, as the country grew rougher, there were plenty of books. One might take a volume, read it along the road, toss it out, and take another from the next abandoned box of reading material. The roadside was one vast circulating library. Perhaps I should limit the last statement to the gold-rush days. The emigrants soon learned to bring only what was necessary to them: the Bible, a dictionary, a grammar, a hymn book, a simple arithmetic, and possibly some scientific literature pertaining to their professions. The universal plea then, from trappers, station keepers, or dwellers in any isolated spot, was for some-thing—anything at all—to read.

To the early Oregonians the rolling dunes, seen over banks of brilliant blossoms, were black with buffalo, but when the Forty-niners traveled the Platte Valley it was dotted with bleaching bones, pathetic remains of giant brutes killed wantonly for sport or for a few pounds of tender meat. The great herds which had galloped across the plains, undulating like the waters of the ocean and seemingly almost as vast, were fast diminishing, and the remnants tended to remain away from their customary summer feeding ground along the Platte. The Argonauts watched with necks astrain for days before they were rewarded by sighting the herds grazing peacefully in masses or lumbering in single file down the deep-worn, foot-wide trails that ran—a dozen or so abreast—to water. Instantly, with guns roaring and wild shouts, they rode at them, wounded and killed many and drove the rest away. By the middle fifties a herd was seldom seen.

We will consider the picture as it presented itself to the wagon trains of—well, say 1846, the year of the Donner Party Expedition. Buffalo were thick along the Platte, especially in the neighborhood where Fort Kearney was later established. The bulls were grazing slightly apart from the cows and calves (as they did in the spring and early summer) and might be found singly or in small groups. As long as the clumsy creatures merely lingered aimlessly within view, the emigrants were not especially exercised but accepted their presence as we might accept a bunch of wild cattle in the neighborhood of a summer camp. True, they seemed to have been created needlessly large and senseless, but ordinarily they could be han-dled. The women even shooed them from the wagons by running out and waving their aprons until they lumbered away in a panic.

If hunted, the bulls rushed to the protection of their families and formed a rear guard which turned now and then to snort defiance and paw up large chunks of turf. Soon, as some of the animals were wounded and the smell of hot blood ran with them, the whole herd formed a rush-ing mass of hooves and horns weighted by tons of living flesh—a great force of nature set in blind and resistless motion. They actually dammed the river as they crossed. The thwarted current rose and flowed above their backs with a rushing noise heard for a mile or more.

The responsibility of starting a stampede of buffalo by shooting one was almost as great as that assumed by one who sets off a blast in a snow-banked mountain side. The act, once committed, could not be rectified. Once put in motion, the resulting avalanche swept on over rivers, cliffs, sluggish ox caravans, whatever lay in its way. Nothing turned it except the desperate expedient of shooting enough animals in the van of the herd to cause the rest to slant off to one side, clashing their horns with a weird rattle heard above all the din.

Fortunately for the emigrants, their acquaintance with the buffalo came while the young calves were running with the cows. The bulls at this time of the year were not moved to display too much interest in the welfare of their families and made no objection to the passing wagon trains; whereas the Santa Fe caravans, traversing the country of the Arkansas, during mating season in August, sometimes found themselves so surrounded by belligerent buffalo bulls that it was dangerous to move.

Bulls were seldom killed except in such an emergency, in ignorance or pure wantonness, as both flesh and hides were far inferior to the product of the cows. This was, of course, a major factor in the extermination of the species from the plains.

Much has been said and written about the vengeance of the Indians upon the emigrants as a result of killing the buffalo. This is perfectly true, but it gives only a small portion of the picture. Granted that the emigrants killed many and frightened away more of the Platte Valley herds; but the hide hunters and the Indians who sold skins to them carried on wholesale slaughter everywhere on the plains. The clumsy animals were nowhere safe from these two groups. The emigrants (bound, as they were, to a certain track) always remind me, in their dispute over right of way with the buffalo, of a small, battered interurban streetcar we once saw near Philadelphia. On a large sign, covering most of its front elevation, was this sensible appeal: "Automobiles: You can turn out. I can't!" The hide hunters on the contrary could and did follow the buffalo wherever they might be found, and destroyed them by the thousand until at last the countless myriads that had blackened the prairie were gone, taking with them the independence of the plains Indians, and clearing the way for the relentless spread of civilization. Then, when no more money could be made from killing, their destroyers returned, gathered up the weighty skeletons, and shipped them by rail to eastern markets, thus squeezing out a final modicum of profit.

Having been the mainstay of the Indian for generations, the buffalo, at the last of their career, made one outstanding contribution to the white race. Practically speaking, they made the emigration possible. It is hard to see how the overland journey could have been successful in the early years without them. In the Platte Valley, just where the herds were thickest, there was a stretch of two hundred miles without one stick of timber —no dry grass, no sage, no anything that would serve as fuel except buffalo chips. Often nearly white with years of exposure, dry to handle, and light as feathers, this age-old deposit of the herds burned like charcoal with little blaze and less smoke. It boiled the night guard's coffee, warmed the baby's milk, heartened them all with hot meals night and morning. It was of such importance to the domestic economy of the emigrants that the canny mules learned to pull up and stop hopefully at any spot where the droppings were thick, and even the most finicky of the women vied with one another to collect the driest.

Unless incapacitated, members of families using oxen walked most of the time. Even the owners of horse teams, which made twenty-five miles and over on good days, walked whenever they could do so without falling behind. These pedestrians, young and old, carried bags and, no matter what else they did on the long day's walk, they industriously gathered fuel. Never was manna in the wilderness more truly a godsend than this remarkable substitute for wood, which providentially appeared only where wood was not.

By the time the Platte Valley was reached the travelers were tired of salt meats and looked forward with real anticipation to the first taste of the much-vaunted buffalo tenderloins. Conscientious meat hunters could use the greater part of a young buffalo (by remaining in camp a day to make jerky), but the great delicacies were the hump, the tongue, the tenderloin, and the marrow bones. The tongue was taken by setting the animal's head with the nose in air and horns deep in the ground to steady it; a large slit under the jaw was then cut, through which the desired member might easily be removed. Marrowbones, buried in coals of buffalo chips for an hour, were considered to be especially rich and delicious. The treat may seem a trifle concentrated to us; but then, we are not living on beans and biscuit. Old mountaineers even used portions of the male buffalo which the emigrants never disputed with them. When the hunters were through with a carcass the Indians gladly ate the offal, and the wolves picked the bones. There was no excuse for waste.

To "jerk" buffalo meat, the camp constructed a large rectangle of boughs or wooden strips, like a rude picture frame, and laid poles thickly across it. Then they elevated the sketchy affair on four legs and built a smudge beneath it. Small sections of meat pulled from the carcass were hung over the poles to cure in the smoke. The white man soon improved on the original Indian procedure to the extent of cutting his meat into thin slices, sometimes small, sometimes the size of shingles, but the name "jerky" was always used. A day or two cured it sufficiently to keep indefinitely. The resulting tidbits varied somewhat as to edible qualities, but were always tough and had an unappetizing tendency to retain small sections of hairy hide. Jerky could also be dried by hanging on ropes outside the wagon covers for several days. When it had become hard it was packed, alkali dirt and all, in bags. This, to their sad surprise, many of the women were glad to eat before they reached the Sierras. Large chunks of buffalo meat also kept a surprising length of time—some said weeks—protected by a hard crust formed by the dry air.

Pemmican was the stand-by of the plainsman, but not so often used by polite society—even in wagon trains. It was made by pounding the dried jerky into powder and filling receptacles about half full. Melted buffalo tallow was then poured over it until the amount was sufficient, and the whole unappetizing concoction stirred up together. It soon hardened. If no other container offered, buffalo skins were tied into bags for the purpose. This confection was used after other supplies were gone, but it was said that a man could do a harder day's work on pemmican than on any other food.

The emigrants of the forties, taking a leaf from the book of the fur traders' caravans, counted on stocking up with buffalo products at this point in their journey; but their degree of necessity was as nothing compared to the urgent need of small companies of trappers crossing from one river to another, out of food for days and just able to drag across the long waterless stretches. A stray buffalo was both food and drink to men whose demanding thirst outweighed delicacy. They cut into the stomach, drained off and drank the water which the accommodating animal had obtained at the river and carried a day's journey to meet them. Trappers and mountain men made shallow-draft boats of buffalo bull hides by drying them over frames of willow limbs. In like ingenious manner they made pants for themselves by skinning the bodies and hind legs of sundry buffalo calves—each man using his own frame for drying purposes.

In addition to all the other debts owed to the shaggy king of the plains, half the migration were gratefully spending the cold nights wrapped in buffalo robes. Indeed the travelers were always appropriating something belonging to this much enduring beast.

Notwithstanding these blessings the valley of the Platte with its wandering wild herds brought its own peculiar worries to the muleteers and bullwhackers. The most unwearying vigilance was necessary. Hitherto temperate and unsusceptible cattle were beset by a sudden nervous affinity for the roving herds and were frequently swept away on the tide of a running band of buffalo. The early Oregon pioneers learned that it was better to make camp, tie their animals, and remain overnight, than to cross the fresh track of a buffalo herd.

*   *   *

The modern highways and cities of the Platte Valley are on the north side of the river. Plenty of emigrants traveled the north bank (of which more later), but the main Oregon road was south of the Platte; and here we also remained day after day. We were able to keep on the approximate course of the trail, which the state has liberally punctuated with markers. At varying fractions of a mile to our left, rose the "grass-covered sand hills" mentioned by Delano, while to the right the river wound through the flat bottoms at a constantly changing distance of more than a mile— too far off to be of interest.

Before the day of the cornfields and shade trees, the slow-moving ox trains found the scenery monotonous. Unless something happened to break the spell, today looked just like yesterday and tomorrow. But the valley had several surprises in store. In spite of the sameness of its level bottoms, it was not apt to afflict its travelers with boredom. In the first place they were apprehensive about Indians; frightful stampedes and runaways were common; and the storms encountered here were considered something unique even by such specialists in dirty weather as the emigrants had become. Witness the following excerpt from the journal of Joseph Hackney, on May 30, 1849: "last night was one of the stormiest i ever heard tell of the rain fell in torrents and covered the ground a foot deep in water—the wind also blew a perf[ect] gale, driving the rain through our tents and wagons covers like as though they had been paper there was not much chance to sleep without you could fancy wet blankets and a torrent of water running under you when we got up in the mornin our cattel wear scattered to the four ends of the earth—every camp that we saw had lost cattel."

Alonzo Delano also described the event, adding: "In this dreadful storm hundreds of cattle were lost, and some trains were almost ruined; some lost half, while others had only one or two yoke left; and for several

Storm in the Platte Valley.

days after, we met many persons who were searching for their cattle, unable to proceed. No situation can be more deplorable than that of being left upon a broad prairie, hundreds of miles from aid, without the means of locomotion. We found families, with women and helpless children, in this sad condition, and yet we were without means to give them relief."

On June 26 of that year two men who had taken refuge in a light wagon were blown over a bluff and, fortunately tumbling out en route, gazed down at the total wreck of their vehicle projecting from the turgid Platte.

These were not isolated occurrences. Almost every diary mentions bad storms. Louisa Rahm, a calm woman of few words and fewer punctuation marks who traveled the trail in '62, was on the Platte when they had a little spell of weather. She wrote briefly, "cold this morning and cups and teakettle mashed flat with hail in a camp below us there was two men knock down with it cuting gashes 3 in long in the head."

Father de Smet, in the year 1841, wrote definitely: "I have seen some hail stones of the size of an egg. It is dangerous to be abroad during these storms. A Sheyenne Indian was lately struck by a hail stone, and remained senseless for an hour."

Well—enough of storms. Even though the valley still can produce a few outsize hailstones, which, only a few years ago, went blithely through the old-fashioned auto tops, we never happened to encounter any in the days before our steel-bodied vehicle afforded ample protection.

As the emigrants approached Plum Creek, which was considered as the very center of the buffalo country, the wagons lurched squarely across dozens of deep and parallel paths—some scarcely a foot wide but close together, like plowed furrows—which the great beasts had made single-filing over the grassy dunes to the river. The busy wind has left no trace of these characteristic trails, but throughout the emigration they were a major difficulty on the otherwise good Platte road.

In staging days Plum Creek Station was a well known stopping point and was the only station left undestroyed between Fort Kearney and Julesburg in the uprising of '64—a pleasant circumstance which was supremely unimportant to its dozen or so inhabitants, who were all scalped. Their near-by grave evidently is seldom visited, but in the center of the plot stands a massive stone monument inscribed, "The Pioneer Men and Women who Lost their Lives by Hostile Indians in the Plum Creek Massacre, Aug. 7, 1864."

It is no more than right and fitting that their burial place should be signally and outstandingly marked. They paid a heavy price that some of the government services which we take for granted might be firmly established. Had it not been for the communicating stage lines and mail service, our western country might have had a far different history. This connecting chain was composed of many links which must hold fast if it were to endure. The stationmasters and stock tenders with their wives and families were these links. They lived rigorously at best, and often lost their lives at their posts. There can be no doubt that they helped to preserve the Union as surely as any soldier who died at Gettysburg.

*   *   *

Eighteen miles west of Plum Creek we found the slough often mentioned as a good place to camp. It makes a pretty picture even now. White-faced cattle stand knee-deep in luxuriant grass, while behind them spreads the shining water, ragged-edged, and shaded here and there with bold lines of heavy reeds. Against the pale horizon dark trees, singly and in solid lines, look like the dots and dashes of the Morse code. The Platte bottoms are very wide at this point.

Bill, who always becomes map-conscious just before mealtime, here announced that not too many miles ahead was a bridge over the Platte leading to Gothenburg (and presumably lunch). The road to Gothenburg proved to be soggy and covered with the debris of a recent local storm and our dusty car took unto itself a top crust of mud spatters. We crossed the river and came immediately onto the transcontinental Lincoln Highway in front of a tourist restaurant. The parking space was full of heavily packed cars which, from their shining appearance, might never have seen a dirt road. We added our disgraceful specimen, and went in to lunch.

In Gothenburg we invaded the emigrant trail lying north of the Platte, which we traveled with interest from end to end at another time. Space does not permit giving its many characteristics in detail, but I will take the opportunity here to summarize it briefly. When the Mormon exodus from the States commenced in 1847, it was not exactly a new idea to travel the north bank as far as the Rockies; but it was not being done that year. Instead, the emigrant parties were starting near the mouth of the Kansas and reaching the south bank of the Platte at what is now Grand Island. The Mormons, wishing to have a route of their own, sent a small pioneering party along the opposite side of the Platte. This party was immediately followed by the large migration of Mormon families, and every succeeding summer for years the north-bank trail was traveled by Mormon converts from Europe and the States. It soon became recognized as the Mormon Trail and is so known to this day although about a third of the non-Mormon emigrants also used it.

Travelers using this trail started from the early Mormon settlement of Kanesville, or later from Council Bluffs on the Missouri River. The

Mormon elders, calling the "saints" together early in the spring of '49 in preparation for the yearly trek to Salt Lake City, stated in their newspaper that Kanesville would be the starting point, it being two hundred miles closer to Fort Laramie than the starting points of the other routes. The saints responded, but so did the gold-seekers. Not only did they come from Iowa and the northern states; doddering stern-wheelers, pushing on up the Missouri from St. Joseph, where the side-wheelers turned back, poured prospective gold miners into the Mormon Trail. The population of the little frontier towns swelled overnight until almost any general description applicable to the camps at Independence and St. Jo might be used in relation to Kanesville (or Council Bluffs) without detection. And then the printer's ink really sizzled as the Mormon elders warned the converts to keep off the river and denounced the steamboats as carriers of whisky, wanton women, and cholera—all of which was true.

Across from Kanesville at Trader's Point the Forty-niners found Sarpie, trader and frontiersman, almost the only inhabitant. Later a city grew up on the western bank, and travelers of the sixties outfitted there, calling it by its present name, Omaha.

The Mormon Trail was well chosen. It was direct. For some unaccountable reason, it had a more vigorous growth of grass. True, it was timberless, having one stretch of two hundred miles broken by a single cottonwood called the Lone Tree; but the south bank was little better. Best of all it had comparatively few river crossings. The Elkhorn and the Loup Fork of the Platte had to be negotiated; but the Loup was soon equipped with a ferry, and the Elkhorn was no more to be dreaded than the Big Blue. Neither the South nor the North Platte had to be crossed, nor Laramie River sometimes called the Middle Fork of the Platte, nor the Kansas with its tributaries. On this account alone travelers of the north-bank trail gained time and saved animals.

There were no forts nor trading posts on the north bank of the Platte in early days, but nearly always a horseman could swim the river to the Oregon Trail forts for mail and supplies. The disadvantages could not outweigh the benefits.

With a discriminating hindsight, assisted by the knowledge of what actually happened to several thousand gold-seekers, I certainly would pick for any Argonaut ancestor of mine an uneventful trip on the north-bank trail in the auspicious year 1853.

9

Keep the Wagons Moving

WE WERE SOUTH OF THE RIVER AGAIN, and the bluffs were closing in. The valley was gradually getting higher and drier and was exclamation-pointed with tubular, whirling dust funnels. For the first time we could see the detail of the dunes across to the north, and each separate knoll looked as if it had been pulled to a point by giant fingers, like the crown of a ten-gallon hat. The line of southern dunes was also taking shape. Soon they would be steep hills, a natural phenomenon which many of the draught animals and some of the emigrants had never seen.

This was a sort of no man's land between the Pawnee and the Sioux. The Indians never fought in the winter; but unfortunately the weeks the emigrants spent in the Platte Valley each year corresponded with the annual recurrence of hostilities between the two tribes, in which the young braves naturally went to war for the simple purpose of bringing home enough figurative bacon to set up housekeeping.

It was no easy matter to maintain apparent calm while driving past a line of forty or fifty painted Sioux whose scheme of decoration somewhat resembled the top of totem poles and seemed (I quote the women) almost as far from the ground. They were generally headed for the unfortunate Pawnee and, beyond an occasional question in sign language, rarely deigned to notice the trespassers on their path—padding past single-file in utter, and usually nude, dignity. Nervous moments, yes, but helped a lot by the well known fact that visible Indians were apt to be good Indians.

On May 26, 1852, a young wife, Mrs. Francis H. Sawyer, wrote: "A large party of Pawnee Indians passed us this morning going on to their hunting ground after buffalo, and this afternoon we met them returning. They had met a party of Sioux, and the result was a battle took place. The Sioux had whipped them, killing and scalping two of the party and wounding several others. The Pawnees were very angry and badly frightened. Some were armed with bows and some with guns. I met some ladies that saw the fight, and they said that they were scared almost to death themselves. The Pawnees had made a poor fight. There were only thirteen Sioux and they whipped sixty or seventy Pawnees. When we came to where the battle had been fought, Mr. Sawyer and I drove off the road a short distance to see one of the Indians who had been killed. It was the most horrible sight I ever saw. Four or five arrows were sticking in his body and his scalp was gone, leaving his head bare, bloody and ghastly. I am sorry I went out to look at him. I have had the blues ever since."

About fourteen miles west of Fort Kearney there was a wagon ford across the Great Platte. There was no pressing need to cross. The travelers on the north bank need never negotiate a foot of Platte water, while those on the south bank might continue for a couple of weeks and then cross the north and south forks separately. Still there were always some who for one reason or another just *must* get on the other side.

On May 27, 1852, Lodisa Frizzell stood and looked first at the mile and a half of rushing water between her and the far bank, and then at a smug little signboard which announced unfeelingly that the ford was safe. Two horsemen were testing the route, setting willow poles deeply in the sand bars to mark the way. A single team was following their directions; but, as the animals were swimming and therefore invisible, the wagon bed looked like a tiny boat adrift in rough waters. When it had safely arrived at the south bank the captain of Lodisa's company questioned the driver and decided to ford to the north side. His twenty wagons took the water one at a time. They were two hours in crossing and made a line from shore to shore. It was impossible to see bottom at the depth of one inch, so that the foaming river looked as dangerous as the Missouri running bank-full; and the noise of the sand-laden water rushing through the spokes was deafening.

Eight days later Udell crossed at, or near, the same spot. He labeled it as two miles wide with a quicksand bottom full of deep holes. His companions were six hours in water to their necks and in constant danger of drowning.

Eighty miles west of Fort Kearney the emigrants found a spring surrounded by cottonwoods. Near it the ravines were filled with scrub cedar. It was always a favorite camp and later became an important stage stop with the unimaginative name Cottonwood Spring. The cedar wood was

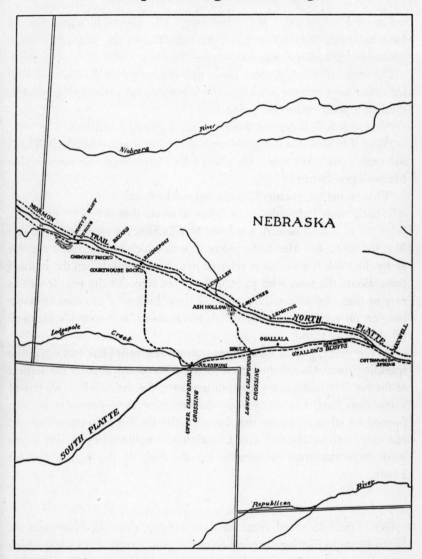

freighted by ox train for a hundred miles in each direction to supply the stations, and cottonwood logs were cut and hauled for building purposes. When the Indians became troublesome Fort McPherson was established close by; and we saw its flag, high and tiny but unmistakable, long before we arrived within sight of the buildings. The stage station disappeared long ago, but the fort remains, surrounded by the beautifully kept grounds of a national cemetery.

The superintendent greeted us—a massive man, newly appointed, and for that reason delving a bit into the history of the place. He gave us at random a good many interesting facts.

"Where was Cottonwood Station?" my husband asked him.

"Why, I believe it was slightly west of the fort, toward Maxwell. That's the next town, you know." He chuckled. "How would you suppose that Maxwell got its name?"

"From some early settler?" hazarded my husband.

"That's what I thought at first, but it seems that the place originally belonged to a man named, I believe, McGlachlin. Anyway he was called Mac for short, and Mac had a splendid well which became quite popular along the road. It was always referred to as Mac's well. When the railroad came along, the man who painted the depot sign did the rest. It was as easy as that," he finished, hitching his great bulk to a more comfortable position on a chair some few inches too narrow, "and now it's Maxwell till the end of time."

On the shady, gravestone-studded lawns many sprinklers sent out a fine sparkling spray. One of the largest monuments commemorates the victims of the horribly unnecessary Grattan massacre, the site of which we passed a few days later. For many years the bodies of these twenty-eight men formed an effective wedge that forced wider the rift between white and red men. And yet, buried with Christian and military impartiality a few yards from the great monument, lies the body of the Indian, Spotted Horse.

*   *   *

Out of the hills ahead, from the right and left, came the North and the South Platte to join together and form the great, erratic river along which we had moved ever since arriving at the site of Dogtown. The junction was known as the Forks of the Platte and was seldom recognized by emigrants owing to the number of islands which caused similar forklike divisions in the current.

In 1842 the Frémont exploring expedition, guided by Kit Carson, crossed the South Platte here and camped on the point of land between the two branches. Lieutenant Frémont was planning to divide his party, sending one group up the North Fork, while he himself took the remaining men up the southern branch. Even though they were to travel through Sioux and Cheyenne country, they arranged to meet at Fort Laramie, miles ahead in unmapped mountains; and they arrived according to schedule.

Because the early trails followed the rivers, the spot of land at the forks was simple to describe and to find. Frémont wanted to dig a cache and leave some salt pork here for the return trip, but his party was accompanied by a group of friendly Indians. He wrote: "It was impossible to conceal such a proceeding from the sharp eyes of our Cheyenne companions, and I therefore told them to go and see what it was they were burying. They would otherwise have not failed to return and destroy our cache, in expectation of some rich booty; but pork they dislike, and never eat."

Three years before, on the same spot, the American fur traders under Harris were camped at the forks when they received warning of the approach of some two or three thousand Ogallala Sioux. They immediately buried their alcohol barrels and waited for them to pass. Instead the embarrassingly friendly Ogallalas camped alongside, held some sort of function, and howled all night in celebration; and only when the last Sioux had gone did the traders dare to dig up their stock of alcohol and move on. A few Oregon-bound missionaries who were in the camp were both gratified and amused when the traders, wholly against their wishes, rested on Sunday.

In 1850 another scene was enacted at the Forks of the Platte: not comedy this time—purest melodrama. It was early evening and, in a large corral formed by prairie schooners, emigrants were going about their suppertime activities, when "down the river came a sound, as of distant thunder, yet more terrible to the ears of the practiced emigrant on the plains. Instantly every man was on his feet listening to the approaching sounds. Faintly above the noise could be heard the cry of stampede! stampede! and a dark mass enveloped in the dust could be seen moving—with the speed of the wind."

E. S. Ingalls, when the excitement was over, wrote graphically of the experience in his journal. The danger was serious, for approximately a hundred fifty horses, mules, and oxen came sweeping down upon them.

Now a stampede is like a snowball. It collects new material from every point of contact, and gets bigger as it rushes along, so that their first horrified thought was for the stock grazing outside the camp. Unless the course of the stampede was deflected, every living thing without the protecting circle of the wagons would be swept away or injured. A frantic rush was made to get the animals inside, and Ingalls wrote, with humor hardly to be expected under the circumstances, that the mules, of course, resisted every effort to get them to walk, and had practically to be moved by sheer muscle power.

One can well imagine the mothers distractedly calling the roll of the large families of the day. It was not, as a rule, possible to collect them all in the short time available in emergencies, and no help was to be expected from the fathers, whose first duty was to the animals. A mother never knew until the danger was over whether or not her children had all found shelter.

In this case, the rushing animals turned when but a short distance away and, surging over the shoulder of high land that lies between the rivers, crowded into the point of land where Frémont had camped, which now lay like a half-finished picture before us, waiting for imagination to fill in the detail.

Stampedes and the fear of stampedes were in the very air of the Platte Valley, and more occurred near the Forks than anywhere else. From whatever trivial cause, the animals were struck to frenzy as you strike fire from a match and broke away somewhere almost every night. Over splintered wreckage of wagon wheels, torn remnants of muslin tops and impeding groups of frightened humanity, plunged the sheer driving fury of hoofed hell on the loose, causing not only immediate danger, but long continued embarrassment and helplessness. Unless the animals were recovered the deprived wagons were paralyzed. Moreover the danger seemed never-ending. It was not unheard-of for the stock of a company to go crashing through all barriers several nights in succession.

When the wild urge to run was spent the gregarious instincts of farm-raised oxen and hitherto cherished teams of genteel horses led them, unless buffalo were near, to some camp or, in the sixties, to a Platte Valley ranch.

Although the night episodes were ghastly it was in the daytime that lives were lost. Picture three entire trains on the march—trains which harnessed a total of two hundred animals—oxen plodding patiently with tails aswitch, big slow-stepping mules with noses to the ground, scattered horsemen, women and children riding in the wagons or walking by the roadside, bunches of loose stock. Suddenly something shatters the over-wrought nerves of just one team and, without preamble, the plodding procession is a wild stampede.

Behind the crazed animals each great wagon leaps from rut to rut and rock to rock like a five-gallon can tied to a terrified dog. Horsemen pound furiously after disappearing stock or hold to the bits of frantic leaders. There are practically no brakes and few reins. The distracted passengers would jump except for the thundering teams behind.

Here a man rides desperately to overtake a pounding wagon, driven by his half-grown boy. Here an animal falls and is dragged till dead. Here a man hangs to the horns of a plunging ox while behind him his invalid wife is dashed helplessly about in the bed of the van. Here a fallen ox with horn caught beneath a root breaks its neck but serves as an anchor to save its great land ship. Here and there a child falls out, or possibly, lives to tell a tale like that of nine-year-old Maggie Hall whose careening home on wheels was trailed like a jerking kite tail behind six running oxen. One by one they dropped and were wrenched loose, until exhaustion stopped the last two, Bright and Lion—one on the bleeding stumps of the other's horns—with nobody in sight, and not a sound but the children crying.

Katherine Dunlap cites in her diary the finding of a grave. Its occupants had evidently been buried by strangers, for the small board at the head was inscribed simply, "Two children, killed by a stampede."

* * *

We traced our steps from the ford at the Forks back to the trail proper and proceeded toward the next, and more popular, crossing. Between us and the river (which was now the South Platte) lay Frémont's Slough. It was some distance north of the trail, but many a caravan deviated from the strait and narrow path long enough to enjoy its plenty for a night.

We passed the marker on the site of Bishop's Station and soon came to the first of the famous trail landmarks south of the river: O'Fallon's Bluffs. This unspectacular elevation was only remarkable in being the vanguard of the sandstone formations. At its very foot the South Fork lay torpid in the sun, bulged around the contours of Isaac Dillon Island like a snake that has swallowed a rabbit. We went up and over the flat top of the bluff just as the emigrants had been forced to do. When it was practical to get down into the narrowing valley, the trail descended again, and battalions of clean-washed little sunflowers turned their faces steadfastly toward the west with us, for the sun was low.

Here our Express map blew out the window and was rescued on an anthill—a circumstance which, unimportant in itself, opened up a conversation on the subject of ants, at one time very numerous along the South Platte. Their mounds were like inverted milk pans, six to eight feet across and six inches high, and often held a fair amount of Indian beads about the size of the tiny pebbles ordinarily used in the construction of their underground cities, and much easier to carry.

These anthills were an invaluable asset to the plainsman. I quote an inelegant but informative paragraph from "The Overland Stage to California": "It is a notorious fact that many of the overland stage drivers and stock tenders, between three and four decades ago, were inhabited by a species of vermin known as pediculus vestimenti, but on the plains more vulgarly called 'gray-backs.' During the hot weather of midsummer, when the vermin were rapidly multiplying, it was the custom of the boys at the station to take their underclothing and blankets in the morning, spread them out on the ant-hill, and get them late in the afternoon." The ants, it seems, solicitously searched out and killed the last socially unmentionable insect. This polite attention, plus the intense sunning thrown in for good measure, constituted the dry cleaning of the plains.

The river crossing was our next objective. From the moment that they had passed the junction of the rivers the emigrants were fired with only one thought: to get across the South Platte. The Colorado gold-seekers of '59, Pikes Peakers as they were called, might remain comfortably on the south bank, but travelers to Oregon and California and, later, to Montana and Idaho must ford this large watercourse which unaccommodatingly swung too far to the left for their purpose.

Many crossed immediately above the forks, following Frémont's example. There were also several little-used fords, but the great bulk of the migration crossed four miles above Brule, Nebraska, at a spot called the Lower California Crossing, although in the late fifties and the sixties the Upper California Crossing at Julesburg, Colorado, became a rival.

The stage line went that way; but it was more than twenty miles up-stream, and the emigrant-train captains were anxious to cross at once and have it over. The stories that your grandfather, grandmother, or Great-Aunt Hannah have told of the dreaded South Platte ford probably took place at the Lower California Crossing near Brule.

We went to Brule (very comfortably on a modern bridge) and were unhesitatingly directed to the automobile repair and blacksmith shop of Art Anderson, whom we found disembowelling a car. Abandoning the operation at its most critical stage when we mentioned Oregon Trail, he gave keen opinions on all disputed points about the crossing and the near-by stretches of trail on both sides of the river. He had an interesting collection of pioneer relics in his shop, including one of the very rare wooden jackets for the glass insulators of the telegraph wires. These were a needful addition in the second decade of the transcontinental telegraph line, and kept the Indians from splintering the glass with their arrows. At first the red men seldom molested the line because they had been told that the trooping telegraph poles marched direct to the White House and that the wires belonged exclusively to the Great White Father in Wash-ington. But as time went on, and the distrust between the races deep-ened, the telegraph, too, was subjected to insult. The easily broken glass insulators were favorite targets. Mr. Anderson's wooden insulator jacket had come from Diamond Springs, a home station on the overland stage line, the site of which we soon passed, two miles west of Brule and south of the river.

There are many farms along the south bank, and we made inquiries here and there, traversing miles of level ground where in the old days the emigrants had camped if the day was too far spent to permit cross-ing. A farm road brought us to a long, one-way bridge—very old and very quaint. We are assured that it is as nearly as possible at the site of the old ford. The river is now quite ordinary. By no stretch of imagina-tion could it be called a quarter of a mile wide, and yet none of the pio-neers estimated the South Platte at this point at less than a half-mile; some said three-quarters, some a mile, while a few, remembering how long they were in the water and how far away the distant shore had looked, said confidently a mile and a half.

This was disconcerting, and before leaving home we had been consid-erably annoyed by the apparent exaggeration. It was inconceivable that any one who had crossed a channel a mile and a half in width should underestimate it by two-thirds. We were forced to believe that many of them had overstated the case, which raised the important issue as to whether we could believe other data which we might gather from these writers. However, as we read more diaries and learned to know the history of the river, we found that its width varied greatly from week to week and even from day to day. In the decades before farming reclaimed the land along the banks and stabilized the channel, twelve hours of warm rain on the mountain snows could, and did, add whole new runnels to the river so that emigrant camps made on dry land far from the regular course of the stream found themselves afloat by morning. The river at such times actually *was* a mile or more in width.

Another item which made an exaggerated idea of the river's width excusable was the fact that the wagon trains never traveled straight across: they went down with the current to about the middle of the distance and then if able turned and came up diagonally against the current. One train which found the river about three-quarters of a mile wide, traveled a mile and a half in the water in a great semicircle. Some wrote that this was unavoidable owing to the strength of the wind and current; others that it was done wittingly to prevent the swift sand-laden water from striking the wheels broadside. Those who could not make the curve landed as much as two miles downstream.

Everything considered, the crossing near Brule was the greatest ford of the Overland trek. True, there were trains which, from choice, plowed through the Great Platte in its entirety—a much more stupendous feat. There were also wagon trains which, instead of ferrying, forded or attempted to ford the rapacious flood of the Green River on narrow and unstable gravel bars—an undertaking incomparably more dangerous to human life; but these exploits were few and far between. On the other hand, there were hundreds of wagons each day during the season, which must get through the quicksand of the South Platte ford or give up the journey. It was one of the few dangers of which they had definite advance notice. They could, and did, worry about it from the time they left home. Other large streams were ferried or bridged, but not the South Platte. Its great width, yielding quicksands and lack of large timber near at hand effectively prevented bridging for many years, while its shallows and sand bars prevented the operation of a ferry. From the days of the first fur trappers, on through the Oregon migration and the California gold rush, it was in everybody's way.

The very early fur traders' parties and the exploring expeditions had their own method of crossing which was entirely useless to wagon caravans. They made bullboats. The rules were like the old recipe for rabbit stew which began, "First catch your rabbit." The main essential was fresh, or "green" buffalo hides, which necessitated first catching a few buffalo bulls—the bigger the better. The green hides were sewed together and put, while still soft, over the bed of a cart (if they had one along) or a framework of green willow poles, conveniently bent by driving both ends in the ground. The hides were then allowed to dry and shrink. This

Bull boats.

process supplied a large strong boat that would carry several men and their dunnage, and drew only a few inches of water.

The average emigrant knew nothing of this, and it would not have helped him anyway. His problem wasn't the baggage; it was the wagon. If necessary he lightened the load by repacking it on animals and sending it across first; then the wagon was less likely to sink in the quicksand and easier to pull, although more apt to be floated out of a true course. Generally he let the load alone, but raised it above water level by means of blocks put between the beds and the bolsters. Ten and fifteen yoke of oxen were sometimes hooked to a wagon. When, as occasionally happened, they balked in midstream and started back, the ensuing mix-up was full of possibilities.

The river, of course, was peppered with sand bars rising at unpleasant angles. It was also full of equally sudden holes. Moreover the bars and the holes had an uncalled-for habit of changing places. If the quicksand proved too bothersome, the loose stock might be driven back and forth to pack it; but this is seldom mentioned, and never by emigrants traveling in a large emigration. Each year as the summer advanced, the river grew narrower, the water shallower, and the sand more firmly packed. Late trains were then able to go straight across with no preliminaries and little real danger. But few of them ever realized their good fortune.

Think of an average crossing in mid-season somewhat as follows: The river is spread over an irregular section some half-mile wide. It has a violent current but is not over a man's shoulders except in the holes, and a week or more may go by without loss of life. The banks on the south side are covered with wagons, bunched stock, and hurrying men. The women sit still and tight-lipped with their children around them. Their work will commence when they get their drenched belongings on the far shore. Some of the men are using "Dutch courage," and the air fills with loud jokes, shouts, and great bursts of profanity. Others are frankly worried or else oversilent.

Some wagons have cholera cases aboard, for this is in the midst of the infected stretch. Some, who have seen the stunning swiftness of the cholera's attack, dread the crossing most on account of the two or three hours' enforced absence from a doctor's care; and some will die for that reason.

The captain of a given train has now decided his course through the water. It will not be exactly where the last train crossed, for their wheels have cut the sand and the swirling current has sucked it out to leave large holes. Anxiously he has grouped his wagons to take the water—his best driver and team first to encourage the rest. They move forward to the bank. There is a four-foot drop, and the team balks stubbornly. After an interval of fruitless struggle to pull or push them off, a horseman rides a wise old mare across and ties her in plain sight (but as if seen through the wrong end of an opera glass) on the opposite shore.

They now try again and the team goes off into the river. The wagon stands on end, holding the wheelers under water. The team is entirely lost to sight and the terrified women and children penned within the hooded wagons see nothing through the foremost hoop but the swirling, muddy current. If this is a team of six oxen, six horses, or mules (and it had better be), the leaders are free to pull, and they soon lurch the whole outfit into motion. The hind wheels come down with a terrific splash. The wheelers struggle to the surface. The women, looking through the foremost hoop, see daylight again and, squinting their eyes against the sun glare, make out the reassuring figure of the old white mare half a mile away across the shining water. The crossing has auspiciously begun.

The chances are also highly in favor of its finishing in the same manner. It is seldom that all of a six-horse team are swimming at once. The noise of the sand-laden water rushing through the spokes is terrifying, but its most irritating result is to cut into tatters the trousers of the men who must wade. If a boy who cannot swim "plunks off into a hole," the swift current probably sweeps him to shallower water before he can even start to drown. Men and animals sink and come up separately, and then wade out. Soon the whole line of wagons is lurching, splashing, or floating in a great half-moon whose ends touch either shore.

Large companies provide extra horsemen who ride here and there among the wagons, pulling and beating the teams into breasting the tumultuous current that continuously forces them downstream, and keeping them in motion, for the grasping quicksand, while not very fast in action, is strong if given time.

None dare to stop. Keep moving if you value your animals, your property, your family, or your life. "KEEP THE WAGONS MOVING."

A mule down! A wagon overturned! The rest of the line is relegated to unknown detours hastily piloted by horsemen. The spectacle of the plunging animals and the pandemonium of yells and oaths add to the difficulty of controlling the near-by teams—and controlled they must be.

Two women are handling an ox-drawn wagon. The wheel ox founders and starts to sink resignedly. Desperately one clambers down the front elevation of her schooner and jabs him hard in the rear with a goad. He plunges and struggles to a firm footing, and the wagon is saved.

Not so fortunate is the man whose oxen plod into a larger swirl of yielding quicksand. Their short legs are imbedded at once, and inch by inch they and the wagon disappear from sight. In a little while the broad river sweeps on its way, "sunny, sparkling, placid, without a ripple to mark where a lonely man parted with all his fortune."

And still it is probable that no one drowns, though the wrecked wagon is left—an invisible pitfall for tomorrow's traveler among the many whose weather-beaten bows remain above water to chart the course.

Crossing the South Platte.

When snugly dry and in order again, the pilgrims left the South Platte for good and all and began to climb the rough, high land between the forks. They called the first steep pull "California Hill." Deep ascending ruts still mar its surface. A tiny school sits squatly on the rounded hillside like a flea on an elephant. Not much else has come to change its look from the days when the drivers cracked their whips like rifle shots to urge the dragging ox trains up the slope.

To those who stood at the river's edge, fresh from its last surmounted danger, the undulating line of ascending prairie schooners was a soul-stirring sight. As the little puppet figures with their great white-topped wagons mounted the high crown of the hill crest, each tiny manikin turned to look its last at the river; but the wagons rolled steadily over and down—gleaming white canvas last to disappear—as the land ships vanished from sight.

10

Ash Hollow

THE HIGH LAND BETWEEN THE FORKS is not a series of gentle, dumpling hills, but eminences that occasionally drop off into small but jagged canyons. To many of the pioneers canyons were a new experience. In past weeks the prairie swells, intensifying into the roly-poly dunes of the Platte, had accustomed those animals hailing from the flat country to pull together on an incline, so that the wheelers no longer strained at the load while the leaders backed, and vice versa. On the down slopes the drivers had learned to chain the wheels so that they served as brakes, and felt that they had the matter well in hand. Still, the few abrupt declivities they had seen were short drops into deep-set prairie streams and probably did not exceed twenty feet. These broken hills were different. As the emigrants took their wagons past the brink of rain-gutted canyons, a couple of hundred feet deep, their heads reeled; and one woman wrote that the eye could scarcely carry to the bottom of the frightful abyss. The wind blows mightily up here; and, even on the balmy July day of our first visit, it shrieked around the pre-streamlined corners of the family automobile with unnecessary energy.

"I never did see an abyss," Bill (who was practically raised in the Sierra Nevadas) said accusingly. "Can't we stop and look over?"

"Well, of course," his father said, "I *am* stopping. Must be the wind rolling us." The hand brake jerked in no uncertain terms, and he and I got out to walk the rest of the way across the high ground to the point where the old road drops into Ash Hollow, leaving Bill and Dr. Neff to detour with the car and meet us later.

In years past, the space on either side of the road may well have looked like a junk yard as fresh batches of easily dispensable articles were discarded. Many stoves carried hopefully thus far were left to rust by the wayside, for Ash Hollow was midway of the treeless area. The term, which was more or less relative as applied to the south bank of the Platte, was so literally true of the north side that it was told as a solemn fact that the Lone Tree, nearly opposite Ash Hollow, was the only specimen for two hundred miles.

Let us consider for a moment the condition of the emigrants of any typical year as they contended with their first real hills. Beyond a doubt, they were much wiser as to trail technique and camp customs than when they left the Missouri almost a month before. One woman who had lightly left a luxurious home wept to think how comfortable her father's hogs continued, while, on the other hand, certain chronic invalids were much improved. Ladies whose fastidious appetite had, at home, been entirely dependent on tidbits now ate burnt biscuit and boiled beans and counted mush and milk a delicacy. The trains were somewhat lightened as to loads and (barring loss by accident) still possessed a full quota of animals. Most of the rolling stock held firm. Provident men had paid high prices for wagons of the best hard woods and had reason to hope that they would last the journey through. Poor or careless men, starting with cheap wagons in bad repair, so far had been able to postpone the beginning of their disintegration by generous soaking in the river after each hot day. This tightened the spokes in the hubs and swelled the felloes so that the tires did not become loose. The backwashes of the Platte River had, so far, afforded endless facilities for this treatment, and the incipient one-hoss shays were still with the procession as it trailed over the hills to Ash Hollow. One might say that the journey had done the caravans little harm *unless* (and it was this "unless" that made all the difference) it happened to be a cholera year.

Some of the so-called cholera cases were only cholera morbus. Emigrants were constantly warned not to eat overly fresh game, especially if it had been run before killing, but the men were tired of salt meat and many pooh-poohed—until the unpleasant consequences followed in good time and had to be endured.

Cholera morbus laid them low, but it was not to be mentioned in the same breath with its deadly namesake, Asiatic cholera; and we have the testimony of physicians of the day that it was the genuine, simon-pure article which filtered up the Mississippi on the river boats from the port of New Orleans. Up the Missouri it traveled, and into the trail outfitting towns, whose cemeteries grew apace. Out to the prairies it marched with the emigrant columns, reserving the full strength of its attack until it struck the Platte Valley, where crowded camp sites and polluted wells provided a fertile field for its spread. Here it reigned supreme in its terror, for while it raged the Indians gave the camps a wide berth.

The year 1849, with many times the traffic of previous seasons, was the worst for cholera. Except that a pitying Providence provided that it should be one of the most favorable years for grass within the memory of the white man, it is hard to imagine how the stricken companies could have managed to drive their animals far enough from the trail to find forage. The camp work and care of the teams were heaped upon those who were still on their feet, regardless of age, sex, or strength. Women harnessed and drove, got their own water and fuel, cooked, packed, nursed, and worked shoulder to shoulder with the men.

The onslaught of cholera was sudden and violent. In extreme cases a traveler might get up as usual in the morning and be buried at the noon stop. It was made more mysterious and dreaded by the utter ignorance of the emigrants as to what caused it. Physicians and thinkers advocated the use of swiftly running river water instead of the polluted wells; but the general knowledge of the action of germs was still in the future, and few, if any, consistently boiled their drinking water. Some guidebooks recommended it, and, in reminiscences compiled many years later, a few pioneers have written that they did so; but I suspect that most of them merely made coffee or tea as being more palatable, and that boiling the water was incidental.

Journals were almost invariably irregularly kept or entirely neglected during a virulent attack of cholera, but that of John Wood carries on, day by day, through his illness and gives more detail about the progress of the disease through his company than any other diary we have seen. I will endeavor to give in brief his story of the happenings of the fortnight beginning on June 6, 1850. In order to get the entire picture, we must bear in mind that the train was in a state of despondency from two consecutive stampedes and a night in which they had tried to sleep in six inches of water. On the morning of June 6th, Robert Duncan was found to be suffering from cholera. This (we can imagine the train captain saying) made everything complete. The sick boy wanted a hymn sung; but the men of his mess were not equal to vocalizing, and it was read instead, after which he relapsed into helpless misery and lay at the brink of death. The next day John Wood himself and two others were taken sick. June 8th, at noon, John learned that they had buried his two comrades near Plum Creek. The company was on the road again by three in the afternoon and, before evening Ellis Dixon lay dead in his wagon. Some brave soul put his body in a tent and straightened it for the grave. Robert Duncan was past hope, but John Wood was recovering and was able to write: "We are not alone in the calamity, thousands are around us sharing the same fate. The sick and the dying are on the right and on the left, in front and in the rear and in our midst. We, ourselves, are nearly all sick—I feel very weak myself. Hundreds are on their way home, faint-hearted and terror stricken. Death is behind as well as before. Many are stalking their way through pestilence, unmoved, while others view each step with perfect consternation. A number of our company now feel determined to go home."

The next day four more boys fell sick and Robert Duncan died; and on the next, June 11th, they started again on their "sickly course to the promised land" and seemed to be traveling through a great graveyard. A doctor advised them to drink as little water as possible and to get it from the muddy river—a most unpopular idea and one not always put into practice. The situation was terrifying and seemed to John like balancing on slippery rock, not knowing when the footing would give way. During the morning Robert Hendrickson died, and they buried him at noon, adding another pitiful handful of human ashes to the stupendous total already enriching the sands of the Platte Valley. On the 12th nothing happened, and on the 13th, all the sick were better—a good thing because on the next day another stampede occurred and two of the hitherto unaffected men were run over. On the 15th they slowly negotiated the difficult crossing of the South Platte, and Jackson Stuart, who had been without the service of a doctor while in the river, died as a result.

Death was all around them—and scenes more saddening than death itself. John was now able to take care of himself and occasionally to lend a hand to others, so that, hearing a child sobbing, he left his wagon to investigate and found a little boy beside the unburied body of a man. He was completely alone, and the cry, "Father, father, what will become of me?" rang for days in the ears of hearers helpless to comfort him.

On the night of June 17th, the company camped in Ash Hollow. The dreadful agony of cholera caught Wesley Mahan, and John sat up all night alone with him while the wolves howled. Toward morning he died. "Oh, God," John wrote desperately in his diary, "shall I ever see such sights again!" and in the dawn attended the hasty burial. This, except for a man who lingered two weeks and then succumbed, was the complete tally of the cholera victims in John Wood's company.

The cumulative effect of such scenes, many times repeated, was tremendous. Some of the travelers worked themselves into such a frenzy of fear that they drove their animals day and night in a growing crescendo of terror. Some grew so callous in their mad flight that they would not stop to give adequate assistance to the dying, but rushed on, carrying them helpless and unattended in the wagons. One party, arriving at the evening camp with two dead men, admitted having abandoned a living sufferer by the side of the road. This was a common happening, and nothing constructive was ever done about it although much indignation was both written and expressed. Sometimes a note might be found beside the abandoned sick man, asking that he be given food and water. In other cases the sufferer was simply left behind when the train pulled out in the morning through lack of any one sufficiently concerned to brave the terror of the epidemic by caring for him.

These facts were harsh, but the emigration had to face the fact that there were worse things than mere abandonment, which at least gave the invalid a fighting chance. Desertion was an open action and the company so doing had to face the storm of criticism which followed. On the contrary, if the members of the victim's mess neatly did the burying themselves, there was no publicity at all. In one instance a woman, left alone by the death of her husband, was probably helped out of the embarrassing predicament of being desperately ill in a company of frightened males by having her grave dug and an overdose of laudanum administered. Other cases equally incapable of proof are mentioned.

Such proceedings were acknowledged wrong, but even the right and ethical way to handle a cholera case in a well regulated train of miscellaneous men was sufficiently heartless to chill the blood. The dying person, doubtless in great agony, was left behind in charge of two men who kept their saddle horses with them. They did what they could for him, but their important duty was to dig the grave, and they dug it at once—necessarily within sight of the doomed man. Then they waited—waited impatiently, for if either of them was taken sick before he caught up with the train his own chances for life were slim. One dying man, who had sunk into apparent coma, got strength from sheer desperation to protest against premature burial on the very brink of the new-dug grave. Sheer terror prompted much of the cruelty, necessity the rest; but it was a stark, raving, maniacal period which the emigrants experienced in the plague-smitten Platte Valley.

Turning to softer, but no less moving, aspects of the unhappy visitation, we find records of people who tended and buried the abandoned; carried sick strangers in their wagons, took orphaned children or mothers with families, maintaining them out of their own scanty supplies clear to the Pacific coast. These disconsolate and bereaved families were perhaps the saddest sight that the Overland Trail had to offer; crushed and stupefied by their loss; hurried along willy-nilly in a company of strangers, with their nearest and dearest left for the wolves to dig up and devour.

Coffins were not to be had, unless some one could spare the boards from a wagon bed, and the heartsick relatives had only to look around them to know that, by tomorrow, there would be a burrow or two, like giant rabbit holes, leading down into the grave and pathetic fragments would tell a tale of horror. The very name, "wolves," was horrible to any one who had buried a friend or relative and, to defeat their ghoulish appetite, children were often interred in the metal or rawhide trunks which had contained the extra clothing. One woman was so filled with loathing on her first trip across the plains that, when necessity forced her to make a second journey while in poor health, she carried a metal coffin—a forehanded gesture which was justified by her death and burial at Fort Laramie.

Sanity was retained in such cases by the irrevocable fact that the survivors *must* go on. Quiet or hysterical, hazy or all too keenly agonized, the bereaved army made its mileage daily, focusing its scattered wits on immediate problems such as proper food for an orphaned baby rapidly yelling itself black in the face, or how to prevent a dead boy's dog from turning back to his grave.

They must go on living, but they never forgot. Through half a century a certain flower scent brought back to an orphaned daughter the day when she left her mother among the roses of the Platte.

*   *   *

"That settles it," my husband said dolefully as we found an exception-ally fine rut. "I was in hopes that we were on the wrong track. Where are the precipices, I'd like to know. Show me one abyss. Somebody said that they couldn't see bottom in the dreadful canyons, didn't they?"

"'The eye is lost in space as it endeavors to penetrate its depths,'" I corrected amiably. "At least that's what Fanny Kelly said."

The trail had forked some distance back, and now each branch frayed out into short ends and approached the next rise from many directions. We selected one and followed it until, without any death-defying leaps or undue exertion, we simply walked out to the brink of the hill over-looking Ash Hollow where we had a bird's-eye view of our familiar car already waiting below us. We were on a quiet stretch of bluff top—wind-swept, remote, and empty; and we learned (as had the emigrants many years before) that these hills do not slope gradually down to the river, but break off into something resembling modified cliffs. Below the steep, ragged slope was the rounded end of a tree-dotted "Hollow" which invades the high land for the distance of a mile so circuitously that it seems to have screwed itself into the hills. On our right the high-way swung down to its floor and zigzagged in white, shining loops out to the North Platte Valley. To our left was the easiest descent: a fat, bare hill that sagged evenly, without broken gullies, to the level of the hollow. Its smooth, clean-cut brink formed the horizon and, beginning at the sky line as if made by chariots from heaven, the old ruts rolled off the top and spilled obliquely down.

"So that's the terrible Windlass Hill!" I exclaimed. "If those people had only known what they were going to go over before they got to the Pacific, they'd have thought this was easy."

"Maybe—but getting down to Ash Hollow wasn't exactly a snap at that. How would you like to start a heavy wagon with no brakes over the top of that hill?"

"I wouldn't be afraid to bet it would get down," I replied cagily.

"Yes, wrong side up," answered my understanding husband, "and it wouldn't be the first one by a whole lot."

"How *did* they get down, anyway? They certainly didn't drag trees behind them. The supply wouldn't have lasted a week." I glanced cal-culatingly at the sparse growth of scrubby little conifers that graced the bluffs and then at the hilltop again. "Oh, I know!" I'm sure my simple countenance brightened as the light dawned. "So that's why they called it Windlass Hill. Where was the windlass?"

"Each company rolled its own. The men staked a big wagon tight to the ground on top of the hill and left one set of wheels running free. Then a long, strong rope was wound around the axle, and the loose end tied to the wagon which was to go down. The men held back on the spokes of the turning wheels and paid out the rope by the foot. There was always one pair of animals hitched in front of the descending wagon to hold up the tongue, so everything was under control, unless—"

"Unless the rope broke," I surmised.

"Exactly—unless it broke."

"And if it did break, then what?"

"Well, if there were enough men with the wagon they could probably hold it back. If not, it pushed the team off their feet and everything rolled down sideways."

"H'm-m. And then they shot the animals with broken legs; mended the wagons, repacked, and went on. Was that it?"

"That was it."

Silence followed which I presently broke. "Ash Hollow must have been a lively place in its day. It's quiet enough now, though. I haven't even seen a car on the highway. Let's go down."

We started along the rough slope toward our car, which stood below us near the ruin of a small stone house. There was no other sign of life.

My husband looked across at the descending ruts. "That hill really isn't so bad," he announced. "It would have been simple to build a road winding down on an easy grade. If all the men who were in this hollow in one day, in 1849, had gone to work on that road, they could have pulled out the next morning and left the place perfectly safe for everybody that came later."

"But they couldn't," I objected. "The duty of every captain was to his own people."

"Yes, I know," he said. "If they worked for a day, two or three hundred wagons might get ahead of them and eat up the grass. Any captain would rather let the whole emigration fall down Windlass Hill than have that happen."

We found Bill and Dr. Neff prowling around the little ruined hut. It is the successor to the original trapper's log cabin that stood there in the first days of the migrations and was used as a sort of emergency post office. Notices of lost cattle were posted, and messages to friends traveling a few days or weeks behind. Letters to families left east of the Missouri were pinned to the wall with a coin and a note begging that some eastbound trader or straggler returning from the column ahead would take them back to "the States" and mail them there.

All of the hollow, or ravine, is visible from the highway, so we got into the car and rode toward the North Platte. On the west side of the broad opening which widens out into the river bottoms is a tiny trail cemetery on a grassy knoll containing the grave of Rachel Patterson who died here in 1849, at the age of eighteen. The pathos of her youth and the accessibility of her grave have made it one of the best known along the pioneer route. A local legend has grown up to the effect that it was in reprisal of an attempt to kill or capture her that the battle of Ash Hollow was fought. This in contradiction of the fact that she had been dead for several years when the fight occurred.

On the right of the highway are rush-filled ponds, fed by the spring which made the mouth of Ash Hollow a famous camping ground and backed by porous cliffs full of swallows' nests. Beyond the hummocky flat to our left was a group of ranch buildings. Creeping plants grew scatteringly on the whitish earth, giving it a beachlike appearance which extended unbroken by garden or porch, clear to the house door.

The rancher had in his possession a handful of Minié balls and a leg bone in which an arrowhead was imbedded—souvenirs, he believed, of the Battle of Ash Hollow, which inglorious and much misunderstood engagement happened in this vicinity. The battle was the indirect result of the Grattan Massacre, the site of which is many miles west, near Fort Laramie. To describe it now is to cite effect before cause; but the only rule I can follow in this erratic chronicle of the events of many years is to keep the geographical sequence and let chronological order go by the board.

In order to make clear the whys and wherefores of this much decried battle, I will try to give in a few words a picture of the conditions obtaining in the Indian country at the time. It seems that, early in the fifties, the government of the United States and the Indians of the upper Platte region entered into a treaty which provided an annual stipend to be paid the Indians in return for the use which the whites were making of the great emigrant trail and for other encroachments in their domain. This payment was contingent upon the cooperation and good conduct of the red men, and the standard of good conduct was necessarily left to the Indian agent. Even after the goods had been sent out by the government, the agent might withhold them. It may be seen how liable to abuse this privilege was, and it may also be said in passing that the Indian agents of later years were not more incorruptible than other men.

The word "Indian" (either good or bad) along the upper Platte Valley usually meant the Sioux, a nation of many tribes, each under its own chief. They were rightfully called Dakotas, and despised the nickname Sioux, originally derogatory, pinned on them by the French trappers; but the nervous emigrants, attempting to be casual, polite, and indifferent, continued the insult unknowingly. The better class of Sioux contained individuals over whom the travelers waxed poetic. There were splendidly built men of great dignity; women with slim, finely shaped feet and ankles and some elements of beauty; and perfectly formed children. They had the ready ability to learn so generally manifested by our modern educated Indian neighbors and, according to their lights, were honorable. Honor in the abstract meant other things to them than to us. The quality that was important and must be above question was a man's courage. Strength and prowess in battle were greatly desirable. Craft and wisdom set some wizened individuals in positions of tribal importance; but the ability to "take it" was the criterion of a man's worth. An Indian would do well by his friend; but, even among the highest types, there was no thought of playing fair with an enemy. It was not expected.

Practically all tribes had one devastating code that threw out ordinary calculations. If an Indian wronged another tribe and its members could not even the score against him in person, they were in honor bound to wipe out the stigma by taking revenge on some other member of his tribe —something like a tong war or a feud. The whites soon learned that the nature of their reception by any Indians met en route depended, not upon themselves, but upon the conduct of the last party of white men with whom said Indians had had contact. Such conditions gave food for thought to a worried President and a non-understanding Congress, and the government, confronted by the irresistible westward sweep of civilization, made solemn contracts with the red men only to find them impractical or impossible to fulfill.

The treaty with the Sioux was, however, satisfactory for a few years. The government assigned to the various tribes specific territories for their villages which in no way modified their hunting rights in other sections, and some of the branches of the Sioux Nation felt that the annual payment from Washington recompensed them for a certain loss of their original wild freedom. Others did not. This difference of opinion resulted (from the white man's point of view) in good Indians and bad Indians. Most were good Indians with a canny desire to have no interruption in the yearly payments of food and goods. They even went so far as to return to the emigrants cattle that had been stolen by other tribes—the methods used in recovering them being kept off the record.

The Indian agent, supposed to advise and control the various intertribal factions, had headquarters at Fort Laramie.

Without, at present, going into the details of the unfortunate Grattan Massacre, it may be said that inexperience and accident should jointly be blamed for its inception. The Indians, having drawn blood and got their dander up, went on to the murder of a government mail party and to other things which could not go unrebuked. Some months passed. A new year came, and with it a new Indian agent at Fort Laramie.

Something must be done.

The position of the agent was unpleasantly like that of a lion tamer armed with a chair and a whip and with a pile of raw meat ready to reward his dangerous charges after they had done his bidding. The chair and whip could hardly prevent their walking over him to get the meat, should they all get temperamental at once. There must be enough riflemen handy to control the situation. Unfortunately the forts along the Platte in the fifties were few and far between. Moreover they were poorly manned. There was little to prevent a rebellious tribe from wiping out the agent and seizing the supplies which he was supposed to refuse them on account of bad behavior.

The new agent, Thomas Twiss, was a man of resolution. If he had qualms he concealed them nobly. He consulted with the friendly chiefs of the Ogallalas and Brûlés and, in accordance with their ideas, sent runners throughout the tribes stating that the Indians guilty of the murders were known and asking the head men to give them up. Nothing happened. To say that he was in an embarrassing position is an understatement of the first water. He thereupon gave out an ultimatum. The North

Platte was set as the dividing line, and the murderers and their supporters were forbidden to cross it. All those repudiating the incident and wishing to show their friendship to the government were invited to come to the south side.

The next day or two was a prolonged nightmare of suspense. Would they come, or had he made a foolish and costly decision? He waited while the Sioux chieftains moved slowly and with dignity.

First came Chief Big Partizan with his portion of the Brûlé tribe. They crossed and took the station allotted them by Twiss on Cherry Creek about ten miles from the fort. The Ogallalas under Man-Who-Is-Afraid--of-His-Horses, crossed in small bands about nine miles up the river at the Ward and Guerrier trading post. They were assigned, and took, a camping site twenty-five miles up the Laramie Fork. And so Thomas Twiss did with others until some four thousand souls had reported on the side of law and order.

Meanwhile Chief Little Thunder, who some say was concerned both in the Grattan and the mail murder affair, brought his band of recalcitrant Brûlés to the river, near Ash Hollow but on the north side. Instead of crossing the river—a very simple matter to Indians—they camped in plain sight on the north bank. The small tributary of the North Platte, at whose mouth they raised their lodges, was called (in order to make things complicated for future historians) the Little Blue. It was the third stream of that name so far encountered on the trail.

Had there been a casual observer, this simple Indian village would have seemed most inoffensive. To those in the know, it was as deliberate an insult to the government as if they had thumbed their noses from the far shore. It was also an insult to the Sioux south of the river. It could not be overlooked. Uncle Sam had either to punish these foster children or lose face with the rest. General Harney and soldiers were ordered to the spot.

The government reports say that General Harney went to "chastise" them. Biased champions of the red man have used the word in bitter irony; but, to do justice to his memory, that is exactly what the expedition was expected, both by the government and by the Indians, to accomplish. The chastisement killed many and put the rest to flight. It seemed needlessly severe, and earned him the mortifying nickname of "Squaw Killer," but what else was he to do? Government mails had been stopped, government employees murdered, a governmental treaty broken, and there sat the perpetrators of the crime defying him to do anything about it. Both the good Indians sitting smugly south of the river and the bad Indians sitting tight on the north bank expected that a brave foe would act as he did. They looked for such treatment from an enemy, or, failing to get it, thought him soft and unmanly. They did not understand mercy. It is now too late to decide whether or not they might have been better taught by different handling.

General Harney's procedure put an entirely new face on the one-time sport of defying the government's right by treaty to insist on good conduct. The killers decided to give themselves up for the good of the tribe. Possibly the tribe helped a little in the decision, but the fact remains that they arrived voluntarily at the fort, singing their death chant as they rode.

They were imprisoned for a short period only. Those in authority thought rightly that the disgrace was, to an Indian, the worst punishment.

*   *   *

As soon as we had left Ash Hollow the friendly little highway, that had served our purpose so well, shook itself and dived into a large bridge whence, across the river, it made its way townward. But we were able to keep directly on our course for some miles by staying on a ranch road which had taken the way of the old wheel tracks because it was the easiest thing to do.

In the fifties the going was very heavy and the wheels sank eight or ten inches in sand. Indian lodges, singly or in groups, dotted the river banks. Quaint sandstone formations jutted out in unexpected quarters, and layers of hoary rimrock outlined themselves against the sky. Stone of any description was still novel enough to be interesting to the travelers who had come on the south bank of the main Platte, while in the case of those who had traveled the north bank, the section opposite Ash Hollow contained the first real rock of their journey.

If the emigrants had the "white man sickness" in their ranks, they rarely saw an Indian; but if things were progressing normally, they found progress somewhat impeded by the adjoining tribes and, as a result, nerves were so taut in the camps that a false alarm sent bullets whizzing into amazing places, such as camp kettles, wagon loads of powder and totally unoffending barrels of crackers. Sioux war parties continued to pad past in single file. Sioux burial parties brusquely blocked the way until ceremonies were over, and so thoroughly frightened the wagon trains that they corralled and prepared for attack, and were astonished when the Indians dispersed quietly. Large parties of Sioux were met in more holiday mood at the fords, where, presumably, they were amused at the predicaments of the wagons. In this lighter frame of mind they were presented with a tin whistle apiece or, in one case, a bushel of jew's-harps, and tooted to the last man, with great enjoyment.

Sioux, both men and squaws, invaded the camps to trade and soon found that moccasins were an open sesame. The footwear they made and sold was neither as neat nor as durable as that of other nations, but the whole emigration bought them as a conciliatory gesture. When Elisha Brooks passed through in 1852, a number of squaws arrived to visit and remained to make moccasins for the children. They squatted around the camp an hour or two; completed the socklike articles and were rewarded by the small close-fisted traders with seven pins apiece. They were delighted but when, after leaving, it developed that one of their number had mistakenly received eight pins, the whole line solemnly filed back for one more.

Common articles of everyday household use, and tawdry trinkets of no value whatsoever were a constant delight to the Sioux, who lived too far from the border ever to see them, except in the possession of the emigrants or traders. They were especially fond of clothes, which they used entirely for adornment, warmth or so-called decency being entirely out of the picture. In this newly attained rough country whole trunks of extra clothing were discarded by the roadside, and it was never wasted. The braves especially admired the effect of a vest worn with the buttons down the back or a high white collar and not much of anything else. They donned bonnets or ladies' hats and they *loved* umbrellas, which they protected carefully beneath their blankets when it rained. One woman wrote that a bulky young Indian arrived in camp wearing the steel frame of her discarded hoop skirt, like an overlarge bird in a small cage. They enjoyed finery but disliked to be bound in any way, and it was a prevailing custom among all Indians from the Missouri River to the coast, to cut the seat completely out of any pair of trousers they happened to acquire. They then wore them with both pride and comfort.

The emigrants often found a Sioux village of from fifty to three hundred tepees in the stretch between Ash Hollow and Courthouse Rock. It was always friendly—otherwise the tepees would not have been pitched near the trail. In the village, as in the communities of any race—white, brown or red—there were all types, from high to low; and some of the diarists noticed here for the first time that the more degraded Indians were renting their squaws to the white men of the migration with rather less concern than they would have displayed over hiring out a pony.

We read, however, with some satisfaction, that there was one village where the predatory white man did *not* intrude—a large encampment of "Minnesota" Sioux compassing more than three hundred lodges. As the emigrants passed, they turned out en masse, braves, squaws, papooses, dogs, and polecats. They were greasy, almost naked, and smeared with an oil which they procured from the last named household pet. The effluvia rising from the village scorned the feeble efforts of the English language.

* * *

We were fortunate throughout this section of the trail and stayed either in or very close to the old ruts as far as the Courthouse Rock. Sometimes we had to circle, as best we could, corrals and barns and fenced fields; but we were always able to rejoin the old road and adjust our car, with rather delicate nicety, to the deeply worn wheel gouges and the high center of heavy grass. There are always plenty of things to slow one up on the trail in addition to the sheer physical difficulty of making progress; the main time-killer being the constant need of explaining one's uninvited presence in other people's back yards, and why one is bumping uncomfortably over hay roads, foot trails, and unbridged gullies on what is very likely private property, when somewhere within a few miles is an expensive highway provided for and by the taxpayers. Our experiences on such occasions have been undeservedly pleasant, and the people whose privacy we have invaded have been so uniformly helpful that we are happy to count many of them our friends, and have returned again and again.

At a little white house we stopped for a cool drink from the well and the explanation which was their due. Then, painstakingly we picked our way through pasture land, where black-eyed Susans crowded together to watch us pass, and groups of cottonwoods, too young for memories, whispered softly together; where everything was freshly green and warm, and even the fragrance of the earth seemed new. Curious prairie dogs sat up firmly on one blunt end, as if sawed off for the purpose. Rabbits, unused to any necessity for fear, remained erect with long ears pricked; twice pheasants crossed the slender, crumpled ribbon of our pathway. Now and then we passed sod houses, as completely a part of the natural beauty of the scene as squat white boulders waist-deep in grass. A herd of yearling Herefords, with the overpowering curiosity of young cattle for anything strange, followed us for a mile, sampling the canvas cover on our trunk and effortlessly keeping pace with our slow progress.

It was an all-too-short space of time, simple, enjoyable, easy, one which we love to remember. Late in the afternoon, when the evening sky was lemon-colored and placid, we distinguished the dark bulk of Courthouse Rock outlined against the sunset and knew that this day's journey was ending, as hundreds had ended in years past, within sight of the first great monument of the Oregon Trail. Tomorrow we would imitate the thousands of encamped travelers who took time out for a jaunt to "the Courthouse" intending to see for themselves how far away in the deceptive prairie distance it might be. No well conducted tour of the Emigrant Trail, either now or one hundred years ago, would be complete without the inclusion of a pleasure excursion on the side to Courthouse Rock.

Characters and Landmarks of the Trail

ON THE SOUTH FORK OF THE PLATTE RIVER, nearly opposite the mouth of Lodgepole Creek, stood, from the late fifties, a flea-bitten collection of shacks—unpainted, unwholesome, and thoroughly unlovely. It was called Julesburg, and its presiding genius, Jules Beni, was a hulking French-Canadian trader as ill favored by nature as his chosen place of residence. At first it was an isolated ranch and trading post, but it was not long before the stagecoaches (instead of fording the South Platte at the Lower California Crossing) continued up the left bank as far as "Jules Ranch," which was then logically known as the Upper California Crossing. The dirty little settlement looked like a wart on the bare face of Nature, but its importance was enhanced because the roads forked here and the stages and mail destined for the recently discovered gold diggings near Pikes Peak left the "Old Trail" at this point and followed the south bank of the South Platte without the necessity of fording.

A stage station was established at the forks of the road, and Jules was appointed stationmaster. Because he knew his prairie and his Indians and seemed to make money for himself, it was thought that he would do equally well for the company. This was a mistake. Jules, who was a rogue, a liar, and a horse thief, spent much of his time drinking and continued to make money for himself instead of for the stage company.

I have gathered here and there (notably from Root and Connelley's "Overland Stage to California") a few facts about the evolution of the mail and stage routes and have condensed them into the next couple of pages. They belong somewhere in this narrative, and Julesburg seems a logical setting. They may be of interest. If not you can skip them.

The first mail route over the Rockies had its inception in the need of the Mormon settlement at Salt Lake City. A monthly contract was let in 1850 to a Mormon by the name of Woodson, who in August, 1851, sublet the western section from Fort Laramie on to Salt Lake City to the firm of Little & Hanks—also Mormons. The people of California, quick to realize that here was a faster method of getting mail from the east than by the steamer routes, started a service between Sacramento and Salt Lake City. This was handled for some time in the early fifties by George Chorpenning. In July, 1854, a contract for four years was let to William F. McGraw to carry mail from the Missouri River to Salt Lake City. He expected to carry passengers and make it pay, but the trip took over a month each way; expenses were too much for him, and he failed in 1856. The Mormon firm of Kimball & Company took over the contract. One of the Mormon firms had become unpleasantly involved with the Sioux near the various stage stations. The Indian agent at Fort Laramie sent written objections to Washington, supplemented by the dispossessed mail contractor's complaints and denunciations from some of the federal judges stationed in Utah. Meanwhile throughout the long hard winter the mail service was discontinued, and no word came to or from Salt Lake City. It was a perfect setup for misunderstandings. The United States government sent troops to quell the Mormon "revolt." They quartered near Fort Bridger during the winter of 1857–58, and naturally wanted mail service. Equally naturally it could not be carried by a Mormon firm. The government rescinded the contract and itself sent out a monthly mule-team mail service which also supplied Fort Kearney and Fort Laramie. This, as well as its predecessors, went by way of the old pioneer trail.

Early in 1858 by agreement with Brigham Young and his elders, the United States troops under Albert Sidney Johnston passed through Salt Lake City without stopping and settled down peacefully enough at Camp Floyd in the Salt Lake Valley. A contract was let to John M. Hockaday to get mail to and from the army once a week. The route started at St. Joseph, Missouri, went by Salt Lake, and ended at San Francisco; and for it the government paid real money and lost heavily.

In 1859 Hockaday disposed of the business to the firm of Russell, Majors & Waddell, who then consolidated with the Leavenworth and Pike's Peak Express which had been run by Jones, Russell & Co., and in which they already had heavy interests. It ran from Leavenworth to Julesburg and then along the South Platte to Denver. They also united with the line already operating from Sacramento to Salt Lake City. The consolidated company was heavily weighted with the name "The Central Overland California and Pike's Peak Express" and formed a through line from the

Missouri to the Pacific coast. However, in June, 1859, with public interest in the Utah situation abated, the government decided that weekly news was too luxurious. It lengthened the intervals between mails—and thereby hangs the following tale

During the late fifties, just before the Civil War, when the South had the balance of power, every effort was made to keep the North from having a well organized mail route to the Pacific coast. The sympathies of California were still in doubt and were considered vitally important. As early as June, 1857, Congress had advertised for bids on conveyance of mail to the Pacific coast. Nine bids came in, but no northern routes were considered although shorter by many miles. The inclement winters were given as the reason.

A company including John Butterfield, William G. Fargo, and D. N. Barney was the successful bidder and commenced service on September 15, 1858. It was routed south through Texas to Fort Yuma and then north to San Francisco, was splendidly equipped, and carried passengers for the fare of $100. It was known as the Butterfield Overland Mail Company. It operated, as you will notice, throughout the same year as the northern mail route to Johnston's Army; but the latter was a temporary matter of extreme necessity, and the government cut down the service as soon as possible.

When the upset in politics evinced itself by the election of the Republican President, Abraham Lincoln, the northern route came into its own. Early in 1861, after the start of the Civil War, Congress authorized the abandonment of the southern route, and the mail was forwarded along the Platte Road where John Butterfield apparently made use of the facilities of Majors, Russell & Waddell's "C.O.C. & P.P. Ex. Co.," now in financial difficulties and known facetiously as the Clean Out of Cash and Poor Pay Company. The owners had been borrowing heavily from a western financier, Ben Holladay, and in March, 1862, he took over full control of the entire company, reorganizing it into a mail and passenger service surpassing anything of its nature that the world has ever seen. For a few years the splendid northern stagecoaches swung along a route which lay partly on the old overland trail and partly on newer roads and then, after the war, dropped off station by station as the railroad stepped its rapid way across the continent to completion in 1869. Shrewd Ben Holladay sold out to Wells, Fargo & Company while staging was still in its heyday, and it was the last-named company that weathered the leaner days to come.

The short-lived, privately owned Pony Express began in April, 1860, and ran eighteen months, or until the completion of the transcontinental telegraph rendered it slow by comparison. It almost bankrupted its originator, William H. Russell, and its financial backers, Majors and Waddell, but did its picturesque bit to preserve the Union.

So much for the background of the stage and mail routes.

Getting back to Julesburg and the reprehensible Jules, we find him still brazenly cheating and stealing from the company which had hired him. An upset took place. A new general manager undertook to remedy the chaotic conditions and to make the line pay. He began at Julesburg, which was the plague spot of the entire outfit, by appointing a division superintendent and telling him to reorganize.

The new superintendent was Joseph A. Slade, often spoken of (behind his back) as Jack Slade. He had served in the Mexican War, but the title of Captain, upon which he invariably insisted, seems to have been a private addition. His unsavory reputation was as redolent and apparently permanent as the smell of Limburger cheese.

Slade went at his new job with the tremendous energy that characterized all his actions, good or bad. One by one, he picked out and killed leaders of the notorious gangs that had terrorized the vicinity. He caught Jules in his thievery and forced him to return some horses stolen from the company. The last item was an unbearable insult. Jules hid behind a door and shot Slade with his heretofore trusty shotgun. They say that he made the irremediable mistake of skimping on buckshot, and Slade was able to get to St. Louis and have most of them dug out.

Meanwhile the manager, arriving on the next stage after the shooting, hanged Jules by the neck until he was pop-eyed and purple and, having no further interest in the matter, went on to other affairs. The grotesque semblance of what had been Jules was cut down.

"Had been" was a little premature. The short arm of frontier law had relaxed too soon, and the swollen, snarling caricature on the ground was still Jules.

He gathered together a few choice spirits who were also unwelcome in Platte Valley society, retired to the wilds of Rocky Ridge and began a long crescendo of raids on the stock and property of the stage company.

He also sent word that he was entirely and happily prepared to shoot Slade on the occasion of their next meeting.

But Slade had the law on his side. He went to Fort Laramie and obtained a verbal agreement from the officers that there could be no security along the division until Jules was removed by one method or another. Then Slade personally saw to the removal; but his method was bizarre even for Julesburg. Jules was hunted down, wounded, and, by Slade's orders, tied to a post in a corral while the latter went somewhere to "liquor up." Some say that Jules remained there throughout a long, icy Colorado night, while Slade drank himself into a cold frenzy of revenge, and that, when it was light enough to see, the latter entered the corral and commenced target practice. He was a good shot, and Jules lived some time. Eventually, however, the bullet-riddled body was cut from the post, and Slade went on to other pursuits.

An old history of Larimer County, Colorado, tries to give a dispassionate account of the killing. It does not hold with the version stating that Jules' fingers were shot off one at a time but admits that his ears were undoubtedly detached and turned up later in Slade's pocket, from whence they occasionally emerged to be thrown on a saloon bar with the request, "Give me change for that"—a sardonic jest calculated to curdle the onlooker's beer.

As division superintendent, Slade did such sovereign work with a few well directed bullets in clearing up complications in the staging business that he actually left the stage lines in better working order by reason of his sojourn. While sober, he was courteous, mild-mannered and efficient, as the readers of Mark Twain's "Roughing It" will remember. When drunk, he was a blood-crazed killer, devastating and deadly as the old-fashioned Judgment Day. Upon the advent of Slade, wall-eyed and looking for trouble, the saloon doors and windows discharged alarmed citizens, bolting like rabbits for the nearest hole. The few who remained did so at their own risk, and the soul who braved him usually trembled very briefly on the brink of eternity.

Old Julesburg had a famous cemetery filled with the graves of defunct gunmen who had made slight miscalculations at critical moments, and it is said that it owed much of its congestion to the regrettable tendencies of Mr. Slade.

After a holocaust of this sort, he would emerge the next day in a more or less contrite state, depending on whether he happened to be fond of the person or persons expunged, and he sometimes paid damages. He was moved to new fields of action several times, both to put them in better condition and in the hope that he himself would take a new start. But the habit of drink was out of all control, and he became more and more feared and hated. With him, wherever he went, was his beautiful and loyal wife; and when, finally and inevitably, he was discharged, she accompanied him to the newly discovered gold mines in Montana. Here he went from bad to worse, and he seems to have been the next thing to a road agent when his misspent energies finally brought him to a rope's end in the hands of a vigilance committee of Virginia City of that state. His death was that of an utter coward.

Spurning every one and disdaining to bury her husband in the earth of Montana, the grieving widow put the body of what had been the best known and most feared man between the Missouri and the Pacific on one of the company's stages and took it to Salt Lake City, where it seems to have been buried in the potter's field of the old Mormon cemetery. The career of "Jack" Slade, with its deeds and misdeeds, has been writ so large upon the history of the West, and so many places claim the doubtful honor of his residence that the casual tourist would suppose him to have been an honored pioneer.

The settlement where he once lived and worked, crazily dividing his Herculean energy between constructive and destructive efforts, had a checkered existence as anomalous as his own.

The first small stage station at Jules' Ranch soon gathered about itself more buildings, some of cedar logs hauled over one hundred miles from Cottonwood Spring, and others misshapen, weird-looking arrangements built of broken-up wagons, brush, and sod—patchwork hovels whose uncompromising ugliness began to greet the emigrants of the early sixties as they arrived to cross the ford. The place was as rough and tough as even a staging center could well be—Dobeytown on a larger scale.

West of Julesburg, the trail penetrated what were originally the best buffalo grounds of the Crow and the Sioux nations; but, after twenty years of emigrant travel, the herds were few and scattered and the Indians restive and dangerous. There was no protection except by the handful of soldiers at Fort Laramie, many miles west on the North Platte. It was absurdly inadequate, and so, in the fall of 1864, Fort

Sedgwick was built. The builders used sod or adobe bricks primarily because there was nothing else at hand; but they were found ideal for use along the trail. The thick walls were impervious to heat in summer, cold in winter, and the arrows or bullets of the Indians. The indisputable fact that the Platte storms filtered through mud roofs in the disconcerting likeness of porridge lost point when set against the item that a burning arrow could not set them on fire.

The fort was five miles west of Julesburg, but in plain sight, and was built just in time to save its motley citizens while the Indians, under Chief Spotted Tail, burned the settlement into complete annihilation.

But—ho for the first Julesburg! It was down, yes, but not out.

Maybe it was too tough to die. At any rate its energetic citizens simply moved a mile or so from the blackened ruins and started over, only to be faced with the unpleasant fact that they were in the wrong spot. A railroad had been surveyed close by, but not close enough. Some places would have died a sad and lingering death, but not Julesburg. It moved again, bag and baggage—this time across the river—and became for a short time the terminal town for the Union Pacific. By 1869 it was well established and was roaring again in good earnest, a whirlpool of conflicting currents where eddied the flotsam and jetsam of railroad, stage line, and trail, huddled together for a few hours but soon to be spewed out and to drift God alone knew where, borne by the resistless human tides that swept on and on without ceasing. Surveyors and railroad laborers, soldiers newly released from Civil War service, soldiers still in uniform on their way to this fort or that in the Indian-infested West, gamblers, freighters, Mexican horse traders, dealers in buffalo bones, Indians—all these, and more, made Julesburg what it was.

Charles A. Messiter, hunter and writer, has left a good description of Julesburg in 1868, when it was the temporary terminus of the railroad. In the space of a few months it had grown from the tiny crossing settlement to a town of three thousand people, most of them "offscourings." Two buildings out of three were saloons, gambling dens, or dance halls. The rest were shops. There was no hotel. The unfortunate transients slept in a lean-to which was built against an eating house. It was divided into pens seven feet square, in which the would-be sleepers contended with discomfort and noise, unwelcome intruders, and insects of varying degrees of unmentionableness—one variety of which Mr. Messiter politely calls "B flats." The roofs which divided these pens from the extremely leaky heavens of the Platte Valley were of boards laid on loosely, and innocent of nails. When it rained the "roomers" collected in the dining room and slept on or under the tables.

There were hundreds of men working on the railroad for what was then high wages. Moreover all the miners of the surrounding country, who must go back home for the winters, passed through Julesburg on the way to the trains. It was a bumper harvest for the gamblers. Many of the miners lost the profits of a year's work in a single night. Walking marathons put on for prizes attracted men to the gambling halls, where free-for-all brawls and unnoted shootings resulted frequently in death. Mr. Messiter, Indian fighter and buffalo hunter though he was, was very wary of Julesburg after dark and agreed with his unknown neighbor at the boarding-house table that "the place was only removed by the thickness of a sheet of writing-paper from a certain hot place—which shall be nameless."

Even though passenger trains now snorted along the Platte, the stage-coach still claimed a large share of attention and excitement. Giant freighters, also, although diminishing in number as their business was gradually absorbed, lumbered through its streets for many years, adding their gleaming white canvas and long jerk-line strings of mules or oxen to the picturesque ensemble that was the Julesburg of the early seventies.

* * *

Into this edition of the town, grown older and ultramodern, we drove late one sultry evening.

A slight detour to Fort Collins, Colorado, had added to our numbers and efficiency. We brought back with us Mr. Charles W. Cox, who had been giving a course at the summer session of the Colorado State College in that city, and whose energetic enthusiasm knows neither meal-time nor bedtime. Also Mrs. Cox, an expert in extracting information from reticent sources. They planned to travel with us for a few days, until next week's lectures necessitated their return, and our two cars rolled into Julesburg about ten o'clock on a Friday evening.

A terrific storm had lashed all the country around the forks of the Platte and was now staging a grand exhibition of fireworks before its final exit; but we stored our suitcases at the hotel and sallied forth anyway to collect such information as we could get at that late hour. The Upper California Crossing was, of course, our next objective, and it would be easier to make an early start if we knew in which direction it lay.

We were lucky. Within an hour we found a kindred soul who drew us a map in six lines so that we could drive right to the crossing. He was in charge at the Julesburg depot, and he certainly knew his history. On the nearest corner we clustered under a street light to view our prize and to take counsel.

"The only trouble is," my husband said, "that this plagued storm has been whooping in the mountains for a week. The river rose, of course, and three days ago the South Platte bridge got tired and quit. We'll have to do some detouring, but Mr. Lytel has it all planned out for us."

"That's fine," Dr. Neff said, "then we can lay off for the night and go to bed."

My husband opened his mouth to answer, but his words were inaudible. An earsplitting clap of thunder rolled peal after peal over our heads as if the heavens were a great tin roof being pulled asunder.

Truly, what with one thing and another, we found Julesburg almost as roaring as its old-time reputation.

*   *   *

The sun rose bright the next morning, as if it had always been so, and began industriously to warm the east side of all the sheds along the road —a fact evidently appreciated by several tramps who had emerged to dry out after a damp night. A bridge at the edge of town was still intact, the flood was ebbing, and we crossed with no difficulty. On the south bank, where we turned west and roughly paralleled the river, our progress was continually impeded by the fact that we had to drive around the bridges instead of over them. We negotiated the muddy washes, which they had spanned, on pontoon bridges of logs and straw contributed to the general good by some person unknown. The trail paralleled us along the river. On the site of the short-lived second Julesburg was the ranch of a Mr. Carlson, but without stopping we went straight to the immediate object of our morning expedition—a large monument which stated briefly that so many hundred feet from here, etc., etc., might be found the site of the original settlement and staging center where Jules and Slade had lived so tempestuously.

I must say that we were somewhat dashed to find it nothing but a cornfield with most of the corn washed out and a bridge, which had washed in, sitting irrelevantly in the middle of it. Nothing is left of the hard-boiled old town—not even a board or a crumbling wall. Spotted Tail did a thorough job, and the Platte Valley weather has taken care of any minor details omitted at the time.

On this particular day a man was rather disgustedly plowing the remaining rows of corn and incidentally turning up everything from teaspoons to bullets and buttons. The storm, which, he told us, had put three feet of water in his house, had washed several inches of surface soil from the old village site, and things long buried were in the light of day at last.

The emigrants had camped in this flat, and we explored it pretty thoroughly, Mrs. Cox and I hopping around on the dry places like curious robins, and the men wading when necessary. There were evidences of two main traveled routes leading toward the river, and certainly there was room enough here for hundreds of wagons.

We were at length able to reach the water's edge at about the point we had set for an objective, and were reassured by finding a lonely old marker a few yards away—a little waist-high post stoutly asserting to those few who might still care to know that here was the upper ford of the South Platte. It was a turbulent gray-brown river that I gazed at dizzily as it rushed swiftly past—not nearly so broad as it is recorded in trail diaries, and apparently much deeper; and this spot at old "Jules' Ranch" was the one considered by the staging company to be the best wagon crossing. If it has not entirely changed with the years, the hard-packed gravelly beaches tell the tale and show plainly why it was preferred to the abrupt drop from the dirt banks of the Lower Crossing.

Once again on the road, we soon passed the site of Fort Sedgwick. It existed briefly, justified that existence, and was dismantled. At the time of our visit, the first house south of the road after leaving the large marker stood where the protecting walls of the fort once saved the lives of Julesburg's pioneers.

On a road that had been under water and was still puddled we circled through the town of Ovid. A few rods away from trail and highway gleamed the silvery trace of Lodgepole Creek like a shining scimitar— a solid phalanx of trees, made dark and sodden by the storm, forming the heavy handle. The same high, bony shoulder of land that we had crossed on the way to Ash Hollow rose now before us, for after leaving the Hollow we had detoured to pick up Mr. and Mrs. Cox and returned to the South Platte again in order to see the Upper Crossing. Blown sand was piled whitely against the fence lines, and sparse, whiskery green vegetation added color. The highway is almost superimposed on the old trail and stage road on this portion of the "Pole Creek Road"; and as we blindly followed what was left of the deeply gouged ruts to a higher and higher elevation we unconsciously traveled through a corner of Colorado and back into Nebraska.

The Lodgepole Creek road was unknown until 1857 and was used very little until '61, when the government routed the new mail stages that way. Within a year or two the Indians grew so belligerent that the mail was rerouted to avoid the Sioux country along the North Platte. The stages then crossed the South Platte at Latham Station instead of Julesburg and went over what was known as the Cherokee Trail across the Laramie Plains, over Bridger's Pass and through the Bitter Creek country, intersecting the old trail at Fort Bridger. By this plan the company abandoned some three hundred miles of overland trail (up the North Fork, the Sweetwater, and over South Pass) previously used as thoroughfare for the stages, and the Pole Creek Road stepped out of the staging limelight as abruptly as it had stepped in. Its few years of intense activity, running the gamut of Civil War drama, romance of the mail coach, swarming tumult of the emigrant trail, and the horror of Indian warfare, have won for it a permanent place in history.

Coming down the north slope of the shoulder, we got our first sight of Courthouse Rock—named by an early party of emigrants from St. Louis who thought it looked like their own new courthouse with its rounded dome.

Bill was sitting next the window.

"These must be the hills where old Jules stayed after he shot Slade and was hung for it," he hazarded, peering out at the rough horizon where nothing moved but a windmill picking at the cloud edges.

" 'Hanged,' " I corrected absently. "Men seem to have been frightfully recuperative in those days."

"They certainly were. Say," Bill said changing the subject abruptly, "Courthouse Rock does look like a building with a dome on it, doesn't it?"

Mrs. Cox accommodatingly leaned out the window. In her relations with Bill perfect cooperation is given and expected on both sides. "Looks more to me like a mandarin's cap with a big button," she objected. "What's the smaller rock beside it?"

"Probably Jail Rock," her husband answered logically. "They say it used to be part of the big one."

"That's right," my husband confirmed, easing the car to a stop, "and the Courthouse was the first important rock formation of the trail. No doubt it's covered with names and dates. When we get there we'll find . . ." He was firmly astride his hobby and off to the races.

Dr. Neff, arriving from the second car, insinuated a burr beneath the saddle. "It isn't going to be so easy," he said. "The highway doesn't go there."

Sure enough, the old stage road from Julesburg was leaving us, moving across the fields in well defined but impracticable ruts in order to pass between the monstrous rock and the North Platte. Our own road made off at a tangent.

"What shall we do now?" Mrs. Cox wanted to know.

"Just what the emigrants did," said Bill rather grumpily. "Walk, I suppose."

"Possibly—but not this evening," his father decided, swinging the car into the highway again, and we moved toward the river, where the Ash Hollow route traveled upstream to its junction with the road from Julesburg.

On the way we became involved in the small city of Bridgeport, where Dr. Neff, Bill, and I succeeded in inveigling the three less orthodox eaters into a properly vitamined repast. We emerged from this into an evening emblazoned with the lemon and gold and scarlet of a summer sunset. All we wanted now was a place to sleep. Tomorrow would be time enough to see the Courthouse—late tomorrow, I decided unambitiously, standing on one foot to rest the other. Maybe if we looked around right after breakfast we could get some rush cleaning done; maybe I could get my hair washed; there might be time to do a little mending or to press my one linen dress; maybe . . . Pshaw! I knew better.

Dr. Neff's devastating habit of rising at crack of dawn and Mr. Cox's supreme indifference to lunch, combined with my husband's passionate determination to see every hill and dale along the overland road, made me feel like some harmless little gadget on a Ford production belt—guaranteed to be found present and accounted for at the end of every steam-roller activity the day had to offer.

We should see the Courthouse thoroughly, I knew, and see it early.

*   *   *

In the Broadway Café, at Bridgeport, the morning air smelled excitingly of bacon, and my easily agitated appetite responded like a flag to a breeze. Our group of six, having separated for the night, were leisurely reassembling at this prediscussed spot for some breakfast before beginning the day's prowlings. Mrs. Cox came hurrying in ahead of her husband and slipped into a chair. She is constructed by nature to take three steps to his one and usually does hurry. He strode in after her, absentmindedly gave her chair the requisite shove, and inserted two-thirds of his long person under the table. "Why all the excitement about the Courthouse?" he demanded, unfolding his napkin. "From a distance it looks like a good enough rock, but I don't see that it's any better than the Utah formations."

My husband rose to the occasion. "Yes, but your Utah formations and practically all the rest of the rocks are west of here. Courthouse Rock was the first outstanding one the emigrants saw on the trip. In fact some of them had never seen *any,* and you've got to admit it's quite a boulder by anybody's standard."

"The landscape so far," contributed Mrs. Cox, who was attempting a working agreement with her grapefruit, "has been conservative to say the least."

"And I suppose that week after week of flat land would get monotonous sooner or later, no matter how lovely and green it is," I added.

"Especially when you and an ox are skimming over it at two miles an hour," Bill put in scathingly. "A chance to treat your eyes to a good healthy rock at no extra expense must have been quite an occasion."

The enormous rock under discussion juts up from a large expanse of pasture land near Bridgeport. It is visible for a great distance—some diarists said thirty miles, but they found it difficult to estimate owing to the deceptive clearness of the air.

We ourselves found it to be twice the distance we had anticipated, but half an hour after we had finished breakfast we arrived at a point almost opposite the most accessible part of the Courthouse where a gateway broke the miles of solid fencing. Beyond the gate was a farmhouse whose barnyard and corrals stretched back toward the rock. A pink-sunbonneted woman walked out of the house, separated us from two bits with an accustomed air, and disappeared again with finality. We were perfectly willing to pay for the privilege of using her road, but in two subsequent visits, we have found the ranch house empty and have passed through the open gates unchallenged.

Ahead of us the Courthouse, inhuman masterpiece of Nature's architecture, stood out against the absolute emptiness of earth and sky. The cactus-studded grassland swelled to meet it so evenly that we were able to drive within a few yards of the base, where we parked the cars and separated into groups. Bill and his father and Dr. Neff started a tour of the larger rock at ground level and then went over to its small satellite, Jail Rock, always keeping a wary eye for names and dates.

Mr. Cox, whose overwhelming impulse to be at the very apex of each hump encountered equaled that of any mountain goat, started for the rock top. Mrs. Cox and I, following more conservatively, stopped about two-thirds of the way up and were satisfied to walk around the rock on top of the second layer. Heaped above us, toward the center of the upper portion, was the higher mass of stone that from a distance resembles a dome. We had no desire to climb it but, looking up, could see on its very crown the long legs and diminishing perspective of Mr. Cox, outlined against the sky. The sunlight lay rich and warm, almost tangible to the touch, on the pinkish sandstone. Energetic little weeds burst through crevasses in the weather-split rock which crumbled beneath our feet as we walked slowly along a balcony-like ledge on the brink of the Courthouse walls. For many miles to the south spread the quiet summer fields that slope up to the divide between the forks of the Platte. In their midst, less than a mile away, was the wavering silver line of a small creek like a carelessly flung tinsel ribbon.

Comfortably we rounded a bulwark of the wall and then brought up short for startled consultation. Just ahead of us, and yawning out to the narrow ledge which was our only possible pathway, was an opening—half fissure, half hole—into which disappeared the fresh tracks of some animal.

"That's rather a big hole for a rabbit, isn't it?" said Mrs. Cox, executing a masterly bit of understatement. "What do you suppose lives there?"

"I don't know a thing in the world about animals except zebras and giraffes and the rest of the genteel kind that live in zoos. He's big though, or at least his tracks are."

"Yes, and he just went in—that's plain enough."

"Well, I suppose it's just an overgrown coyote, but, if so, he has feet like a St. Bernard. You know—these rocks used to be full of prairie wolves, the real big boys. I should think that there might be a few hold-overs. Anyway I wouldn't like him, no matter what he turned out to be. What do you think about it?"

She looked ahead to the end of the Rock. From that direction came the voices of Bill and his father, far below, in one of their interminable discussions. She looked back along the tedious way we had come. Only a fraction of its total lay within sight, but we knew that three full sides of the Rock had to be negotiated by that route before we could join the rest of the party. "I'm scared," she said simply, "but I'm not as scared as I'm lazy."

I was, perhaps, a little scareder, but we scuttled past the hole and went on as fast as we dared to move on the slipping, disintegrating rock. Of course nothing happened, but while we picked our way along the remaining distance I told her the story of Carlisle Abbott, who was trapped by wolves and crouched all night on a shelving rock barely out of their reach while the long shadowy bodies leaped, missed, fell, and snarled morosely. His one charge remained in his muzzle-loading gun. At first he was afraid to discharge it for fear that some wolf, more active than the rest, might make the leap successfully. Later his hands became too cold to reload and, toward the end of his long vigil, he was in more danger of freezing than from the wolves.

Some men admitted to the mute pages of their diaries that they were far more afraid of wolves than of any Indians the trail produced.

Mrs. Cox looked straight ahead while I told my hair-raiser, and visibly defied anything to make her nervous; but I was bringing up the rear and pretty well succeeded in scaring myself.

At the eastern end of the Courthouse we looked down upon Jail Rock. Two of the men were just completing its circumnavigation and called to us that most of the names and dates were obliterated—"Marshall McAllister," sprawlingly inscribed, being far the best preserved. Mrs. Cox scrambled down to join them.

I stayed where I was. It was a fascinating spot in which to conjure up past scenes; to think of the scores of venturesome youths risking their necks on the sides of the rock, and of the lovers who had wandered around the base selecting the spot on which to carve their names. Courthouse Rock, standing as it did slightly away from the Lodgepole route and ten or twelve miles from the Ash Hollow road, was not visited except at the cost of some exertion. For that reason it reechoed to the lighter aspects of trail life, and the trip was viewed as a sort of pleasure excursion. The weary or anxious stayed away; the sick could not make the ride. Here came only the young, the adventurous, and the livelier spirits of the expeditions, keen for the wild, free gallop over the rolling bottoms. Many of them, who were without riding animals, walked. Some of these realized what an undertaking they had attempted. More were deceived by the clarity of the atmosphere and the curious circumstance which causes the Rock, when seen from the Ash Hollow road, to appear as if sitting squarely on top of a much nearer swell of ground. A gay undertone of long-gone voices seemed to hum an obbligato to the irrelevant conversation of the men below.

Circling to the south to see the rear of the Rock, we crossed the small creek whose shining thread we had admired in the distance. It proved to be an unglamorous watercourse of the deep-set variety with the unromantic name of Pumpkin Creek. From this new vantage point it was evident that the Courthouse is not so isolated as it appears from the highway, but is really a part of the bluff-dunes of the Platte and is the jutting end of a sloping height of land that traverses the fields from west to east. On the north side of this incline, between it and the river, a large area of swampy ground makes the going uncertain, and Chimney Rock, the next famous landmark, looms ahead like a beckoning finger to encourage the traveler.

Here the prairie schooners held to a trail along the gently sloping higher land rising from the marshy meadows. A few miles west of Bridgeport the Lodgepole Creek route joined the Ash Hollow road. We were told by local residents that the junction occurred at Clark's cabin camp, three miles out. The highway between the two landmarks lies south of the river, and one may ride in comfort with the course of the trail in plain sight much of the way.

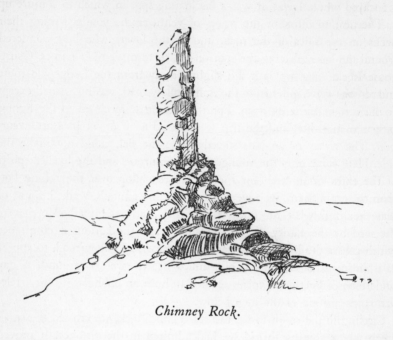

Chimney Rock.

Except in cholera-ridden years the pioneers reveled in the beauty of the rich green meadows starred with black-eyed Susans and in the gorgeous sunset coloring of the broken cliffs. The very loveliness of the scene made for enthusiasm and exaggeration. Some journals record the height of the Chimney as four hundred or even five hundred feet, but the government report, made by Preuss of the Frémont Expedition in 1842, read: "It consists of marl and earthy limestone, and the weather is rapidly diminishing its height, which is now not more than two hundred feet above the river. Travelers who visited it some years since placed its height at upwards of five hundred feet." Jim Bridger explained this phenomenon by the supposition that it had been struck by lightning, stating that he had passed it standing intact on one of his trips to St. Louis and had found it broken on the way back to the fort. More credence might be placed in this ingenious explanation if the explainer had been any other than the well known Jim. Local tradition has it that a company of soldiers once camped near by, and, needing a target for their cannon practice, displayed the excellence of their marksmanship by knocking off about forty feet of the famous old column.

The Chimney Rock stands just across the valley from Bayard, Nebraska, where a one-way bridge tempts the motorist to cross the island-studded Platte and view this great limestone shaft. Here the recurring cholera epidemics of 1849 and 1850 were at their worst, and the Chimney stands guard over the long chain of hasty graves like Nature's own monument to their memory, visible for miles, a fit symbol of the wild and throbbing romance of the trail.

*   *   *

The third of the soft stone landmarks is Scott's Bluff, slightly more than twenty miles from the Chimney. For most of the distance the highway thoughtfully keeps on the course of the trail. On the left, looping to the south, is a semicircular ridge of rocky knobs of which the Chimney is the eastern point. These are tinted with delectable shades of ocher and soft pink, and, when aided by unusual light effects, are gloriously beautiful. Reams of glowing descriptions attest the emigrants' appreciation of this landscape so novel to them.

Scott's Bluff owes its name to an incident of the fur-trapping days. There are several versions of the story, but the following seems to be generally accepted. Scott, it seems, was employed by the American Fur Company, and fell sick on his way home from the mountains. It was, for some reason, necessary to overhaul another party and, in order to make speed, the leader of Scott's group went ahead with his men, leaving only two to bring Scott down the North Platte in a bullboat. It was agreed to meet at this distinctive bluff.

The boat was wrecked, and there was no easy way to take Scott along. The two men deserted him, expecting that he would obligingly die quietly where they left him. In fact they reported to their party that he had done so, and the entire company left the bluff and returned to civilization. The unfortunate Scott, meanwhile, struggled along toward the assigned meeting place, a distance of some sixty miles. After untold agony of body and mind he arrived to find the unmistakable evidence of their departure. Hope was gone. He relinquished his soul to its maker and his outraged body to the wolves; but his bones remained—his bones and some identifying trifles by which they were recognized the next summer and the whole sordid story was exposed. A memorial tablet has been erected near the spring where he spent his last hours.

The river lapped at the very base of Scott's Bluff. The wagons must go inland. This was the more difficult because the bluff is not an isolated rocky formation, but the end of a line of hills. Several more or less parallel canyons break through, and of these Mitchell's Pass, used by the highway, is the best and shortest and lies nearest the river; but it was not passable to the early migrations. Probably it was obstructed by fallen rock and debris. Instead the wagons toiled through Robidoux Pass the next canyon to the south.

Fortunately we decided to go first to the more obvious Mitchell Pass where we found a museum full of interesting relics and historically minded young engineers from whom we learned an amazing amount of helpful local information. The word "amazing" is used advisedly. Ordinarily the exact information on any given historical locality is contained in a library at least a hundred miles away, and the nearer one comes to the spot the less anybody seems to know about it. Through Merrill J. Mattes, located here, we obtained a detailed map of the Lodgepole route upon which he himself had done the research work; also some valuable maps of the Oregon Trail through Nebraska by Paul Henderson.

Before we left, Mr. Mattes told us how to find Robidoux Canyon, also the grave of the notable French trader Papin, some six miles due south of the museum; and we took our departure with those objectives in view.

Robidoux Canyon or Pass is reached from the town of Gering. One proceeds first over a decided rise and then down into a large circular valley of loose sandy loam. The emigrants' columns raised storms of dust through which the southern exposure of Scott's Bluff showed fitfully until they reached the canyon and entered its obscuring walls. The dust was bad for the lungs and equally so for eyes. Helen Carpenter's little dog became entirely blinded and caused her mistress some bad hours by getting lost in the billowing clouds that smothered the teams. Many stated that they suffered more acutely from eyestrain and from cracked and bleeding lips than from any other cause.

Graves grew thick and thicker. They were no longer approached on paths worn smooth by inquiring emigrants who trudged up from the road to read the crude marker and learn who lay below. Now the travelers were too intent upon their own discomfort to bother, and indeed they might have had trouble by reason of the (un)professional advertisements painted over the original inscriptions "in bright red keel." It seemed an unnecessary insult, for the poor shallow graves were already disarranged by wolves and strewn with scraps of burial clothes. One had portions of a uniform and some bloody bones; another, the whole front of a "waist of Dolly Varden goods, made in musk-melon style and gathered into the old fashioned long piqué." On the headboard, inscribed with the name of the woman who had been so lovingly dressed in her best and laid reverently to rest, "Dr. Noble" had advertised again and some disgusted reader had scrawled "is a Jack Ass" after his (probably self-assumed) title. And still the westbound families camped near and, unless the smell was offensive, even *on* the graves in stoical disinterest.

The diarists raved about the distant beauty of Scott's Bluff. It gave off romance in practically visible emanations, but they seldom mention being comfortable there.

In the canyon, by the big spring, those travelers who passed between 1848 and 1852 found a blacksmith shop displaying the sign: "Tinware, by a. Rubidue." Doubtless this was Antoine, one of the famous Robidoux brothers. It was a real home, meant for permanence, and many diaries mention it. On June 22, 1852, Mary Stuart Bailey arrived in the canyon. She wrote: "Passed a Frenchman's blacksmith shop. His wife, a squaw of the Sioux tribe, sat in the door of their hut rolled in a scarlet blanket. Looked rather sober but well. Another squaw was on horseback chasing a drove of horses and mules. She was only half dressed." The casually covered Indians were still slightly annoying to eastern women.

Only a few days after Mrs. Bailey sat writing in her diary the peaceful little cabin was destroyed. Either the blacksmith shop or the Sioux wife was a tactical error and the Kiowas burned up the place and made other arrangements. "a. Rubidue" simply moved one canyon south and built another shop and trading post.

The sun was curtained and the canyon cold and gusty as we drew opposite the bronze plaque marking the site of the blacksmith shop.

"There were several trading posts along here," my husband said, "—that is, between here and Fort Laramie; but this must have been the first one to cater to the emigrants. The rest were to catch the Sioux's trade and maybe the Cheyennes' and other friendly tribes'."

"Why did they come clear out here to trade when they were practically stepping on Indians all the way from the Missouri River?" Bill wanted to know.

"Because the Indians out here had no normal contact with civilization."

"Then it wasn't because the Pawnees and the Pottawatomies and the rest of them back there were higher types?"

"Not a bit, but they knew from experience a lot more about what things were worth. You wouldn't find a border Indian trading a prime buffalo robe for a paper parasol; but a Kiowa or a Sioux might, because paper was a novelty and a parasol that went up and down would just tickle him to death."

"Or a five-cent jew's-harp would be just as tempting," Mrs. Cox put in, "and cost even less."

"Maybe it was after they parted with all their buffalo hides for a dozen jew's-harps and a few pints of whisky that they came over and burned the joint," Bill suggested reasonably.

"I don't think they'd pick on just this one when there were three or four others," I remarked. "I've read in an early journal that one of the rugged Robidouxs was rather peremptory with his squaws. Possibly that was it."

12

Fort Laramie

FROM THE MOMENT when Robidoux's red-blanketed squaw burst upon the consciousness of the emigrant women, they had a new interest in life. For Robidoux's establishment ushered in a long sparse line of solitary trading posts and trappers' hangouts (also presided over by Indian wives) which extended to the Pacific coast. Make no mistake—the fur-trading industry, besides being romantic and furnishing our pioneer grandmothers with a little much-needed gossip interest and our grandfathers with high beaver hats, accomplished plenty in its day and generation. Witness the two-thousand-mile trail found ready to hand when most needed. Witness the efficient guides available for emigrant companies. Witness the presence of the Sioux Nation on the emigrant trail (of which more later) and also, by all means, witness the alarming fact that the pioneers found the Indians amply supplied with both ammunition and whisky.

Recorded history of the section immediately west of Scott's Bluff begins about the year 1818 when Jacques La Ramie, a French Canadian, built a trapper's cabin near the junction of the North Platte and the Laramie River. He was trapping in the vicinity of Laramie Mountains when the erection of the tiny dwelling established him as the first permanent resident of the section. Four years later the Indians clinched his claim to permanence by leaving his bones to bleach on the headwaters of the river that bears his name.

A decade passed: ten years of good business for the fur traders. The Indians had not yet realized that they were being robbed of their priceless heritage of furs for the paltry recompense of a few gewgaws and guns. Clashes occurred now and then but, on the whole, the tribes tolerated the traders and came to depend on them for such commodities as needles, beads, knives, cloth, and ammunition. The dispensing of liquor was always frowned upon, and the better companies did not deal in it except when it was necessary to prevent less scrupulous trading posts from scooping in the cream of the fur crop in return for a few barrels of whisky.

In the year 1832, two events occurred that proved to be of paramount importance to the fur traders: The silk hat was invented to take the place of the high beaver tile and Nathaniel Wyeth, an extraordinary young man from New England, made his advent into the affairs of the Far West. Wyeth organized and led an inexperienced trading expedition to the Pacific coast at the mouth of the Columbia, and returned with no financial profit. The established concerns regarded him with tolerance and, on his way back in 1833, he succeeded in getting a contract from the Rocky Mountain Fur Company authorizing him to bring a pack train of goods to the next summer rendezvous on Green River. The contract was elastic, as Wyeth could not be sure of prompt arrival, and forfeits were provided in case of nonfulfillment.

So it happened that, at the proper starting time in the spring of 1834, Wyeth and his party set out for Green River with every intention of delivering the goods. Close behind them traveled Robert Campbell and William Sublette, brother of the man with whom Wyeth had the contract. They were similarly equipped with a pack train of supplies and were also bound for the rendezvous.

Somewhere on the Platte they circled Wyeth's party and hurried on to get first chance at whatever profit might be had from trading with the Indians along the way and, also, to reach Green River a few days ahead of the other train. At Laramie River the trading was excellent. Sublette left Campbell to hold down the situation and hurried on. Campbell, getting help, built a small trading post consisting of a high stockade of pickets and a few tiny huts inside. This was a combined fort and dwelling and was some protection from the wandering bands of Crows and Pawnees on their occasional forays along the Platte. He named the place Fort William, after his partner; but in two years, it evolved into what history knows as Old Fort Laramie.

In the meantime Sublette arrived betimes at the rendezvous and sold his goods. When Wyeth's supply train arrived the contract was repudiated, and Fitzpatrick, acting for the Rocky Mountain Fur Company, paid the agreed forfeit. But Wyeth was indignant. With the avowed intention of becoming a thorn in the flesh of Fitzpatrick and his partners, he continued on to the valley of the Snake River, then called Lewis Fork, where he commenced the erection of a trading post of his own. It was named Fort Hall. It is hard to imagine how the early emigrants could have fared through to their destinations without the support and confidence given by these two sturdy outposts. They seemed, indeed, like the buttresses of some long, tenuous bridge, sustaining the slender footway of the trail.

Meanwhile, because of growing Indian resentment, silk hats, and other contributing causes, the days of trapping were not what they used to be. Companies broke up, and other combinations were formed. In 1835, William Sublette and Campbell sold Fort William to Jim Bridger, Milton Sublette, and Thomas Fitzpatrick. This new firm quickly dissolved, and the partners became agents of Fontenelle, head of the firmly established American Fur Company. Fort William passed into the same hands and was rechristened Fort John after John B. Sarpy, an officer in the company.

A United States Army report indicates that in the same year, 1835, the company sent emissaries to the north Black Hills to invite the Sioux Indians to come and hunt and, for convenience in trading, to pitch their tepees near the fort. The emissaries returned with over one hundred lodges of Ogallala Sioux under Chief Bull Bear. This, says the report, was the first appearance of the powerful Sioux in the country which they later overran. At first they had no horses; but stole and traded for them and soon learned their use. By the year 1849 the whole country from the forks of the Platte to Horseshoe Creek, forty-three miles west of Fort Laramie, was claimed by the Sioux in conjunction with the Cheyennes and Arapahoes with whom they were friendly.

In 1836 the American Fur Company deserted the stockade of Fort John and built a better one a few hundred yards up Laramie River on a small plateau. The name went with it but "Fort John on the Laramie" was soon corrupted to the simple "Fort Laramie" that has remained in use ever since. It was of adobe, copying those forts farther south that had been built with Mexican labor.

The two divisions of Frémont's 1842 exploring expedition met at Fort Laramie on July 15th after separating eight days earlier to follow the north and the south forks of the Platte. Charles Preuss kept the records of the North Platte division and wrote that Fort Laramie was "a quadrangular structure, built of clay, after the fashion of the Mexicans, who are generally employed in building them. The walls are about fifteen feet high, surmounted with a wooden palisade, and form a portion of ranges of houses, which entirely surround a yard of about one hundred and thirty feet square. Every apartment has its door and window—all, of course, opening on the inside. There are two entrances, opposite each other, and midway the wall, one of which is a large and public entrance; the other smaller and more private—a sort of postern gate. Over the great entrance is a square tower with loopholes, and, like the rest of the work, built of earth. At two of the angles, and diagonally opposite each other, are large square bastions, so arranged as to sweep the four faces of the walls."

Preuss' detailed description is well supplemented by that of Frémont, who circled in from the South Platte country and struck the North Platte thirteen miles below the fort. He wrote: "Issuing from the river hills, we came first in view of Fort Platte, a post belonging to Messrs. Sybille, Adams, and Co., situated immediately in the point of land at the junction of Laramie with the Platte. . . . A few hundred yards brought us in view of the post of the American Fur Company, called Fort John, or Laramie. This was a large post, having more the air of military construction than the fort at the mouth of the river. A cluster of lodges, which the language told us belonged to the Sioux Indians, was pitched under the walls."

It was because the trade around Fort Laramie was too brisk to remain long without competition that Fort Platte was built. John Bidwell, passing in 1841 with the first caravan bound for California, wrote of it as "another fort, within a mile and a half of this place [Fort Laramie], belonging to an individual by the name of Lupton." In view of the quotation from Frémont's report just offered it would appear that the post changed hands at least once (in accordance with the uneasy status of the fur-trading business in the forties) before lapsing into obscurity. It was abandoned in the summer of '45, probably in favor of Fort Bernard, eight miles down the North Platte.

Francis Parkman visited Fort Bernard in '46 on his way to Laramie Fork and wrote that it was "a rough structure of logs . . . a little trading fort, belonging to two private traders; and originally intended, like all the forts of the country, to form a hollow-square, with rooms for lodging and storage opening upon the area within. Only two sides of it had been completed." In charge was the hair-trigger, whisky-running Richard, a little, swarthy black-eyed Frenchman more or less in bad odor with the American Fur Company, who disliked the practice of selling liquor to the Indians, even though they thought it impossible to discontinue its use as long as their competitors handled it.

Fort Bernard is said to have burned sometime during the fall and winter of 1846–47; if so it was evidently rebuilt, for E. A. Tompkins, who saw it in the summer of '50, said that it was an assemblage of log huts surrounded by great piles of buffalo hides, the size and shape of eastern haystacks.

By the year 1845 the fur traders dealt mostly in buffalo robes, beaver having passed gradually from its position of importance, and although the other forts did a brisk business, the preeminence and prestige of Fort Laramie was unquestioned. Parkman wrote of the American Fur Company at Fort Laramie that they "well-nigh monopolize the Indian trade of this whole region. Here their officials rule with an absolute sway; the arm of the United States has little force; for when we were there, the extreme outposts of her troops were about seven hundred miles to the eastward."

In 1847 the Mormons opened their road on the north bank of the Platte but, through some misapprehension of the route ahead, felt that it was the lesser of two evils to ferry the river at this point, use the Oregon Trail on the south bank as far as modern Casper and ferry again there. The Forty-niners using the Mormon road did the same. This unnecessary avoidance of the north bank west of Fort Laramie was fostered by at least some of its occupants who told highly colored stories of impassable mountains and advised the use of the rude ferries. The Argonauts of '49 firmly believed that these men secretly owned the ferries and were only lining their own pockets in complete carelessness of the numerous fatalities that occurred among the hurrying travelers while swimming their stock. In 1850 this opinion had gained such weight that one or two daring companies refused to ferry and continued their journey north of the river. In a few days, when it was apparent that they had not been forced to return, they were followed by Franklin Langworthy's wagon train and others. The north-bank road was open.

The lack of governmental protection mentioned by Parkman was felt so keenly that in the summer of '49 the United States purchased Fort Laramie and garrisoned it for the avowed purpose of giving advice, protection, and the opportunity of buying supplies to the emigrants. It had a monthly mail service, and the marching thousands moved perceptibly faster for the last few miles, hoping for a letter from home. Comparatively few were received, for they were apt to be longer en route than the would-be recipients; but the myriads of letters sent eastward fared better, and, if the addressee stayed long enough in one place, they arrived in the fullness of time.

The fort kept a register, and train captains were supposed to enter the names of all adult members of their companies. It was necessarily inaccurate because there was no way to enforce the registration, but on July 5, 1850, Henry Stine wrote home from the fort that so far that season there was a record of 37,171 men, 803 women, 1,094 children, 7,472 mules, 30,616 oxen, 22,742 horses, 8,998 wagons, and 5,720 cows. He added that it was too great an undertaking to look up the name of any one person who had gone ahead.

Besides handling registration, the soldiers maintained boats for ferrying, saw to it that a bridge was soon built over the Laramie River, and, in years of disturbance among the Utes, organized small wagon trains into large companies for better protection through the dangerous areas farther west.

Laramie Fort was beautifully situated, but was never improved, during early trail days, by the softening touch of green fields, orchards, and growing things. Experimental plantings were tried at different times, but crops were not easily grown. They needed plenty of water and much hard work, two things which had no appeal for the trapper and very little more for the soldier. In addition, the Indians objected strongly to the look of cultivated fields as indicating an encroachment of civilization on their domain, and, in one or two instances, took strong measures to return the land to its native state. In 1849 and the three or four years following, the grass itself vanished early each season under the trampling feet of thousands of foraging animals, and the whitewashed buildings of the fort were left stark against the naked ground.

*   *   *

When we left the fantastic reaches of Scott's Bluff and started the fifty-mile trip to Fort Laramie, we went through Mitchell Pass rather than Robidoux Canyon. It was a later route, shorter and closer to the river and led us over knolls where the horizon was almost under the radiator cap and each spear of grass pricked its separate way into the sky. Kiowa and

Horse creeks proved to be neighborly companions and meandered lazily between cushioned banks bright with scattered sunflowers and patches of lavender daisies. They come from widely separated beginnings but flow into the North Platte only a mile apart. Mixed with the heavy vegetation and bright flowers on their banks the emigrants found tiny bushes of soft, velvet-gray sage, little unnoticed prophecies of what they would encounter later when prairie grass and flowers had been left behind—the countless miles of sagebrush on the Great American Desert across the Rockies.

It was at Horse Creek in 1846 that Parkman interrupted the noon rest of a moving Dakota (Sioux) village under the stately chief Old Smoke. His chief men and elders stood haughtily near him, while each lazy warrior sat under a temporary shelter (erected by the old and discarded squaws) with some youthful and bedecked beauty at his side, while before him, on a tripod of three poles, were displayed his shield, bow and quiver, lance, medicine bag, and pipe; "the whole scene had an effect too lively and picturesque ever to be forgotten."

Five years later, in 1851, the Sioux again congregated on Horse Creek. This time a treaty was consummated between the Sioux Nation and the United States government whereby, for the value of $50,000 in goods each year, the emigrants were given the right to travel unmolested through Sioux territory; so that the next season's travelers were half relieved, half irritated to find that the Indians of the vicinity loved their white brothers with an intense and discommoding fondness. This peaceful interim lasted about three years.

At the Torrington depot, those interested will find, as we did, the grave of William Guerrier, "Indian Trader and Noble Gentleman"; then, after the town is left behind, they may take the highway and see the course of the trail in perfect comfort simply by looking across the river to where it once wound its uninteresting way along the south bank. This procedure satisfied us for a while, but we arrived presently at a bridge and started for the south side again. It was a very long and ancient bridge, too narrow to permit two vehicles to pass except at the center, where there was a turnout.

At the end of the bridge we turned to our right and drove along the south bank. We were so close to the river that by wadding our tinfoil gum wrappers into little hard balls we could toss them into its roily cur-

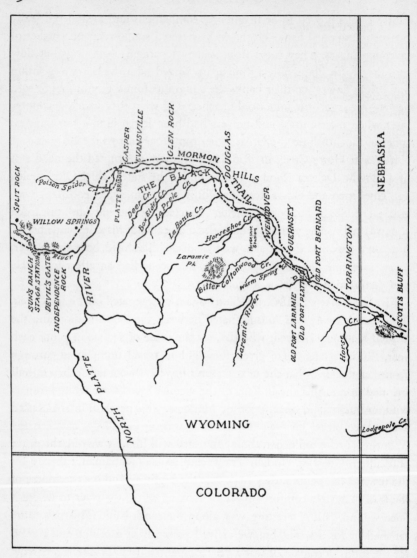

rent. The worn and rounded ruts, grass-grown for fifty years, cut and recut across our way and sometimes disappeared into our own thoroughfare, which was, by the way, optimistically constructed of adobe and looked as if it would be a nonconductor when wet. We met only one car on this stretch, and the driver stopped as a matter of course to visit.

We passed the site of Fort Bernard close to the line of greenery on the river and, when six miles east of Fort Laramie, were immensely relieved to strike a gravel road, for by this time slow clouds moved swollen and heavy in the south and it was a certainty that it would soon rain. The improved road proclaimed the vicinity of the monument commemorating the Grattan Massacre. It is often visited and not to be slighted by an adobe approach. The site of the massacre is not so easily accessible, being in a flat plain about a half-mile north of the road.

The massacre, sad and incredibly unnecessary, occurred in 1854 and effectively broke up the friendship between the whites and part of the Sioux Nation. It was the immediate cause of much trouble, including the battle of Ash Hollow—not the deep and underlying cause, but the springboard which projected the Wazzazi and Brûlé tribes into difficulties with a morbid thump. Because it had such far-reaching consequences, we later made an intensive search for accurate data, and finally laid hands on the annual reports of the Commissioner of Indian Affairs. In the volume for 1854 we found the statement of the trader, Bordeaux, who was an eyewitness.

Bordeaux was no scholar, and the tedious business of writing his statement had to be delegated to one Samuel Smith who, with six others, witnessed the laborious document. It is too long to be quoted in its entirety, but the gist is as follows:

On August 17, 1854, a train of Mormons passed along the flat plain where the marker now stands, and found there the villages of the Brûlé, Wazzazi, and Ogallala bands of the Sioux. A man walked behind the train driving a lame cow. The cow became frightened and ran into the village where, Bordeaux states, it would have been quite safe for the man to go after her. He was afraid to make the venture by himself and went on, abandoning the cow. A stranger Indian, sojourning with the tribe, killed the cow, and it was eaten. In the course of time, the man reported the loss at Fort Laramie. Young Lieutenant Grattan, quite unaccustomed to Indian ways, with twenty-nine men and an interpreter, started out to arrest the offenders. Ordinarily a petty theft would not have been handled in such a drastic manner. The government disliked any tangle with the Indians along the trail and had overlooked much more important matters than the present whereabouts of the beef from an abandoned Mormon cow.

The soldiers went to Bordeaux first and asked his opinion. He recommended that they go to the chief and have that dignitary tell the culprit to give himself up. Good advice because, if they could get him to give the order, all the consequences would normally be laid at the chief's door. They were successful but, possibly because the instigator of the beef barbecue was of another tribe, the chief's request met with nothing but an unlimited amount of status quo. The young officer was really in an embarrassing position. He had thirty men and a cannon and was supposed to uphold the dignity of the garrison. He inquired from Bordeaux the location of the lodge of the offender and his men fired on it from sixty yards, wounding one Indian. Even then the old men of the village urged the young braves to stay their arrows, saying that possibly the young officer would be satisfied with the blood of one. Although the interpreter supposedly translated their words, it is said that he had been drinking and was in no condition to be tactful. No cow thief came forward, and Lieutenant Grattan gave the order to fire the cannon and the muskets. The following is a direct quotation from Bordeaux's statement: "Accordingly the chiefs that had gone with the soldiers to help make the arrest, ran, and in the fire they wounded the Bear Chief of the Wazzazies; and as soon as the soldier's fire was over, the Indians in turn rushed on the soldiers and killed the lieutenant and five men by their cannon, and the balance of the soldiers took to flight and were all killed within one mile or so from the cannon."

The Wazzazies then rushed Bordeaux's house, intent at first on making a clean sweep of all white men present, but thought better of it and contented themselves with entering the buildings of the American Fur Company, and taking by force their annual payments, now, of course, forfeited for bad behavior. This, with the addition of some petty thieving which they were constitutionally unable to resist, completed an eventful day. Bordeaux's statement ends quaintly: "So no more at present, Yours truly James Bordeaux."

The wounded Wazzazi chief, Bear That Scatters, soon died, and the fat was in the fire which, after smoldering darkly for ten years, blazed into the disastrous Indian uprising of 1864.

The ill-omened Sioux village was situated in a large, flat valley. Between it and the fort were barren hills through which the wagons wound to their first view of the stockade. Beginning in '49, with the military regime, the compact, walled trading post was supplemented with first one building and then another—barracks, stables, powder magazines, and whatever else was necessary for a garrison. Emigrants of later years, pushing through the low hills, saw quite a settlement.

Robert Campbell had cannily built his picketed stockade in the angle of the two rivers, so that all who approached from the east must either ford the Laramie or ferry the North Platte. Both projects provided plenty of exercise and some risk. Those companies who had attained the west bank of the Missouri River at Independence, St. Joseph, Nebraska City, or near-by ferries, and who consequently traveled south of the Platte now must ford the Laramie. And the Laramie was deep, swift-flowing, and ice-cold. Those who ferried the Missouri at Kanesville or Council Bluffs, and remained north of the Platte were now faced with the thankless job of ferrying to the south side only to cross back again just west of the Black Hills, where the river swung too far south for their purpose, and the road left it definitely and forever. They did so up to and including the year 1849.

There was no necessity, as it later proved, for any man to risk (and sometimes lose) his life in ferrying the Platte at Fort Laramie: there was an easy route on the north side. The officers were suspected of giving out misleading information to induce the emigrants to cross—at first, on account of the profit they could make from selling supplies at exorbitant prices, and later because they ran a government ferry at five dollars per wagon and had unlimited opportunity to line their pockets. Complaints of this nature are most frequent in journals written in the first year or two of the garrison's occupancy; but these same years, '49 through '53, saw the great westward push, and more trail journals were produced then than in later years.

Modern-day travelers cross the North Platte at Fort Laramie on an iron bridge—very slim pickings as to iron, and only wide enough for one vehicle. We were told that it is a fine specimen of the old bowstring girder type, and it bears the date 1867. The original crossing from the north bank to the fort, made famous by the Mormon migration of '47 and perpetuated by their popular guidebook, was a few yards upstream from this bridge. Here men ferried their shrinking (and probably shrieking) families in wagon beds. The ferry later run by the soldiers was just downstream. There was no provision for animals. The owners, not very optimistically, shoved them off the bank to swim. One man shoved too hard, lost his balance, and was swept by the current into a hole where his heavy boots held him down. A living chain was formed from the shore, and the ninth man succeeded in reaching him. Pure melodrama lasting less than a minute.

Carlisle Abbott mounted his favorite horse, Old Pompey, to lead a band of floundering horses across the flooded Platte. He was soon forced to swim, hanging firmly to Pompey's tail. Soon the milling herd pushed him under their churning hoofs. Fortunately he came up unharmed and, grasping a flowing mane, pulled himself high enough to see that the whole band was drifting helplessly toward an angry whirlpool. He gave up hope for the band and, in a desperate effort to save himself, jumped from one horse's slippery back to another like a lumberjack riding a log jam, then dived and swam deeply as long as he could force himself to do so. When he came up he discovered, to his joy, that Pompey, swimming high and strong, was leading the other horses safely across. Some soldiers from the fort had rushed a few saddle horses to the bank; Old Pomp rolled a sagacious eye in their direction, picked up his course and made a landing with all his band in tow. Mr. Abbott was still in desperate plight until, being swept under a bush, he grasped a branch no bigger than a pencil and hung exhausted until the soldiers, rushing to his aid, cut the branch and pulled him in. They carried him to an Indian tepee, where a squaw rolled him in her buffalo robe before the fire and the soldiers rubbed him back to warmth and consciousness.

He was very grateful to be alive, even if close contact with an Indian buffalo robe was a matter which gave any white man pause for thought, and plenty of occupation for the next day or two.

In its trading-post days previous to '49, almost every visitor to Fort Laramie spoke of the tepees all about the walls. They were occupied by the in-laws, for most of the trappers took Indian wives to whom they were reasonably faithful, at least to the point of seeing that they were fed and had plenty of work to do. It was not contrary to Indian ethics if they stretched a point and took two or even more wives; and this was sometimes convenient to the trappers, for each found his chief guarantee of safety in the large number of his wife's shiftless relations who were camped about his establishment.

Besides these permanent residents, early travelers found large detachments of various tribes camped at the fort, trading or, sometimes, just visiting—a pursuit of which they were inordinately fond. Father de Smet, passing this way in 1841, found forty lodges of Cheyennes and wrote in his journal: "The principal warriors of the nation invited me to a solemn banquet, in which three of the chief's best dogs were served up to do me honor. I had half of one for my share. You may judge of my embarrassment, when I tell you that I attended one of those feasts at which everyone is to eat all that is offered him. Fortunately, one may call to his aid another guest, provided that the request to perform the kind office be accompanied by a present of tobacco."

The Sioux were excessively fond of sugar and coffee and spent a good deal of time dickering for them, but they had an intense dislike for acids. Fanny Kelly told an amusing incident where a few Ogallala braves acquired some jars of pickles. Tasting produced howls and wry faces, but their desire to eat was unquenchable. They decided that cooking might improve the flavor and clapped the glass jars into the fire. An immediate debacle ensued. The jars exploded and the Indians registered a complete disgust for the "white man's kettles."

Many journalists speak of the personal comeliness and dignity of the Sioux around the fort. The men were well formed and tall, with clear and surprisingly delicate skin. The young, unworked women were not bad to look at, with well formed bodies, ankles, and feet; kept their hair smooth (if not clean) and were ornamented like the proverbial plush horse. The majority of the pioneers took them in their stride, but persons who had had unpleasant experiences with Indians along the trail found their numbers somewhat staggering.

On the evening of July 4, 1849, when the recent garrisoning of the fort had relaxed all tension, a startling incident occurred on the stripped camping land outside the fort. The emigrants were having a celebration and had chosen for Goddess of Liberty a young girl with the appropriate name America West. Under her gentle rule the camp hummed with music and the rollicking laughter of women so often eulogized in the diaries of solitary travelers. Their merrymaking was halted by a wild-eyed woman and a frightened child, tattered and half starved—the wreckage of a family.

The mother, whose name was Martha, told their story. Three days previous, their wagon had halted to bury two cholera victims, the husband

and the sister of the hysterical woman. Their company plodded straight ahead, leaving her with her brother and her two children to bury their dead. They were then to catch up, if possible, by forced marches. The body of the sister had been lowered into the open grave when the Indians swept down upon the helpless little group. The context of the story does not suggest any particular animosity on the part of the red men. They were opportunists; they were passing by; and here were clothes and food and scalps for the taking. Somehow the woman and her five-year-old daughter crept into the brush unobserved, but the last thing which her straining eyes photographed on her brain was her little son being dragged away. Her brother had been busy at the grave, and she mourned him too as dead.

She passed three days in the rough country of the Black Hills with only a dead fish and a chance-killed squirrel to feed her little girl, frantically terrified of the wandering groups of Indians. In consequence of her mad rush into the hills, they were now between her and the trail. She worked her way back within sight of the fort, but was afraid to run the gantlet of the far-flung tepees. There could be no doubt, of course, as to her fate had she encountered another group of prowling braves; but a few lodges of Ogallalas or Brûlés under an older chief conceivably might have helped her on her way to the fort, and the squaws would have seen to it that she stood not upon the order of going but went at once. They were extremely jealous, and each objected strongly to the presence of a white woman captive for fear that she might catch the roving eye of her polygamous lord and master. Indeed the horrible mutilations inflicted on women captives were as a rule caused by the squaws, who proceeded in the traditional way to wipe out any affront to their pride. The hair of the captive, strange-hued and fine, was torn. Eyes of blue or hazel, gray or brown, were burnt with coals in retribution for the admiration of the braves. White skin was scored and scorched, lips cut off, any offending beauty of face or person ruthlessly destroyed. Undoubtedly it was safer for any woman to risk starvation.

The little girl might have been kindly treated, for the Sioux were fond of children and badly spoiled their own. They liked especially little girls with long curls that snapped back into shape when pulled, and curly *red hair* provoked flattering offers for the coveted child—there are cases on record of tribes following certain trains for days.

The woman knew nothing of all these traits. She knew simply that she would rather encounter a tiger barehanded than another Sioux.

Starvation drove her in at last under cover of darkness, and she effectively broke up the party.

Two days later the train, peacefully moving west through the hills, came upon the scene of the tragedy; but the dreadful duty of burial was shirked for fear of contagion, and the bodies were left to the elements and the wolves. For many days, they feared that Martha would lose her reason.

To a few of those less intimately concerned, it was a matter of grim satisfaction that the vandal band, eating animallike whatever they could find around the camp, were doubtless, by this time, stricken with cholera. The Indian habit of disinterring the dead for the sake of their clothes often laid whole bands low with smallpox or other maladies to which they had built up no racial immunity or resistance; and any white man's disease, even measles, was almost always fatal to an Indian.

For the sake of continuity, the rest of the strange story may as well be told now. Martha, devoting herself to the children of her benefactors, entered California by way of the Humboldt Sink. Another woman in the company, Mrs. Haun, whose manuscript reminiscences give the story, separated from Martha in Nevada and took the roundabout Lassen route into California. She was, therefore, a month later than Martha in arriving at Sutter's Fort. It was one of those providential happenings that make one suspect the presence of a special guardian angel. Mrs. Haun and her husband had gone to bed one night when, out of all the hundreds that tramped along, half frozen and short of provisions, one man came to sleep by their dying campfire. In the morning he told his name, and proved to be Martha's brother. He had slipped away in the heavy shrubbery supposing that the little boy had gone with his mother. When in three days they had not returned, he made up his mind that the Indians had killed or captured all but himself.

The Hauns gave him word of his sister, and he started out to rejoin her. Then, incredibly, he found his little nephew on a creek bank where they had both gone for water. The boy told his uncle that the Indians had offered him to some emigrants in exchange for a horse, and they in common Christian charity had parted with one of their animals and had taken on an extra mouth to feed without question. So it appeared that the Sioux had not killed any one after all, and that the boy and his mother had been only a few miles apart all the way to California. The story of Martha ended better than it began.

Just without the circle of military buildings at Fort Laramie stood, in the late sixties, the burial scaffold bearing aloft the remains of Chief Spotted Tail's daughter. The rather odorous practice of lashing their dead on scaffolds or in the so-called "burial trees" had badly disconcerted more than one gold-rusher who too hastily camped beneath their welcome shade. The rougher element among the soldiers and emigrants often raided the buffalo robe wrappings for the simple treasures of the dead placed there for use in the spirit world. And the disturbed bodies falling apart because of the rough treatment gave the tribes concerned just cause for resentment. The young Indian "Princess" is said to have entertained a fondness for one of the young officers. Later, developing tuberculosis, she spent six months in the tedious business of dying, and requested that she might be "buried" at the fort. The officer in charge of the garrison, to conciliate the Indians, permitted it. With the combined dramatic effects of a military funeral and of Indian wailings her body was elevated to the open-air scaffold, where it remained Indian-fashion, for years.

The old fort has passed its hundredth anniversary, and the once teeming buildings are historic ruins now. The fine picturesque cavalry barracks stand by themselves. The officers' quarters are brave skeletons of houses facing a deserted square, as do the sutler's building, the guardhouse, and the rest. Among these buildings, famous old "Bedlam"—two-story clubhouse and quarters of the bachelor officers—still stands, defying the winds. Creaking ox teams brought its timbers eight hundred miles from Fort Leavenworth, and it has endured the years better than its adobe neighbors.

In Bedlam famous visitors were entertained and dances held—Fort Laramie, for some reason never attacked by Indians, having been a gay and spirited post. Not all isolated forts were so fortunate. One Christmas night during the last years of its occupancy, "Portugee" Phillips stumbled into the midst of its festivities, half frozen from a four-day ride through blizzards along the tops of the mountain ridges to avoid hostile Indians. He was revived and managed, as his spent horse died outside the door, to tell of the Fetterman massacre and the peril of Fort Phil Kearney.

At the north end of officers' row is a timeworn adobe building containing (according to old-timers of the vicinity) a fragment of the trading post erected on this site in 1836. It is a section of adobe wall forty inches thick including one doorway, and is still stout enough to justify the workman who hauled it a hundred yards or so for use in the new post office and sutler's building. This was in 1852.

In amplification of this tradition I offer an incident that occurred ten years later. It is given briefly in the official report of Assistant Surgeon H. S. Schell of the United States Army made in 1870. He wrote: "A portion of the old adobe fort was standing until 1862, when it was entirely demolished and the adobes used in the construction of the front portion of the magazine." But, no matter in what building the peripatetic adobe bricks may now be found, the old trading post, as an entity, disappeared long ago, crumbling into the high land near the river, at the southeast end of the forsaken parade ground.

There was a mere handful of men gathered here under the Stars and Stripes, and it was little enough that they could do to make safe the hundreds of miles over which they were, at first, the sole protection. But it was a gallant gesture. And, just as a Canadian Mountie does his dangerous job unsupported save by the unseen but strongly felt power behind him, so the few men who each morning unfurled Old Glory five hundred miles from the frontier, in the heart of the Sioux Nation, remained and did their duty unmolested.

13

The Black Hills

THE NIGHT THAT WE STAYED at Fort Laramie it rained; but the day dawned crisp and sparkling. The sky, unbelievably blue and massed with menacing cloud stacks, stared down at its own reflection in puddles the size of small lakes. It was a poor day for field work, but we dutifully stopped short of the quaint bridge beckoning us to the highway across the river and turned instead into a vague unworked road leading up the south bank—the successor to the south-bank route which the pioneers followed from the fort to the next night's camping spot at Warm Spring.

It was soggy and mud-filled but easy to trace, being faintly green on a drenched yellow background. Sage was abundant in the grass, and scrubby trees smudged the mountains ahead—were, in fact, responsible for the name Black Hills. The era of the despised buffalo chips was over.

And what, we may well ask, did the later travelers use for fuel in the years after the buffalo had been driven from the Platte Valley, especially throughout the treeless two-hundred-mile stretch now ending? The question has been answered by the veteran stage man and freighter, Alexander Majors, of the famous firm, Majors, Russell & Waddell. He writes: "Strange to say the economy of nature was such, in this particular, that the large number of work-animals left at every camping-place fuel sufficient, after being dried by the sun, to supply the necessities of the next caravan or party that traveled along. In this way the fuel supply was inexhaustible while animals traveled and fed upon the grasses. This, however, did not apply to travel east of the Missouri, as the offal from the animals there soon became decomposed and was entirely worthless for fuel purposes."

The road leading west from Fort Laramie was anathema to the overloaded Argonauts, for it marked the beginning of the Black Hills, whose low, rough summits shouldered the sky line just ahead. The travelers had lost much of their cocksureness during the seemingly endless struggle with the sand and waters of the Platte. They were tired and (in cholera years) badly frightened. Their sense of values had changed. Things that had been great treasures when they were carefully packed for transportation to the new land, were now only extra weight wearing out the suddenly precious draught animals. Men as well as women were offenders. In spite of warnings from those who had gone before that furniture and implements might better be shipped around the Horn or purchased on the west coast, farmers brought their plows and farm machinery; dovetailed them into the wagon with the pieces of heavy carved furniture from which their wives had not been able to part, and with solid little rawhide trunks of fine clothes. Now they all went out, and many a walnut whatnot and four-poster sat by the roadside—but not for long. Everything that could burn, was burned, from one end of the trail to the other.

Excess supplies of food were thrown away here, too. The wagon masters had repacked at Fort Laramie, but it took the pressure of actual present necessity to key them up to the wholesale abandonment that was now in progress. One Forty-niner wrote: "We begin to see the preparations made by the overloaded trains for crossing the black hills— piles of bacon lying by the roadside, some must have had 2000 or more lbs, beans—corn—all kinds of iron implements & cook-stoves etc—etc— One train we passed told us they threw away over a ton of bacon— several barrels of bread—six dozen steel shovels—axes, hoes etc—etc— amounting in value to nearly 1500 dollars."

Even for us, following in their wake nearly a century later, the going was hard. Our course lay practically on the trail and was full of small ponds with no guarantee of a bottom. In one we got the front wheels crossways and slid for twenty feet, almost denuding it of water and coating our car and the landscape with mud; whereupon we dodged the next with a speed and verve that had us all climbing for the high side.

"Made it!" exulted Bill.

Dr. Neff discouraged any elation. "Well, I can *see* six more puddles, and there are ten miles of them that I can't see between us and anything ahead. We either need a canoe or cars with more clearance. We'd be wise to go back and wait around the fort another day—that is, if we *can* get back."

A masculine delegation strode to the rear to give their opinion of the water holes just navigated. Through the back window the decision appeared to be adverse to an extreme degree. Dr. Neff left them and walked ahead some distance to where the road ceased to be soupy and stiffened into mud. I sat quietly and admired the bright reflected blue and floating white clouds beneath our wheels.

When we get out of here, we can brag about it, I said to myself. But please don't think we're bragging yet, I added hastily to my guardian angel.

A hail from the doctor interrupted my soliloquy.

"Tracks ahead!" he called back. "Somebody has been on the road this morning."

And sure enough, in the firmer mud ahead, tracks of small tires had held their shape. This brightened the outlook considerably, and the consensus of opinion immediately veered to the vainglorious attitude that if any one could get through we could.

"That is—if he *did* get through," said my husband doubtfully; "but if he didn't we'll have company."

The road gradually grew a little better, as the sun and breeze dried the mud. Our allegiance was now hopelessly divided between the big old historic ruts and the little muddy new ones. When the latter took to the water we followed unhesitatingly; but when they circumnavigated a rain-water pond by circling out into the sage we were often stuck. The car ahead seemed to have had unlimited clearance and to have taken debris and boulders in its stride.

When other plans failed we sent some one ahead to sound the untried ponds, and then splattered the indignant sounder solidly with mud as we roared past in low. The sounding and splattering lasted perhaps half an hour.

"Buildings ahead," announced Dr. Neff, as he got out to take his turn.

"If it's the ranch where that fellow with the car was going we're coming to a dead end," Bill reasoned.

"We'll soon know," Dr. Neff told him. "Here come some fellows on horseback."

"Maybe the Sioux have risen," I contributed.

"Hi!" my husband yelled, rightfully ignoring me. "Does the road end here?"

"Yes, it does"—cheerfully as they galloped up. "Good thing you turned back."

"Turned back!" This from Bill. "Who turned back? We're still going." But they had loped on past.

"I think," Dr. Neff said slowly and with clarity, "that this is considered a dead end from the other direction. We'll find a lane or something beyond the house."

We were glad to get our long-suffering cars onto a decent roadbed again and, by dint of some walking, continued to get a good idea of the trail. Mr. and Mrs. Cox, my husband and I presently disembarked completely and started off on foot, sending Dr. Neff and Bill on with the cars to meet us later. For the better part of a mile we kept to the edge of the bluffs, separating and spreading over a wide strip of territory as we hunted for the place where our maps showed that a right-hand fork of the trail made its descent to the river bottoms.

It was lonely on the rolling, cloud-curtained plateau extending back over a countless succession of dips and rises to Old Fort Laramie. Windswept and apparently limitless, it linked the two horizons. In the solemn silence, made even more intense by tiny insect voices, it seemed to breathe as if it were mysteriously living and must remember those crowded years of activity when one of the most amazing human tides the world has ever seen flowed across its broad expanse. As if some spirit of the mighty pageant of men and beasts must cling there still—some echo of the thunder of hoofs and the rolling of wheels on wheels.

The men were first to find the descent, which is merely a steeply washed break in the bluffs. But it bore evidence that the wagons had descended at this point and is called (we found later) Mexican Hill. They at once started an intensive search for ox shoes or other scattered hardware—the foot of a hill being a likely place for such finds.

I forget how wide the river bottom is just here—maybe half a mile. The wagons had been all over it, for it was a perfect place to noon. As our wanderings carried us far enough from the bluffs to give perspective, we could see that they were low but abrupt and projected toward the river in enormous points. We walked at least a mile between the jutting cliffs and the water, separating again to cover more territory.

Ahead of us and to the right was a ranch. The corrals backed up to the sandy waters of the Platte. The low-roofed, sprawling buildings looked homy and comfortable. A small winding of smoke issued from the great squat chimney. In front of it was a peaceful meadow harboring many quietly feeding cattle. I was among them before I realized it. Also among them was one tremendous old bull, who would have suited me better if he had been harbored somewhere else.

The presence of so many cattle pasturing on the grazing land surrounding the old emigrant trail has been, to me, its major drawback. I am not really very much alarmed by cows, although I find their bony structure uncomfortable for close contact, especially about the hips; but the bull is my *bête noire*. And doubtless I am not the only woman, by many hundreds, who has walked timorously along these dusty miles, for the modern trail follower encounters few by comparison with the herds that traveled in its heyday. The wagon-train emigrants remained for months cheek by jowl with more cattle than they had ever seen before; rode behind them; walked ahead of them; took their dust; drank milk from tired cows; ate beef from lame oxen butchered to get the last ounce of use from their faithful carcasses; slept on stormy nights with them tied restlessly to the wagon wheels while their horns poked bulges in the canvas tops; desperately kept themselves and their children from under stampeding hoofs—or sometimes despairingly failed; endured cow hair on their clothes and in their food; drank water sullied by cattle and by buffalo; cooked with their dried droppings; and everlastingly—day and night—lived with the noise and the smell of cattle.

The lord of this particular herd stopped eating and looked me in the eye. Across the stingy interval between us I could practically hear him revolving the problem of my presence in his stubborn bull head, meanwhile almost dislocating his neck in abortive efforts to produce a really satisfactory bellow.

I made for the first object resembling a fence—a length of ancient chicken wire pegged to the ground in front of the bluff to keep people away. It was doing a good job, too. There are few things more insurmountable than a wabbling, eight-foot chicken-wire fence. Finding no way of getting into my haven short of burrowing under it like a rabbit, I cast a quick look behind me to estimate how fast I should have to dig, and saw his bovine majesty still consuming grass with the smooth forward sweep of a power lawn mower. My usual poise returned in good order, and I turned back with some curiosity to the cliff which had been thought worthy of such protection. It was literally covered with names and dates.

Later investigation proved that the jutting points of the bluffs all had initials, and sometimes full name and address and date, carved upon the soft stone surfaces. They are called Register Cliffs and lie directly across the river from Guernsey, Wyoming. Until very recently they have received little publicity but are among the best of the "guest-book" rocks of the old overland road. It may fittingly be remarked, just here, that the hurrying, tired travelers who passed this way did not spend their time carving names for the fun of it, nor risk their necks to put their carving in the most conspicuous place possible for the thrill. The imperfect hieroglyphics gave reassurance to the friends and relatives who came, possibly, a few weeks later. Finding the one beloved name meant that its owner had reached this stage of the journey alive, and presumably well. It was one of the surging joys of the anxious journey.

We moved slowly along the base of the cliff, stepping into holes and falling over clods, with our eyes fixed steadily on some name about fifteen feet up, which we wished to decipher before losing. Now and then we passed the field glasses from one person to another. My feet hurt from unwary walking among rocks, and I had a crick in my neck when my husband became interested in a group of names having a very similar appearance.

"Come look at these," he invited us all.

"I can come, but I can't look," said Mrs. Cox reasonably. "I can't bend my neck any more."

"If it's important I can try," I conceded. "What's on your mind?"

"Well, these names all look alike. You can see it best on the vertical strokes. They are exactly the same width."

"They were made with the same instrument," Mr. Cox said with real interest. "See, it must have been a half-inch bar of metal, broken, and with one sharp projecting splinter that made a groove deeper than the rest."

"But these names have different dates," I objected. "There are two or three years between them."

"They left it here, then. Maybe they tied it with a string like the old tin cups at watering troughs."

"Maybe it's *still* here," my husband said idly, without, I'm sure, a thought in the world that it could be so. He kicked the dead weeds, sticks, and fallen debris from the cliff to one side with the toe of his shoe. And there it was.

We still have it: half of a four-inch link from a hand-wrought log chain—the kind that they threw away in quantities all through the hills. The breakage had occurred lengthwise of the link, and offered a perfect handhold, leaving a free end shaped like a giant fishhook, with which to scrape out the names. The sharp projection which we had known must be on the instrument was in plain evidence and fitted correctly into the telltale groove in the carven letters.

Near one of the great rounded points of the cliff a group of forgotten pioneers sleep in unmarked graves. We passed them on our way to the ranch house for information. Farther along, and out in the open, is a large Pony Express marker. No name is given on the plaque, but it commemorates the old Point of Rocks Station.

It is not very far from the cliffs straight across the bottoms to the ranch buildings, and the foreman had evidently had his eye on us for he met us in the big, clean outer barnyard. Every well ordered Wyoming ranch seems to have one, and it is the generally accepted point of disembarkation for visitors who come in cars. But we had no car. Dr. Neff and Bill had left ours at a convenient place and joined us on foot. Wyoming is not accustomed to pedestrians, and the good-looking young foreman gazed at us very inquiringly from under a huge soft hat.

When he understood our errand he thawed to the melting point and showed us courteously around the place. The rambling hewn-timber house was in an enclosure to the left. On the right were the long low sheds, their roofs studded with relics of the trail. From where I stood the row of inverted kettles on the edge of the flat sod roof of the nearest shed reminded me of hobs on the upturned sole of an old shoe.

Among the young foreman's answers to more or less relevant questions was woven the romantic story of the homestead. The first Mr. and Mrs. Fredericks to arrive in Wyoming had come, it seems, as bride and groom, in a wagon train. They camped at Register Cliffs and their names are still legible, carved in the sandstone; but when the rest of the company went on, their wagon remained out of the line, and no argument sufficed to get it in again. They established their home and raised their family right here near the protection of the fort on the Laramie. It is still the Fredericks Ranch.

* * *

We stayed in Guernsey that night, and the next morning said goodbye to Mr. and Mrs. Cox, whose week-end holiday was over. After breakfast they started off—down the highway, too, as an added insult—while we, after waving an answer to their last honk, headed again for the south side of the river. The inevitable Platte! It was becoming almost a ritual with us, owing to the fact that the trail lay south of it while seemingly all the available food supply was north.

Conscientiously we connected with the trail at the spot where we had left it yesterday. Some two and a half miles west of Register Cliffs virtue was rewarded with the unexpected discovery of the most amazing cut on the whole overland road. It was at least shoulder-deep in solid sandstone and barely wide enough for a wagon. The bull-whackers and muleteers, who walked beside their teams, had kept to the right and left. They themselves, through the years, had worn two narrow footpaths deep into the rock. Doubtless, at the beginning, the wagon passage and the muleteers' paths must have been side by side, curving in a gentle arc over the top of the little hill. But the wagons had all the best of it in their ability to wear down and gradually grade a roadbed through sandstone. The footpaths were left high and dry, with the feet of the bull-whackers stumping along about the shoulder level of the plodding oxen.

* * *

"Warm Spring is the next campground according to the map. Does anybody know where it is?" asked Dr. Neff, who likes to have a few facts in advance.

"No, nobody that I asked knew anything about it; but when we get to the mileage indicated on the trail map we'll get out and hunt," my husband said cheerfully. "We'll find it if it's still in the same place."

A knoll wedged itself between us and the river. On the summit was a conspicuous new monument, and we went up to look at it. The cement gravestone was just completed and had been built with the evident purpose of attracting attention. Sunk into a glass-fronted recess in the cement was an ordinary irregular rock. Its still legible inscription read: "Lucinda Rollins—Died June '49."

Some family, in those far-gone days, stayed in this beautiful spot long enough to lose a loved one, to bury her, and to drive on. Some one in this family could not bear to leave her in an unmarked grave, and so it has borne a headstone—small and insignificant, but miraculously remaining for all these years. The marked graves are greatly in the minority. In years when the trail was crowded, the trains were so hurried and sickness so prevalent that common decency could hardly be observed. Bodies were hastily deposited in shallow holes—by strangers, it might well be—and dug up within a day or two by wolves. There was no time to cut an inscription in rock. And, even if at first the grave bore some pitiful data, scratched on sandstone or painted with axle grease on a barrel stave, it only took one careless person out of the thousands who passed by to remove the sole remaining link to human memory. It was during the small migrations at the beginning and at the end of trail history that deaths occurred singly and a burial was a special and tragic ceremony. Because the wagons were few and the trail at the mercy of marauding Indians, the graves had need—a dreadful, ghastly need—to be completely obliterated.

Picture a trail-side camp in the early morning. In the trail itself a grave has been dug in the night. Wrapped only with blankets and soft buffalo robes the precious contents are gently lowered into it. If the neighborly occupants of near-by wagons have been able to find cactus, a layer of its protecting spiny joints is carefully tamped in next to the beloved dead and a shuddering prayer breathed that it may be enough. Next, the earth is packed above it firm and smooth. The bereaved family must go on. There is no help for it. The wagons are loaded and ready, and wait for the word which must be given. It *is* given. The slow-moving oxen move forward and onward. The creaking, rambling wagons lurch and roll. The whole inexorable march, from this moment on, flows westward over all that was mortal of their loved one—forever obliterating the last resting place and effacing it from the memory of man.

The river, at Lucinda Rollins' grave, begins a great sweep to the north, but the wagons cut straight northwest across the bend and allowed the stream to leave them. One after another, as in the game of follow the leader, the ungainly wagons rolled into the canyon of a small creek, an insignificant tributary of the Platte. Up this canyon we expected to find the Warm Spring where so many emigrants camped. Well within its confines we passed a sheep corral and, in ten minutes more, arrived at a grove of cottonwoods whose huge ragged spread of bough and foliage was incongruously shedding a drift of fragile, downy fluff. It got down our necks and up our noses. The air was full of it.

In the middle of the grove was collected quite a pool of warm water. The supply came from somewhere up the canyon and we drove beside, through, and in it for some time before finding that it had its source in a most satisfying spring that gushed from the hillside. The Mormon migration camped here in 1847, and Apostle Orson Pratt wrote on June 5th: "The name is 'Warm Spring'; the water is not so cold as one would expect. The quantity is nearly sufficient to carry a common flour mill, being very clear. By our road it is fifteen miles from the junction of Laramie River and North Fork."

It may be said in this connection that about three weeks earlier, on May 16th, the Mormons had installed a crude but effective "roadameter" on one of their wagons, and that their mileage was surprisingly accurate.

There were, in all, four routes west from Fort Laramie: a river road and a hill road on the north side of the North Platte, and a river road and a hill road on the south side. They all had their disadvantages— there never was a royal road through the Black Hills; but, of them all, the north-bank river road was decidedly the best and the north hill road the worst. The wagons on the south side struck a happy medium of difficulty, the hill road, remaining in the rough upland away from the river, being the shortest of all. Both of the south roads availed themselves of the good camping facilities at the Warm Spring.

Beyond the spring was a lime kiln established and used by the soldiers from Fort Laramie. The evidences are still visible. Still farther along and on the left, the south hill road made its way through weird wind-carved gray cliffs, pocked with holes and alive with swallows, and came down the bluffs to join the river road at the spring. Near its descent we found the canyon home of a bachelor who had an extensive collection of hardware picked up on the trail. He informed us that there were three places where the wagons left Warm Spring Canyon for their cross-country run over the ridges to rejoin the Platte. Of course all three exits were over the right side of the draw as one faces toward its head: There was one beyond his house—one just west of the sheep corral which we had passed as we entered—and one, most used of all, had left ruts almost a foot deep in the lime rock on the east side of the corral. Unless a wagon train wished to camp, it had no need to enter the canyon as far as the spring.

The next important stopping point, according to the diaries, was the Bitter Cottonwood Creek. Maps located it at Wendover, Wyoming, a railroad stop—but, in the year 1934, not very easily reached by road. We drove out of one sand-rock gully into another about, I should say, three days after a cloudburst. The memory of those miles is still with us, but there is no point in stressing them, for in 1937, when for the second time we arrived at this section of the trail, we found a perfect setup for lazy historians: an automobile highway laid out by C.C.C. boys which follows the trail very closely from Guernsey to Wendover. On this we flowed over the swelling hills like syrup from a pitcher. From the green crest of the divide we could look back at the chalk-white, rocky ridge standing guard between us and the tepid canyon of Warm Spring. Ahead the depressions were dark with small, runty pines. Many miles to the left, Laramie Peak loomed high—the most famous single mountain of the trail. We surmounted the last swell. Down in the valley ahead of us was sketched in crayonish green the feathered line of trees that marks the Bitter Cottonwood.

On our first adventurous trip into Wendover, we walked down the last hill on the trail itself. *We* walked, and I have no doubt that the thousands of pioneers who used the route walked too. It would not be a pleasant ride. Squarely across our way, at the hill's foot, ran the railroad tracks. Beside them stood a trail marker. It was little and old. The usual group of railway buildings surrounded the depot, supplemented by a couple of houses. A sturdy grizzled man was coming down the tracks at a good clip. He was the only soul we saw in this metropolis then or later.

I have since thought that he couldn't possibly have known how good he looked to me. We had had a fiendish time getting there, and I needed somebody to be surprised and congratulatory—somebody to tell me that it wasn't everybody's idea of a vacation. I waited for him to come into the short breadth of road crossing that lay on the tracks. He didn't stop, and I trotted along beside his unslacking stride.

"We're on the old emigrant trail here, aren't we?" I inquired, as a conversation opener.

He turned steel-rimmed contemplation in my direction momentarily. "Yep. Go as far as you like," he said adequately, and left me behind.

We gaped after his firmly disappearing back for some moments and then took his advice.

The name Bitter Cottonwood came, they say, from the narrow-leaved cottonwoods of bitter taste along the banks of the clear, pretty stream. It was easy to ford. We tried it with the car and no one was inconvenienced except a Plymouth Rock hen who was gargling on the spot where we wished to exit. Camping was good, but the fast horse and mule outfits went on to Horseshoe Creek where the feed was better.

We went several miles on the trail itself before having to circle. Some one, a very long time ago, had made and stacked adobe bricks near the spot where we were checkmated. We found that it was just possible to get the car into the faint sled marks left by this defunct industry. Slipping and twisting, we put yard by yard of the tracks behind us; went up and over the edge of a hollow and arrived among the dingy outbuildings of a ranch. Farm machinery dotted the fenced inclosures. An automobile of an outdated model stood near by as if some one had left it there for a moment. The house was of roughly squared logs, as were also the barn and several of the sheds. The buildings were scarcely higher than their own doors and were backed up against the earthen banks of the hollow so that they might be finished off in the rear as dugouts. It was hard to tell from the front how much of these peculiar structures was log, and how much cave.

We went to the house to explain our unheralded approach from the wrong direction. It was empty and abandoned.

We pushed the heavy sagging door ajar. Squalor greeted us, and the smell of the small animals that had moved in when the family moved out. Magazines and a calendar said 1913. A cobwebbed trunk with tightly fitted lid was unlocked. We opened it. It was full of women's clothing, nicely ironed and folded, house linen uncreased and clean, and some letters. We opened one. It was also dated 1913 and showed that the recipient was probably the schoolteacher. We found the contents of the trunk neat and undisturbed just as the unknown owner had packed it so many years ago. We closed and left it that way and drove out from the ranch through more scattered farm machinery. The family had simply walked out leaving the place intact. What in Heaven's name, I often wonder, can be the story back of that solitary, log-faced hole in the ground which once sheltered a cultured woman.

At the time I hadn't much opportunity to think, for, after passing through what had been their front gate, we went up a hill and found that the trail was with us again. A wide trail now, taking off down a precipitous white slope in a cut worn five feet deep. We were delighted to find it with so little exertion, and the driver seized the opportunity to take a good look as we drove slowly across a little bridge, knowing that the guard rails would prevent any deviation from the strait and narrow path. Because of this quite reasonable faith we went dribbling off an abrupt eight-inch drop at the far end with two thuds that jarred our teeth and made omelet of our possessions. A quick check-up showed all present and no bones broken, and so we went on at once—gingerly at first, then, as nothing fell to pieces, with more assurance.

With us went a tiny thread of water, the beginnings of the Bitter Cottonwood, whose several easy crossings had lightened the hard journey of the wagons with shade and water. We left it presently and went up a short, rocky lift—exactly on the trail—reached the top and, looking over, saw that it was a long way down. Slowly and majestically we slid, with all brakes set, clear to the bottom. The short cut was complete. We had reached the Platte Valley again.

A young fellow and a dog came out from a cluster of ranch buildings near the foot of this masterpiece of trail architecture and watched us sliding down, detouring fearsomely around the boulders. This amazing young American remains unique in my memory in that he took it for granted that we should joy-ride on rocky canyon sides instead of on concrete highways if we so desired, and merely pointed out that we had missed a trail marker on the way down.

With a sigh of thanksgiving that we *had* missed it, we looked at it through the glasses and let it go at that.

Now markers on the trail generally mean the approach of a better traveled road, so that we were not surprised to find that one came in as far as the ranch buildings from which the young man had emerged. A mile of travel also disclosed the fact that the trail had folded up like an umbrella in the maddening way that it has, and had vanished.

We seethed back and forth for a while, but our findings had more loose ends than a horse's tail in a high wind. Somebody was going to have to curry them into shape for us. There was nothing for it but to go back for information. In fact we went back several times. It took three different trips to get this particular stretch straightened out.

To the best of our knowledge, this is the solution. Not all of the wagons went down our pet hill among the great boulders. Probably the majority took the next canyon to the right. Ranch buildings stand at the foot, and the descent is now known as the Diamond A Hill. From here the wagons turned slightly to the right to pass Twin Springs, about one-quarter mile off the road.

The original Oregon Trail then turned to the river and remained with the south bank of the Platte. It meandered along the spacious current, past historic Bridger's Crossing (near modern Orin) and its travelers ultimately arrived at the upper crossing of the North Platte, near Casper, without much discomfort. However, they lost time. Almost as soon as they struck the Platte it had the bad taste to commence a huge shallow sweep to the north. This was roughly divided into two nearly equal bulges like an old-fashioned Cupid's bow. The grim necessity to save time spurred the men of the march on to the breaking of a trail straight across the bulges in a direction corresponding to the bowstring. A number of fine creeks running into the river from the south took care of the always serious question of water and grass. For the sake of clarity we usually refer to this short cut (on no one's authority but our own) as the Bowstring Cutoff. We haven't found, as yet, who used it first, nor the exact spot where it breaks away from the river route; but in a short time more and more wagons went that way, until it became the most traveled of the four routes through the Black Hills, as it was also the shortest.

That portion of the Platte Valley into which the wagons dropped after leaving the Bitter Cottonwood was a common stretch on the two roads south of the river and afforded the best grass the pioneers had seen since leaving their own planted meadows. With the possible exception of Bear River Valley, Carson Valley, Fort Bridger and the Fort Hall Bottoms, it was the most luxuriant of the two-thousand-mile trek. It extended no doubt from the lovely meadow near Bull's Bend to Horseshoe Creek and beyond. Men diarists, especially, wrote of it in glowing terms, for it gave the animals a much-needed "chirking up" right in the middle of the hard grind of the Black Hills.

We discovered the ruts again in a stack-studded hayfield belonging to an English gentleman, Mr. Foxton. We found him tall, lean, charming and no longer young. After fifty years of residence in Wyoming he still pronounced "been" as if it were the canned variety. In a field just outside his garden was the site of famous Horseshoe Station, used by Jack Slade as a headquarters from which to operate the adjoining division of the stage line. The spot had been identified for Mr. Foxton by one of the two men who survived its burning by the Indians. The same man had presented him with a document containing a bald and unadorned statement of some of the grimmest facts it has ever been my lot to encounter about Indian fighting. He wrote that, as the Indians succeeded in setting fire to the building and it commenced to blaze high and hot, all the men within made a run for it, except himself and one other. The men who ran were slaughtered and then mutilated with all the ghastly originality that the fertile mind of the red man could supply. The two who remained buried themselves under the earth in the cellar and safely allowed the building to be burned over them.

Mr. Foxton took us to see the place. We found an irregular pit overgrown with scraggly sage and tussocks of grass. Half imbedded in the ground are segments of old and rotting timbers, all that remains of beautifully situated Horseshoe Station where so many transcontinental stage passengers stretched cramped and weary legs and gazed in self-effacing curiosity at the redoubtable Mr. Slade.

* * *

In years when the Sioux were peaceful, those travelers who had no responsibility for the animals enjoyed the Black Hills. The pure water restored health. The pure air uplifted morale and seemed like heaven after the contagion and contamination the emigrants had experienced along the Platte. Mountain cherry, currants, and luxuriant tangles of wild roses grew in the sheltered spots while giant brush strokes of blue flax, larkspur, and tulips streaked the slopes with color. Pine and cedar braved the bluff points and showed a gratifying tendency to produce knots for campfires and tar for the wagons. Frequent rains washed through the hills, and the air was permeated with sweet-scented herbs and pungent sage. The rocks and scrubby timber teemed with highly variegated wild life: antelope and black-tailed deer, panther, rattlesnakes, and the cunning "frogs with horns" are mentioned. Solitary buffalo bulls, outcasts from the herds, roamed the ravines and gave rise to a sudden access of manly enthusiasm for the chase, for buffalo of any description were not usually plentiful through the two hundred miles of Sioux territory just traveled. The occasional tough specimens encountered were shot down by the united efforts of so many amateur sportsmen that it was the greatest wonder they didn't bag one another instead of the bulls.

For some reason children strayed away during this week's journey. Some were found again after hours of the most desperate anxiety. Some few were actually abandoned to their fate as their particular wagon trains were forced, for the safety of all, to forge ahead. I do not remember any account that attributes the disappearance specifically to the Indians, or indeed gives any explanation whatsoever.

From Horseshoe Creek to La Bonte (sometimes called Big Timber Creek) was fifteen and a half miles by the Mormons' roadameter. The casual estimate was two to three miles longer, and the road varied somewhat from year to year. It mounted a ravine to the crest of a dividing ridge, where the emigrants had an inspiring view of Laramie Peak, and crossed in the course of the day four or five lovely little mountain streams. One of these was the Elkhorn, and it was here that Heck Reel's freight outfit loaded with beer and flour was attacked by Indians and the wagons burned, adding a bizarre touch of beer-keg hoops to the grim austerities of the Black Hills.

The rocks of this section were particularly vicious and abrasive. They wore the animal's hoofs to the quick, cut and otherwise lamed them. So far the road had been full of large ragged chunks, but the last five or six miles before reaching La Bonte were packed hard and smooth, "equal to McAdam roads" or, as some said, like pounded glass. Arrival at La Bonte was equivalent to a victory. The worst pulls of the Black Hills were now behind. But, in years of heavy travel, the grass supply was not adequate and many drove on to greener pastures or camped sketchily only to move at daylight.

Our own arrival at La Bonte was toward evening, so that we took the shortest road to the near-by city of Douglas to spend the night.

"Are you going to see Mr. Bishop while you're here?" I asked my husband.

"Absolutely. I wouldn't pass up L. C. Bishop—although," he added in surprise, "I really don't seem to need any information this time."

"Those maps he drew us last year came in handy," Bill reminded us. "You practically wore them out."

"Well, we won't bother him with maps this year," his father promised. "We'll go to his office for a while after dinner just for fun."

Luck was with us, and we found him there. After an hour, as we were leaving, Mr. Bishop had a sudden idea. "Say, do you know," he said abruptly, "there's another man in town you should talk to—that's E. B. Shaffner. I saw him just this afternoon, so I know he's back. He was over at Laramie this last week."

"We'll look him up," my husband assented cordially. "Is he interested in trail history too?"

"He knows a lot about it. You couldn't do better than to see him."

"It shall be done," we promised, and said good night.

But it wasn't so easy to do. He wasn't anywhere that we had been told to look, and we finally decided that he had left town again.

Early the next morning we did various things not usually bracketed in the tourist's itinerary. By ringing four doorbells and imposing upon the courtesy of half a dozen people, we succeeded in accompanying the custodian to the Public Library, where I made a freehand copy of a map we needed which, I trust, will never have to be disclosed to public view. At the Historical Museum or Pioneers' Building we spent half an hour copying a fine picture of the old Platte Ferry which hung on the wall and consequently got a very late start back to La Bonte.

We were speeding up toward the outskirts of town when we saw a weather-beaten car parked casually, half in the street and half in the gutter. It was little and old and solidly mud-plastered from stem to stern. An intent-looking individual was readjusting boxes on the seat. Suddenly, for no reason perceptible to the rest of us, my husband jerked our car to a stop, looked joyously at the antiquated vehicle like Balboa sighting the Pacific, leaped out of the car and into action.

"Are you by any chance Mr. Shaffner?" he asked the energetic individual's back.

"Why, yes," was the amazing response, accompanied by a raising of eyebrows that meant "Who are you?"

Later we tried to analyze why, out of a town full of people, he had unerringly selected the one man he wanted most to find. It was, he said, the mud that first attracted his attention and then the tires. He recognized them at once. He had followed that pattern, unrolled into a muddy ribbon miles in length, from Fort Laramie to Mexican Hill. Nobody but a dizzy historian would have taken a car on that road for any reason whatever. Mr. Shaffner had just returned from Fort Laramie. Mr. Shaffner bore the reputation of a historian than whom there was none more apt to be out cruising in a shallow lake, car and all. In short, here was the puddle-jumping automobile, and it belonged to Mr. Shaffner. *Quod erat demonstrandum.*

He got in with us, and we went back the river road past Bridger's Ferry; circled and arrived on the west bank of La Bonte. He showed us where had stood, in staging days, La Bonte Station. Showed us the two fords of the creek, one circling somewhat in order to pass by the station, and the other bearing straight across in the shortest possible way. Showed us where the trails from the two fords came together on the near side of the creek, and got us started west, paralleling the old wagon tracks, and headed for the succession of creeks which the pioneers had crossed in the next three days' journey.

The first was Wagonhound. Few knew the name, but none ever forgot the creek, and it could always be identified by description, for it was red. The soil and the rock were almost audibly red, from the burnt hue of Mexican pottery to the clear vivid tone of a madrone trunk. Between three and four miles of the road were deep with what appeared to be brick dust. It rose in billows and hid the teams. One woman was so impressed by the lurid color and the general look of drastic upheaval that she painfully crawled to the top of one of the "mountains of red stone" and inscribed upon it, "Remember me in mercy O Lord."

Within sight of the trail Grindstone Butte juts up from the rolling uplands—an isolated stony bulk where a few diarists mention gathering rock for whetstones. It was easy to see why the animals became lame and somewhere in this stretch of rocks the humane train captain took measures to protect them. Lydia Waters wrote: "The hoofs of the cattle became so worn they had to be shod. Now the amateur blacksmiths had to show their skill. George became quite proficient shoeing both horses and oxen— To shoe the cattle a trench the length of the animal and the width of the shovel was dug. The animal was then thrown and rolled over so that its backbone lay in the trench and all four legs were up in the air. In this position it was helpless and the shoes were nailed on readily." In very bad cases protectors made of buffalo hide were tied clear up over the hoofs like bags. Even dogs had leather moccasins. A few owners hardened their animals' hoofs with alcohol and omitted the footwear.

A stream just beyond Grindstone Butte, modernly entitled Bed Tick Creek, was apparently nameless to the emigrants; but it furnished water and a little much-needed grass. Next came La Prelle, the first large stream after La Bonte Creek, boasting a natural bridge of rock.

After La Prelle came Little and then Big Box Elder. One summer day in 1864 a small wagon train forded the shallow waters of Little Box Elder and started the ascent of the opposite bank. It was the sunset hour and was getting cooler. As the water dashed musically through the spokes of the great wheels the cheerful little party sang with gusto, "Ho, for Idaho!" Even tiny Mary Kelly, the "star and joy" of the whole party, joined with the older voices. The song broke off, the last words dying in constricted throats as the most dreaded sight in America confronted them. A Sioux war party was waiting silently at the top of the bluff. Fanny Kelly, the mother of little Mary, tells the story in her book, "My Captivity Among the Sioux Indians." There were at the bluff head some two hundred and fifty Ogallala Sioux under old Chief Ottawa, and, after hypocritical preliminaries which did not deceive their victims, they tried to inveigle the frightened train into driving within the confines of a rocky glen. Meeting with an obstinate refusal to stir another inch, they made their attack then and there, killing or disabling most of the men on the spot. Because they were still in the open four men escaped, two badly wounded, and two unhurt. One of the latter was Mr. Kelly, Fanny's husband, and he determined to preserve his own life in order to devote all his energies to ransoming his wife and child.

He was forced to hide in a clump of rocks and sagebrush within earshot. The noise of splintering wood came to his ears as the Indians used their tomahawks to force open the storage boxes of food. He listened to their harsh accents calling back and forth, hoping, in an agony of grief and terror, to hear his wife's voice or little Mary's; but no sound came from the prisoners. He lay motionless for a long time, and presently the Indians began to hunt for possible stragglers. It was now past dusk. Footsteps came closer and closer in the dark while he huddled in breathless silence. Just when he thought discovery inevitable a rattlesnake close beside him raised its blunt head and gave a warning rattle. It was answered by others. The footsteps retreated, and when it seemed wise he rose unharmed and went swiftly to the east, where he found a large wagon company. The other unhurt man came running in soon after. As quickly as possible the whole train proceeded to the scene of the attack. The wagons and the cattle still stood there. This had been a war party and needed only horses. Flour and feathers heaped the trail and dribbled off on every puff of wind; for partly in sheer exuberance of spirit and partly to get the cloth, Indians on the loose seemed always to slit the pillows and the featherbeds, and liked nothing better than to gallop fiercely about the sagebrush waving the torn ticking and leaving a fluttering comet's tail of choice goose feathers behind them. After a careful search the two wounded men were found and cared for, but the women and children were gone.

Mrs. Kelly was a brave and resourceful woman. She had kept outwardly calm and quiet. When at last the war party was mounted and ready to start she held out her arms for the little girl and was allowed to keep her. Watching her chance, she gave the child whispered instructions as to how to find her way back to the road and, under cover of darkness, dropped her gently from the horse. Mary found the trail and was seen there by three or four soldiers who were returning from Fort Laramie. They mistrusted that she was a decoy placed by the Indians. While they were still hesitating and undecided as to what was best to do, a band of Sioux appeared, and the soldiers fled on to Deer Creek Station. The Indians put three arrows into the little body and took her shawl and scalp. The mother later recognized the bloodstained trophies at the Ogallala camp where she was held prisoner as a sort of nurse for the aged chief who had been wounded. She was five months with the Indians, and many times was in immediate danger of violent death, especially by reason of the jealousy of the old chief's wife who at last drove her from the wigwam at the point of a knife and, failing in her murderous intent, stabbed the chief himself.

When the frightened captive was caught and brought back to dress her patient's wounds, the old squaw had disappeared forever. Mrs. Kelly wrote:

"True, the Ogallalahs had treated me at times with great harshness and cruelty, yet I had never suffered from any of them the slightest personal or unchaste insult. Let me bear testimony to this redeeming feature in their treatment of me.

"At the time of my capture I became the exclusive property of Ottawa, the head chief, a man over seventy-five years of age, and partially blind, yet whose power over the band was absolute. Receiving a severe wound in a melee I have already given an account of, I was compelled to become his nurse or medicine woman; and my services as such were so appreciated, that harsh and cruel as he might be, it was dangerous for others to offer me insult or injury; and to this fact, doubtless, I owe my escape from a fate worse than death."

Her captivity was given wide publicity. Her husband's frantic efforts and the little girl's death caused such public sympathy that perfect strangers coming past on the trail offered large sums of money as ransom. Other tribes tried to buy her from the Ogallalas as a profitable investment, but, with the courage of his convictions, old Chief Ottawa hung on to her.

The wagon trains on the road were now guarded by soldiers. On September 5th the Ogallalas surprised a large train escorted by Captain Fisk and his men. They killed fourteen and came back to the village loaded with spoils and crazed with victory. They greatly coveted the rest of the horses but were afraid to attack while the company was circled and ready. It would be easy to ambush them if they moved. They waited impatiently three days and then insisted that Mrs. Kelly write a deceitful letter to Captain Fisk telling him that it was safe to break camp. The Indians were suspicious of her and counted the words as they dictated them. It was easy to run two and three words together and thus add extra phrases of warning, but very difficult to reread it to the watching braves. She was actually risking her life, but she accomplished her purpose. The wagon train took precautions and got safely away, but all attempts to ransom her resulted either in the death of the messengers or in nothing at all.

The Sioux Nation with several other kindred tribes remained at enmity with the United States all through the fall months of her captivity; but with the approach of winter their spirit cooled. Indians do not fight in the winter. The Blackfeet asked for peace and were told by the government to secure the white woman from the Ogallalas and bring her safely to Fort Sully. Then, and not until then, could peace terms be made with the white man. So the Blackfeet went to the Ogallalas. Fanny Kelly wrote, "They held solemn council for two days, and at last resolved that the Blackfeet should take me as a ruse, to enable them to enter the fort, and a wholesale slaughter should exterminate the soldiers."

She remembered that she had been allowed to send the letter to Captain Fisk and had never been suspected of duplicity. She had a messenger at hand. An Indian, Jumping Bear, who had once saved her life came to her, reminded her of what she owed him, said that he liked her and wished to be "more than a friend." She persuaded him to take a letter to the fort as a test of his affection and made all arrangements in it for him to be well recompensed and protected. Some young squaws, not yet soured by a hard life, helped her in egging him on to show his independence and bravery. They probably thought her letter had to do with plans for ransom and would come to nothing.

It all worked out like clockwork. She was at the point of death on the way to the fort from a faction who wanted to get rid of her and wash their hands of the whole thing, but, that crisis past, all went according to her letter. She and the chiefs accompanying her were admitted into the fort and the gates were suddenly slammed on the rest. The Blackfeet were shut out, and she was free. Her letter was credited with having saved Fort Sully.

Thus, throughout the sixties the wild wind-swept slopes of the Black Hills, where the cholera-crushed masses had been healed and purified, were deadly traps through which the pioneers, knowing well the danger, must take their families and all their worldly wealth. The garrison at Fort Laramie did not permit small parties to leave, but held them until a large company had been formed. This made for safety but occasionally worked great hardships. Lavinia Porter wrote that in the year 1860 she, with her young husband and baby were herded into a company with an unkempt and quarrelsome crowd from Arkansas and Tennessee. The slatternly women continually chewed on short sticks which "they occasionally withdrew and swabbed around in a box containing some black powder, while a muddy stream oozed from the corners of their polluted mouths. It was evident to the most casual observer that they were snuff dippers." Besides these eye-offending habits they had other unseemly characteristics. They fought grimly, men and women alike, using horsewhips and cudgels, and their language was unbearable. The near vicinity was no place for a lady. Lavinia's husband was rightfully worried. It was true that a Sioux brave had several times offered to trade a few ponies for his wife, but when it was made plain to the red man that it was not merely a question of more ponies he had withdrawn in good order. Mr. Porter decided to take a chance on the Sioux. By feigning illness they managed to remain in camp at the last minute. The Tennessee train went on without them, and he and his wife and baby were alone in the Indian country.

They had no trouble. At one camp she showed a group of Sioux the first mirror they had ever handled, and in no time they were all over the camp like sugar on a doughnut. The uglier the Indian, the more passionately he desired to see himself. Again, they had four strayed oxen returned by a strange Indian. At another place she found one of the braves with a raging toothache. Of course the Porters seized every opportunity to strengthen their position, so they got out the toothache drops and packed the cavity. They made a snappy stay and moved along while the deadening effect lasted, for the trail Indians resembled children who like to be helped or pleased or entertained, but fall quickly into fits of temper if disappointed. After some time they looked around and found, to their great distress, that they had a traveling companion.

This new encumbrance was a taciturn Indian who said little, ate enormously, and held his blanket on by mesmerism. He rode near them in the daytime and slept under their wagon at night. For three days Lavinia politely tried to fill him up while the flour supply visibly dwindled. At the end of that time, seeing certain preparations that indicated he might be leaving, she filled a bag with bread for him. He turned back and returned the way they had come. They were later informed, by those who knew the country, that the Indian had personally conducted them through, and safely out of, a very hot spot indeed.

It is quite likely that their phlegmatic guide left them somewhere in the neighborhood of Box Elder Creek or in the four miles that separated the ford of Box Elder from the Platte. For, in the sixties, there were forts and soldiers along the river, and even a bridge to take the place of the scattered ferries. The Indian would no doubt have turned back to his people and let them go on alone.

Through all the years it was a great moment for the throngs of emigrants as they struggled over the last elevation. Behind them, low ridge after low ridge, in serried order, marched the Black Hills. Ahead, the Platte twisted through the lowland, gleaming silvery on the curves: a strange river, blurred and gray and untrustworthy, whose long pale waters hid their spoils; a deadly river and hard to conquer; one that, through decades, lipped softly at the makeshift ferries and whispered along the sandy shores, causing sensitive travelers to shudder at thoughts of drowned bodies cast up upon its wooded islands, never found and never buried. The groaning wagons lurched down the last slope and reached its banks. Once more, and for a last encounter, the emigrants were to match their strength against the Platte.

14

The Ferries of the North Platte

FROM THE TIME THAT the wagons left the Black Hills behind until they had either crossed the North Platte or had been bested in the attempt, the emigration was really functioning on all sixteen cylinders. Progress was faster, and the sore-footed oxen were urged to more miles per bushel as the wagon masters speeded up for the ferries.

They encountered the first doddering specimen near Deer Creek five miles from the point where the Bowstring Cutoff rejoined the Platte. It was a poor affair, too small for its burdens, creaking and rheumatic. It staggered painfully across troubled waters broken out in an eczema of froth and foam, but the travelers were incomprehensibly optimistic. They either inserted themselves, complete with vehicles, into the confines of the crazy craft and ignored the impersonal antagonism of the river, or dared the dirty gray flood in their own, just-calked wagon beds.

Franklin Langworthy, already on the north bank, was an interested bystander. He wrote: "We perceive today that many of the emigrants are crossing in their wagon beds to our side of the river and we hear that men are daily drowned in these operations. If one of these frail boats oversets, all on board are lost. Not one in a thousand can save his life by swimming, no matter how expert a swimmer. The water is cold, being formed from the melting snows, and the current rolls, boils, and rushes along with tremendous velocity. The goods and passengers are ferried across, and the cattle and horses are forced into the water, and compelled to swim the raging torrent. The animals are exceedingly loth to enter the stream, and have to be pushed in by main force. In this process the men frequently wade in so far as to lose their footing, are swept down by the tide and drowned." C. A. Kirkpatrick arrived at the mouth of Deer Creek in June of '49 and was horrified at the setup. "Already within our hearing today," he wrote, "twelve men have found a watery grave while crossing with their stock and effects; and yet this makes no impression on the survivors." In the same week Alonzo Delano described the breaking of a ferry rope and told of the attempts, lasting half a day, to get another across the implacable current so that the jumble of humanity, rolling stock and hungry animals that had been piling up on the grass-stripped south shore all day, could make a start toward the greener pastures of the north bank.

What seems to me to be the crowning tragedy of the Platte crossings is told very simply in the autobiography of Theodore E. Potter. It was in the summer of '52, and the valley of the North Platte swarmed with emigrant companies and their herds. During the ordinary traveling hours of the day those on the north side moved steadily along upstream with very little regard for the vicissitudes of their less fortunate brothers across the river. But toward evening they camped by the water's edge and anxiously watched the ferries as they spun dizzily in eddies or withstood the battering-ram attack of logs borne swiftly on the flood waters. Sometimes, in the late evening light, the campers were hard put to it to keep small groups of dripping cattle, swept by the current beyond the immediate control of their owners, from joining their family circle.

It was in such a setup that fourteen Mormon men with a herd of about one hundred cattle arrived one evening on the south bank. Two of the men established their wives on a ferry which was about to cross and, rejoining their comrades, succeeded in launching the cattle into the swollen current. They then rode their horses into the water and followed the cattle at a safe distance. All went across in reasonably good order and, as the herd began to find footing across the river, another large drove was driven out from the south shore. The emerging herd, however, was encroaching upon the domain (real or fancied) of some conscientious watchdog. He barked furiously and drove them back into the river where they turned tail and started for the place they had just left.

The horsemen, caught between the two churning bands, hadn't a chance. All fourteen were drowned, and their bodies carried downstream within full view of the two wives.

The tragedy was one of the few which seem to have aroused widespread interest. A thousand people attended the funeral of the first five bodies recovered. Then seven more were found and buried, and a search party was sent out to locate the remaining two. Theodore Potter started out with the party but discovered that he was in excellent hunting territory and bagged first one elk and then another. Happening by chance to come across one of the objects of the search, he arrived back in camp at the end of the day with the bodies of five elk and one man; and the entire camp partook of the funeral baked meats.

The dun-colored river often retained the bodies garnered at the ferry crossings, tossing them out again far down the river—bulging masses of rotted flesh in sodden homespun. It was possible to mistake these dank, drowned bodies for water-soaked logs. Joseph Batty, selecting a nice clear spot from which to dip his drinking water, stepped on a yielding sponge-like specimen and temporarily deranged his digestive functions.

It was a commonly accepted premise among the emigrants that the well-to-do trains ignored the Deer Creek ferry and, trekking two more days upstream, crossed at the Mormon or Upper Ferry. Sometimes large and efficient companies built their own rafts, afterward leaving them behind for general use; and yet, at the peak of the traffic, wagons poured so fast along the overland road that there was a complete stoppage of two or three days at any ferry with a hundred or so wagons and their attendant stock around each landing place. No wonder, with the grass gone and a score of dead cattle lying here and there to greet the newcomers, that worried captains took a chance on ferrying in their wagon beds.

Near Deer Creek the highway traveler may visit a grave marked "A. H. Unthank, Died July 2, 1850." It comes as something of a shock, for his is one of the most legible carvings on Register Cliffs, about a three-day journey back. He certainly had no conception when he inscribed his name so carefully on the sandstone bluff that it would figure next on his headstone; but such was the case, and the last miles of his life, gritting slowly beneath the heavy wheels, brought him here for his long rest.

It was one of the little ironies which Fate deals occasionally from the bottom of the pack that the wealth-seeking Argonauts were at this point heedlessly rushing over riches beyond anything they dreamed of finding in California. Today's traveler sees great companies of derricks marching stiff-legged across the rolling dry knolls, acres of muscular machinery engaged in a profitable St. Vitus's dance, and squadrons of tanks; sees all the fascinating sights and smells the not-so-fascinating smells instinct in a great oil field. But the Forty-niners were hurrying for the ferries. The grass was gone, and they felt, with some reason, that the sooner they emulated its example the better.

*   *   *

Twenty-eight miles from Deer Creek was the Upper or Mormon Ferry of the North Platte, near modern Casper. The earliest travelers found it, of course, in a state of nature and were utterly dependent upon their own efforts. Tradition tells us that the crossing selected in pre-prairie-schooner days was three miles down from the later ferry site. It was a favorite with the Indians, who would make rafts of their lodgepoles, pile them with household goods and attach thongs of buffalo hide, with which swimming braves towed them across the river.

The fur traders usually waited for a favorable day and crossed with their goods packed in bullboats, floating the heavy carts. The early emigrants were not versed in the virtues of bullboats and made rather heavy going of the proposition. Father de Smet, well loved Catholic missionary who came west with the migration of '41, gave an amusing description of their adventure. Seeing their Indian hunter lash his year-old baby to a colt's back and lead it into the current, they were emboldened to ride their own horses across the river. Father de Smet reached the north shore safe but dripping, and turned to look. "On one side appeared the American captain, with extended arms, crying for help. On the other, a young German traveler was seen diving with his beast, and soon after both appeared above water at a distance from each other. Here a horse reached the shore without a rider; farther on, two riders appeared on the same horse; finally, the good brother Joseph dancing up and down with his horse, and Father Mangarini clinging to the neck of his, and looking as if he formed an indivisible part of the animal. After all our difficulties, we found that only one of the mules was drowned." Evidently the papoose arrived according to schedule.

In 1847 the well organized Mormon migration faced the river. They built light pine-pole rafts capable of carrying an empty wagon, and went, hammer and tongs, at the task of getting across. By afternoon of the fourth day, when they were all on the north bank, it was brought to their attention that two wagon trains from Missouri had arrived at the crossing. A bargain was struck by which the Mormons ferried the Missourians for $1.50 per load and the privilege of buying provisions at Missouri prices.

The workability of this infant enterprise was not lost on the Mormon leaders. Several of the brethren were left at the spot to "keep a ferry until the next company of Saints came up, by which means they hoped to make enough to supply a large company with provisions." By these simple be-

Ferry Across North Platte.
(From an old print in the museum at Douglas, Wyoming)

ginnings the businesslike Mormons established a system of ferries, profitable both to them and to the coast-bound emigrants.

There were those here, as at any ferry, who could not or would not pay the price and who used self-constructed substitutes. To these novices the strong west wind was an additional hazard—a twin current flowing above the river. It caught and rumbled in the capacious bellies of the white-topped wagons, swelling them into sails that flung the rafts downstream. Pulling men were dragged into the current. Ropes snapped. Rafts capsized. Wagons tipped overboard and bobbed along to be rescued at the next curve with cargo gone. The river was a watery sarcophagus of biscuit and beans. One experience was enough to teach every one present to remove the wagon tops during a ferry trip in a windstorm; but the next playful breeze, sneaking up after a two- or three-day calm, would catch a new group unprepared.

Regular travel on the south side of the river ended at the Upper Ferry. Practically every one crossed. The women went over on ferry, raft, or wagon bed and then took up their vigil on the north bank. There was nothing (because of their commendable forethought in having been born females) that they could do about navigating the cattle except to scream advice across the river, while hitherto conservative husbands cast themselves into its unresponsive bosom in a way that no wife could readily condone. The time had come—could no longer be postponed—somehow each man must reassemble his family, cattle, and goods on the far side of the dangerous, snow-swelled Platte.

At this spot, in the year 1850, a band of horses were lined up for the crossing—the same animals whom Old Pompey had led across this flooded stream at Fort Laramie, one hundred twenty-five miles back. Carlisle Abbott watched the stock driver just ahead meet his death midstream, and then quietly led Old Pompey to the water's edge prepared to cope once more with the Platte. He undressed and slid into the water, getting a firm grasp on Pompey's useful tail. In his free hand he carried a long stick to rouse that deliberate animal to the necessity of keeping well ahead of the swimming band. The men of his company had begged him not to make the attempt, but he and faithful Pompey won through the heavy current and into the lightly fuming eddies of the north side. Pompey's forefeet struck the long beach on the opposite bank, "I mounted him," wrote Mr. Abbott, "and rode up the bank, the band following, while the men on the other shore sang or yelled: 'One more river to cross!'"

A simply worded climax to another trail melodrama.

Had Mr. Abbott known that his first-hand impressions of trail life and incidents would come to be of such interest to future students of western history, he might have soared to climactic heights. Perhaps, as the lady journalists of the fifties would have phrased it " 'Tis better thus." If the hundreds of persons who kept trail diaries could have had an inkling of the erudite institutions that would some day cherish them in fireproof vaults, nine-tenths of them would have forestalled the attention by personally burning the diaries in the last campfire. And letters! Imagine the tired women snatching a moment here and there to write home. If they could have had a prophetic vision of the incipient Ph.D.'s of the future hunting bits of useful information wedged in between what they thought of the dirt and what probably ailed the baby, the letters would have been edifying homilies but sadly lacking in authority. As it is, the majority of the daily journals kept by the pioneers are about as subtle as a dose of poison oak, and hold inexhaustible funds of good solid information. From them we gather that it was indeed a fortunate company that crossed the North Platte and continued intact on its way.

*   *   *

Considered historically, the year 1858 is the beginning of the end of the picturesque extravaganza at the river crossing. First a prosaic military encampment, known as Mormon Ferry Post, appears in the picture. Then, in the winter of 1858–59, a bridge presents itself apologetically for our consideration.

The little fortress antedated the bridge by a few months only. It was located about two hundred sixty-five yards southwest of the bridge and ferry site and was equipped to maintain a hundred soldiers. The bridge was long, narrow, unbeautiful, and supported by piers made of log cribbing filled with rocks. It waded slowly across the Platte on these bulky legs and was finished in time for the migration of '59.

In '49 a few travelers noted a precarious bridge three miles below the site of the later bridge near the ferry. It had been built by a fur company and was apparently of no importance or use to the emigrants. Diaries of the sixties, however, mention an Upper and a Lower Platte Bridge, placing them six miles (and two hours' travel over a heavy sand hill) apart. Probably the lower bridge was constructed at a better location in the meantime.

One fine July day in the first year of our field work, we arrived at the spot where the southern approach of the bridge built in '59 used to be, and parked the car near a monument commemorating the fort, which, in its short life of less than ten years, was known by three titles. The first name, Mormon Ferry Post, was supplanted naturally enough by Platte Bridge Station; but its final appellation, Fort Caspar, was bestowed after the heroic death of Lieutenant Caspar Collins, and is the one which comes proudly down through history. There are no ruins. There is nothing of the fort left to see. We came to hunt for the remains of the bridge piers.

The dry details of how we came there and how we had annexed the well known Wyoming historian, A. J. Mokler, are unimportant. The vital item is the fact that we arrived on the spot in his company. Under his guidance, we left the car and walked from one to another of the evenly spaced hummocks of earth covered with straggling bushes which are all that the years have left of the bridge supports.

Mr. Mokler was pleasantly informative. "You can see," he said, "that the piles of cribbing gradually rotted and disappeared. Then the rocks inside sank down and in time became so mixed with sand and earth that they look like natural mounds. There's no path here. We'll have to do the best we can." He proceeded to set a good example.

"Can we see the high lights on the original river trail west of the ferry today?" my husband asked, as we approached the car again.

"Yes, indeed." Mr. Mokler planned efficiently. "Then tomorrow, when you leave town, you can take the Emigrant Gap Road out through the hills. It wasn't used until after 1865, but it saw a lot of traffic in its day. Perhaps you can drive on it clear to the Sweetwater River."

"How far would that be?" Dr. Neff asked.

"Over fifty miles; but I think it is passable. The older trail runs into it about twenty-five miles out, so that you will approach Independence Rock and the Sweetwater just as the early emigrants did."

"Well, if the old one starts right down the river, we may as well begin with it." Dr. Neff concluded the conversation briefly and stepped on the gas.

The first spot of interest was the place where the wagons, having just pulled off the ferry or crossed the bridge, joined the north-bank trail. In gold-rush days plenty of excitement attested the importance of jockeying for position as the intruders from the south side attempted to cut in on the north-bank wagons. Ear-cracking pops from the twelve-foot rawhide whips, the tortured creak of axles in drying, sand-filled hubs, the call of the drivers to the lead horses, unprintable streams of unique profanity from the bullwhackers, nickerings and bawlings from the harassed animals, all punctuated with the inimitable voice of the mule, formed a kaleidoscope of noise, a broken pattern of continually changing sounds, the stirring diapason of an emigrant trail never repeated to so great an extent in human history.

"Roughly speaking," Mr. Mokler said, "the road north of the river is called the Mormon Trail from the Missouri River to this point, although of course you know that the first Mormons crossed the North Platte at Fort Laramie and arrived here by way of the south bank."

"That didn't last very long, did it?" Dr. Neff asked.

"No, it didn't. After 1850 the Mormons kept their own side of the river pretty consistently, but the people bound for the coast used both roads."

"About a third of the west-coasters took the Mormon Trail," I volunteered. "I took a sort of straw vote once. Out of 135 non-Mormon journals and reminiscences picked at random, 41 were written on the trail north of the Platte."

"What do they call it from here west?" Bill asked with an unusual urge to garner information.

"Oregon Trail is the usual term for the northern fork," Mr. Mokler told him, "and of course the entire trail, from the Missouri along the north bank of the Platte and over the mountains to Salt Lake City, is called the Mormon Trail. But they are coincidental over the Rockies."

"And who traveled them?"

"Probably as many people bound for California as anywhere else," his father broke in with some amusement.

This finished Bill historically for the day.

Mr. Mokler laughed. "It is confusing, but after the transcontinental wires were strung, the river road west from the bridge was called the Telegraph Road. Maybe you'd like that better. At least it means what it says."

Called by what name you will, the trail was now concentrating for the ascent of the Rockies, where, for a few congested miles, there would be no alternate road. From the north end of Platte bridge it followed in the general direction of the river for about twelve miles—twelve deadly miles if the Sioux chose to make them so. On July 26, 1865, their hostility reached a climax at the approach of a train of three wagons under the protection of Sergeant Custard and twenty-three soldiers.

Mr. Mokler told us the story.

The party was moving eastward from the Sweetwater River toward Platte Bridge Station and the most grueling anxiety was felt for its safety. Early in the morning a thousand or so belligerent Sioux and Cheyennes moved into ambush on the river-bank trail. About a hundred men were in the fort. Lieutenant Caspar Collins volunteered to take twenty-five and go to meet the wagons. It was a forlorn hope, but they accepted it as their duty. Half a mile from the north end of the bridge, they were attacked by some four hundred Cheyennes and completely surrounded. Holding the reins in their teeth, the soldiers fought their way back to the fort with the loss of but eight men, one of whom was Caspar Collins.

While the Cheyennes were taking care of the Collins attack, the Sioux sent some five hundred fighters to capture the fort. They were repulsed "with the unintended aid of the Cheyennes who were firing at the retreating Collins men," but whose erratic bullets topped them and laid low some Sioux braves. Somewhat disconcerted and decidedly disgruntled, the two detachments retreated to the hills where they had a private tiff. Others fell to mutilating with their lewd surgery the men who fell on the retreat, and the fort was temporarily forgotten.

All this happened early in the morning.

At eleven o'clock, the men of the fort saw the wagons coming far in the distance and fired the small brass cannon to warn them. It was all that they could do. Four miles out on the Telegraph Road the train was attacked and held out for five hours against fifty times their own number. But it was over at last. The survivors were tortured on the spot and when, during the afternoon of the next day, reinforcements came from Deer Creek Station, the Indians went away. The nineteen mutilated bodies found with the charred remains of the Custard wagon train were buried in one long grave. It was not marked, Mr. Mokler told us, and the exact location is not known. Monuments to their memory have been placed at an arbitrarily selected spot which we passed as we circled back from our survey of the first twelve miles of the old river route. The massacre is often called the Red Buttes fight from the famous trail landmarks of that name near by.

15

The Approach to the Rockies

No ONE, I HOPE, will ever depend on me for guidance across the continent, as my acquaintance with good roads is sketchy. In our necessary contacts with the larger towns we usually make a flourishing entrance by way of the city dumps and a grandstand exit past the slaughterhouse. We left Casper, with regret, by necessity and a back road. I have no idea where the highway goes. We encountered it again with something of a shock about forty miles away, toward Independence Rock. Meanwhile we gathered up the thread of our trail philanderings and followed its lead, out from town and over the hills toward Emigrant Gap.

Just out of town we discovered a perfect cemetery of historical markers indicating the place where the wagons from the south side of the river angled into the north-bank (or Mormon) trail. From here on, the two great roads that had come all the way from the Missouri as separate entities were united. Of course there would still be minor splits and alternate routes covering a few miles here and there but in a large sense they were now one. The spot is so significant that no regular putter-upper of markers could afford to ignore it.

Our road started uphill and rose higher and higher, but very gently. Wyoming makes less fuss about its elevation than any place I know. To our left was the wide sandy pass used by migrations of the sixties. A later generation of indigenous Casperites have named it Emigrant Gap, one of a long series of Emigrant Gaps that punctuate the trail clear to the Pacific coast. The highway uses a parallel pass near by. Just beyond it we found Poison Spider Creek, all the wrong colors for respectable water and very scummy, but wholesome in comparison with the neighboring supply, for the emigrants now had a new trail bugbear—alkali.

The travelers had seen alkali water along the Platte but, with the river running near by, the discolored pools were little temptation to the cattle. Now the migration wallowed in billowing dust (also tinctured with alkali) that choked and almost blinded the animals. Their ears, eye rims, and nostrils were coated an eighth of an inch thick, and the implacable brassy sun baked it solid. Anything that looked like water caused a rush in its direction. The continuous herding tried the vigilance of the lax and shiftless emigrants and was too difficult for the tired and sick. The slough-ing carcasses of their animals lay all about the gruesome little pools.

And here again it was all a matter of preparedness. After the enormous migrations of '49 and '50 had learned what not to do, later comers han-dled the fifty-odd miles of semidesert much better. After all there *was* good water at short enough intervals to preserve the stock if they could be kept from the poison pools between.

By either the Emigrant Gap route or the older road it was in the neigh-borhood of fifty miles from the ferry to Independence Rock on the Sweet-water River—a forced march of two days. The emigrants of both routes softened this somewhat by making a short drive after crossing the river and camping at the last drinkable water, so that repellent Poison Spider Creek was populous if not popular in its day. Both routes led to Willow Springs on the second night, and from there it was possible to make the Sweetwater by the end of the next afternoon.

We left the Poison Spider about the middle of the morning, heading for the next noted landmark, Rock Avenue. It proved satisfyingly true to its advance advertising—a hideous stretch of deformed rock strata burst-ing jaggedly from the torn earth—and formed a real point of interest for the travelers in the midst of the sprawling sage-studded grayness. We left the car to look it over. A pushing wind flowed like swift, deep, warm water across the plateau. Its force on the west side of the upthrust points of rock was surprising. It was difficult to walk or even to breathe when facing it.

"This has been an easy morning's work," Dr. Neff remarked. "The full length of the river road would have taken quite a bit more time."

"I wonder where it comes in," Bill said. "Do you suppose we can see it from here?" And we were lost in a flood of conjecture. To end it I dug out the dirty and dog-eared Paden Encyclopedia and commenced to flip the pages.

"Leaving this Emigrant Gap road out of the picture," I said, "there were two old roads from the ferry. There was a river road, of course, and then you could always depend on the Mormons to find a hill road. How-ard R. Egan wrote about it in '47. Here is what he said:

" 'The first six miles we traveled after leaving the ferry was about a west course, over several high bluffs where the road turns to the south and rises a high bluff about a mile long. The whole face of the country as far as the eye can extend from here appears to be barren and very much broken. The descent on the south side of the bluff was crooked and uneven. We halted about a quarter of a mile from a good spring, which is about eleven and one quarter miles from the ferry. The Red Buttes are nearly opposite this place, in a southeast direction. About twelve miles from the ferry there is a lake, supposed to be supplied by the spring. We proceeded on our journey from this spring, bearing a southwest course over a rolling prairie. About eight miles from the lake there is a steep descent from a bluff, and at the foot there is a ridge of sharp-pointed rocks, leaving only a narrow space for the wagons to pass, and the road is very rough.'

"Mr. Mokler said," I went on, "that the descent has been named Poison Spring Creek Pass. There are lots of names carved around on the rocks. Udell's second journal says that the right-hand or hill road had a better roadbed than the river road but less water and grass, and I guess it was rough enough at that. One of the rises was called Rattlesnake Hill. The water of the spring and lake was not considered good; but they were quite a feature of the landscape, and travelers on the river road wrote as if they were sorry to miss seeing them. Henry Mann states that the river road left the Platte at the Red Buttes, went one mile to an alkali lake, next to a sulphur spring and lake, and then to 'Rocky Avenue'; and Mr. Mokler said that the two older roads met at the Poison Spring Creek Pass, and the wagons from both hill and river roads went through Rock Avenue together."

"Was the river road the same one we were on yesterday?" Bill asked.

"Yes. Some wagons left the river just across from the Red Buttes; but the earlier companies hugged the river until they had crossed Iron Creek, about twelve miles from Casper."

"I wonder why they called these rocks an 'avenue,'" Dr. Neff said. "It looks a great deal more like a ragged wall."

"They rode *in* it, with a ridge of rocks on each side," I explained. "Sawyer said his wagons 'entered' Rock Avenue, and Dinwiddie wrote very clearly that his company proceeded for a quarter-mile between the rocky walls on a roadbed just wide enough for a wagon, but very even and good."

"I'd like to hike along the Avenue of Rocks until we find that place," Dr. Neff remarked.

I listened hopefully, for to tell the truth, I was more interested in the older road than in the one we were on; but my husband had embarked on an enterprise and was not to be deterred.

"Some day we'll come back," he promised vaguely. "Right now I'm concerned about hitting Independence Rock and the highway before it gets dark. Pile in."

From Rock Avenue the wagons rumbled and bumbled down a steep pitch onto a six-mile stretch of intermittent alkaline puddles and swamps. The animals were thirsty, and this hodgepodge of impossible water was torture. Steaming marshes alternated with pestilent pits of semifluid that shook and smelled like spoiled meat jelly. Mineral springs of complicated parentage comprising salt, soda, and sulphur exuded warm and indescribable odors. Some, if undisturbed, lay clear and brandy-colored. The loose stock got into these and often died as a result, although the antidotes for alkali poison had the merit of being simple. Gobs of bacon pushed down the gullet with a blunt stick and swigs of vinegar saved many—temporarily at least, for these weakened cattle fell easy victims to the rarefied air of the mountains just ahead.

The fifty miles between the ferry and Independence Rock brought to the harassed travelers uneasiness and discomfort so sharp that it became fright. There was no surcease anywhere in the dust-blanketed and scorched sage of the plateau. Nebulous horizons heaved out of saucerlike depressions that strung along, one beyond another—meaningless horizons which, when surmounted, gave way to others exactly similar in the dusty, deceitful distances. Crawling crickets, as fat and loathsome as if there had been anything visible to eat, crunched under the wheels, and the exhausted thousands, plodding in a dust-obscured crowd, laid their blistered feet like so many cornerstones across the sandy waste.

In time they passed out of the poison-spring region, went over a snappy ridge, and came to Willow Springs at a distance of twenty-six miles from the ferry. In years of little travel it was the perfect oasis, pure water in a tiny willow grove surrounded by untainted grass. During heavy migrations the grass soon disappeared, and the cattle of the poor or improvident man went unfed at the end of a grueling day's work. The water never failed.

Another mile brought the emigrants to the summit of Prospect Hill. Often they had spent the night near Willow Springs and climbed the hill in early morning, thus getting their first view of Sweetwater Mountains, the vanguard of the Rockies, by the optimistic rosy light of dawn. A full twenty miles still separated them from the Sweetwater River, and they could catch no glimpse of it.

*   *   *

If we can judge by her simple and unstudied reminiscences, Lydia Waters was a splendid specimen of the healthy, hearty pioneer women who baked and washed and milked and helped to harness up and still had energy to spare. Lydia journeyed west in the touch-and-go year of 1855, and at Willow Springs her camp was roused by an Indian scare. Some shots were fired, and the Indians (sixteen of them counted against the sky as they went over a hill) departed unrewarded for their efforts. The next morning she was rather enjoyably relaxed as she drove an ox team during an interlude in her wifely duties of herding loose stock. A guileless pup in search of coolness who waded into a white-edged alkaline pool caught her eye. While she watched he fled as if bee-stung, yelping with pain from the biting alkali. Greasewood Creek was a welcome sight, a rapid ten-foot stream, midway of the twenty-mile stretch, where the oxen sunk their muzzles deep and drank as they crossed. After a slow five miles more the alkali lakes came into view—paper-flat deposits of a pure, fiery-white soda that ate the soles from the shoes of the luckless herder who must go among them after cattle. The biggest one was called Saleratus Lake. Here the cooks replenished their supply of cooking soda and sometimes encountered the wagons from the Mormon colony at Salt Lake shoveling it up for home consumption.

Today Lydia drove the last wagon and for that reason led all the saddle animals belonging to the company tied in a long string behind her. Looking back through the wagon and out the flapping tail sheet, she saw a long vista of plodding horses. She also saw an antelope. She called, and one of the men took a heavily loaded gun out of her wagon hoping for a shot at it. He was too slow and put it back on the seat beside her, muzzle to the rear—inadvertently leaving it cocked. From that indiscreet moment things happened fast. Lydia caught her pocket on the hammer; there was an ear-crashing din; and she had baptized the animals with fire. They bolted—her cherished horses—full of buckshot. The wagon top began to blaze. Lydia, generous soul, had given away the last of her water, but the tea pot was close by for solace later in the afternoon. She emptied the soggy tea leaves into her bare hands and held them on the flames during those first crucial seconds, scouring the burning edges of the white drill covering between her palms. She was successful and the wagon was saved; but she did no more driving with her blistered hands for two months, and it took longer to find and extract all the slugs buried in the horses.

It was four miles and more from the end of the alkali stretch to the Sweetwater River—a beautiful mountain stream, swift, clear and full, which received its name from the accidental loss in its waters of a pack containing all the sugar of an early-day trading expedition. When the travelers had drunk and bathed they went up its bank a mile to Independence Rock, the most famous of all the landmarks—the first and almost the only trail bulletin board of names and addresses that absolutely everybody had to pass. For the first time since leaving home the migration was now in one set of wheel tracks.

*   *   *

We were almost all day going the fifty-odd miles from the ferry to the rock, remaining for the most part in or within sight of the Emigrant Gap trail. Sometimes we varied the gray monotony by searching under the old telegraph poles that had come this way along with the overland stages. We had a feeble hope that we might find one of the glass insulators with its curved wooden protector, but had no luck, then or later, and only succeeded in delaying our arrival at the rock.

Once we saw the shining ribbon of the highway, and crossed it almost at right angles. Our tiny thread of roadway was too insignificant to merit any sort of a filled approach, so we bumped up onto the pavement and down again on the other side, glad to be done with it.

Wild life abounded—sage hens with their young broods, prairie dogs, antelope, and the long-eared jackass rabbit. It grew sandier all the time, with the dry gray sage everywhere. In marked contrast was the vivid green greasewood and the blinding white patches of hungry alkali whose corrosive mud ate the soles from the pioneers' shoes.

From the last intervening rise we saw Independence Rock just ahead, lumped down among the sage like some inert monster, hips and shoulders high, its swayback saddle scarcely seventy feet above the ground. The long anticipated Sweetwater River flowed briefly toward us from around

Independence Rock and the Sweetwater River with the Granite Range and Devil's Gate in the background. (Adapted from a painting by William H. Jackson)

the huge shoulder and then turned away to the south in a mighty sweep—clean, pure, sweet water at last! The sun was declining in the blank, electric blue of the July heavens and the imminently looming mountains towered darkly to a clean-cut edge. The nebulous gray expanse of rolling sage land ended here, abutted against the outer guard of the Rockies.

Like the emigrants, we approached the rock from the east side—a lusty monolith, a mile in circumference, and seemingly one solid piece of gray granite. No wonder that this tremendous outpost of the hard-rock country struck sparks from the sandstone-weary migration. For that matter there is nothing frivolous about the Sweetwater Range, or, as the emigrants called it, the Rattlesnake or Granite Mountains—a substantial little item rising in full view to the right and flaunting its nakedness in the teeth of the Rockies. It is a bare ridge of solid rock, and on the occasion of this, our first visit the knuckle ends of its protruding bones were slowly mellowed by reflected light from the vast copper bowl of the gathering sunset to a pale polished coffee color.

We left the car by the markers that disseminate information at the base of the rock, and ascended the rounded granite saddle. It was not too difficult on the east side, but very slippery and bulging. At the top I stopped out of breath, enraged that any glacier should have spent thousands of years and Heaven only knows what amount of horsepower polishing so much rock to so little purpose. The wind from the west was close to a hurricane, and it was hard to maintain a firm footing; but we sidled around, gasping a breath now and then with faces averted from the wind, and came to a shallow recess in the rock that Mr. Mokler had described. Here was held the first Masonic meeting in Wyoming. Certainly it was an isolated and appropriate spot, something not so easy to find around the populous camps, and on July 4, 1862, about twenty Oregon-bound Masons utilized its privacy to conduct lodge.

Most people know that Independence Rock is called the Great Register of the Desert. Even so, a few facts about it and about the thousands of names that at one time appeared upon it, may not come amiss. From earliest days it was noted as a landmark and a camping place for the fur traders' expeditions. Not a man among them but knew every foot of its surrounding country. Many of the early travelers thought that its name might have been evolved because of its sturdy isolation; but Asahel Munger, a missionary Oregon-bound in 1839, was told by Harris, well known mountain man, that the name Independence was bestowed upon it in 1830 by trappers of the American Fur Company who happened to spend the Fourth of July camped in its shadow.

Until after 1849 the Sweetwater ford was immediately at the rock, and the companies stopped automatically to prepare for the crossing. John K. Townsend states that he was encamped there on the Sweetwater on June 9, 1834: "Here we found a large rounded mass of granite, ... called Rock Independence. Like the Red Butes this rock is also a rather remarkable point in the route. On its smooth perpendicular sides, we see carved the names of most of the mountain bourgeois, with the dates of their arrival. We observed those of the two Sublettes, Captains Bonneville, Serre, Fontinelle, etc., and after leaving our own, and taking a hearty lunch in the shade of the Rock, and a draught from the pure and limpid stream at its base, we pursued our journey."

Father de Smet also wrote in his journal about "the famous rock, Independence, which is detached, like an outlook, from the immense chain of mountains that divide North America. It might," he continued, "be called the great registry of the desert, for on it may be read in large characters the names of the several travelers who have visited the Rocky Mountains. . . . On account of these names, and of the dates that accompany them, as well as of the hieroglyphics of Indian warriors, I have surnamed this Rock 'The Great Record of the Desert.' "

John C. Frémont, in his entry of August 13, 1842, wrote: "I obeyed the feeling of early travelers; and left the impression of the cross deeply engraved on the vast rock, one thousand miles beyond the Mississippi, to which discoverers have given the name of Rock Independence." By the summer of '49 there was not a trace of the cross left. Mr. Jaggers of that year's migration searched carefully without avail. As a possible explanation Mr. Mokler called our attention to the fact that there was an emigrants' celebration at the spot on July 4, 1847, in which the impetuous patriots filled old wagon hubs with powder and exploded them in crevasses of the rock, thus turning over onto the ground a huge segment of granite weighing several tons.

Few names are now legible. Most of them were painted on with wagon paint, axle grease, or gunpowder mixed with various incongruous liquids. The enterprising Mormons sometimes had a man or two at the Rock who would undertake to inscribe a name and date for varying prices up to five dollars, depending on the location. Probably they fulfilled their contracts, but the uncompromising granite was hard to carve and then abused the confidence of the carver by weathering off all the faster by reason of his efforts to leave an enduring message. Still, all the laborious autographs lasted long enough to serve their purpose of cheering the few friends and relatives who followed, and entertaining the thousands of strangers.

* * *

With the arrival at the Sweetwater River the caravans entered the fringes of the country of the Crows—"notorious rogues," Captain Bonneville called them, "jockeys, and horse stealers, and errant scamperers of the mountains." Their gorgeously beautiful domain lay to the north, on the eastern slope of the Rockies, and included the valleys of the Yellowstone, Powder, and Wind rivers. They loved and were justly proud of it. Their chief Arapooish once said: "The Crow country is a good country. The Great Spirit has put it exactly in the right place; while you are in it you fare well; whenever you go out of it, whichever way you travel, you fare worse." The emigrants had just tested the truth of this statement before entering. They would prove it again in no uncertain terms when they should leave.

The pioneers seldom found an encampment of Crows, but occasional moving villages angled in from the hunting grounds and moved up the Sweetwater in company with late stragglers of the migration. The people of this tribe were short, almost squat, very black, and possessed a devastating sense of humor. They were not especially noted as warriors but stole with a verve and flair that placed them at the top of the list. Their skill at this profitable diversion was a proverb among mountain men. A band of Crows meeting a band of trappers habitually flung themselves upon their white brothers in a collective embrace out of which the trappers expected to emerge with empty pockets and missing buttons. With few exceptions they were tolerant to the emigrants.

In 1852, Mrs. Brooks, with six children under thirteen years of age, started west to join her husband. At first she had for a teamster a hired ruffian of whom she was afraid and the children had the measles. In the course of time both of these hindrances faded from their lives and they were free to stumble along under their own feeble power. A son, Elisha Brooks, later wrote: "On the Sweetwater River, we came across a band of friendly Crow Indians moving camp in search of better hunting grounds. They traveled with us a week or more, marching by day in our front and on our flanks and erecting their wigwams near us at night. We presented a strange and weird scene in camp, and a motley and picturesque procession en route: red men in rich robes of bear and panther skins decked out with fringe and feathers; red men without robes or feathers, and unwashed; favorite and actually handsome squaws in elegant mantles of bird skins, tattooed and adorned with beads; unlovely squaws in scanty rags and no beads and unwashed; papooses rolled in highly ornamented cradles grinning from the backs of their ancestors; toddling papooses without a rag, and unwashed; ponies hidden under monumental burdens; packs of dogs creeping under wonderful loads; and, bringing up the rear, an old ox team with six wild, ragged children and a woman once called white, and sometimes unwashed, for we could not always get enough water to drink. We were a Wild West Show." This is another, and an interesting, instance of the tolerance of a large party of

Indians (not, of course, actually at war) for a single inoffensive and obviously unprotected family.

In marked contrast is another case where Indians (in this instance Sioux probably accompanied by Cheyennes) did escort duty up the Sweetwater. It was the year 1842, and the Oregon-bound columns were just slightly ahead of Frémont's South Pass Expedition. At the spot where the emigrant wagons struck the Sweetwater some one pulled a cocked gun out of a wagon and shot young Bailey, their blacksmith, through the body. He died, and they remained there to bury him. Consequently this particular company passed Independence Rock without loitering. Lansford Hastings, later sponsor of the Hastings Cutoff that was the undoing of the Donner Party, and A. L. Lovejoy, one of the founders of Portland, were both anxious to inscribe their names on the rock. They let the columns pass on up the river and remained behind with a can of paint to finish an artistic job. The Sioux encircled them before they could get to their horses. There seemed to be hundreds of Indians—so many that the white men attempted no resistance.

To their surprise it appeared that they were not entirely without champions. Certain haranguing went on, that was apparently in their favor, and a chief sat near Hastings and gave him some protection. What happened to Lovejoy seemed not to be within the chief's jurisdiction, and an excited brave placed a pistol against the despairing man's chest and pulled the trigger. It missed fire and called forth a raging flood of oratory. Some of it was in their behalf, and the offending Indian was driven away. Meanwhile the howling mob concentrated on the job of killing Hastings' dog and worked themselves into a frenzy by spear-thrusting and kicking its carcass.

It was nearly sundown when the big chiefs and elders of the tribe arrived. They looked things over and readily shook hands with Hastings, who was spokesman. A French Canadian with the tribe served as interpreter and, upon promise of many presents, the whole assembly got under way and marched in beautifully regular formations up the Sweetwater.

Many of the braves wore small looking glasses hung about their necks. The reflection of the declining sun, glancing from them in flashing gold lancets, could be seen a great distance. Fitzpatrick, noted mountain man and trader who was guiding the emigration, knew the meaning of the strange heliographs and put his camps on guard. The Indians were somewhat nonplused to find everything prepared for defense, and when the white men proffered presents the red men accepted, after which they proceeded to stay around while the head men went into council with Fitzpatrick. It was touch and go. Most of the emigrants never knew how much they owed to Fitzpatrick that night; but he handled the mercurial Sioux with a master's touch, and they withdrew peacefully.

The route taken, both by the volatile Crows with their ragged American protégés and by the Sioux with their two captives, lay along the southwest bank of the Sweetwater for some five miles after leaving the rock. Here they must negotiate a passage through the Sweetwater Range. For the Indians and the emigrants this was not difficult. Even the prairie schooners moved up into the low unimpressive pass without stress or strain. But the river made heavy going of it and chose a near-by gap in the range, so tremendous and so narrow that it seemed to have been hacked through the low mountains with two strokes of a giant cleaver. The inadequate opening and the damming cliffs lashed the water to a raging frenzy, as wild as it was short-lived. The shining segment of western sky, visible through the narrow gorge, extended in a slim wedge to the very base of the solid granite mountain. The emigrants saw this slit in the horizon—fourteen miles away, so they said—and commented on it with interest, for Devil's Gate was one of the major landmarks of the trail.

Most of the pioneers took it for granted that the gate itself was impassable and let it go at that—it was not of the slightest importance; but to the dare-alls of the migrations it was a continual challenge. One young fellow undertook to write his name high on the perpendicular wall and clambered to his selected point at constant peril of his life only to drop his writing material into the raging torrent below. Parties went constantly to the easily accessible brink of the southern overhanging cliff only to find that no one (even when a human chain had been formed to support the outside man) could be found to peer over the overhanging lip of the four-hundred-foot drop. The clamor of the goblin waters in the black depths below, the pull and suck of the powerful air currents uncovered unsuspected funds of fear in otherwise brave men. Still we must admit that it was all in the viewpoint. The diary of a twelve-year-old girl mentions casually that she and two younger children climbed to the brink by themselves and tells what they saw over the edge. She tells, however, in more detail and with a much greater sense of its importance, what they got when they returned to camp again. So opinions differ.

George E. Jewett gives the dimensions of Devil's Gate as one-quarter mile long, four hundred feet high and just wide enough to let the water pass. To me, exploring the gorge, it seemed that any one who thought it wide enough for anything to pass was an optimist: I never was jostled by any such amount of brutal-looking water. Noisy too, a regular gangster of a river, shouting defiance down its own dark alley—very different from the normal aspect of the Sweetwater, which, when uncoerced, is a very good citizen indeed.

It was a relief to get back to where we had left our car on the Casper highway just short of the wagon pass. The unmistakable scars of the wagon wheels traveled companionably beside us as we mounted the hill. We were crossing the sloping shoulder that rose to make the beginning of the Sweetwater Range. It had not yet swelled to its full height when, only a short distance away to our right, the Devil's Gate scarred its gentle even line—if anything so solidly granite could be termed gentle.

Just short of the low pass we stopped, as we did innumerable times in a day, and looked back. Probably nine-tenths of the pioneers did so, consciously or unconsciously. Their eyes carried along the curling river, lazying now in the flat after its terrific struggle; carried past the tremendous bulk of Independence Rock, seeming from this angle like a huge stone turtle; carried miles and miles across gray sage to where the low hills were misty and unreal on the eastern horizon—hills that hid loved graves lying untended in the valley of the Platte; memorizing the unforgettable picture since they would never return. Then, moving on ten paces, they followed the plodding teams over the turn of the hill. To each driver the low rounded ridge formed a hemming horizon at his wagon's endgate, and held him firmly to a new course—the valley of the Sweetwater.

*   *   *

Objects of interest found in the stretch of trail between the Mormon Ferry and the Great South Pass of the Rockies were better known and more publicized than any other landmarks between the Missouri River and the Pacific. The reason was simple since this was the only portion of the northern road with no alternate route and every traveler had, perforce, to view its beauties and curiosities whether he liked it or not. Of these landmarks Independence Rock and Devil's Gate were by far the best known; but two others, Three Crossings and Icy Slough, remained to be visited in that order as we moved up the Sweetwater River. Other points, not so well known but notable enough to merit close attention, would also present themselves; in fact the first one wigwagged us by means of a small roadside sign, just after passing Devil's Gate.

This modest marker, labeled "Martin's Cove," indicated a little recess in the hills where in 1856 an unfortunate company of Mormons were caught by early snows and suffered from exposure and starvation. A great many died. Just as the Donner party epitomizes the sufferings of the California-bound emigrants, so this story of a handcart brigade is the crowning tragedy of the Mormon Trail. The party was largely composed of converts from Europe and elsewhere who had arrived at the Missouri by rail or steamboat. There they were supplied with facilities to reach the Mormon settlement. Some wagons were furnished, but, owing to the size of the migration, approximately six hundred persons were forced to be content with handcarts. Winter set in early that year, and a wagon party was sent out from Salt Lake City to meet and succor the endangered company. They found the vanguard along the Sweetwater and the rest straggling through the sage desert east of Devil's Gate. There were some twelve hundred souls. The elevation was above five thousand feet; there was little wood and less feed, and the formidable Rockies lay just ahead.

The suffering Mormons congregated at a little blizzard-swept trading fort about a mile west of the Gap where trappers and their cattle were wintering. During the next week some two hundred of the Mormon beasts died and the winter-famished wolves gathered in packs to feast upon their carcasses. Later, when the attenuated caravan had struggled on up the mountain, the wolves remained to menace and harass the isolated trappers.

Daniel W. Jones, one of the advance guard of the relief party, met the handcart brigade under command of Edward Martin as it crept across the uneven, wind-swept sageland east of Independence Rock. He wrote:

"A condition of distress here met my eyes that I never saw before or since. The train was strung out for two or three miles. There were old men pulling and tugging their carts, sometimes loaded with a sick wife or children, women pulling along sick husbands, little children six to eight years old struggling through the mud and snow. As night came on the mud would freeze on their clothes and feet. We gathered on to some of the most helpless with our riatas tied to the carts, and helped as many as we could into camp on Avenue hill. . . . Such assistance as we could give was rendered to all until they finally arrived at Devil's Gate fort, about the first of November. There were some 1200 in all, about one-half with hand-carts and the other half with teams.

"The winter storms had now set in in all their severity. The provisions we took amounted to almost nothing among so many people, many of them now on very short rations, some almost starving. Many were dying daily from exposure and want of food. The company was composed of average emigrants; old, middle-aged and young women and children. The men seemed to be failing and dying faster than the women and children. The hand-cart company was moved over to a cove in the mountains for shelter and fuel; a distance of two miles from the fort."

Of course as many unfortunates as possible crowded into the fort buildings where, in their freezing condition, they cut the walls for fuel until the roof caved in. The storm lasted in the neighborhood of a week; and, when it ended, the remaining wagons and teams went on as the common property of all. Behind them remained a desolation of wolf-picked bones and shallow graves where the snow blanket lay in great protecting bats over huddled bodies of adventurers to the promised land who met the greatest of all adventures at Devil's Gate.

*   *   *

At this stage of their journey, especially in the headlong gold-rush years, the pioneers experienced a general unhingement. Teams heretofore considered indispensable were dead. The migration would have been face to face with impossibility except for the canny traders who appeared at strategic spots with fresh animals to sell and to swap for tired ones. Two or three exhausted horses, for instance, could be exchanged for one in good condition. A few weeks on good pasturage in the mountains put them in shape to be retraded. It was a lucrative proceeding and ethical enough from the trader's point of view. Kit Carson was one of the first to anticipate this crying need and was mentioned by several trail diarists —never, that I can recall, in terms of recrimination. This was not true of other traders encountered, who were often cursed up one side of the calendar and down the other. Nevertheless, with their expensive help, the emigrants reorganized their teams, often changing from horse or mule power to that of the stronger and more easily cared-for oxen. Just one little blessing had resulted from the alkaline marshes and hot sands—infections and hoof-rot had now disappeared from the feet of the animals.

They had here another spree of discarding weighty articles. Out went the assorted hardware that had survived previous holocausts. Heavy ox chains were the main sacrifice, the lighter ones being kept with the general, if unspoken, idea that by the time they wore thin and parted another team would be dead anyway.

And so order was brought from chaos, and the prairie schooners went cruising leisurely up the Sweetwater.

I really hate to mention this, but there were two parallel roads west from Devil's Gate: a river road and an inland road. The river road was popular with the dust-choked travelers—not that it was free from dust but it presented the relief of good water at hand. The inland, or "table road," was shorter. We took the latter.

We used the highway from Muddy Gap to Lander as our life line, making short dashes on foot into the fields at our right to keep the trail corralled and everything under control. At the end of three miles or so the highway and the trail converged. The sage-scented morning was inspiringly beautiful. The sky was a lucid aquamarine. The naked tops of the Granite Range seemed glazed into smooth, shapeless lumps like chinaware that has gone through a fire. Respectable, portly prairie dogs sat at their thresholds and kept unwavering gaze on us as long as they could, and then went back to whatever morning chores Wyoming prairie dogs have to do. An unseen bird sang from a greasewood clump and, delicately nibbling at the bunchgrass, were three antelope. They raised their heads to stare; we honked; and they floated off with the deceptive appearance of flying low over the ground, often mentioned in diaries and caused by the disproportionate slenderness of their swiftly moving legs. As days went by we became indifferent to the big white powderpuff tail of the antelope, which flares in a highly intriguing manner when they are startled; but at that time it vied with the prairie dogs for first place in the amusement field.

After crossing Willow Creek we commenced to watch for Dry Gulch where, so we had been informed, a large rock marked the junction of the table and river roads.

At the proper time, between us and the river, appeared a large sloping rock which might very easily have been the one in question. It was along this road and past this junction rock that young Buffalo Bill Cody rode for the Pony Express. His run was exceptionally lengthy and ended just ahead at Three Crossings Station. The ox trains of 1860 took so long to negotiate the distance that he passed and repassed them several times on his biweekly trips. He was a gallant, handsome youth, they wrote, and very friendly, often shouting news items of national import over his shoulder from out a whirling cloud of dust. On one occasion, at the end of his usual run, he found the man dead to whom he was authorized to entrust the mail sack and rode another 85 miles to Rocky Ridge Station, where the next relay waited. Without resting, he returned at once to Red Buttes, making a continuous ride of over 320 miles at an average of 15 miles an hour, one of the longest runs ever made on the Pony route. The pioneer children trudging toward Three Crossings who turned at the sound of pounding hoofs, snapped their heads back as the pony rocketed past, and then followed it with their eyes while it topped the next sagy rise—these children never forgot the slim youth with flying scarf and upflung arm, but told and retold the incidents of each passing to their own grandsons as treasured anecdotes of the great trek to the West.

The Three Crossings hid their pitfalls within a narrow gorge formed by the true range of Granite Mountains and a projecting spur of like unyielding temperament. The gorge is now dammed, but in trail days the evenly flowing waters of the river did not completely choke the passageway. They abutted against first one rocky wall and then the other, leaving for the most part room for a wagon to pass on the shallow side. In order to take advantage of these stingy little beaches the wagons, with beds blocked high above the water, forded the river three times.

There was no need to go to all this trouble. A heavy sand road completely circumnavigated the gorge. But the travelers were hot and dusty, the river cool and tempting, and the gorge itself, like the "dizzy depths" of Ash Hollow, had a sort of fearful charm. It is not a cause for wonder that many chose to soak themselves, their wagon wheels, and their hot and thirsty animals for a few hours even though the proposition turned out to be a tougher one than they had bargained for.

We elected to take the sage-hill road and proceeded to encircle the gorge. Then, true to our well defined propensity for eating our cake and afterward having it even to the point of indigestion, we decided to see the gorge anyway and turned back, heading for the west end.

The ruts run through the meadow of the J. J. ranch—splendid specimens, probably somewhat washed by rains but not eroded out of shape, and deep enough to conceal a person lying prone.

Pony Express rider in Sweetwater Valley. Split Rock is in the background.
(Adapted from a painting by William H. Jackson)

As we neared the place where the trail emerges from the gorge, we found ourselves fighting through thick growth massed over muddy backwashes of the river and skirting steamy bogs where the water had but lately receded. The mosquitoes were thicker than we had ever before observed—and our observations, both visual and vocal, have been extensive. They got so bad that we even stopped complaining for fear of swallowing one.

It was nearly noon when, hiking eastward down the stream, we found the most westerly of the three crossings. The gorge lay just ahead, was, in fact, already closing in around us. We stood on the right bank at the exit from the river where the wagons crossed on a slant upstream. The slope was very gradual and lent itself admirably to the purpose. The great schooners had groaned and heaved out of the current and strung along the mud-filled ruts in good order, their heavily laden beds propped up on twelve-inch blocks against wetting. The drivers would be glad when they could take the blocks out again and let the load down—top-heavy enough without raising the center of gravity. They eased the lumbering wagons along into what is now the open pasture lands of the J. J. ranch and restored them to their original status.

As to the other two crossings one guess is as good as another. The modern dam backs up the water so that it spreads unnaturally among the shrubbery and, in the gorge proper, extends deeply from wall to wall. Somewhere, far beneath its lakelike surface, the old wagons rolled, stuck, upset, pulled apart, and exhausted the gamut of unpleasant possibilities while their waterlogged owners wished mightily that they had stayed with the sage. But then the dusty trudgers on the sandy detour regretted with equal fervor that they had ever left the river.

* * *

Occasionally, in the rolling gray miles, there would materialize from out the scrub a farmhouse of the small insignificant logs in use throughout this tree-starved country and rarely shaded by a tree or so much as a cabbage plant. Often the house was deserted. Once we stopped on the indefinite summit of a foothill swell to look our last at Split Rock, one of the less known trail landmarks. From this distance, it was merely a small excrescence among other similar bumps on top of Granite Range, different only in the cleft that split it vertically through the middle.

The day had somehow crept away from us, and it was late afternoon as we watched the attenuated highway unroll ahead of us over the slopes toward Lander. The altimeter, which had worked loose and was bobbing like a seine cork in a most distracting manner, registered six thousand feet. Our way led through a series of huge, shallow bowls, where we could see nothing but the gradual lift of the ground on all sides to meet the cupping sky. Deep wheel scars showed where the wagons had rolled, making heavy going on the almost imperceptible slope of the Great Divide. A young elk, startled, lifted his weighted head and stood poised for flight, straddling one of the well defined gouges. We drove steadily on, making no change in speed, and he remained immobile. The road continually

crossed and recrossed the conspicuous ruts left by the caravans which at
this point had saved weary miles by cutting off a bend of the river. Men
and women both, and especially children, here had looked forward with
the keenest anticipation to the hour they would spend at Icy Slough.

We have many descriptions of this place, for inevitably it proved a
diversion. Delano wrote that they here encountered a "morass, perhaps a
mile in length by half a mile in breadth. Some of the boys, thinking that
water could be easily obtained, took a spade, and going out on the wild
grass, commenced digging. About a foot from the surface, instead of
water, they struck a beautiful layer of ice, five or six inches in thickness.
. . . To the unsophisticated," he continued, "this may look like a traveller's
tale, but it is easily explained upon natural principles. We were now at an
elevation of about six thousand feet. The morass was either a pond, or a
combination of springs, covered with turf or swamp grass, and at this
high altitude the temperature of winter is very severe, converting the
water of the morass to solid ice. Although the sun of summer is intensely
hot in these mountain valleys, the turf and grass intercept the intensity of
its rays, and prevent the dissolution of the ice, on the principle of our
domestic ice houses."

The astonishing part is not that they found ice, but that they were surprised by the discovery. Its presence was well known. The Mormons noted
it in '47, and most of the guidebooks featured it. Companies planned to
noon there for the sake of the genuine enjoyment afforded. The travelers
could use a little diversion; and, as a morale booster, Icy Slough, the last
of the trail landmarks that every one must pass, had few equals.

There is nothing striking in the appearance of the place. It is merely
a shallow swale or immensely wide, dry slough running roughly at right
angles to the Sweetwater. Two small bridges take care of the winter
downflow, but on our several visits the heavy dead grasses of midsummer
filled the flat bottom from bank to bank. We left the car at the sign "Twin
Bridges" and turned right. Immediately in front of us, straight across the
bottom, a wire fence line supported its dissolute and staggering posts in
the ease to which they were evidently accustomed. Across the far end of
the slough (as I remember it now, possibly a mile away) ran the willow-
bordered river. Beyond it rose the Granite Range, looking like a carved
board set on edge to keep out the wind.

The many people whom we have asked on many occasions are unanimous in stating that there has been no summer ice for years. We pass on the information as we received it. At the same time we feel obligated to say that we didn't dig up the slough to find out, and we don't think they did either.

Over the Great South Pass

IT IS ALL PART AND PARCEL of the unsatisfactory nomenclature of the trail that South Pass is by no means in the south.

The descriptive title was first used by trappers who had moved into the untimbered, Indian-infested prairies along the northern reaches of the Missouri River. In 1823 trouble with the Arikaras closed this route, and a picked group of William Ashley's mountain men, desirous of reaching the new trapping fields of Green River, set out to locate the strange, smooth gap through the Rocky Mountains of which they had heard from the Indians. It lay to the south, in the country of the Crows, and they spoke of it as the South or Southern Pass. Directions of a kind were obtained at a Crow village and, after wintering as best they could, the trappers left the headwaters of the Sweetwater River, moving west across the mountains. The country was oddly flat, but sometime in March, 1824, they discovered to their joy that the creeks were flowing westward under their sheaths of ice, and knew that they had reached the Pacific watershed. From this date the pass was known and used by white men.

The crossing of the Rockies was not dreaded by the emigrants, who knew from their guidebooks that the grade was easy and the summit flat and unbroken. That there might be exigencies on a mountain top beyond the danger of falling off did not occur to travelers to whom an elevation of seven thousand feet was an unheard-of experience. It was with as few misgivings as the uncertainty of the trail ever permitted that the wagon trains ascended the valley of the Sweetwater on their way to the pass.

For that matter I was feeling quite elated myself as we bowled along beside the Sweetwater one morning just at daylight. It was a drought year in Wyoming, and we had decided to attempt to drive our car over the South Pass along or near the trail—"we" meaning, in this case, just the three Padens, as Dr. Neff had not been able to leave his practice.

My husband was optimistic. "If this hot spell holds one more day, I believe we can get across," he opined. "This has been the driest year in these parts since records have been kept. More than that, there has been a steady wind for two weeks. The marshy places below the snow-sumps should be nearly gone."

"Yes, it's almost unbelievable good luck for us," I agreed, "when you stop to think that we couldn't possibly plan in advance on weather conditions."

"Tomorrow night will be time enough to talk about good luck," Bill interposed gloomily. "The man at Muddy Gap last night said that he had been a 'cow poke' in the Sweetwater Valley for twenty years, and that nothing had ever been driven over South Pass anywhere near the trail except possibly supply wagons for the sheep camps."

"But there's never been such a good opportunity," his father defended the proposition, "and I'm certainly not going to pass it up."

Accordingly we filled our gas tank at the little dot on the map called "Hudson's" and shamefacedly asked the Hudson family for advice. They refused even to consider the possibility of reaching the pass by staying in the vicinity of the trail, repeated all the warnings we had heard before, and added a few novel ones of their own. They agreed readily that if we could surmount the east slope and arrive at the great flat top of the mountain we should find a good road to take us across and down the west side, but said flatly no car had ever made the trip and, that beyond the Ellis ranch which lay part way, we had better go prepared with one or two yoke of oxen. Furthermore they offered, with true Wyoming helpfulness, to come up and look for us unless they received a phone message of safe arrival from South Pass City within twenty-four hours. We refused the proposition, probably foolishly, but we couldn't burden them with such an obvious uncertainty: we might easily be delayed beyond reach of a telephone without being in need of a rescue party. So we cast off with no strings attached.

At a small but well defined turn-off we left the Lander highway. Unless we got lost, this thoroughfare would take us to the Ellis ranch where we were supposed to make further inquiries. There were no signs of automobile travel—just the narrow bite of iron-tired wagon wheels—and for eleven miles we made brisk progress through the struggling early-morning sunshine. Then our one set of wheel tracks forked into two. Here was a pretty how-do-you-do. We got out and tried intensive detective methods.

Traffic seemed to be about equally divided. Each road had one set of wheel tracks which had been made since the last rain. While we stood there considering, Bill found a small board sign leaning against a bush a few yards up the right-hand road. Signs of that type can always be depended upon to fall down and usually lie prostrate at the crossroad where they mean anything or nothing. We mentally thanked the unknown somebody who had at least propped this home-lettered finger post on its own road.

Briefly but firmly it read, "Mines."

"Mines are always up canyons," my husband decided arbitrarily. "We will have none of them." And he swung to the left with outward assurance.

The narrow deep-cut tracks of wagons turned off occasionally, all of them old and rain-washed, but our chosen route was still the main stem of traffic. By this time our right wheels were riding the high road center and our left wheels were out in the sagebrush.

The amount of earth and sky in view at once was rather appalling. Something familiar about the situation kept ringing a bell in my memory, and suddenly I audibly recalled the "tiny moving speck of humanity in the great, rolling waste of sage," without which no self-respecting western novel can get past its first page. Thus oriented into the picture, we went on slowly in approved style.

In the course of time and miles we attained the top of a swelling headland on the gigantic mountain side and overlooked a previously hidden valley to the left—a deep, abrupt valley containing the incongruous patches of green that meant cultivated fields. Buildings were readily visible. We afterwards found one to be an enormous log barn.

"There's the Ellis ranch," my husband affirmed, "and we can get on the trail again. We've been above it for quite a while."

"Well, I certainly hope it will prove more amenable to automobile traffic than it has in the past," I remarked, "for the road ends at the ranch, or I'm greatly mistaken." And we set out in the rutty wheel marks, sliding off the eyebrow of the mountain and down toward the green pastures.

At a lazy curve of the Sweetwater we crossed a tiny, one-way bridge with the old-time peaked railings and turned toward the low ranch buildings; being now on the trail, which led directly through the hayfields. We stopped in the corral. My husband went on foot to a small vegetable garden near the house where a man in boots was getting remarkably wet and muddy in the occupation of irrigating. Bill and I remained at the car, quite overpowered by the stupendous barn.

"Must be why there aren't any trees left around here," he hazarded, and really it was a problem where all the wood had come from.

"Well, I'm going to find one pretty soon and eat lunch under it," I informed him. "It's nearly noon, and my appetite is better when there are people in sight."

A saddled horse stood comfortably within the open barn door. Our voices disturbed his siesta, and he shifted weight expertly, delicately balancing the other hind foot on its toe. Outside the fence a couple of overstuffed lambs lifted their absurd baby faces and added the last peaceful touch to an interlude made doubly enjoyable by the sense of relief that, so far, we had come right along without wasting time.

My husband returned. This *was,* it seemed, the Ellis ranch, and permission to stay with the trail as far as practicable had been readily given. We found it in a meadow, leisurely meandering upstream, and apparently used sometimes as a hayroad. Soon the river made a generous curve in our direction; the meadow pinched out into a small flat between the water and a low bluff topped with rock, and the trail was forced to make another of its numerous crossings of the Sweetwater River.

In the flat was a small marker for the site of old St. Mary's stage station, usually referred to as St. Mary's Crossing. Two buffalo horns, gray and scaly from long exposure, lay beside it. A scrabbling noise made me look up, and there on the bluff, closer than we had ever seen one, was an antelope peering down at us curiously from the rimrock.

There are no evidences remaining of the old station house; but tradition at the Ellis ranch places it in that particular spot, and we saw no reason to doubt the accuracy of the marker. Getting out the robust lunch which had been put up for us, we sat down in the full sunshine and, with some difficulty, ate it.

After we had returned home, a letter arrived from a middle western university asking if we had succeeded in relocating the site of St. Mary's Station, which, it appeared, had been lost to historians for a long period. My husband replied in the affirmative, adding, in effect, that it was probably the historians who were lost; but, at the time, we consumed our thick sticky bean sandwiches in unhappy ignorance of having done anything

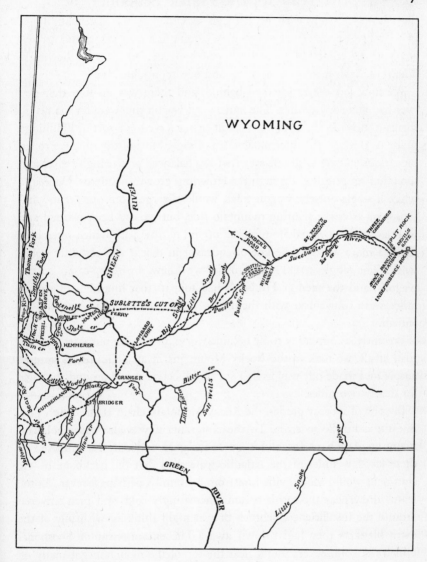

impressive. What we couldn't choke down, we left for the coyotes to worry over; then, photographing the marker, we started out again.

We commenced operations for the afternoon by trying to force a passage up the mountain more or less on the course of the trail; but it was much too steep and overgrown. We gave it up and eased the car back to the flat—fortunately with no damage—returned to the ranch buildings, backtracked on the road we had used coming into the valley, and arrived again at the point from which we had had our first view of the ranch. The trail, having come straight up and out, soon joined us.

We now left the ranch road behind, and there was no sign that cars ever had gone any farther. The narrow-cut wagon ruts were far too rough for us to drive in the customary manner but served as a sort of life line to guide us through the interminable sea of sage. Most of the time we rolled precariously along with one set of wheels balanced on the high center and the other set grinding through the crowding growth beside us. Once in a while a single ancient wagon track would diverge from our "road" and mosey off over the slanting mountain side, but we had been warned and were not to be diverted from our strait and narrow path which resembled many a more worth-while line of endeavor in that it was certainly uphill work. The single tracks were made, we knew, by sheep-camp supply wagons, and the men at Hudson's had told us that hundreds of square miles were cobwebbed with them in a maze guaranteed to bewilder an Indian.

Presently, as our crazy route became worse for driving purposes than no road at all, we took to the Rocky Mountains in an unimproved state of nature and made our way as best we could, between and around the sage, for nearly two miles.

In spite of its easy grades, the Rocky Mountain chain at the South Pass is quite a hurdle to cross. To the emigrants it was also a symbol, and many an Argonaut forgot his quest for gold and only remembered in these last few miles of the Atlantic watershed that the backbone of the continent would soon divide him from his family, perhaps forever. As the teams drew near the top it became increasingly cold, and men shivered around the insufficient sagebrush fires at night thinking wishfully of the extra blankets they had thrown away. The encampment of Shoshones which the gold-seekers found near the top of the mountain got many requests for buffalo robes.

Snowbanks filled the gullies crossed by the prairie schooners and stood beside the trail. It was hard snow, glazed on top, soiled with mud and twigs and with the tracks of animals. Rivulets of melted ice trickled from the downhill edges and watered patches of green, starred with brilliant yellow flowers and clumped with iris. Because the mountains of the Atlantic seaboard are low, these wanderers had never seen summer snow—had never experienced dust and seepage mud at the same time. To "lie over" at noon in a meadow so hot that their new-made butter melted and to find great banks of snow available for refrigeration purposes was a new and

A Shoshone squaw moving across South Pass. (From an old print)

pleasant adventure. But with a storm imminent the seven thousand feet of elevation weighed heavily, the curtaining clouds above the huddled wagons pressed too close for comfort; and when they were torn by jagged tridents of lightning the whole flat mountain top was incandescent with excruciating, blinding light. Stupendous crashes of thunder followed with disturbing promptness, sometimes deafening the hearer for hours. It seemed to the hapless lowlanders that they had ventured to the roof of the world and stood in the immediate presence of the Almighty.

Clouds were gathering over us also—majestic masses that rolled slowly up from behind the high horizon and into the very zenith of the curving sky. Another branching set of ruts left our chosen thoroughfare, and another and yet another. Some of them were eighteen inches deep in stiffening mud, for the spots where the great snow patches had lain were scarcely dried. The body of the car was racked and creaking as we eased one front wheel down in a hole while the other rolled lurchingly up and over a clod—to be followed instantly by the rear pair—every ten feet or so. During the afternoon we successfully passed over several of these slopes where the snow sumps had drained, investigated the site of Burnt Ranch Station, and gradually came up on the level sweep of the pass, which I believe is considered to be some eighty miles long and twenty or twenty-five wide. The wagon tracks imperceptibly changed to the marks of truck tires, and we were able to enjoy the luxury of looking out the windows without fear of knocking in our teeth. Naturally our absorbing preoccupation with the weather vanished. Let it rain now if it would—we could manage. The trail was distinguishable by several tokens, but most readily by the enormous sage along the old line of march.

At a large sheep camp manned by Basque herders we made connections with the small, noisy truck engaged in supplying them with food and (especially) drink. Its occupants offered to guide us out to the main road. We accepted thankfully, but they had joined so whole-heartedly in the celebration caused by their arrival that I was grateful when our tandem procession of cars got loudly under way. At the end of an hour's hectic progress they had grown so much louder that we took advantage of a wide spot to circle the weaving truck and put on a burst of speed. We called our thanks as we roared by; and, although they produced a reserve of power which I certainly thought would be the death of them, we saw to it that they never caught up with us.

Our next informant was an Indian on a pony—a wilted little animal, almost eclipsed by its rider's fat body and dangling legs. This was the first real Indian brave we had encountered on the trail, and experience later proved that the modern trail follower is not apt to meet any east of the Rockies. A large black hat perched as if accidentally on top of a rag tied around his head. His heavy hair hung in braids on either side of a countenance the shiny, greenish black of stove polish. His moccasined toes hung immobile within inches of the ground. His unfaltering dignity was beyond words.

An emigrant meeting an Indian at this point would have expected him to be a Crow or a Shoshone, either of whom would be friendly. We determined to ascertain his tribe and to get some necessary road information.

It was of no avail. He either had no English or didn't choose to use it, so we made elaborate gestures calculated to find out where we should meet the graveled highway. This resulted in wrist maneuvers on his part that looked like a Siamese dance and meant a great deal less—at least to me. My husband said that they were really remarkably lucid, and that he followed the pantomimed directions implicitly for twenty miles. As the next hour's movements entailed nothing more complicated than staying with the road, I have consistently doubted it, which is merely a wifely privilege and has nothing to do with facts.

It commenced to rain—a matter now of but little moment. With each mile, our spirits rose and our confidence grew. The highway from Farson to South Pass City fell in our way, and we took it. Far to our left, on the rim of the pass, the Oregon Buttes raised their rugged crests. The name, when given, was descriptive, for in early trail days all the shaggy wilderness that lay between the mountain top and the mouth of the Columbia *was* Oregon. Before us, through the flat sage land, the great emigration road unrolled in an enormous ribbon one hundred feet wide. We paralleled its resistless onward sweep. The omnipotent Artist who created this mighty picture used bold strokes. The swelling summits on each side are too huge for detail. Mile after mile, their cushiony tops roll high under the sky, unrelieved and simple in their immensity—overwhelming in their sheer colossal bulk.

So much earth; so terrifically much sky; and so close together! The first few wagon trains across the God-given pass feel that they are squeezing between the two. It is a halfway milestone—a place of parting. From this point on old ties are gone and pilgrims look ahead, not back, for even the raindrops draining in the wagon ruts run westward now. From this tipping mountain slope, without choice or change, the very waters move on to the Pacific; and so must they. Each hour the lurching wagons roll more easily. The oxen cease to strain. The plodding thousands lift their eyes and gaze across the valley and beyond, where other mountains rise mysterious and vast—a mighty country soon to be their own; and the cry goes up, "Hail, Oregon!"

* * *

On another fine July day the Paden family stood again at the summit of the Pass. Two years had gone by since our circuitous trip down the mountain at the tail of the little truck. Dr. Neff was with us. We were equipped with another car and were prepared to take time enough for details. We had waited two days at Farson at the foot of the west slope hoping for suitable weather, and this particular morning seemed perfect. Before us, the Pass stretched out level and unexciting. "Can't you just imagine," my husband queried, "Kit Carson and John Frémont arguing about where to find the summit? The story goes that it took them quite a while."

"If it did I don't blame them," I agreed. "It certainly looks flat. I wonder which one decided the question: the woodsman or the engineer."

"We don't need either one," said Bill practically. "The curve shows up in the telegraph wires."

"I'm afraid that didn't help Frémont any," my husband said; "he was here twenty years ahead of the telegraph. But I'll tell you who did get the breaks. Just look at that monument to the first women over the Pass, and their husbands didn't even get an honorable mention."

"Narcissa Whitman was a bride," I told him, "and you know nobody ever talks about the groom. For that matter Mrs. Spalding had only been married about a year when she set out for Oregon, and the four young couples that were sent out two years later by the mission board were all married expressly for the purpose. Can you imagine a girl leaving civilization completely behind with a man she barely knows?"

"It wasn't easy for any of them," my husband acknowledged. "It took a year to get an answer to a letter, or, if they happened to think of something to say after the traders' caravan went east, they waited a year to post the letter and *another* year for an answer."

"And if they needed a new pair of shoes—well—" The sentence lapsed for lack of adequate words.

This terrible inaccessibility is perhaps best illustrated by the communications that passed back and forth between Narcissa and her family during the years just following the birth of her daughter and the little girl's death by drowning at the age of twenty-seven months. By the first traders' caravan Narcissa sent word of the birth; months later, by another caravan, she sent for several pairs of little shoes. Then tragedy struck, and the baby girl was buried. The next westbound traders' party brought congratulations, and the following year the shoes arrived. The grief-stricken mother was forced to wait until a third season for her letters of condolence.

Willingness to endure the difficult journey was the least part of the contribution made by the six women missionaries who had traveled overland into the Oregon country by the fall of 1838. Each of these women undertook, for the sake of her religion, to cut herself free from every familiar tie—in some cases to accept as a husband a man only recommended to her as God-fearing who needed her as she needed him, for an essential partner in missionary work; she undertook to marry him and within the day leave family and friends—too often forever; to travel two thousands miles dependent on the rough (and sometimes grudging) hospitality of the traders' expeditions; to live the rest of her life surrounded by Indians some of whom would always be hostile; to be submissive, loyal, and loving to her new and sometimes difficult partner; to bear his children and to raise them in the wilderness; to feed, clothe, and educate her family by her own exertions, and to devote a fair portion of her time to similar duties among the children of the tribe to which she and her husband had been allotted.

Narcissa Whitman and Eliza Spalding came with their husbands in 1836, two years before the others. They were the first white women to cross the Pass and continue overland to the Pacific. Mrs. Spalding was not especially robust, and the hardships of a new country might have been expected to react on her more adversely than on her companion. Instead the case was exactly the reverse. The Spaldings were assigned to the country of the Nez Percés, where they were made welcome, helped with the necessary manual labor, and allowed to live in relative peace of mind. She became so beloved that it was told, in years after her withdrawal from the field, that the Nez Percé prayers sometimes ended reverently, "In the name of Jesus Christ and Mrs. Spalding." It was Narcissa who drew the short straw in this lottery of fate; who, with her gifted husband, made her home among the recalcitrant Cayuse Nation, and eleven years later was destroyed by them.

The imprint of Marcus and Narcissa Whitman, missionaries, upon the development of the West was fated to be political rather than spiritual. The activities of the forceful Marcus and his invaluable assistance in opening the Oregon Road to wagon trains are closely centered about Fort Hall and will be taken up at that point in this disjointed travelogue. But South Pass, beside the rough monument graven with their names, seems a fit place to pay a small tribute to the memory of these loyal, much-enduring women.

For the Whitmans in 1836 there was no puzzling decision to make upon leaving the South Pass. They were committed to the fur traders' trail leading southwest. The Forty-niners, on the contrary, must make a choice between two routes: the just-mentioned trail and the much shorter Sublette's Cutoff which recently had been found practical for wagons. In the early fifties the matter was complicated by a third important road designated Lander's Cutoff which left the main trail near the last crossing of the Sweetwater and led north through the mountains, crossing Green River at a point much nearer its source than the other two. The three prime necessities, grass, water, and fuel, were better distributed on Lander's Road, and it was pleasingly free from tolls; but it never carried the amount of traffic that streamed over the other two during the height of the westward movement, and was therefore lonely and dangerous.

We ourselves were not to be tempted from the original Oregon Trail—not, at any rate, so early in the game—and set our faces toward Fort Bridger. Later we would investigate Sublette's Cutoff, which carried the bulk of the gold-rush trains.

Two miles west of the summit we emerged into a meadow. The Pass was at our backs. To our left stood a cluster of weather-beaten log buildings. Before us, sunk in a green fold of the stupendous gray slope, a small stream with a bright grassy border flowed steadily westward. Pacific Creek—no doubt, its clear water eventually to reach the Green, then the Colorado and the western ocean.

A casual, low bridge spanned the water, and on its irregular edge of jutting planks sat a most attractive girl, apparently looking at her own reflection. I approached the bridge alone and rapidly, by way of a rude fill of brush and rocks on which my feet crunched loudly.

She looked up, and her startled glance jumped from me across the fill to the men and indicated plainly her opinion that the sagebrush was becoming overpopulated. It is our misfortune always to arrive unheralded and unsung, and it leads to an unlimited variety of social dilemmas.

Without pausing to preserve the amenities (which, whatever they may be, seem to need considerable help) I went right to the subject in hand: "Is this the first water that runs west?"

"Yes, this is Pacific Creek," she answered pleasantly, "and the spring it runs out of is just a hundred yards or so away."

"Can I get over to it?" I asked uneasily, as I caught the glint of standing water here and there in the marshy ground, and noted that the men had turned back toward the buildings.

"You certainly are very welcome to try," she said, with an amused little smile.

Well, I tried, and remembered how the emigrants watched their horses in order that they might not sink in this glorified boghole. The turf looked firm enough but was really nothing but matted grass pocked with seeping pits of icy water. Hopping from one tussock to another, I got pretty wet, and had to give up many yards from the spring. In its mossy border it looked like a huge mirror flush with the turf.

Most of the early-day wagon companies planned to camp here on account of the abundant grass. The spring with its accompanying boggy meadow and cheerful little brook occupied a long soft depression like an elongated hollow in the fat thigh of the mountain, and as I looked this way and that across its moist richness to the confining hills of sage, pictures came to mind: camps of encircled wagons spaced throughout the hollow; cooks, both men and women, discovering volubly for the first time that it takes longer to cook rice and potatoes at a high altitude; traders' lodges pitched on the slopes near by; hobbled horses drifting over the bulging mountain top; tossing invalids ill with mountain fever; men whose animals had died along the Sweetwater sawing up their wagons to make amateurish pack saddles; men running in the long late evening as the unearthly scream of a wolf-torn pony shatters the air; wagons emptied of great heaps of disorderly duffel for repacking or abandonment; Lodisa Frizzell's brave little diary receiving its last notation from her failing hand:

"We are hardly half way. I felt tired & weary. O the luxury of a house, a house! I felt what some one expressed who had traveled this long & tidious journey, that, 'it tries the soul.' I would have given all my interest in California, to have been seated around my own fireside surrounded by friend & relation. That this journey is tiresome, no one will doubt, that it is perilous, the deaths of many testify, and the heart has a thousand misgivings & the mind is tortured with anxiety, & often as I passed the fresh made graves, I have glanced at the side boards of the waggon, not knowing how soon it might serve as a coffin for some one of us; but thanks for the kind care of Providence we were favored more than some others."

The little book is put away forever—Lodisa has written her last entry. Around the fires men sit in their greatcoats, whittling. Now and then one gets up to stamp his booted feet, for it is bitter cold in camp and the sagebrush fires, although quick and hot, leave no comforting coals. They whittle purposefully with their hunting knives, paring down the massive ox yokes so that the fast-failing beasts may have less weight to bear, for tomorrow they intend to start on Sublette's Cutoff and some of the animals will die.

Many, including all who go to the City of the Great Salt Lake, stand firm for the Fort Bridger Road. The camp at Pacific Spring belies its name and becomes electric with argument and dissension over what shall be done, so that men grow grim as they whittle, and women weep.

Whatever the decision of each group, they are soon gone. Seldom is an earthly stage so completely cleared of its cast. By the time the sun has risen over the smooth sweep of the Pass, it may be that the entire personnel of this shadowy drama has departed, taking the stage furnishing along and making a final exit over the next sagy hump to the astonished admiration of a large audience of antelopes.

All the time that my brain was wandering in this pleasant fog of confused ideas, my feet were carrying me out of the troubled times of '49 and into the comparative luxury of the sixties (for the log houses, toward which my gregarious husband started some time ago, date from staging days, when they constituted the important Pony Express and stage station called Pacific Spring). There are four buildings—two on each side of the old road—widely spaced so that they form the four corners of a rough rectangle. The house faces the old store and bar. The blacksmith shop stares across at the stables. It is now the John Hays horse ranch, and the buildings are in everyday use.

In front of the store a sheep wagon idled in the sun, and near it stood the pretty girl, accompanied by two husbands—hers and mine. Dr. Neff, at some distance, was peering sharply into the dusky interior of the blacksmith shop dimmed with the soot of more than half a century, as if hoping to surprise some loiterer from that long-gone historic parade.

Our questions met with few helpful answers—which was entirely natural, for our friends were young and far more concerned with the future than with the past.

From Pacific Creek the modern road roughly parallels the trail to Dry Sandy Creek. This disappointing watercourse is ordinarily all that its name implies; but we, like the Forty-niners, were regarding it in the summer of a wet year, and the hot, sandy bottom between steep banks boasted a string of unappetizing stagnant pools.

The emigrant ford is right at the bridge, and the trail, continuing north of the road for some time, angles to the south side and meanders through a wide curving gap toward the Little Sandy. In the gap Sublette's Cutoff splits from the original trail and wanders down the mountain, keeping to the right. Well within our view as we stood on the mountain it strikes the sage flat, passes the small rocky trail landmark called Haystack Butte and goes on and on interminably through a dreary waste.

We came to the forks and paused there, realizing that the solid unit of trail, which had come up the Sweetwater so heavily burdened with wagons and stock, had again frayed out into loose ends. First the long thread of Lander's Cutoff had unloosed itself toward the north, and now the main cord was parting into two strands. As we had planned, we bore left with the road to Fort Bridger where the light soil of the mountain side was, in the old days, so pulverized that gusty dust clouds often hid from the bewildered driver all of his team except the wheelers.

Between mountain and desert the emigrants found the Big Sandy, lovely dependable stream that it was, and went hunting for rabbits and sage hen and big plump gooseberries for pies. The ford was at modern Farson just above the junction of the Little Sandy. We returned there late in the afternoon. The day had darkened, and a wind-driven phalanx of clouds rushed over the sun as I went down to sketch the crossing. The dulled river looked like a dampened slate, and the ford had evidently not been selected for its beauty. I finished quickly and walked back up the hill to the hotel. Before I reached the stairs one or two persons greeted me in passing, but the delay was only momentary, so that, on reaching the second floor, I was somewhat dashed to meet my new straw hat trundling down the hall apparently on its way to the bathroom. A gale had arisen in the three minutes that I had been indoors. Like the Platte Valley this Wyoming sage land encompassing the Green River has a character and temperament all its own. Quick-changing, sometimes dangerous, its weird beauty, like that of any desert, grows on one.

In the night I listened a long time to the changing tempo of the wind. From my window I could see a heavy cloud mass with gilded edges. Behind and above it the screened moon gave inverted lighting to the lustrous arch of the heavens cupped like a dark polished bowl over a carved ebony world.

The bright immensity of the sky added to the shadowy mystery of what might lie ahead in that waste of utter blackness. Meanwhile, insistent and savage, the wind screamed out of the emptiness, slapped at my face, snapped the ends of the bedclothes, and rattled the windows fiercely before finally tearing off around the corner of the house to increase the night's unrest.

When, in due course, tomorrow's dawn swept over the Pass, we crossed the Big Sandy on a new bridge just north of Farson and, at once, turned back and faced southward, paralleling its course. Every little way our road crossed dry washes running to the river, and down most of them old camp roads headed for the water. The Big Sandy was, of itself, clear and wholesome, but during rush years was fouled by the rotting flesh of animals that died trying to fill their baggy hides with green willow from the banks. Tiny beasts like a cross between a squirrel and a gopher had dashed across the dusty road ahead of the oxen in exactly the same exasperating way that they would jerk their short twitching tails out from under our wheels and bounce into seclusion behind some handy bush. "Little zoological whisks," an amused pioneer woman called them, and added that they looked too much like rats and tasted too much like fish to be popular. George McCowen spoke of them with more restraint—or maybe he was hungrier. "This morning we had an extra dish for breakfast," he said. "Learning that the traders called these small animals (which are so plentiful) squirrels I took the revolver and killed a mess, if they had called them rats they would hardly have been palateable, as it was we relished them considerably."

Just where the Fort Bridger road swung over to touch the Big Sandy for the second time, the emigrants of the fifties found a fork in the trail. By turning right they might travel Kinney's Cutoff, favored above the Sublette Cutoff because of its commendable manner of arriving at water every fifteen or twenty miles. At the fork was a trading post of logs elegantly roofed with poles and brush, and from there to the Green River was sixteen miles of dry and lusterless desert growth. "There is not enough grass to keep sheep," Mr. McCowen wrote, "much less oxen that have to work. One of our boys came in quite blue after seeing so many cattle. He prophesied death and destruction to be the fate of our little team."

One other landmark caught our attention on the trek toward Green River—the graves in the stretch of river bank where the coulee of Simpson Hollow opens out to the Big Sandy. We were on the bridge over Simpson Hollow when we saw, coming up the gulch, a flock of soft dun sheep that blanketed the rolling banks on either side like a spread cloth of nubbly wool. A herder followed—a glum person whose battered hat rose and fell with the steady mastication of his "plug-cut." He was apparently glad for company and left his dogs in charge while he walked back with us along the way he had come, through the stifling dust barrage left by his blatting band. We emerged at the river. Yes, there were graves there—quite a lot, he told us, getting more and more indistinct as years passed until now he only remembered where to find one or two. As a boy he had considered it almost a trail cemetery.

And how did the travelers know that it was ahead? Well, the word of tomorrow's travel and what it would bring seems to have sifted throughout the whole line of wagons, probably from those favored trains who had guides or from travelers who had crossed the continent before. So, because of the overwhelming need to leave their dear ones in some place which they might some day find again, they sometimes carried them many miles to be buried at this accepted spot—where a stretch of hardbaked sage land at the end of a smudgy coulee still holds the now forgotten dead.

17

The Ups and Downs of Old Fort Bridger

FIRST TRADING POST ERECTED FOR THE EMIGRANTS

THE TROUBLE WITH THE Green River Desert was not lack of water. There was plenty, but it was all in the Green River—"by far the most formidable stream to be met with on this entire journey," said William Johnston, whose company was well in the forefront of the gold rush. He found it in full flood, a rushing torrent three hundred to four hundred feet wide and ten to twenty feet deep. This was in June, but well do we know from personal experience that the Green makes no promises, flooding if it jolly well feels like it clear to the middle of July.

The traders' caravans and the early wagon trains skirted the desert proper to the southeast, remaining timidly near the Big Sandy until well within the angle of its confluence with the Green and then striking up the east bank of the great river about twenty miles to a crossing near the mouth of Slate Creek. Later companies crossed almost at the mouth of the Big Sandy at what was called the Lombard Ferry.

Although we sleuthed determinedly in their tracks we saw nothing between Simpson's Hollow and the river but gray clusters of sheep with their herders, and scraggly sagebrush jittering in the heat waves.

Instead of sheep the emigrants saw mirages, vague representations of rivers, lakes, and lines of leafy trees toward which their oxen tried to turn and were restrained by force. They themselves were not misled by the visions; but the sight tempted them to empty their canteens more quickly, and (unless a detour was made to the Big Sandy whose dependable current paralleled them on the left) their water receptacles would not be refilled until the Green River was reached.

The Green in the month of June is a rare sample of a watercourse born of perpetual snowbanks. Its swollen current, racing down from icebound peaks and crisp and sparkling upland meadows, arrives in the hot sage flats swiftly but ponderously, and as cold as Greenland's icy mountains.

It is almost unimaginable, but on this torrential sluice ordinary men, butcher, baker, and candlestick maker, launched their wives and young families in wagon beds. Taking such a liberty with the Green was surely the quintessence of something or other—maybe heroism, maybe just fool-hardiness. But with the unfathomable drive of any great instinctive migration the westbound pilgrims, like spawning salmon or southbound birds, pushed on through all impediments alike, and hurled themselves into whatever danger lay between them and their goal.

Later there were ferries, but the earliest pioneers had to do with substitutes: catamaran rafts, made of braced logs dug out to hold the wagon wheels; ordinary rafts constructed hastily of any small timber available; sheet-iron or wooden boats fitted with wheels and previously driven in the caravans as vehicles; and, most common, wagon beds calked tight and with the naked bows stripped of canvas. Helpless passengers gripping the arching bows while their cracker-box boats whirled downstream were a commonplace: a woman with two children lashed to her body; a small girl who clung precariously with one hand and held a baby sister with the other; a wife whose crazy craft sank and left her to flounder while her practical husband ignored her screams and rescued the mules. Indignant bystanders saved the drowning woman; erected a tripod of three wagon tongues and she was resuscitated barely in time to prevent a lynching. Countless such incidents made up the unbelievable melodrama of the Green River crossing.

There were one or two fords, but they could be used only before the spring floods, or late in the summer. The professional guides could force the wagons through the current by tripling teams and using a dozen or so mounted outriders. So narrow was the "safe" strip of gravel bar where they felt their precarious way that a deviation of ten feet meant loss of the wagon and a forced dunking in swift, icy water for its occupants.

And then, in the summer of '47, came the ubiquitous Mormon and his ferryboats. By '49 several were needed at the main crossings. It was a money-making venture, but the prices were ordinarily fair, ranging from three to four dollars a wagon. Certain journals show variations ranging to eight dollars and more, but it would be unjust to say definitely that such tolls were exacted on Mormon ferries. There were many other ferries created by the excessive demand whose owners asked and got all that the traffic would bear.

As the years went by, the ferries improved; but there was no royal road for the poor cattle nor for the men whose duty it was to see that they swam across safely. Besides the danger of drowning, the stock drivers suffered from cramps in the icy water, and illness followed, almost as a matter of course, any prolonged immersion. Some were invalided and confined to the wagons all the rest of the way to the coast.

The crossing used in later years by the wagons bound for Fort Bridger became known as the Lombard Ferry, and is so named on historical maps. In order to get to its western landing we made a detour of many miles by way of a bridge and arrived sometime in the afternoon, easing down into the scattered cottonwoods on the low bank that edges the river bottom at this point. Leaving the car in the shade, we were obliged, for a time, to join what the pioneers called the "Foot and Walker Company" and hiked briskly through groves where, during the summers of almost a quarter-century, emigrant camps had elbowed one another for room. After a half-hour's search we found the place we were looking for. It is marked by the ruins of several stone buildings and a snubbing post to which the ferry ropes were attached. The wagons landed here, and their path was plain before them over the low bluff toward Fort Bridger.

From the original Oregon Trail crossing, some twenty miles up the river, the early wagons converged toward what was later the Lombard Ferry trail. The two routes form a wedge like a slice of pie, of which Green River is the fluted crust and the point is at Blacks Fork. Near the point Hams Fork cuts diagonally across as if severing the first crooked bite. The whole section of country between the two routes is a broken, barren prairie, covered with sand and gravel. The emigrants often found it difficult. We found it almost impassable: it had recently rained, or perhaps I should say "cloudbursted." The inefficient roads had been washed over by torrents just strong enough to carry perfectly strange boulders as far as the middle of the wheel tracks, but under no conditions able to take them on across. Here, our trail work was sketchy. We touched the trail when and where we were able, visioning its course as well as we could from one high point to the next.

By late afternoon, when each tiny round sagebrush threw an elongated shadow so that the plain looked like a parchment covered with exclamation points, we found ourselves near Blacks Fork. Sunset caught us on our little back road just as we bumped up to a shining straight stretch of the Lincoln Highway. The temptation was too great. We turned east to the city of Green River to spend a relaxing evening and a comfortable night. This part of the country is seen at its best either at sunrise or sunset. When traveling east we often stay all night at Green River and leave very early in the morning in order to enjoy the really exquisite light effects on the weird castlelike rock formations that are its dominant feature.

It was in the midst of a dazzling pageant of color that we made our unspectacular entrance into the town and secured for the night half of a large double cottage in a camp whose damning location near the railroad tracks was not readily noticeable.

Already installed in the other half was a lovable little old couple. She was tiny, fragile and retiring. He was fussy but competent. His mottled shiny dome had the opalescent luster of an old tea set. The comfortable curve of his façade indicated the excellence of his wife's cooking, and a row of ornamental buttons rode the crest. With the neatly hemmed remains of one of his wife's silk print dresses, he was carefully dusting the last speck from their shiny black Ford. Beside it our big dun-colored equipage was in a perfectly disgusting state of dirt that made me wonder at his demeaning himself to speak to us.

Their excited pleasure over this vacation excursion to see a married daughter was very appealing, and I hoped silently, as I watched them, that everything would go well on their long looked-for trip.

"You are not going far tomorrow," my husband told the little lady, "so you won't start early. We have to be up before daylight, but we'll try not to disturb you."

"Oh, I'm so glad you are," she beamed on him. "Father and I prefer to travel early. There's not so much traffic. But Father broke the crystal in his watch and it isn't running. We'll get up when we hear you." So it was settled, and we went to bed but not to sleep.

Miles and miles of groaning freight train dismembered itself in our backyard. Each time a car was dropped the engineer closed the gap with a series of reverberating crashes that began under my pillow. Between times—but not allowing interim enough for us to get to sleep—the engineer evidently went off for a midnight snack.

Finally, tooting more and more faintly, the freight took itself into the distance, and we breathed great sighs of relief—quite prematurely, for the rumble gradually grew louder again and presently the concussions and repercussions began as if they had never left off

"What did it come back for?" I asked hopelessly.

"It didn't come back. It met another one," returned my husband in a raucous whisper. And we settled down to await the pleasure of the new engineer, hoping that he wouldn't want two cups of coffee.

When the cars were distributed (one in particular being practically at the head of my bed) the second train snorted out of town. With any luck we might now go to sleep. Acting on the normal impulse to give a last check-up, I pressed my thumb on the flashlight, noted that it was two o'clock, and turned the light through the open door on Bill's bed. It was empty.

This was an unheard-of occurrence for, compared to Bill, Alice's dormouse was a mere amateur. I got up quietly and went to reconnoiter. Our three rooms and bath were open for all to see, but still no boy. The screen door was latched on the inside, the windows impractical as exits. If ever I had had any faint desire to sleep it was gone now.

An alarmed word to my husband, and he joined me. It took us a full minute to discover that our missing heir had simply rolled out of bed on the wall side, taking a blanket with him, and remained impervious to external conditions.

It was no light job to rouse him, particularly as we were trying very hard to be quiet; when it was accomplished we took time to be disgruntled.

"We might as well have gone to a party instead of to bed at dark," whispered my husband crossly. "I haven't been asleep at all. What's that?"

There was no need to ask, for we both recognized the thud of large spattering drops on the roof.

"It's just one of those little showers," I told him. "It won't last ten minutes." Then, with the wifely habit of mentioning the one item that is most uncomfortable to consider at any given moment: "Did you close the car windows?"

"You would bring that up." He paused hesitatingly halfway between his bed and the door. "Oh, well, I guess I had better go fix them before the seats get wet."

Very carefully, he unlatched the screen and stepped outside. The wind was brisk and businesslike, but the shower was already passing. A cynical moon stuck its fat face through a rent in the ragged cloud blanket with an especially knowing look. Inadvertently he let the door slip, and the wind slammed it sharply. Verbal fireworks followed, much cramped in scope and power by being executed in a whisper. Then he descended the cement step, stealthily opened the car, and got in.

Briskly the door to our adjoining apartment swung wide, letting out a flood of light, and he was joined by father, complete even to the vest buttons and carrying a suitcase.

"Good morning—*good* morning," he greeted my speechless husband. "This is fine and dandy. Yes, sir. This is fine. The best start we've had yet."

The revitalizing aroma of coffee stole out into the night, and through the thin wall I heard Mother cheerfully rattling pans.

Once more the screen door closed.

"Okeh," said the partner of my rather exhausting life. "Get your clothes on. We're starting."

*   *   *

It was thin, gray dawn by the time we had found an all-night restaurant and were ready to move on, so we napped a bit in the car and waited for the sunrise on the castlelike buttes that guard the town. Then we struck out for the valley of Blacks Fork and the trail we had left yesterday afternoon.

The wagons had various routes as the years went by, but these all tended to center near the confluence of Hams and Blacks Forks. Both the original trail and the later road from Lombard Ferry crossed Hams Fork first, just above the junction, and then negotiated the more difficult Blacks Fork which curved like a frightened snake as it hastened through the low sage. Its waters were swift, cool, and deep, and the wagons turned and followed up its south bank, sometimes close to the stream but oftener out in the hot sage and choking dust. The abundance of small green willows surprised the sage-accustomed cooks with very little fire and a terrific smudge—which was not without its uses, the mosquitoes being recorded as smaller than hummingbirds but decidedly larger than crickets.

The emigrants of '43 and the next few years found Jim Bridger's fort on Blacks Fork and then went northwest, through a long draw and over a flat benchland studded with heavy-trunked junipers; across the Big and the Little Muddy, turning west on the north bank of the latter; through the Bear River Divide to Twin Creeks near modern Sage, and over to the Bear River. The very early Oregonians had pursued an indeterminate route through the Green River watershed, depending on where the fur traders' rendezvous was held in that particular year, so that this old road may be called the Oregon Trail from the time that wandering thoroughfare became static. We found it fascinating, but space will not permit detail. Vital in its day, it became an alternative route in 1846 with the opening of the ill-fated Hastings' Cutoff used by the Donner Party; was less used after the Mormons founded Salt Lake City in 1847, and ceased to be important with the wild rush of gold-seekers through Sublette's Cutoff in '49.

The majority of the migration arrived at Fort Bridger in the month of July. It was July also on this gorgeous morning when we found ourselves approaching the fort. The valley of Blacks Fork is beautiful out of all reason, like a charming but improbable stage setting, for which the snow-topped Uinta Mountains provide a magnificent backdrop. Apparently from sheer altruism the river divides near the head of the valley and sends its cool waters through this lovely flat land in several clear-flowing channels which unite again some miles below, forming a group of islands. On the westernmost of these we found the fort.

When, in the early forties, Jim Bridger built his first rude cabins at this garden spot and fenced them in with a stockade of small logs, he executed quite a stroke of business. There was, so he thought, money to be made here.

There is evidence that he had completed something in the way of building by the summer of 1842, because an eccentric minister, Williams by name, returning from Oregon, passed on July 3rd of that year and made mention of reaching Bridger's fort.

By December 10, 1843, Bridger, who could neither read nor write, had a letter sent to Pierre Chouteau, Jr., the head of a large fur-trading company in St. Louis, announcing: "I have established a small fort, with a blacksmith shop and a supply of iron, in the road of the emigrants on Black Fork of Green River, which promises fairly. In coming out here they are in need of all kinds of supplies, horses, provisions, smithwork, etc. They bring ready cash from the states, and should I receive the goods ordered, will have considerable business in that way with them, and establish trade with the Indians in the neighborhood who have a good number of beaver' among them." We may infer from this that the post was reasonably complete, and that Bridger was ready to lay in his stock by the end of 1843.

Dirty little log outposts of civilization such as this, chinked with mud and roofed with sod, were the first exponents of a new type of business, the emigrant trade, which rolled merrily along throughout all the years of the migration, amassing fortunes for those who embraced its opportunities. Fort Bridger was the first trading post west of the Missouri built especially to cater to this business, and it was a blow when the opening of Sublette's Cutoff to wagons drew thousands of prospective customers away. In the summer of 1849 Bridger's partner, Louis Vasquez, with a retinue of Indians camped at South Pass, trading with the emigrants and trying to persuade them to go by way of Fort Bridger.

Captain Stansbury visited the fort that same year and wrote in his diary that it was "an Indian trading post . . . built in the usual form of pickets, with the lodging apartments and offices opening into a hollow square, protected from attack from without by a strong gate of timber. On the north, and continuous with the walls, is a strong high picket-fence, enclosing a large yard, into which the animals belonging to the establishment are driven for protection from both wild beasts and Indians." In designating the "offices" and "lodging apartments" Stansbury was considering merely the uses of the so-named cubicles and not, by any means, trying to aggrandize them. An office was a place where business might be transacted, and contained the necessary rough furniture. A lodging apartment was a cubbyhole or room in which one might sleep. If it were sufficiently elegant to have a floor, the owner probably could provide a stack of buffalo hides for a bed; if not, the favored portion of ground occupied by the sleeper was frequently pulverized to form a more yielding surface, and the occupant made up his bed each night with the hoe.

William Johnston also saw the fort in '49. "I visited several of the apartments of the fort," he wrote, "among others the rooms occupied by the families of the proprietors, through which we were conducted by Mrs. Vasquez, who entertained us in an agreeable and hospitable manner, notably by inviting us to *sit upon chairs,* a situation somewhat novel, one to which for some time past we had been inaccustomed. Opening upon a court were the rooms occupied by the Bridger family. Mr. Bridger with a taste differing from that of his partner who has a white wife from the States, made his selection from among the ladies of the wilderness—a stolid, fleshy, roundheaded woman, not oppressed with lines of beauty."

In spite of the preference for white helpmates shown by Johnston and others, the trappers themselves preferred Indian wives, as being used to the life of the wilderness. They took grueling hard labor as a matter of course, indeed were proud to do it. Besides all the camp work, including packing the horses and putting up the tepees, they took full charge of the furs and hides—no light task. A really first-class buffalo skin, for instance, was always cured by patiently working the great beast's own brains into the raw surface. The squaws did this by the hour. They never asked favors, fully expected their hard-bitten spouses to get drunk, and took a little beating now and then in good part. There were a few cases of desertion of course, in which the docile creatures went unprotestingly back to their own village where, apparently, they were received without loss of caste. Their half-breed children fared worse and were sometimes abused by the tribe. I think it may be safely stated that soldiers at frontier forts were more often the offenders in cases of flagrant desertion. If a trapper took an Indian wife, or even two or three, he selected them more for endurance than for speed and beauty, considered them as assets, and thoroughly intended to keep them.

Such was not the case with the Don Juans of the emigration, but every now and then an amiable brown maiden entered into an affair in all good faith, after which she arrived, pack on back, at the wagon train with the embarrassing intention of accompanying the man of her choice to California. It cost one sheepish young (and previously gay) Lothario several bad hours and all the property he had to extricate himself with a whole skin.

The beautiful and fertile valley of Blacks Fork, with Fort Bridger standing squat and picturesque in its midst, was well known to the Mormons. The first small Mormon advance party passed near it in 1847 when, by reason of bloody clashes with their gentile neighbors in the States, they left the Missouri River for an unknown haven near the

Great Salt Lake. They were closely followed by the great Mormon migratory caravan, who took careful note of the trading post just east of the passage leading through the Wasatch Range. It must be confessed that they also took note of the histrionic Mr. Bridger and recorded him tersely as a man who did not tell the truth.

There he was, however, firmly ensconced on the best piece of pasture land between Salt Lake City and Horseshoe Station, and so situated that whatever the Mormons required from civilization, whether mail, freight, or converts, must pass within a mile of two of his door. The setup was far from satisfactory to Brigham Young.

At the time the Mormons chose their new homeland on the Great Salt Lake and settled down to farm, their colony was in Mexican domain several hundred miles beyond the jurisdiction of the United States, while Bridger and Vasquez held their lands, totaling nine miles square, under a grant from the Mexican Government. Within a few months the terms of peace at the close of the Mexican War threw them all into United States territory.

Distrust and dissension prevailed between Mormon and gentile, aggravated by lack of definite information and the growing gossip concerning polygamy, then an intrinsic part of the Mormon religious custom. The colonists had once been forced, if they wished to continue its practice, to leave their homes, and they felt that their freedom of action was again threatened. Any gentile settlement near them was unwelcome.

The facts and issues are clouded by the passage of many years, but the two conflicting stories are somewhat as follows: Jim Bridger contended that the Mormon leaders had no particular grievance against him but simply coveted his property; that they sent a group of their "avenging angels" to do him bodily harm; that he barely escaped into the willows and, with the aid of his Indian wife, was able to make his getaway, abandoning everything to the Mormons. The Mormons claimed that Bridger was furnishing guns to the dangerous Utes, with whom they were at war. Both are nice healthy arguments and are not at all incompatible. This happened in 1853. The Mormons took over Fort Bridger, and its namesake and founder, who then appeared to be in his middle fifties, took himself back to Little Santa Fe to make a new start on his ranch there. Fort Bridger became a Mormon outpost. (Church records show that, after some time had elapsed, Bridger was at least partially reimbursed.) Many changes were made, one of them an outer wall of small round rocks set in mortar, of which a small fragment remains.

A word or two about the unpleasant predicament into which circumstances had forced the Mormons will make the subsequent history of the fort a little clearer. As soon as they found themselves living once again in United States territory, they held a meeting, revowed allegiance to the Constitution and organized their own independent state, calling it Deseret. This was in 1849, so it will be readily understood with what curiosity the gold-seekers visited the Mormon colony. In 1850, Congress (which had ignored the state of Deseret) created the territory of Utah, cleverly appointing Brigham Young its governor. He accepted and took the oath February 3, 1851. Several of the district judges in the new territory were gentile and, like the Indian agents, were not always above reproach. This was true also (by their own standards) of some of the leading Mormons. There were recriminations on both sides, and unfavorable reports were sent to Washington, including the letters from the Indian agent at Fort Laramie, and from the dispossessed mail contractors already mentioned in connection with Julesburg. When President Buchanan took office, he completed a purge of Mormon officials and sent out an entire new set of territorial officers—accompanied by an army of twenty-five hundred men as a slight reminder to treat them with courtesy.

The news reached the Mormons during a grand celebration on the tenth anniversary of their arrival. About two thousand souls were present, among them Governor Young. With his usual vigor he hastily organized a plan of defense, and the "war" was on.

When it became known back in the States that the soldiers would be denied entrance to the Salt Lake Valley, everything came to a halt. If there were to be trouble the troops must be provisioned for a winter campaign. It was September, 1857, when Colonel Albert Sidney Johnston took command and left Fort Leavenworth, Kansas, to join the first detachment which had already started. Wagons and troops were strung out almost the entire distance in an attenuated line too thin to be impregnable. The Mormons resorted to guerrilla warfare and flung their ragged but determined Utah Militia on a weak spot. By this old and effective method they succeeded in destroying three wagon trains of supplies and, without actually resorting to bloodshed, caused the troops no end of grief and were themselves torn between elation and apprehension.

The little-known Rocky Mountain country could be terrifying in winter. While Johnston's men were still east of South Pass the temperature dropped below zero, and blizzards set in. There was reasonable safety in the numbers and equipment of the troops; but, even so, the animals died in droves (five hundred in one night, it is said), and progress was almost halted. Meanwhile the Mormons had burned Fort Bridger and retreated west to new fortifications in Echo Canyon, leaving only the stone wall of their own construction standing empty and alone in the valley of Blacks Fork. It took the troops fifteen days to worry through the last thirty-five miles, but eventually, like a slow tide, they reached and overflowed the ruins of Fort Bridger.

A day or two before their arrival Johnston's men were joined by the last detachment of the invading army under Colonel Philip St. George Cooke. With it came Mr. Cummings, the newly appointed Governor of Utah, who, unwelcome as he must have felt by this time, had put his hand to the plow and was gouging right along to Salt Lake City. Some of the other new officials were also on their uncomfortable journey to the Mormon settlement, but one of their number had reached his journey's end at the fort. The new post trader, William A. Carter, unpacked his cases of goods at what was left of Fort Bridger to join in its restoration and to spend the rest of his life there.

All of that severe winter Johnston's army remained at and near Fort Bridger, advised as to ways and means of existing comfortably by Jim Bridger himself and upheld in health and morale by the wisdom of their commander. And winter with its discomfort was the worst that they had to endure. There was to be no war. Sometime during the intervening months Brigham Young had sent Thomas L. Kane to President Buchanan as an emissary, and, on February 25, 1858, he arrived in Salt Lake City, having traveled back by ship to California and thence overland. Colonel Kane then met Mr. Cummings at the army camp and induced him to leave for Salt Lake City, where he was recognized by Brigham Young as Governor of Utah; and the two men eventually became friends. By early summer a peace commission from the government had arrived and the difficulty was ironed out.

For a long time the troops maintained an uncertain tenancy at Jim Bridger's old trading post, and through it all William Carter remained in a sort of patriarchal state. Naturally much building was necessary; and, with the fade-out of hostilities, timber was brought from the Uinta Mountains, and barracks, officers' quarters, guardhouse, etc., were all constructed around and about a large square parade ground through which flowed one of the most beautiful of the tiny channels of Blacks Fork. Far to one side of these were the stables, used later by the Pony Express. It is the back wall of these stables that the modern traveler sees as he rockets by on the highway. It will richly pay him to stop and go in.

In all probability if he goes in he will proceed straight into the museum. Here he will sign a register presided over by a dignified curator who receives us each year with resignation. He will then look at the relics, buy a postcard or two, and depart, since, let us hope, very few have my rather feverish mannerism of taking the framed maps off the wall and frantically copying them before leaving. In the same inclosure which includes the museum he will find the stables used by the Pony Express riders, still (when last seen by us) unstuccoed and unrestored. Some old freighters with enormous wheels have recently been put under shelter after having weathered many a winter in the yard. Even the vague and musty smell of horse that lurks in shadowy corners is gloriously historic.

From this section, which was once the spot where civilian and military affairs met and mingled, our traveler may proceed over a stile and past the old officers' quarters toward the parade ground. He will go slowly, for it is a most delectable spot. Thick, vivid green grass, more than knee-high, is starred with lavender daisies. Above his head the leaves of the white-trunked aspen trees swim in the little breeze, like pages of blurred printing. Curving through the aspen grove flows the clear brook, perfect in its setting and landscaped inimitably by the consummate Artist.

Beyond the grove lies the parade ground, plushy green and still faced by several well preserved buildings, whose squat walls seem to have been grown rather than built into the scene.

To the buildings our traveler now comes; skirts them carefully, and continues to their rear. Carefully protected under a specially constructed roof, he finds the remaining fragment of the Mormon wall, but he may look in vain for one memento of Jim Bridger's old trading post which it once inclosed. Not a board nor beam remains. Not two sticks nor stones together. Just a small, uneven, weedy patch of worthless ground—where much history was made.

18

Sublette's Cutoff

SUBLETTE'S CUTOFF, the mountainous short cut from South Pass to Green River and west to the Bear, was certainly never meant for lumbering prairie schooners, cattle, milch cows, women, and children. Still the Forty-niners were in a hurry, and thousands went that way.

It split from the old Oregon Trail in the gap between the Dry Sandy and the Little Sandy, and the caravans that took it rolled down the mountain to the Big Sandy, where they made camp to rest the teams. Occasionally it rained or even snowed on the Green River desert. In that case the dreaded trip was simply another fifty miles, no worse than the last fifty, and was accomplished in the daytime. Oftener it was hot. Then everything possible was filled with water—bottles, kegs, and breadstuff barrels which had been gradually "eaten empty" for just such emergencies. Around four in the afternoon the wagons started. The dimly seen hills in the west, visioned through the mocking witchery of heat waves, skipped and danced in a weird travesty of those of biblical persuasion.

The wagons passed just south of the Haystack Butte, crunched and cut the arid beds of some partly dried, alkaline lakes, and at last began to drag over low, gravelly rifts. The latter were unexpected, for the expanse looks level, and were none the more welcome for that. All night they moved steadily, the road winding like a snake out of one sandy depression into another while those who were physically able plodded ahead of the teams.

At dawn an hour's rest was allowed. The oxen were unyoked, fed and watered out of supplies carried in the wagons. Grass here was nonexistent, and the normal amount at the Big Sandy had been stripped so bare that it took a man all day to gather a sackful. The resourceful emigrants got around this emergency by feeding their animals flour and water or even baked bread—a grain product which they were able to digest.

The morning came on hard and hot. Sometimes they had days of baking heat when they smothered in their dust blankets. Sometimes they had galelike headwinds; stinging particles drove into eyes, nose, lungs, and the animals struggled for each foot of progress as against a heavy current.

Well disciplined, fully equipped trains led by experienced men generally did well enough. Trains led by novices, even though properly stocked, suffered mightily on the march to Green River and often lost valuable animals. Shiftless, poorly equipped companies without sufficient water kegs, with weak stock and disintegrating wagons (and there were many such) were headed straight for disaster.

We hear little of the families to whom "crossing the plains" brought complete shipwreck. Their journals, if begun, were never finished. The survivors during long lives could not bear to talk of the experience that cost the life of father, mother, sister, brother, friend, sweetheart—or all of them together. We only read in the diaries of more fortunate travelers that they encountered the remnants of the broken companies returning home, or plodding westward if that were the less desperate alternative. On the Green River desert they went west. It was too late to return.

Naturally the earlier companies contended with a general ignorance of the country, and the route was hazy and confusing. In '49, when the laboring, panting, exhausted line of animals and dust-caked humans arrived within ten miles of Green River, they found broken country and no definite road. They must push and tug at the heavy wagons in the full heat of blazing noonday. Many collapsed and were loaded in the wagons by companions almost in like case. The poor beasts fell, were hastily cut loose, died, and added their bit to the discomfort of next week's caravans. The only solution possible was to double-team and abandon some of the wagons, and this section of the cutoff was one of the two or three places of the whole overland trail where no one had time or reason to burn them.

Five miles from the river the Forty-niners were faced with a three-hundred-foot descent and had to remove the animals and let the wagons down by ropes. By 1850 a better grade had been found. Two hours of travel beyond this descent found the caravans of any year upon the river bank. That is, the emigrants were on the bank, the animals were in the river, and it had taken a struggle to prevent the wagons from going with them. It was dangerous to have any dealings with a team of thirst-crazed oxen after they had got wind of water. They often ran the last mile in spite of all handicaps, and it took a brave man to unloose them. Sometimes after seeing the stock strike the water the men flung themselves down, utterly done in, and their cattle wandered loose for hours searching for forage along with the loose stock of others exhausted like themselves.

Some journal keepers, more observant than others, record that the cattle cooled themselves, completely submerged in the icy current with just their muzzles thrust up and out, before they began to drink. Considering the lack of control exercised, astonishingly little is written of the effect of unlimited ice water on the overheated animals.

And here again, with the desert well behind them, the victory was to the strong, for the near-by islands in the river furnished safe and sufficient pasturage for the stock of those who were ingenious enough and had the remaining strength to get them there.

No matter how jaded the travelers or how weary the saddle animals, some one from each train must mount his horse and ride to the nearest crossing to sign up for ferry passage. This would brook no delay, for the ferryman kept a register and took each in turn. Although the cutoff branched into several terminals at the Green, five of which we know, the ferries were not of necessity near any one of them. The terminals came over the cliff where it was easiest to get down and then made straight for water. The ferries crossed where river banks and current would permit. In early days it was usually two to four miles from the spot where the teams rushed into the river to the nearest ferry. Others of the train must collect the stock and drive them several miles to pasture unless they were equal to the task of getting them onto an island. This was vital. It might be a day or two before their turn for ferrying would come. So, in a few hours, through pressure of necessity, the tired men and women took up the burden of their duties, and life snapped back to normal.

When they had time to write in their journals again, the guidebooks came in for a great deal of caustic criticism. The cutoff was listed as somewhere in the neighborhood of forty-two miles (Delano's party had expected a little jaunt of thirty) while the grim actuality, measured by the strength of dragging mules and dying oxen and by the stumbling feet of those who walked to save the animals, was sometimes fifty-two miles from water to water. But this time the guidebooks were not wrong. William Sublette guided a party across the cutoff in 1850, and E. S. Ingalls kept a diary of the trip. Their route across the desert, measured by roadameter, was forty-one miles. Ingalls mentioned that Sublette was looking for a little-used short cut of thirty miles but failed to find it. Now if the great Sublette himself, who had practically raised the Green River from a creek, couldn't find a road for which he was looking, what chance had the inexperienced and ill qualified emigrants from the cities? Perhaps, early in the season, some wagon master missed a turning in the dark or followed an old trapper's trace. Others shaped their course by his and a new road was born, not to be discredited, it might be, for weeks, or until some returning traveler put a note at the crossroads. It happened in other places —why not here?

* * *

We picked a hot week in the drought year of 1934 to arrive at this portion of Sublette's Road. We made headquarters at Farson on the Big Sandy and dipped tentatively into the sagy flat on foot. *Very* tentatively would be more accurate, for it was sunstroke-hot, and a group of civil engineers who were staying at the hotel squashed firmly any budding attempt to try sage-hopping in the car. "If you got ten miles from here and the car got stuck, which it *would*," one of the boys told me, "you'd have a sweet time walking back and we'd have a sweet time getting the car out." There was good reasoning in it. I mentally increased the ten-mile hazard to the extreme limit of forty and decided against it. Quite independently my husband had already reached the same conclusion, which increased my chance of cancelling the sage-hopping expedition by just 100 per cent.

When it was plain that we had to detour in one direction or another, we circled north for a change through badger-burrowed flats, salted with alkali and peppered with blackbirds, leaving the quivering horizons of the Sublette country for the grassy meadows and swift cold creeks of the upper Green River.

At Pinedale, a lively widespread town capitalizing on the fact that it is farther from a railroad than any other settlement in the United States, we turned northwest to connect with the La Barge highway. In front of the comfortable ranch houses were piles of bleached elk horns crammed down, one on another, in a bewildering intricacy of interlacing prongs. These amazing stacks, ranging up to fifteen feet in height, are one of the features of the country and furnish the simplest way of disposing of the huge antlers at one time shed so freely over the valleys.

We stopped half an hour at the site of old Fort Bonneville, where, in 1832, stood Captain Bonneville's tiny and unsuccessful trading post; but there was nothing remaining to detain the curious, and we turned abruptly south in the direction of Big Piney. At a faded and almost indecipherable sign on the highway we turned up a small gulch to see the monument erected on the spot where Father de Smet called together the trappers with whom he was traveling and held the first Catholic service between the Rockies and the Pacific coast.

In time we emerged from the canyon, and the sun, coming from behind a cloud, shone on a strange and unforgettable scene.

Along the top of a broken cliff that stepped up suddenly from the glassy, jade-edged windings of Green River, was a company of kneeling men and women. Their heads and shoulders loomed startling against a background of bluest heaven and silvery white cloud, fantastic and unreal. Before them on the cliff edge was a flower-decked monument. On its stone base and facing them, a young priest stood with uplifted arm.

We instantly halted where we were and shut off the engine. A great hush settled over the cliff top, broken only by the slow voice of the priest and the deep-toned responses. A bird, inspired by this startling invasion of its domain, began to sing and supplied a thin, piping treble to their thunderous bass.

Possibly for five minutes the spell lasted. Then the people got up and the priest got down. As he moved back a pace or two beside the monument, I held my breath for fear a few false steps would land him in one of the wriggles of Green River just below. The crowd broke ranks and pressed toward him. We slowly moved in also.

Uncannily we had arrived during the mass which is said once a year at this spot, always on the Sunday nearest to July 5th, the original date. The little company broke up slowly as if indisposed to leave, knowing that until another year had passed this historic spot would remain empty and meaningless.

Meanwhile the wind, to which time is nothing, had swept down from the Tetons and carried out over the valley of the Green the sound of many voices congregated in Christian worship, just as it had last year and the year before—and on the memorable occasion when Father de

Smet himself and his rough company had gathered for the same high purpose, many years ago.

* * *

At La Barge we had a very good, if slightly informal, Sunday dinner at a tiny hotel called, apparently with no attempt at humor, La Barge Inn.

"How far down the river was the Mormon ferry?" my husband asked our hostess as she came in with the dessert.

"About six miles."

"How will we know the place?"

"Oh, you'll recognize it easily enough. The bluffs are covered with names and initials. They call the place Names Hill, you know."

"Is that right at the crossing?"

"Yes, although the ferry's been gone now for years and years. There's nothing to see *there*. But Names Hill has Jim Bridger's own signature on it. You can't miss it. It's been blacked in so it will show when it's photographed."

After we were in the car again I said speculatively: "I wonder about that signature business. Jim Bridger was illiterate, wasn't he?"

"Yes, of course; but so was Kit Carson, and I think he enjoyed carving his name more than most people—once he had learned to do it. At least," added my accurate husband, "we can't say he didn't put it there, so let's enjoy it."

Six miles brought us to Names Hill—a precipitous, almost overhanging cliff made of great, jutting, flat-surfaced, and sharp-edged rocks. At the base sage grew raggedly. We easily found the inscription, "James Bridger —Trapper—1844," while many other names crowd the available space. In its day this quiet and almost deserted spot saw much joy and much sorrow but, above all, much action; and many men were launched into eternity from below Names Hill who didn't die in bed.

It was not the river alone which demanded its pound of flesh. "The Elephant"—that fantastic name for the heaped-up terror of the trail—took its share as well. The horror of cholera, fear of Indians, dread of deserts and quicksands, dangerous currents, and precipitous bluffs—these did terrible things to a man's nervous system. Add the gradual wearing down of resistance through overexertion and lack of proper diet, and the deadening, hardening effect of the constant sight of agony—deserted and dying animals, bereft wives and orphaned children, men with shattered outfits unable to care for their families, illness without medicine, amputations without anesthetics—it sickened a man to the very soul.

All this apprehension of suffering, and then its terrible realization, which was what the Argonauts jestingly called "seeing the elephant," brought out the latent tendencies in any man—unsuspected nobility or lurking meanness. If nobility, then its display was always welcome (and all too often unnoticed). If violence, then even the hard-bitten Argonauts sometimes stood aghast at its display.

About the 1st of July in 1849, among the hundreds camped on the west bank where we now stood, was a man named A. E. Brown. It may be that the vicinity of so much water gave him an idea, for he suddenly decided that he needed a cake of soap. Instead of doing anything about it himself he shouted at young Bonner Lapet, who happened to be cooking for his mess that day, and demanded that he fetch it. Quite naturally the young man told him to get his own soap. So far, quite simple and unvarnished. Sounds like home, in fact, to most of us. But cause and effect were quite unrelated on the trail. The presence of "the elephant" gave strange and macabre twists and endings to normal situations. Brown rose up and stabbed the young man dead—through the back.

The Brown case was a famous trail murder. A court was assembled, but imperceptibly merged into a liquorous Fourth of July celebration, and the criminal went free. Occasionally in such cases, forceful leadership was lacking and no trial was held. More often an impromptu meeting was called with all the poise and authority which are the birthright of a typical American assemblage of men, and which so astonished European travelers of the day. Jurors and counselors were chosen, witnesses called, and sentences carried out with a cold impartiality that might well have been (and probably was) a strong crime deterrent. Sometimes the penalty was banishment; sometimes flogging; occasionally hanging, but a gun furnished the quickest and most characteristic weapon of punishment.

At Names Hill the bottoms are wide, but just below it the cliff presses close to the river for a short stretch and the modern road has been blasted through at the water's edge. Where the bottoms suddenly widen again we found a group of ranch buildings between us and the river. Our maps showed an old ford at this point, and we drove in.

We had no trouble in annexing a couple of men and numerous small boys as guides to the river bank, and one of the men said that he had heard of a ford and thought it used to be back of the sheep corral, where we presently arrived. Near the fence stood the stone slab that marked the ford. It was dirt-encrusted and forgotten—so forgotten that our guide had had an argument with his family before leaving the house as to whether it had ever been possible to cross the river except on the ferry.

"Where did the wagons go from here?" my husband asked the owner of the place as we trudged back.

"By golly, I don't know! West, I suppose."

"What lies west of here—up on the plateau?"

"Fontenelle Creek, about six miles over. Does that help any?"

"It most certainly does. In fact it makes everything dovetail." And it did help, too, for Fontenelle Creek was the pioneers' next objective after leaving the Green River bottoms. They had little trouble getting up the bluffs, for there are soft and sloping earthen breaks in their structure, the one at Names Hill leading up and out from the ferry being particularly well marked. The several roads ascending the bluffs then united on the rough plateau through which the Green has cut its channel. Six miles more or less brought the emigrants to pretty Fontenelle Creek, and the wagons rumbled along near its bank for a couple of miles, forded, and took to the barren sandy ridges. Ten miles brought them to some springs where a few trees, crowded at the foot of a bluff, made a good stopping place; and the travelers sometimes found an encampment of Indians perched on the side hill. The caravans, since crossing the Rockies, were in the territory of the Shoshones, who were often called the Snakes but much preferred their rightful title. They were peaceable and for years were controlled by their honest and friendly chief Washakie, who proudly wore on his hat a silver coffin plate engraved "Our Baby." The emigrants rather doubtfully gave the Shoshones the edge on structural points over the Crows (who appear to have been disruptingly ugly) but freely admitted they had never seen anything so filthy.

Besides being peaceable and dirty they were affectionate, the women especially being affable to the point of embarrassment. If a Shoshone squaw fixed her temporary ardor upon a respectable man in the pioneer camp (which she was all too apt to do) he might as well make up his mind to an uncomfortable sojourn and being the laughingstock of the whole company for a week.

From the camp at the grove the wagons surged up the swelling eastern slope of a snow-patched mountain studded with small clumps of thick-set balsam firs—a mountain from which may be had a comprehensive view of country broken into every conceivable form of deep canyon and ravine. In these fastnesses the hunters, circling for game, killed elk and mountain sheep. Loomis informs posterity that the ascent here "was steep and verry lengthy, tyreing our teams more than two days travil on good roads."

Along the scalloping ridges between these ravines meanders the wispy and nebulous gray line of the old Sublette Road. It descends to the head-waters of Slate Creek and there coincides for a few miles with the Kinney Trail. It passes Emigrant Springs—yes, another one—runs through mountain country preempted by a ranch or two, and emerges finally on Poplar Ridge and the brow of the west slope of the mountain range where the travelers had a bird's-eye view of the valley of Hams Fork, or instead could look across to the top of a range, higher yet, which they must surmount.

Part way down the west slope is the small, almost deserted, settlement of Sublet—the same idea, you see, but spelled more economically. It erupts from the mountain side, dry, hard, and unsightly, but, at one time in its career was quite a town and boasted a large boarding house catering to trail business. Here the lumbering land craft of the Argonauts hung poised and then catapulted breathlessly to the valley below.

Hams Fork at last! Synonymous with water, feed, and comfort.

Because of its situation the trains seldom camped, but "baited" there for a good long nooning instead. They forded the famous watercourse which was "too small to be called a river, and too big to be called a creek," by raising the wagon bed on blocks, unyoked the animals to graze, and spent an hour or two fishing. Mountain trout were, at that time, found only west of the Great Divide and were a novelty to the emigrants, who bought them frequently from the Shoshones for some trifling present—a few pins, a tin cup, or a pair of hopelessly dirty socks.

Emil Kopac, who has devoted years to a study of the Sublette country, says that both Sublette's Trail and the later Kinney's Trail fork into two divisions before entering the east side of the valley of Hams Fork.

The two sectors of Kinney's Trail join again at the river so that there are but three crossings. We are satisfied to take his findings, which we cannot hope to equal while spreading our efforts over so much territory.

The northern of the two branches of Sublette's Trail crossed Hams Fork at the confluence of Robinson's Creek and followed along its course a short distance. The southern ascended a ridge but soon joined its fellow, and they went on together, steadily, up and up to where the highest mountain of the travelers' experience swelled gray and dun to meet the lowering sky.

We have succeeded in managing most of our field work well enough by automobile with a lot of footwork thrown in, and had no difficulty in jaunting all over the valley of Hams Fork; but the mountains between Hams Fork and Bear River which are the actual divide between the watershed of the Colorado and that of the Great Basin, defeated us each year until three had gone by. There were roads of sorts, but the clearance bothered us.

Finally, the fourth year, we borrowed a truck at Kemmerer, Wyoming, persuaded Mr. Louis Jones of that city to guide us, and started out just at daylight. Under his direction we circled through Pomeroy Basin, where a velvety meadow spread out in a sort of oasis, with the tree-dotted river winding snakelike over the flat bottom land. Farther upstream, we later found it quite different, with ordinary dry banks only sparsely studded with small brushy trees.

We didn't stop at Hams Fork today but circled miles and miles by way of the high land that encloses Pomeroy Basin, and met the trail near the summit of the next big rounding mountain. Our road led by the Lone Pine Ridge, and, from one point and another, the eye could carry the course of the trail. It was visible from Sublet on the ridge to the east, down and across Hams Fork, on through the valley, up Robinson's Fork, and several weary miles up the mountain to the point where we joined it, near the famous Bear Head encampment at the aspen grove.

Dr. Wayman said that, in 1853, it rained on them every day but one from South Pass to the Bear River, such being the nature of this Rocky Mountain country. It now began to look as if a spectacular command performance were going to be put on for our benefit.

While we watched, a huge white thunderhead with an ominous leaden center came sailing over the high sky line to the west, trailing daintily

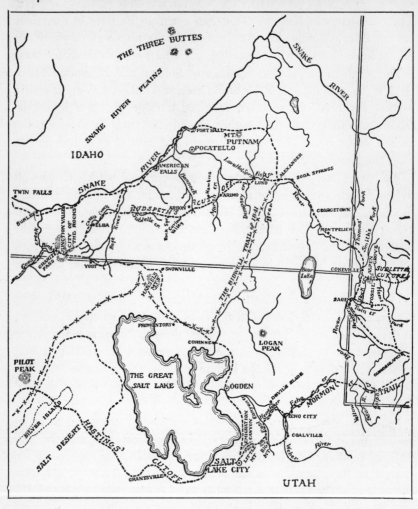

deceptive misty streamers. Our course now joined that of the trail, just below the lovely aspen grove. On this day of odd and bewildering light effects the grove was transcendently beautiful. The luminous flat gray of the sky just above the horizon shone like tinfoil between the dark tree-tops. Their white trunks, defaced by emigrants' initials, were picked out in high relief by a vivid ray that had speared its way through the tumbled clouds.

From this grove the trail led over the top of the immediate range, traversing a fir grove, dropped into the canyon of Watercress Creek, and progressed on to Rock Creek (often called Stony Creek in the old writings), whose current becomes muddy and milky before it leaves the mountains. Farther still is the last summit the wagons had to surmount before glimpsing the Promised Land of Bear River Valley.

By this time Mr. Jones was legitimately concerned with getting us and the truck off the mountain before the storm struck, and we turned back; but we felt justified in detouring to a certain cabin for information. We could see it—in this sky land of magnificent distances—as a small speck north of east on one of the wind-swept promontories.

In half an hour we reached our objective. The truck jerked to a stop, shuddered, and was quiet.

I crawled down, stretched my bruised person gingerly, and looked out and around me at the sky. It was magnificent, exciting, and rather scary. There are no words to describe the wind-blown glory of these mountain tops before a storm. Below us, crawling gradually up a brush-choked canyon, was the trail, rising to meet the aspen grove, which was on our level but behind us to the west.

We turned to the house, a squat and extremely solid log structure. It was a line cabin of some ranch, but the owner, Mr. Connely, chanced to be there. He came out and made us welcome.

"Yes," he answered us reflectively. "There are several graves still recognizable among these mountains, but the one you mean is undoubtedly Nancy Hill's."

"That's the one," said Mr. Jones. "They say some one shot the date right off the old stone. It does seem as if they could have found a more suitable spot for target practice."

"Drunk probably," said Mr. Connely succinctly. "But we know the date anyway. It was 1847."

This led to quite a discussion. He and Mr. Jones told us a good bit, and I filled in the rest of the tragic story from two old newspaper clippings which were given me to read that same evening.

In the year 1900 Ed Sutton, whose ranch we had passed about two hours earlier, was visited by a stranger—a Mr. Wright. He had been at the last resting place of Nancy Hill and had come down to this neighbor to enlist friendly interest for the lonely grave on the mountain. He was to have married her, he told them, and had traveled in her wagon train. In the fifty-three years that had passed since he helped to bury her he had returned three times to see her grave: once in the seventies, once in the nineties, and now again.

The pioneer cavalcade in which they traveled had fallen on evil days, he said. Her death was not an isolated tragedy, but only one of many. The train was hag-ridden with fear and apprehension. The terrified travelers never knew what the day would bring forth. In the morning the companies would leave camp in their regular order. At night one or more wagons were oftentimes missing, while the worried women called to one another for news of who might possibly be ill in this wagon or that. Later, when the belated teams came slowly into camp, the sick were dead—and already buried.

Nancy Hill was a goddess of a girl, close to six feet tall and magnificently healthy. She was well in the morning. She was dead at noon. She was barely cold when they buried her. The wagon with her grieving relatives went on. What else could they do? Their whole future and even present safety was bound up in staying with the relentlessly moving caravan. Her lover remained. He was mounted and could catch the wagons. He stayed a day or two at the grave trying to reconcile himself to the inevitable, but eventually rode after the train and arrived in the west without his bride-to-be, and with the whole course of his life changed.

Close to this grave Mr. Wright knew of seven more. Others, bringing the total of recognizable graves near a dozen, are scattered over the mountain. The only other two identified are those of A. and J. Corum.

On this occasion (as involving less wear and tear) we had decided to travel down the trail instead of coming up on it; so, as soon as feasible after leaving the cabin, we turned the truck into the old ruts and started, for better or for worse, back down the slope to Hams Fork. We soon came to the grave, at the head of Robinson's Hollow. It was about fifty yards from the road. Small gray sage and greasewood but a foot high crowded close to cover Nancy Hill, and delicate flowers, very frail like baby blue-eyes, grew near her head.

We looked to the rear and saw the separate and patchy groups of trees gradually merging into the semblance of one big grove with a line of cliffs beyond it. Over the cliffs the clouds grew momentarily blacker and more threatening. The line cabin still showed tiny and distinct. Then we took off over the bulging brink and went down and still down, sped by clashing thunder. When the torn clouds finally released their heavy cargo, it was not rain that came in wind-borne shining streaks like knitting needles, but hail.

The rising gale caught up with us and shrieked past, pulling at the corners of our robe. It was making far better mileage than we dared dream of with a borrowed truck. Meanwhile it hailed with grim thoroughness.

I slid forward off the seat, removed my hat, and pulled the robe over my head, mentally pigeonholing my impressions for future jottings; but, as they were limited in scope by my temporary eclipse, I just never did jot. And so were lost, no doubt, many valuable data. Meanwhile my husband stoically drove the truck, buoyed up by the well grounded Paden belief that the family will be found present, and still animate, at the end of any given episode. It was icy cold; the trail was rough, and the truck springless. I remember that it occurred to me, as often before and since but never with such conviction, that woman's place is really in the home.

19

Green Pastures and Beer Springs

FROM THE SUMMIT where the travelers of Sublette's Cutoff commanded such a heartening view of Bear River Valley, the road went down on a slant, winding around the mountain in order to maintain a passable grade. Wheels, hoofs, and feet soon pounded it into dust knee-deep. At the bottom they struck the headwaters of Muddy Fork of Bear River and often camped, for there was still a steep hill between them and the main valley of the Bear. On the right of the road and dribbling down so as to be easily accessible were some poison springs; and in the first few years the emigrants lost many of their cattle at this unforeseen danger spot. Even though the guidebooks contained terse warnings the stock drivers were not sufficiently on guard. Later they learned to start the loose animals hurrying down the hill and to drive them past the springs on the dead run, watering them a few miles farther on at Smith's Fork.

Before arriving at Smith's Fork the cutoff came into the old Oregon Trail from Fort Bridger, and companies who arrived by it during the years while the old road was still in constant use were keenly interested to see whether they had gained or lost ground by their decision. Major Cross, commanding the mounted riflemen who crossed in '49, thought the cutoff was the better way, but Henry Mann, who had passed Cross and his riflemen in the mountains, was disgruntled. He wrote: "So the cut off was no great affair fix it any way we will. Teams that left the junction of the California and Oregon roads on the 5th are ahead of us and we passed the same place on the 3rd they taking the old route. Messrs. [word undecipherable] Sublette and Co. get a great many curses on all sides."

It is noticeable in the diaries that the curses were all left on the east side of the divide, for the summit was beauty itself and the descent not too difficult. Bear River Valley, when reached, was knee-high in heavy grass; the Indians proved friendly, the sluggish river stayed on its own side of the road, and the wood and water situation was ideal. Then, too, the epidemics were over and the few cases of mountain fever improved as the elevation became lower. Morale rose like a thermometer in the sun.

Little things helped too—the little things that loom so big on such a journey. First must be placed the welcome change in diet—berries and game. Bear of course, for the river was not named lightly, elk, mountain sheep, and antelope. The companies who maintained hunters divided with those who did not. The women made stew, and the men brought in pocketfuls of wild onions for seasoning. Then they had stores of balsam gum from the fir grove traversed on the divide. It was not only good to chew but healthful. And (very important to their happiness) they could easily collect wood enough for campfires. Out came the violins again and the jew's-harps.

Balanced against these advantages were the mosquitoes. Travelers crossing the divide early in the season spoke of them as the heaviest cross they had to bear. Even to those following a month later they ranked with alkali dust and split lips as one of the great triumvirate of irritating discomforts.

Marshy spots and places from which the snow had recently melted produced millions of them, ravenous and peevish. Pack mules and saddle animals became frenzied and rolled in the mud, loads and all. No one was exempt from their attacks, and no year was free of them. Cholera was bad during the gold rush and grew less. The plains Indians were reasonably friendly during the gold rush and grew worse. Wolves were gradually frightened from the trail. But the mosquitoes went on forever. Even Father de Smet's flowing robe was not proof against them. He lamented sadly: "I have suffered so much from them that I cannot leave them unnoticed. . . . There is no defence against their darts, but to hide under a buffalo skin, or wrap oneself up in some stuff which they cannot pierce, and run the risk of being smothered."

The sun-soaked valley of the Bear is opulent and beneficent, full of hollows weighted with tasseled grasses and dotted with smacking-fat meadow lands. Down through the years this long slow valley has come unchanged as to its essentials of comfort and well-being. On either side the mountain slopes reach up to summer skies. Its fruitful flats produce an inexhaustible abundance. It saved the emigrants from disaster.

An observant man wrote home to his brother in 1853, "If the railroad ran through Bear Valley I would not exchange a section I could pick out there, for twice that amount I ever saw anywhere."

When the wagons had trekked down the bottoms four miles they came to Smith's Fork. Within their sight it obligingly came out of its deep rocky course through the cliffs and flattened out for their convenience. More than that, like Blacks Fork, it divided its current among several channels, thus making it barely possible to ford them all. Many authoritative journals disagree on the number, and I have managed to disagree with myself. My notes taken in 1935 record four crossings, while in 1938 we modestly contented ourselves with three. They are seasonal, no doubt. The second fork was considered the worst to cross. Even though the wagon beds were blocked up on bolsters, water splashed in on the load; and the going was very rough because of large boulders which had fallen from the cliff.

A majority of the emigrants did not see Bear River until they had traveled down its bottoms some ten miles beyond Smith's Fork, or in the neighborhood of Thomas' Fork. They then noted it as dull, sluggish, and unlike any other large river they had seen, with dozens of Shoshone lodges nuzzling close to the brown current.

Thomas' Fork is about a mile across the Idaho border. The stream is deeply cut and carries a full current. The wagons were worried across with ropes and plenty of man power, occasionally turning turtle on the up pull. The distress of the Forty-niners at this contingency was faint and amateurish compared to the scorching indignation of the travelers of the fifties who found toll bridges erected over Smith's and Thomas' forks, and who could not afford to pay the charges. It was only human to feel much worse about being stuck in the mud part way across a ticklish river when the plutocrats of the trail were driving levelly and safely over bridges. So where the Forty-niners took the crossings in their stride and wrote comparatively little about it, the diarists of the fifties who had to ford felt really hurt and said so redundantly on many pages.

Beyond Thomas' Fork the valley narrowed and the wagons were forced over a large grass-covered hill. Bluejoint, wild oats, barley, and wild rye grew profusely, and the bright blue blossoms of the flax added to a lovely picture. At the summit, some thousand feet above the valley floor, they looked right down upon Bear River again. Nothing was gained by this toilsome climb. The hill was merely an obstruction in their road.

The wheel marks on the down slope are very pronounced, showing plainly from the highway, and we found several places where the wagons had ground distinct grooves in solid rock. At the foot of the hill we passed some rotting log houses and came to the river. Its olive-green windings are close to the highway with a smoothly rippled surface like crinkled glass.

At the place where the trail and river met, the Argonauts of '49 encountered a Shoshone village whose curling, plumy camp smokes had been visible from the mountain. It was a scabrous collection of tepees, littered with snarling dogs and overfed children. Grotesque crones were there, whose sagging bodies attested years of hard labor, but whose lease upon life might well be canceled, each by her own relatives, should a hard winter make food scarce. There were grinning old men and squat, solid hunters whose long straight hair, bushing around their shoulders, was full of bits of brush, feathers, small clods, and most of the lesser fauna pertaining to the unwashed aborigines. The all-too-friendly younger squaws completed the tally. As imperfectly suppressed as a raided burlesque show, they bobbed up again after each rebuff. It was an almost naked, lousy, itching mob, but human and even kindly.

The emigrants were well received by this motley assembly who laughed easily and heartily, meanwhile parading around, out of sheer exuberance and almost everything else except a leather waist thong, a precarious strip of buckskin, and some miscellaneous vestments. A few presented themselves, completely unabashed, without even a gleam of raiment, an unforeseen circumstance which amused the men and caused the temporary retirement of the New England ladies.

The nonchalance of their eating etiquette exceeded (if it were possible) that of their sartorial habits. One old Indian politely passed around, after the manner of candy or salted nuts, a cluster of rats swung by the tails to his belt. If by chance one had been accepted he would have expected presents in return, but it appeared that no one in the party had any use for rats, rather sketchily boiled whole without removing anything which had ever been of use to the animal. When he was sure that they were no good as bait for presents he registered a dignified disappointment and ate one himself with good appetite—feet, face, and all.

The emigrants always tried to lie over in Bear River Valley, especially if Sunday happened to fall in the two or three days they spent in its rich windings. The Sunday rest was a sincere gesture in most cases— a reverent acknowledgment of the Sabbath by a generation who considered travel on the seventh day next door to wickedness—but, as a matter of fact, only the animals got much in the way of relaxation. That the latter always showed marked improvement after a day out of harness was perhaps in itself enough to persuade many otherwise not over-scrupulous companies to rest one day in seven. For the preservation of the stock was the crux of the migration's success, and stanch God-fearing people, who did not hesitate to separate from their caravan in Indian country and remain camped alone upon the Sabbath, were later forced by the starving condition of their oxen to harness up on Sunday morning and set out for better grass.

It was sometimes possible to hear a sermon. There were many preachers in the wagon trains, and they did their best, often going from one camp to another for the better part of the day and picking up a sort of trailing audience like a golf tournament. They gave their exhortations as best they could in the center of the wagon circles, while the miscellaneous congregation washed, baked, greased harness and wagon wheels, and, in general, did whatever must be done before the next day's march. Meanwhile the proximity of the Indian villages added a flavor of their own which was distinctly not the odor of sanctity.

The Shoshones of Bear River had splendid horses, but they would neither sell nor trade, being completely under the domination of the traders of the vicinity, of whom Peg-leg Smith was the chief and kingpin. The Forty-niners described him as a portly, round-headed man of about fifty-five who had lived with the Shoshones for twenty-five years. He, with his wives and numerous offspring, must be considered as constituting the first family of Bear River Valley. Their headquarters consisted of four log cabins and a profusion of Indian lodges twenty-five miles down river from Smith's Fork, making it somewhere in the stretch opposite Dingle. (This fork was named not for him but for the better known Jedediah Smith, who made the path-breaking journey across the Mojave Desert into California in 1826.)

The emigrants found Peg-leg friendly, hospitable, and apparently innocuous; but, in his younger days, when he trapped and traded to the south, he did not scruple to steal Indian children from their parents and even nursing mothers from their babies for sale to the slave trade in Mexico. His wooden leg was said to be the product of his own skillful knife, which, supplemented by a saw, he is credited with using to remove his own limb, taking up the arteries with a bullet mold—not the only instance of self-surgery performed by lonely trappers.

Isaac Wistar, who encountered him at Independence in April, 1849, describes a fight that took place while Peg-leg, Sublette, Hudspeth, and other mountain men were waiting to take the trail west. It seems that Peg-leg, although quiet when sober, was not to be trifled with when drunk; and, in that reprehensible condition, he was temporarily locked out of the barrooms of Independence. "He therefore," according to Mr. Wistar, "blew off the lock of one of them with his rifle and entered upon four border-desperadoes, deep in the fascination of 'poker,' who instantly opened fire. 'Peg-leg's' gun being empty, he promptly jerked off his hickory leg and at one blow extinguished all the candles on the table and began feeling for the enemy. The general net result of the engagement was—two men killed by the wooden leg, another hors de combat, and the fourth, shot with a captured weapon as he was making his way out. Having been variously wounded in the encounter, 'Peg-leg's' blood was now up, and he was for remaining to fight the town, but his friends applied the 'similia similibus curantur' and with the aid of more whiskey, managed to get him away among the Kaw Indians across the boundary and no one in Independence hankered for the job of capturing this famous character on the open prairie."

Against this lurid character sketch we must weigh the testimony of John Minto, who saw him at Fort Hall in '44, neatly dressed in navy like a steamboat captain, and watched open-mouthed while Peg-leg paused respectfully for a blessing from a traveling priest.

From the bottom of the "Thousand Foot Elevation" the trail runs along the valley floor through Montpelier and Georgetown—not at any time far from the highway. At Montpelier was a trading post, now commemorated by a marker. There is a local tradition (substantiated by deep wheel gouges) that some of the wagons came down from the hills directly at the marker, but, to the best of our knowledge, this route was not a main stem of traffic.

In the secure haven of the valley the travelers explored here and there at a distance from the line of travel. The women picked berries and made pies again. The men went hunting. One excited Nimrod chased an antelope on the bell mare with the pack mules in full convoy behind him and the packs flying apart.

Probably because the Indians resisted all attempts to trade, the Argo-nauts were correspondingly determined to break down the barrier. A few prime buffalo robes rewarded their efforts, and, soon after, one of the men discovered his shirt literally crawling with lice. Everybody pooh-poohed but everybody investigated and a very shamefaced company built huge fires and boiled their clothes. It didn't take long for the Indian to discover that the white man had a strange distaste for the gregarious and (from the red man's point of view) nourishing louse, and that if he could snatch a hat and cram it on his busy head, he was more often than not permitted to keep it. It was shortsighted for the white man to accept such a defeat, though, and the wise emigrant snatched it back and burned it as an offering on the altar of prejudice.

Beyond the trading post at what is now Montpelier there came a long, rather dry stretch, broken by Black Mud Run which seemed to be seasonal. And so the wagons came at last to the much talked-of and discussed Soda Springs and, in the fullness of time, we in our turn approached the modern town bearing the same name and occupying the same site.

The Soda Springs of modern days is a small place. The main street makes a T with the highway, and business centers along the two wide thoroughfares. From this nucleus, cottages stray up toward cushiony hills and down toward the river—their comfortable yards set with myrtle, hollyhocks, and marigolds. In the hills the springs are of the pothole variety, but we were told that toward the river we should find them more impressive.

We turned riverward, where the waters of the Bear are now backed over many acres of flat land by a modern dam, and came to a struggling golf course. Scraggly junipers grow plentifully and provide snappy haz-ards, but they share honors with great cones of porous rock, ten feet high and more, formed by mineral deposit and containing the famous springs. The water rises to increasing heights, as the walls gradually build up, and laps out over the top or runs through crevices and spills sloppily down the sides. Lydia Waters came equipped with lemon extract and sugar and had an epicurean morning among the springs while her company lay over to recruit. She broke off some of the spongy yellowish deposit and took it with her. At first, she said, it had a color and texture like jelly cake; but in a week or so it turned pure white. Others, not prepared for the novelty of soda water, wondered how liquid could boil and not be hot. The very early wagon trains used it successfully in place of yeast.

A mile or two farther, on the bank of the river was the notable Beer Spring. Lydia writes: "Its water looked exactly like Lager Beer, and tasted as if it were, only flat." It formed an important stopover in the summer itinerary of the fur trappers. In fact these inelegant but graphic travelers always spoke of the place in general as Beer Springs. It was so known for years, and at least one innocent lady of the migration expected to find the land flowing with free drinks on the house as a current substitute for milk and honey.

Of them all, the only hot spring recorded was the famous Steamboat Spring, which puffed and snorted at the river's edge as its gaseous contents boiled in and out. Reams of paper were used in describing this eccentric landmark. Both Steamboat and Beer springs are now submerged under the dam.

We drove back past the main business block and toward the uphill edge of town. Ahead of us a man with a demijohn was striding away from a still chugging automobile toward a green dimple in the hill. We got out and followed him on foot. A pothole spring occupied the dimple. When we arrived he was filling the demijohn from a tomato can and made certain polite motions as of giving us precedence. We waved him back, and he went on dipping and pouring.

"Twice a week," he said, "I take a demijohn full to an old lady who can't get out to get any, and she gives me a quart of buttermilk in return."

"They're both crazy," whispered my unappreciative son just back of my ear, as he took one swallow of the cupful he had dipped.

I liked it very much, and so did some of the ladies of the migration, but then, as Mr. Mann wrote: "These women are strange beings, and would drink anything that is called fashionable."

If so, they were beyond doubt entitled to their idiosyncrasies, and we can only be glad that the Soda Springs formed for them an intriguing climax to one of the most pleasurable interludes of the overland journey.

20

The Parting of the Ways

Six miles beyond Soda Springs the men of the migration stood opposite the dark, forbidding bulk of Sheep Rock and watched Bear River curl around its unyielding base in one of the most spectacular curves known to the rivers of the continent. The heretofore philanthropic river was in the very act of leaving them flat.

There could be no complaint. It had seen them through a vital period in their journey; in fact its great hairpin bend had swept so far north to meet the caravans that it seemed as if an all-wise Providence had directed the course of this erratically flowing river far out of its ordinary course in order that the greatest migration in the world's history might be made possible. But now, full, deep, and unchangeable, it was headed south. And so the early travelers trekked within a few hundred yards of the great rock across the river, took a hungry look and a few ineffectual shots at the mountain sheep poised upon its summit, and turned northward toward the watershed of the Snake. Thus matters were cut, dried, and stacked for the Oregon emigrants who followed in their tracks.

There had been only a few groups of western settlers over the trail (and they mostly missionaries) when, in the summer of '41, the Oregon-bound wagons arrived at Sheep Rock. With them traveled a small group of nonconformists who didn't want to go to Oregon; they wanted to see the storybook land of California.

Now the bend of the Bear was as well known and as easily described as the forks of the Platte. They decided to make it their point of departure from the stereotyped road to Oregon, and, as they wished to travel in a general southwest direction, to remain with the lavish river. And so the rearward glance of history sees a small, thin line of wagons turn and go south with the Bear—the wagons of the noted Bidwell-Bartleson party, first to reach California overland from the United States. The Bear did well by them for a few days and then betook itself ponderously into the Great Salt Lake and left them to struggle around the rim of the desert, down the Humboldt River, and across the Sierras. They were in sore straits by the time the land of promise was reached. Future emigrants took warning, and no more California-bound wagons turned south at Sheep Rock.

From that time until 1849 the travelers for California continued with the Oregon trains another week, making a detour to the north to touch Fort Hall and the Snake River, and returning south on Raft River and Goose Creek. It was in the gold rush, when detours and delays were unthinkable, that a wagon train dared to attempt the route straight west from Sheep Rock. The trial trip was successful, and the new road was soon known as Hudspeth's Cutoff. Thereafter the traffic was divided; the wagon masters had a choice to make, and, when the day came that we also must choose, we elected to follow the early wagons and turned north toward Fort Hall.

It is on the eastern edge of a large valley that the Bear River makes its hairpin turn and the trail divides. The whole landscape is messy with evidence of volcanic action like the spilled ashes and charred debris of some untidy smoker. As we turned north, we saw that the trail penetrates the low land between two mountain ranges, and chose a small road that had apparently been used as gangway for a cloudburst since the last passenger traffic. Tawny, wind-blown grass lay flatly along the hillside like fur on an animal's flanks. Fat little sheep in bulging clusters seemed like distended ticks living on its bounty. Ahead of us a mountain barred the way, snow-smeared and dreary.

"That's Mt. Putnam," Bill said instructively. "We have to get around behind it, haven't we? On the north side, I mean?"

"That's the general idea," his father told him. "We'll go through the low place in the hills just to the right."

"I see the mountain and the low place, all right," put in Dr. Neff, looking disapprovingly at the mangy patches of stubbly growth ahead, "but I don't see any sign of a trail. I'll bet anything we're lost."

He was undeniably right. For a valuable hour of late-afternoon daylight and eleven mountain miles we were very lost indeed, but eventually we made connections with the Port Neuf and brought up with a jerk on the abrupt, grassy bank of that surprisingly crooked river. On the far side were the faint grass-grown gougings of the trail. Spanning the river, partly in and partly out, were the remains of what had been a bridge before the last high water. On the wrong bank were we and a belligerently curious band of full-grown steers.

We decided to take a chance on fording; and, as the bridge would safely take foot passengers, all got out but the driver in order to decrease the weight. He picked a spot about fifty yards downstream for the attempt, and the car took off from the bank like a diving mud hen. If she had waggled her tail lights the illusion would have been perfect. For one long moment she stood on end while my husband gunned into the engine every ounce of power it possessed, then graciously accepted the challenge and rolled on across.

A flowery meadow succeeded the river crossing. It made a tempting camp, but those who circled their wagons here regretted it. The dried grasses of the side hills agreed better with their cattle than the wet herbage of the meadow—not to mention the mosquitoes. Next came a particularly slick and slippery clay summit, and we were over the divide. The battered face of old Mt. Putnam looked down into the sheltered Fort Hall bottoms while we in our dingy car rested like a disregarded gnat on its whiskery cheek. Below us the trail slithered down a hoary wrinkle and, resolutely, we steered along. The long July day was slipping into evening. Trailing down from snow-filled gullies, aspens shivered while the wind whined among them in a whisper. The tiny unworked road was so runneled and undermined as to be almost impassable.

Presently the far-away buildings of an Indian reservation swam dimly into sight; and the faint baying of Indian curs blended with the wind. Ahead of us and across the great Snake River stood the Three Buttes— purple cardboard mountains pasted against a murky gray flat and a tinsel sky, just as they had looked to the Oregon missionaries a century ago— ancient landmarks to tell us we had reached Fort Hall.

*   *   *

We stayed the night in Pocatello. It was off our route, but we needed information about the site of old Fort Hall, which well informed authorities seemed to agree had been inundated by the waters of the American Dam project. For months we had been regretful that this should have happened to a site so vital to the upbuilding of the West, but we certainly intended to get a boat and see what the submerged ruins would look like.

The next morning was Sunday, and we found no one who could tell us where to start; but there was a welter of information as to the early history of the place, some of which had better be considered in order to clarify the picture as a whole.

In the early 1830's, when the no man's land of Oregon held the uneasy attention of both England and the United States, Nathaniel Wyeth, a plain young man from New England, became a figure of destiny. Wyeth, without plan or premeditation, built a trading post and implanted himself on the overland thoroughfare to Oregon—a post which, by virtue of its strategic position, gave aid and succor to the westbound American settlers and helped to checkmate the plans of England. He named the post Fort Hall in honor of Henry Hall, head of the company which had backed his venture.

The small adobe structure was home for almost two years to Wyeth and his trappers, and its visitors included hunters, Indians, scientists, missionaries, and explorers. On July 27, 1834, just a few days after its founding, Jason Lee delivered at the fort the first sermon heard between the Rockies and the coast of the Pacific, followed the next day by a funeral service. It was, of course, a Protestant ceremony, and the Catholic trappers, in order that every one should feel it had been properly done, added a Latin chant which the Indians supplemented with prolonged and well meant howls.

By 1836 the Hudson's Bay Company had taken over the fort, and until 1843 the men in charge were able to persuade all emigrant companies to abandon their wagons and go on as pack trains—a most discouraging proceeding. It is understandable also that they should have attempted to divert to California the increasing thrust of Oregon-bound homesteaders. Probably in some instances they succeeded—to the ultimate gratitude of the American Nation, for Oregon capably handled her own destiny through the medium of the early settlers of 1843 who stubbornly drove on to the Columbia; while California, held by Mexico (then in the midst of her short period of hostility) and populated by a well intrenched Spanish-speaking people, needed every available man to win through to an eventual union with the United States. This was accomplished by the treaty closing the Mexican War only a few months before the discovery of gold in 1848. Meanwhile (we must gratefully certify) the Hudson's Bay Company, with but few exceptions, consistently aided their rival settlers whenever politeness and humanity so dictated.

Throughout the hectic year 1849 and on into the fifties, Fort Hall, although in United States territory, remained the property of Hudson's Bay Company, while the fur trade became of less and less importance and the trail was thronged with westbound Americans. In 1855 the company abandoned it, and the material of the walls was soon torn down and utilized again in the construction of a stage station known as "The Adobes" some three miles distant at the Spring Creek bridge. The great flood of '62 finished the razing of the fort, and its location gradually faded from the public memory. When, in 1906, Ezra Meeker raised money for a monument to mark the site it was erected mistakenly at the Adobes. Ten years later Mr. Meeker relocated the exact site, which he considered to be one of the most significant spots on the entire trail; and, in 1920, the monument was correctly placed with some ceremony.

Then the public forgot it again. The waters of the American Dam project backed up in the Fort Hall Bottoms, and indignant historians in distant universities said that it had been flooded and what a pity it was. In 1934, the centennial of its founding was celebrated in Pocatello with all the furor imaginable but with no mention, as far as we could find out, of its actual location.

In the summer of the next year we arrived in Pocatello on a Saturday evening, bought pamphlets and special centennial editions of the paper (now a year old), and spent the next few hours looking through them for geographical information. We were, of course, unable to get in touch on Sunday with our usual sources of information, the Chamber of Commerce, the Public Library, and the college, and so we milled around the city for an unprofitable hour and then started out toward the Fort Hall Indian Reservation to see what we could find out for ourselves.

Sunday or no Sunday, the reservation store was busy. Tall Indians with long black braids and dingy hats decorated with bright feathers strode along impassively. A darkly handsome chap with bright green silk rodeo shirt and yellow metal belt gave evidence of the younger generation's changing tastes but got small notice from us compared with the rapt attention bestowed on the stolid ancient who wore a white muslin nightgown tucked into his capacious pants. It had long, full sleeves, finished at the wrists with frills that seemed to afford him some pleasure, as he occasionally glanced down at them.

Cottages, originally neat, stand on farms of about twenty acres. But the fundamental inability of the Indians to keep things shipshape (due, perhaps, to racial nomadic habits) soon brands them, and often the real habitation is a tepee in the back yard. Much effort has been made to give them adequate instruction, and some of them farm their acres well; but too often, if they succeed in wresting a living from Mother Earth, it is because of her maternal instincts rather than undue exertion on their part.

We passed, without hailing, a number of intelligent-appearing Indians whose imperturbable dignity, as they rode slowly on small dirty ponies, or in big dirty automobiles, precluded light or unnecessary conversation. Instead we stopped a car containing two couples and a baby. One of the young wives was Shoshone, good-looking, and cultured to the point of causing all the Paden family's casual speech habits to vanish. She offered to show us the old wagon trail, and we set out in their wake as closely as the clouds of dust permitted.

When the road arrived at the short, steep bluff that edges the bottoms it plunged directly down to the flat. The trail did the same a short distance to our left, having come straight across the valley from where we had left it at the foot of Mt. Putnam. The young Shoshone girl then showed us the old ford over Clear Creek and pointed to wagon ruts running straight down the bottoms, paralleling the river. They continued, she said, to where Fort Hall lay submerged but visible under the waters of the dam. We, in turn, reiterated to them our determination to see the ruin if we had to float over it in a rowboat; got into the car, and started out to fulfill our rash promise.

At six o'clock that evening, we returned to Pocatello disillusioned. There weren't any boats, nor any people from whom to rent boats, nor apparently any people of any sort whatsoever in the Fort Hall Bottoms on a Sunday. Nothing but mile after interminable mile of wheat grass studded here and there with willow thickets, currant, and wild rose, through which we caught occasional glimpses of the great, curving river.

We might have wanted to tour the Arctic Circle for all the progress we made.

The next morning at nine, we moved in on the Chamber of Commerce determined to get some definite information.

The pleasant-faced woman in charge gave it her attention. Dr. Howard might know, she said: Dr. Minnie Howard. A telephone call produced the information that she was on her way downtown. A hasty sortie at the door discovered her just passing the corner.

Thus easily did we annex Dr. Minnie Howard—not to return her until she and we had stood within the foundations of old Fort Hall, submerged under nothing at all but wheat grass.

Dr. Howard was a physician, wife of a physician and mother of several sons, all physicians; but at heart she was a historian—a true one, painstakingly accurate, eager to gain more knowledge and to share her own. The cumulative wisdom gained in years of professional service among the Indians made her contributions so valuable to us that I put her in the front seat with my husband, grabbed my notebook, and climbed in the rear to try to get it all down.

All day she talked with power and passion and an unshakable knowledge of her subject; but the item most pertinent to this record was that in 1916 she and her husband, with an Indian and a local cattleman, had accompanied Ezra Meeker when he succeeded in locating the site of Fort Hall, and that they had definitely identified the place to their complete satisfaction. The old Indian, who had been familiar with the fort in the days of its usefulness, recognized the particular curve of the river and, from that point, worked inland through the shoulder-high wheat grass to the foundations. Once there, he had told them just where to look for the well—which they found without difficulty.

Many years had passed, and Dr. Howard was uncertain as to the exact location of the foundations; but she was positive that they were not under water, and that she would recognize the vicinity if she ever got close enough. For the rest of the morning and on into the afternoon, we bumped here and there through the outspread unreason of the Bottoms with the fullest expectations of getting results.

Mainly we stayed in the open, paralleling the river, but every now and then we attempted to crash through the heavy willows and shrubbery to the flat banks where we could see the course of the wide, still river. Dr. Howard was closely watching its contours, hoping to get her clue from them. With unflagging optimism (and utter disregard of our paint job) she insisted on tilting at impenetrable masses of willow growth, and, failing, had us move on and try again. Her vivid, warm energy was contagious, and we kept hard at it.

Old wood roads led off at sixes and sevens through the shrubbery.

They were flanked with tall nodding goldenrod. Dr. Howard interrupted herself to inquire professionally, "Does anybody here get hay fever?" and then went right on with her illuminating monologue, without waiting for an answer. Finally we became tightly wedged in an amazing trail growth of wild roses which met above our top, and almost forced themselves in at the windows.

The men squeezed out and went to reconnoiter. Dr. Howard, being confronted with manna in the wilderness in the shape of rose berries practically in her lap, ate a half-dozen as a slight collation and slowed up the historical treatise enough so that I stopped to sharpen a pencil. My fingers were acutely and achingly weary, and my powers of comprehension had sprung a slow leak. I absent-mindedly polished and chewed down a berry and leaned limply against the cushions.

The men came back. It was no thoroughfare. We backed out; moved on to the next wood road and tried again. A clearing strung itself like a bead on our latest set of wheel ruts, and then another, and another. Small log cabins and tiers of chopped wood indicated that people sojourned there, but there were no gardens or other sign of occupation. A short period of excitement punctuated our search as we found and explored the excavations at Loring Cantonment, the old military post which we knew to be about three miles from the fort.

My always nebulous ideas of geography had completely curdled long since; but as we crossed for the *n*th time the great swale of the old trail and found that it had turned sharply and was now going purposefully toward the river, it occurred to me that this might be the place where the wagons had turned in toward the fort. Just then Dr. Howard caught a glimpse of the point of willows ahead on the next decisive bend of the river. She evidently recognized them and asked my husband to stop. None too soon, for, as it proved, we were within a hundred yards of our objective.

We might easily have passed it, for there are no walls remaining, and the site was hidden under a four-foot growth of wheat grass through which we breast-stroked our way to a partial clearing where stood Ezra Meeker's monument. The old fort itself was located, in its day, on a very slight elevation a few feet distant. We pushed through the tall waving grass stalks until we thought that we were about at the line of the wall and then each made for himself a spot in which to work by trampling down a circle of grass and sitting on the heap. This completely submerged us in the warm jungle.

"Here is a hole," said Dr. Howard in high excitement. "I'm sure it must be—yes, it *is* the place where we dug in 1916."

With every one pulling grass, we had it cleared in no time.

"We wanted to get all the proof we could," she continued; "so, after we checked the size and shape of the outline of the walls and the position of the well and what Ezra Meeker called the rifle pits, we dug to see what we could find. They let me choose the spot, and I picked the inner angle of the walls. You know how it is in a ruin with the roof caved in. Things get shoved or rain-washed into the corner. So we dug there and we found," she went on with satisfaction, "buffalo bones with knife hacks in them, great bolts from the wagon door into the fort, lime, fragments of stove grate and some bottle glass. But the most interesting find was some broken pieces of blue English china and a piece of a bronze luster bowl decorated on the outside with apple blossoms."

"Do you think they belonged to the factors?" my husband asked.

"Well, you know how the English are. A man in authority thinks it pays to keep up appearances, no matter where he lives nor how crude the place is. Mr. Meeker and I both thought it was a definite possibility."

We had no shovel with us, but by poking a bit we found the rotted wooden foundations and more bones with knife hacks in them. The men also, under some difficulty, managed to pace the length and breadth of the structure and checked the position of the well and the rifle pits. There was no doubt that we stood within the confines of Fort Hall itself, of which not a wall remains, close beside the hungry river which ever laps out toward it.

The channel of the Snake has changed in the last hundred years, hasn't it?" asked my husband. "The old fort was supposed to be a mile from it."

"Certainly," said Dr. Howard crisply. "We know it has changed a lot upstream near Ferry Butte. There used to be an old ferry there, and the bank where it landed on this side is now completely washed away. A big river can do a lot of moving in a hundred years. Never you mind the river. Here's Fort Hall."

And, after all, that was the main thing.

*   *   *

After we had traveled three or four miles Dr. Howard pointed toward a tangle of willow and undergrowth that lay between us and the river.

"There's where old Chief Pocatello was buried," she said, "if you can call it being buried."

"Who was he, and what happened to him?" Bill wanted to know.

"He was a Shoshone chief," Dr. Howard commenced obligingly, "and you can imagine that he was quite a character around here or the city wouldn't be named after him." After which she went on to give such a fascinating story of his mother, his birth, and his career that I shall give the bare outline as a sort of thumbnail sketch of the Shoshone Indian, his ways, his woes, and his wrongdoings, at about the time the trail was coming into extensive use. The details were supplied to Dr. Howard by the chief's granddaughter, who was at one time a maid in her house.

About six months before the birth of Pocatello, his mother, her younger sister, and her tiny daughter were taken prisoners in a raid by a distant tribe. The young mother connived at the escape of her sister, stoically remaining behind because her child would surely cry and betray them.

When the warriors returned, one claimed her as his prize and, not wishing to bother with the child, wrung its neck and gave her back the dress, which was a nice one of buckskin.

On the way to the distant village a warrior died of his wounds and was left under a buffalo robe with his knife and bow and arrows.

When she reached the village she found that she was a second wife, but the warrior soon transferred his warmest affections to her. The first wife became bitterly jealous and each day sent the young captive some distance to a stream to cut and carry wood. With her went the little daughter of the first wife, too young to tell what she saw.

The young Shoshone girl laid her plans. Little by little she dug under the overhanging river bank until she had a dry cave stored with stolen dried meat. Then, as she knew that her baby would soon be born and that she must get away quickly, she killed the little girl as a parting gesture of revenge for her own child's death and hid in her cave.

Several days she lay there frightened and cramped before she dared to leave by night. Even then she had a narrow escape from a returning search party. She had no weapon, and so slept by day and walked by night. Her food gave out, and she was hungry and could hardly go on, but she remembered all of that terrible march between her home and the warrior's village and knew where the dead Indian had been left under the buffalo robe. She found the place, and when she had the knife and the bow and arrows and had cut the buffalo robe to make a pack and moccasins, she felt much more secure; but best of all, she found a skin bag that had dried meat in it, left for the dead man's journey to the spirit world. With new strength she kept on many days into the Raft River country and saw a lone tepee in the strange valley now called the City of Rocks. In the tepee were an old Indian and his wife whom she knew. They told her that just over the hill was her tribe in camp, that her mother and father had cut their hair for her death, and that her husband was not yet re-married.

So "she found peace with her husband again" and the child was born, named Dono Oso—that is, Buffalo Robe. No wonder that the character of this boy was dark and stormy, and that later the Indians renamed him Paughatella, or He Does Not Follow the Road.

"And what finally happened to him?" Bill asked after a few silent moments spent in hushed tribute to such an efficiently deadly woman.

"Well, he grew up to be a bloodthirsty, renegade Indian. The whites had reason to hate him, and he was a constant worry to the tribe. As he got older and times changed, of course he wasn't a menace any more, and he grew to be a comical old rascal—part of our local color around here, you might say. He wore any old thing for clothes but always managed to top it with a dilapidated silk hat."

"And how did they bury him?"

"Oh, yes, how did they bury him," repeated Dr. Howard with a twinkle. "Well, they dumped him in a bottomless spring—him and his ponies. You see, the Indians knew he had made enemies and they thought he had better have a little help on his way to the Happy Hunting Grounds so they gave him a good start and plenty of horses."

* * *

From Fort Hall, the wagons drove nine miles and crossed the pretty Port Neuf, whose abundant beaver made it a trappers' paradise. Next came the wide-bottomed Bannock, where thin dark rushes stood wind-slanted like pen-stroked shadows in a sketch. From here on, down the Snake River, were Bannock Indians, originally quite honest and friendly. Captain Bonneville saw fit to trust them with the pasturing of his horses and credited them with the safe return of every one. Of course it might be said that they wasted more horseflesh than if they had stolen one or two, for invariably the animals had been used in buffalo hunts until they were gaunt and poor. It has been suggested—pertinently, I think—that the Scotch traders named this tribe from their habit of forming all their food—mashed berries, camas roots, dried grasshoppers, everything—into little cakes, or bannocks. (R. Ross Arnold, on the contrary, in his "Indian Wars of Idaho" says the word is derived from the Shoshone word *bampnack,* meaning to throw backward, and was applied because of the long forelock of hair which the Bannocks wore thrown back over the crown of the head.) In the fifties this tribe was greatly dreaded, and in '78 the Bannock War was the last major Indian uprising of the Northwest; but the first travelers found them amusing and helpful.

In very early trapping days a boatload of American trappers were caught in the pull of a fifty-foot fall on the Snake River and plunged over to their death. Because its thunderings could be heard for a mile or so along the trail, the place was an often described landmark. The name American Falls commemorates the tragedy, but in the parlance of modern Idaho it indicates merely a town and a dam site.

Below the town, some two miles, the trail crosses the highway at an angle, going into the knolls which lie away from the river. It passes a spring surrounded by a maze of old camp roads, goes near the Indian Springs Hotel (where, on the day of our visit, a sheep was odorously dead on the roof of an Indian dugout) and winds out to the sagy rolling flat again. Some half-mile to the right, the Snake River cuts deeply through the lava, forming such high and abrupt cliffs that the majestic current can be glimpsed only at the curves. The "escarpments" described by Frémont, commencing here, for days on end presented their formidable barrier between the emigrants and the water supply of the great river they followed.

About ten miles from American Falls, we drove squarely between the Massacre Rocks. Like Scott's Bluff, these giant boulders formed an ideal spot for ambush and must have been an almost irresistible temptation to the Indians, used since time immemorial to supplying themselves with necessities by warfare of this kind. The particular incident which gave the rock its name happened in the summer of '62. The Indians were restive, and the train captains carried a leaden weight of apprehension; but still they traveled on, trusting themselves and their charges on the brittle surface of self-control and expediency which had briefly crusted over the undisciplined passions of a people unused to curbing their primitive desires. About four miles west of American Falls on the day of the massacre an ox train was nooning. One of the train later wrote his personal experiences as follows:

"A man came riding at full speed from down the river. He told us the Indians were robbing the train in which he was traveling, at a point about four miles from our noon camp. He had escaped with a horse and ridden back for help. When we came to the place of the attack with the teams, we saw a pitiful sight.

"There were eleven wagons in the train all of which had had the covers torn from them, the people's feather beds had been ripped open and the ground was white with feathers. Practically everything was taken from their wagons including all provisions and clothing. The only clothing they had left was what they were wearing, some of the men just having a shirt, overalls and boots. All their stock had been stolen, in fact out of 65 head of cattle and 11 head of horses the only animal saved was the one ridden back for help.

"It was a small train of only 11 teams and there were not less than 200 Indians that made the attack. There were only 25 men in the train and a few women. They killed one man and wounded one woman that was shot in the neck. We made arrangements to take them along with us and hauled their wagons to a suitable camping place about four miles distant. Here we found a horse train of about 12 wagons that was attacked at the same time the other attack was made. Eight of their horses were stolen and two of their men killed."

The woman who had been wounded died the next day. Two men were missing and never returned. Six others had been killed, and ten were lying wounded in the various wagons. The trail through Idaho was not a path of roses in the sixties.

Two miles from Massacre Rocks, down in a hollow, is the old Rock Creek Camp. The wagons crossed the streamlet at the foot of the descent, traversed the little flat, and pulled out again up several deeply cut gorges. Jutting up in the hollow are rocks which fairly exude names and dates. Among others we found the one word, Mann. It interested us principally because Henry R. Mann's unpublished diary had helped us over many a rough spot in Sublette's Cutoff.

Another four miles and we crossed Fall River—called Beaver Creek by many of the pioneers—a stream of great natural beauty. In July, 1850, Margaret Frink wrote that the campfires along its banks were as thick as city lights. We found the river a clear, transparent golden brown under shadowy trees; its glassy water full of sunken rowboats and a rusty automobile or two.

Fall River was the last camp of the combined migration, and now the pioneers were actually marking off the miles on the day's trip that would mean many a goodbye. For the forking of the trail at Raft River was the parting of the ways. The ones who took the right-hand turning arrived eventually in Oregon, while those who turned to the left finished their journey (if they were lucky) in California. Each step of the oxen took them farther apart, probably never to meet again. Sometimes, as the plans and objectives of a man changed en route, the plows for prospective Oregon farms, which had been hauled with such difficulty thus far, were pitched overboard and the owners plunged into the left-hand line of gold-seekers.

Youth turned toward California. Turned also the hothead, the adventurer, the gay ne'er-do-well, the invincible optimist, the gambler.

This must not be interpreted to mean that great and good men were not among them. Most of them were of the highest type, men who went to California for health, for business opportunity, or for the sheer, crashing adventure of it; but they had poor companions. On the contrary, the solid, dependable, steady line that turned to the right was here purged of most of its riffraff and undesirables.

We joined the contingent of sterling citizens and started for Oregon.

21

In Mormon Territory

ON THE THIRD DAY of a brand-new summer vacation we turned up again (no doubt to the curator's distress) at Fort Bridger. This time the fort was not an objective in itself. It was just the jumping-off place for the emigrant road leading to the valley of the Great Salt Lake. We got our usual early start, and for half an hour drove briskly along the Lincoln Highway between the yellow clover patches and natural meadows of the valley where the old trail looked as if it had been made with a gang plow. Then we turned up a draw into sage-covered foothills, completing what would have been a long morning's haul for the ox teams. Twenty minutes later we had left the highway, and a flourishing growth of junipers proclaimed the summit of the first ridge.

Impressions remain of this little-visited region: a sagy draw, studded with tall cottonwoods and watered by a very unimpressive piece of the Big Muddy; a beaver-felled tree, roughly tapered by strong teeth; a barn, enormous out of all reason; antiquated oil derricks; an old store with a false front far away across a meadow, in company with an incongruous modern hotel which might have been empty for all we could tell; a peculiar roadbed where we bowled along easily—very narrow, beautifully graded with long, painfully exact fills and absolutely no traffic; a meadow bottom full of rotting railway ties; and finally the idea becoming fixed in our minds that we were on a railway grade, never finished and never used. With us, all the way, went the trail, sometimes plainly marked for a half-mile at a time by reddish ruts through cover-weeds and sage.

Presently we picked up Sulphur Creek, a yellowish thread of water that one might step across, and went along with it through round, naked hills toward the Bear River. Along its course we found a motley collection of buildings and corrals—what I call in my notes a "pole, sod, and rawhide" ranch—and a number of ruined stone kilns where sheep bed down at night. A small sign up a canyon called attention to Stovepipe Oil, bringing to mind the fact that the guidebooks listed a tar spring within a mile of the Bear River ford where the wagon masters could refill their swinging buckets of axle grease.

Sulphur Creek, the trail, and we, all arrived at the edge of the Bear River bottoms within a few yards of one another. The trail went steeply down the low bluff and across the bottoms to a ford on the Fred Myers ranch. The Bear, nicely bedded down in cushions of big green trees, is not nearly so large at this point as it is where the travelers on the northern roads encountered it at the end of Sublette Cutoff. It was, so we gather from trail manuscripts, of somewhat the same temperament and character as the Weber River—a mountain stream, full of big round rocks and the devil in general. In stormy weather it was difficult. "Forded Bear River," wrote Franklin Langworthy one rainy day in 1850. "The most terrific stream to cross we have yet encountered. . . . Indeed it is a perfect sluice running down the side of a mountain, the top of which is covered with snow. Our cart, by happening to steer precisely the right course, came safely through, but a wagon was swept down, upset, and all baggage lost." We weigh against this crushing evidence the fact that Mr. Langworthy, although truthful, never minimized a danger, and the fact that it was the mildest of mountain streams when we saw it.

Practically every one camped here overnight, but it was the part of wisdom to ford before unharnessing. For one thing, it was hard to persuade a mule to take a river "in a cold collar," and second, it was never safe to wait until tomorrow. The stream might well be impassable by that time.

The boots of the bullwhackers were still seeping with Bear River water when Yellow Creek presented its peculiarities for their consideration. It had a bad reputation, and the ford was boggy; but the women admired the curious cliffs just above the crossing where round rocks were cemented together into a conglomerate mass culminating in freakish spires and pinnacles. Their admiration would have been perhaps greater if all the rocks had been content to remain in the cliff; but these were rolling stones, and many of them appeared to be in the creek bed trying to disprove the old adage about moss.

The teams lurched and fell on the slippery, uncertain footing and, as the wagons of William Johnston's mule train took the water, the drivers, one after another, were yanked from their seats by the jerking of the fallen lead mules and soused precariously at the heels of the wheelers. One man, who seemed to be quite a character among them, decided that he, for one, would not get soaked to make a Roman holiday for the laughing crowd of men who uproariously lined the creek banks. He removed his clothes and carefully piled them inside the wagon, taking the driver's seat in a state of nudity in the full faith that he would be pulled into the water long before the stream was passed.

The lead mule of this team, as it happened, was itself rather a character and had been endowed with the descriptive title Lousy. We are informed that it could scratch its ear with "the hoof of its hinder legs." Unfortunately Lousy used such beautiful judgment in charting a course among the rocks that the wincing driver was borne in unwilling triumph clear into camp across the creek, as, of course, it was beyond thought to jeopardize such good fortune by stopping en route.

Some marshes where the wagons mired—a difficult ravine and a steep descent—accounted for a few more miles, and the headwaters of Echo Creek were reached. The emigrants found the upper part of Echo Canyon very disconcerting. They had never (except for a few hundred yards at Three Crossings and Ash Hollow) been hemmed in by natural walls. The diaries go into amazed details about the natural properties of a canyon very much in the same fashion that the depth of Ash Hollow was overstressed. In the next three days the pioneers had completed a college education in canyons and were going on to postgraduate work; but now even the shadows distressed them. Only during the middle of the day could they actually see the sun. The cattle and mules, too, were uneasy. They lowed and brayed continually, to be answered tirelessly by the multitudinous echoes which gave the place its name. Lonely eagles soared over cliffs which were dotted with caves and dripped boulders. The narrow bottoms were prolific of springs and vast heaps of rocks fallen from the crags above; but in spite of hazards the caravans wound for eighteen miles down the crooked canyon, crossing the stream about once every mile.

The west end of Echo Canyon is today, perhaps, one of the best known stretches of the pioneer trail. Both highway and train parallel the wagon route, and many hundreds of modern pilgrims ride beside the old wheel tracks without a flicker of interest.

The health of the migration had improved, but the roadside was not without its quota of graves. Thissell tells us that on July 25, 1852, a lonely group of three wagons camped in the canyon—a terrible place to be attacked because of the high cliffs which commanded every foot of its floor. The setup was too tempting and the Indians yielded to their old-time method of getting glory and a few groceries. Not a person was left alive. They were buried by the next train in six large excavations. In 1853, when Thissell passed the ill-fated camp, the wagons still stood guard over the graves.

Even though some voted Echo Canyon the worst road they had so far encountered, it had its advantages. Besides its marvelous springs of fine water, it provided the luxury of a mountain sheep steak—if the train could spare a hunter to go after one. "Mountain hens" made good potpies, and the women had ample time to cook while the wagons were being wangled across the unaccommodating creek bed. They also picked service berries and wild currants, which provided a much-needed dietary change. So little did the wagon trains get in the way of fresh fruit that the children—and men too—had to be carefully watched to prevent sickness from overindulgence in this abundance. Rosebushes massed heavily along the creek, and, as the men cut brush to fill in the marshy spots, the women literally walked on paths of roses.

Eventually the canyon ended. Echo Creek was swallowed up by the sweeping, dangerous current of Weber River, and the pioneers were faced with another choice of routes. Weber Canyon lay across their way, and they might go either up or down.

We took a couple of days for each route.

To go up Weber River a motorist may turn left at the Echo Reservoir and pass through Coalville and Hoytsville, where seemingly each modern home has the original log cabin somewhere in the yard; then over a high sage plateau to the Kimball Junction. He should then take the highway leading west. The trail is just below it, humping along the creek and gradually worming up to the top of the ridge. It crosses the summit near the Beehive Inn and starts down through thick groves of aspens. The upper reaches of East Canyon Creek presented themselves at this juncture as a way out of the dilemma, and the prairie schooners went over the brink into the ragged, steep ravine much as a man might step out of an upper story window if a fire were at his back. Franklin Langworthy took this nerve-racking chute into Salt Lake Valley. We will let him tell the story, with due apologies for his being a trifle overwrought when he wrote it.

"We then descended ten miles," complained Mr. Langworthy bitterly, "through the most ragged and frightful cañon in all this region. I think we descended three or four thousand feet in the course of the ten miles. Down this fearful declivity rushes a small river, at the bottom of the cañon roaring loudly, as it tumbles over a succession of cataracts. We have to ford this stream thirty-nine times, and no crossing can be worse. In the mean time the mountains on each side are nearly perpendicular, and in some places the towering cliffs seem actually to impend over the traveler's head.

"In several places, the mountains of naked rock from each side come down at so sharp an angle, that the only road is the channel of the river itself. Down this we go, pushed along by the current, and floundering over huge boulders in the stream. The road resembles a huge flight of stairs, like Jacob's Ladder reaching from earth to heaven. The path consists of small rough stones, mingled with dry dust, and at the sharp pitches the wheels are locked, and the carriage slides from top to bottom. In many places barely chaining the wheels is not sufficient; in such cases, a strong rope is fastened to the hind axle of the wagon, a number of men take hold of it, and, by holding back, the carriage is steadied down the hill."

To explore down the Weber River the motorist turns right at the Echo reservoir and proceeds about a mile to Echo City. Exhibit A is Pulpit Rock, where, so the townspeople told us, Brigham Young stood to preach to his followers in 1847 on the way to their new home in the Salt Lake Valley. From the confluence of Echo Creek, the Weber flows six miles through velvety meadows starred with wild flowers and then slips into the mouth of a rock-bound canyon where, in trail days, the wagons could not go. The railroad and the highway, by the aid of up-to-date engineering, are able to follow the river, and the traveler will most easily recall the canyon by reviewing the postcard he bought of the famous Devil's Slide which disfigures its left-hand wall.

Somewhere in the six-mile stretch preceding the canyon mouth the emigrants had to get across the Weber, and the sooner the better, for it picked up small tributaries along the way. It is definitely a mountain stream, and the early parties—those, for instance, who arrived before the end of June—found it dangerous. A horseman who carried a rope end across the stream wrote in his diary: "Its great resistance to the current almost dragged me from my saddle. Had I been pulled into the stream my only hope of escape from drowning would have been in clinging to the rope until drawn ashore." Another incident to weigh in the balance against the quiet midsummer beauty of Weber River is the story of the old lady who was swept from her wagon into the tumbling current and rolled along struggling and more than half drowned as far as the next bend, where an agile stranger climbed on a jutting rock and fished her out.

The emigrants left Weber River near the mouth of the unfriendly canyon, and stayed with timid little Henefer Creek its few feeble miles up the rough hillside. Beyond its headwaters the great wagons rolled and thundered through Pratt's Pass on the summit of a low divide. Down another steep hill the wagons pitched while all hands and the cook held back on ropes and on the wheels; along the bed of a tiny streamlet, crossing and crisscrossing it for two or three miles down to East Canyon with its steep rocky watercourse known variously as Canyon, East Canyon, or Kenyon Creek. Here they really learned the meaning of the word "trouble."

Small shallow East Canyon Creek had to be forded ten or more times; the trail was crooked beyond reason and thick with amputated willow stubs, testimony to the Herculean task accomplished by the Reed-Donner party in forcing a passage through the mountains at this point in 1846. The Mormons, traveling in their footsteps a year later, accomplished the thirty-five-mile trek from Weber River to Salt Lake Valley in three days; but they recorded that it took the Donner party sixteen days of hard labor to win through to the valley. For years the cut willow stubs remained, and the animals baptized them with blood from torn hoofs and gashed legs.

From East Canyon the trail led up a ravine worn down by a narrow and precipitous creek full of bottomless mire and huge boulders "over which mules and wagon wheels had to be pulled or lifted constantly." William Johnston continues: "Thus in labors inconceivable and altogether undescribable we toiled up the well nigh inaccessible heights of the Wahsatch of Utah range—our night camp was in the ravine and never before had the men, mules and wagons been so closely huddled together, for on either side we were hemmed in by precipitous walls."

When they reached the top of this four-mile climb the wagons were at the highest elevation of their entire journey so far, and about two thousand feet above the point where they had entered East Canyon. Here, on the fir-crowned summit of Big Mountain, the migrating Mormon columns had their first view of the promised land.

A mile and a half down, and down. No animals were left on the wagons but the faithful wheelers remaining to hold up the tongues. Every available man held back on a rope. By '49 the timber had been cut for the building of Salt Lake City and the caravans twisted here and there between the jagged stumps down to a small, sheltered hollow known as Mountain Dell. It was a lovely meadow, but miry. The wagons often celebrated their return to the horizontal by stalling in the mud with promptness and precision, and the tired travelers, admitting that they were sunk, gave it up for the day, camped, and fought mosquitoes.

*   *   *

We needed a map—a map of Big and Little Mountains—so we went to the Mormon Church offices in Salt Lake City. Mr. Jenson, the church historian, was most cooperative and allowed my husband to hunt through their old map files.

After a two-hour search, he found one. The two men then checked its detail with the daily diary of Brigham Young and found it quite correct.

Armed with a hastily made blueprint, we started the next morning to conquer Little Mountain. I shall pass over the difficulties of getting there, and commence at the top.

We were afoot at the moment, and, as we stood on the summit, Mountain Dell lay below us on the east. To the west a steep descent and a long canyon led to the valley. Little Mountain swarmed with surveyors plotting the route for a new highway, and their camp spread white-tented and efficient, crowding the hayfields of the ranch that occupies the Dell. Somewhat to the north were the ranch buildings with a line of sheets draped across the yard like a row of fat Roman senators engaged in aesthetic dancing. Beyond them was a Pony Express marker.

Many companies camped on top of Little Mountain and rested before attempting to descend, but Mary Ackley recorded that her company made a bad error of judgment and started down in the evening. In no time all the able-bodied men were clinging to ropes that steadied the wagons, for they were appallingly difficult to control and manifested a giddy tendency to fling themselves tail over tongue. Hours passed, and still they could find no level place on which to stop. It was the middle of the night when they crossed a secure spot, drew the wagons out of the trail and lay down supperless and exhausted until morning.

On July 12, 1852, John Clark went down the west side of Little Mountain, "the steepest, roughest and unchristian like road to be seen in any country." He continues: "We alighted in safety and camped at the foot of the mountain where we had a good and full view of the tide of emigration as it came tumbling down the steep sides of the mountain. Sometimes the wagons would get before the teams which it would drag after until brought up by some hoary headed rock, when wagon, oxen, women and children would all tumble together in one confused mass of matter amid the wreck of which would soon be heard the screams of women, the yells of children and the swearing of men." Seven miles yet intervened between these recklessly intermingled people and the City of the Great Salt Lake, most of them in narrow, rock-bound, brushy Emigration Canyon.

Between Emigration Canyon and the city the wagons slowly filed past the spot, now called Journey's End, where Brigham Young spoke the well remembered words, "This is the place." Just ahead the "City of the Saints" spread before them, three miles in each direction.

"It is divided into large squares," wrote Franklin Langworthy in 1850, "by broad streets crossing each other at right angles. Through each street runs one or two small canals of pure water, and they run with such velocity that their rushing sound may be heard in all parts of the city. Water is thus brought to every man's door, and can be easily turned so as to water all the gardens and lots in the city. But a small proportion of the city lots are as yet improved, and the whole place resembles rather a neighborhood of farmers and mechanics, than a city, and the number of inhabitants may amount to five thousand.

"There is but one place of public worship, and this is a mere temporary edifice, called the 'Bowery,' the length, one hundred feet, and the breadth sixty. The walls are ten feet high and made of unburnt brick. The roof is covered with boards, overspread with earth, and supported by a great number of posts or pillars, which are the rough bodies of small trees. It is seated with rough benches, and will contain, perhaps, two thousand persons, and is generally thronged on Sunday."

The Bowery was soon replaced by two permanent buildings.

The twelve-foot wall which inclosed the ten-acre Temple Square was built in 1853. The granite Temple was begun at the same time and took many years to complete. It is never open to Gentiles, but the interior of the quaint, squat, dome-roofed Tabernacle is included in the tourists' sight-

Mormon handcart.

(From a bronze casting in Salt Lake City)

seeing tour. Just about the time your feet get tired, you are led gently but firmly into this oddest of buildings; seated lonesomely in a space designed to hold ten thousand people, and told to be still while the organ plays. And you are glad to be still, for the unique instrument composed of hand-made wooden pipes, lovingly fashioned by old-time Utah artisans, is said by musicians to possess the sweetest tone of any organ in the world, and the building, made without nails and held together with rawhide thongs and pegs, has perfect acoustic properties.

In the Temple grounds stands a monument gratefully erected to the memory of the gulls that, attracted by unlimited food, flew inland from the Great Salt Lake and saved the irreplaceable seed crops from locusts in the first few months of Mormon residence in their new home.

To the Argonauts of '49, the Mormons were a fascinating enigma. They had declared themselves an independent state and were functioning in that status; but actually the group was a more or less benevolent dictatorship with Brigham Young at the head, and he, partly from the exigencies of the situation and partly from temperament, would not tolerate adverse comments.

To the men of the migration who kept journals (rather a superior group on the whole) this gag rule was the most offensive item encountered. For the kindly and helpful people as a whole they had very little but praise. The Mormons were quite destitute of comforts, but industrious and thrifty. Furthermore they were determined to succeed. What little they had, they shared with those who needed help, and many an invalid remained in Salt Lake City to be nursed back to health. The chief elders were masters of budget balancing. They carefully trained their people to turn the needs of the migration to good account, and blacksmith shops and vegetable gardens brought marvelous returns. At first they refused coin, which had no value to them, and would only accept in trade articles that were "hard to come by." Coffee and sugar are most often mentioned, but by 1852 they had sent to France for the sugar beet and had it under cultivation.

To the women of the migration this large settlement of adobe houses was a welcome sight, and the reassuring glimpses of ordinary women like themselves at home in neat kitchens gave them confidence. Of course they had a perfectly human and rather excited curiosity about a community where the men might have all the wives they could support, and where spinsterhood was unknown. Some women of the wagon trains, both young and old, went no farther west.

Lucy Cooke, arriving July 8, 1852, wrote to her sister: "I was very pleased with the appearance of the city. It seemed such a treat to see houses again, and to hear the chickens crowing as we entered the streets— we camped opposite a boarding house, and Pa, wishing to give us a treat, ordered dinner for our family, and oh, when we sat down to the table I thought never did victuals look more tempting! We had roast beef, chicken, green peas, potatoes, pie, cheese, bread and butter and tea. I thought the bread and butter seemed the greatest treat; and then it all looked so clean, and the house was so trim and neat. But you will laugh when I tell that so unused were we to chairs that on entering the parlor we each and all dropped down on the floor and thus sat until one of us remarked the situation, when we all laughed, and forthwith arose and took chairs."

Many emigrants spent the winter in the city, as the story of the Donner party (much embellished with untrue detail) had given every one a wholesome dread of the snows of the Sierra Nevada Mountains which lay ahead. William and Lucy Cooke with their baby girl were among those who remained, mingling with the inhabitants of the community, sharing their hardships and their pleasures. There was no tallow for candles. They spent their evenings by firelight. They laid in for the winter supplies of potatoes, squash, and sugar beets (delicious eating, they thought). Variety was not to be had, and flour and breadstuffs were the greatest luxury; but they were young and together and never complained. Meanwhile Lucy continued to write to her sister about themselves and about the Mormons. "William got a small piece of bacon once or twice," she exulted, "and we stood over it marking it off into sections for each day, to see how long it would last. And sometimes he stood over me and begged just one little piece more, for it was good." As to their Mormon neighbors: "So far as we have seen," she wrote, "they are very hospitable and kind to us 'Gentiles,' though we understand matters enough to be guarded in our speech respecting them or their doctrines, for there seems strict surveillance kept over all outsiders."

One old fellow, whom she had known as a non-Mormon in the East, indicated to her that it would be much better if she and her baby would leave her husband and come under his protection, but he received scant courtesy for his pains. "You can imagine how this proposition was received by me," she wrote to her sister. "The old scamp! With his slipshod gait and lank figure; with his long unkempt hair, almost down to his shoulders—a rare prize, he! How William did laugh when I got home and told him the offer I had."

Grace Greenwood in her book "New Life in New Lands," published in 1872, writes of the Englishwomen who came out as Mormon colonists and found human nature to be much the same the world over. One paragraph particularly appeals to me as an interesting thumbnail sketch of the situation: "A man who will beat his wife under Victoria, will not always have the grace to spare her under Brigham. Ill-used wives frequently appeal to that power which is absolute and ubiquitous in the Territory, and whose action is usually prompt and decisive. They carry all their intolerable burdens to the Lion House. So these Mormon wives declare that at the worst they are better off here than in the old country, where there was no division in the beatings, and no Brigham to appeal to."

Irrefutably, the Mormon doctrines attracted undesirables as naturally and unavoidably as adventurers followed the lure of gold to California, and often it was these low-minded masqueraders who brought contumely upon the whole colony. But, in the main, the people themselves were kindly and well ordered.

*   *   *

The day arrived when we were to skirt the north end of the Great Salt Lake. It had to be done, and we might as well get it over—especially, so my husband reasoned, as it was a cool week.

And so we turned north, out of the city.

This time we were deliberately passing up Hastings' Cutoff, which passes south of the lake, crosses the white hell of the Salt Desert and joins the regular California trail far ahead on the Humboldt River. In general, the first part of its course across the sand approximates that of the Wendover Cutoff Highway, and it is well described by Edwin Bryant in his book, "What I Saw in California." It was first blazed by Kit Carson guiding for Frémont in 1845; was traversed by a few famous caravans, best known among whom was the Donner party, and at the last carried a stream of deluded gold seekers who mistakenly dared its ninety-mile waterless desert in their mad rush to gain time. It was the most deadly stretch of road between the Missouri River and the Pacific and was totally abandoned after 1850. Hastings' Cutoff has many points of interest, is still miserably hard to negotiate and merits more space than I can give it. It was never a favorite route.

We turned our backs, or at least sundry cold shoulders toward it as we took the road to Ogden.

We had barely cleared Salt Lake City when we passed the warm spring that furnished the hot running water for the early Mormons' baths: women on Tuesdays and Fridays; the more favored males on the other five days.

For some miles we sped through a panorama of fertile farms where in the fifties the Mormon settlers charged five cents a night per animal for grazing privileges and gradually diminished the popularity of the Salt Lake route. To the right the Wasatch Range stood straight up to dizzy heights. It was dusty, and the walking women sank below their shoe tops. Weber River, now quite mature and well behaved, boasted a Mormon ferry which parted the travelers from four dollars per wagon; and near it was a settlement, named Odgen for the famous fur trader and officer of the Hudson's Bay Company.

About forty miles from this ferry, near Corinne, Utah, the ubiquitous Bear River again crossed their pathway on its way to the lake. Shuttling across its calm expanse was another Mormon ferry at three dollars per wagon, while hidden in its depths were, so the impoverished migration unkindly but firmly believed, pits dug by the ferryman to prevent any possibility of fording.

We got out to look at the gray river moving steadily on to an unpleasant death in a young inland ocean of brine.

"It's funny," said my husband thoughtfully, "that the Bear River was such a boon to the emigrants who took the Sublette Road—just about saved their lives I guess, and they never had to cross it either—while to the ones who came by way of Salt Lake it was always in the way. A bad ford at one place and a pay ferry at another, and they hardly needed it for water at either place."

"Maybe we'll wish we had it with us before this trip is over," said Bill, who had listened with much distaste to our plans for the day.

"It looks to me as if we would get plenty of water if that's what you mean," said Dr. Neff with a glance at the sky overhead.

We now left highways and the fertile, well tenanted land, and cut southwest toward the north end of the lake. Far ahead strange mountains rose from the mist, only the tops accepting light enough to show the deep worn ravines. We were directing our course to pass between the lake and a bare, yellow shoulder of hills that jutted down from the north. A storm had just preceded us, and we traversed marshy green flats patched with seeping white spots like festering sores. Fuming sulphur springs polluted the air. Black, long-legged, and long-beaked birds paced jerkily here and there, and a flight of graceful gulls passed above.

Erosion, both of wind and of water, has been busy here. Evidences of the trail are not so deep and unmistakable as elsewhere; but, to balance this difficulty, there has been no extensive fencing and no cultivation, and the roads have always followed the tendency to go as straight as possible from one water hole to the next. We were often in the trail itself, and never far from it.

At the point of the mountain shoulder we came to some brackish springs and Blue Creek flag station. A few lone freight cars stood there and made me wonder whether they had brought something to this desolate spot or had come to take something away. The trail, without circumnavigating the shoulder, crossed over its gradual slope, and we continued west with the railroad.

Most people remember the stirring history of the race between the Central Pacific (laying its tracks furiously from west to east) and the Union Pacific, coming madly to meet it. Of how the two construction crews finally met at Promontory Point and of the gold spike that was driven there. It was only natural to leave the straight course of the trail for an hour in order to detour to the Last Spike Monument.

A scattered collection of a dozen desolate houses was Promontory. A storm had struck here recently in concentrated fury. Damp debris clung in the fences and against the steps, and even now the day was dark with a heavy and portentous cloud overriding the sun and the atmosphere dank and weighty.

We left the car on a high, dry spot and, true to our small-town beginnings, picked our way down to the store for a little gossip. It was flooded out and closed; but the monument was in plain sight down the tracks, and we plodded through the clinging mud. As a triumphal climax, Dr. Neff picked up a bona fide railroad spike at the very base of the monument.

Twenty minutes took us back to the trail. We were now in "the rising seven miles" mentioned by Langworthy's conveniently verbose diary and modern grain fields had been inserted into his well described landscape. We completed the rise through the fertile acres of the enormous Sunset Valley Ranch. At the top was a view, unbeautiful but weird and exciting. To our left a sun shaft scintillated from the northernmost waters of the great inland sea, stained and distempered to a yellow tone. Ahead, the trail went straight down to a white, unhealthy-looking flat, while, pounding by us in the sage, swept the most spectacular pageant of horseflesh I have ever seen. No circus, horseshow, or cavalry parade has ever thrilled me as did this band running uncurbed and free, led by a gorgeous golden stallion. Palominos, they shone in a chance sun ray like gilt. In this isolated spot there is no need to guard them and no inferior breed with which they can mingle.

As the last golden beauty thudded down the hill we turned again to the glimmer-white flat spread below us, horribly cut into ditches and ridges by the fury of the cloudburst. We soon found this to be a slightly descending plane of about six miles.

The car rode the ridges like a tightrope walker but came to grief when we had to cross the narrow washes. Our front wheels each time went down obediently to the bottom and started up the other side. At about the halfway mark we formed an involuntary bridge. The rear wheels then dropped in with a thud and the rear bumper buried itself in the flourlike earth. Various things happened after that, but mainly we pushed. Somehow we always got through.

In the course of time we shoveled and grunted our way across the gutted flat land to the next group of brackish springs and continued all morning across unestimated gray miles under an angry sky. About noon we came to Hansels Mountains whose springs water a line of green fields. At the north end of this range we came to Snowville, now the biggest settlement in the vicinity, but known to the emigrants only for the big spring which was the source of Deep Creek. Deep Creek lasted six miles, and the emigrants followed it every step of the way to its sink on what is now the Rose Ranch, where it spread out and watered a square mile of luxuriant knee-deep grass.

The stage road in later years came, as we had come, around the end of the range, but the trail (so we were told locally) cut through a low, unexciting pass known as Monument Gap. We backtracked on this latter trail for many miles and became convinced that it is of much later date than the one described in the many diaries which we have read, and which are practically unanimous in declaring that they followed Deep Creek the whole six miles from the spring to the sink.

Every one camped at Deep Creek Sink, which was later known as the site of the Curlew Valley Stage Station. To us after our day's trip, heading across the Idaho line apparently into the center of the gathering storm, it seemed a perfect haven.

From the sink the wagons rolled on to Pilot Springs and then to Emigrant Springs near Strevell. From there they held the benchland short of the hills to the left and headed north through a gap into rougher country, having traveled west along the present Utah-Idaho line for close to forty miles.

From our position on the high slope after negotiating the gap we could see a town in the far distance. It was plainly, tantalizingly visible, like something seen through the wrong end of an opera glass, but our road seemed to have no relation at all to towns, and meandered maddeningly in a great half-circle back into the rolling sage foothills of Utah.

The trail kept right on across the valley toward the village, but we were helplessly bound to our vagrant little raveling of a road winding along through the tough, scrubby side-hill growth. Vague impressions of the next hour or two remain—of log houses, sod-roofed and flanked by green meadows occasionally emerging from the dull gray; of a large barnyard where my husband, getting out to make inquiries, was promptly treed in a hay-wagon by a young bull and had to be rescued by driving the car up to its very wheels; of a flat-faced cow with fetching white eyelashes that stared through the window at me during the process; of the road getting rougher and the sky ahead getting blacker, of a last and final inquiry, shouted at some men who were madly hauling hay, for a place— any place—to stay; of their shouted directions to go to "Grandma Yost's," and of our desperate race to beat the elements.

We were directly in front of her neat two-storied house when the clouds broke just over our heads and let their tons of water down.

Tucking my notebook under my sweater I bolted up the bordered pathway where the herbs were beaten flat, to the porch-sheltered kitchen door and, looking back, could scarcely see the car.

Grandma Yost opened the door hospitably, and the scent of warm earth and herbage becoming suddenly wet, drifted stingingly up to mingle with the pleasant homely smell of a wood stove.

The house was perfect of its kind. My room was small but very clean. Crocheted lace a foot wide flared showily from the pillowcases. A washstand complete with pitcher set and bowl had an embroidered splasher tacked to the wall behind it. An abalone shell held the soap. A self-conscious calendar of the year 1905 hung beside the splasher. The light came from a blue glass kerosene lamp sitting accurately in the center of a fluffy worsted tidy, which I had for years considered to be as extinct as the pug dog. Something bulky on the foot of the bed resolved itself into four patchwork comforters, thick and weighty, that sat squarely on top of the counterpane like stacked toast, and refused to tuck.

Night settled stormily down. Rain thrummed unceasingly on the slanting roof above our heads. As the hours advanced the howl of wind, the crack of thunder, the untold tons of water splashing, spinning down, united into a unique nocturne, slowly swelling to a mighty crescendo. And it rained and rained and rained. Toward four o'clock it cleared. Morning came fresh, crisp, and sparkling under a businesslike July sun. There was strong, fragrant new life in the herb beds fairly bursting in vivid gold-green.

After a short wrestle with the domestic problems presented by well buckets and wood stove, we got along famously and soon set on the table in the cozy kitchen an assorted meal of everything we could find, including cake, lettuce, and green onions, of which the pièce de résistance was a large plate of fried cakes.

These toothsome twists of fried piecrust disappeared like ice cream in an orphanage and were capable of variation according to the tastes of the company—Dr. Neff liking them stiff, and my husband limp. Whenever the supply ran low, Grandma Yost fried another installment, alternating the two varieties. The last batch were limp. Dr. Neff and I left my husband trying the effect of a green onion with his coffee and went out to talk to a man who was driving cows to pasture.

"Can we get into the City of the Rocks from here, with the roads as they are?" I asked. Not that it mattered. We should turn up there anyway after a while, I knew. I have a touching faith in my husband. "It will be bad for a while," he told us, "but the roads dry quick enough if they get a chance. The trouble is that it has rained every afternoon for a week and probably will again."

"That's encouragement enough for us," Dr. Neff opined, as our informant disappeared beyond the dripping trees. "We'll either be there or hopelessly bogged down by afternoon." And we went in to pack.

In the full flood of morning sunshine, the situation looked very different from that of the last night. A good road went straight toward the town we had so helplessly wished to reach. It proved to be Almo. Two big dome rocks, skyward at the left, were (we knew from previous visits) southern sentinels of the City of the Rocks, through which the Fort Hall road must come to meet us.

Winding rivers and dottings of conical hills make this section of the Idaho border distinctive, while the network of emigrant trails and old stage roads that mesh across the flat land, avoiding the hills, would fill a blueprint. We were now skirting the southwestern edge of the large flat Raft River Valley, watered by three branches of Raft River with their tributaries and traversed by three of the main routes to California: the Fort Hall Road, Hudspeth's Cutoff and our present line of travel, the Salt Lake Road.

Twenty miles wide from east to west and, on a hazy day, without apparent bounds to the north, Raft River Valley was always good for a few sentences of astonished description in any trail diary.

Yesterday, while the storm threatened, the Salt Lake Trail had annoyed us by wavering uncertainly back and forth near the state line. It had now made a dash into Idaho and was scurrying across the southwest corner. Its emigrant travelers took at once to the mountains, following a branch of Raft River for nine miles and then turning up a small creek into an open valley. It is cultivated now and blanketed in summer with golden grain. At a solitary farmhouse in the midst of the rolling fields a young woman responded to our request for information.

The Fort Hall Road came down from the City of the Rocks, she said, right across their ranch. The trail from Salt Lake City came up a canyon from the southeast (whence we had just accompanied it), and the two met in the open valley. Joining, they went west up the fast steepening slope (we turned and looked in the direction of her pointing finger) and disappeared over the horizon where a few scattering aspens marked the beginning of Granite Pass.

"It's really funny," she added, looking around her at the mountain swale filled with modern grain fields, "for it must be nearly a century since the name had any meaning, but we still call this hollow Junction Valley."

22

Cross-Lots with Mr. Hudspeth

SIX MILES FROM SODA SPRINGS, at the bend of the Bear, Hudspeth's Cutoff broke away to the west, cutting straight across four mountain ranges to connect with Raft River. The rounded elbow of road reaching north to Fort Hall and back was thus eliminated. An old Indian camped by the soda springs illustrated the difference in length and character between the two roads by showing the emigrant women a bucket. He ran his finger around half of the circumference, supposed to be the Fort Hall route, and showed them that it was longer than the diameter, representing the cutoff. Then he raised the bail in his slender (and very dirty) brown fingers and said "This—road." When the bail lay down along the rim it was flat, but when he raised it over the diameter it arched up in the middle. "All same," he said earnestly, and grunted an end to the interview.

The cutoff was opened in 1849 and soon drained the California-bound traffic from the Fort Hall road. When Fort Hall was abandoned the Oregon settlers, too, followed the majority, and by the middle fifties the older route was almost deserted.

Hudspeth's or Myers' Cutoff derived its two names from the men who first committed the colossal imprudence of taking a wagon train across its uncharted mountains. The date of its opening is neatly fixed by the unpublished diary of Mr. Mann. When he passed Sheep Rock on his way to Fort Hall, the first wagons had not yet ventured from the beaten path. Shortly thereafter Myers and Hudspeth turned their teams sharply west in an effort (so it appeared later) to drive directly across to the Humboldt River in Nevada. Train after train fell in after them, shearing from the regular road and toward the mountainous horizon with an abandon only to be likened to sheep short-cutting off the edge of a cliff. Ordinarily careful men took their families over four roadless ranges on the off chance of arriving at the Humboldt ahead of the teams then on the Fort Hall road.

Meanwhile Mann reached the fort and, in the course of time, Raft River. He journeyed up its sluggish current to the point afterward known as the junction of the two roads, and there, on July 24, 1849, he saw the dust of the approaching Hudspeth train. "Messrs. Hudspeth & Myers, of the Jackson Co. Mo. Co.," wrote Mr. Mann that night, "have just made their appearance through a gorge in the mountains. They left the main road at the point where we left Bear River, going west to a gap in the mountains—they intended to come out at the head of Mary's River but not understanding their true latitude have struck the old road before it crosses the dividing ridge to the Basin. They would have made some 200 miles on the old road had they succeeded but as it is they have made nothing. They were almost thunderstruck when upon inquiry, they found they were only some 70 miles from fort Hall."

It might have consoled Messrs. Hudspeth and Myers somewhat could they have known that the broken tracks left in the wake of their heavy wagons were deepening hourly as more and more, and still more hastening trains grasped the promise of ungrazed grasses and shorter mileage; and that these same tracks were soon destined to become the main stem of traffic for the gold-bound thousands.

The saving in mileage was estimated at anything the optimistic writer of any given journal happened to guess. Ninety miles was a favorite figure. It was actually in the neighborhood of twenty-five.

On August 9th, when the cutoff had been used for three weeks, Elisha Douglas Perkins arrived at Sheep Rock and wrote: "Came to the fork in the road the left hand being the cut off of which we have been told. Found that it had been considerably traveled by wagons also our Masonic company decided to use it too so we all started on together. At the 'Forks' we found several notes and cards innumerable stuck up for the benefit of various companies behind, several of which we read stated that 'by this cut off it is only 100 miles to Humbolt River.'" The fallacy of the notices was, of course, inspired by the original purpose of its explorers. They are also a proof that no one was turning back; else, in three weeks' time, they would have been corrected. Once the Rockies were behind them it was easier for the travelers to continue, no matter what misfortune thinned their ranks.

All these data and many more, we had collected and carried with us as we left Soda Springs and moved six miles west to Sheep Rock. Here the tiny settlement of Alexander is practically at the spot where Hudspeth's wagons took off into unknown difficulties.

To the right, turning northward, was the road we had taken to Fort Hall some weeks before. To the left, extending southward, the route taken by the Bidwell-Bartleson party pushed down Bear River toward the Great Salt Lake. Somewhere, radiating west from Sheep Rock, surely there would still be traces of the cutoff. We spread out fanwise and commenced to circle through the heavy growth and scattered lava rock. We were rewarded by a small, *very* small, back road, polka-dotted here and there with jagged black rocks the size of one's head—an almost deserted road bravely insisting on its integrity amongst gigantic and encroaching sage, and, what was more important, following the course of Hudspeth's wagons.

The first eight miles led straight across a level valley floor broken into spasms of lava and dominated by two blunt and hollowed cones known as "the craters." We climbed one of them. It is ordinary and harmless now, even grass-grown down its previously convulsed interior.

We passed through the town of Central and, after an interval, came to Lund at the far edge of the valley backed up against Fish Creek Divide. Just short of the latter, the trail split. The left branch was visible, heading for a depressed spot in the hills known as Low Divide, while, ahead and slightly to the right, the more venturesome had urged their cattle to a saving of five valuable miles by climbing straight up and over High Divide. Their wagons, moving through a spatter of round black junipers, stirred clouds of smoky white dust until, having gained the crest, they were rewarded by nothing more reassuring than a prospect of tumultuous heaving mountains. A good secondary road took us between the two branches and, for the most part, within sight of both.

Half a mile down the west slope the trail from High Divide crossed our road and slanted off to the left to join the road from Low Divide and slither down the little canyon of Fish Creek. They and we both struck the Port Neuf River at the bend near Lava Hot Springs. We took our car across the river and brought it back into the trail just beyond the town. The emigrants did not have to cross the Port Neuf but touched briefly at the bend, sometimes using it for a camp. Its green banks under sheltering trees were a picture of cool serenity, but in 1850, a printed placard marred their beauty. It stood over the grave of one John Dennis, late of St. Louis, and had been placed there by a party who found him dying by the roadside. They gave him the best attention and help that they could and, when their best was not enough, buried him decently on June 29th. Just another high-hearted adventurer who had left loving arms at home to try his luck in the emigration; had found the emigration careless and cruel and had died, lonely and frightened, in the midst of thousands. He wanted his family to know (the little notice said) that his company had abandoned him. I wonder if they ever got the news.

A mile or so beyond the bend Dempsey Creek flows in from the south. The wagons, wallowing in rough ravines, managed to cross it and continued through hills covered with scrubby conifers and occasional clumps of aspens toward Arimo. We were able to stay very close to the wagon ruts clear to the crest of the second range where the wind screamed over the hilltop driving sand endlessly over the misshapen shrubs, scouring and polishing the very rocks.

One large boulder was worn to an unbelievable smoothness, pale mother-of-pearl in its coloring, and slipped beneath the hands like glass.

From its vantage point the course of the Port Neuf was in plain view to the rear while ahead a friendly little country road wound ankle-deep in dust and sand down the sunny hill slope into Arimo.

The early travelers, dropping into this goodly valley, found a large swamp, or, as some called it, a bulrush pond, feeding a sluggish creek full of reeds, and teeming with water fowl. The camp cooks were often encouraged at this point to attempt duck stew—a laudable ambition frustrated only by the lack of suitable fuel. It was quite possible to boil coffee or fry bacon over a sage fire, which was exceedingly quick and hot; but any optimist who attempted to boil beans or stew anything wore a path between his fire and the nearest sage patch.

The modest, square-steepled church at Robin swam into view and was presently lost again as we approached a gash in the mountain spur ahead known locally as the Gap. It is very like Devil's Gate, only narrower and minus the river. If the evil one himself had cleft it through solid rock with one blow it couldn't look worse. It sucked us through, however, safely enough, and spewed us out into Hawkins Basin.

The prairie schooners could not use this freakish passage, which probably had to be cleared of debris with a few well placed sticks of dynamite, and so they crossed the spur a few miles to the left. It took us two hours to pick up their tracks within the narrow end of the basin, and while tracing them out again we saw ahead of us an interesting phenomenon.

In the soft olive shadow of the hill slope, whitewashed in great brush-strokes down the steep declivity, were streaks showing the course of the caravans. The wheels had cut through a substratum of limestone and dragged it to the top, much as if each wagon had carried a leaky flour barrel leaving its telltale trace behind. The stained hillside was on our right as we went up a rocky, sagy draw to the summit. If this were a road it was never traveled, for a spring gushed across it, using the ruts for a runway. There was one miry spot of indeterminate depth which, under ordinary circumstances, would have demanded probing, but the road (Heaven save the mark) proved unbelievably sideling. The slipping mud made it dangerously so. We drove into the spring hole gladly as a spot of safe anchorage and lurched through, coming almost at once to Malad Springs, the first good camping spot since Hawkins Basin. Here aspens in tattered bunches made some effort to cloak the shivering mountainside, and the white faces of staring Hereford cattle dotted the shadows under the trees.

Bill rode the running board and frequently checked the height of the mound between the wheel ruts, lying flat on his stomach and gauging the amount of daylight remaining between our crankcase and the current bump. Finally there wasn't any more daylight between them and he got in. The top surface was soft and we sheared it off without doing any particular damage. Occasional holes and small logs across the road varied the monotony.

After a half-hour's advance into the purpling hills ahead the hare-brained little road quit for the night.

Our car stood perched on the brow of a hill which dropped sharply, sloughing off into a canyon.

In the weird half-light the blurred, black rounded trees below seemed a bubbling witch's brew in which we were about to be completely submerged. A narrow ditchlike gully presented itself as the current substitute for road, and slanted straight for the canyon.

"Well," said my husband with decision, "if we go down there, we'll stay down. Nothing short of an army tank could get up again."

I looked around with distaste. The canyon might not be tempting, but I didn't care much for my present surroundings and said so.

"Yes, but you can," argued Bill, "at least get back to Soda Springs from here, and you can't from down there."

"That's just it," said his father. "We aren't sure we can get anywhere from down there. On the other hand it must be fifty miles back to Soda Springs."

I rocked on my heels and looked down the absurd little shell-shocked gully which in 1849 had successfully landed the prairie schooners right side up at the foot of the hill. I was too tired and hungry to be discreet. "Which way is closest to dinner and bed?" I inquired shortly.

"Straight ahead, of course, even if we have to walk," said my husband. He hates to backtrack.

Well, we risked it, sometimes sliding with all brakes set and once anchoring a wheel against the inside bank while we charted the remainder of our course. In five minutes we had arrived intact at the foot of the declivity and started foot by foot and yard by yard to follow the canyon.

Nobody said much, for it was gradually sinking in that this was an ill judged proceeding. We were entirely lost. Our maps meant nothing, and if we had to walk it was doubtful that we could find a town that night.

It was almost dark when the trail merged softly into plowed ground and we knew that we had found a farm. The astonished family told us that we had just negotiated a section of the old trail known as Turkey Tracks. Sheep wagons sometimes come that way, the rancher said, in a poor year when they need feed badly; but they have to tie trees behind the wagons in order to get down the hill. He helped us to relocate ourselves geographically and said that the nearest accommodations for the night were more than thirty miles ahead in Curlew Valley. We turned gladly into the county road that went past the ranch and, pulling a great spreading tail of dust like an unexplained comet, put on an unaccustomed and welcome burst of speed.

*   *   *

The land of the Shoshones was now passed, and the country of the fierce Utes and the ubiquitous and utterly pitiable Shoshokoes, or Root Diggers, was ahead. The valleys and mountains of the cutoff formed a sort of borderland between the two.

As a race the Root Diggers were degraded and unpresentable, with a physique alarmingly overemphasized in spots. Tremendous swollen bellies topped shrunken limbs, and mops of hair which "looked as large as bushel baskets," full of sticks, dried grass, dirt, and other impedimenta perched on spindling necks. Their lives, even in summer, were one long effort to survive. How Providence preserved them through the winters (and why) was a moot question. In summer they slept like animals in hollowed dust holes scooped beneath the sage, remaining, it was said, until forced to move by their own accumulated filth. They lived swinishly on roots, eked out by a few piquant items such as wood grubs, grasshoppers and lizards. Fish and rabbits, they snared when and where they could get them; but the stronger tribes kept them away from the good streams and hunting grounds, and the timid Diggers ranged in the arid sections.

Occasionally, under favorable circumstances, they rose to the high excitement of an antelope drive. In preparation for this event the men slept in magnificent leisure for a week while the women piled up great hedges of sagebrush about three feet high and inclosing perhaps one hundred acres. After this the women watched and waited until the antelope entered the great trap by its single entrance. When enough were inside it must be presumed that some one woke at least one man who entered the circle and chased the antelope until he was tired. His place was taken by another and another and another. When the antelope were exhausted they were easily approached and clubbed to death. They never seemed to jump the hedge, probably because of its extent. Remains of these great windrows of sage were seen and described by various emigrants.

With the first appearance of this little people who sometimes congregated in large numbers but who, if alarmed, vanished each to his own hole, an itchy uneasiness spread throughout the emigration. Even though none were in sight, the crowding hills might be full of them and their very hunger made them dangerous.

Totally impervious to slight, the braver ones made social calls garishly attired in a single rabbit skin judiciously tailored, and were received without cordiality by women who afterward failed to digest their meals.

To eat—preferably to eat too much—was their driving ambition; and it must be admitted that, in years before they learned to distrust the white man, they would share their hard-gotten supplies with any who were so far reduced as to need them. But, above everything else, even more than food itself, these disgustingly misshapen, foul little people begged for mirrors, going into perfect paroxysms of eagerness "for the smallest fragment in which they might behold their squalid features."

All the valleys of the western half of the cutoff had been sporadically overrun by the Root Diggers, and as we left Curlew Valley the next morning we went through country which had once been open to them. We soon joined the trail, for it had docilely tagged along somewhat to the north of our last night's route and was plainly visible crossing the flat land.

After a rough passage, during which the component parts of our entourage exhibited no cohesion whatsoever, we arrived at Twin Springs. These were rather mildewed in appearance and stingy as to water. Below them a determined little bridge clamped tightly over a dry creek bed.

The road reaches this oasis through a peculiar ravine called the Narrows, but the trail comes straight across the level land. The emigrants were not hunting any tight-fitting ravines full of Diggers.

After walking around a bit we decided that, in the old days, the springs were often dry; for a waterless stretch occurred along here, variously estimated from twenty-two to thirty-one miles.

Because of local misinformation we missed the next short stretch of trail over the mountain top (one of the few gaps yet to be filled in); but from many diaries we know that the wagoners who took their outfits up this ridge utilized a dry watercourse—very narrow and rough. The wagons were wrangled up one at a time by the full force of men and draught animals. At the top the available flat surface was barely wide enough for a wagon to stand. In spite of this handicap the men must hitch all the animals except the wheelers to the rear axle hoping to prevent its turning "tail over head" on the terrific descent, which was the worst the travelers by way of Sublette's Cutoff and Bear River Valley had had to negotiate.

Lydia Waters' amusing reminiscences tell of her attempts to get the loose stock down this hill. The men had all gone ahead with the teams, leaving her, as usual, with a tough job to do. Now Lydia was perfectly capable of driving stock—she had driven them day after day and had taken her regular turn at driving the wagon; but this rocky descent was different. "As soon as I'd got one ox a little way down," she wrote, "I'd go back up after another. Then the first one, afraid of the steep decline, would follow me back up again. I would have been there a lifetime if George, after he had driven down, had not returned to help me."

Once started, they went down as if they had been poured out of a bucket; then on, through a mile of water-cut gorge twenty feet deep and seven wide, where the axles scraped the sides and the oxen must be driven from above; where rock ledges ran across the bottom of the chasm, binding fast under the axles of the enormous wagons so that they must perforce be lifted over them by wedges. One at a time, they brought the wagons through this ordeal, collected them again into an orderly caravan, and went on to Rock Spring.

We also came to the west side of the ridge not far from Rock Spring. We left our cars beside a log cabin where a small engine was put-putting away and a woman in a crisp pink dress was wiping a clothesline. To her we propounded the usual routine questions.

"Suppose the spring she spoke of isn't Rock Spring," I suggested in a small voice, as we moved off in the direction she had pointed.

"I've got way beyond the stage of supposing," replied my husband stonily. "It had better be Rock Spring."

Then we saw it up the next draw—a husky, devil-may-care stream of water welling out of a rock pile on the hot side hill, steady and never-failing. In trail years it was, without exaggeration, of vast importance, reigning supreme for one whole day in each of thousands of lives as the most vital item of their existence. It lay to the right as the wagons came down the hill. Without fail they groaned and creaked to a stop, watered the dust-parched animals, and filled the kegs, for the camping spot was a half-mile ahead, where the canyon flattened out. Dr. Wayman described the place, mentioned that wood and grass were scarce—two self-evident facts—and concluded by commenting testily on the soft road cut through sage. "By Ging, it beats everything in the dust line," quoth Dr. Wayman. And by this time he should have been a good judge.

The whole hour we spent at the spring was punctuated with the yapping of coyotes. As we returned (by a different route) toward our car the charivari grew louder and more earsplitting until we, from curiosity, traced the outlandish noise to its source—seven coyotes in a cage built against the face of a rocky bank.

My first reaction was surprise, but I soon became interested in the cageful as a sort of stage property—an appropriate orchestration for the drama of the gold trail.

For the coyotes, or small prairie wolves, were the bane of the whole emigration. Their yappings and lugubrious howls were the unwelcome lullaby which accompanied the tired pioneers' attempt to sleep. They sat hungrily outside the camp circle all through the night and, as soon as it was vacated in the morning, rushed in for the scraps and refuse. This was not so true during the gold-rush years, when the trail was solidly packed with teams; but the early Oregon migrations and those in the years later than '53 had always to reckon with the "wolves."

There were also more imposing wolves, large gray or white individuals encountered most often on the eastern half of the journey. They ran in packs but were often seen singly, skulking over the next rise or loping with deceptive swiftness along the flat land of the Platte. The smell of

Trail wolves.

them and their infernal howlings caused sedate mules and staid buggy mares to take French leave and depart for home; and their presence, much more than that of Indians, rendered a lost child an object of frantic anxiety until found. Both types could scent the taint of blood an incredible distance; and whenever a kill had been made, either of game or of domestic cattle for eating purposes, they made the night hideous. A shot or two would quiet them for a time; but during the Indian uprisings few camps cared to advertise their presence unnecessarily at night.

A fact, amazing but vouched for by good authority, is that wolves seemed never to touch the flesh of a Mexican. Whenever a Santa Fe caravan was attacked, dead Mexican muleteers littered the plains beside their comrades from the States. But when the escaped survivors brought back help and the roll of the dead was called only the Mexicans were left to be buried. The bodies of the others were so scattered that identification of the fragments was quite impossible. Various speculations were rife as to why this should be so. Some thought it was on account of the smell of cigarettes which the Mexicans smoked incessantly. Others insisted that it was because they were so saturated with red pepper, which was an important part of their diet.

From Rock Spring the trail strikes the open country and, meandering along a natural swale in a plowed field, passes just back of the barn on the Commons Ranch. We kept it in view and soon got the cars into it, winding up a ravine heavily padded with the usual scrubby growth of the Idaho mountains. The ravine grew to large proportions but the bottom remained V-shaped and narrow. We stayed in it until we reached and passed over the low summit. The landscape now presented an entirely new face, which, it might be added, was somewhat in need of beauty treatments.

Unhealthy bare spots in the thick growth gave the uneasy impression that the mountain might be beginning to moult. In one of these mangy clearings two foul, bare saucerlike springs were set like expressionless eyes. For sheer ugliness the place was prize-winning. Their trampled, oozing rims were a leprous gray-white. The slime-begotten contents were nauseating to look at and worse to smell. These staring holes, so we were informed later, are called Sublette's Troughs.

We hurried on: past the gleaming white bones of defunct log fences; past silent cabins falling quietly apart, past small aspens in unostentatious groups to acres of greasewood in full flower that spread a brilliant yellow mantle over the shoulder of the mountain. The trail was always near us.

The pass is some fifteen miles through and is very gradual. The emigrants described it thankfully as an easy road. Feed was fair, and springs were sufficient. They found time and energy to write along this stretch of road, to describe the view or to speculate on what lay ahead. Lydia Waters devotes a paragraph to the description of a traveling companion:

"An old Mormon camped with us. . . . He had a dashing turn-out; a cart with two wheels of different sizes, a wooden axle on which he never put any grease, a tongue made of a sapling with the bark still on, and his team consisted of a horse and cow with its calf. Whatever filled the cart was covered with rags. He sat on the front with his feet on the tongue, and when the wheels would give a terrible screech, he would turn his head first to one wheel and then to the other. That cart could be heard easily a mile away."

For five and a half miles we drove through interminable draws; past thirsty cattle nuzzling empty troughs; past a solitary woodcutter in a clearing; past several springs but little feed; through a circular gray flat which had been oozy and putrid before drying into a smooth cracked surface. In this arena (while I voiced genteel objections) the men, exhibiting a vulgar gusto nothing short of atavistic, proceeded to promote a bullfight.

And all the time the old cutoff, so long disused that full-grown aspens grew between the ruts, ran with us.

We had now come to the streamlet so much appreciated by the emigrants that they drove beside it for more than five miles. It is called Sublette Creek but was known in trail days as Muddy Creek. We felt that if we might remain with it until it made an exit into the valley below, our trek through the last of the four ranges would be over; but modern conservation methods were against us. Some one had built a dam in the canyon. The trail, of course, went through, but on a high curving line like the rim of a bowl our road could be seen taking its way around it. The roadbed proved an exciting foot or two too narrow, so that I made myself as adhesive as possible until, half an hour or so later, we completed our circumnavigation and were back with the trail beside the little creek.

Its canyon opens out into Raft River Valley, and some twenty miles or more of flat land lies between the emerging traveler and the point where he will enter the range of mountains to the west.

As we stood on Sublette Creek looking down and across the expansive Raft River Valley, the first car we had seen all day crept slowly along below us, sending up a plume of dust. Many a pioneer has paused just here to catch his breath, with the dust of his companions ahead rising like a land fog to blind him; but, if he could find time or space to step aside and gain a clearer forward view, he saw two other curling lines of dust across the valley: one hovering over the wagons from Fort Hall, the other springing from the feet and wheels of those who had turned aside on the Little Sandy to see the Mormon city of Salt Lake. With slow surety these two roads were now converging with his own. The wagons from Fort Hall, after separating from their Oregon-bound companions, had followed the west bank of Raft River and could be seen to meet the dust-cowled wagons from the cutoff at the mouth of Cassia Creek Canyon across the flat valley lands. The caravans from Salt Lake City did not continue so far to the north but disappeared into the western range and met the united northern routes in mountain-encircled Junction Valley.

A later trail, well marked for miles and running along the western edge of the valley, connected the two routes and made what was in effect a crossroad running from Salt Lake City north to Oregon; but in early trail days it was seldom, almost never, used. Seemingly no wagon ever deviated from its course. Just as the three forks of the Raft River unite to make one, so these three roads met and mingled their streams in a mighty flood that flowed inevitably west.

Straight ahead, in the middle of the valley, the three large branches of Raft River converge from widely separated sources to form the main stream. The apparent inaccuracies in different diaries telling of the Raft River crossings are explained by the geography of the valley and waterways. Diverging a scant mile or two to right or left, a wagon might cross one river or two or three. Some writers, more meticulous than the rest, mention the two little branches of the main forks, bringing the total up to five. In fact the material previously available gave us mental indigestion until verified by this day's field work.

Helen Carpenter arrived at Raft River in August, 1856. The Utes were troublesome that year, and all through the mountains her party found roadside messages warning them to take care. They believed themselves to be the last company on the road. There were only four men, with four women, three boys, and three young children. "Such a mere handful of humanity!" she wrote. They were justifiably frightened, and had even exchanged shots with some Indians by the time they came into the broad valley of the Raft. They were afraid to start crossing the river that afternoon and risk having dark settle down with part of the wagons on one bank and part on the other. They were also far too terrified to have lights or a fire, but put up their tents to deceive the Indians and then lay behind a barricade of ox yokes at some distance. The next morning they made the crossing and set out, hoping by forced marches to catch up with the next train ahead. Three or four days later, in Thousand Springs Valley, they did so with consequences that will be detailed at that geographical point in this travelogue.

The wagon bosses found the crossings of Raft River deep and narrow, with oozing, muddy beds. From there on, the few remaining miles of the cutoff lay straight before the wagons, thick with flour-white dust, but fully as good as many an eastern turnpike.

In the gold-rush years the marching columns of the cutoff met a comparable number from Fort Hall at the junction near Cassia Creek. Companies came together who had last parted at the bend of the Bear, and when they compared notes it seemed usually to be the man who had taken the older road who was interested in justifying his choice. He always managed to do so. It was longer, he would freely admit, but had more feed and fewer hills. Notwithstanding all arguments the cutoff (harder but shorter) absorbed the traffic, and by the later fifties the Fort Hall road was virtually abandoned.

Up Cassia Creek Canyon through rolling hills the two routes went on as one. Over rough roads in rougher mountains with strange steeplelike formations, the wagons shook and jolted, but those weary riders too young or too old, too tired or too sick to walk were promised rest and comfort when the City of the Rocks was reached.

Rocky City, Circle City, or Pyramid Circle: it had many names, but none of them was adequate. Its first amazing vista was gained, like a child's penny-peeper show, through a single steeply cut notch in the hills scarcely wider than was necessary for the wagons to enter. Here the weary crowd from the northern roads squeezed in to camp in an unbelievable pixy place—a large circle of slender crowding rocks, great monoliths stuck on end around an emerald meadow watered by a tiny crystal stream. Throughout the meadow were other stupendous rocks perched carelessly, here and there. By an accumulation of geological accidents the Rocky City is a place of unusual beauty—a sermon in stone. Its pyramids, like great bastion towers, protect the serenity of its sheltered meadow.

The City of the Rocks is now the cattle range of the Circle Ranch. The house is at the lower end near the gap through which the lumbering wagons entered, and we were told that the entire acreage within the rocky circle is fenced with but a few hundred feet of wire. But the carved and painted names and dates that smear the isolated rock masses are a reminder of the time when this natural stockade was held by an army of continuous occupation for a quarter of each year; each company remaining only long enough to mend its broken wagons and ailing bodies, then moving on to make room for the next. Without exception they entered its portals with joy and cherished its memory with affection. No—on second thought I will except the family whose infant boy was born there and departed from its walls and out into Junction Valley and all points west weighted for life with the unique name, Pyramid Alenso.

In leaving the circle, the wagons curved up among the rocks to the left and struck a smaller and less spectacular basin which they quitted by a gap between two rocky portals scarcely wide enough for two of the great schooners to pass together. Once released again to the outside world the columns descended gradually, drifting past the two Steeple Rocks and making for the valley where the lines of wagons from Salt Lake were flowing steadily along toward the great junction that would write "Finis" to a chapter of progress for both contingents and would, of a certainty, not immediately lead to anything better.

23

Along the Curving Snake

Just as the climax of the western movement into California is found in the mad tumult of the gold rush, so the high interest of the history of Oregon came six years earlier with the "Great Migration" of 1843. In order to comprehend the significance of this influx of almost a thousand settlers from the States it is necessary to have some understanding of the rivalry between the nations (narrowing down to England and the United States) for possession of the Oregon country. England, represented by the Hudson's Bay Company—oldest chartered organization in the world— held the Hudson Bay region and much of Canada, and her trappers spread out along the watercourses like the branching roots of a mighty tree. The United States staked her first claim to the West on the discovery, in 1792, of the Columbia River by Robert Gray who sailed from the port of Boston around the Horn, and anchored safely within the mouth of the great river which he named for his ship, the *Columbia*.

In the winter of 1803 the Louisiana Purchase was consummated, and the United States acquired from France all of the Mississippi Valley. Immediately the land neighboring it on the west became of paramount interest, and President Jefferson authorized the Lewis and Clark Expedition to explore its possibilities. The two men and their cortège started in 1804 and spent the winter of 1805-1806 at the mouth of the Columbia, having traveled by way of the upper Missouri River, through North Dakota and Montana and down the Snake and Columbia rivers, a route not afterward used. After an absence of two and a half years they returned with favorable reports of rivers filled with beaver. There was an eager market in China for all the pelts that could be shipped, and the enterprising John Jacob Astor grew interested. He had already amassed a fortune in the fur trade and now decided to expand his business to the Pacific coast. He sent two parties to the west. One, under command of Lieutenant Jonathan Thorn, sailed around the Horn and arrived at the

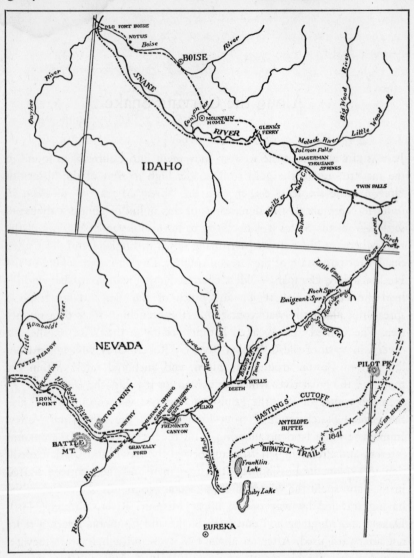

mouth of the Columbia, March 22, 1811, where it promptly established a trading post at Astoria. The other party, commanded by Wilson Price Hunt, proceeded overland. He expected to follow the route of Lewis and Clark but, in fear of the dreaded Blackfeet, left his planned course and went through the Wind River country. The party endured terrible hardships, touched at places what was later the Oregon Trail, and straggled into the little fort at the Columbia's mouth in the spring of 1812. Thorn's men were wild with joy and, in spite of the fact that the experiences of the Hunt party might well have dissuaded any one from attempting a return trip, Robert Stuart and five men were selected to make their way back to the States with dispatches telling Mr. Astor of their arrival. Stuart's route, with two or three deviations, probably including an unlucky circuit around South Pass, was practically that of the future Oregon Trail, and he and his men arrived at St. Louis in April, 1813. But history had moved faster than they. The War of 1812 brought Astoria into the hands of the British, who renamed it Fort George. It was a technical "capture," and the Treaty of Ghent which ended the war stipulated that all points taken by either side should be returned. Astoria became once more a part of the United States. In 1819, by a treaty with Spain the United States purchased Florida and renounced all claim on Texas; and Spain on her part gave up all claims to the Pacific coast north of the forty-second parallel based on early Spanish explorations.

On these premises the United States staked her claim to Oregon.

England did not concur, but in 1818 the two countries arrived at a working agreement that all lands between the forty-second parallel and 54° 40' and west of the Rockies should be open to both nations until a final settlement. The Hudson's Bay Company established headquarters of its own on the Columbia at the mouth of the Willamette and called it Fort Vancouver. From its position this settlement became of paramount importance to the American settlers, whereas Astoria was nearly a hundred miles too far west to afford assistance.

In 1832, Captain B. L. E. Bonneville, on leave from the United States Army, and Nathaniel Wyeth, a New Englander, with their parties made separate and unsuccessful trading expeditions into the Oregon country—financial failures, yes, but great successes in information gained and in historical results. The trail to Oregon, which had been almost as imaginary as the equator, was now a definite track through the wilderness.

In 1834 Nathaniel Wyeth left the Missouri River on his second unsuccessful trading expedition—the one ending with the building of Fort Hall. With him traveled the first party of missionaries to Oregon. They were Methodists and included Jason Lee, a big, well liked, companionable man, his nephew Daniel Lee, and three others. On Hams Fork the company came up with the hunting party of the English nobleman Captain Sir William Stewart, out after buffalo, grizzlies, elk, antelope, and other specimens of the big game of the new world. They went on together, and near Sheep Rock were overtaken by Thomas McKay with a band of Hudson's Bay trappers returning to headquarters. It happened that Captain Bonneville's exploring party was encamped near by, and the resulting festivities probably qualify as "romance of the trail." The personnel of the four parties, plus an encampment of amiable and hungry Indians, formed quite a gathering, and (so wrote a member of Wyeth's party) Stewart and Wyeth almost demolished Captain Bonneville's supply of diluted alcohol and honey, then termed metheglin. Bonneville left them, but the three remaining parties went northwest to the confluence of the Port Neuf and the Snake, where the winters were more moderate and the forage plentiful.

On the Snake (sometimes called Lewis Fork) Wyeth built Fort Hall and tucked his party in for the winter; but Stewart and McKay with their following started toward the Columbia. The missionaries went with them. There was genuine distress at parting, for friendship formed under such circumstances was often so deep and lasting that men seemed like brothers; but all these people had parts to play in setting the stage for the drama of the next twenty years. Wyeth, in constructing Fort Hall, built what might be termed the "take-off" for the last lap of the Oregon journey. Jason and Daniel Lee, in founding the mission at the Dalles, furnished what was for the first few years the finish of the overland trail, the terminus of the wagon road, the place where the emigrants' household goods were loaded on hastily constructed boats for the voyage down the Columbia.

The next year, 1835, when the traders' great caravan under Fontenelle came west to the rendezvous, they brought two other famous men, Samuel Parker and the young Marcus Whitman, both ministers. Men of the cloth were unwelcome among the rough packers, and at first their resentment took the form of petty annoyances; but cholera struck the party, and Whitman, besides being a man of God, was a doctor. He worked tirelessly, saved several lives, including that of Fontenelle himself, and cemented a lifelong friendship with many of the traders and mountain men. At the rendezvous he made an incision in Jim Bridger's back and removed an Indian arrowhead which had been embedded in the flesh for some years. Many a trapper who had never expected to get medical help short of a visit to St. Louis received advice and simple medicines.

The two ministers were astonished at the ease with which the traders' wagons crossed the Rocky Mountains. It would be possible, they felt sure, to bring women and household goods to Oregon and establish real mission homes. So they changed their plans and separated at the rendezvous, Parker to go on to the Oregon country and reconnoiter for suitable sites, Whitman to go back with the returning caravan, get more missionary families, and return the following year. He was successful. Narcissa Prentiss, in whom he was already much interested, consented to marry him and join in his work. They were given three companions, Henry and Eliza Spalding and a young man named Gray who from the beginning was slightly *de trop*. They made ready and came West with the traders' expedition of 1836, and this time it was Narcissa with her lovely blond hair and sweet singing who was the popular member of the party. The mountain man, Joseph Meek, was her devoted friend as long as she lived, and many others were won to sincere admiration of the consecrated little group.

The Spaldings were allotted to the friendly Nez Percé nation and lived too far from the trail to influence its future history in any marked degree. But the Whitmans, assisted by Gray, built the mission at Waiilatpu on the Walla Walla River twenty-five miles above the Hudson's Bay Company's fort, which was situated at the mouth, and commenced there their strenuous term of service with the sullen and resentful Cayuse Nation. The mission was forty-five miles from the emigrant trail, but the wagon columns detoured that way until after 1845, and individual companies did so until its destruction in '48.

Wyeth, meanwhile, gave up the unequal struggle and sold Fort Hall to the Hudson's Bay Company. He had departed before the missionaries, piloted by a guide hired at the rendezvous, arrived at the fort; and so it happened that the first white women to travel overland to the Pacific coast were received by a man whom he had left in charge. From then on the Hudson's Bay officials played host to hundreds of miscellaneous Americans traveling through for the expressed purpose of preempting the choicest lands. They received them kindly or, at the worst, politely; dined their leaders and captains; bought some of their discarded wagons for which they themselves had no particular use, and sold them provisions that were hard to replace. Many of the emigrants gave them, in return, gratitude and real appreciation; the rank and file of the migration took it all in their stride; but the disgruntled few thought it hard that there were not more provisions for sale, and that they cost so much.

The summer of 1841 saw a few families arriving in Oregon, and 1842 brought a real migration of one hundred fourteen souls. It brought also a letter from the American Board of Commissioners for Foreign Missions to its Oregon missionaries suggesting the abandonment of two of their holdings and the return overland of Mr. and Mrs. Spalding.

The mission personnel was aghast at the thought of curtailing their endeavors, and, besides, the American Fur Company had disbanded. Caravans no longer returned to the East each year. How could a man with his wife and small children hope to complete such a trip alone? The missionaries gathered at Waiilatpu for a formal meeting on September 26th, and Whitman made the proposal that he himself should go East that fall to intercede with the Board. The others agreed, and went back to their various headquarters to consider the proposition prayerfully. Dr. Whitman, on the contrary, was accustomed to praying and acting at the same time. He persuaded A. L. Lovejoy of the just-arrived emigration to travel back with him, and they departed for the East on October 2nd, leaving Narcissa alone to manage the Indians at the mission. Only a few days later, McKinlay, in charge at Fort Walla Walla, came and took her, with the children then in her care, to the fort for the winter. There can be no doubt that Marcus Whitman made his perilous trek through winter snows on mission business, and not, as has often been suggested, for the purpose of bringing more settlers to Oregon and saving it for the United States. Still, once back in civilization, he was besieged with questions, and was unflagging in his exertions to promote the migration which was to leave within a few weeks.

The days passed, and it was well along in May when the caravans of 1843 started for Oregon—an assemblage of nearly a thousand souls. Dr. Whitman caught up with them in time to render yeoman service at the crossing of the South Platte. From then on he was guide, counselor, physician, and friend. He did everything from locating the fords to delivering the babies. His "great experience and indomitable energy were of priceless value to the migrating column," wrote Jesse Applegate; and, notwithstanding that "he was clad entirely in buckskin, and rode one of those patient long-eared animals said to be 'without pride of ancestry or hope of posterity,'" he was an arresting figure. With characteristic lack of care for his own material comfort he started his journey with no provender but a solitary ham and ate his way (a welcome guest) through the various companies of the caravan, beginning with the "cow-column" commanded by Jesse Applegate at the rear of the migration which he naturally overtook first. By the time they sighted the squat adobe walls of Fort Hall he was in the vanguard of a great aggregation of people, most of whom knew and trusted him.

Captain Grant, commanding Fort Hall for the Hudson's Bay Company, was worried by the great wagons of household effects, women, and babies and gave forcibly and with apparent honesty the same advice that he had given to the handful of travelers in 1841 and the hundred-odd emigrants in '42: they had better leave their wagons at the fort—it would be imposible to get them through to the Columbia.

But Whitman was like one inspired. Wagons *had* gone through. His own cart, abandoned in '36 at Fort Boise, together with another selected from those more recently left at Fort Hall, had made the trip. These two battered vehicles driven by Joseph Meek and Robert Newell, seasoned mountain men, had come safely over Blue Mountains and down to the Columbia at Fort Walla Wala in 1840. If two wagons unsupported could complete the journey, Dr. Whitman argued, how much more easily could two hundred or so, backed by the man power of the whole season's migration!

The company captains had learned to trust his judgment, and he prevailed. With the title now of official guide Whitman left Fort Hall and turned his face toward home early in September. The Great Migration of 1843 had crossed its Rubicon and, complete with wagons and household goods, was on its way to settle Oregon.

* * *

We found the old road down grassy Fort Hall bottoms mosquitoish but charming. The sad change comes near American Falls, where the winding, verdure-bordered Snake shuts itself up in a precipitous gorge of basalt. Half the time our casual glance carried well across to the far bank several hundred feet above the river, which stormed along unseen at the bottom of its rocky crevasse.

Sometimes the pioneers traveled the sage-studded flat where fifty steps taken from the brink of the cliff removed the river from their sight, and where drinking water was acquired at the price of an hour's climb down

Gorge of Snake River.

and back. Sometimes they traveled within the crevasse, picking their way timorously along a dizzy ledge trail with the river roaring and eddying below. The stock was tired from the short, sharp ascents; valuable oxen fell and were killed; provisions were running low; game was too far afield; fish were too far below and the travelers were bitten severely by the mosquitoes.

Between Raft River and the city of Twin Falls, Idaho, traces of the old road are lately erased. The first patchwork effects of cultivated squares edged by native sage gradually give way to the luscious solid green fields of one of the garden spots of the world. Thousands of jack rabbits live in the unirrigated wastelands and nibble at the edges of toothsome acres. Enormous silvery canals slip silently, bank-high, through the fields and

have so reduced the Twin Falls of Snake River that scarcely enough
water jumps the double brink to make worth while the fatiguing scramble necessary to see them—especially as they were not included in the
emigrants' itinerary.

We spent the night in Twin Falls and made a nice early start. We were,
I believe, discussing the enormous dugout warehouses that hold the
potato wealth of Idaho when we encountered Rock Creek on the outskirts of town; and we didn't get any farther until noon. It is a chasm
of columnar rock. The pioneers, cutting across a bend of the Snake, came
to it far upstream, turned down its east bank, and skirted the steep brink
for eight miles before a suitable place was found for the descent. The
creek itself was but twenty feet wide, and they forded without notable
trouble.

The country is a colorful ensemble of individual, yet related, items.
Prosperous farmhouses delight the eye with vivid gardens like picture
postcards of old England. Feathery groves shelter clusters of red cattle.
Low board bridges almost touch the silky, silent canals they span, while
beneath and beyond all is the green, green, green of a land that never
fears a drought.

It is absolutely impossible to envision the fodderless, foodless, almost
waterless men and animals who plodded here along the course of the
Snake, keeping well back from the brink to avoid irregularities and short
curves, and pressing on toward Salmon Falls, hoping to purchase from
the Indians enough fish and berry cakes for a full meal.

Besides the several falls in the actual flow of the river the emigrants
descending for their evening supply of water were amazed by falls
springing without apparent source from out the basaltic cliffs and foaming downward to swell the impetuous current. There are many such, and
Frémont described one in detail in his report to Congress, inclosing a
skillful sketch by Charles Preuss. "Immediately opposite to us," he wrote,
"a subterranean river bursts out directly from the face of the escarpment,
and falls in white foam to the river below. In the views annexed, you will
find, with a sketch of this remarkable fall, a representation of the mural
precipices which enclose the main river, and which form its characteristic
feature along a great portion of its course. A melancholy and strange-
looking country—one of fracture, and violence, and fire."

For miles below the one described, similar beautiful falls are strung along the north wall of the Snake. Several are in plain view from the highway, just where Salmon Falls Creek joins the river, and were called by the early missionaries "the Shoots." It is generally believed that these falls are the waters of Lost River, which disappears into the lava over a hundred and twenty-five miles to the northeast, near the Craters of the Moon.

Below the highway bridge the river is interrupted by islands, and the banks become rather low and grassy. Pioneers describe it as split into various rocky channels, but a dam now diverts part of the water into a large new runway which guides it to a modern powerhouse. Salmon Falls itself is simply a glorified rapids, with a drop of seventy feet in a mile and a half.

Whether because of the amusing, talkative Indians or the plentiful fish which, in season, might be caught with the hands, arrival at Salmon Falls was an event to the travelers. The river is quite open and the dwellings of the cheerful, if lowbrow, natives were perched in niches up and down the banks like swallows' nests. Large pots made of something like brick clay seethed with fresh fish soup. Its characteristic odor curled tantalizingly upward to greet the hungry pilgrims. The grinning Indians were hospitable and generous, and the squaws set fires in the sparse grass to drive out lizards, crickets, and grasshoppers so that there might be a goodly supply of these, made into cakes, which they were always willing to give away, or to sell for a fishhook.

Although the Salmon Falls Indians were the most cheerful and uncomplaining creatures imaginable, the travelers noticed that they had scarcely enough clothing to keep them from freezing. Buffalo robes were not available. Deerskins (the staple of the plains Indian) were scarce. They depended on the skin of the humble jack rabbit for their main cover against the cold. Bare brown shoulders and bosoms shivered above scanty fur garments; fingers and toes of almost naked fishermen were pinched with cold on mornings when ice coated the soup kettle. Naturally articles of clothing were readily accepted in trade; but next after a shirt or a pair of breeches, with its double temptation of warmth and adornment, a big fishhook was of the most compelling lure. In the watershed of the Columbia it was a main staple of exchange. In fact fishhooks, with a supplementary line of pins, being both cheap to buy and light to carry, formed the entire stock in trade of many a foot traveler. One man actually made the trip from the Missouri to the Columbia on a job lot of hooks and pins and $2.50 in cash.

It was a great pity that the placid state of mutual helpfulness between Indian and emigrant could not endure; but, as years went by and thousands of settlers trekked past the birds'-nest village on the river bank, relations grew strained. The emigrants took the Indians' fish to eat, the Indians took the white men's horses for the same purpose—fair exchange in the Indians' reasoning; but to the white man horse stealing was a shooting offense, and shooting followed promptly. By the fifties the Indians along the Snake River were so unfriendly that massacres occurred, and, in retaliation, peaceful Indians were shot in the back while fishing.

Below Salmon Falls the trail strikes definitely out into an unappealing dry stretch that cuts off another bend of the river. At the end of the cutoff was the ford over the Snake, or in later years, Glenn's Ferry. The highway disdains the dry stretch and crosses the river; passes Hagerman Valley's exclamation-point poplars and comes to the Malade River. The name, meaning sickly, immortalizes the sad experiences of a band of fur trappers who dined upon beaver that had just fed upon poisonous roots. By the highway it is not far to the town of Glenn's Ferry, where we crossed again to the south side and went back to pick up the thread of the trail.

24

On Toward the Columbia

THE OREGON TRAIL comes across the waste land south of the Snake in apparently indestructible gouges. When we saw it the sage had been burned so that pathetic black arms stretched out jaggedly. The earth between was covered with wispy, short straw-colored grass without a particle of life. A transverse sand gully was almost our downfall, but in time we arrived at the cliff top where the trail breaks through a sloping gap and winds down to Three Island Ford.

"I guess we can call this a pretty good afternoon's work," Dr. Neff said in a mild sort of triumph, as we all stood and looked at the long sweep of river below us. "Not very many people bother to come here."

"That's quite evident," said Bill shortly. Then: "There are the islands all right: all three of them, flat as flounders. Do you know I always had a picture of the prairie schooners climbing over big fat islands like plum puddings in the middle of the river?"

"Heavens, no!" I told him. "The islands were just sort of level safety zones."

"H'm-m—maybe," my husband said doubtfully. "But at that the crossing was never *too* safe. I suppose you have just reams and reams of information in your notebook."

"Plenty—but Frémont gives the most interesting description. Probably he was sitting right over there across the river when he wrote it, too. This," I continued, opening the book, "is from his report to Congress: 'About 2 o'clock, we arrived at the ford where the road crosses to the right bank of Snake river. An Indian was hired to conduct us to the ford, which proved impracticable for us, the water sweeping away the howitzer and nearly drowning the mules, which we were obliged to extricate by cutting them out of the harness. The river here is expanded into a little bay, in which there are two islands, across which is the road of the ford; and the emigrants had passed by placing two of their heavy wagons abreast of each other, so as to oppose a considerable mass against the body of water. The Indians informed us that one of the men, in attempting to turn some cattle which had taken a wrong direction, was carried off by the current and drowned. Since their passage, the water had risen considerably; but, fortunately, we had a resource in a boat, which was filled with air and launched; and at seven o'clock we were safely encamped on the opposite bank, the animals swimming across, and the carriage, howitzer, and baggage of the camp, being carried over in the boat. At the place where we crossed, above the islands, the river had narrowed to a breadth of 1000.049 feet by measurement, the greater portion of which was from six to eight feet deep. We were obliged to make our camp where we landed, among the Indian lodges, which are semi-circular huts made of willow, thatched over with straw, and open to the sunny south.' "

Fortunately, so far, all the Indians westward from the Rockies spoke the Shoshone or Snake language, and some of Frémont's men were able to converse with the comical inhabitants of the small village with whom they shared the river bank. They were well disposed, wore occasional isolated garments such as a greatcoat or pair of pantaloons and made frequent calls heralded by the cry, "Haggai, haggai," indicating that they had fish to trade.

The Snake was the first deep river encountered whose waters were crystal-clear, and it led to underestimation of their depth. "Snake River," wrote Father de Smet, "having such limpid waters that the bottom can everywhere be seen, could only be dangerous to incautious persons." He was wrong, as his next statement shows: "Brother Charles Huet found himself all at once on the border of a deep precipice, too far advanced to return. Down went mules, driver and vehicle, and so deep was the place, that there scarcely appeared any chance to save them." The priests were escorted by a band of Flatheads, and they performed "prodigies of valor" in diving for Brother Charles, pulling him out of the wreckage, raising and refloating the wagon, and swimming after goods. They all, including women and children, repeatedly risked their lives. In the end they lost what they had considered most safe: the mules. These had been cut loose to swim ashore but had gone under and given up, at once. "It is said," wrote the good priest, "that these animals always perish when once they have had their ears under water."

Not all travelers, either in early days or later, crossed the river near Glenn's Ferry. The Snake was merely accomplishing another wriggle, and those who stayed on the outside of the big loop as it wandered south and back had no need to ford or ferry at all; but the fur traders, who first plotted the road, were careless of the dangers of the river and wished to save the long, deadly dry trek around the bend even though it meant fording the river twice.

Not many days either before or after Frémont was writing his famous report two young men, Overton Johnson and William H. Winter, essayed to cross at the ford, failed, and took the road around the bend, through God-forsaken country of which they wrote: "Twenty-seven miles below the Salmon Falls, we came to the crossing: where the companies, which preceded us, had passed over to the North side, which is much the nearest and best way; but we, having attempted the crossing and finding it too deep, were obliged to continue down on the South. This is, perhaps, the most rugged, desert, and dreary country, between the Western borders of the United States, and the shores of the Pacific. It is nothing else, than a wild, rocky, barren wilderness, or wrecked and ruined Nature; a vast field of volcanic desolation."

As the wagons pulled away from the northern end of the ford, they crossed the future highway near the marker put up by the Boy Scouts. It would be a two-day drive, and a hard one, to the Boise River. They climbed steadily until they attained an elevated plain some six hundred feet above the river, passed the hot springs, and came to Canyon Creek. Here was the site of the original settlement of Mountain Home, and I received an explanation of a name that had always seemed to me as if it must be a misnomer. There was, according to local tradition, in the early eighties a Commodore Jackson, and Mountain Home was just what its name implies—his home in the mountains. After some years it became a stage and freighting stop, and he ran it as he pleased; a post office became desirable, and the Commodore ran that also just as and how he thought best, without orders from any one. The hour arrived when the government, distant but displeased, requested reports and, failing to receive them, sent a rebuke by mail. But the government's displeasure was a feeble thing compared to the Commodore's, and he picked up his town, post office and all, and moved it over to the new railroad, leaving the stage line flat but keeping the name, of which he appeared to be fond. They say that the government remained uninformed for months.

After Canyon Creek and Old Mountain Home, the wagons crossed a little tributary, Rattlesnake Creek. Then Squaw Creek (dry when we saw it), Ditto Creek, Indian Creek, and Black's Creek, site of Black's Station. When the trail strikes the modern New York Canal it turns and follows its south bank as far as the Desert Edge Service Station, crosses it and proceeds to the Boise River. The trail comes in sight of the river long before they join forces—to be exact, about eight miles east of Boise City, where that mountain stream "debouches into the plains." I am quoting Frémont; other travelers, evidently using his reports as a guidebook, unconsciously used the same word, and we grew curious. What does a river do, anyway, when it debouches? We decided to backtrack from Boise City and see. Following first this lead and then that, we milled around town until our various bits of information led to Mr. Peasley.

Now Mr. Peasley is a busy man; but he knows his trail and loves it, and he wanted to go along and see the Boise debouch. When we returned to the car we had him in tow.

We left town on the trail—paved now but still narrow and called Boise Avenue; soon turned on Broadway and started back toward Glenn's Ferry. The countryside is a series of great steps composed of thousands of acres each, of which the bottom lands around the city of Boise are the lowest level. The trail comes down into this bottom land at the Desert Edge Service Station, right at the New York Canal crossing, and may be seen in the V of a deep, sandy gully moving along diagonally toward the river. We took the trail south of the canal on the second level and at once started to backtrack on an abandoned ranch road where we accounted for several miles quite easily. In the lee of Lucky Peak we met the old trail leading down from the third level. It is picturesque and steep, and I walked up behind the car, thoroughly enjoying it. Barker Dam now was below us, and, at the mouth of a canyon ahead to our left (where Boise River did indeed debouch from as ugly stone portals as any one could ask for) was the New York Canal Dam. The ruts were grass-grown and spread all over the landscape, maybe a dozen abreast. The hill soon flattened. The road was not fit to be called one.

"I certainly hope we don't have to go back the way we came," whispered Bill, who was driving, while the men were temporarily out of the car moving rocks from the thoroughfare.

"Don't worry," I reassured him. "I don't think it could be done."

"What a trip to take in a new car!" he groaned, thinking of the automobile's resplendent paint-job.

"You may be glad of all the power you have before you get up that next little incline," I told him. "It looks bad to me. The wagons must have used ropes coming down."

When we reached the top I got in, and we lurched along. The sage closed in on us and rasped on the fenders. I took time to hope that it would not be necessary to return by the same route.

It was on this level that we met a party of surveyors in a station wagon driving out the way we had come. They were facetious at our expense (for which I didn't blame them), but when we continued on they yelled a good unmistakable warning that the hill ahead was impassable for touring cars. They even ran a few steps after us. Mr. Peasley was calm. "It isn't impassable," he said, "I've been up myself in the last few years. Of course the car had lots more clearance than this one, but you'll see she will make it."

I don't know yet how it was ever accomplished, but the men picked a continuous groove between the rocks for the transmission and let the wheels go where they had to. I hung out the window on the up side for ballast and Bill drove while Mr. Peasley calmly encouraged us all to "ride it out," and my two other relatives did intensive road work at a tempo which may never have been equaled. The crisis came when both right-hand wheels dropped into holes between the rocks so that the weight of the car had to be hoisted straight up. We polished the near side of those rocks till the smoke streamed out, but the big car slowly raised itself and a quarter-minute of floundering brought us to the top of the next hill and a better prospect.

We turned into a stage road of the sixties, high under the curly clouds. Surely sage was never more aromatic. The trail lay just on our right. Lytle Gulch was at our left with the site of Lytle Ferry at its foot, and the mountain promontory called Bonneville Point lay dead ahead. When we had attained this massive bulkhead we found that the travelers obtained their first view of Boise River from its point. Here, so historians more or less agree, is where Captain Bonneville's party exclaimed in

French over the lovely wooded river ("rivière boisée") that lay ahead.

A massive monument to the memory of that first moment of discovery crowns the flattish point and, as Mr. Peasley observed truthfully, very few people ever see it.

Back in town, we went to the Hotel Boise for a late lunch, taking Mr. Peasley with us. He is elderly enough to be a very privileged person, and seemed to know every one in the place. As I washed the accumulated dirt of Lytle Gulch, Bonneville Point, and way stations off my hands and face, and saw a faultlessly groomed lady next to me gaze unbelievingly while the water rolled blackly down the vent, I, who never apologize for necessary oddities, was at least moved to an explanation.

She looked relieved, I thought. "If Mr. Peasley started out to take you anywhere, I'm sure he did it thoroughly," she said, and laughed affectionately. "He never does anything by halves."

* * *

From the time that the emigrants of 1843 came down into the Boise bottom lands until they reached what is now the town of Notus, they kept south of the river. In these days it is nearly all cultivated; but, on the Johnson ranch a mile and a half below the town, the ruts used to be visible swinging down to the ford and then up from the river through a field on the north side. They have long since disappeared.

In very early years the Bannocks had a fishery on the Boise and sold bales of dried salmon weighing about eighty pounds each. Their squaws hunted for berries, which they beat into a paste and shaped into little cakes about four inches across. When dried these kept well; and the travelers were glad to get them, for by this time they were regarding fish as one of the Creator's lesser blessings and were actually in great need of a variety in diet.

John Minto, later one of Oregon's well known citizens, wrote that when he traveled down the Boise in '44 he and his comrades came upon the camp of a solitary Indian family. The young brave made signs to trade, but his timid little wife picked up the long papoose-basket containing the rigid figure of their fat offspring and fled to a safe distance. The men paused to see what he had in mind and were amazed when he seized a stout stick and pushed the fire to one side. Further excavations revealed a fine salmon baking in the hot sand underneath, but still he dug. At last, a foot or two beneath the salmon, a beaver skin was exposed. Beaver were rare by the forties, and this one pelt was the Indian's prize possession. He had placed it in the safest spot he could devise, for no one in this hungry country would ever get beyond the smoking salmon.

In the mouth of the Boise River, at its junction with the Snake, is a large delta island—flat and exactly like the surrounding country. In the summer of 1941, it was almost all cultivated and little cottages bowered in trumpet vines and hollyhocks sat smugly in the midst of crowding haycocks. We had no difficulty in finding the trail to Oregon and in learning that there had once been a dreadful massacre on the "Watson Ranch" resulting in the burying of thirteen bodies within their quiet acres. Trying to locate the various evanescent channels of the Boise River was another matter, and we got so lost that I began to think of scattering fragments of my petticoats out of the rear window to help us get back.

There had been a fort. We knew that. Diaries, from 1836 on, all agree perfectly that there was a fort at the mouth of the Boise, but the proposition was complicated by the fact that we had just found out that there were three forts in succession, and that the Boise's two mouths (one each side of the delta island) were in the habit of moving frivolously about. We were armed with several very usable maps drawn for us by Mr. J. Neilson Barry of Portland and with the findings which he had compiled from the available source material, and our gratitude to him increased with each hour. By noon of the second day we had also enlisted the help of Mr. James Hedges and Mr. and Mrs. C. S. Burton, residents of the island, and had straightened ourselves (and the forts) out somewhat in this manner: in fur-trading days the largest mouth of the Boise lay south of the delta island, and the tongue formed by its confluence with the Snake was an important bit of land—easily described and easily found. Here a trader named Reid built a fort and, with nine other men, was massacred by Indians in 1813 or 1814. In his honor the Boise was first known as Reid's River. Trader, men, and fort might be gone but the land was still important. Donald McKenzie tried to rebuild the post in 1819; but the Indians were too much for him, and the place lay idle until 1834. In that year McKay, probably on his return from the accidental meeting with Bonneville, Wyeth, and Stewart, built a trading post for himself in what had been the horse corral of the Reid fort. The Whitmans and Spaldings were entertained here in '36 on their way to the Columbia, and refer to it in their journals as Snake Fort. It was apparently a private venture of McKay's, and a year or two later Hudson's Bay Company built Fort Boise slightly below the smaller mouth at the north side of the island. The emigrant ford was immediately below this fort.

It was to the Hudson's Bay Company's Fort Boise that early travelers came, firing their muzzle loaders into the air to show that they approached in peace with empty guns. It was to this Fort Boise that the emigrants of 1843 and Frémont came to buy provisions, to exchange tired animals, to borrow or hire the enormous dugout canoes for transporting wagons across the river, and to plead for the all-important dairy products and vegetables. They found in charge a stout, good-natured Frenchman named Payette. The fort flourished until the winter of 1853, when a heavy flood crumbled the adobe building into the Snake and it was lost to history; but the name lived on. It was still desirable for the emigrants to cross Snake River, and so a new Fort Boise was built at the narrows just above Goose Egg Island, and in 1868 the Keenan ferry was established there. Even now, where the old county road to Nyssa crosses the Snake, may be seen the trees that shaded the buildings of the ferry settlement and a portion of the old cable.

To the student of western history "Fort Boise" means the Hudson's Bay Company's ill-fated building, and so, unless otherwise specified, it will be understood in this travelogue.

The ford of the Snake was just below the fort, but "ford" must not be taken to mean that teams pulled the wagons across. It was simply that for years there was no ferry. It was sometimes possible to borrow the dugout canoes from Fort Boise, and of course there was always the good old wagon bed. Narcissa Whitman and Eliza Spalding were placed with their saddles in a crude misshapen boat made of willows and rushes, just large enough to float them, and two mounted Indians towed them to the far shore.

Mainly the emigrants were not sorry to leave Fort Boise, for the whole place stank of fish and, what with the salmon leaping noisily in the river and the Indians howling joyfully on shore, there was little sleep to be had. The Indians of the Fort Boise region were of an exceptionally low type, corresponding somewhat to the Shoshokoes or Root Diggers of the

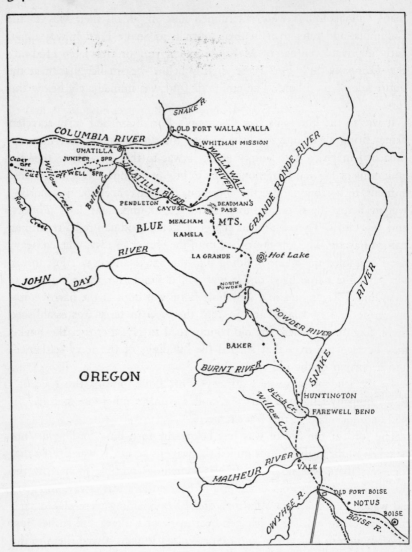

Humboldt country, and lacked even the providence of a squirrel. Frémont wrote: "Mr. Payette informed me that, every year since his arrival at this post, he had unsuccessfully endeavored to induce these people to lay up a store of salmon for their winter provision. While the summer weather and the salmon lasted, they lived contentedly and happily, scattered along the different streams where the fish were to be found; and as soon as the winter snows began to fall, little smokes would be seen rising among the mountains, where they would be found in miserable groups, starving out the winter; and sometimes, according to the general belief, reduced to the horror of cannibalism—the strong, of course, preying on the weak. Certain it is, they are driven to any extremity for food, and eat every insect, and every creeping thing, however loathsome and repulsive. Snails, lizards, ants—all are devoured with the readiness and greediness of mere animals."

Frémont was unfair. They ate everything, it is true, but were not too low in the scale for discrimination. They greatly preferred ants to locusts as being more oily, and collected them in large bowls to be eaten *au naturel*.

Opposite the mouth of the Boise the Owyhee River runs into the Snake from the south. It was of no interest to those who had crossed at Three Island Ford and traveled down the Boise, but the wagon trains trekking on the south bank of the Snake negotiated a crossing near the mouth. It is no exception to the practice, general among early trappers, of calling a river by the name of some one who lost his life there. Two Sandwich Islanders brought over by Hudson's Bay Company were killed in its neighborhood and the name is a phonetic version of the word Hawaii. From here we pursued our route up Cow Hollow, and Cow Hollow more nearly persuaded us that the road to Oregon is indeed a long, long trail than anything we had experienced for some time. It seemed interminable. Modern Cow Hollow runs to corn, but, creeping along under the fence lines, were easily identified ruts. Eventually Cow Hollow Creek gave up the ghost, and the long valley petered out in a draw where the wagons had concentrated and the sage-grown ruts were beautiful to behold. It is a very good place to see what is left of the Oregon Trail. Presently, after rounding the points of some rocky and dry hills, we came to the Malheur River at the town of Vale.

It was seldom that any one wrote in a pleasant vein of the Malheur. Its very name means "mishap," and commemorates a calamity of early trapping days when an important cache of furs and food was found and stolen by Indians. In 1845, because of hostile Indians, a family including an expectant mother was left here to await the coming of the new Oregonian while their company hurried on toward safety. Large and telltale fires were not to be thought of, and they were greatly helped and comforted by the plentiful hot water from a large boiling spring.

The spring was nowhere in sight, but we spied a laundry building and trudged up the side hill to look behind it. There, half hidden by lumber and pipes, snorting and bubbling like a witch's caldron, were the hot springs of the Malheur. Never ornamental, they are still utilitarian.

Beyond the river the trail goes fourteen miles among barren, grayish yellow hills, passing to the left of rugged Malheur Butte which looks, so the emigrants said, as if it had scarcely cooled. The wagons crossed Willow Creek, passed the alkali spring, and struck Birch Creek, down which they traveled seven miles. Four miles more, across a hilly point brought them to the Snake River at Farewell Bend. The gray waters of the constantly enlarging river shine between flattish banks as it turns from the trail forever and slips into the mountains. At the bend, marked by a level, useless island of sand, camped at different times the Astorians, Wyeth, Bonneville, and Frémont. The ruts here are good and are close to the highway. They lead over naked, dead hills into the valley of Burnt River, which here, according to Frémont, "looks like a hole among the hills." The hole is now Huntington, a dingy but interesting red-brick railroad town full of chugging trains. We set our watches back an hour to Pacific Standard time, realized that we had an extra sixty minutes before lunchtime, and felt aggrieved.

Burnt River was not at all what we had expected from written descriptions. It was hard to reconcile its moderately slanting canyon sides with the fact that one of Peter Skene Ogden's pack horses fell off the trail on Burnt River and broke nearly every bone in its body. Probably the early-day traders' caravan was not following exactly the later used route. For wagons, it was easy to see that the firmly compressed canyon would always be difficult and rough.

I leaned out the window, deeply interested, and checked our progress with Mr. Barry's maps. We passed through Lime, featuring a large kiln and long lines of overhead buckets, and into the higher part of the canyon. Near Weatherby the trail turned up Chicken Creek to get around a large yellowish elevation known as Gold Hill and then into the valley containing the town of Durkee. Pritchard and Alder creeks made good camp sites, but most of the wagons continued up the hill to the right. At Troy House the ruts turn up a steep, sandy and sage-grown swale to leave the waters of Burnt River—the first place where the early Oregonians were forced to double teams. It is noteworthy that the very early settlers, having no reason to hurry and a sufficiency of grass for all, came by a route avoiding all of the dangerous grades. From the summit they went through Virtue Flat and struck the down grade to the Powder River Valley, which they entered by way of modern Flagstaff Hill. The evidences there are fair.

We couldn't find the famous Lone Pine Camp at the first crossing of Powder River. We know that we saw it from Flagstaff Hill because the whole valley was laid out before us, but just where is for some one else to say. The trappers called it *l'arbre seul,* and loved the great pine which stood alone in the valley, but Frémont (just behind the 1843 emigrants) found it felled and lying partly used. It may be that the company who cut it felt justified; but, for many years, those who came after mourned its absence and execrated the "wretch and vandal" who had destroyed it.

Powder River is small and very winding. The travelers crossed it at whim, seeking the splendid pastures of the valley. It was here in the neighborhood of North Powder City that the Dorion baby must have been born, the poor little mite, offspring of the French guide of the overland Astorians, whose Indian mother traveled uncomplainingly on horseback with an older child slung to the saddle. But speaking of the advent of any one baby on the Oregon road is like going down a street in a one-time populous town and remarking with pride that once a child was born hereabouts. The Oregonians were a family people. Each year's migration was a little community on the march, and babies were born there just as elsewhere. There is a record of one small company, in the year '47, in which five babies arrived en route. The Dorion baby, however, is entitled to fame as the first infant in whose veins flowed white blood, to be born on the Oregon Trail.

*   *   *

By mistake we came down into the Grande Ronde Valley by way of Union and the old stage road instead of on the trail, and had to turn back up Ladd Canyon in order to find it. Here Mr. William Benton put us straight. He is quite accustomed to the process, for he has lived his eighty years where the wagons dropped down off the mountain into the valley. We found him irrigating the vegetable garden just conveniently below the trail descent. The telltale marks are easy enough to see—always providing some one shows you where they are. Grande Ronde Valley is well named. It is large and it is round, and in 1843 it was one immense field of redtop. The luxuriant, feathery grass was a thrilling sight to prospective farmers—orchids would have been a mere drug on the market beside it. The men were immensely cheered. There was a tendency to loiter along the road while the loose stock sampled its bounty and men called optimistically from one wagon to another. It was customary to camp twice in the valley, just after the descent and again on the Grande Ronde River just before starting up the next range. Every one had a breathing spell, and the animals could eat their fill and rest up for the tough ascent—the dreaded Blue Mountains at last.

At daylight the next morning they commenced to pit their strength against inflexible heights ahead—appallingly big and dark and solid. For the emigrants of 1843 they were the major obstacle of the journey. Phalanxes of trees trooped forward to meet them. They grew so thick and with such gusto that they scraped hide from the stock and tore the horsemen's breeches. Tangled scrub and matted huckleberry barred the way. Lovely open dells of brilliant flowers contrasted with dead trees like black goblins. It took forty men five days to clear a spindling, circuitous track through the heavy growth so that the first wagon might work its way to the top, heeled, of course, by all the rest.

Because of the slow progress and the lower elevation there was not nearly the loss of stock on Blue Mountains that had discouraged the travelers on South Pass.

Dr. Whitman was no longer with them. While still in the Grande Ronde an Indian messenger arrived with word that the Spaldings were critically ill with scarlet fever, and the caravans lost their guide at once. As a substitute Whitman left them the Indian, Stickus, who faithfully brought them on. He spoke no English, but Nesmith writes, "He succeeded by pantomime in taking us over the roughest wagon route I ever saw." This method of communication left something to be desired, however, as Nesmith later discovered. "I once dined with Stickus," he writes, "in his camp, upon what I supposed to be elk meat. I had arrived at that conclusion because, looking at the cooked meat and then at the old Indian interrogatively, he held up his hands in a manner that indicated elk horns; but, after dinner, seeing the ears, tail, and hoofs of a mule near camp, I became satisfied that what he meant to convey by his pantomime was 'ears' not 'horns.' "

It may be as well to state that horse and mule meat, although disdained by the wagon companies, were always part of the menu of early exploring and trapping parties, having the advantage of speed and serviceability as long as it remained on the hoof. A young horse was said to taste like venison. The Whitmans, finding no other meat available, used it at the mission and ate up twenty-three wild horses in the first three years. "This will make you pity us," Narcissa wrote to her mother, "but you had better save your pity for more worthy subjects. I do not prefer it to other meat, but can eat it very well when we have nothing else." Mr. Nesmith was merely amused by the mule-meat incident. The joke was on him.

Old Stickus endeared himself to the migration in more ways than one. Every morning and evening he gathered his family together as he had been taught to do, and they raised their lusty voices in song and prayer. On the evening when they had won through to the summit and could look down the untimbered western side, his thanksgiving was so picturesque and so devout that a skimming of slightly embarrassed piety transferred itself to the entire group. And indeed it was an inspiring sight that presented itself to the exulting Oregonians. To the north and south no bounds were seen. To the west the great wall of the Cascades stood like a fortress, from which rose the white-capped towers of Mount Hood and Mount Adams. Against this majestic backdrop stood the figure of the Cayuse Indian with arms uplifted, singing, in a weird minor, the hymns he had learned at the mission. If some day a truly great painter transfers this moment to canvas, American art will be the richer.

* * *

The emigrants' route had been in general northwest from the time they left the Snake River at Farewell Bend. The trail used by the early comers over Blue Mountains went from the camp on the Grande Ronde River, to Pelican Creek, to California Gulch, to a point just northwest of Meacham, to Emigrant Springs and on to Deadman's Gulch, where the 1843 emigrants went to the right (splitting from what was the later trail) and came down Poker Jim Hill. The later trail went along the shoulder of Cabbage Hill near Pendleton, and is plainly visible to the right of the highway.

Beginning with the hard-won wagon path of '43, there have been many roads over Blue Mountains. There was the rough prairie schooner trail of the forties and fifties, the Meacham toll road of the sixties, the many ramifications of the county roads, and the modern highway. All of them travel directly across the mountain range. Added to these is a very useful thoroughfare of a special nature: the forest rangers' road, which often runs at right angles to the others. We used this latter as a convenient means of cutting across the trail and the toll road.

From the early sixties all traffic—prairie schooners, heavy freighters and what have you—came by way of the Meacham toll road. It rejoiced in the name "Blue Mountain Wagon Road Consolidated" and was probably the best known stretch between Fort Boise and the Columbia.

We arrived at the little mountain settlement of Meacham earlier than we ordinarily stop for the night, and in the combination store and restaurant we met Mr. Ross, who made a splendid guide to local points of interest.

"Suppose you people tell me," Mr. Ross suggested, after much had been said on both sides, "just what you want to know."

"It's a large order," my husband said. "We want information about the trail that the Oregon emigrants came over, and the Meacham toll road that succeeded it. Where do they run, and how far apart?"

"Why, I couldn't possibly describe them," he answered reasonably enough. "They cross each other and recross and sometimes run concurrently. Suppose we go and look at them."

Nothing on earth could have suited us better, and we started at once. Within a few hundred yards our guide steered us through a modern gate and onto the old toll road. Small, even trees pressed in tightly—I have forgotten whether pines or fir or both. There was no undergrowth to encroach, but the sparse dry weeds grew impartially among the trees and across the roadbed.

"The Meacham road used to be wide enough for two teams to pass," our guide told us. "The trees have moved in because for years one wheel track took care of the traffic. Miles and miles of it are corduroyed, too. Do you know what a corduroy road is?" he asked me suddenly.

I nodded, with vivid recollections of bumpy rides over the dislocating contours of old corduroy roads when I wondered if my infant bones would ever be the same again. "Indeed I do. But this certainly isn't one. There isn't a log in sight."

"There's dust and dirt over them now," he said, "but there *is* a layer of small logs underlying the wheel tracks all along this stretch—thousands of them between here and the Grande Ronde," and proceeded to prove his point with his boot heel. "They had to keep the road free of bad mudholes because they charged toll: a dollar and a half, I think, for a four-horse team, and other things in proportion. The main point of deviation from the highway is on top of the ridge between here and the Grande Ronde where the old roads go through the next gap to the northeast. We can drive up there and get oriented. Then you can, so to speak, come back into Meacham with the wagons."

Half an hour later we were on the ridge.

"Hello," said my husband sharply, braking the car to a standstill, "here's something interesting—an intersection of the trail and toll road." Sure enough, in an open, cushiony slope, the two lanes of pilgrimage approached, crossed and departed: the emigrants' wagon trail keeping the devious course of least resistance; the toll road boldly diving into the dark forest. At Mr. Ross' suggestion we turned into the latter and bore toward the Grande Ronde.

"It's not far down into California Gulch. I want you to see it while the light holds, for, if I remember correctly, it's a dark place."

"How did it get its name?" Dr. Neff wanted to know.

"Haven't the faintest idea. It's about as far removed from California or any thought of California as any place in the state of Oregon. Some forgotten incident pinned the title on it, probably."

Five or ten minutes brought us to a break in the forest in which lay (for it could not be seen to flow) a shadowy watercourse—just a gloomy strand of opaque water, black but glistening with a weird, bloody reflection of the afterglow, high and remote above—a ghostly stream densely bordered with trees, on which I should not care to be caught out after dark. If the uneasy spirits of the many miscreants of the migrations are wont to gather anywhere, I felt that they must haunt California Gulch.

"From here going eastward," said Mr. Ross, "the toll road meanders along until it comes into the highway near Five Point Service Station. It practically goes through Kamela, which, by the way, is the Umatilla word for a low pass between two hills. It touches Pelican Creek, goes near Hilgard and down into the Grande Ronde River. You have seen most of that?" We told him that we had—or, at any rate, enough to follow his descriptions intelligently. "Well, then, let's go back toward the west. There are some other things I want to show you, and I'll be busy tomorrow."

And so we went west "with the wagons" to Meacham. "This was an important place in the days of the old Blue Mountain Wagon Road Consolidated," our guide said reflectively, "and Meacham himself was quite a character: six foot four with red whiskers, and the type that legends just naturally build up around. Swing over by the depot, and I'll show you where he lived."

Past a railway corral full of blatting sheep my husband slowly swung the car in a wide circle and doubled back on a lower road parallel to the highway. "The first emigrants came over the hills along there"—our new friend pointed a brown finger—"just diagonally beyond the present hotel. The toll road came right where we are. There was a famous old eating house here, but it's been gone many years."

"This was a regular stopping place then," Dr. Neff said tentatively.

"Oh, yes, one of the best. The flat meadow beyond that large shed was Meacham's corral. Drive on, just across this little bridge. Now stop. See that leaning post? Well, right there they excavated the bodies of a man, woman, and little child who had been buried in their wagon. There was nothing to identify them but some buttons and the fact that the wagon still showed that it had been painted blue and yellow. A common enough tragedy in those days."

"A lonely grave in a busy spot," I said. "It probably lost its marker in a month, if it ever had one, and after that of course it would be tramped down and forgotten while some family back East waited the rest of their lives for a letter." It was not a pleasant thought. "What's on up the road?" I added quickly.

"The old Meacham house used to be," our guide answered me, and we drove on a short distance before receiving the signal to stop. "It was here to the right of the road. The car is standing on what used to be the rock causeway or paving where the freight teams pulled up. You can see part of the cellar excavation."

The heavily grass-grown meadow sloped to meet us from the edge of the crowding forest, but close by the roadside its cushiony contours were broken and cut to the shape of a cellar noted in its day for outsize piping and the luxury of real plumbing.

"This is the place he called home when he was alive, and I think I can find his grave if you have time to prowl around a few minutes." Following directions, we turned through the first gate to the left, parked the car, and, moving between great blossoming spikes of the homely skunk cabbage, came to a pine thicket where, in an unmarked and almost unnoticeable grave, lie the seventy-six inches of one of Oregon's outstanding pioneers.

We left Meacham early the next morning, but Mr. Ross had taken his departure even earlier. We soon discovered that the two old roads and the highway twine like rope strands on the west slope. The toll road apparently incorporated whatever stretches of the wagon trail proved useful and left the rest to nature. Every now and then, spaced in between clearings, barns, thick wooded patches, and old worm-fenced corrals, we would see a short span of distinguishable thoroughfare marching straight through the thick even growth of trees.

"Of course the road is worn down," Bill said. "I can see that. But wouldn't you think that twenty years of the heaviest kind of hauling would gouge it into holes? It's as smooth as a floor."

"I asked that same question yesterday," Dr. Neff said. "It's on account of the soil being so light. The winter frosts make it heave up and the spring thaws mush it down again and smooth out any marks that have been made on it during the year. And," he added, "it's been a long time since any have been made. No wonder it's smooth."

We passed a sign, "Emigrant Spring."

"Was this Emigrant Spring a night camp or a nooning place?" I asked as we left it behind.

"Both—that is, for individual wagons. Small emigrant parties straggled along at all hours. But they told me last night," my husband said doubtfully, "that before the spring was augmented it was probably too small to water a large company. The freighters, I believe, camped at Two Mile Creek near Meacham."

Just then a band of five or six horses thudded across the highway directly ahead of us. "Somebody has fine stock," said Bill, swinging the car around the last one, "but he doesn't seem to care much what becomes of it."

"Oh, those belong to the Cayuse," his father told him. "They've always been noted for their droves of horses, and, of late years, the government has given them some good stallions. Haven't you noticed the loose stock in the clearings and alongside the road? They tell me there are several hundred."

"Well, some day they're going to get hit, and there'll be a bad smashup."

"That's what the authorities think. It seems they sent word to the Indians that horses and highways don't mix—or, at least not pleasantly—and requested that the horses be moved. The neighboring tribes held a conclave and agreed that the situation was bad, but said the horses had been there a long time and they would recommend that the authorities move the highway."

"What happened then?" Bill slowed up for a splendid bay mare.

"I don't know that anything happened. Both the highway and the horses are still here."

Presently the two tangled old roads went through Deadman's Pass, and down the brusque declivity beyond, and I became hopelessly entangled in notes and annotations. It wasn't until we had made the journey down into the Umatilla Valley ourselves and worked the trail backwards that I got the strands straightened in my mind.

The bare western slope of Blue Mountains breaks up into massive jutting shoulders tapering down to the flat lands from which, on this bright Sunday morning, haze rose softly as if the earth lay and perspired in sheer lassitude. The great shoulders form the least precipitous descents and have been striped with Indian trails from time immemorial. The 1843 emigrants, led by Stickus and bound for the Whitman mission, are believed to have come down one of these buttresses now entitled Poker Jim Hill. The trail used by the emigrants through the late forties and fifties is plain to be seen from the highway, wandering down a similar slope called Cabbage Hill in the vicinity of Pendleton. The Meacham road we later found midway between the two.

Far to our right, as we descended, we glimpsed the modest ensemble of the Catholic Mission snuggled against the mountain; took a small dirt road leading in that direction, and eased inconspicuously alongside the main building. It was not yet eight o'clock, but Father Steele, in charge, made us welcome and said that the mission, although modernly entitled St. Andrew's, used to be called St. Joseph's and is the successor to the old mission, mentioned by the emigrants. At his suggestion we took a small road leading north, and immediately crossed the tiny stream where the original mission stood. A few hundred yards more brought us to the Meacham road coming steadfastly and straight from mountain to valley between its own two fence lines.

After a short, dusty ride—say about four miles from the mission—we came to Poker Jim Hill pushing its way out toward the Umatilla. With the last mountain at their backs, the gallant companies of 1843 guided their cherished wagons down this slope to the uncertain reception awaiting them at the Cayuse village on the river. Those battered wagons! Rolling and pitching steadily along in line, they were a source of unspeakable wonderment to the Indians, and the whole population turned out en masse to see the "horse-canoes."

The Cayuse were sulky and suspicious; but they raised potatoes, and soon learned their value. The early emigrants actually gave their shirts for the precious brown nuggets. There was no waiting for mealtime. So starved for starch were their systems that men actually got up at night and cooked more potatoes to satisfy the craving. Young Minto and his companions, in the vanguard of '44, came to the Cayuse village down the easy but unbroken descent of over two miles, sometimes within sight of the faint tracks left by the migration of last year and sometimes in the deep-worn horse trail of the trappers. It was his birthday, and the boys sacrificed a shirt for six potatoes. But the surly Cayuse, informed by his chattering squaw that the garment was thin in places, returned with that insufficient article and demanded his potatoes back. Now he could have had almost anything else in the interests of peace but *not* their birthday dinner. They said as much, probably in unmistakable sign language, and he uncoiled a lasso and got ready to go into action—eliciting, instead of the potatoes, four loaded guns that induced the prompt but vituperous withdrawal of the Cayuse family. This was a typical encounter.

There is still an Indian village. Its name is still Cayuse—and there we went.

It was a pale, milky day, as if seen through white chiffon, and we drove between still, silvery-gilt fields. Presently the road dipped to the river and we found the dingy collection of small frame houses that is modern Cayuse. There seemed to be a paucity of Indians. In fact we didn't see a single one, so we pulled up in front of the shady little store that served the village and went in to inquire. It was dark, cool and old-fashioned. I took my root-beer bottle and strolled outside, hoping to find a child or a woman. I like Indian women, and I can get them to like me if there is plenty of time for the purpose. I parked the bottle on a box and walked slowly toward the houses.

A little man was coming down the road. He looked friendly. "Where is everybody?" I asked him. "We hoped that some one here would be willing to talk to us for a while."

"Oh, yes," he said, "you mean the Cayuse. Well, they're having a pow-wow down the river. Umatillas too, and Walla Wallas. Now and then they get together and have sort of a convention."

I remembered the calm executive session that had suggested the removal of the Blue Mountain highway and nodded in full comprehension.

"If that's the case," I told him, "they'll be quite a while and we won't wait. I'll just take another look at the river before we go"—and I walked back toward the bridge.

The shady banks were tree-lined, and the clear water splashed rhythmically below me as I leaned over the railing. The Umatilla! It meant to the early travelers that the last mountain, cowled in forests and almost impassable, lay behind them. The rest was easy.

*   *   *

From the Cayuse village the emigrants of 1843 and one or two later migrations detoured to the Whitman Mission as a matter of course. After '45 it was not customary. The Lee Mission at the Dalles was on their direct route, and by this time there were many settlers to whom they could go for advice. The general plan of these few later years was to proceed down the Umatilla River and across the forty miles of benchland, shadeless and arid, through which the river found its way to the Columbia. From the mouth of the Umatilla the wagons remained on the south of the "Great River of the West" as far as the Dalles. As soon as the incoming settlers became better informed as to the terrain they learned that there was no point in blindly following the Umatilla north and then turning west on the Columbia when the hypotenuse of the giant triangle afforded water. We have evidence that Dr. Whitman himself, who was in the habit of meeting the later emigrants at the foot of Blue Mountains, recommended this new road along the foothills.

We had been many times along the Umatilla, but never before had we circled to the Whitman Mission site. This time, with the century mark so close, we were interested mainly in the hard-won road of the 1843 emigrants and set out on their course.

Wide rolling spaces lay toward the Walla Walla River. Wheat stood thick upon the land and rustled like a taffeta petticoat. Farmers worked in pea fields spread wide and green on sunlit slopes. Cattle standing on the knoll tops seemed children's cutouts against the sky. Here the early travelers, riding through barren country unrelieved by trees except at the

Whitman Mission at Waiilatpu. The buildings from left to right are: the mill, mansion house, blacksmith shop, and mission. (From a drawing in W. A. Mowry's "Marcus Whitman")

watercourses, met Indians who asked grace before meals and insisted that they stop to wash both hands and face before approaching the mission that the Whitmans had built on a lazy curve of the Walla Walla.

The Indians called it Waiilatpu, the Place of the Rye Grass, and the river looped about the land in a fashion that enabled three hundred acres to be inclosed with but eighty rods of fencing. Here, in the summer and fall of 1837, Marcus Whitman built his home of adobe mud with wooden doors and window frames, and beds made of "boards nailed to the side of the house, sink fashion"—a haven henceforth open to all the homeless and needy who passed their way. Here their baby girl, Alice Clarissa, born on her mother's twenty-ninth birthday and loved by the Cayuse, a real bond to hold their interest, was drowned at the age of twenty-seven months. They never had another child, but, by the year 1848, they were raising eleven: children of the mountain men and of emigrants who died on the plains.

There is no need to recount the tragic history of Narcissa and Marcus Whitman. Others have done so in detail. Clifford Merrill Drury, from whose carefully written book "Marcus Whitman, M.D." I take most of the following facts, is a reliable authority. The missionaries never won the confidence of the Cayuse people. The Indians could see that Dr. Whitman favored the white men who came to settle the land; that he went back beyond the great mountains and brought more white families. What they asked themselves, was there in that for the Cayuse?

Matters were already on an uneasy basis when, in the fall of '47, the arriving column of emigrants spread an epidemic of measles. The whole mission was laid low, but, what was immeasurably worse, the Indians were stricken. Dr. Whitman did all that even his indomitable energy could devise; but a red man who became feverish could not be restrained from jumping in the river, and the results were fatal. Meanwhile the doctor and Narcissa, working day and night, saved most of the white patients. The Indians were both frightened and angry. Egged on by their chief men and especially by a half-breed called Joe Lewis, some of them entered the mission house on Monday November 29, 1847, and killed Marcus, Narcissa, and eight others—all men. During several days of terror they killed three more men, and two girls died from illness compounded with fright and unavoidable neglect. One of these was Joseph Meek's little daughter Helen. Forty-seven, including Jim Bridger's daughter, Mary Ann, were taken captive. A few escaped, and the horrible story came to the ears of Hudson's Bay Company. A party of men under Peter Skene Ogden were sent with goods to ransom the survivors. They succeeded and brought them all back to Oregon City, a remarkable achievement considering that some of the girls had already been taken as wives by the chief Indians. Mary Ann Bridger died three months later.

On the day following the massacre, the Indians allowed one of the captive men to dig a large shallow grave. The next morning Father

Brouillet (a Catholic missionary recently arrived to found a rival mission) braved the Cayuse and came to Waiilatpu. He was reasonably safe. The Indians favored the Catholics. Although the two men, after the bigoted fashion of the times, had exchanged recriminations, Whitman had visited the Catholic mission the day before he died and had had tea. It was a horrifying thing to find him murdered and his mission a shambles. The priest gritted his teeth and gave the mutilated bodies a Christian burial. Before many days wolves dug them up. They were covered again, but the wolves were equally persistent. The ransomed captives were then taken away, and the bodies left to the elements.

At once the scattered settlers of the lower Columbia commenced to gather an armed force to mete out retribution and on February 24, 1848, over five hundred men started for the scene of the tragedy. They pursued the fleeing Cayuse to no avail, but the tribe did not dare to return. Meanwhile Joseph Meek, having found and buried the body of his daughter and cut a strand of Narcissa's blond hair, parted from the rest at Waiilatpu and rode east to ask the government's protection for Oregon settlers. The spring migration of 1848 met him, riding alone, to bring the first news of the massacre to civilization.

The Cayuse tribe wandered in the mountains for two years, and then five braves gave themselves up. They were tried, found guilty, and hanged on June 3, 1850. Joseph Meek, who was then United States Marshal in Oregon, served as executioner.

And what came of it all? What in the inscrutable ways of Providence resulted from the sacrifice of this devoted pair, unsuited by temperament for a life where tolerance and adaptability were necessary, but held to their posts by an unfaltering sense of duty?

In the last week of his life, when danger was fast closing in, Marcus said to Henry Spalding, "My death will probably do as much good to Oregon as my life can."

They were true words. Joseph Meek, a rough and arresting figure, arrived in Washington on May 17th. Congress took action, and by August 13th had approved the bill creating Oregon Territory. The United States crossed the continent as an immediate result of the massacre.

And who shall say what imprint the life and death of Marcus and Narcissa left upon the hearts of the Cayuse? To die for your belief was simple and direct, something they could understand and respect. It is said that, when the five Indians were awaiting execution, one of them was asked why they had given themselves up, and he replied, "Did not your missionaries teach us that Christ died to save his people? So die we to save our people."

The Whitmans, with the other victims, were finally interred in a small plot slightly up the hill slope from the mission site. The spot commands as much reverence as any shrine. They were true martyrs in the cause of God and of old Oregon.

25

Oregon for America

AT THE MOUTH OF THE Walla Walla, near its barren confluence with the Columbia, stood a small Hudson's Bay Company outpost manned by half a dozen men.

The country round about was sandy and sterile, the wind screamed like a cat with its tail caught, and the heroic outlines of river and shore were unrelieved by so much as a single tree. In point of age the small stockade at Fort Walla Walla was much the senior of any fort so far encountered. It was about two hundred feet square, and was built tightly of timbers set on end. At opposite corners, square bastions, supported on sturdy legs, projected out beyond the enclosure so that the small cannon and other firearms mounted at loopholes commanded all sides of the fort. Here, for the third time, the Oregonian-to-be invaded the hospitality of their courteous British rivals; and here travelers (beginning with Wyeth's party in '32 and ending in the early forties) found cordial P. C. Pambrun in charge.

Two miles before reaching the fort the pilgrims passed the lip-smacking vegetable garden where beets and melons were shouldered by bumptious cabbages and where, no doubt, they often saw the docile Mrs. Pambrun surrounded by her six sturdy half-breed children pulling turnips for dinner.

The men of Hudson's Bay Company, from high rank to low, took wives from among the Indian women. It made both for comfort and for good business. These marriages were entered into with some thought both for the pulchritude of the Indian girl in question and for the probable fur harvest of her village. They were usually solemnized at Fort Vancouver, were considered definitely binding, and the husband was expected to care for and, if possible, to educate his children. Every effort was put forth to make these marriages a lasting link with the tribe to which each wife belonged. It was sometimes difficult to explain to the expectant relatives that the white man neither bought nor sold his females, but they usually accepted the honor and endured the financial loss with good grace.

The Whitmans and Spaldings found haven at Fort Walla Walla in the first week of September, 1836, and the two bastions above the high walls were allotted to them for bedchambers. Narcissa was so delighted to hear the familiar and homely sound of a rooster crowing that the loaded cannon by her bedside was passed over as a minor detail. She wrote: "We consider it a very kind providence to be situated near one family so interesting, and a native female that promises to be so much society for me. She is learning to speak the English language quite fast." Later, when Narcissa's baby was born, it was Mrs. Pambrun who came to her aid.

Four years after the arrival of the Whitmans and Spaldings, two mountain men of superior intelligence and personality obtained the precious cart the missionaries had been forced to leave at McKay's fort on the Boise. These two, Robert Newell and Joseph Meek, drove it (together with another wagon obtained from Fort Hall) over Blue Mountains and arrived with great fanfare at Fort Walla Walla. No more wagons followed until the great migration of '43, and by the time its first companies under the leadership of Peter Burnett reached Fort Walla Walla a new post commander, Mr. McKinlay, ruled within the eighteen-foot log walls. The first division of wagons was trailed by the straggling cow column captained by Jesse Applegate, and the leaders of the emigrants went into a discussion of ways and means with the factor of the post that lasted several days. Meanwhile, into the hodgepodge and confusion of the emigrants' camps near the fort came the United States Exploring Expedition consisting of Brevet Captain John C. Frémont with his associate scientists, and "the people," as he always called his beloved coterie of trained mountain men. Mr. McKinlay rose to the social aspects of an occasion such as had never before presented itself. He invited Captain Frémont, representing the American government, and the captains of the wagon trains, representing unwanted American settlers, to a good English dinner, and every one was exceedingly polite to every one else.

As a result, Mr. McKinlay made a proposition that any emigrant so desiring might leave his weary stock at the fort, taking an order for a like number to be delivered by Hudson's Bay Company from their herds in the Willamette Valley. Probably both sides were satisfied with the deal. The stock driven overland from the States, once rested and sound again, was immeasurably better than the scrawny long-horned California cattle from which the Company had been recruiting its supply. On the other hand it was a long dangerous journey to the valley of the Willamette by way of the foot trail and the animals were already exhausted.

Wagon train by wagon train, the emigrants made their decisions and trickled out of camp. The Applegate family decided in favor of the Hudson's Bay cattle, disposed of their animals, and remained to arrange boats for themselves and their baggage. Frémont, leaving the migration to do as it pleased, began his long trek down the south bank of the Columbia and found it definitely wearisome. His men greatly envied the Applegate party, who soon passed them, gliding swiftly down the smooth current with apparently nothing to do but steer the boats.

At first the river was broad and placid, and the banks were studded here and there with a few willow thickets in which later travelers concealed their camps to avoid the overfriendly Indians. The ruse seldom succeeded, and the odorous and beaming aborigines arrived at all hours. They brought their own food, over which they asked loud blessings, and ate their well aged rabbit and spoiled fish in company with their shrinking white brothers in spite of all the latter could do. The emigrants complained at so much affection from the mission converts; but infinitely worse to meet were the deadly brown-skinned opportunists who bided their time at the river crossings to watch for stragglers.

The wagon companies of the first few migrations crossed the Umatilla near the mouth, unaware that many travelers of the future would first strike the Columbia at that point. The banks of the great river along this open stretch have always been fertile fields for fire, and the men were warned at Fort Walla Walla that miles of pasturage might disappear in a day.

Twelve miles beyond Willow Creek, near modern Arlington, the banks of the Columbia which for miles had been swelling and cracking into barren gullies, broke out in an eruption of scabby rimrock; but the indomitable pack trains invaded the canyon and stayed with the river. Soon the narrow pack trail ran about midway up the cliff with a dizzy drop of one hundred feet to the river and another hundred feet of basalt bulging out over their heads. The wagons could not use this shelf trail and moved along the bluff tops, but were forced to descend a steep hill in order to ford the John Day River, lying peaceably at the bottom of its sunken

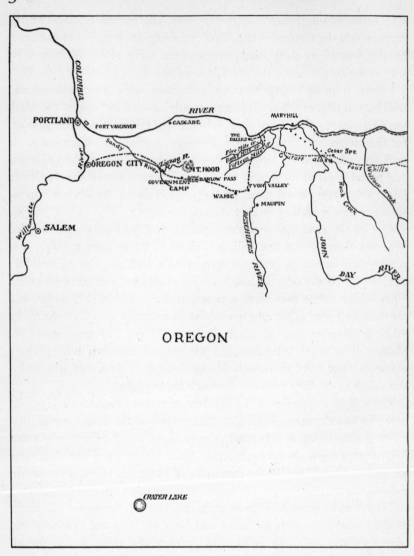

valley. They crossed without difficulty and had a long pull up and out before proceeding along the bluffs again.

Two years less than a century had passed when we, with a copy of Frémont's reports in our hands, traced his day-by-day progress, supplementing it with all the miscellaneous items I had been able to gather into the "Paden encyclopedia" about the experiences of the early pioneers along this section of the river. Looking across the broad expanse of water to the bare north shore, we could see miles and miles of fires burning unheeded in the sparse grass. The warnings given at Fort Walla Walla in 1843 still hold good. A flatboat carrying cars blundered out into the smooth strong current, and a sign tabbed it the Maryhill ferry. Just beyond it we came to a trail marker. Here, the inscription said tersely, the emigrants had their first glimpse of the Columbia.

For us, who had just followed their trail along the river all the way from the Walla Walla, this required explanation; but it turned out to be true in part. Some of the emigrants did *not* see the river until they got here. The sign is right as far as it goes, for it marks the end of the cross-country trail that went along the foothills, and that came into the river-bank trail here.

Actually the last few miles of the cross-country trail were very little used. Most of its travelers never saw the Columbia at all because, about the time the wagons started going cross-lots along the foothills, a man by the name of Barlow worked out a route to the Willamette Valley that turned sharply back from the river along one of the creeks just east of the Dalles. For a year or maybe two, the emigrants continued to come to the river here and turn right back south again to get on the Barlow road. That seemed rather useless, so after a while they stopped coming to the Columbia at all and simply cut across.

The ford of Deschutes River was the next uncertain quantity, and the Indians hiring out as pilots might be classed similarly; but there are recorded cases where they undertook to swim the cattle and did the job well and cheaply. It was never advisable, however, to become separated from the company or to allow animals to stray while fording, for unfriendly Indians lurked behind its trees and rocks. It was noted as a dangerous crossing.

The beauty of Deschutes River, named for its many cascades, is no small feature of the picturesque grandeur of the Columbia and ushers in the interesting portion containing Celilo Falls and the Dalles. Frémont called the former "the Falls of the Columbia" and failed to send a description to Congress on the ground that they had been many times seen and praised. He was disappointed that he could not wait and watch events during flood season, when the river was apt to back up and submerge them and the Canadian voyageur found no difficulty in passing over them in his canoe. On the contrary the Dalles were negotiable in low water but were entirely impassable during flood season. Frémont wrote:

"The whole volume of the river at this place passed between the walls of a chasm, which has the appearance of having been rent through the basaltic strata which form the valley rock of the region. At the narrowest place we found the breadth, by measurement, 58 yards, and the average height of the walls above the water 25 feet; forming a trough between the rocks—whence the name, probably applied by a Canadian voyageur. . . .

"In the recent passage through this chasm, an unfortunate event had occurred to Mr. Applegate's party, in the loss of one of their boats, which had been carried under water in the midst of the Dalles, and two of Mr. Applegate's children and one man drowned."

Just below the Dalles at the modern city of that name, Daniel Lee, nephew of Jason, had built a mission settlement which, with the scattered wooden huts of the Indian village, "gave to the valley the cheerful and busy air of civilization." The Indians of this section were shockingly indolent and dirty. They looked to the river to supply all their wants, and, as nature had failed to place fur on the salmon, they went unabashedly without clothes. They were, however, amenable to kind treatment and easily became active in religious observance.

The place where the mission used to stand was our main interest at the Dalles, and the population singly and collectively thought we were balmy. After a while, in spite of some would-be directors and because of others, we stood on the Twelfth Street hill just back of the high school and were told that the Lee mission was built thereabouts. A jagged rocky fragment entitled, as might be expected, Pulpit Rock stands in an intersection of two streets and was pointed out as the first place where the missionaries preached to the Indians. The old mission springs still flow in the school yard. It was here that John Minto, arriving tired but exultant on a Sunday, camped up against the mission and was but coldly received because he had traveled on the Sabbath and thus set a bad example to the heathen. In later years, a trifle amused, he admitted that the emigrants were not much help to the missionaries as shining exponents of Christian training.

Another significant spot, and one of much more interest to the run-of-the-mill traveler, is the historical museum of the city. It is well up on the hill away from the river, and was built in 1856 as the surgeon's quarters at old Fort Dalles. The building is quite pretentious and of an almost indescribable quaintness. Two or three rooms are crammed with exhibits, and many things of interest lie here and there in the yard, including a large dugout canoe and the bell from the mission.

Until the fall of 1845 the Oregon Trail ended at the Dalles. Frémont wrote to Congress, "Our land journey found here its western termination." He left Kit Carson in charge of the camp and, with three others, hired a canoe and Indian paddlers to take him to Fort Vancouver and back again. "The last of the emigrants," he wrote, "had just left the Dalles at the time of our arrival, travelling some by water and others by land, making ark-like rafts, on which they had embarked their families and household, with their large wagons and other furniture, while their stock were driven along the shore." We are told that the only trail to the lower Columbia at this time was the horse trail (probably of Indian origin) used by the missionaries to bring cattle from the Willamette Valley. It passed through a forest of such weird density that day appeared almost like night, and, leading its travelers north of Mount Hood, struck straight for the Falls of the Willamette.

It seemed hard to the contingent toiling along where the first few miles of the cattle trail paralleled the Columbia, to watch the river craft sail past so easily; but the time came when, had they known it, those on foot were in better case than the ones on the log rafts, often so heavily loaded that the current ran strongly three or four inches above their floor. Where the great river breaks through the Cascade Mountains the current became roughened and terrific headwinds filled the air with flying sand. At the Cascades a difficult portage was necessary for the baggage, while Indians ran the empty craft through. Sometimes, instead, the travelers found Hudson's Bay Company's boats waiting. It was often impossible to make way against the gale and they were forced to tie up for days at a time. The food supply of the '43ers was low and, of course, the boat parties had no cattle to kill. Things looked rather desperate when James Waters with a few men came upstream to meet them with a boatload of supplies from Fort Vancouver and, in all probability, saved much suffering.

Ninety miles above the fort, and one hundred eighty miles from the ocean, wrote the pioneers of '43, the boats came to tidewater, with its ebb and flow, and progress was still more impeded. The first sign of civilization seen by the expectant emigrants was a small sawmill on the north bank. Six or seven miles beyond was a considerable prairie on which, set well back from the river, the emigrants found a large stockade, or fort, surrounded by farm lands. On the river were the Hudson's Bay Company's sloops. Many Indians paddled idly about in their canoes singing, while wild fowl in great numbers flew overhead. On the gently sloping north shore a village of more than fifty houses was arranged in even rows to form streets. One building, larger than the rest, proved to be a hospital, while a boathouse hugged the water line. It was a settlement sheltering in all some eight hundred people. The travelers had come at last to Fort Vancouver.

Wyeth's party in '32 found Dr. McLoughlin, chief factor for the company, in full command. He was a kingly figure of six feet four inches, a courtly, kindly gentleman ruling his territory with a firm hand. There was not, so they wrote, a white woman in all of Oregon, but the men were well cared for by their Indian wives. Dr. McLoughlin and his clerks lived in separate houses within the stockade where, if one includes the storehouses, were some forty buildings. There were cannon on the premises, but, as the fort was always peaceful, they were mainly to lend an air of preparedness. In the village by the river lived the French trappers with their families, the laborers, and the servants from the fort. Outside the walls fruit trees flourished, and grain fields colored the slope. Cattle had been brought from California, and the herd allowed to increase. Only one bull calf a year was killed in order to provide rennet for the cheese making, and some four hundred head were said to graze within sight of the fort.

The "good doctor" never allowed desire for profit to blind him to the best interests of the Indians or of the voyageurs, his devoted servants. No liquor was traded for furs. He himself was most abstemious and drank but once a year, on the day when the trappers' flotilla returned down-river bringing the men back to their homes.

A decade later the pioneers of 1843 found a similar picture with Dr. McLoughlin the same stately figure of authority. His compassionate nature still embraced all humanity, and could not see their needs without taking measures to alleviate them. It was not the policy of England nor of his company to encourage emigration from the States; but to him the new settlers were just human beings in distress. He fed and clothed them.

He gave them work. He put them on their feet in the new land to which they had blindly trusted themselves. He did this increasingly, as each year brought new people and new problems, until his greatness of heart put an end to his career and brought immortality to his memory.

*   *   *

The pioneers were glad to reach Fort Vancouver with its orderly peaceful village at the river's edge and its air of well established comfort and safety. It was a haven; but it was not their goal, and they must hurry to complete their journey. For until each traveler had found a home on fertile land, or an opportunity to earn money in one of the tiny communities, he was still "on the road."

In '43, '44, and to some extent in later years the prospective settlers simply took boats and drifted down the Columbia six or seven miles to where the broad Willamette enters, and pulled their way up the latter. Navigation headed at the Falls of the Willamette, and a prosperous industrial site seemed assured by the unlimited water power. The newcomers established a budding settlement on a narrow shelf of land between bluff and river and called it Oregon City.

Soon afterward Portland was laid out at the mouth of the Willamette by Mr. Pettigrove and the same A. L. Lovejoy who had been captured by the Indians at Independence Rock with Lansford Hastings and who later in the same year traveled East with Dr. Whitman. They flipped a copper for the privilege of naming it. Mr. Pettigrove won and called it Portland, but only the thickness of a coin stood between the future metropolis of Oregon and the name Boston.

Oregon pioneers being what they were, one might guess that a short cut to the Willamette Valley would be found—or, if not found, hacked out—before long. As a matter of fact only two migrations had taken their wagons apart for the long boat trip down the Columbia when, in 1845, the family of S. K. Barlow arrived at the Dalles and camped to consider the matter. Separating his wagons and stock did not appeal to Mr. Barlow, to say nothing of parting from his family. He determined to take his teams intact to Oregon City. The east side of the Cascade Mountains, he heard, was easy. The west side was swampy and thick with undergrowth. Very well—then the west side would have to be reconnoitered. He took the bull by the horns and moved his party of nineteen adults with thirteen wagons out of the Dalles, southeast to Five Mile Creek and thence some thirty miles south to Tygh Valley. Meanwhile William H. Rector and his wife joined them and, on a separate occasion, a small wagon train under Joel Palmer.

A semipermanent camp was established in Tygh Valley, and Mr. Barlow, accompanied by Mr. Rector, set out to locate a possible wagon route over the Cascades. The first fifteen miles was on a plainly marked Indian pony trail. During the absence of their leader the other men set to work, with dull tools sometimes augmented by the use of fire, to widen the trail for wagons. The cattle were driven ahead, and as the Indians had never bothered to make a wider passageway than would just accommodate their small ponies some of the larger animals were crippled and even killed between the trees. As the road was finished the wagons were moved, and the two leaders, returning almost starved from their reconnoiter, found them considerably west of the spot where they had been left. Mr. Rector refused to expose his wife to the vicissitudes of the proposed journey and returned to the Dalles. The rest went climbing slowly toward the summit of what is now called Barlow Pass. This was just one year after the first teams got across the Sierras into California and four years before the gold rush of '49. A century ago!

We made our simple preparations and left the Dalles for Tygh Valley.

Pretty little Five Mile Creek did not see much emigrant traffic, so we took a look also at Ten Mile Creek—as its name indicates, ten miles east of the Dalles. Later travelers left the Columbia at this point, to save the extra mileage into the Dalles, and trekked almost twenty miles along its course. While climbing Tygh Ridge we passed through a countryside of golden wheat, dead ripe; but beyond the summit the grain land gives way to rough uncultivated canyons where cow trails slanting down in both directions form a mesh like stretched fishnets over the scrubby hillsides. Beyond the canyons Tygh Valley opens, long and winding. Within its confines is a town of the same name, where I bought the best peanut brittle imaginable and we were told to drive to Wamic and to take the Forest Service Road from there up the mountain.

On and on, up and up. Here was the portion of the route made from the old Indian trail. Over the pathfinders towered noble, white-crowned Mount Hood. The years do not change it. It watches over the tawny wheat fields of modern Oregon as impersonally as it looked out over the tangled oak and sage slopes of long ago. It watched over us as we scrambled toward it, just as it did, in magnificent detachment, when two determined men trailed by a small equally determined wagon train, set out to hew the first road through its swamps and forests.

In timber almost impenetrable the old road crept up to Barlow Summit and started down. The small dirt thoroughfare now labeled Barlow Road is not the original but often intersects it, and we were able to keep in touch. At the summit of Mount Hood Loop Highway the interested motorist may notice the original road, crossing at the Hood and Clackamas County sign. The modern Barlow Road is about a hundred yards distant.

Sliding downhill through the timber, the old road looked much more attractive than it had when toiling up the slope. My husband and I suddenly decided to walk down to Government Camp, sending Bill and Dr. Neff around by the highway with the car.

It was a marvelous hike, short, downhill, and shady. I recommend it to any one who would like to get away from the beaten track and retire a hundred years into the past. The old road leaves the summit at the Clackamas County sign and comes into the highway again at the Pioneer Woman's grave. I don't think it took us more than half an hour, and it is the only short section that is so definite in its directions.

The mountain is thickly wooded with red fir and mountain white pine, and hundreds of trees were felled to let the wagons through. Sometimes they are piled in a hodgepodge like jackstraws. Sometimes they are laid neatly, one on top of another, on each side of the road, almost like a great solid fence. Long sections of the roadbed are bottomed with rotted corduroy, and sometimes rocks the size of a man's head fill it from rim to rim. The wagons had driven for a distance along the bed of a tiny creek, and we hopped from rock to rock until dry land was available again for walking purposes. Sometimes the long ribbon of open space hemmed by solid timber was bedded with wild strawberries, sweet and ripe, and the decayed tree trunks piled along the way were clawed apart and strewn about the road in spongy brown strips by bear, hunting the hideous white wood grubs with which they are filled. Once we saw a doe mincing daintily at a thimbleberry bush. We startled her, and she bounded from the slender clearing and disappeared. Nowhere did we see a place that looked wide enough for two prairie schooners to pass.

* * *

For a while after leaving Government Camp we followed the highway and commenced playing at cross purposes with the Zigzag River. The travelers of the Barlow Road, too, found it continually in their way. It is a beautiful mountain torrent, swift, deeper than it looks, and full of smooth, glassy boulders that played havoc with the horses' legs. The highway keeps close to the old road along this portion. Laurel Hill was the landmark most often mentioned, and usually ushered in trouble for the stock. Grass was scarce, and the cattle were used to browsing on cottonwood branches as an acceptable substitute. They needed continual watching, for the leaves of the laurel tree poisoned them. The Barlow company lost a horse from this cause and had become so apprehensive of a serious food shortage that the hams were severed from the body and saved for emergency rations.

The rangers at the Zigzag Station drew us some maps and added plenty of advice, for the old road had commenced to deviate from the highway. They turned us at once across a bridge and past a C.C.C. camp. Two more bridges appeared in quick succession; the first was a quaint suspension that spanned another "zig" of the Zigzag, the second was an old covered bridge over a big, swift, and exceedingly dirty stream, laboring under the shopworn title Big Sandy. Some three hundred yards beyond we turned sharply to the left on the Brightwood Road, and used that as a base of operations. It partly coincides with the Barlow Road and runs hand in hand with the river. Big-leafed maples, shading sword-fern thickets, edge the little backwoods lane, and in the sunny spots are fuzzy, dry hazelnut bushes and hedges of wild rose. Sweeping fir forests shelter fine log cottages, and over the clearings march four-foot magenta spikes of fire plant which only flourish in soil ravaged by conflagration. Along the first stretch is a large up-thrusting rock, noted landmark and camp site, and then the little old Marmot Post Office claims attention for its historic memories.

The original Barlow party was unincumbered by wagons as it toiled down the Sandy, for the leaders had decided to leave their belongings and wagons for the winter and come back for them the next spring. By the time the tiny cabin was built five miles east of the summit, provisions were so low that only one man could be outfitted, and William Berry remained on guard alone. It was December, and there were twelve inches of snow on the ground: a bad time for a mixed group containing children and elderly women to be afoot. The whortleberry swamps at the base of the mountain were desperately hard to skirt and, even in later years, were considered the worst mud of the two thousand miles. The Barlow and Palmer parties climbed onto their miscellaneous livestock and rode.

There seemed to be unlimited masculine Barlows. James A. and John L. undertook to go ahead and bring back much-needed food. They disappeared down the mountain. The rest of the party ate sparingly, shivered, and made three to five miles per day. Several days passed, and William Barlow and John M. Bacon set out afoot to try their luck. There was so little food that, after feeding the children, the older members of one family had a cracker apiece. It was imperative to get help.

There was no fear of losing the way after striking the Big Sandy; but, for men afoot, there was danger at the numerous crossings. William felled a tree at one swift and deep ford, but it washed away before they could use it and left them hungrier and more tired than ever, to pass the night as best they could. In the morning William decided to make use of an island planted cockily midstream. He cut himself a pole, took a long run and vaulted across to it. Here he was more handicapped in take-off, but managed to land in shallow water and started posthaste toward Oregon City, leaving Bacon where he was. In eight miles from this last crossing of the Sandy, he came to the ranch of Phillip Foster, well known as the first habitation to be reached in the Willamette country, and in twenty-four hours had found his brothers, finished organizing a supply party, and was on the way back.

Meanwhile the remainder of the company had not sat down to wait for rescue—not they! The young men met them on the evening of the first day of the return trip trooping steadily forward, mounted on the animals which had formerly drawn the wagons—horses, oxen, bulls, and with old Mother Hood on the faithful cow she had ridden clear from the Dalles. This was the 23rd, and on Christmas Day they arrived at Oregon City, having been eight months and twenty-four days on the road from Illinois.

And the future order of events on the Barlow Road gravitated every year into much the same channel. As each fall's migrations neared the bottom of the mountain slope, enthusiastic Willamette Valley settlers came out to meet them. Meat and flour were dispensed with equally lavish hands to those who could pay and to those who could not, so that all fared alike. And for years Foster's Ranch was their immediate objective and Oregon City their Mecca.

In the summer of '46, Mr. Barlow was granted a charter to improve his road and to collect toll by the provisional government set up in Oregon by the pioneers of 1843. He was not a man to dillydally, and by early fall when the caravans arrived at the Dalles they found it ready for travel; about two-thirds of that year's migration used it. Mr. Barlow kept it as a doubtful source of income for two years during which promises to pay were taken as readily as cash, and then turned the charter back to the government for a free road. Naturally it fell into disrepair. The government granted another charter to Foster and Young, and later still another to Honorable F. O. McCown of Oregon City. In one way and another it was kept open to the wagons until there was no longer any need for it.

The thriving community at the Falls of the Willamette soon became choked on its shelflike river bank and crawled to the cliff top for room to

Oregon City in 1845.

(Adapted from a sketch made by British Naval Officers, found in Joseph Gaston's "Centennial History of Oregon, 1811–1911")

stretch and expand, but the stores and buzzing business centers still hugged the churning water's edge. Here at Oregon City the tired but exultant emigrants who had just conquered the forests and swamps and snows of Hood Mountain met again both those who had sailed down the Columbia and the travelers of the missionaries' cattle trail. Anxious families were reunited and, looking around them at the old settlers of a week or a year, realized that they themselves were unkempt and shabby beyond belief. Joseph Watt, later an influential citizen of Oregon, wrote that he was the first to arrive in Oregon City in the year 1844. He was penniless and had earned his way down the Columbia by sitting in a Hudson's Bay boat and singing to the oarsmen—an accomplishment he was unaware of possessing until necessity forced him to try. His walnut roundabout was worn and dirty; his knee-length buckskin pants were bunchily patched with antelope hide; his woolen hat was mainly brim, worn to shade his eyes and requiring dextrous balancing to prevent its suddenly becoming a necklace; and, around his shoulders, he clutched a red blanket. Suddenly he came face to face with Dr. McLoughlin—an imposing presence with a mane of white hair flowing almost to his broad shoulders and the carriage of a man born to command instant obedience. The factor gazed distastefully and compassionately at the apparition for a moment and then ordered him completely outfitted.

And, in just such fashion, the good works of this great man continued. As chief factor he was never unfaithful to the Hudson's Bay Company, with which he had so identified himself that it was his very life. He never deliberately encouraged American settlers; but common decency demanded that he give help where help was so desperately needed, and through his humanitarian example the commanders at the three lesser forts along the trail did the same for many years.

Of course, economically speaking, it might have been better for the Hudson's Bay Company if the first comers from the States *had* been mistreated by the Indians or had starved to death; and a distant headquarters felt that abstractly he had failed to protect its interests. The handwriting on the wall was plain to be read. In 1845, the same year that the Barlow party struggled over the mountains, he resigned from the company and built a big two-story house of clapboards at Oregon City.

The Indians had been peaceful throughout his long firm domination of Fort Vancouver and the middle and upper reaches of the Columbia. His overthrow did not mitigate their growing unrest. Neither did the closing, in 1844, of all the Methodist missions—in the Willamette Valley, at the mouth of the Columbia, on Puget Sound, and at the Dalles. The Methodist Board could see that the missions were very expensive, that they made few converts, and that their chief asset was the ability to give confidence and a helping hand to the new and uncertain settlers. They did not feel justified in using the Church's money for secular purposes.

By 1847 the Indians were out of hand. The Whitman massacre resulted. The volunteer soldiers went up the Columbia, and white man was arraigned against red man in the Oregon country. It would have happened anyway. It was the inevitable story of the westward strides of civilization. These incidents were merely bundles of straws on the proverbial camel's back.

The years of adjustment have now passed. The Indians are both increasing and advancing. They live the year around in comfort and for the most part in dignity and integrity. It is very doubtful if any of them regret the former winters of semistarvation and summers of spoiled fish endured by the ancestors whose unenviable attributes have been recorded in history.

In 1849 Dr. McLoughlin became an American citizen and lived on quietly in Oregon City, not acclaimed nor especially appreciated. Like many another saddened man his reward came posthumously, and now the whole Northwest proclaims him blessed. On the bluff edge at Oregon City the white rectangular house, all the more beautiful because of its simplicity, still stands above the broad Willamette to mark the end of the road to Oregon.

26

South with the Big Goose

"The Junction! Here they come!"

Down from the mountain fastnesses of the City of Rocks came the wagons of Lydia Waters, David Cosad, Helen Carpenter, Alonzo Delano, Leander Loomis, and many, many others, each in his own year and with his own company. Up a curving canyon to the south, elbowing a small branch of Raft River, came the wagons from Salt Lake, creeping quietly into Junction Valley and bringing Franklin Langworthy, John Clark, Lucy Cooke, James Abbey, William Johnston, and the fellowship who had elected to go by way of Salt Lake City, each in his own time and season.

The two lines met and fused. It was one of the significant events of the journey west.

A mile or so back on the road that led down from the mountains, were three symmetrical sugar-loaf rocks, all that the Salt Lake contingent saw of the wonders surrounding the City of the Rocks. Delano estimated them as sixty to eighty feet high. We neglected to estimate, and so we will let Mr. Delano's figures stand.

As the California-bound wagons entered the wide grassy spread of Junction Valley their owners cherished no illusions. Not only was the approaching descent into Big Goose Creek one of the worst of the journey, but they knew that the remaining third of the overland trek was by far the most dangerous and uncomfortable, with bad water, absence of feed, dust and heat in the daytime and extreme cold at night. In addition to these disadvantages, very few early guidebooks covered the rest of the journey to California. The gold seekers had left the beaten track of the Oregon Trail and were disturbingly on their own. It was counted sixteen miles from the junction, over Granite Mountain and down to the Big Goose Creek. A small stream known by some as Sleet Creek comforted them on their way for a mile or so, and they often baited at noon beside Mountain Spring, snuggled just below the summit on the near side.

A good modern road leads straight to the pass, and the trail is plainly seen, especially as it lifts above the valley land and passes the spring. A few weather-beaten aspens crown the summit, and the view down to the west is picturesque and extended, with the massive bulk of the "Flatiron" mountain occupying a prominent place.

"A prospect bounded only by the power of vision, now burst upon the sight," wrote Langworthy, ". . . one of the most sublime pieces of mountain scenery I have as yet surveyed in this region of wonders. We now descended five miles a fearful steep, and in many places, we had to chain all the wheels, and assemble all our force to hold the wagons back."

It was the last week in July when our party stood on the summit of Granite Mountain. The take-off is really steep and leads down a grassy ravine filled, even in the late summer, with wild flowers. The ascent has been short and uneventful. The descent is long and dangerous. It is divided into two parts, and it was from the vantage point in the middle that the full extent of the tumultuous mountains ahead burst upon the view of the emigrants. Caroline Richardson made the journey in 1852 after the trail had shaken down into some sort of permanent grades. "I thought I had seen mountains," she wrote, "but what I had previously seen was merely a prelude." After winding over hills and rocky defiles her company came to a steep mountain called, so she said, "The Devil's Grave." They were lucky enough to reach it while daylight held. Many did not. They also reached bottom in safety. And many did not. This was the place where the Forty-niners let their wagons down with ropes and, according to Mrs. Richardson, was worse than all the bad places of their previous experience put together, having perpendicular stretches of twenty feet at a time, besides being deeply gullied. In spite of all their efforts a wagon went tail over tongue to the first landing, losing a hundredweight of flour and ruining a large water can. Lucy Cooke wrote later of the same hill, "My wagon seemed as though it stood on end."

"Was this the place where a driver fell off the seat and over the rest of the team onto the lead mules?" Bill asked doubtfully.

"Somewhere on the down grade, yes—and the wagon probably tipped over right afterward," Dr. Neff answered. "The center of gravity was up in the load. Those old schooners and Conestoga wagons were built for clearance. Some of them had six-foot wheels."

"What the emigrants needed was tanks," Bill said flatly.

"No, the wagons were pretty well adapted to their job," his father disagreed, "and they were safe enough if the drivers didn't allow themselves to be rushed in dangerous spots, and if the animals didn't get frightened or balky or any of the *if*'s that killed people every day. I'll bet there wasn't a grave marker on the whole Oregon Trail that couldn't have had an inscription beginning with 'if.'"

The journey down the mountain to Big Goose Creek was loosely noted as seven or eight miles, the last of which were along the course of a little tributary known today as Birch Creek. It is the driest, sagiest little gully imaginable and is barely passable for an exploring car. White, chalky cliffs are everywhere in evidence and supply ample reason for the ghostly effect of the valley. Fantastic rocks, cone-shaped by wind erosion, fringe the right-hand bluffs, and the canyon opens opposite the Horseshoe Ranch.

The Goose Creek country should be seen for the first time at twilight, as the emigrants saw it from the top of the Devil's Grave, in order to get the benefit of the weird lighting effects for which it is noted. Instead we struck it flatly at noon with a storm brewing, and found that the big rolling clouds cast perfectly ordinary shadows over the barns, houses, and pastures that lay before us.

We drove through the ranch gate and approached the house in time to see the men rush out on the double quick for the hayfield to beat the rain. The women invited us in, said that they felt like sitting for a few minutes over their coffee cups, and hospitably offered lunch which not one of us was strong-minded enough to refuse.

"Are we far from the Utah Construction Company's ranches?" my husband asked as he helped himself to sugar.

"They're just south of us," one of the women answered. "Miles of them, running along the Utah-Nevada line. A Mr. Bowman is the manager: Archie Bowman. He lives at the San Jacinto Ranch over on Twin Falls Highway."

"Gracious!" The younger woman stopped with the coffee pot poised over her cup. "If you want to get there, you'd better go back to Oakley, then to Twin Falls and take the highway to Wells, Nevada. The way you're heading, it's fifty miles to the highway and then at least twenty-five more back north to San Jacinto."

"Besides, I'm not really sure the road is passable except maybe for trucks," the older one added anxiously.

"We don't have to see Mr. Bowman," my husband explained. "Fortunately we found him at San Jacinto on our way east and he gave me a letter to the foremen of the other ranches. We'll just stay along with the trail as far as we can. If it's impassable we can always come back."

And so it was left.

The Big Goose proved upon investigation to be a narrow, winding willow-hidden watercourse flung carelessly in verdant green loopings. From its edges gray sage sneaked up on the flat-topped whitish hills smudged with junipers. Higher and sharper peaks loomed pale and ghostly in the distance while, just behind the Horseshoe Ranch, Flatiron Rock jutted black against the cloud-massed sky. We turned up the valley and went south. Whenever an occupied ranch appeared the men were busy haying.

The valley, even in these days, is not overpopulated. For a while we crow-hopped along a channeled thoroughfare which was evidently a sort of no man's land between the ranchers who do their trading in Idaho and the ones who make occasional visits out to Wells, Nevada. The washes were so bad that we built aprons of rock to let the car slide down into them and made our mileage, while the afternoon waned, by a succession of infant engineering feats.

It cleared presently, but strings of tiny water beads still slanted across our windows as we, traveling with the trail, came to Goose Creek again.

There's no blinking the fact that this valley, in trail days, was not a good place to be. Its irregularities consisted more of discomforts and uneasiness than of active dangers: heat, cold, bad water, dust, and ugly little Indians. But beyond all this its worst characteristic was the lowering of morale, both in the travelers themselves and in their stock. Animals became jittery, teams were difficult to control, and hitherto docile bossies became as impossible to milk as the wild antelope. Maybe it was because of their resemblance to wolves that pet dogs caused so many runaways, but they had always been a disturbing factor and were especially so along Goose Creek. The cattle were developing exposed nerves that twanged like banjo strings at the very sight of a pup.

The emigrants had found a few dead animals in the Big Sandy, but it was in Goose Creek that the stock really formed the habit of dying in the only available water supply. In places the current was dammed with disintegrating carcasses, and the creek crept on as a foul and slimy stew. Beside it the corrupt earth was strewn with nauseous hides and wolf-gnawed bones while the drainage from a hundred camps reeked in the hot sun.

The caravans had the heeby-jeebies. Fear crept in, as indefinable as the dust and as inescapable: fear fused of weariness, illness, and uneasiness. Qualms of aversion, too: aversion to the fetid air, loathsome water, and revolting sights. Every sense was offended. Brittle outbursts resulted in antagonisms, and former partners were now ranged grittily against each other.

It must be, one might think, that the romance of the trail died and weltered away on Goose Creek. But no—the records tell us that it did not. For here, at the ford, a wedding took place. Not just a marriage, but a real wedding with a supper, kissing of the bride, and tears from the sentimental. Here in Nature's chapel, carpeted with half-pulled roots from which the heavy dried grass had been eaten, upholstered in cattle carcasses and embowered in willow to which clung clusters of crows like strange shining bunches of dark fruit, Lavinia Pond was given in marriage to Isaac Decker while the members of the emigration of 1853, then present, looked on and approved mightily.

The wagon sheets were spread on the ground to form a table; the bridal couple took their places on an ox yoke at the head, and forty members of the couple's own train sat around it. Besides the ordinary fare they had roast duck and custard pie, for the boys had found a nest containing fourteen eggs still fit for use. The festivities continued until daylight, when the little Indians came timidly into camp to see what the war dance was about.

The Indians! We may as well consider the subject, which, from here to the sink of the Humboldt, was never far from the minds of those who trod the trail. The emigrants called them all Diggers. Actually there were two types, as far apart as the poles.

The Utes, a dangerous, implacable nation were not often seen except in horse-stealing skirmishes. They ranged up and down Utah, lower Idaho, and the upper part of the Humboldt River, had a more or less permanent village near Battle Mountain, and used their horses to ride. The other kind were small, timid, and excruciatingly filthy. They were not a warlike people, and their chief use for a horse was to roast it whole and fill their always empty stomachs. Goose Creek Valley specialized in this latter variety, whom Captain Bonneville had called Shoshokoes. Both were found on Hudspeth's Cutoff, on the Fort Hall Road, and on tributaries of Raft River; and caused plenty of trouble. Through the years Goose Creek was the scene of some brutal killings by the Utes, but the Shoshokoes' chief vice was their appetite.

A Shoshokoe never got enough to eat. Sunflower seed and dried berries were scarce. Owls, lizards, and snakes furnished tidbits which they now and then offered to share with some shrinking female who had given them bread. Lice were not very satisfying and took time to catch, but any Shoshokoe had plenty of both commodities. Antelope drives, previously described, furnished them with an occasional gorge, but the best hunting grounds and fishing streams were preempted by the stronger tribes so that they were always at a disadvantage. Fortunately crickets and grasshoppers were numerous. The squaws either burned their legs off by setting fire to the grass and then picked them up by hand, or else dug a big hole and enlisted the help of the men. A very large circle of Indians was formed, and thousands of crickets were driven into the hole by the gradually narrowing ring of flailing Indians. In some cases they merely added hot rocks and served at once, in others they allowed the insects to dry and ground them into a coarse meal for cakes.

They had no reason to love the Americans. Captain Bonneville's trappers, the first men with white skins the tribe had ever seen, shot them for robbing beaver traps and then shot many more to prevent the news from spreading. Nevertheless a Shoshokoe was not unfriendly. He was just hungry. If anything was proffered him, he bolted it whole—even chewing tobacco. He sometimes hung around a night or two for the sake of the handouts, even submitting like a dog to a good scrubbing in order to qualify; but when he left, all the portable property handy vanished at the same time.

The Shoshokoes' incessant struggle for food made them a constant adverse factor in the experience of the emigrants. An ox, found in the morning pincushioned with arrows, had to be killed, and the watching little people were sure of the offal. Sometimes they ran off cattle at night (but most cattle running can doubtless be attributed to the Utes). When they did make a raid they preferred horse or mule meat because it made better time before butchering; and they would stop to kill, cut the warm meat in chunks, sear and eat it almost under their pursuers' disgusted noses. A white man, they knew, wouldn't take away a dead horse. They could come back for the rest after he had gone.

Our impressions of this afternoon's dusty miles remain as vague recollections of haggard gray flats upon which various ranchers unknown have tried the decorative effect of rectangular tin houses—now empty; of distant ghostly mountains like smudges of rubbed chalk; of one or two fords of the Big Goose, massed with heavy green willows and merely threaded by the glinting silver of the water; of the old trail in worn, hard-beaten gouges and the thrashing of wind-whipped sage; and finally of coming to a hollow full of flowering greasewood and the comfort of a decent ranch road.

Our attention was soon caught by some curious white cliffs known since the fifties as Record Bluffs. They were full of queer, shallow holes like a salt lick, and one of them was crowned by a malevolent hand-carved head. On the face of the cliff, among others, we found the name "Mann"—presumably the Henry Mann whose manuscript notebook we have read many times.

Near the confluence of the Big and the Little Goose we left the trail to find the Grande Ranch, where we spent the night.

The foreman greeted us with the friendly enthusiasm of a man who hasn't been in town for a long time, selected a site where we might pitch our tent, and invited us to dinner. After a while the men emerged from the bunkhouse and came in groups over to the main ranch house to eat.

Six capable sentences from the foreman took care of introductions and disposed of the possible thought that we might be tourists strayed from the paths of orthodoxy. Then we settled down to business, and a mighty quiet settled down on us. The table was pleasantly crowded with fried veal chops, potatoes browned whole, chopped lettuce and sugar, melted cheese on crackers, marvelous spongy slices of homemade bread, green onions, sour pickles, apple sauce, and a plate of he-man tarts that looked like big biscuits and were full of mincemeat.

Here was a crowd that strained the dining room at the seams and a dinner that would rouse enthusiasm in any one—but no conversation. Maybe we were cramping the party. From pure altruism I started in to help out.

They took turns listening with perfunctory courtesy, while the un-obligated remainder ate in concentrated silence. Once in a while I received a monosyllabic reply. It was a bit stiffish, and after six or eight minutes it dawned on me that my audience was barely tolerant. My next laboriously conceived idea was stillborn. I glanced at my husband. He was swiftly finishing his dessert, and his face expressed simple pleasure in my struggle. I looked around the big rectangle of empty dishes. Every one was through except the last unfortunate who had been answering my questions, and about one minute more would take care of him. I hadn't even made a dent in my good food. My blush was practically audible, and I tried to match him forkful by forkful. No use—he finished, and the time for eating was past. Each man shoved his chair back and picked up his dishes. I slid a tart into my sweater pocket and did likewise, depositing my plate and cup with the rest on the kitchen sink, and went out into the evening with, at any rate, plenty of food for thought.

I joined the Paden family at the tent, and my husband grinned. Bill was happily unconscious of any contretemps. His successful absorption of a second helping of food during the time allotted must be set down to native talent, for he and I had shared a common ignorance of ranch etiquette. And I date from that day my realization of the fact that a farm (with which I was and am perfectly familiar) is *not* a ranch.

"Mr. Paden!" The foreman's voice was raised from the vicinity of the gate.

"Yes, I'm at the tent."

"How much gas have you in your car?"

"Plenty, I guess. Mr. Bowman told me not to worry, that, if we reached the Eccles Ranch in the early afternoon of July 2nd, we could get refilled there. That's tomorrow and it can't be more than fifty miles."

"That's funny. There's nobody at the Eccles Ranch this year. You're sure that's what he said?" By this time he had reached the tent.

"Yes—absolutely. Mrs. Paden made a note of it." I tried to feel efficient. The business of being the official note taker has distinct disadvantages, like being President or one of the New York Giants. After a while the responsibility gets you. I wondered uneasily if I could have made a mistake.

"Well, if he said so, that ends it." He dismissed a possible Paden gas shortage from his mind. "There's only a gallon or two here, so I can't take my car, but I'd like to show you something down on the Emigrant Trail."

"We'll take mine," my husband said quickly, and they did so. Bill ran the intervening distance and swung into the back seat as they turned around, and soon the throbbing of the engine died away in the twilight.

I sat alone at the tent where the sweet, milky smell of cud-chewing bossies drifted over from the cowsheds, and seized this first moment of privacy to eat my tart.

A hill sweeps up directly from the ranch buildings. The next morning we waited while the empty hay wagons swung upward at the heels of their galloping teams. When the road was clear we took our departure, and proceeded again to the confluence of Big and Little Goose creeks.

The trail here is worn so deep in yielding soil that it is like a dusty canal bed. In fact the Utah Construction Company has bridged it for the convenience of the hay wagons, and my husband parked his car and took us across on foot, leaving his hat on the running board.

Here, on a knoll overlooking a great shimmering flat, head and foot stones mark a little grave. "Our Jessie," the headstone announced firmly, but was a trifle uncertain as to just how many years had slipped by since loving hands had placed it thus on guard, and contented itself with a blurred "5 . . . ."

"Here's where we came last night," Bill told me. "That's how Dad knew he might as well leave his hat."

"That's right," his father assented. The Grande men are proud of Jessie. They manage without really making a point of it, to keep the grave from getting overgrown and littered. I was told that when the flowers bloom around the streams some of them are apt to take a short horseback ride and wind up here with a bouquet, just as a little delicate attention.

Lucky Jessie, whose soft influence lives on and on. What other unknown girl, dead almost a century, could accomplish so much for good?

Right here the trail turned and followed the Little Goose across the open flat commanded by the knoll on which Jessie lies—followed it into an ill-omened canyon of all manner of disaster. The place looked like hell upset or the aftermath of a bombing raid. The way of the wagons led along, beside, over, and in the water—but mostly over. Led along on the top of great rocks that seemed to have erupted from the creek bed. The noise from the crashing, thundering wheels and plunging horses was flung back at the worried travelers, harsh and heavy, from the sloping canyon walls. Wheels dropped into gashes in the welter of rocks, like buttons into buttonholes, and came off with a wrenching jar. Animals fell and were injured, but all obstacles were ineffectual against this mighty procession whereof the rearward drove the forward on for all the world like a herd of buffalo, even though the hindmost ranks must starve.

Along the walls of Little Goose Canyon the Indians lurked watchfully, creeping through the rocks. They had learned a lot under the white man's tuition and, once in a way, their chance came. Then the rocky passageway dripped blood from men and animals, but only just enough to stop the solitary wagons that had been chosen for attack. The Utes seemed to have no particular pride in scalps and often failed to take them. A wounded person feigning death might be left quite unmolested, while wounded and dead animals, being too hard to move on the great rocks, were disregarded. A surprise attack that netted them many horses and no dead and wounded among themselves pleased the Indians best.

From out the mouth of Little Goose Canyon the pilgrims emerged to a dry stretch and plodded fifteen miles to the narrowing neck of the valley. Great billowing curls of dust like half-furled feather fans blinded them and caked the tears of the bereaved. Soft contours of the hillsides suggested a gathering of plump ladies in gray fur coats. Gradually these moved in more closely about the marching columns until only a small space was left through which to pass. The dingy wagons rumbled through the opening in single file and found the waters of Rock Spring warm but sweet and safe.

Here George McCowen and his company were confronted by a better class of Shoshokoe who offered a five-foot water snake with the arch pride of the family cat presenting a rodent. He did not drive an easy bargain and demanded much bread in return. They passed on snakeless. Along the road were written notices of Indian depredations and urgent warnings to emigrants still on the road.

We found Rock Spring flowing freely but preempted by two excessive bulls that looked as if Rodin might have hewn them out in his more intense moments. Almost at once we swung free of the hemming horizon and into the first section of the valley of Thousand Springs. About five miles beyond the bulls we saw Emigrant Spring running down a rocky and discolored side hill. We went halfway up, sat down, and, with our heads under a "cedar" and our feet in the water, ate our lunch. This is a lusty, gusty spring, and it runs into a fat distended valley dotted with cattle. Four miles farther lies flat, pondlike Mud Spring—marshy, and swarming with deer flies. In trail days rotting carcasses nuzzled the reedy brink, so that the passing travelers were practically gassed by the stench. Lonely travelers of the late fifties were so afraid to build fires in this valley that the night guards were chilled to the bone and complained that they would rather be a target for Indian arrows than to die from exposure. Others, equally frightened, built fires and then stealthily moved the wagons by hand to some other spot, hoping to deceive the Indians.

Our only worry was that we might not be able to find the Eccles Ranch, and we blew along like a summer gale. The old trail had been near us all the time. Now it crossed our road on an angle and, looking ahead, we saw buildings, a parked truck, and a man mending a fence. Our gas tank was in no shape to boast about, and I looked hopefully at the buildings. They were obviously untenanted. My heart sank, and I was trying without success to think of something cheerful to say when suddenly the light dawned in one comprehensive burst of appreciation, for this was the San Jacinto truck and even now another man, hitherto unseen, was unloading a tin of gasoline.

This type of cooperation has been given us from one end of the cattle-ranch section of the West to the other. We always *think* that we can paddle along under our own power, but it's not a fact that seems to be universally accepted, and every one we meet gives us just one more helpful boost.

The valley narrows again into a pass. The trail concentrates, and in places is one hundred feet wide and six feet deep. The pass is merely an insignificant little neck between two valleys. Once through it, the adventurer is greeted by rising curls of steam from the hot springs in Thousand Springs Valley proper.

It would be more correct to say that the steam is visible only in the cool of morning or evening. On a hot day all the well-like springs, both hot and cold, bore a refreshing but deceptive similarity. It comes down through the years as sober fact that a company of men drove through a stretch of grassy-edged wells one blistering-hot noonday in '49, and that one of their number decided a quick, dust-removing plunge would be worth the effort. He stripped off his clothes, threw them in the moving wagon and, running to the nearest pool, jumped in. It was almost boiling, and he popped out on the rebound. "Drive faster, Joel," he shouted to his brother on the driver's seat, as he ran after the wagon. "Hell ain't far off."

The grass was as thick as could be imagined, and hung heavily over the deep well-like springs so that eager horses missed their footing and fell in. Many of the wells were so clear that discarded refuse from the camps was visible on the bottoms. It seems incredible that any one should have willfully contaminated the few sources of pure water found along the way, but I must record the fact that it was the rule and not the exception. A stove that had made the trip thus far in spite of all handicaps was thrown into a crystal-clear well at Thousand Springs and left to rust. Maybe some distracted man threw it at the mosquitoes, which according to advance notices were as big as crows but were "actually no bigger than fair-sized grasshoppers."

Helen Carpenter has been mentioned many times in this hop, skip, and jump travelogue, and especially in connection with the fact that her company was almost if not quite the last wagon train through the Goose Creek Mountains in the year 1856. They had noted the blowing feather piles marking the scene of recent massacres; had exchanged shots in broad daylight with skulking Utes; had put in lonely and terrified nights, and finally had made a terrific effort to travel faster and catch up with another company. They did so in Thousand Springs Valley.

It was not a very large or cocksure wagon train whose camp smokes they hailed with such joy, nor was it in Thousand Springs Valley for pleasure. It was stalled as a result of having supplied the diligent Indians with sixty head of its best stock. A premature baby was the result of the scrimmage and mother and child lay close to death. A few horsemen went out, grimly promising to return with enough animals to move the wagons or die trying. They succeeded in rounding up over half of them.

The women took odd moments out to worry about the men, but mainly they had troubles of their own. After hours of frantic efforts to revive its feeble spark of life, the tiny baby died. The mother's condition was doubtful; but they continued their efforts to revive her, while another of their number took to her hard bed in the wagon and waited her dark hour almost unattended.

Before night fell men and rescued stock pounded into camp to find that another red-faced infant, strong and kicking, had been added to the floating population of Thousand Springs Valley. Both mothers remained in a serious condition for many days, but the two parties consolidated and went on as best they could.

The matter of babies was not a subject of so much thought and preparation by the members of the migrations as it would be to young mothers in these days of supersanitation. Except in the womanless gold rush it was taken for granted that families should travel as a unit, and that babies would be born on the plains; but statistics for 1849 show that the women remained in the States and homesick men, ill and near starvation, wrote in their diaries phrases wrung from their very hearts. One ran: "I hope my dear wife is having a happier Christmas day than I am. May God keep her in good health. Should I never return to her, and should chance deliver this journal into her hands, she will glean from these pages that she was never far from my thoughts and that my heart will beat for her to the last." On New Year's Day of 1850 he added, "Blessed New Year, dear wife and perhaps child." It was a perplexing question whether the women were better at home in the anxiety of mind that was the natural accompaniment of such a separation or sharing the fortunes of their husbands.

Given a normal year, a well equipped company, and plenty of wagons passing by to give a sense of security, a birth caused little commotion. Competent Lydia Waters took charge of such an event within a few days' journey of Thousand Springs. She stopped the train, heated some water, and told the crowding Diggers that the woman had smallpox, all of which measures were effective. A fine healthy baby was born, and Lydia wrote briefly, "Could not have done better anywhere else."

*　　*　　*

The ranch house of the H. D. is just beyond the well-like springs, and we went there to double-check our facts. We struck a snag at once. The attractive young wife of the foreman had never heard the name Thousand Springs, but she couldn't imagine where else there would be enough water holes to warrant such a title.

My husband was visibly crestfallen. "It's got to be here," he insisted. "I can't manage at all if it isn't."

The young woman laughed lightheartedly, and put her arms around her two little daughters. "We'd like awfully to fix it up for you, but it's a fact I've never heard that name in all the years I've lived here."

"You wouldn't," my husband told her severely. "You're too young. Isn't there somebody over seventy around the place?"

"No, there isn't, but I'll tell you what I can do. I'll ask Mr. Bowman. He's a great one to study, and he knows the history of the country about as well as any one. Honey, take that big fat lamb of yours out of the way so I can get in the door."

The lamb, bumptious and obstinate, was removed. We went in, introduced ourselves all the way around, and Mrs. Ihrig moved over to the box telephone on the wall. She revolved the crank with a terrific rasping, and I should not have been surprised to see freshly ground coffee filter through onto the floor; but nothing ensued except an answering hello from San Jacinto.

"Where's Thousand Springs Valley?" she inquired dutifully. "There's a man here hunting it."

The answering voice of Archie Bowman came clear and distinct, "You're sitting on it."

*   *   *

From the H. D. Ranch buildings we went south, up the valley, toward a line cabin. Part way we passed a chuck wagon surrounded by saddle horses and lounging riders, one of whom warned us against a bad hole in the road.

"This road's more for trucks—not for cars like yours." He gave our equipage a critical glance. "If you don't watch for that drop I'm telling you about, you won't have a spring left."

The drift of gray hills ahead showed that we should soon forsake the spacious watered valley. A phalanx of cattle plodded with their tails to the wind which poured over the quivering horizon. We saw the hole in the road before us; eased down into it; across and up—and it was the old prairie schooner trail itself, worn wide and deep, headed for the high land that still divided it from the Humboldt Valley. On the lower slopes it (and we) crossed the neatly paved ribbon of the Twin Falls and Wells highway, stretched stiffly over the curved breast of the hills. It was so disturbingly out of the picture of things as they used to be that I felt as if a few medals and a stiff shirt would be in order.

Over these new hills, now drenched with the glow of a late Nevada afternoon, the wagons came to another choice of routes: they might turn to the right through a rough canyon in the hills, or they might circle the range past some poison springs where stock must be well guarded. The Mormons who went to California in 1848 were credited with opening the road through the mountain pass. It is called Bishop Canyon.

Most of the wagons went by way of the canyon because they reached good water many miles sooner and did not have the difficulty of avoiding the poison springs. And, just in case it concerns any one, it was here at the canyon entrance, on August 14, 1850, that S. F. Clements of Ohio was abandoned to die. He was buried at the spot by strangers who marked his grave.

The wagons crossed Bishop Creek eight or nine times, and at the upper end it was considered to be almost as rocky as Little Goose Canyon. But, where Little Goose has been left in a perfectly outrageous state of nature, Bishop Canyon has been cleared for a modern road. We went in at the west end and took our car almost through. A warm spring within its confines gave the pioneers a chance for comfortable soaking of the rheumatic joints engendered by icy nights.

In steady sequence the emigration moved through the constricted passage and came out upon an elevation overlooking the valley of Humboldt Wells. Most of the wagon masters elected to continue to the west with Bishop Creek. Some few chose to turn back to their left and recruit a day or two at the wells which are immediately on the outskirts of modern Wells, Nevada. They would meet here the outfits that had circled the hills to avoid the canyon, many of them tending stock sickened by the poison springs. Here the animals rested and grew less gaunt, invalids recovered, and an atmosphere of laughter and gayety returned.

27

Yea, Though I Walk Through the Valley

THE HUMBOLDT RIVER, along whose penurious banks the wagon trains trundled for over three hundred miles, was and still is a queer proposition. It comes from small beginnings, grows to a river, and then peters out ignominiously in the hot sands of Nevada, producing, so the pioneers wrote, a sort of whiplash effect with a long substantial middle and two tapering ends. Even its course seems contrary to nature, very few long rivers in the world flowing westward parallel to the equator. Yet if, like the Bear, it was a special gift from Mother Nature, it was a stingy handout—more like a famine than a feast—and barely served to keep life in the strongest of the draught animals. They might all have starved and made an end of it except for the grassy marshes at Winnemucca, Rye Patch, and Lovelock. Finding the last-named right at the edge of the desert was the one thing that made emigration by the Humboldt Valley possible.

Many of the travelers, as well as their stock, suffered from fatigue and heat during the two or three weeks that they were dependent upon the meager Humboldt; but most of the actual illness occurred in the last seventy-five miles and was caused by the increasing alkali and filth content of the river. The lower valley of the Humboldt was one long sequence of calamity working up in a consistent manner to the crowning catastrophe of the great desert.

In order to see the headwaters of this notable stream we drove out from Wells in the early morning. The day was heavenly, the one perfect specimen in weeks of just weather. Ugly frame houses took on new and unexpected beauty from the bath of apricot-colored sunlight in which they were immersed. It was one of the rare moments when the earth and the contents thereof seem in perfect focus. The sky looked positively smug as it contemplated its own handiwork.

Upon our arrival in the vicinity of the wells they proved to be in somebody's pasture, and we detoured for permission to enter.

The home to which we turned was a "tie house"—a small foursquare building methodically built of mud-chinked railway ties in much the same manner that logs customarily are used, and of a type favored in Nevada for its economy, coolness in summer, and warmth in the long cold winters. It was occupied by a hospitable Mormon family who were particularly well informed on local road conditions, and the lady of the house was ironing.

I stood beside her folding aprons and tea towels while we got our geography unknotted, and listened to a thumbnail sketch of the Bishop Canyon road. Conversation drifted after a while to the early history of her own family, and she told simply and without elaboration a story whose few words covered years of heartache: the story of an aunt who, as a child, took refuge in a stranger's wagon during the confusion of a skirmish between the emigrants and the Utes and could neither find, nor be found by, her family until forty years had passed.

When, at last, we set about the business of finding the wells, they proved gratifyingly different from ordinary springs. They are all sizes, from a foot to forty feet across; are set hit and miss in a thick, turfy tangle of pasture land and look like rush-bordered pools; but it is highly inadvisable to go wading, for they are deep—some, in fact, used to be considered bottomless. They made a splendid recruiting ground that, like the City of the Rocks, practically always buzzed with people in a relaxed and mellow state of mind. Only the presence of a girl or two was necessary to promote a celebration, and the tall reedlike grass was often cut away to form a dance floor. If the next day chanced to be Sunday, many stayed over. There was a kind of incorrigible sanctity about the Sabbath that insisted on recognition and may be felt even in the uneasy notations of the travelers who broke it.

The wells were teeming with minnows, which could be scooped out in the hands, and the Diggers often came to offer some for trade. The culinary dainties proffered by this misshapen little people at one time and another merit consideration. They ranged from assorted roots and simple game such as lizards, coyotes, sea gulls, pelicans, crows, and screech owls to more adventurous concoctions of tiny frogs, ants gathered before the thaw of sunrise, and the large disgusting worms peculiar to the shores of the Great Salt Lake. Serviceberries were exposed on deer hides (green side up) to the utmost effort of the sun, flies, and the Indian curs, and then were mixed with dried and pounded crickets. All things considered, the impoverished Diggers were offering of their best when they proffered minnows, boiled whole, and furnished a certain amount of amusement to any whose stalwart stomachs permitted an objective viewpoint.

When we left the wells we started straight down the valley, moving over gentle swells. A tiny, sparkling thread of water, almost hidden beneath rank entangled grass, was doggedly flowing west. I could and did step over it. "Don't tell me this is the Humboldt?" I begged.

"Well, naturally it isn't the whole thing," Bill said, "but it's one of the heads."

"Yes, and Bishop Creek is another," his father supplemented. "There are a couple more, but those two are all we have to worry about. Mary's Fork comes in at Deeth, about eighteen miles down from Wells, but all that the wagons got out of *it* was a bad crossing. None of them followed it. We'll have to take a look, though. The Humboldt had so few branches that we can't afford to miss any."

Taking our way through sepia-hued protuberances that might just come under the tolerant heading of mountains, and then cutting north of the last peak of Ruby Range, we came in an hour to Deeth, a straggling little town built around a railway station. There was snow within walking distance, and drift fences of sagebrush protected the highway. On the edge of town Mary's Fork comes in from the north—a slow, ditchlike stream fairly hidden in massed willows. The first travelers called the entire river from wells to sink Mary's, or sometimes St. Mary's, River. It was Frémont who bestowed its present title in honor of the noted traveler, the Baron Humboldt.

Between Mary's Fork and the slow, treeless windings of North Fork were eighteen miles in which the emigrants became increasingly aware of the presence, continued but usually unseen, of the belligerent Utes. They seldom had any pacific dealings with the American encampments except, now and then, an attempt to trade fish or game for guns, ammunition, and American horses. As the answer was almost invariably "No trade" and the crestfallen savages often attempted force, the meetings could hardly be rated as social events.

Their headquarters were south of the river, and it became dangerous to send small parties over to cut grass, to hunt, or to pasture stock. The Indians, on the other hand, although partial to the south side, were never pig-headed about it and would cheerfully cross if they thought it would be profitable. Written notices of stock thefts and of murder garnished the camp sites, with fresh graves to point the moral. Unburied bodies of stray hunters or stock drivers stared with glazed eyes at the men who first passed that way in the morning. Stolen teams forced the down-on-his-luck, improvident man, whom no company had wanted, to take his gun and brave the unknown canyons alone—and he had the necessary quality of stolid grit to do that very thing or he wouldn't have been on the Humboldt.

And what of the wives who waited one night—two nights—three nights for the husband, or husband and sons who never came back. They had nothing to offer in return for help. What good to any one were wagons without animals? Rolling stock was a drug on the market, abandoned in every camp and left all along the day's march, and no sooner deserted than broken up to boil the next train's coffee. Money could not buy transportation. Strong animals were beyond price even if the forlorn women could have handled them alone. There were many such helpless trail widows, and they were always cared for, fed, and comforted by some kind Samaritan who already had far too much burden for his staggering mules to pull. A woman with seven children was left in this manner to the charity of strangers.

One night's raid on the draft animals might cause two or three such tragedies, but in spite of danger the recognized answer to the problem was a determined posse of twenty or thirty men starting at once. Occasionally they caught up with the Indians and taught them a lesson. More often they never saw the thieves but found a portion of the stock, abandoned when the chase got too hot. They were seldom entirely disappointed, and were likely to come through unscathed.

Here again the large well organized company had its innings. It had plenty of men for guard duty, and plenty for defense. It was not so likely to be attacked and could do more about it if it was. It might even dare to take its cattle away from the road to where the grass showed green around some spring on the slopes of the hills, and so keep them in better shape than those of the man with four or five wagons and a small party, who must stay where the crowd was thickest.

By this time the travelers of the fifties were running out of provisions. The Forty-niners had brought food for months—even up to two years, and (generally) had some left. But later emigrants had been warned not to overload the wagons, and many were on short rations.

"There is one thing Sertain," wrote Joseph Price to his wife as early as June 26, 1850, "that the People were most too mutch in lightened this year they did not carry a nuff flower for there appitites." Such undoubtedly being the case, they sadly missed the game they did not dare to hunt along the Humboldt. Rabbits and ducks abounded, and fish were plentiful in the stretches of river remote from the trail, but the swarming Indians were everywhere.

There were a few instances in which the Utes, as well as the Crow and the Sioux, forbore to make trouble for defenseless people. Bennett writes of a man, the solitary remnant of a small train, who was living comfortably by catching and smoking fish. His one animal was an old bull, too tough to be of interest to the Indians when they could do so much better.

Another interesting story was of little May Philly's cat who caught rabbits in spite of the Indians. Heat, bad water, and fatigue had sapped the child's vitality until her appetite was too jaded for the continual salt meat and frying-pan bread; but there was nothing jaded about Jip. The willow clumps intrigued him, and he commenced to hunt. Every morning for two weeks he arrived at the door of her tent stepping high and carefully around the limp body of a rabbit; and he was credited with saving the child's life.

Such incidents were exceptional. In most cases the rabbits and trout were as safe as if they had been at the Antipodes.

Beyond the big green valley of the North Fork the up-thrusting brown mountains close in. Ranges appear meaninglessly and end without reason. Modern travelers see snow fences marching beside the highway to tell them of the elevation. The emigrants simply knew that they were cold at night, that water froze, and that the men on watch thought they were going to do likewise. Those standing guard with the grazing animals on the south bank had the most unenviable time. They got wet swimming the river and then, because Indian fires crowned the heights in all directions, they dared have no fire to dry themselves, nor any kind of light, but fumbled around from one animal to another in pitch-blackness and a bitter wind until their watch was over.

Wet years were not welcome in the Humboldt Valley—a strange anomaly for a dry country but understandable, for grass was found mainly along the river, and if the bottoms were flooded the pasturage suffered. The weather conditions in 1849 were such, all along the overland road, that the mountain men wondered at the unusual quantity of feed. It held true on the Humboldt. Not only was there an abundance of grass, but the wagons were able to utilize miles of river bottom road. The year 1850, on the contrary, began adversely with a late spring on the prairies that held the wagons on the Missouri River a full three weeks before the grass began to prick; it ended (as far as the travelers were concerned) with the results, in the Humboldt Valley and the Sierras, of a heavy winter and a sharp, hot spring that cooked the tender feed and melted the snows. The Humboldt River flooded. Bottom roads were minus, and pasturage was stirred and soaked into a black smother of mud that trapped the animals. Dozens of unfortunate beasts (some said hundreds) sank and suffocated in the miry pits. It was not much better early in the season of '52. "The mud at the banks of the forks of the Humboldt was so deep," wrote Lucy Cooke to her sister, "that at one place nine yoke of our cattle had to be put on one wagon, and then it was a dreadful pull, and chains broke pretty fast. Yesterday William called me out of my wagon to come and see an ox down in the mud. Nothing was visible but the top of his back and head; his nose even was covered." The later months of 1852 were very favorable, and the grass turned out well, making it much like 1849, and a good year to travel.

In spite of mire in the bottoms there was good pasturage along the sloughs of the upper Humboldt and wheat grass in the meadows. Thus far, no matter what the year, no company should be in actual want unless the animals had been raided. And so they came opposite to the hot springs where the town of Elko is now.

They are not often mentioned by journalists, but Franklin Langworthy wrote, September 17, 1850: "At ten in the morning, saw numerous columns of what appeared like smoke, rising over the bushes, at the distance of a mile to the left, and near the river. We supposed it to be a large Indian encampment, but moving on around a bend in the stream, we perceived that the smoke was nothing but steam that arose from a great number of boiling hot springs." Here also, the columns of vapor from these springs are more noticeable in the cool of the morning than during the heat of a summer day.

About eight miles beyond the hot springs is the site of the first regularly used ford. It is in the midst of an open valley filled with the vivid, impudent green of greasewood. To the south rise the snow-spattered, jagged peaks of the Ruby Range. In front of them yawns the rugged canyon of the South Fork. The Bidwell Company and the Donner party both came through this unfriendly gorge, as well as the horde of unhappy people who, in 1849 and 1850, chose Hastings' Cutoff from Salt Lake City. Out to the Humboldt Road they poured, afoot or with an animal or two, often stripped of all their possessions and starving—another staggering burden for the travelers of the more conservative Goose Creek route. This ford in the vicinity of South Fork, like the three or four others to follow, was only used in dry seasons or after the flood waters had subsided.

The valleys narrowed almost at once and the yellow sphinxlike rocks of Frémont's Canyon rose on either side of the river. It was passable for wagons in dry seasons, but (once within the grateful shadow of the gorge) they had to cross and recross the stream. The fords were rough, and rolling stock upset that had remained firmly on its four wheels all the way from the Missouri River. For periods of high water or for the duration of the resultant sticky mud, there was a long unpleasant detour over the hills to the right. Lacking guidebooks, the company captains sometimes took the tiresome mountain trail from ignorance when they might as well have forded in the cool canyon and spared their teams. It was dubbed the Greenhorn's Cutoff.

Five or six miles after the thirsty travelers of the detour had rejoined the river, they were forced away from it and into the mountains for a second day's dusty journey. This time the Humboldt entered a truly impassable canyon. Fortunately the emigrants didn't want to go that way, for it was sweeping broadly to the south in an arc twenty-five miles across. They watched the life-giving water disappear into its abrupt and rocky defile and climbed disgustedly into the hills again.

Near the point where the river deserts the trail, stands modern Carlin, utilitarian railroad town with large antiquated gray sheds and a single black smokestack belching equally black smoke. We went with the wagons, straight ahead into the hills over a road called (and again I can't do a thing about it) Emigrant's Pass. Up to the year 1941 the trail was visible for miles, sometimes on a hogback and sometimes in a curving swale between rolling hills. The present ultramodern superhighway has obliterated all but a few scattering traces of the wheel ruts and, indeed, is often sprawled on top of the old road.

Modern tourists on Nevada's splendid highways can have no conception of what torture such a simple thing as dust could be to the emigrants. C. A. Kirkpatrick wrote here on August 8, 1849: "In passing through a narrow pass the dust rose so thick that neither myself nor companion could see the cattle and I had to send my dog in to hunt and drive them through till we could see them. After dark it was still worse. Not being able to see the road we sometimes got into the dust knee deep and often found ourselves rolling in it." Many tied handkerchiefs over their faces, while in later years they wore goggles. They were dun-colored and dust-caked—"a strange looking army." "Are obliged to swallow dust all day in place of water," wrote Caroline Richardson, "for which I have suffered more this afternoon than all my sufferings put together."

A short distance west of the summit are the Emigrant Springs. They held fair sweet water, so one woman wrote, but were too easily "roiled." Rank bunches of wheat grass and tall greenery grow around the springs, and a few yards down the hill is a cabin camp owned by Mr. Primeaux, son of Antoine Primeaux who trapped with Jim Bridger.

The convenient placing of Emigrant Springs made it possible for well equipped trains to continue straight across the southward bend of the river and eventually to arrive on the north bank near modern Dunphy where they might continue on the same side of the stream, if they so desired, all the rest of the way to the Sink. It was only the companies who tried to take advantage of the more abundant grass and occasional shorter mileage on the south bank that forded painfully back and forth. It was practical to remain on the north side from Humboldt Wells to the Great Desert.

Meanwhile the river had completed its circuit to the south through the impassable canyon and was about to make a similar wriggle to the north. The regularly used route crossed the river to cut across the resultant bend. It separated from the north-bank road while still in the mountains west of Emigrant Springs, and the wagons reeled down a steep hillside to famous Gravelly Ford, scene of many snappy skirmishes with the Utes and also of the fateful event in the history of the Donner Party when James Reed and John Snyder quarreled, Snyder was killed, and Reed expelled from the company.

In order to see the ford we took a side road from the highway to Beowawe, nine miles away on the railroad.

Near the town sagebrush made way for farm lands. A nice meadow with haycocks and a creek adjoined the road. The hay was just cut and very fragrant and, although I must admit that it smelled better than the creek, we enjoyed the little valley. At the shady gate of the Horseshoe Ranch we stopped to read the data we had with us and sat for a while in full view of another set of hot springs terraced on the foothills across the river.

"They certainly had plenty of Indian fights at the ford," I summed up from my hasty perusal of the Paden Encyclopedia. "It seemed to be a hot spot."

"I imagine that it lay down between the hills where it was impossible to get the wagons into a circle and hard to make any speed with them. Besides," my husband added, "it was a common trick for the Indians to attack the first few wagons to cross a stream while they were isolated from the rest."

I turned a page and continued to expound.

"Here's an account in Helen Carpenter's diary of a skirmish at the ford where eight white men were killed. They buried five in one grave and three in another."

" 'Skirmish' is a mild word," commented Bill. "Did they get the Indians?"

"Yes, quite a lot. The Indians weren't very good fighters from a white man's point of view."

"That's the truth," his father confirmed. "They never attacked unless they had a big advantage. Ten to one or something in that neighborhood. And another thing: did you know that the popular idea about Indian night attacks is wrong? They didn't like night fighting. Oh, they stole at night, and all that, but if they intended to make a real issue of it, they usually waited until daylight."

"So they could be sure that they *were* ten to one or better," Dr. Neff summed up.

"Ten to one!" I gave a ladylike hoot. "Here's a fight where one man held off twenty-six Indians right out in the open. With just one shot in his gun, too, and they knew it."

"Well—who was he, and how did he do it?"

"Davis Burris was the man, and I took these notes from the manuscript account at the Bancroft Library. He and another emigrant were on guard duty when the Utes rushed them. Burris was slightly ahead of the other and took steady aim at the first Indian with his old muzzle-loader. The Indian couldn't face the buckshot and turned and ran, followed by all the rest. But they knew that Burris had only one charge and wouldn't use it unless he had to, so they soon stopped. An Indian, who happened to have a gun, aimed carefully at Burris, using his ramrod driven in the ground for a rest. He missed his mark and hit the mule of the second man on guard duty which promptly bolted for camp, guard and all. The Indians charged again, but the leader couldn't face that gun aimed so steadily at him, and ran back again with the rest of the mob churning around him. While they were still shuttling back and forth the men of the company came hurrying out to rescue Burris, and the Indians scattered."

"I hope he managed to accelerate the retreat," Bill said.

"That was the trouble with the old muzzle-loader. Once you had shot you were helpless until you could get it reloaded; but it was pretty effective as a threat as long as the charge was in the barrel."

"What happened then?"

"The Indians went on to another camp and wounded two men. Then, at the next stop, they really netted a haul—sixteen horses; but they lost a brave."

"There must have been *two* guns in that camp," Bill commented.

"Well, anyway the Indians were as indignant as if the emigrants had thought up the whole thing, and so they surrounded and captured a family, including a woman and a little boy. They told her that the boy was to be killed in retaliation, but they relented after a while. None of it was as blood-curdling as you might imagine. The next day the family caught up with Mr. Burris and his company. They had been robbed of everything and were almost naked, but none of them had been killed and the Utes had even given the woman a scraggy pony to ride." I closed the book and put it away.

"I suppose," Bill said, "the Indians considered that real kindness."

"It was a whole lot better than being skinned or burned alive," Dr. Neff reminded him.

And at that point we left it: The Utes of Idaho, Nevada, and Utah were both better and worse than the Pawnee and Sioux encountered farther

east: better because scalps were not at such a premium and torture is seldom mentioned; worse because guerrilla warfare on the wagon trains
was an accepted summer job at which they worked industriously each and
every year.

We received efficient directions at the Beowawe store. There had been,
it seems, a sort of run on Gravelly Ford, and the owner had sent several
parties there in the last five years. The instructions proved to be much
better than the road. For five miles the car swerved and bucked like a
bronco in the rain-washed ruts until it seemed wise to leave it and walk

Grave at Gravelly Ford.

the rest of the way. Half a mile brought us to a hillside sloping toward
the river. Beyond the stream, as we had expected, were the railroad and
a grave heavily becrossed by the Southern Pacific in the interest of the
traveling public. Two other graves were immediately ahead of us on the
hill. They were packed with rocks, and the one nearer the river was
marked at the west end with a heavy cross deeply sunk. A more flimsy
one had fallen and lay on the second grave, broken and useless.

"Here's a funny thing," Bill called before the rest of us could get there,
"the big cross has a flat tobacco can nailed to it—the kind you can carry
in your hip pocket."

"Why, it's upside down, too," I exclaimed, coming up the hill beside
him. "It couldn't be for flowers, even if it were big enough."

"It's upside down to keep the rain out," Dr. Neff reasoned. "It must
have something in it."

My husband had wasted no words. He pried open the tight-hinged lid, inserted an exploring forefinger and dug out two notes. They were very short and had been signed by Captain Charles E. Davis, U.S.A., and (with a sort of witness effect) by one Emile Cote, and dated 1927. We made careful note of the contents before leaving the graves. I wish now that I had copied them verbatim, but did not think of it at the time. On return to the car I rewrote them from memory and believe the wording to be quite accurate. The significant information was, of course, contained in the notes taken on the spot. The first note ran about as follows: "This paper pertains to the grave twenty feet north. It is the grave of John Snyder, young member of the Reed-Donner Party bound for Sutter's Fort and buried here in 1846." The other paper said in effect: "Please keep these graves up as they are difficult to locate."

"Interesting—very interesting if it's true; and I suppose it could be," my husband said with slight skepticism.

"Jim Reed killed Snyder at Gravelly Ford, didn't he?" Dr. Neff asked. "And Snyder was beating the oxen up the hill when Reed interfered, so it was on this side of the river—probably right near here."

"A man who would kill a friend for beating his team," Bill commented, "*must* have been jittery."

" 'Jittery' was the word. They had seen plenty of the 'elephant' coming across the desert from Salt Lake, and when they got to the Humboldt they found that it offered still more."

"You still haven't told me why and how it happened." Bill insisted on satisfactory details.

"Well, Mrs. Reed saw that her husband and Snyder were going to come to blows and ran between them in hopes that they would draw back. She was just in time to get a cut from Snyder's stock whip. Snyder swung the whip back for another blow, and Reed was so angry that he used a knife."

"So then the party expelled James Reed," I took up the story. "Of course they were terribly broken up about it. Snyder had been a favorite, and Reed was an accepted leader; but they had to do something, I suppose."

"Some people think that if Reed still had been with the party when they arrived in the Sierras he would have hustled them on over the summit before they got snowed in," Dr. Neff contributed. "One company who saw a portion of them near Truckee, warned them to hurry and then went on up the mountain themselves and got over. The storm commenced, but they made it."

"Reed might have managed it," my husband said, "he and the man who rode with him got over the Sierras all right although they had a pretty bad time toward the last."

"And he finally got back to Donner Lake with a relief party," I added. "Personally I think he was a resourceful man. It may have been the incident here at Gravelly Ford that settled the fate of the Donner Party, but of course we'll never know."

"And nobody will ever know who's in that grave, either," Bill said stubbornly. "For all you know the five men Mom was talking about are in one grave and the three in the other."

"Yes, and maybe Captain Davis found an old headstone or some other evidence," his father defended the proposition. "When I get home I'll write to the War Department and find out where he is. Then we can get in touch with him."

But he wrote and wrote again and consulted army authorities without avail. No such Captain Davis could be found. It was two years later, on a visit to Sutter's Fort, that we accidentally mentioned the name to the late Harry Peterson, then director of the fort and museum. He had been acquainted with Charles Davis, a retired sea captain, who for years and for his own pleasure had explored the Nevada reaches of the old trail, always accompanied by some younger man for company and to help with the routine duties of the trip. He had faithfully reported his sundry findings and theories to Mr. Peterson, leaving at one time and another reams of maps and papers, but never, so that gentleman assured us, any proof that the body of John Snyder lies beneath that particular cross. He was out of touch with Captain Davis and believed him to be dead. Some day, we hope, possibly by reason of this publication, the reasons for marking that particular grave may come to light.

*   *   *

In my own mind I always think of the stretch from Gravelly Ford to the great tule beds near Winnemucca as the middle or transition period between the comfortable, grassy upper Humboldt and the starvation rations of its last seventy miles. There were roads on each side of the river and for a while it seemed to me that no matter which bank the pioneers were on they never rested until they got on the other. A little study let more light into my supercritical brain. Each side had its points, upon which the travelers all too often found themselves impaled. For instance the south bank seemed to have a little more grass along the way, though lacking the large meadows. Also it was shorter. These two advantages outweighed, to a company of well armed men, the disturbing fact that the Indian encampments were near by. They could, so they figured, always deal with the Indians if they had to, and could either cross to the meadows on the north bank or cut grass and ferry it in their wagon beds.

Timorous companies felt more comfortable on the north side and patiently detoured around its purposeless bends while the great prairie schooners curtsied politely to one another from the small summits. There were very few landmarks for the north-bank parties, Stony Point being the only place mentioned by a majority, and we have never decided to our satisfaction which route proved the safer. Udell, who made three trips, recommended the north side. One thing only is sure: it was never safe to be both inexperienced and poorly equipped. Good equipment might make up for inexperience, and experience for poor equipment; but to lack in both was disastrous.

The pioneers never attempted to cut across the big northward bend of the Humboldt which has the tule marsh at Winnemucca for its apex. It was too great a stretch of mountains and waste land to undertake. They stayed with the river, cutting off small segments here and there, struggling with short identical sage deserts, but continually returning to water. At some of these camp sites, the stream might, in normal years, be forded, and the wagon trains seemingly made haste to cross to whichever side they were not already occupying—apparently convinced that any change must be for the better. In this they were all very much mistaken, as they found to their cost.

Many fine journals of the year 1850, including those of Sawyer, Loomis, and Langworthy, show that their authors were south of the Humboldt as it started its giant swing to the north. The last, having been delayed at Salt Lake City, arrived late in the season and was able to stay near the river. His notation for September 20th reads: "We move upon a very fine road, upon the south side of the river. This stream is now about sixty feet wide, and not more than eighteen inches deep upon the ripples. In the

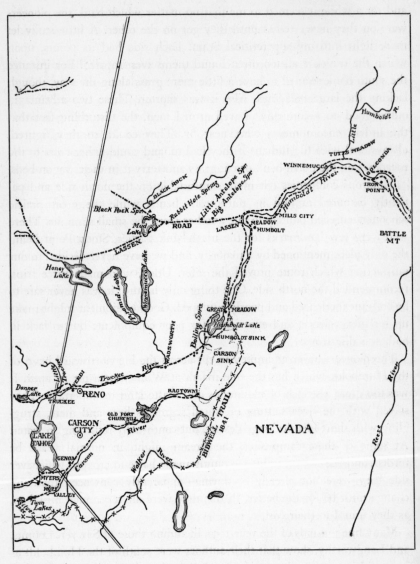

fore part of the season, this river was a turbulent stream, and gave the emigrants great trouble in crossing, and in it not a few were drowned. ... Where we stop, at noon, are twelve wagons; besides which, are two men packing upon ponies, and two others who carry on their backs their provisions and camp equipage. Men are so bent on going to the land of gold, that they travel on, whether properly prepared or not. I hear of two men now on the way to California, and who are ahead of us, one has a handcart, and the other a wheelbarrow."

In a day or two Langworthy's company had passed dark Battle Mountain (not yet named), its strange canyons melted bare of snow. They were in the great bend of the river some sixty miles from Gravelly Ford, and a desert lay before them wavering in a voodoo dance of heat waves. "About ten in the morning," he wrote, "I discovered the corpse of a man lying about six rods from the road. He had been shot through the heart with a bullet, was stripped naked, and had been some eaten by wolves. His scalp had been taken off. It appears, that after he was shot and scalped, he was dragged about two rods, in order to remove him from the blood, preparatory to stripping off his clothes. He lay on his back, among the sage bushes, upon a hard, smooth piece of saleratus ground, and in his death struggles had with his heels gouged two holes in the ground, nearly twelve inches in depth, and with his fingers had scratched up the earth as far each way as he could reach. We judged that he had been dead about twenty-four hours. Twenty rods from the body, we found a piece of a pocket-book, containing a paper, from which we learned that his name was Huttenbaugh, from St. Louis. We buried the corpse, and I wrote a statement on a slip of paper, put it in a split stick, and placed it at the head of the grave." This account, even to the written statement and the split stick, was entirely characteristic of the middle section of the Humboldt Valley.

The company camped that night near Iron Point, where the river enters the east end of a canyon. The next morning about ten o'clock it passed two miles north of the hot springs at Golconda. It was still cool enough for their heavy column of steam to be visible for miles. "Along here," wrote Mr. Langworthy, "the river runs a very serpentine course, through a valley twenty or thirty miles wide. The road proceeds in nearly a straight line, touching upon the stream only at the bends. The Humboldt seems to grow smaller as we follow it downwards." They must have camped at the end of this day somewhere in the vicinity of Winnemucca.

Differing from Langworthy, who came late, Leander Loomis found himself south of the Humboldt early in the flooded season of 1850, just where the river makes its great sweep to the north. He was a likable young chap, evidently a clear-headed, cool thinker, and his company seems to have been well equipped and efficient. Punctuation was a little out of his line, but he worked hard at it and, by throwing in plenty of commas and a few extra capitals as a sop to convention, came out very well. His entry for July 16th reads in part: "Today we were told by some Packers, who overtook us that a large train stoped yesterday at noon to graze, and soon after turning their horses, out, twenty of them were taken by the Indians, and run off among the mountains, they followed on and tracked them about 10 miles to their Town, the Indians being to numerous for them they returned to camp, and let, the emigrants along the road know their situation, and the Packers said that when they passed them they had 100, men, well, armed, and willing to Stand by them to the last,—they said they intended to go out and demand the horses, and if they would deliver up, well and good, but if not they would kill evry Indian in the Town. this is the present report, we are waiting to hear the result, whether there is any truth in what we have heard." It is quite likely that this engagement was the celebrated battle which endowed Battle Mountain range with its present name. George A. Crofutt, who published "Great Trans-continental Pacific Railroad Tourist's Guide" in 1870, speaks of a battle "between the Indians and whites—settlers and emigrants—which gave the general name of Battle Mountain to these ranges." He then supplies details: "A party of marauding Shoshone [probably Ute] Indians had stolen a lot of stock from the emigrants and settlers in this region, who banded themselves together and gave chase. They overtook them at this point and the fight commenced. From point to point, from rock to rock, down to the water's edge they drove the redskins, who, finding themselves surrounded, fought with the stubbornness of despair. When night closed in, the settlers found themselves in possession of their stock and a hard fought field." It is likely that this was the engagement of which Loomis was waiting to hear final reports. It is noticeable that he makes no overstatement and puts no undue faith in hearsay. Not wars nor rumors of wars ever seemed to sweep his adequate little company from the calm pursuance of its way. Fortunately there were hundreds more like them on the Emigrant Road. Their example, strength, and material assistance sustained the weaker and more unfortunate travelers through the ordeal of the Ute country and through bad days to come on the deserts.

Certain pictures come to mind, among hundreds of similar incidents, as characteristic of this middle section of the Humboldt. A stalwart negro woman marches along with an iron Dutch oven topped by a blanket perched jauntily on her head—it contains everything that she owns in the world. Men in silent groups look at what is left of an unfortunate straggler, shot through the heart last night and cut open by the economical Utes to salvage the bullet. A gaunt ox faithfully reports for duty with an arrow buried ten inches in its shoulder. Mormon parties and packers returning from California are centered in rosettes of questioning emigrants and display an occasional teaspoonful of gold dust. A large company of men from California, waiting for their families, have with them some Mexican and Indian packers who are proficient with the strange new weapon called "lasso." John Clark's cantankerous mule lies down in a mudhole and is lassoed and pulled out by one of the accommodating strangers to the obbligato of much excited comment. Insolent Utes take three stolen horses up a hill in plain sight while the indignant young owners rush headlong after them—coming down again much faster than they went up with bullets whizzing past their heads. A man just bitten by a scorpion embalms himself ahead of time in a pint of straight whisky and becomes delirious. An amazed crowd measures a dead pelican with a wing spread of over seven feet. Three or four young fellows, clothed only in willow branches and water blisters, stagger across the desert to rejoin their wagons, which had unexpectedly left the river carrying all their clothes while they were bathing. Some dirty little Diggers, watching from the willows, give the thoughtless youths old moccasins to save their feet from the unbearably hot sand. Wagons rumble down the river, drawn by reliable milch cows pulling in the yokes vacated by their stolen or dead mates, while their morning's milk, ungrudgingly yielded into a tin bucket, is hanging beneath the endgate churning into butter. A man trudges in the line wearing a woman's sunbonnet; he is almost blind from the brilliance reflected by the sand. Countless gold seekers, swimming through billows of alkali dust, have swollen, bleeding lips that will scarcely open, and the tender membrane cracking from the inside of their nostrils. The anxious driver of a faltering team consents from common humanity to take in a sick stranger who can no longer sit his horse. Men, ill and crippled with rheumatism, wade thigh-deep through sloughs, cutting the tall thin grasses with hunting knives. Destitute and half-starved refugees from Hastings' Cutoff make soup from the bodies of dead oxen found beside the trail. A young Californian arriving to meet his promised bride finds that she has married on the way and gets out his gun to do a little shooting. The children of a mother gradually becoming insane are cared for by sympathetic women. Lonely men, standing in the river camps at dawn, watch the wagons of their companies roll doggedly away into the sterile heart of the next sage desert while they remain perforce with a sick comrade or saddle animal, hoping against hope that they may catch up with them in a day or two. And, toward the end of this middle section of the Humboldt, certain strong teams may be seen returning with loads of grass for the animals too weak to reach the next meadow without food and rest.

And so, across the plaster-white plains, the travelers come to the tule meadows at the northern apex of the big bend of the Humboldt, where they must all recruit for the next seventy miles of assorted hell.

* * *

It might be interesting, while at this haven and breathing spot, to see in what circumstances and condition various of our trail friends find themselves by this time. Carlisle Abbott, for instance, hero of the frightful night in the wolf den on the Platte and of several dangerous river crossings—he still plods along on faithful Pompey. His party is small now, just a few young horsemen. Along the middle Humboldt his brother is stricken with cholera, and all except a doctor and himself take French leave. These two build a cart, probably of abandoned wagons, and carry the sick man along; but the ravenous crowd from Hastings' Cutoff steals most of their supplies. The doctor limits each to a gruel made of one spoon of flour, one spoon of meal, and one-half ounce of dried beef. On these starvation rations they travel, nurse, and take turns keeping guard at night, during which duty one sees an Indian cutting hobbles and mortally wounds him, getting a retaliatory arrow through his own shirt collar.

Henry Stine, who took passage in a passenger train as a thoughtless boy, is now a man of character and decision. His company have given so much to the destitute that they are on half-rations, and Henry insists on crossing the river to hunt rabbits. Suddenly the sage erupts dozens of Indians, and he runs, fortunately finding a ford. The red men find other hunters a mile ahead and drive their horses into the deep mire. Henry gets assistance from his company and rescues this party, returning to find his own wagons and carriages in the center of a mob of three hundred Indians. The men of the company form a close line and ostentatiously display all their weapons, and the Indians decide to leave. No one has been hurt, but a note in a split stick by the trail tells of two killed here yesterday.

And Margaret Frink, who sat up all of her first night on the prairies for fear of Indians, to be sure that the guards stayed awake—how has she endured the attentions of the ubiquitous Utes? Well, Margaret has just survived the most agonizing episode of her life, beside which that first timorous vigil might be considered pleasant. Her young son has been lost all night near the Battle Mountains with five hundred hostile Indians known to be near by. In the morning he is handed back by a stranger who has taken part in the search. She and her family then try frantically to ford the river, swim it, or cross in any way from the south side; but the flooded stream is impassable. At last they take a leaf from the book of their earlier experiences and ferry the river in their wagon beds. Margaret thankfully sits in the flimsy, improvised boat with her feet in the washtub to keep them dry, and arrives safely at the meadow where, after her soul-racking experience, she is able to view mere trail discomforts with philosophy.

At one of the meadows Margaret meets the attenuated remains of the Mount Morris Company with whom she camped on Bear River. It is reduced to four young men and a perfectly composed woman, Mrs. Foshee. The Indians have stolen all their animals except two ponies, and they are reduced to painfully short rations; but this woman left to their care by adverse circumstances has proved a tower of strength for the past week. Food would be provided as they needed it, she was positive; and her courage was steady. Sure enough, one hungry day just as everything eatable was gone, a young cow walked from the willows straight into the trail among them. A note was tied rakishly to her horns. "This cow is only footsore," was the God-sent message. "Use for food." The next day she found a sack of flour—luxury of luxuries—abandoned where a team had given out. The young men gradually came to appreciate her faith and steadfast fortitude, and by the time they arrived at the meadow they were making her welfare their chief concern. Now they are trying to induce some one—any one—to give her passage room in a wagon. The day is August 11, 1850, and it is evidently Saturday for, while they are talking the situation over, a minister comes into camp to say that he will preach on the following day. The young men suggest that he practice instead of preaching and add that, if he will give up his (more or less) comfortable seat in a passenger carriage, they will give him their two remaining ponies. After hearing the story he gives Mrs. Foshee his place, takes the ponies and disappears completely from their knowledge to fend for his unaccustomed self. The four young men, now without animals of any kind, start to walk the rest of the way to California.

And John Wood, whom we followed through a two weeks' nightmare of cholera—how is he? Well, as usual, things could be better with John. In the first place he took the Hastings route, on which he suffered unspeakable torments of thirst; afterwards he spent a day or so carrying water back into the desert for the suffering whom it seemed impossible to abandon. When he finally went on, he and his fellow travelers had three skirmishes with the Utes. In the first, they killed several Indians. In the second they stood off forty mounted redskins and an estimated hundred on foot with two guns and their tent poles until relieved by a hastily gathered rescue party. An organized band of thirty-five men then went back and killed fifteen Indians for a lesson in manners, and the vicious circle was kept spinning. After that the travelers gathered in a bigger crowd for protection and began actually to starve. For several days before reaching the meadow John has lived on the hearts and livers of sick and abandoned cattle and even of carcasses found by the road. On the heartbreaking stretches of sage desert away from the river, he has thought desperately that he could drink his own blood. No, things are not too good with John, and they will be worse before long.

Leroy Kidder has traveled the Humboldt Valley very early in the season of 1850, without miring or drowning, and arrives at the meadow with no further mischance than having to combine with the next wagon in order to have enough draft animals. In this necessary merger he is forced to take on the person and effects of a maiden lady of uncertain age, Florinda Washburn by name, and those of the boy she is taking to California for half of his first year's earnings. Her brother is of the party, and fraternal sparks fly freely when, in the transfer of baggage, it is found that she has the component parts of a milliner's shop including a "tailless goose" or tailor's heavy pressing iron. In spite of protests Florinda, who has a mind of her own, hangs on to her property, and the goose goes along.

Conditions get better on the marshes of the Big Bend as the years roll on. The year 1852 finds more grass, better roads and fording places, and a few trading posts. And in August of '52 Caroline Richardson is pleasantly surprised at finding less destruction of wagons and goods than she has been led to expect. The river is dark, though, and looks thick. She suspects it of being "sickly," and there is illness both in her party and at the trading post.

No matter what the year or the conditions, a day's rest must suffice, for each team passing means just that much less forage along the awful seventy miles between these grassy marshes north of the bend and the providential meadows that precede the sink of the river.

*　　*　　*

The course of the wagons was southwest. They had rounded the "elbow" of the river and now furrowed through deep and blistering sand that pulled at the wheels and at the scorching boots of those who walked. "This portion," wrote Joseph C. Buffum, "has the appearance of having been literally consumed by fire. The earth is ashes and the rocks are cinders." From a distance naked brown hills looked out at gaunt flats where the sodden river wandered, slowly sucking the polluted blood of the sinister valley into one corrupt channel. Lower and lower it sank between steep white banks like a fungus growth: banks that trapped abandoned cattle seeking water and kept them there to die and bloat and rot in the filthy water; banks so graceless and so barren that the thick and torpid river lay between them like swill at the bottom of a trough.

It was the only water. The emigrants dipped the ill-smelling stuff in buckets and lugged it up the banks for the stock. For themselves, when it was at its worst, they soaked blankets in the least offensive spots and wrung them out into containers. On August 20, 1850, Henry Bloom wrote: "The river water which we have to use is detestable; it is fairly black and thick with mud and filth; but there is one advantage one has in using it—it helps to thicken the soup which would be rather thin without it." Henry listened to the crickets singing and thought of home and "the abundant fruits of the earth" which those he loved were enjoying. "I pray

God," he wrote, "they may never know what it is to want for food, though I starve myself, and there is a tolerably good prospect of it right now. What would I not give for some bread, butter and milk!"

The seventy miles of desolate emptiness choked in dust took them from three days to a week. Sometimes they traveled at night; but usually they gave it up because of the inability to get any rest in the daytime. For forage they cut the scrawny willows and a few blades of weak, sun-burned grass. At an indefinite distance (say twelve to fourteen miles) from the place where the road rounded the elbow of the river and started on its southward course, there was a stretch of bottom land where, in favorable years, the wagons might follow the stream, but where most of the emigrants missed the turning because it was less traveled. The fortu-nate few found dark red cranberrylike fruit growing profusely on tall thorny bushes with pale green leaves. Both E. P. Howell and Alonzo Delano enjoyed them in '49, and Caroline Richardson made inroads on the bushes in '52. "In addition to our usual traveling fare," wrote Mr. Delano, "with an excellent cup of coffee we had a delicious pie, made of a nameless (to me) fruit, which grows in abundance along the river in this part of the valley." His company were still in fair condition, thanks to the extraordinary grass supply of '49 and the fact that the emigrants of that year carried a great deal of food. The Forty-niners suffered mainly from a lack of water, which struck its peak a week later on the great desert. Disturbing reports of the holocaust on the new road across Humboldt Sink to the Carson River were filtering back along the trail and reaching the party daily. They decided to turn from the Humboldt River trail at Lassen's Meadow, striking due west to Rabbit Hole Spring (the Applegates traveled this cutoff first altruistically seeking a safer route for Oregon emigrants) and crossing Black Rock Desert on the way to the Sierras. From there they would find their way to the ranch of Peter Lassen at the edge of the Sacramento Valley near modern Vina (old Benton City). The route was known to lead into Indian-infested mountains but was believed to have sufficient feed and water and to be shorter than the old road. All these concepts proved wrong except the prevalence of Indians, and the title "Lassen's Cutoff" was such a misnomer that parties taking the route arrived at Sutter's Fort weeks behind their comrades who stayed with the Humboldt River. It is estimated that most of the '49 emigration were gossiping about this alternate new route, as they came southward around the bend of the river, and were weighing Indian against desert, with the result that at least half were making ready to go by way of Peter Lassen's ranch. They could have no feeble conception of what lay ahead. Near modern Rye Patch they came to Lassen's Meadow, strung like a brilliant green locket on the dirty gray thread of the trail, and camped to cut grass for their journey.

The next day, some five miles beyond Lassen's Meadow on the north-bank road, the wagons came to the junction. Sheer necessity had created a post office consisting of a barrel where those who turned from the stereotyped road might leave word for friends behind them. Each man was his own postmaster and patiently went through the entire content of the barrel until satisfied that there was nothing for him, or until he found the letter that might change the course of his journey.

Year by year, the majority of trail journals do not mention Lassen's Meadow or the cutoff; nor do they speak of any surcease of anxiety for the animals. "Lost our Jim horse last night," wrote Henry Bloom, "just laid down and died." And hundreds more did likewise. "This morning," Loomis inscribed sadly in his diary, "old Charley being so weak, we thought best to shoot him,—he has been a good horse, and served us well,—Peace be to his ashes." "If there is any worse desert ahead than we have found for seventy miles back, I don't know what it may be," E. S. Ingalls wrote as he neared the end of the sterile and stinking sand stretches. "I have noticed several dead horses, mules and oxen by the roadside that had their hams cut out to eat by the starving wretches along the road; for my own part I will eat the lizards which infest the sage bushes, before I will eat the stock that died from the alkali. The destruction has reached its height now. Hundreds are entirely out of provisions, and there are none who have any to spare, and but very few who have enough to carry them into the mines."

From the junction of the Lassen road the great cavalcade struggled along for more than thirty miles, moving in the early morning and the late afternoon and evening; struggled through sand that rose in a solid sheet with the wheels and poured from the tire tops—hot sand that burned through hoofs and thick boot soles and lamed the marching multitude. At night they camped on the filthy river and fed whatever hay they had been able to bring from the tule marshes. When that was gone branches of tough dry willow must suffice, for there was not one blade of grass for the patient animals, and the continual lowing of the cattle was almost more than a humane man could endure. All who were able walked apart to avoid the sight of such suffering.

A half-day's journey before reaching the great meadow the teams reached a shallow slough containing the only good water of the lower Humboldt—a spring of slightly sulphurish taste but cool and free-flowing. Every company watered here and filled kegs for use later on. It was the last good water for sixty-five miles. "It was here the mule we called the 'She-Devil,'" wrote Jasper Hixson, "took her first drink in all this dusty, hot week's travel. She would never drink out of a bucket, and the bank of the river here was too steep and the bottom too miry for the animals to get to water." Fifteen more miles brought them to the end of their difficulties for the time being, but in this day's journey James Abbey counted one hundred dead horses, thirty mules and sixty oxen, also twenty deserted wagons. He, as well as two more of the justifiably worried gentlemen just quoted, traveled the Humboldt Valley in 1850, the year that went down in history as the great debacle.

There was a little feed around the springs, and the teams were greatly revived by the cool, healthful water. With renewed strength and hope they plodded through another difficult half-day before sighting the green flats ahead, today the fertile fields of Lovelock: grass, armloads of grass, wagonfuls of grass, acres and acres of grass! grass which, coming as it did on the edge of the desert, was in the eyes of the emigrants the supreme and life-giving miracle of the waste lands. They had reached the great meadow of the Humboldt.

28

Of the Shadow of Death

AT THE GREAT MEADOW OF THE HUMBOLDT every one relaxed into simple comfort—something to which the emigrants had been strangers for days; and those who dared to take the time flung themselves upon the spongy turf and lay as if they never expected to get up again. The wide spread of grassy land, although covered with camps, was far more marsh than meadow, was cut by winding sloughs into thick saturated islands and feathered with a rank growth of cane, flags, and reeds. When the new-comers had recovered sufficiently to concern themselves with the morrow they rose and joined the army of men and boys who waded waist-deep for grass. All manner of receptacles were filled, from sacks to floating wagon beds. For the most part the animals were not allowed to graze for fear of miring or of being lost in the tall flags; and hay, even for present feeding, must be cut and carried.

The respective arrivals of the migrations of 1849 and 1850 were perhaps the most interesting as, beyond doubt, their difficulties had been the greatest. Before '49 the available pasturage had taken care of the small caravans, and after '50 the trading posts and traveling purveyors of water relieved the thirsty travelers of their worst discomfort. But in those two years, as stumbling, hairy skeletons dragged in the heat-cracked wagons and landed their split-lipped, glare-blinded passengers in the greenery of the meadow, many tragic, dramatic, and even funny episodes were recorded in the dirty notebooks in which the daily diaries were kept.

With the sudden relief from pressure of sheer bodily discomfort the travelers perked up and began to take thought for their own well-being and that of their neighbors. The meadow was as much as eight miles long, and so without fail they moved to a better location than the spot where they happened to pass the first few hours of recuperation. They hunted for better water than that of the brackish sloughs, and many diaries record the springs where bright little water snakes drizzled endlessly in and out of the dipping buckets and became involved in the ladies' petticoats. They butchered oxen, or even horses they could ill afford to spare, and cut them up "while still kicking" for the benefit of the destitute who waited hungrily for their handout of the warm flesh. They met with helpful sympathy the exhausted man who had left his wife and his outfit beside the Humboldt and came creeping in from the scorching sands with two half-dead pack horses and three small children. They fed and doctored up their animals and took time to shed a tear for the family pets they now shot for mercy's sake.

The Indian situation was well under control. The implacable Utes had been left behind. An easy-going tribe called Paiutes frequented the oasis and, having no horses of their own, were amiably willing to cut hay all day for the doubtful privilege of wearing the white man's dirty shirts. They are not spoken of as a problem but seem to have been cheerfully underfoot all the time. They traded fish. They sold wild ducks. They herded stock. If the emigrants butchered an animal, the ever present Greek chorus of Indians threw the entrails into the fire for a slight, and almost unnecessary, warming and ate them in the manner of hors d'œuvres before dinner. In return they passed a dainty of their own preparation—sugar from the peculiar coarse cane growing profusely in portions of the marsh. Groups of busy red men, as naked as Adam before the apple episode, were here and there, thumbing off the sweet, honeylike liquid which exuded in dewy drops and acted on the insect population very much as would an equal amount of flypaper. This natural property so detracted from its popularity among the camps that unwary eaters were afterwards, upon enlightenment, quite ill. To the Indians it was merely a satisfactory way of increasing the calorie content.

The great meadow, like the other two, changed arbitrarily through the years. By 1852 it had several trading posts selling liquor (bad, of course) and beef, sickeningly sweet from a sugar-cane diet. It had also a network of well beaten roads. The two main westbound stems separated and went to the north and south of the large lake into which the marsh finally resolved itself, meeting again in the desert beyond.

The emigrants called this large body of brackish water Humboldt Lake or sometimes (mistakenly) the Sink and took a full day to travel its length. The margin lands produced some grass at the beginning of a season; but, except in flood years, the surface water was undrinkable, having the look and taste of dirty soapsuds after a hard day's wash. Some, more ingenious than others, dipped usable water by sinking jugs to the deepest parts, but, if they could have seen the miscellaneous collection of discarded humanity that lay on its sandy bottom, they might not have been so thirsty.

It seems that, years and years before the coming of the white man, a tribe of Indians lived in the caves on the south side of the lake. When an important person died he was laid in state, with a suitable number of his possessions, upon some sort of float or raft—possibly of tules. The raft was towed out on the lake and stacked with rocks, brought a few at a time, until it sank. Generations were duly, and in proper sequence, laid, towed, stacked, and sunk. And then, in modern years, somebody drained the lake. Its bed now extends dry, white, and dusty for miles just west of Lovelock. On its surface lie, in peculiar groupings quite foreign to their environment, the heavy rocks that once weighted the burial rafts and, with them, the bones of the former occupants.

We drove right out on the lake bed, crossing the railroad at a little flag stop. A car can go anywhere on the hard-packed white surface, and we had no difficulty in finding the bones of a member of one of Nevada's first families; but he had a dismaying tendency to come apart, and I was glad to know that the next dust storm would probably retire him into decent and select seclusion again.

Both highway and tracks skirt the northwest edge of the old lake bed, and, in its palmy days when miles and miles of brackish water stretched between the hills and smelled like salt marshes on the ocean's shore, the trail was in much the same place. The men trudged a long, hot, weary day from dawn to the late August sundown to cover the distance between the ragged border of the meadow and the western end of Humboldt Lake. We drove it easily in half an hour. The lake bed at our left looked as flat and innocuous as an empty dinner plate, but on the south side dust in a solid curtain with fringed edges hid the mountains of the Humboldt Range. Ahead of us, to the west, the white expanse terminated abruptly, against a low ridge of earth like a natural dike.

"Get out the Paden Encyclopedia," Dr. Neff demanded, "and read us what you have about the lake before it was drained."

"As it happens I haven't very much," I told him. "Here's something from H. C. Thompson's diary when he went past in 1859: 'As we neared the sink of the river, it broadened out and had the appearance of a lake, while at the extreme lower end there was a ridge, or sort of dyke, through which there was a channel some thirty or forty feet in width. Through this channel the water poured with great force, emptying itself upon a wide boggy piece of country surrounded by sand and sage brush, and here it all entirely sank out of sight.' So you see," I concluded, "the Sink was beyond the lake and separate from it."

"And there might or might not be water there now"—Dr. Neff took up the subject and polished it off—"because the river doesn't always run into the lake bed any more, let alone pouring through the dike."

"Then what," Bill complained, "did we come all this way for? I thought the whole river disappeared down a hole somewhere. Now two to one it will be just more sand and sagebrush."

"You can omit the sage," I told him. "Just more sand."

* * *

Until 1942, the dike had limited our explorations toward the desert. It is not a place that one invades lightly in the summer. In fact there is only one month in the year—September—when the sink of the Humboldt may be reckoned as reasonably safe for cars off the beaten track. In spring the sink is a lake and the surrounding sections are swampy. Summer is most unsafe on account of heat and translates the swampy sumps into greasy slickings deceptively coated with a brittle crackling crust. In October the rains begin again.

It was September 1st, and we were unadventurously at home nursing the family tire supply when my husband received a telephone message from Robert Allen, State Highway Engineer of Nevada. In effect it stated that the weather was favorable, the sink as dry as it was apt to be, and that (to his competent judgment) it was now or after the war for us to cross the forty-mile desert north of the Carson River.

Dr. Neff was in San Diego catching up the slack in his practice after the summer holidays. Bill was at college. My husband and I, hastily persuading a friend, Charles R. Bromley, that it would be a nice change for him and would do him no end of good, enticed him into our car so early the next morning that (even at 35 miles per) we arrived at Carson City right after lunch.

We enjoy Carson City. It is the kind of town that steps up and takes you by the hand; is very, very historical indeed; and has always forgiven us that, deeply, inexcusably, and with no valid reason, we wanted to cross the sink on the trail. It is a relief not to be considered a bit unhooked. Mr. Allen, besides being an expert on the whimsies of highways, is historian enough to be in sympathy with our wishes and acknowledged a keen curiosity to know what might be found there. Instead of the maps we had expected, he assigned us one of his staff, Mr. Frank Garaventi, with the specific job of seeing that we struck the right road into and (with luck) the right road out of the desert. What happened in the interim was on the knees of the gods.

We picked him up on the stroke of five the next morning and started the long circle that would bring us to the dike and the beginning of our day's journey. Having him along was great luck for us. He proved to be pricelessly well informed on pertinent subjects. In addition to his other qualifications, he had wanted all his life to cross the sink.

The sun leaped to its task as we progressed on roller bearings and superhighways toward the old bed of Humboldt Lake. Warmth reached out and closed in behind us. The stiff and desiccated rabbit brush rustled gently as the desert filled its lungs for a new day. We turned in at the first road west of the dike and drove to its broad damlike top—it might be 150 feet high and 200 feet across—a healthy obstruction to be there accidentally.

Leaving the car, we scouted around until we found the trail that skirted the south edge of the lake bed. We had had a wet late spring this year, and the low spots still held a skimming of shining water moving sluggishly toward the break in the dike through which the Humboldt Valley slowly bleeds to death in the desert sands. The wagons had gone up and over the south end of the barrier, and we did so also, soon finding ourselves in the curve of the slough after its exit through the dike.

In trail days, when the profligate inclinations of the sordid river were allowed full sway, the unclean stream that broke from the lake and gushed through the bunghole of the dike crept six or more bitter, alkaline miles before it ceased to fertilize the resentful desert into salt-encrusted reeds and brackish marsh grass. When all perceptible current had died away it spread wastefully into elongated, stagnant sumps—the "sink" of ill repute. The six miles of barely moving water was called the "slough."

The slough made a giant letter C projecting west and south from the end of the lake. That branch of the trail skirting the northwest side of the lake crossed the top arc of the C into its center, where it was at once joined by the branch which had come around the southeast side, keeping between the water and the razor-edged Humboldt Range, and creeping between the lips of the C-shaped slough without necessity of crossing it. My husband went on foot to keep the course of the north-bank trail, slowly tracing it to meet Mr. Garaventi and me where we faithfully held the way of the south-bank road. We met according to schedule midway of the curve of the slough and went on together. The channel has been dredged and now turns somewhat to the north, but the original slough may be seen turning southward. The joined trails crossed this dry wash and started off in earnest. Now Mr. Bromley's hobby is geology (to my mind the only adequate reason why he had consented to come along) and he is a great deal more interested in basaltic flows, diatomaceous earth, and suchlike wonders than in any signs the efforts of man have left exposed to view on the desert; but, as we returned to the car, we found him transfixed over a little heap of rubble. "This is odd-looking stuff," he said, and looked questioningly at Mr. Garaventi.

"Oh, yes," Mr. Garaventi remarked as one who knew, "the Indians made arrowheads here long years ago, out of glass. See this." He picked up a roughly shaped triangle of thick bluish glass, opaque from long exposure. "They collected it along the trail. Evidently they spoiled this one."

"H'm-m-m!" My husband put two and two together mentally. "Now I know what those very rare ruby-red ones are."

"Danger lights from the railroad switches," Mr. Garaventi acquiesced. "They liked nothing better."

We now did some juggling with the car and wound up on the small road that serves the two section stations on the stretch of overland railroad across the desert. We crossed an alkaline seepage ditch full of reeds and fat ducks and came to a white salt flat, poured out like blancmange and without a spear of any growing thing. At the first station we found a young woman with two small children who went to school every day in a specially fitted car drawn up on a spur track. She had never seen the trail.

For a while we drove through the peculiar knolls topped with greasewood clumps that so annoyed the wagon masters. Each bush, it seems, catches and holds the wind-blown sand, growing taller and taller as necessary and forming the nucleus for a hillock five or six feet high. Presently we saw the trail and turned into it, hitting for the point of the Mopung (Mosquito) Hills to the left, the salty crust crunching loudly beneath our wheels.

The ruins of an old saltworks loomed below us.

"Buildings *must* mean water," my husband said. "If those old sulphur wells that the emigrants dug are anywhere about, they should be here." He looked at the disappearing figure of Mr. Garaventi, who was hitting for the railroad tracks to identify the milepost, and at Mr. Bromley, bent contentedly over a pile of rocks. "Let's hunt for them. I'll go to the right, and you take the left."

He strode down the gentle slope in the direction he had chosen, and I started for my objective; but, as the last few yards pinched out, a smell arose that made me kink up at the corners, and I saw two pools of filthy, slime-infested water just ahead. They were evidently not natural springs, but had been dug and sided with boards; and they teemed with drowned and swollen rabbits like a Halloween tub with apples.

I knew that it was incumbent upon me to find out for a certainty that the water was of sulphurous extraction; but, although such incandescent vapors rose that it had practically a graveyard glow, the trend was overpoweringly rabbity. One injudicious stirring with a long stick, and I was more than stopped. I was routed. It devolved finally upon Mr. Garaventi to make the decision, and they *are* the sulphur wells which the emigrants found to be the last water of the desert possible to retain in the human stomach.

The day was not too bad. The sun was incredibly hot, but a fluctuating breeze sang faintly as it passed. We moved slowly up to the shoulder of the low Mopung Range, above which hunched a disagreeable mountain —rugged and queerly red, with its nose turned up and the corners of its mouth down. It was often mentioned by those Argonauts who still took an interest in their surroundings. Incredibly there were many such.

The streamliner crackled by like an electric spark on the gleaming steel rails, and the engine crew, seeing a car where no car was likely to be, leaned out of the window to wave and gave us a mighty blast of the whistle. The sand was soft with a stiff crunchy top raised an inch above its surface as we came to the last crossing of the slough. So shallow and so transparent was the water that a wading sandpiper left a semipermanent trail behind him in the soft mud. The wagon crossing had been rendered practical at some time by stones brought from a distance, and they are still scattered from one bank to the other.

Immediately beyond the slough was the fork of the two desert routes. The left road ascended a low and easy slope and bore off southwest through a gap toward the Carson River. The right climbed the rough ascent to the plateau on which the highway now runs and continued west over a range of low-slung hills to the Truckee. It was longer but not so hard on the teams and had the advantage of drinkable water halfway. They were wise who took it. From the forks, the anxious travelers, giving scarcely a thought or glance to the comrades who had turned away, plodded ahead on their chosen pathway, intent upon putting as many miles as possible behind them before morning.

We found the left-hand road without trouble and, picking up a modern one that paralleled it, went on toward the Carson. The hard-packed earth was the sickly white of a fish's belly and bubbled with tiny knolls three to five feet high. Here the clumsy schooners plunged and dipped while their seasick passengers watched the end of the purpling Humboldt Range slip by on the port side. We soon were forced to leave our road for the trail itself and occasional piles of hardware from burned wagons punctuated our progress until we came to a pure white salt plain having a giant tank beyond, like a beacon in the distance. It looked as dry as a legal document and foolishly we drove straight onto it—almost the car's length, before we broke through its sterile crust and nuzzled cozily into the muck below. Fortunately the rear wheels retained some traction and, by the addition of muscle-power, we backed out at the first try.

Then we circled back, south across the railroad tracks and on again, through a dirty, gray-white flat bordered with luscious mirages, to Parran —a section house with five or six yellow buildings and four tank cars of water on a siding. Mrs. J. M. Wheeler, whose home it is, presented Mr. Garaventi with the only perfect emigrant ox chain I ever saw to take back to Mr. Allen. She had picked it up near the spot where we struck the slickings and turned back.

After three or four false attempts we were successful in circling the wet spot, which was several miles across and, moving cross-lots between large dunes thatched with greasewood, nosed up to the railroad fill again. Here, leaving the certainty of our direct return neither to hap nor to hazard, we parked the car where by the simple expedient of walking the track we should be sure to find it again; crossed the fill and started west on the trail afoot.

I believe we counted the remains of fifteen burned wagons in the distance we walked. Stoneware jugs abounded, for they were heavy and the horsemen threw them away as they became empty. They are always broken from having filled with water in the winter and burst while freezing. The only particles of wood remaining are the little circles, warped and bleached, that were the bottoms of the water kegs. I may have walked three-quarters of a mile—not more—when I realized that I was tired. "Don't mind me," I called to the men who were milling through the heavy greasewood. "I'm starting back. I'll make for the tracks and stay with them so I can't get lost."

A stretch of deep bare sand intervened between me and the tracks. It was hot sand, too. At each step I sank over my instep. My enthusiasm seeped out, and a large moth fluttered in my stomach. With beetle-browed determination I hoisted my knees, one at a time, until I had reached and climbed the railroad fill, where I stumbled like a spavined horse for what seemed like miles and miles. At last I saw the car ahead. My legs lasted until I got in its shade where I fell, rather than sat, on the sand.

In ten minutes I knew that I should eventually recover and began to feel consciously noble, something like a human guinea pig in a scientific experiment. If heat and deep sand had such an effect on my own not especially enfeebled physique, what about the women of the migrations weakened as they often were by illness, lack of food, overfatigue, anxiety, and, most of all, by thirst? If I couldn't take it—not two miles of it—how did they stand forty? And many of them walked the entire distance.

The men returned eventually, and once again we circled to the trail ahead, stewing humidly in the hot panting breath of the desert while the sun went with us, a polished brass ball in a skim-milk sky.

In trail days it was different. The wagons left the last crossing of the slough in the late afternoon, and long before they reached thus far black night had hovered down and nested in the dunes. Each straining company was isolated in the eerie darkness where the desert was drained of its daytime heat, and bitter wind sucked down from the snowy mountain tops. No wonder that when exhaustion of the animals made it necessary to abandon wagons they were fired to warm the travelers a little and to serve as beacon lights along the line of march. Each company rested an hour toward midnight by a burning wagon, and if it was possible to salvage a wheel they wrenched one off. The coffee pot containing a few cups of precious water was set on the hub, the spokes filled in with splinters from the wagon bed and kindled, and they had the comfort of a cup of hot coffee. Then, throwing out part of the load and rearranging the teams, they went on under stars low-hung and enormous toward the next flare of light.

A group of salt wells, filled with a fair imitation of pickling brine, tantalized those who knew their water supply to be insufficient. The more desperate of the wayfarers, pedestrians, and solitary horsemen, lay in them to soak in at the pores what they did not dare to drink. Two of these, who had not slept nor eaten since day before yesterday, saw a man in the near-by darkness mixing flour with water to "slime" the stomach linings of his animals in the belief that they would not feel so thirsty, and offered gold from their belts for a small portion of what he was feeding the mules. They went on hungry and thirsty. He wasn't heartless. He just didn't dare, for his family's sake, to part with even a little.

They passed the hard, white conical hills some twenty-five to fifty feet high and, near dawn, came to the thick sand which made the last ten miles of the desert so deadly—heavy sand like iron dust that was lifted on the rims of the wheels and poured from the sides and tops. Oxen on all sides faltered and gave out. Wagons stalled hopelessly, and all the available animals were harnessed to the remaining rolling stock. Of course it was the heavy housekeeping wagons that had to be left, and it was here, in Destruction Valley, that the family treasures were abandoned: the Bible, the hymn book, the daguerreotypes, the dead baby's shoes. But the women had no time to mourn. The sleeping children must be hustled into another wagon, and their clothes thrown in after them. Then the water must be garnered; every pint that each had tucked away in bottles and jars and even in the big washing pail, tied under a rubberized cloth— every drop must be conserved like so many diamonds. A hasty round of the faithful animals now lying limp upon the sand, to be certain that each mercy bullet had been swift and sure, and they went on in a dawn that gave promise of blistering heat—walking ahead of the remaining wagons. "Don't feel so bad about leaving your things," each husband told his hollow-eyed wife. "We can't be far from the river, and we'll come back for them." But they never did.

Such wagons as struck the deep sand at dawn were lucky—companies that had not lost animals to the Utes and still had strong wagons. It took only a broken wheel or axle arm, or a sick animal if irreplaceable, to delay the unfortunate owners beyond the limit of safety.

At Destruction Valley the sun flung into the sky like a projectile while despairing walkers prayed to halt its course. Night had hidden yesterday's victims, but this coming of the light was like entering hell. "Who will accurately describe the desert at this time?" E. S. Ingalls asked hopelessly of his diary as he sat at last on the river bank, and then, seeing nobody better able, went on to do it himself. The following is his notation of August 5, 1850:

"Imagine to yourself a vast plain of sand and clay; the moon riding over you in silent grandeur, just renders visible by her light the distant mountains; the stinted sage, the salt lakes, cheating the thirsty traveler into the belief that water is near; yes, water it is, but poison to the living thing that stops to drink. . . . Burning wagons render still more hideous the solemn march; dead horses line the road, and living ones may be constantly seen, lapping and rolling the empty water casks (which have been cast away) for a drop of water to quench their burning thirst, or standing with drooping heads, waiting for death to relieve them of their tortures, or lying on the sand half buried, unable to rise, yet still trying. The sand hills are reached; then comes a scene of confusion and dismay. Animal after animal drops down. Wagon after wagon is stopped, the strongest animals are taken out of the harness; the most important effects are taken out of the wagon and placed on their backs and all hurry away, leaving behind wagons, property and animals that, too weak to travel, lie and broil in the sun in an agony of thirst until death relieves them of their tortures. The owners hurry on with but one object in view, that of reaching the Carson River before the broiling sun shall reduce them to the same condition. Morning comes, and the light of day presents a scene more horrid than the rout of a defeated army; dead stock line the roads, wagons, rifles, tents, clothes, everything but food may be found scattered along the road; here an ox, who standing famished against a wagon bed until nature could do no more, settles back into it and dies; and there a horse kicking out his last gasp in the burning sand, men scattered along the plain and stretched out among the dead stock like corpses, fill out the picture. The desert! You must see it and feel it in an August day, when legions have crossed it before you, to realize it in all its horrors. But heaven save you from the experience."

He might well have said "smell it" also, for the clustered bodies of dead animals would, it was said, if laid in a line have bridged the entire desert. No man who was on his feet or lying in the shade of a greasewood bush received a second glance; but a man who stumbled and lay in the sun might well be dying, and some Samaritan would, after a time, be sure to go to him. One of these "was left there by his messmates," wrote E. S. Ingalls, "without food or water, and when found, his hands and face were so blistered by the scorching sun that the skin all peeled from them, leaving them as raw as a piece of beef. Poor fellow! When found he was crying in the most excruciating agony for a drop of water." In all probability he had just fallen, for as long as he kept going he would get no help.

The so-called "luxurious" passenger trains could find no royal road to the Carson River, and the plodding family caravans (who were doing best of all) took time to notice the rolling stock of one—wagons and carriages, all bunched together. Every animal had been unhitched and driven to the river. In one of the carriages in the seat formerly preempted by the minister who had given her his place sat Mrs. Foshee—alone, composed as usual, and firm in the faith that some one would return for her since she had been unable to walk the distance to safety.

The remainder of David Cosad's company, having used the five gallons of water with which they started, were in serious trouble. David strapped their empty containers (two canteens and a coffee pot) to his saddle and started on a forlorn attempt to ride to the river and get back with water, roweling the sides of his well loved mare until they were "a gore of blood." In his absence two of the company became crazed by heat and thirst and tore the top from the wagon; but one, retaining his good judgment after strength had gone, dug the hot sand out from beneath a straggling greasewood bush and lay down on the cooler layer thus exposed to wait for help. Another comrade, Samuel Cosad, twisted his hand in the tail of the strongest mule and beat him desperately through the desert with the ramrod of his abandoned gun. They were all rescued, one at a time, by a man who had crossed the desert four days before and had remained to save what lives he could. For three days he had ridden steadily under the pitiless brassy sun, carrying as much water as his horse could bear up under and ranging as far from the river as he dared.

Not every wagon was burned in the last ten-mile stretch of heavy sand before the Carson was reached, as the majority struggled through in the heat of midmorning, and each gaunt and cracking schooner stood as the nucleus of a semicircle of carcasses where abandoned animals had sought its fluctuating shade. It was not always thoughtlessness or cruelty that left them there to suffer. The firearms that might have dealt out mercy were heavy and were thrown away long before the saddle animals went down for the last time.

John Wood thought for a while that he had lived through an attack of cholera only to die on the desert. His company left him and went on to save themselves; but he clung to the last steer, coaxing it, prodding it, lying close to its back for six inches of shade when it fell on sand hot enough to cook eggs, and finally winning through to a water wagon stationed miles from the river. Water was a dollar a gallon. He gave the steer a gallon and a half and they dropped exhausted to wait for evening. For hours he lay under the wagon and learned that its owner estimated that three thousand wagons and three million dollars' worth of property were at that time abandoned on the desert. Toward evening the man on the water wagon gave him some boiled oats to eat, he watered the steer, and they went on. Shallow graves, just heapings of sand, followed one another at distances of a few hundred yards, and the unburied bodies of solitary men disintegrated unnoticed amongst the stench and corruption. For three miles they stayed on their feet, and then the steer went down. "The sight of the dead," wrote John in his diary, "is not so fearful as the living dying. God in Heaven! could human suffering appease thy wrath, the world would soon be forgiven." By a process of tail twisting the steer was forced to a few more short efforts but, when it was twisted out of joint in several places, John left him to die in peace if he could, for it was again night and cool, and plunged on through beachlike sand. As he neared the river he met men going back with water to relatives or to favorite animals who had dropped close by. "Go on, my friend," they encouraged him, "you will soon be through," and at ten o'clock his dreadful journey ended.

As we turned our car onto this section of the trail we found it impossible to mistake. We were surrounded at all times by bones, burned and rusted hardware, and especially by water-keg hoops. It was growing cooler as evening closed in, and we walked a great deal of the time. The earth and sky had blended to an opalescent rosy gray, like the heart of a great pearl, disfigured only by the blackened scatterings of iron. Hoops, hoops, and still more hoops—hundreds; we were never out of sight of them.

Burned wagons at Humboldt Sink.

The sand was deep but thickly crusted, and so far our heavy car had ridden it. A low bare range of sandy hills appeared to our left, marching purposefully toward the Carson. In it lies Soda Lake and the spring of fair water that, from here, although far off the direct route, is slightly closer than the river. Single horsemen often went to it for water to take back to their stranded families. Still we went on over foothill swells from whose summits we could see the trees at the site of old Ragtown ahead. Two miles now and our journey would be over—or would it?

No, definitely it would not. On the next brusque ascent we broke through the crust into deep dunelike sand and were face to face with one of the more disheartening aspects of field work. The remedy was at hand but uncomfortable (for greasewood when broken belies its velvety appearance), and the only disability I garnered on our entire trip was the thorns from pulling brush to throw under the wheels. The tires whined a moment through the heavy sand—lifted—were free—and we drifted back down the hill. Gone was the heartening view of river and trees; nothing but desert again.

We made a nonstop flight of twenty miles, circling by way of a duck hunters' road into the slender thread that leads from Parran to Fallon.

The sun had long fallen below the jagged horizon where the towering Sierras stormed the heavens, but one single golden cloud rested snugly on a bed of snowy white, a topaz on jeweler's cotton. The greasewood clumps were an amazing yellow-green, and the desert edge began to stir with life as lizards scuttled among their roots.

The first water reached is a furtive-looking slough and here (or in one similar) the thirst-crazed walkers threw themselves to drink from between the carcasses of animals who had come this far only to die. Sights hereabouts were not so dreadful. Relief parties financed in California were in operation. Wagons left the Carson River driven by men determined to get water as far as possible into the desert, only to be drained dry within a few miles and turned back for more. Horsemen went out with full canteens and came back with stragglers holding to their stirrups. Rescue parties found some solitary sufferers in time and brought others in for burial for whom they had come too late.

One at a time the oxen began to raise their heads and snuff the air. When more than a mile from the river they broke into a frenzied trot, the stronger pulling the weaker. It became dangerous to halt them, and when the low banks of the Carson were reached they plunged in with the yokes still on and the driver felt himself lucky to have loosed them from the wagon.

Oh, the blessed green cottonwoods of the Carson! Their great outspread boughs were a benediction. Men who had thought never to see a tree again took them in their arms and laid their faces against the rough bark. Women, safe again and comfortable beneath them, thought of the old home left behind and of their keepsake treasures abandoned hopelessly among the rotting carcasses of Destruction Valley; remembered lovingly the oxen and the saddle ponies whose faithful lives were sacrificed in their service and took time to weep at last.

*   *   *

And the Truckee River road, with its almost equal number of anxious-eyed travelers, what of it? Well, a great deal that was uncomfortable, it must be confessed, and a great deal that was dangerous including the rather bizarre need to guard the beef lest it be boiled before butchering. We traveled it, in company with Mr. Garaventi and Mr. Bromley, within twenty-four hours of the time we reached the Carson River. It was noon when we left the forks of the two roads where the sandpiper had waded in the slough.

In the early fifties there was a trading post near the forks, and the trader baked raised bread for the emigration, carelessly kneading in the dirt from his encrusted hands. It was the first bread they had seen since leaving Salt Lake City. He had also for sale a few miserable, green potatoes like big marbles, that, although peeled deeply, cooked up still green and bitter and made the children sick, so that they were whining and uncomfortable as they commenced to wind over the rough hillocks that led northwest to the Truckee River. It was impossible not to look back and notice that the wagons bound for the Carson appeared to be having an easier time; but the choice was made, and they held firmly to their course, coming down, in a few hours, to bottom land in a backwash from the sink. There was water (unfit for any use of course) but no grass for the stock, "and what is still worse," one woman wrote, "they all seem to be sick—and here we are with a 45 mile desert just ahead. We must push on for if we stay here the cattle will die of starvation."

After a short rest they did push on into the low sag of Hot Spring Hills, leaving the sink behind them and Cinnabar Peak on their left. The blanched gray earth was the color of a bilious oyster. Battalions of small dead bushes double the size of a cabbage had baked brown in the slow oven of the arid slopes. But (now about midway of their desert stretch) the travelers were getting ready to cash in on their one big advantage over the Carson road—water! On the slope ahead and to the left filmy wavering columns of steam rose into a day almost as intemperate as they.

To the worried emigrants the Boiling Springs were almost as quiveringly anticipated as their chances of heaven. It might even be said with truth that, as a popular resort, heaven was running a very poor second and the first glimpse of curling steam gave rise to the well formulated hope that arrival at the pearly gates might be postponed indefinitely. As they drew closer it could be seen that the side hill was crudely trenched, and that men were working hastily to guide the boiling water into ditches where it could cool enough to be useful. Children herded the thirsty stock but they were unmanageable and many a burned muzzle added to the general distress. Snorts and bellows of pain came frequently, and once the nerve-wrenching scream of a tortured horse rose above the ceaseless lowing. From the bounty of the nearest spring men were filling hogsheads, barrels, pails, dippers, tin cups, and whatever else was available. One man was seen trying to water his riding mule from a tin plate, his only other choice being a coffee cup. But a woman arriving on the scene observed his difficulty, and her first act, after pulling her children out over the end-gate of the wagon, was to loan him a bucket.

In early years, or during months of moderate travel, when only one or two companies arrived at a time, water was usually found in barrels, placed there to cool by the last passer-by, and it was incumbent upon the user to replace it with fresh. But when the Forty-niners reached this wonder spot of the desert—a milling crowd whose interest in it could be bounded by a three-hour span—they found only boiling water; and so would the constantly arriving stream of wagons until the gold rush should be over and straggling companies arrive one at a time again.

Taking her children by the hand, one woman went up the slope to the largest spring of all. It was about a rod across—deep and clear, and with no outlet that she could see. Every fifteen minutes it boiled with terrific intensity. When the animals were safely tethered and had their small portions of hay to eat, the husband came up to join them. The great pool greeted him with an outburst that startled him, and he wrote: "Of all the wonders I have seen in my life I never have beheld one that made such deep impressions on my mind. It appeared to me when I first stood and saw the troubled movement of the water that I was nearly in the presence of the Almighty." His wife, less philosophical, was horrified at the unconscious vandalism of the anxious, fretting crowd. She wrote, "This was the place of all places, where people left everything but themselves, and not satisfied to merely throw their things away, they dumped them en mess into the spring." The conscious pleasantry of "en mess" points the difference between the Truckee road and the Carson.

They stayed three hours so that the pan of dried peaches which the mother set afloat on one of the smaller springs had time to cook nicely. If the pan had upset it would have been a real calamity for, during the night spent just east of the meadow, the underfed mules had raided the wagon and undiscriminatingly chewed down most of their dried fruit and corn meal. The two little girls squatted in the shadow of a near-by wagon and watched with the zeal of the hungry to prevent any accident. There were several reasons why the mother chose a small spring, besides the obvious one of danger to the children. The most significant was the story passed around from camp to camp (although all first-hand witnesses had moved on hours ago) of a man who from faintness or some sort of seizure had fallen in the great spring during the previous night, and who was supposed to be buried somewhere among the wagons. Another was the disturbing presence under its translucent waters of a large ox and a small dog, both with the hair scalded off and well boiled.

The Boiling Springs, life-giving miracle of the westward migration, are now small, unspectacular Springer's Hot Springs and seldom rate from the highway traveler a second glance: just another set of hot springs in another set of low hot hills, nothing to write home about.

The trail goes on from there across a greasewood-studded flat, through another low spot in the hills, and may be seen close to the old Leete Salt Works. Soon it appears to the right of the highway on the first shelf of the dry hill slope where the ruins of Hoffman Station may be visited at the point of the tapering ridge. The wagons wound between dropsical dunes topped with upthrusting greasewood and the loose boulders of the basaltic flow where feathery bunchgrass still grows in small tight clumps of creamy yellow. At a knobby-topped knoll, on the county line between Washoe and Lyons counties, we left the highway and turned to the right, traveling on the original roadbed of the railroad from Wadsworth, which was laid close to the old trail. The ruts are deep and made heavy going through loose sand of decomposed rock—like beach sand—in which the wagon wheels sank twelve inches. Dead animals lined this stretch in windrows, but the great masses of ruined and abandoned wagons that characterized the Carson road were lacking. A few, yes; but the stretch was only eight miles long, the water kegs had been filled at the Boiling Springs, the situation was not so appalling.

Three miles from the river was a relief station selling water. One man wrote that, when almost there, the cow gave out; but his mules scented the river and could not be held. Loosing them from the wagons, he went along willy-nilly calling back to his family to coax old Sukie to the water station. With infinite trouble and discomfort the wife and children pushed and pulled the stricken animal to its shade and rushed in for water. Their own thirst was relieved, for a price; but there was no water for a cow. It was unthinkable that Sukie, as much a part of the family as any wet nurse, should lie outside and die for lack of a drink. No better proof of affection could be given than that the mother, staying with her babies to work over Sukie, let her two little girls start to the river for water.

No one helped them or offered them a ride. But then, practically no one was riding. After a mile the little one got tired. Her sister left her under a bush and went on alone. Her shoes were hot and full of sand. She took them off and put *them* under a bush. A hundred yards more and her feet were in a sad state. The poor child took off her stockings confident that she had solved the difficulty, and hung them conspicuously by the side of the well beaten roadway. With bare feet she reached the river, filled her container at a bank rendered dangerous by dozens of rushing animals, and returned, gathering up in turn her stockings, her shoes and her sister.

When the mules were fit to travel again, the father brought them back for his family and found Sukie on her feet and ready to live to a ripe, old age; but never again could he bear the thought of a relief station.

The eight miles of sand ended about half a mile upstream from the modern town of Wadsworth, at the beautiful tree-lined Truckee River. The current was turbulent and swift. The water was icy. The mules were easier to control this second time, which was lucky as the water was occupied by fifteen yoke of oxen, yokes and all. Each team consisting of three pair was fastened together with chains, and the whole conglomerate mess was intermingled almost beyond hope in the thigh-deep current.

The Truckee River, like the Carson, was a true mountain stream, pure and cold and crystal-clear. It swarmed with trout, and the best of pasture filled its fertile meadows. No traveler along the Truckee would ever be endangered by alkali, desert heat, lack of forage for the animals or of healthful water for every one. Those troubles were of the past, and, from the moment that the dust-choked emigrant gulped his first long draught of water from the snow-hooded California mountains, he looked ahead to where, in dark inscrutable majesty those soaring peaks held delights and dangers all their own.

29

Ragtown to Hangtown

DAYBREAK AT RAGTOWN on the Carson shed its uncertain light on a gaunt and tottery assembly of human scarecrows. Split-lipped, watery-eyed, tanned as a blacksmith's leather apron, they dragged themselves to unsteady legs and commenced to take stock of the future. The worst was behind them now; shade and water were at hand, but many of the gold rushers lacked food even to satisfy their immediate hunger, let alone the steadily mounting appetite to be generated by the two weeks of carbonated mountain air just ahead.

It was an emergency, and California rushed with characteristic speed into the breach. No prospective settlers should starve practically on her threshold: they were too badly needed. Supply parties were hastily equipped and hurried over the mountains to meet the emigrants where they struck the Carson River. At Ragtown they set up relief posts and dispensed their wares. It has been stated that they also charged for them, and charged highly, which was probably true if the chargee had any money left; but help was never refused to the destitute. Prices were exorbitant everywhere in the West. The newcomers had yet to become used to eggs at a dollar apiece, melons at a dollar and a half, milk at a dollar a pint, and so on indefinitely. The young man who paid fifteen dollars for a shortcake was astonished, but enjoyed it and doubtless grew accustomed to the high rates before the week was over.

The relief stations were of limited duration, but the trading posts soon had the matter well in hand. In a season or two, although healthful food might be scarce and dear, there was plenty of liquor, and Ragtown, like Dobeytown, ran full speed ahead.

There was no incentive to remain at Ragtown an hour beyond the time necessary to readjust to changed conditions; but it was essential to condense and discard some of the traveling equipment. Many men chopped up their wagons to make rough pack saddles and started on foot along the river, leading their animals. The company of Leroy Kidder, it may be remembered, had already discarded rolling stock on the big bend of the Humboldt and crowded Leroy into a wagon with one Florinda Washburn, spinster, and her brother. Florinda was a resolute individual, and her embryo milliner shop was taken along as a unit. To preserve it she had uncomplainingly walked every step of the desert crossing. The wagons of her company were now completely broken up at Ragtown; but the men had learned to respect her grit, and without too much comment they stuffed the delicate materials and implements into packs and put them on a pony. It was a high moment of mutual sacrifice and, not to be outdone, Florinda took the tailless goose under her apron, walked to the river, and came back grim-faced without it.

Some say that Ragtown got its euphonious title from the flapping canvas shacks, others from the long lines of ragged shirts and underwear hung out to the breeze in tribute to a clean and plentiful water supply. There was no set time to leave the settlement. Every hour of the day men took the trail upstream, some mounted, many walking, and the more fortunate still in organized wagon trains. The faded flannel shirts of their comrades, fresh from the (previously) unsullied river, waved encouragement as they turned away and commenced this rather pleasant lap of their journey. They were out of danger but had not yet had time to recuperate.

"A woebegone, sorry-looking crowd," wrote Margaret Frink on August 20, 1850. "The men, with long hair and matted beards, in soiled and ragged clothes, covered with alkali dust, have a half-savage appearance. There are but few women; among these thousands of men, we have not seen more than ten or twelve.

"The horses, cattle and mules are getting gaunt, thin and weak, almost ready to drop in their tracks, as hundreds of them have already done. . . . The once clean white wagon tops are soiled and tattered, and grimy with two thousand miles of dust. Many wagon beds have been cut off short to lighten them, or sawed in two to make carts. They go creaking along the dusty roads, seeming ready to fall to pieces, drawn by weary beasts hardly able to travel, making up a beggarly looking caravan, such as never was seen before. The great splendid trains of fifteen, twenty, thirty wagons have shrunk to three, four or at most half dozen, with three fourths of their animals missing. Their former owners now trudge along on foot packing on their backs the scant provisions left, with maybe a blanket, or leading skeleton horses that stagger under their light burdens. One of the 'passenger trains' left most of its carriages by the side of the road, the passengers having to finish their journey on foot."

For the first two or three days, depending on their speed, the caterpillar-like caravans found it more advantageous to remain on the south side of the river, cutting off the curves by crossing two large sand and sage plains and returning to the stream for rest and refreshment at night. On one of these returns Florinda Washburn's pony refreshed himself too impulsively by jumping from a bank into the river where he soaked both himself and the millinery-shop-to-be quite impartially. I must be excused from repetition of Florinda's expressed views of the matter, but the men were sympathetic to the extent of rescuing and helping to dry and pack the materials. Early the next morning, the trail-worn finery was under way again and headed for California. As this is our last encounter with the redoubtable Miss Washburn, I will include a jotting from the end of Leroy Kidder's reminiscences in which he notes that the strapping youth never made himself nor his sponsor rich by his efforts at the diggings, but that the millinery shop took in over $100,000 and Florinda was rated as a capitalist in later years.

The ragged columns passed the spot where Fort Churchill later guarded the stage road and, on the third or fourth day, crossed to the northwest bank of the river. Gold Canyon (named in later years) here opened into the river bottoms, and they moved wearily across it soon to emerge in the lower end of beautiful Carson Valley. Any one who has ever tried to count the enormous haystacks that blotch the flats like a bad case of measles will realize that the valley was born and raised to be an oasis. The men compared it favorably with the valley of the Bear, which was their criterion of fertility.

Such persons as share with my husband a mania for old tombstones positively must turn aside as they follow the windings of the river and climb the little knoll that holds aloft the ancient cemetery of Empire City. Tiny plots the size of a large desk top are elaborately fenced with hand-wrought iron fences made in patterns to match the beautifully sculptured gravestones. Money a plenty was made in Nevada, and most of it was spent.

Neither can the motorist afford to pass Carson City, self-captioned the smallest capital in the United States.

Wandering along the warm sidewalks of the charming tree-shaded little town, one comes to the most unexpected of historic landmarks for so small a community—a pretentious brick building that once housed the fittings and wealth of a United States mint and is now a museum. It has recently acquired a most historic trophy, the Frémont cannon—third item of the three most famous museum pieces known to have been lost in the West,* all recovered during a period of six years.

The story goes somewhat as follows: On Frémont's government-sponsored expedition to the west coast in 1843 he was supplied with a twelve-pound howitzer from the United States Arsenal at St. Louis. It was mounted on a small pair of wheels and was hauled clear to Oregon, south along Pyramid Lake, finally to a point just south of Kit Carson Pass, some thirty-five hundred miles in all, and then was abandoned.

Years later it was found and placed in Virginia City; thence it traveled to Brockway and later to Tahoe City, both on the shores of Lake Tahoe. At the last named it was occasionally unlimbered and fired at Fourth of July celebrations. A controversy arose as to its ownership, and an enterprising California congressman succeeded in obtaining an authorization from the War Department to remove it to his home town. Not a bad idea, civically speaking, but it didn't work out.

The howitzer promptly disappeared and remained hidden for many years. It was somewhat of an impasse, for naturally, while the order remained in force no one took an interest in finding it. Meanwhile historians fretted somewhat for fear that, through death or other mischance, its hiding place might be forgotten. With these conditions obtaining year after year, my husband finally took it upon himself to write to the War Department asking them to rescind the order and to make such arrangements as would facilitate its return to the general public. In time they wrote back to him releasing the little cannon to whomsoever had it in custody. This communication was forwarded where he thought it would do the most good, and (also in time) the cannon popped up in Carson City.

Unlike the funny little Indians of the sand country who were confident that no one would be tempted to covet their territory, the Indians of Carson Valley had a great deal to lose and already had reason to feel that their hold was slipping. For one thing, the Mormons had established a perma-

---

* The Sir Francis Drake plaque found in Marin Co., Calif.; the cap to Frémont's telescope, found on an island in the Great Salt Lake, and the Frémont cannon.

nent settlement at Mormon Station, now Genoa, which was a rankling thorn in their flesh. It was, however, a genuine spine-stiffener for the feminine portion of the early-day cavalcades. There were white women there, the first since Salt Lake City, and real houses with vegetable gardens at the foot of the forested mountain. Franklin Langworthy wrote in 1850:

"At noon, we stopped at a trading-post, called the Mormon Station. It is a large log building, standing in the skirts of the pine grove which covers the mountain side, and at this point extends quite down to the level of the valley. . . .

"This morning, a young man belonging to our train, was sent back ten miles, for the purpose of bringing up an ox, that had tired and had been left on the six mile desert. When he arrived within half a mile of the spot where the animal had been left, he perceived a crowd of Indians, apparently feasting on the carcass of the ox. The Diggers saw the young man coming, when twenty or thirty of them, mounting their ponies, gave him chase for about six miles. The young man threw away his boots, and in his stocking-feet ran for life, striking his course for the river, not daring to keep the smooth road. . . . The Indians soon discovering the object of their pursuit with hideous yells came on with accelerated speed, rapidly gaining ground while ready to launch their winged arrows, and the pursued was about to sink exhausted on the ground and thus surrender his life, when, to his great joy, the lengthy Mormon train came in sight around the point of a hill but a few rods ahead. The Indians stopped short in the chase, and fled with precipitation."

Mormon Station was, to all intents and purposes, a trading post. It maintained a store and a boarding house that served appetizing meals with vegetables and bread. There was even a dinner bell at noon and at sunset. One of the buildings was, in later years, treated to a genteel two-story false front as deceptive as a cheap toupee and as useful, and was the oldest house in Nevada when, quite recently, it was destroyed by fire.

In the late fifties, after the difficulties between the Mormons and the government were settled, harassed travelers found a United States Indian agent in Genoa. Widows and orphans from Indian massacres were placed in his charge to be returned to their homes when opportunity afforded.

Just beyond the town the enormous flow of hot water from what is now Walley's Springs called for comment, as did also the forks of the Carson

River, plainly traceable on the valley floor by their thick margin of green willows. The West Fork was the important one, and the wagons angled to meet it at its unimpressive exit from the mountain canyon. Over the rollicking, rocky little stream the Mormons built toll bridges, which the

Mormon Station.

Indians burned. More were built and for a while the Mormons, afraid to stay so far from the settlement, tried somewhat unsuccessfully to collect their toll in advance at Genoa. In September, 1852, an impostor preempted the first bridge and boldly charged five dollars a wagon. It was directly over the only possible ford, and many indignant travelers (including John Clark) paid the money.

About the middle of the month Colonel L. A. Norton declined to pay the exorbitant toll, backing his refusal with a gun. The jubilant emigrants whose turn came next refused also, and some packers passing on their way east carried word down the line. Not another soul paid a cent, and the next day the disgruntled man burned the bridge and took himself off. It would probably take a patient and able-bodied historian years of his life to dig out all the facts about these repetitious toll bridges. It was a case of now you see them and now you don't.

Many travelers used two bridges. Some found none, and Mrs. Francis Sawyer, traveling genteelly in her carriage in 1852, crossed three. She knew that the carriage was a temporary luxury only to be used until it cracked up, for her husband had packed all her baggage on the animals and a saddled mule was waiting for the hour when she would have to mount. The time soon came, for this was one of the most difficult parts of the whole journey, possibly equaled only by East Canyon Creek on the Salt Lake road. It was not the most dangerous (human lives were seldom lost, although the carcasses of exhausted animals lined the sides of the narrow canyon), but it was the hardest to accomplish. Foot by foot and yard by yard, the wagons were worried over boulders that so choked the bottom of the gorge that the little stream was heard rather than seen, gurgling and leaping along below.

"With nostrils distended and smoking, and flesh quivering in every fibre," the Spanish mules belonging to the train of William Johnston brought the first prairie schooners of the year 1849 up the canyon. The wagons were empty, for they had to be lifted bodily over fallen logs and enormous boulders. Other animals carried the load in packs. Somewhere in the cavalcade was the mule called Lousy of whose exploits we heard at Yellow Creek, and they would all die in harness, so Mr. Johnston wrote, before quitting on the job.

Ahead of them reached the rock-bound Sierras, ledge heaped on terraced ledge, rock piled on rock in a terrifying upward sweep that seemed to meet the tumbled masses in the sky. Here a noble pine soared high, its needles sketched in ink against a blindingly white cloud like besparkled Christmas-tree cotton. Here a fir tree's towerlike trunk, caught by a chance sun ray, glowed brilliant against the blue-black stormy sky. Always the battle of the elements seemed to center above the upper end of the canyon, at the top of the Jacob's Ladder of rock on which they were mounting so painfully to the heavens. Late comers like Langworthy, passing in October, dreaded early snows, and the almost routine afternoon thunderheads of the high Sierras chilled them with apprehension.

Where the last mile or so of the canyon leveled off, the women sat waiting for the wagons amidst the beautiful madder brown, age-old cedar trunks and watching the busy furry creatures of the forest. Down the dark mile still before them the wind could be heard whooshing through each treetop in turn. Having arrived, it shook a cone or two into the rock piles

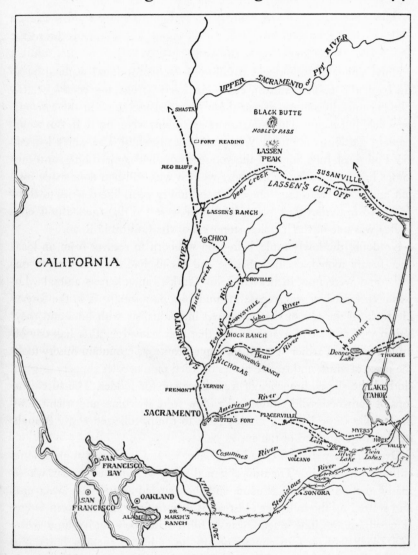

and departed with a swish. Every few minutes a tired team would clamber into view and grind steadily over the level to the cracking of whips and of the dead and fallen branches beneath the wheels. A few routine oaths from throats almost too hoarse to swear fell unnoted on the ears of teams too weary to listen. Three or four minutes, and they were gone, as the watching women knew, toward the end of the canyon where Hope Valley opened to receive them. Again no sound was heard but the rushing, lapping, rollicking noise of the water.

Hope Valley is a mountain paradise of flat pasture land watered by a low-banked accessible stream, clear and lively as clicking crystal beads. The encamped pioneers, except those who had lost stock in the canyon, were cold but happy. The unfortunate exceptions were just cold. But what leaping, glorious campfires! What pine-knot torches! The valley looked like Fourth of July. Some of the younger boys had gone fishing, and the camps had trout to fry, while those women who still had flour made biscuit and doled them out—one each—to hungry men, like cookies to children. No festivities took place. The men were too dog-tired. But Hope Valley was one of the happiest stopovers of the California Road.

No doubt the lowly mule, being too stubborn to recover from an idea once firmly rooted, decided that he and his ilk had died on the canyon rocks and were now in heaven. John Clark's cantankerous animal who was accustomed to seek repose in mudholes now sought it in the forest. He took all the rest of the long-eared individualists with him, and they hid so well and stood so immovably that they gained another half-day of mule paradise. Farther along their rugged route, as mountain misery took the place of grass, and twelve inches of dried pine needles slippery as glass clothed the slopes, branches of trees were cut for fodder. The succulent tops of dogwood, wild plums, and willow were welcome, and truant hobbled mules came hopping nimbly back to camp, collected easily enough by the ringing sound of the ax.

Over a rise lay shallow-edged Red Lake, set at a southwest angle among enfolding mountains. The trail stretched along its southeast border, where many stopped to "bait" at noon, and then circled around the lower end and started up the hill. The old road is easy to find, and the steep ascent is worth seeing. The wagon way is filled with loose and rolling rocks and edged with broken chunks of granite as big as packing boxes. Fir trees, still standing, furnished immovable snubbing posts, and each hard-won inch gained by the oxen was held by men and ropes while the winded beasts slacked their chains and rested. Toward the top we found a large tree with a groove worn knuckle-deep from rope chafing. Soon the roadbed became a series of sidling pancakes of granite where the pulling oxen fell to their knees. It was necessary to lead them to the next place that afforded a toe hold and fill the gap between them and the wagon with long chains. In some cases along the steep Sierra trail they were led over the top of the hill and given a down pull with spliced chains while the wagon still remained below the summit.

Starting as was usual at three in the afternoon, many could not make the top before nightfall, and the mountain side was illuminated by the flaring torchlight of burning pine trees. Equipment, for the time being, was a hindrance, and pack-men whose bloody feet were wrapped around with rags begged a biscuit here and there and went on ahead, sleeping by the warmth of limitless fires.

It would have been bad enough had they all been going in the same direction; but freight, eastbound to Genoa, passed occasionally and proved a definite complication. A string of heavily laden pack mules was dangerous on a narrow ledge trail, for it was impossible for the packers to conduct every mule. Consequently each animal was a law unto himself, and stopped for nothing but individual preference. Lavinia Porter, in spite of the warning bells on every collar, was caught on a narrow ledge against a cliff. She found a niche in the wall large enough for her body and cowered within the partial shelter while the packs from sixty mules scraped her clothing.

Looking back from modern Kit Carson Pass the emigrants could see the lovely valley they had just quitted, with two others, smaller but equally beautiful. A company of Odd Fellows standing there named the three Faith, Hope, and Charity. Then, turning to a large rock near by, they drew the insignia of the three links and added their names. They used something white, white lead perhaps, and each year it grows fainter.

The trail crosses this mountain top a hundred yards or so east of the Kit Carson monument. In 1844, when the famous scout was guiding Frémont across the Sierras, he carved his name on a tree where the monument now stands. The tree fell during a storm in '84, and two young San Francisco hunters chopped out the section bearing Carson's name, took it down to the valley in their buckboard, and placed it in Sutter's Fort.

Through gnarled and twisted aspens, firs and tamarack, and clumps of willow the wagons descended to a valley containing, without much doubt, a lake similar to others in the neighborhood. Some called it Mountain Lake. Langworthy knew of no name for it, but described it as irregular and strewn with islands. He camped at the south end, at the foot of immense piles of granite rock described as "stupendous towers." Two lovely artificial bodies of water called Twin Lakes now occupy the valley, but it was also beautiful in its natural state when the wagons crossed the bed of these lakes. Nancy Hunt buried her invalid husband here. She was glad it was in California, for it made the lonely grave seem closer to her new home. "We laid the body away in the best manner we possibly could," she wrote bravely, "specially marking the grave so that emigrants passing that way for years afterwards would take particular notice of it: in this way we could hear from it sometimes. We could not linger there between the two majestic pines where my husband's body was tenderly laid to rest; there was no grass for the cattle. We must push on."

Few can realize the difficulties of the mountains over which just such pioneers as Nancy Hunt pushed—and they pulled, too, before the day was over. For the Carson Pass of the emigrants is on a windswept hog-back above the timber line, and it reaches an elevation of more than nine thousand feet, higher than any of them had ever been.

The highway has in late years been blasted, lower on the mountain, out of the very brink of a stupendous rocky promontory called Carson Spur. It very definitely goes one way while the old trail patiently plods the other. We had to have horses.

In order to have time to engage them and to do the thing properly we made a separate trip. Dr. Neff, to his intense disgust, was unable to leave, and we (using erroneous inducements) persuaded Mr. Bromley to make his first field trip with us. We obtained the necessary information from Frank Tabeau, a cattleman, whom we found at Plasse's Resort. He even combined business with pleasure and rode a way with us to see that we got started to his satisfaction. After that we were on our own, for there is no modern trail to the summit. We left the highway near the old Kirkwood Hotel and turned toward the mountains to the east. Beyond the feathered grasses and lavender daisies of the meadows, dense forests of tamarack stood across the trail. To the right a rocky wall topped with lava plugs rose high and forbidding. We kept on the trail below the escarpment and rode pleasantly enough through acres of skunk cabbage and dark tree-tunnels of young fir and pine, coming by and by to a rotting log where cattle had been salted. Here our trail was joined by a much shorter trail that left the east end of the Twin Lakes Bottoms and came due south up the canyon. The gaunt gray mountain lay ahead—a craggy eminence with beetling brows and protruding chin. Possibly a half-mile of heavy climbing was necessary—most of it up the rough bed of a snow-born rivulet with its visible beginnings in a dingy but durable snowbank near the top of the pitch. Besides unloading the wagons many of the emigrants now removed the heavy cloth cylindrical tops and sent them up on mules. "The last two miles of the ascent is terrific, being excessively steep," wrote Mr. Langworthy, "and a part of the way so sideling, that it was necessary for several men to brace themselves against a wagon to prevent its upsetting and rolling down the side of the mountain. By doubling teams, and assisting with manual strength, we succeeded in gaining the top of this dreaded eminence by two o'clock in the afternoon. Arriving near the top of the ridge, the road turns to the south, and runs along the summit about two miles."

We arrived at the end of the scramble to find that we had gained the lip of a flattish mountaintop. The handsome postcard view back to Twin Lakes and its adjacent forests was instantly gone as we moved a few yards farther, for the top tilted slightly downward in front of us. We ate lunch in a deep depression near the point where we had gained the top (mainly because it boasted a small snow lake and was out of the wind), but wasted very little time in the process and were soon ready to go along the ridge that rises east of Silver Lake.

There was little snow, and the peculiar rock formations rose stark and storm-scoured on either side. Almost at once our procession threaded in a housewifely manner directly between the Thimble and the Needle's Eye, too well named to need description, and the horses jogged easily along on the soft loose earth, which is protected by immense bats of snow most of the year. The trail continued down the hogback while, on the east side, mists boiled in abysmal canyons. The depths of Horse Canyon were on our left, and Devil's Hole was ahead. Flat boulders with their slopes ground off by the heavy iron tires, some with gradual approaches built of smaller stones, marked the trail.

From the next steep pitch we had a splendid view back to old Summit City and Silver Mountain on the right, Round Top in the middle, and Thimble Peak to the left; then down we rode through Telephone Gulch where (we were later told) the old telephone line ran from Bear River to Blue Lake; out on the far side and up to a summit from which we had our first view of Silver Lake.

We stopped a moment at an unmarked grave and then turned to the left to circle into Martell Flat, knee-deep in splendid grass.

In trail diaries of this high Sierra section it will be found that companies still having animals to care for seldom camped on the road. They took them a mile or two from the trail and put up for the night where the feed was good. We have no doubt that Martell Flat was frequently used for this purpose.

Somewhere near this point Carlisle Abbott and his companions found themselves entirely without food but each in possession of a mount. It seemed only sensible in their extremity to eat one of the horses, and they drew lots. Abbott received the short straw, and old Pompey was elected to die—faithful "Pomp" that had led the swimming animals on every river of the journey. Abbott cried himself to sleep and, the next morning, went hunting through the mountain mists at crack of dawn while the others waited. He killed a deer and was still riding Pompey when his story ends at the settlements.

Of course, not all the wagons using the high hogback road were prairie schooners carrying emigrants. The Mormons greatly improved it in 1850 for their freighting strings, and no doubt the "lengthy Mormon train" met by Langworthy at what is now Genoa, Nevada, came over this first skyline boulevard.

We circled back from Martell Flat to the trail and found another grave, a lonely heap of rocks unshaded and unsheltered by the sparse and storm-torn timber; and then came at once to the site of the old Plasse Trading Post. Raymond Peter Plasse was in business here for a busy nine years, from 1853 to 1862. The hogback is very rocky with a scattering growth of tamarack, but down the hill toward Silver Lake is Beebe Lake surrounded by Beebe Meadows. It is doubtless one of the camping places down off the trail so often mentioned and possibly was the scene of the campfire song-fest and jollification held by Langworthy's company on the night of October 15, 1850. There was still another flat to the left where we found legible initials on the aspen trees—one set dating from the fifties.

Half a mile from the trading post the lurching schooners skirted the east side of a moist flat full of great piles of solid granite, and went down toward Clemmens Meadow, which they also passed on the left. It is as green as a lawn, bordered with tall skunk cabbage and painted with tiny dark blue lupin. The timber is very large. We led our horses down a rocky length of trail and presently saw the shine of a little lake ahead. It might from its beauty be called Mirror or Diamond or Jewel, but I have no desire to blink at facts. It is plain Mud Lake. Old cabins stand on drier ground beyond the meadow and on a large embedded boulder near by we found almost illegible names.

Two or three miles below Mud Lake, Tragedy Spring flows from a bank immediately at the right of the highway. Its name dates back to a summer day in 1848 when thirty-odd members of the returning Mormon Battalion passed on their way to Salt Lake City. Bloody stones and arrows caught their attention, and investigation disclosed the nude bodies of three of their number who had become restless and gone on in advance. A purse of gold lay near by, untouched. The bodies were buried at the foot of a large pine. The soldiers blazed it and carved the names of the victims and a brief account of the circumstances. The tree stood for over eighty years. When it died the segment containing the blaze was removed and taken to Sutter's Fort Museum at Sacramento, and a bronze replica was attached to a boulder. The emigrants seldom camped there. Two miles farther along the trail, the Argonauts who hurried down the mountain late in the season of 1850 passed a sad new grave. It is the last resting place of Rachel Melton of Iowa, and, like Our Jessie's pathetic stone marker on Little Goose Creek, it grows in interest with the years. The traveling public knows it as the Maiden's Grave.

The old trail, naturally, is hopelessly erratic in its windings over the mountains, but it does stay more or less in the vicinity of the highway until both arrive at Corral Flat, where the trail angles off to the right. The old dirt road to Placerville is then the best base of operations, and we took it.

Within two miles a branch road turned left to Leek Spring. It was well labeled; but that was the best thing we could say about it, and we worked out our road tax, all unappreciated, on the way in. The small protected valley was named by the same group of the Mormon Battalion who a day or so later found and buried the men at Tragedy Spring.

Every summer it was modestly bowered in wild leeks and practically every company camped there and ate them. The cows ate them too, and Leek Spring Valley was remembered as long as the milk and butter retained their peculiar aroma. We found old buildings quite deserted. Out in the woods, on the meanderings of the trail, Bill picked up a very heavy home-constructed shoe last attached upside down on a long iron spike. The user could drive it into the ground, pull his shoe on the last and half-sole his footwear with whatever came to hand, and he probably sat on the wagon tongue while he did it. The milder climate of the valley was sometimes mentioned in diaries, and we noticed that the tall, flaunting leaves of the skunk cabbage were bronzed, and that the willows were tinged with a rich green-gold. Autumn was at least a month nearer at Leek Spring than it had been yesterday at Martell Flat.

Hangtown was the immediate objective of most of the journalists who came this way, with Volcano possibly a good second, and at Leek Spring they had a choice of roads. The easiest way to Hangtown was the right-hand or north route along the dividing ridge between the South Fork of the American River and the North Fork of the Cosumnes. This un-adventurous hogback leads, in a slight northward curve but with commendable singleness of purpose, straight to Placerville (Hangtown with a modern veneer), and makes very little fuss about it. The left-hand road took a curve south of the North Fork of the Cosumnes among more irregular and capricious mountains, crossing the fork at Buck's Bar, and its travelers might either complete the curve up to Hangtown or turn off to Volcano. We took the north road out of Leek Spring for two reasons, and it was most fortunate that they coincided—the little dirt road went that way, and so did Langworthy, whose detailed diary we had with us. On another occasion we traveled the turn-off into Volcano; but we have never finished the southern fork to Hangtown in its entirety.

We went straight to the top of the ridge, passing a sign that read, "Placerville—40 miles." The side hills were tracklessly timbered in large red firs and burly yellow pine whose distinctive rectangular groovings made them seem encased in bronze armor plate. The ridge top was narrow in places but was otherwise one of the best and easiest pieces of roadway the pioneers had yet found. Very accommodatingly the ridge gradually lowered. Red fir gave way to cedar, and the twisted, tortured manzanita appeared, interspersed with large-leaved, fat-acorned black oaks. Alder Creek parallels the ridge on the right, and Camp Creek on the left.

A mile short of Stump Springs the original road for some reason deviated from the hogback, turned to the left down a spur, dropped off the steep end of it into Taylor's (now Zumwalt), and traveled the present Gerard's Mill road to Five Points. "Going off at the deep end" was quite characteristic of the old trail. It dumped its passengers into California willy-nilly and had not the slightest interest in getting them out again. When teams began to go eastward with freight for the Mormon settlements and materials for the Nevada mines, the pull up from Taylor's was far too steep, and the easier grade through Ditch Camp and Bryant's was evolved. It left the older road near Five Points.

Not only the overly steep pitches delayed the freighters (who traveled most seasons of the year), but deep snow on the ridge stretching from the Thimble to Mud Lake. They looked for a pass by which they could sneak between a pair of ribs instead of marching straight over the backbone of the Sierras. Johnson's Pass over the Echo Lake Summit was the answer they found. The Pony Express, in 1860, passed up West Carson Canyon into Hope Valley and then northward through Luther's Pass, up to Echo Lake by way of Johnson's Pass, at the left of the highway summit, and down over Slippery Ford to Strawberry. The last-named hostelry belonged to a man named Berry who sold straw under the name of hay and received the unflattering sobriquet of Old Straw Berry. From there the flying riders went to Sportsman's Hall and on into Placerville. Many wagon companies followed the same route. Sometimes they omitted the West Carson and made the difficult climb up the Nevada mountains to Lake Bigler (Tahoe), around it to Yank's Station (now Myers) and climbed to Johnson's Pass direct. Lucy Cooke took this route in '53, the earliest record that I can remember. Her party came out at Roopley's Ranch near Hangtown.

The timber of the lower reaches of the California mountains staggered the travelers and jolted the relatives at home. "There were pine trees," writes Mr. Langworthy (and he a minister), "ten, and even twelve feet in diameter, and towering to the height of three hundred feet or more. These facts we should have been loath to believe without ocular proof.

By the side of such a grove, the stateliest pine forests in the eastern States would appear like humble shrubbery." Truly Mr. Langworthy was born to be a Californian.

Near as the caravans now were to the diggings, the mountains were not safe for small parties. From the mileage, it was probably along Plum Creek that a young couple from Tennessee were walking and driving two oxen packed with their meager belongings when they were attacked without warning. They had no gun, but the man gained a little time and diverted the aim of the Indians by hurling rocks as they drew their bows to shoot. He kept urging his wife to run while he held them, but she would not. At the top of a hill, after dodging a dozen or so arrows, the man received one in the left shoulder blade; and they both turned and fled down the hill. Their assailants for some reason neither pursued them nor stole the oxen, both of whom were recovered with the loads intact. Some favorable chance no doubt distracted their attention. Upon arrival at a near-by trading post it was learned that the eighteen-year-old bride had been severely wounded through the breasts at the beginning of the struggle and had concealed the fact in order to leave her husband as free as possible to help them both.

The Indians of the Sierras were small, scarcely over five feet, and repulsively ugly. When encountered peacefully they were usually gathering acorns from the tall, reaching black oaks, or nuts from the digger pines of the foothills. Great quantities were collected, and the squaws crept around bent double under enormous basketloads. Picking nuts is a two-hand job and, as a defense measure for curtailing enemy activities, the squaws kept their heads thickly daubed with soft pitch. The bucks did not need to do this, as they always had both hands free. They do not seem to have invaded the camps of the emigrants to beg. Probably they knew all they cared to learn about Americans.

As might be expected, trading posts along the Hangtown Road were as thick as hasty pudding. It was the easiest part of the overland route to keep supplied with staples, and the travelers were almost destitute and eager to buy. Men with no equipment could get lodgings at the posts. Others bought meals from them and camped near at hand.

Now and then men and teams turned off to locate at some isolated diggings. Companies broke into units and separated not to meet again for years. Snap decisions were made upon the slightest of foundations—

decisions that determined each man's future and that of his family and descendants.

Upon the whole, though, fewer wagons turned off from the northern fork to Placerville than from the southern, which ran through more broken country, had more deviating byways, and, most important of all, carried the wagons bound for Volcano. Mary Stuart Bailey traveled the

Acorn gatherers in the California Foothills.

endless canyon road in the stifling dust of October. "We arrived in Volcano," she wrote, ". . . the first mining town in California. Took dinner there, had variety of vegetables. The buildings are very rude. Some of logs, others of cloth covered frame. The village is without form or confine." The town never grew after the decline of the mines—quite the contrary; but it will richly repay any one for a visit.

Volcano was fortunate in being on a short offshoot from a main traveled road and could get healthful food, but men went wherever gold beckoned. If they couldn't get potatoes or other vegetables, and the supply of pickles, vinegar, or citric acid gave out, they often fell into desperate stages of scurvy. Small camps in the high mountains suffered, and solitary miners died in their tents because they were unable to make the trip out to civilization. One man's life was saved because, on the previous year, a pack mule had burst a bag of beans along a little used trail. In the spring the young pale green sprouts pushed up. They were found, boiled, and fed to the sick man, who gained strength enough to make the ride out to health.

In one camp of four men the dreaded symptoms of scurvy appeared. They knew that they needed green vegetables but were unacquainted with the native plants. They had seen horses and oxen die from unrestricted browsing along the Truckee Trail, but no one knew which herb caused death. In their dilemma they took a walk and each picked a panful of some likely-looking plant. Each cooked his own, and each ate his own in an effort to see what would prove effective—and also to insure only one death in case some selection should be fatal. None of them so much as sickened; but the one who had chosen the soft little plant now known as miner's lettuce (montia perfoliata) had the best results. It was at a premium from that time on.

The emigrants were used to rattlesnakes. Scorpions they had seen along the Humboldt, but tarantulas burst on their exhausted mentalities as a brand-new nightmare. Some of the expectant miners, fortifying their flagging spirits with potent liquor, and casually meeting a tarantula family out for a stroll, swore off with fervency and looked in vain for a pledge to sign. Mary Stuart Bailey selected only their luxuriant hair for comment, and it really does seem prodigal to waste it on an insect; but her most fascinated interest was centered on the "horned frog." "I should think it something like a crockidile," she wrote, "with a tail, and sharp points all over its body." Truly there was much at which to wonder in the California mountains.

Thickets of the treacherous poison oak lined the roadway. The thick coating of dust, rendering it unattractive where most easily accessible, probably saved enough suffering to make up for the discomfort of the suffocating clouds that completely enveloped the wagons. Miners, clearing and burning the shrubbery to get at their claims, swelled up at all unhandy seasons and were acutely ill. "The disease caused by the poisonous oak" was listed next to dysentery and higher than scurvy in the diggings.

It was immediately following an autumn shower that the beautiful glistening rose madder of the poison-oak sprays were so tempting to the children of the migration. Reaching tendrils of the climbing grape also flaunted rich gold leaves amid the clear soft yellow of the willows. Dogwoods, summer-kissed to a warm peach-blush, flamed in the sun. Dark leaden masses of mistletoe showed here and there through the thinning gold of the black oaks. To the late comers these lower reaches of the mountains had their own autumnal beauty, and the southering sun shone through nature's cathedral windows stained every shade of lime-yellow, copper, raspberry-brown, Spanish red, and pure shining gold. Hills were fronted with wet red banks where the wagons had cut through, and rose gradually to slopes of dried tawny grass stuck wetly into tufts like a licked Persian cat. On the open canyon sides ghostly digger pines waved pendulous arms—irresolute finger tips now beckoning, now waving farewell, and so the caravans moved down toward the foothills.

Fifteen miles above Hangtown the teams reached Pacific House; at fourteen, Bullion Bend, where a stage was held up and loot is supposed to be buried; at twelve, Sportsman's Hall (named from the multitude of card sharks that frequented its tables) where the relay waited for the Pony Express rider on his mad dash. It was the chosen stopping place for teamsters freighting to the Nevada mines and had stable room for several hundred horses. Then they came to Five Mile House and on down to Hangtown Creek with all its water drained out into ditches to feed the "long toms."

There was no grass. John Clark's obstreperous mule, being hungry, took a tentative bite at the company captain's booted foot, which happened to be protruding from the wagon, and found himself in the limelight again. The road beggared all description. "For miles and miles," wrote Clark, "it was full of passengers, wagons, mules, oxen and horses, and dust, I can't pretend to say how deep. It was like traveling through snow up to one's knees. As we came down a high ridge to Hang Town Creek we began to see the miners and their way of working. There were hundreds of them at work, Americans, English, French, Negroes, Chinamen and Hindoos with here and there a Spanish Mexican."

And Hangtown—what of it? Built flimsily at a carefree slant on the two sides of a shallow pine-filled canyon, the log-framed, canvas-roofed buildings of '49 gradually gave way to better arrangements. Men found there was sure money to be made in lumber, and small mills hacked out heavy timbers for warmer houses. A crude but effective line of stores centered the rambling elongated town and soon became a recognized goal for gold seekers. It was the third largest city in the state. And, second only to Sacramento, Hangtown symbolized to the overland Argonauts, their arrival in the West.

A large circus tent, pridefully set up for a saloon, became in a year or two a clothing store, and here we take leave of the optimistic young wife and mother, Lucy Cooke. With the pardonable vanity of a pretty woman in a man's world she took occasion to stop outside the town and put on the neat silk dress that had been the object of her fond concern throughout the entire journey. She then mounted her side saddle and rode into town quite elegantly. But the mare had a touch of colic. Right in front of the dry-goods store she lay down in the middle of the road and rolled. Lucy saved her dress from ruin by a narrow margin, having plenty of assistance, no doubt, from the admiring bystanders. For many years a building occupying the same site has been called the Tent Store.

The settlement started its diversified career under the title Dry Diggings, but was rechristened in honor of its early citizens' well meant exertions in the cause of justice. Two Frenchmen and a Chileno were hanged on an oak in the center of town in January, 1850. Several other executions followed rapidly—possibly too rapidly. The place was irrevocably dubbed Hangtown. When California became a state, later in the same year, the more aesthetic citizenry had its name legally changed to Placerville. In the spring of '53, still struggling for less violence, they narrowly prevented another lynching and had the oak cut down. The top was made into souvenirs, but the stump is beneath a building within a few feet of the memorial plaque.

The biggest buildings in town were, of course, the dance halls—the Boomerang, Trio Hall, the Jenny Lind, and others. Most of the place burned in '56, and the Patton Home was built that year. It is one of the few buildings preserved from that time and is occupied by the Hangtown Antique Shop. The stage station and corrals were opposite. The Raffles Hotel is on the site of the famous Carey House, to which Hank Monk was driving Horace Greeley when he was purported to have said, "Keep your seat, Horace—we'll get you there on time."

Hangtown was a great place for the ambitious tradesman. John Studebaker's first job in California was turning out twenty-five wheelbarrows at ten dollars each. In the course of time he had his own shop near the junction of Main Street and Bedford Avenue, which was the beginning of the manufacture of wagons and automobiles that has continued for ninety years. Mark Hopkins, later railway magnate, brought one load of goods from San Francisco and opened a grocery store. Philip D. Armour was in Placerville four years, from '52 to '56. Then he was just the redheaded butcher, but the products of his stupendous business enterprises later furnished food to people the world over. Whatever faults Hangtown may have had, there was no lack of brains or good company.

If the newly arrived family or group of men intended to stay awhile in town they set up their tents, pulled up their wagons, or otherwise set up housekeeping almost anywhere—under a tree, in the lee of a house, or in the side or back yard of a store. Then they added a few square yards of calico partition and a brush lean-to kitchen and felt well equipped. In such a setup within the elastic confines of Hangtown, Mrs. James Caples found herself, at the end of the second week, the sole support of a suddenly invalided husband. He had to have good food, and food cost lots of money. She frantically cudgeled her brain for the most income for the least expenditure and decided to make a few pies in her Dutch oven. Dried peeled peaches from Chile were available. They had been pressed into forms the size and shape of large cheeses, but she tussled chunks from one and went to work. The butter had been brought around the Horn and was valuable chiefly because one was never tempted to use it, so she tried out fat from salt pork, freshened it, and mixed it in her crust. The men practically stood in line and ate the fragrant concoctions redhot. Before she quit this enterprise she had made as many as a hundred pies a day at a dollar a pie, and a dollar and a half for mince creations. History will always be the poorer that this resourceful woman failed to tell what she put into the mincemeat.

From Hangtown the Sacramento-bound Argonauts went over a steep hill to Weaver Creek, where in 1850 a miner with an eye to business camped by a log that had accidentally bridged the flooded stream and charged fifty cents toll. Occasionally he got it. It has been said that it was the first toll bridge in California. Three miles from town was another settlement, Diamond Springs, where a group of springs were so located that they formed the corners of what some imaginative person felt to be a diamond. One such flight of fancy being all the traffic would bear, the next town, three miles farther, was dubbed Mud Springs. Twelve miles below Hangtown was Missouri House, and beyond it the travelers had their first view of the great valley of the Sacramento, which on an overcast day had no apparent boundaries.

Ghost Town.

Most of the mining camps built up, became prosperous, erected false-fronted guild halls and opera houses, finally petered out, and the residents moved on to the next diggings. Coloma, Smith's Flat, and others were on, or nearly on, the Hangtown trail. Dozens of others bordered the Truckee route, Feather River route, Lassen's or Greenhorn's Cutoff, and the road through Johnson's Pass. Scattered wooden settlements, perched high in mountain fastnesses or chaotically huddled down in dusty canyon depths, were noisy and crowded for a few years. Jackass trains stubbed up narrow trails. Men congregated at the stores to buy and eat, at the saloons to drink and gamble, and in the street to fight or to pass the time of day. For ten, twenty, thirty years the mining camps prospered. French Corral, Indian Diggings, Rough and Ready, Whisky Flat, Port Wine, Jackass Hill, picked at random from scores of whimsical names, were populous and then deserted and forgotten by all but a few. Little faded ghost towns hidden here and there, snow-buried in winter, forest-fire-scorched in summer, they were in their golden heyday the Mecca of the weary Argonauts, the pioneers of '49 and '50.

30

At the End of the Rainbow

On THE FAR BANK of the Truckee River, in the year 1855, stood a trader's house built of woven willows like a champagne basket. The house was empty, but the shallow grave within its shadow was full. Weary emigrants arriving from the desert crossing, whispered to one another that a rival trader from the Carson had sent Indians to remove unwanted competition. The wagons splashed across the lovely stream, their loads remaining a gratifying six inches above the lapping water, and the travelers looked at the pathetic grave. Its murdered occupant should be avenged, they told one another in trenchant terms—but when, where, and by whom? Then they went on and soon forgot. Battle, murder, and sudden death had lost the power to impress. They traveled up the Truckee, for these were the travelers who had chosen to come by way of the Boiling Springs and Truckee Lake Summit instead of Carson Pass. They traveled in a very ecstasy of damp enjoyment, crossing and recrossing the sparkling river at every whim of the current or caprice of the sloping banks. Twenty-eight, thirty-five, forty-nine times—there was no set rule. One day the wagons crossed a half-mile strip of boulders where the noise of the wheels was like thunder, and those who walked wore the boots off their feet.

The river proved to be a scalloped ribbon of silver narrowly bordered with vivid green. It lay flatly and incongruously between the bosoms of tailored beige hills that swelled firmly from its tender hollow. Thirty-two or thirty-three miles brought the wagons, on the afternoon of the second day, to Truckee Meadows, where they halted early to take full advantage of the splendid grass.

Originally the city of Reno depended upon her surroundings—the all-important fertile bottom lands of Truckee Meadows; but now they are all but forgotten and only "the biggest little city in the world" gets mental comment from the motorist. It is a crisp, sophisticated place, and its lawns and freshly painted apartment houses form the greatest contrast imaginable to the dingy sage-studded desert.

We had barely left the city behind when we came at once to the first small serving of dumpling hills, moving on shortly to more and bigger ones. Some of the companies, arriving in Truckee Meadows and looking ahead at the vast Sierras, found that they had no stomach for them. Stories seeped among the apprehensive gossipers of tragedy ahead, of Death crying on the mountaintop, of smothering, blinding snowstorms and of ghoulish Indians. They thought enviously of those who had taken the Carson route and now faced the shorter distance across the mountains. It was probably the Donner catastrophe that turned them aside, for many companies hesitated here and took a foothill route past Steamboat Springs to intersect the Carson road near Genoa, and it is doubtful if they lost more distance in the process than would balance the extra miles wasted by the Truckee route in striking the Sacramento Valley too far north.

It was along the Truckee that the practically indestructible cattle that had survived fatigue, starvation, alkali, the desert, and the Indians began to die. Helen Carpenter saw the veteran, Old Star, sag under his yoke as the wagon pushed him down the slope. She cried for him to be unchained, but it was impossible as well as unsafe to stop. He continued to brake the wagon with his dying body and succumbed at the foot of the hill. Later comers learned that it was wild parsnip that did the mischief, but scores of cattle were poisoned in the first migrations.

The settlement of Verdi is in one of the occasional wide spots in Truckee Canyon. Both highway and trail approach it on the north side; but both cross the river as the current curves around the hayfields of the open patch of bottom land. The highway goes impersonally on its way, but the trail, in its day, crosscut the (then) grassy meadow and unconcernedly forded the river again, back of the present settlement, for what Eliza Donner Houghton wrote was "the forty-ninth and last time in eighty miles." The original trail, first used in 1844, continued up the stream; but an important variant, first attempted in '45 and used for several years, split from the main trail here and took its way into a dusty canyon to the north. It is known as the Alder Creek Trail.

We dropped into second and went along after it. As just mentioned, this hilly detour dates from 1845. The first overland party to reach California from the States was the Bidwell-Bartleson party in 1841. It crossed the Sierras near Sonora Pass but found no desirable route. Then in 1843 Jo Walker guided the Chiles party south from the Malheur River in Oregon, through the mountains into California, but no one left a trail suitable for future settlers to travel. It remained for Caleb Greenwood, at the age of eighty-one, to open the lane of wagon traffic that continued in use for over twenty years and is now paralleled by the transcontinental highway. It was the Stevens-Townsend-Murphy party that "Old Greenwood" guided from Fort Hall, down the Humboldt and up the canyon of the Truckee in the year 1844, driving the wagons in the bed of the stream when the grudging rocky walls impinged on their meager roadway. The Truckee Route was then called North Pass.

The ascent of the canyon was cruelly hard, and, when the emigrants had completed it and the grassy meadows around modern Truckee rewarded their perseverance, they faced the mountain rising sheer and grim ahead. Old Greenwood took his wagons over, but it was too hard for some of the party to face. They thought better to cache their goods, leave some men on guard, and come back in the spring to get them. And so a one-room log house was built where the Pioneer Monument now stands near the shores of Donner Lake. Foster, Montgomery, and a seventeen-year-old boy named Moses Schallenberger remained behind. They had expected to live on game; but soon the snow was ten feet deep, and no game remained. They grew worried and started out for civilization but, upon reaching the summit, Moses Schallenberger became too ill to go on. His companions brought him back to the cabin and, with his free consent, left him and went on to save themselves. Somehow he lived and grew better and went out to trap foxes; and fox meat constituted his main support until the party returned on March 1, 1845.

In that same year, for some reason (possibly high water) the next caravan of settlers was diverted from the canyon of the upper Truckee and turned to the right at what is now Verdi. Thomas Knight tells the story. He and his company were headed for Oregon when, somewhere on the Sweetwater, they met Jo Walker. He told them of the success of the party of '44, some of whom had crossed the Sierras with their wagons. On the strength of their achievement Mr. Knight's party turned for California at Fort Hall and traced the Greenwood route as far as modern Verdi. At that point they entered the canyon to the right, being the first party to do so. The detour necessary was lengthy, but the route was continued by the wagons arriving the following year. Last of this 1846 migration to ascend the river was the Donner party. They turned into the branch canyon in the rear of the other wagons and up a gradual rocky grade to the summit of the dividing ridge between the Truckee and Dog Valley, where they camped.

As night fell, an Indian, with the ostentatious foolhardiness characteristic of a young brave out after laurels, sneaked carefully into a clump of willows near the camp and concealed himself until he had a chance to sink an arrow in each of nineteen oxen. With incredible speed one after the other sang through the air, and each buried itself in flesh. He turned hastily to make good his escape but quick as he was, retribution was quicker. William Eddy had walked the Truckee desert carrying a heavy child, and had watched his wife drag through the same deadly fifty miles with the baby in her arms, because the Indians at the Sink had killed all his animals. He had failed to mete out justice there. He had no intention of failing here. His gun spoke once, and the rifle ball struck the fleeing Indian between the shoulders. The red man screamed agonizingly before he died, but it is doubtful if he got much attention. All rushed to the oxen to stanch the bleeding, and, strange to say, not one was seriously hurt.

The breaking of an axle and other circumstances caused the five Donner wagons and one belonging to the recently widowed Mrs. Wolfinger to drop behind. The rest of the company went on down a steep descent to the grassy depression now known as Stampede Valley. Their road soon turned south, met the Little Truckee, and followed it some four miles before turning away, crossing Prosser Creek, and traveling along Alder Creek, one of its tributaries.

Somewhere in the flat land near these creeks this main portion of the Reed-Donner party was encountered by the company of G. D. Dickenson. Captain Dickenson urged them to make all speed ahead, for the whole sky was overcast and it looked as if one more halt might make all the difference between a reasonable degree of safety and grave danger. His own company struggled up through the aspen woods, crossed Trout Creek, bisected what is now the highway near the Gateway Motel, ate a hasty midday snack near Truckee Lake (now called Donner), and pushed on. Soon snow fell in flakes "as large as saucers," but they were afraid to halt. "In places deep ravines ran down the sides of the gorge, rendering travel almost impossible. The only way of advancing was to unhitch the oxen and drive them over one at a time. The wheels were taken from the wagon beds, after removing the goods, and all were carried over by the emigrants." Trees had fallen across their way. Men relieved one another and axed furiously at the obstructions, and on the sixth day the Dickenson party reached the summit and camped in the snow, whence they made their way in safety to the valley.

On the 28th of October, the forward part of the Donner party reached a flat and saw Truckee Lake spread, a sheet of dull tinfoil under the heavy gun-metal sky. A quarter-mile before reaching the shore they passed the cabin where Moses Schallenberger had lasted out the hungry, terrifying winter just two years before. Two days in succession the worried company tried to surmount the mountain, but without success: five feet of soft snow was insurmountable. Then a terrible storm killed all hope of progress. They turned their attention to cutting logs for winter cabins and erected two, known respectively as the Murphy and the Graves cabins, using also the one found at hand which was from then on known as the Breen cabin.

Meanwhile George and Jacob Donner with six wagons, thirteen adults, and eight children reached Alder Creek and camped about a mile and a half above its confluence with Prosser Creek. The storm caught them with only a few logs cut, and there were not enough able-bodied men to build cabins. Tents were erected and fortified with poles, branches, blankets, and anything else they could find. There was no respite from the snowfall, which here reaches its maximum for the nation. The little shelters were soon buried under fourteen feet of snow and could only be distinguished by smoke curls emerging from holes that otherwise might have been wolf dens. Drifts forty to sixty feet deep, in unexpected places, trapped the animals. The party killed such cattle as had not strayed and saved every scrap like Digger Indians. They ate the meat; they ate the hides, and then they burned and ate the bones. They ate the field mice that came in for shelter, and they boiled and ate their own boots. They starved in interminable crescendos. Their suffering had better not be imagined. Jacob Donner soon died, and George Donner, their captain, was helpless with blood poisoning in his arm. The teamsters died one at a time, leaving only two or three.

Meanwhile, from the camp at the lake, the party of fifteen called the Forlorn Hope set out on makeshift snowshoes made of sawed ox yokes with scarcely rations enough for six days. It consisted of all who were able to stand a journey, and hoped to be able to assist those left behind by bringing help and by lessening the number to eat their slender store of food. Ten men and five women started. Husbands left wives. Young mothers left children. Eight men died on the way and, about two weeks after the departure from the cabins, one requested that his body be utilized to maintain strength in order that help might be sent to his starving wife and children still at the lake. It was done, and, in the awful days to come the dreadful experience was repeated again and again. Still they struggled on through ice-dust storms. The one small incident that brought the survivors through and hurried help to the entrapped party at the lake was a wife's sacrifice for her husband. William Eddy, when almost in the last extremity, found a small packet of dried bear meat concealed in his pack with a note from his wife saying that he was to use it for himself, and that she would try to live and keep the children alive until he should return for them. A little at a time, he used it to keep strength in himself for what was before him, and in the last week he killed a deer when only he of the whole party had strength enough to sight a gun.

And it was William Eddy who brought the five women through to safety at an Indian encampment, for the only other man surviving was temporarily demented. It was January 10th, so they learned afterward, and they had been twenty-five horrible days and nights on the way. They looked like nothing human. The squaws could not control their tears and wept noisily as they made and cooked acorn cakes. The children ran and hid.

When they went on, two Indians supported each sufferer. At every rancheria two fresh Indians took the places of those who turned back. Seven days later they all succumbed except William Eddy and could go no farther. Eddy desperately reeled along on feet swollen and burst from freezing, and at sunset, supported on either side by Indians, presented himself at the house of Colonel M. D. Richey, thirty-five miles from Sutter's Fort. He was placed in bed and fed by sobbing women. A relief party set out at once to bring in the other members of the Forlorn Hope, and backtracked the heroic man for the first six miles by the blood from his feet.

Meanwhile James Reed was frantically trying to raise a relief party large enough to have some chance of success, but was handicapped by the fact that the nation was at war with Mexico, and that most Americans were enlisted under Frémont and the rest didn't wish to leave their families alone. The arrival of the Forlorn Hope put a different face on the matter. The public was deeply stirred, and two relief parties were organized. The First Relief was comprised of thirteen men, including the two survivors of the Forlorn Hope; but William Eddy was not yet strong enough and soon had to be sent back. The party was outfitted at the Johnson Ranch on Bear River, the last outlying American habitation before reaching the mountains. They departed on February 5th, and several days later left the animals with two men encamped at Mule Springs about twelve miles below Bear Valley. Ten men went on, carrying heavy packs of approximately fifty pounds each. Of these, three soon turned back to Mule Springs and, on February 19th, seven reached the cabins on the lake, having crossed snow packs of thirty feet in depth. They found the survivors subsisting on the hides of the slaughtered oxen which had been laid on the cabin roofs. There was no food nor time to waste. They took out twenty-one emaciated people who were supposedly strong enough to walk and free to leave; were caught by heavy storms and were soon themselves in a starving condition.

Ten days later, on March 1st, the second relief organized by Old Greenwood and led by James Reed and William McCutchen, fought its way through the snow. They met the first relief—now with only eighteen survivors—and hurried on to the cabins, where they took out seventeen more. Mr. Reed found his family intact although they had had no cattle to slaughter and were dependent on the generosity of the rest.

The fortitude and nobility of many of these starving people is beyond praise. Charles Stanton and Patrick Dolan, both bachelors and in no way obligated to the company, heroically gave their lives when, each in a different way, they might have saved themselves. The stubborn will to live and mental courage shown by the women with little ones in their care was unbelievable. Mrs. Graves had nine children, but six mothers besides herself had nursing babies. Unhesitatingly she and Mr. Graves divided their cattle among the rest. From all accounts the women never gave up hope, and some never ceased to cheer and encourage the rest. It was finally imperative that the flesh from the dead be used to preserve themselves and the children. It was done, but some of the group managed to cling to life without its aid until relief came, and some died outright rather than touch it.

The Third Relief was led by William Eddy, now recovered. It took out all who remained with four exceptions. At the Murphy cabin were old Mrs. Murphy, ill in bed, and Lewis Keseberg, lame from an ax cleft in his heel. George Donner, dying from the effects of starvation combined with blood poisoning, and his wife Tamsen were at the camp on Alder Creek. One instance of heroism, outstanding among the many, was that of Tamsen Donner who (knowing that her husband was on his death-bed) sent her little daughters with the rescuers and remained alone with him.

In May a rescue party, some of whose members bore a dubious repu-tation, invaded the two camps and brought down a pack train of goods to Sutter's Fort. With them, or rather walking behind them, came Lewis Keseberg, the last of the forty-five survivors left from the original eighty-one. He was reviled and execrated—even stoned in the streets because of the revolting stories of unnecessary cannibalism spread by his rescuers; but within the month some of these were proven entirely false. After many years his wife died, and he lived on, alone with his two idiot chil-dren, shunned and despised but apparently harming no one. Before his death he had convinced the Donner survivors that he had been maligned.

And so ended the sorriest saga of the overland trail.

On June 22, 1847, General Kearny visited the cabins near Donner Lake. Edwin Bryant accompanied the soldiers and wrote that the dis-membered skeletons and other grisly evidences of tragedy were all col-lected and buried in a pit dug in the floor of the Murphy cabin, which was then burned. The body of George Donner was found just as his wife had straightened him for burial and wrapped him in a sheet the day before she died, thus clearing Keseberg of the accusation of having un-necessarily mutilated his body. He was buried by a detachment of soldiers.

Evidences may have been found lately of the Donner encampment on Alder Creek. They include a couple of graves, some rocks laid loosely into a rectangle as if for a foundation, a tree hacked feebly at the snow line by hands evidently too weak to fell it, and a few pieces of hardware.

Similarly hacked trees were found at the cabins. One had hundreds of shallow cuts while, at the base, lay the abandoned hatchet. The great flat-sided rock that formed the back of the Murphy cabin is perhaps the most interesting relic left, but the place where the Graves cabin stood is also marked; and, towering near the site of the earliest dwelling (that sheltered Moses Schallenberger first and then the Breen family), is the massive Pioneer or Donner Monument. There are only three larger bronze statues in the nation than that of the pioneer family topping the stone pedestal. Twenty-two feet above the ground the heroic figures stand today, to mark the height of the snow on which they stood in 1846. They epitomize the sufferings endured and the dangers braved by the early settlers of the West.

*   *   *

From the portentous hour when the 1844 expedition built the Schallenberger cabin, the six-mile stretch between it and the summit held the fascinated interest of the pioneers. Besides the stimulation of its dangers and pitfalls, it has beauty beyond description. The more fortunate companies, passing in late August or early September, drove around the boggy snow-sumped meadows, through stands of giant trees upholstered with brilliant green moss, and came with awe to where the granite torso of the mountain rose naked from the forests. The regular hand-to-hand struggle was waged, and, with a last terrific heave, the wagons lurched one at a time to the shoulder of the dividing ridge and the exhausted men looked directly up to snowy-headed Donner Peak helmeted in clouds.

The wagons of '44, under Greenwood and his sons, used a windlass to draw the wagons to the summit. It was seen standing in the same spot, by Nicholas Carriger and Mary Jones both in '46, and by D. Jaggers in '49, but seems never to have been used again.

It was always afternoon when the wagons reached the top. The men were rushed for time and turned their backs on what is now one of the most publicized views in America, with only the parting courtesy of a few lines in their journals. At the end of a gentle downhill slope a dimple in the mountaintop held a tiny lake surrounded by marshy grass-lined shores studded with brilliant flowers. It was beautiful, but cold and exposed. Few camped there.

The rocky rise beside the lake did not retain wheel marks, and for the first few years the travelers floundered about, hunting the trail. After a mile or two of walking through a granite-strewn ravine, they came, late

in the afternoon, to Summit Valley. One of the headwaters of the Yuba
River has its small beginnings near by and flows through the flat. Its
banks were a rich shining green, star-dusted with flowers such as the
women had last seen on the prairies when they left the Missouri River
in May. It seemed like the completion of a cycle. The caravans set up
housekeeping for the night, and the omnivorous mules made short work
of such beauty as they could reach. The valley at the time bore the name
of the stream. "It is sometimes pronounced Juba," wrote Edwin Bryant
eruditely, "but I think Uber is the correct etymology. How the name was
derived, I never could learn." It was always cold and often stormy in
Summit Valley, and the careful fathers heated a circle of rocks and skillet
lids at the fire so that their families might sleep warmly and well.

The wagons forded the Yuba in the valley and took off over high undulating country, heavily timbered and watered by a chain of small clear
lakes like mirrors in a diorama. The course had been south but changed
abruptly to west as they entered the open gorge of the river. The journals
do not complain particularly of the geography of this section, but—just
take a look at the Yuba River some day and picture yourself in a prairie
schooner nearing the point where the valley deepens into a canyon. Up
and down—up and down on the mountain side the mules or oxen
tugged the rumbling, lurching, tipping wagons, stopping every few feet
to pant and blow. The pioneers made sudden acquaintance with California hornets, saw long-tailed birds which they listed as pheasants, and
ate sweet wild raspberries and tiny bitter "cherries."

The trail stayed near the Yuba until, in the neighborhood of Cisco
Butte, the wagons were forced to leave the canyon and cross a ridge to
the southwest, passing Crystal Lake in a small bottom and returning
again to the ridge top. It is nowhere a long hike from the modern highway to the trail, and in some places they are within yards of each other.
At last the pioneers wound up, high and dry, on a narrow hogback where
was scarcely room for the teams to stand. The modern motorist may see
the hogback in luxury without leaving his car. It lies between the miles
of dingy, blackened snowsheds that shelter the overland trains and the
sunken grassy acres of Bear Valley, and culminates almost opposite the
mountain railway settlement entitled Emigrant Gap.

Any one there will tell you where the wagons were let down—and
seeing is believing. It was one of the two worst descents of the Sierras

Lovely, fertile Bear Valley saw thousands of camps. The women scrambled down at once and picked wild peas and flowers and sampled the fruit of the manzanita, or "little apple," trying to imagine that the flavor reminded them of home. The first tiny thread of Bear River flows down through the valley, and they spent the night in comfort.

The wagons then went two or three miles down the stream, forded, and angled up the opposite ridge for a hard, uninteresting day's march. The ridges of the Truckee route were much more broken and difficult than the ones down which the columns of wagons creaked into Placerville—and more roundabout, besides. The Truckee road continued in later years to carry traffic to Marysville, Grass Valley, and the northern points, but soon lost its popularity as a main stem to Sacramento. Once the summit was reached all its superiority to the Carson route was lost.

Twelve miles below Bear Valley is Mule Springs, where the first relief party for the Donners left their animals. It took them three days to flounder through the soft snow between the springs and the valley. Also in this stretch was the gigantic "Mother Pine" whose bust measure so startled the newcomers. The trail went up Nigger Jack Hill, and about opposite Dutch Flat the wagon masters found their cumbersome caravans riding another elevation—this time between Bear River to the left and Steep Hollow Creek to the right. The descent into the latter canyon was so long and abrupt that journalists wrote in apparent good faith that they and their animals slid for a mile and a half. In early days there was not much to do after sliding down but to climb up the other side. One wagon train could consume what few spears of grass grew in the little meadow at the bottom of the shadowy, cold canyon. The men cut willows for the animals, and the mules learned to come fast and most unmusically when they heard the ax ring against wood. The faithful and hard-worked cows, now pulling in the yokes laid down by the dead-and-gone oxen, were growing into the affections of their owners so that often only death ever parted them. A lengthy rattling of the milk cans served to bring them ambling to the wagons to be milked or fed or yoked. Many a company stayed all night in cheerless Steep Hollow for sheer lack of strength to climb out.

James Marshall's discovery of gold changed all that. The Forty-niners, peering into the depths below them, saw miners squatting among the ferns, rocking rude cradles. The heretofore crystal waters of the little stream ran mud. The Argonauts of the Truckee route had reached their first gold.

Many of the unattached men left their companies and wandered erratically from stream to stream, from diggings to diggings hunting the pot of gold at the end of the rainbow, but few ever found much more than enough to bring the family West. Those who, on the contrary, catered to the wants or needs of the miners amassed fortunes. Little or nothing was required as a start. A man arriving with a wagon and a yoke of steers might knock the wagon into a counter, sleep under it and sell tough steer meat over it for enough to start a butcher shop. A man with a mule might start packing goods to isolated mining camps and, in a year, own a string of twenty animals. It was the land of opportunity for the man with health and brains.

Three miles up from the Steep Hollow Creek the Argonauts found the incipient mining towns of You Bet and Red Dog, but the main column marched on past, heading for Marysville. The very early pioneers found nothing but great quantities of landscape continuing unabated between them and their first known goal, the Johnson Ranch.

Autumn had come to the foothills. Burnt russet weeds rose rustling by the trail side. Old digger pines, twin-trunked to the ground like slingshots, stood in fanciful black tracery against the pale beige of the shining hillsides where silvery wild oats rose and fell in the breeze. The crudely tied ladders of the foothill Indians leaned here and there against the wayward trunks, for the nuts contained in the heavy thorned digger cones are good. At this season the timid tribes came to the hills for berries, nuts, and, most of all, for acorns from the black oak. The squaws gathered them in quantities—enough in a year of abundance to carry them through the next season when the crop would not be so heavy. It was Indians of just such a group who fed and cared for the Forlorn Hope on their way to Sutter's Fort.

The blackish green of small round foothill oaks stretched flatly like apple orchards at the foot of the irregular ridge where the wagons toiled up and down and up again. An elevation slightly higher than the rest rose squarely before the rumbling, weary column, and the first man to top it raised a cry that brought every one who could leave the teams. About twenty miles ahead the enormous flatness of the Sacramento Valley lay spread before them in the lucid afternoon light. The river with its tributaries was boldly sketched in green. A sun of unbearable brilliance declined in a flaming sky. Fifty or more miles away the line of coastal mountains formed a scalloped edge of flat opaque heliotrope topped with a line of luminous crimson. The miniature peaks of the Marysville Buttes shaded to black at the crests and had apparently erupted into a sky of molten gold. The garish, unbelievable, unforgettable chromo that is California sank into their minds and hearts forever.

Two or three hours from the hilltop, where the men of the early trains had cheered until they were hoarse and shaken one another's hands in triumph, the wagons came to Johnson's Ranch.

Johnson, ranking (to the very early overland travelers) second only to the warm-hearted and open-handed Captain John Sutter, was a sailor from New England who had settled down to farm under the shelter of the Sierra foothills. He was a bachelor and lived in contentment among his Indians in a piebald dwelling of two rooms, of which one was constructed of logs and the other of adobe bricks. There was no need for any great attempt at security, and the doorway was shakily filled in with a light wooden framework on which a rawhide had been stretched. Small pens of poles and pickets surrounded the house. Fields of wheat, barley, and corn filled the fertile bottom lands of the Bear, and his cattle roamed a hundred hills. They were valuable chiefly for their hides, and impoverished emigrants were freely given the beef from animals slaughtered for the purpose, or might even butcher for themselves if they would see that the owner received the hides. Flour was harder to come by, being ground in a hand mill by Indians; but the heavy unbolted article was produced for unusual occasions together with small round cheeses and quantities of milk full of chunky cream. Beef tallow took the place of the lard to which the easterners were accustomed; but the newcomers freely admitted that it did well enough, and "Johnson's Ranch" was synonymous with security and plenty.

After a night of rest and relaxation the companies pressed on. Before 1849 the pioneer men were hunting ranches, and the sight of the limitless acres centered by the cultivated Bear River bottoms whetted their desire to secure something equally good before some one else found it. They drove toward the great central valley of California, fording the Bear right at the ranch and following it to its junction with the Feather River. This wide, shallow stream was shining and spacious. Untidy piles of drift strewed the flat islands, topped with vagrant logs in silent reminder of the turbulence of winter. Huge masses of dead weeds bore mute testimony to the richness of the soil. Slender willows, practically sitting in the river, trailed graceful branches in the current. In the motionless backwashes last year's cattails massed—some rank and green, some dried to a rich burnt sienna tone. At the confluence of the Feather with the Sacramento they found the settlement now called Vernon, while Fremont, then Gordon's Ranch, consisting of a house or two, was opposite.

Some families were bound toward the valleys beyond the coast mountains whose strongly molded blunt heads reared dark against the western sky. They crossed from Vernon to Fremont on the first ferry some of them had seen since leaving the Missouri River. From there they scattered widely, depending for a day or two upon the hospitality of such men as Yount or Chiles in Napa Valley or Dr. Marsh in the flat land near Mount Diablo. General Vallejo and his warm-hearted brother Colonel Salvador Vallejo, at Sonoma, were generosity itself. Their wives, although unable to speak English, caressed the children and gave them sweetmeats, and Indians carrying heavy burdens of flour and fruits and chocolate were dispatched to the camps. That the less valued beeves were slaughtered for the benefit of the newcomers goes without saying. Every one had beef in California. The "native Californians"—that is, the Spanish and Mexicans, of whom it is said there were never over thirty-five hundred in the state—were spoken of in highest terms for their unfailing helpfulness.

In and after '49 the picture was greatly changed. The men were not hunting farming land or pasture for their stock, and they no longer headed for the coastal valleys. They intended either to mine, or to serve or exploit the miners, and they headed for the mountains or the newly founded towns. Many dropped away from the columns before striking the valley at Johnson's Ranch, but those who rested here were planning to go to the "northern mines" at Grass Valley, Nevada City, La Porte, Downieville, Goodyear's Bar, and the country around Bidwell's Bar; or if not there to the settlements in Trinity County near Old Shasta. Or if, in spite of the fact that they had taken a circuitous route, they still wished to mine along the American River, they started at once for Sutter's Fort and Sacramento.

It was customary to start late in the afternoon and travel all night, for the road was well beaten and unmistakable and the days were hot. Seven miles from the Johnson ranch a chain of small ponds made a good stopping place. The herds of wild cattle and horses, deer and antelope that originally grazed under the moonlight soon were killed and frightened off; but the wild duck were easily shot, and the yodeling coyotes were practically ineradicable.

They passed Vernon, approximately at the halfway point, and came in the morning to the American River—"Rio de los Americanos," as the native Californians called it. On the south side was Sutter's Fort, in early days the end of the trail and the Mecca for all overland travelers. Generous John Sutter had flour, had beef, had saddle animals and many dependent Sandwich Islanders and Indians. He could and did come ably to the rescue of scores of unfortunate newcomers. His hospitality was too well known to permit of dispute, and he lived among his fat lands like a feudal lord.

What then must have been the emotions of the early comers of '46 to find the fort under United States guard, having just been wrested from Mexico, and the sorrowful Sutter a prisoner within his own walls? They were readily permitted to see him, and, although not privileged to have guests overnight, he was allowed to send them supplies. Beef went as a matter of course, and much-needed salt; but, best of all, were the melons, onions, and tomatoes from the gardens.

He was soon released, but in a few years left his now overrun headquarters and withdrew to the Hock Ranch near Yuba City, where a pair of enormous iron doors from one of his warehouses may still be seen standing beside the Garden Highway.

Gold seekers, passing Sutter's Fort, stopped out of curiosity and explored the famous old hospitality house of Sacramento Valley, surrounded in its decline by the solitude of sun-baked earth and hot blue sky. The buildings, some of them with two stories, were built of adobe bricks and inclosed by a turreted wall. Strings of small cubic rooms like halves of egg boxes were set against sections of this wall and opened on the central court. Here Frémont came to replenish his supplies and to remount his men. Here James Marshall rushed the first few chunks of gold. Here the Donner children were brought to be cared for until homes were found. Here the attractive young John Bidwell lived and served his benefactor so well that he was later offered the hand of Captain

Sutter's daughter in marriage, an honor which he tactfully declined. Here scores of emigrants camped to receive advice and material help. It was, until its overthrow, the Fort Vancouver of California.

The travelers of '49 found a short-lived hotel within its walls; but it was too far from the center of activity to prosper, and the pioneers of '50, who stopped to stare, reported that the old adobe was rapidly going to ruin. The attraction was now at Sacramento, about two miles away, where Sam Brannon, an enterprising Mormon, had started a settlement and (so people seriously insisted) had spread the news of the discovery of gold to stimulate business. From the Embarcadero along the river bank might be seen every sort of motley vessel that could stem the current. San Francisco had been drained of its men. Hundreds of deep-draft foreign vessels that had dropped anchor in San Francisco Bay remained for months, their naked masts like a forest of dead trees, their crews having deserted to the mines. In one case the sailors spent their last few weeks at sea making small boats. When they arrived in the bay, they launched them and set out directly for Sacramento without even the formality of landing the unfortunate passengers. The river at the Embarcadero was abob with odd and misfit craft bringing the soft-muscled, tender-footed sea voyagers from around the Horn and those in but slightly better case from across the Isthmus.

All roads led to Sacramento. The travelers of the Carson route had come from Hangtown down the American River, following its southern bank. Even the disgruntled souls who had made the unfortunate circle northward by way of Lassen's Ranch arrived here eventually, having joined the Johnson's Ranch road near the junction of the Bear and Feather rivers. The ragged pilgrims grew more and more self-conscious as they approached civilization. On the trail every one had looked the same, but now they met men with trimmed hair and beards—men whose shirts had been ironed. Their own appearance shamed them, and many stopped outside of town for necessary repairs.

Once in town, the women looked for a permanent place to sleep—something that wasn't on wheels. Tents were at a premium, and shacks with cloth partitions were put up which, to arrivals of a week later, were old establishments. It was of no moment that the uncontrollable Sacramento River rose periodically and would surely run them out. Probably the builders of the flimsy dwellings wouldn't stay that long. If they did—some one would rescue them. It all worked out. They had gone through too much to worry now. The women of '49 especially need have no fears. They were cared for like queens. One wife and mother of that migration, who afterward came into great social prominence, lived on a small lot between a gambling hall and a saloon. The land was freely given to herself and her husband, and she wrote that an atmosphere of respect and protection surrounded her as long as she remained.

It was food, more than the housing, that distressed the ladies. The pork was terrible when it left New York on its long ocean voyage around Cape Horn. The butter had accompanied the pork in its travels and was brown with age. California teemed with cows, but men were too busy shuttling up and down ravines to realize the gold that lay in sweet fresh dairy products. There was positively none for sale. The flour was sour, and a handful of long black worms could be sieved out of a single quart. Beans and dried fruit from Chile, yams and onions from the Sandwich Islands, with sea gulls' eggs from the Farallones, were the best and most diversified articles of diet obtainable for months. The latter sold at one dollar each. The incoming crowds were starved for flavors, for sweet and sour and salt. One man's first action was to buy for himself vinegar and molasses. Sitting astride a fallen tree near the store, he mixed the two and sopped them up with bread, eating peacefully and undisturbed among the thronging people until his craving was satisfied.

In spite of all these adverse conditions, children came and stayed and flourished. Instead of the rumble and creak of wagons they learned to recognize again the sound of boots on planked sidewalks, the hoarse vibration of a steamboat whistle, the clang of a church bell. Even the bickering sound of a ticking clock was strange to these prairie children. They saw new faces and new types of people, the fur-hatted Hudson's Bay man, bright-shirted miners bewhiskered and belted with heavy guns, sleek gamblers in high hats and glossy white shirts whose guns and whiskers did not appear. They learned that Sydney ducks were not water fowl, but obdurate, shifty-eyed convicts from Australia. They made friends with little bobbing men whose long black braids were wrapped tightly around their heads: men whose yellow countenances split in intriguing grins as they shuffled between the houses, each balancing a pole across his drooping shoulders to bear the weight of two heavy (and often odorously fishy) baskets; men, they were told, from far-off China whose like they had never seen.

"As the gambling houses were the center of attraction," wrote Henry Bloom in 1850, "thitherward I bent my steps, and of all the sights I ever saw, this was the cap-sheaf. More gold and silver than I should ever want; one continual jingle of money! And there were all sorts and kinds of people, from the cute Yankee to the swarthy Chilean alongside the same table. There, also, was the dark-hued daughter of Mexico and her fair-skinned Saxon sisters betting their thousands in all the mad excitement of gambling. Saw also daggers flashing and pistols drawn for deadly conflict." Henry may be a trifle ponderous, but there is no quibbling in the picture he draws.

The settlement on the Embarcadero sprang into affluence overnight and soon had its alphabetical and numerical streets. Luzena Wilson, one of the first American women to arrive, reached its precincts on September 30, 1849, and was able to buy an interest in a hotel which was already a going concern. She and her husband sold their oxen to get the necessary cash and went to look at the edifice on what was soon K Street near Sixth. The first sight was unforgettable. "Imagine a long room," she wrote, "dimly lighted by dripping tallow candles stuck into whiskey bottles, with bunks built from floor to ceiling on either side. A bar with rows of bottles and glasses was in one corner, and two or three miners were drinking; the bar keeper dressed in half sailor half vaquero fashion, with a blue shirt rolled far back at the collar to display the snowy linen beneath, and his waist encircled by a flaming scarlet sash, was in commanding tones subduing the noisy demands, for the bar keeper, next to the stage driver, was in early days the most important man in the camp. In the opposite corner of the room some men were having a wordy dispute over a game of cards; a cracked fiddle was, under the manipulation of rather clumsy fingers, furnishing music for some half dozen others to dance to the tune of 'Money Musk.' One young man was reading a letter by a sputtering candle, and the tears rolling down his yet unbearded face told of the homesickness in his heart. Some of the men lay sick in their bunks, some lay asleep, and out from another bunk, upon this curious mingling of merriment and sadness stared the white face of a corpse. They had forgotten even to cover the still features with the edge of a blanket, and he lay there, in his rigid calmness, a silent unheeded witness to the acquired insensibility of the early settlers. What was one dead man, more or less! Nobody missed him. They would bury him tomorrow to make room for a new applicant for his bunk. The music and the dancing, the card playing, drinking, and swearing went on unchecked by the hideous presence of Death. His face grew too familiar in those days to be a terror."

And so the community grew, as did all California communities. A man who had come yesterday was an old resident to the man who came today; but the man who came today voted with just as good a conscience at the city elections, and every fall the overland trail poured its unkempt hundreds over the mountains in the regular channels to separate and sift into their future environments.

"So we came," wrote a young woman Forty-niner, "young, strong, healthy, hopeful, but penniless, into the new world. The nest egg was gone but the homely bird which laid it—the power and will to work— was still there. All around us twinkled the camp fires of the new arrivals. A wilderness of canvas tents glimmered in the firelight; the men cooked and ate, played cards, drank whiskey, slept rolled in their blankets, fed their teams, talked, and swore all around; and a few, less occupied than their comrades, stared at me as at a strange creature, and roused my sleeping babies, and passed them from arm to arm to have a look at such a novelty as a child.

"We halted in an open space, and lighting our fire in their midst made us one with the inhabitants of Sacramento."

"We are at the end of our long and weary road," wrote John Clark after he had stabled and fed his cantankerous mule, "and it is here that we separate. The bonds that held us together on the long and toilsome march hold us no longer. Each individual has his own road to pick and choose whether for good or evil luck, time only can disclose."

Here at the junction of the Sacramento and American rivers the trail ended. Here the travelers separated to go their various ways—the pushing, rising cream of the nation with a small portion of its dregs. The New Englander with his business acumen, sound horse sense, and background of generations of seafaring forebears; the Southerner with two hundred years of American breeding and culture behind him; the men from the frontier states who were already pioneers and sons and grandsons of westward-moving pioneers. Of these groups only a highly selective, courageous skimming took the trail. In Oregon, the thousand or so Americans who had arrived by the winter of '43, organized an effective government within a few months. In California, the adventurous thousands swarming over the mountains were the stock of which democracies are made. California was never a territory. By the time the heavy migration of 1850 saw their future home the Forty-niners had founded a state.

The California-Oregon Trail peopled the West. Never during the world's progress has there been a concerted pioneer movement of equal magnitude along such a tenuous life line. It stands unique in history.

Bibliography

ABBEY, JAMES, California: A Trip across the Plains, in the Spring of 1850. New Albany, Ind., 1850.

ABBOTT, CARLISLE S., Recollections of a California Pioneer [of 1850]. New York, 1917.

ABBOTT, HENRY L., "Diary of an Emigrant Journey in 1854," *Oregon Historical Society Quarterly,** Mar. and June, 1932.

ACKLEY, MARY E., Crossing the Plains and Early Days in California. San Francisco, 1928.

ADAMS, DAVID MADDUX, A Biographical Sketch, ed. Robt. J. Burdette. Chicago, 1912.

AKIN, JAMES, The Journal of James Akin, ed. Edward Everett Dale. Norman, Okla., 1919 (Univ. of Okla. Bulletin, No. 172).

ALDRICH, LORENZO D., A Journal of an Overland Journey to California. Rensselaer Co., Lansingburgh, N.Y., 1851. Photographic reproduction in Bancroft Libr., U. of California; original MS. at Huntington Library, San Marino, Calif.

ALDRICH, NATHAN, Letters written on the overland trail in 1852. MS. in poss. Mrs. G. O. Fraser, Clarksburg, Yolo Co., Calif.

ALTER, J. CECIL, James Bridger, Trapper, Frontiersman, Scout and Guide: A Historical Narrative. Salt Lake City, 1925.

ANDERSON, DR. CHARLES, Diary and letters written on the overland trail in 1862. MS. in poss. Mrs. Seddie Anderson Daniels, Santa Cruz, Calif.

APPLEGATE, LINDSAY, "The Applegate Route in the Year 1846," *O.H.S.Q.,* Vol. 22 (1921), p. 12.

APPLETON, HORATIO, Letter dated June 4, 1874. MS. in California Pioneer Scrap Book, Bancroft Libr., U. of Calif.

ARAM, JOSEPH, Across the Continent in a Caravan; in *Journal of American History,* 1907, u.l.p. 617–632.

AUDUBON, JOHN W., Audubon's Western Journal, 1849–1850. Cleveland, 1906.

AYER, EDWARD E., Reminiscences of the Far West and Other Trips, 1861; typescript at Bancroft Libr., U. of Calif.

* Hereafter given as *O.H.S.Q.*

BAILEY, MARGARET STUART, Diary written while crossing the plains in 1852. MS. at Huntington Libr., San Marino, Calif.

BAILEY, WALTER, "The Barlow Road," *O.H.S.Q.*, Vol. 13.

BAILEY, WASHINGTON, A Trip to California in 1853. Le Roy, Ill., 1915.

BAIN, READ, "Educational Plans and Efforts by Methodists in Oregon to 1860," *O.H.S.Q.*, Vol. 21.

BAKER, WILLIAM B., Diary written while crossing the plains in 1852. Typescript in Calif. State Libr.

BALL, JOHN, "Diary Written on the Oregon Trail in 1832," *O.H.S.Q.*, Vol. 3.

BANCROFT, H. H., Works: Vol. 26, History of Utah; Vols. 29–30, History of Oregon. San Francisco, 1886–1889.

BANDEL, EUGENE, Diary written on the trail from Fort Leavenworth to Fort Scott, 1857. Typescript in Calif. State. Libr.

BANNING, WILLIAM, and GEORGE HUGH, Six Horses. New York, 1930.

BARLOW, WILLIAM, "Recollections of Seventy Years," *O.H.S.Q.*, Vol. 13.

BARNETT, JOEL, A Long Trip in a Prairie Schooner [in 1859], taken from memo. of John Mellican. Whittier, Calif., no date.

BARRY, J. NEILSON, "First Born on the Oregon Trail," *O.H.S.Q.*, Vol. 12.

——"The Trail of the Astorians," *O.H.S.Q.*, Vol. 13.

BARTON, H. D., Diary written while crossing the plains in 1865. MS. in Calif. State Libr.

BASHFORD, HERBERT, and WAGNER, HARR, A Man Unafraid: The Story of John Charles Frémont. San Francisco, 1927.

BATTY, JOSEPH, Over the Wilds to California; or, Eight Years from Home (ed. Rev. John Simpson). Leeds, England, 1867.

BELL, MAJOR HORACE, On the Old West Coast (ed. Lanier Bartlett). New York, 1930.

BELSHAW, GEORGE, "Belshaw Journey: A Diary Written on the Trail in 1853," *O.H.S.Q.*, Vol. 32.

BELSHAW, MARIA PARSONS, "Diary of a Bride Written on the Trail in 1853," *O.H.S.Q.*, Vol. 33.

BENNETT, JAMES, Overland Journey to California [a diary written on the overland trail in 1850]. New Harmony, Ind., 1906.

BERNIE, ROBERT, Personal Adventures. MS. contained in Calif. Pioneer Scrap Book, Bancroft Library, U. of Calif., Document No. 33.

BIDWELL, JOHN, Address to Soc. of California Pioneers, delivered Nov. 1, 1897, *Soc. of Calif. Pioneers Quarterly,* Vol. 3, p. 10.

——"The First Emigrant Train to California," *Century Magazine,* Vol. 41, pp. 106–130 (Nov., 1890).

——A Journey to California [diary written on the trail in 1841]. Pamphlet printed at Weston or Liberty, Mo., 1842. (Only known copy in Bancroft Libr., U. of Calif. Reprint ed. by Dr. H. I. Priestley, San Francisco, 1937.)

——Letter to Capt. J. A. Sutter, dated Chico, 2nd April, 1851. (MS. at Calif. State Library.)

——"Life in California Before the Gold Discovery," *Century Magazine*, Vol. 41, pp. 163–183 (Dec., 1890).

BIGLER, H. W., Memoirs and Journals. Facsim. of the typescript of orig. MS. made by Hist. Records Survey of Utah, 1936–37, at Bancroft Libr., U. of Calif.

BLOOD, JAMES A., Diary, written on Overland Trail in 1850. Typescript, Calif. State Libr.

BLOOM, HENRY S., Diary, written on overland trail in 1850. Typescript, at Calif. State Libr.

BLOSSOM, ROBERT H., "First Presbyterianism of the Pacific Coast," *O.H.S.Q.*, Vol. 15.

BODDAM-WHETHAM, J. W., Western Wanderings, London, 1874.

BOGG, JOHN, Diary written while crossing the plains in '49. Facsim. at Bancroft Libr., U. of Calif.

BOGGS, W. M., Reminiscences of his father, Governor Boggs of Missouri, and of early days in California. MS. in Calif. Pioneer Scrap Book, Bancroft Libr., U. of Calif.

BONNEY, B. F., Across the Plains by Prairie Schooner: personal narrative by B. F. Bonney of his trip to Sutter's Fort, California, in 1846, compiled by Fred Lockley, Eugene, Ore., 1924(?).

BOURKE, JOHN G., On the Border with Crook. New York, 1891.

BOWLES, SAMUEL, Across the Continent. Springfield, Mass., 1865.

BRACKENRIDGE, HENRY MARIE, A Journal of a Trip Up the Missouri River and Back in 1811, in Early Western Travels, ed. R. G. Thwaites, Vol. 6.

BRADWAY, DR. JOSEPH R., Diary written on overland trail in 1853. Longhand copy certified by a notary, Calif. State Library.

BRAY, EDMUND, Statement concerning the formation of early companies of emigrants and of his trip west in '44. MS. in Calif. Pioneer Scrap Book, Bancroft Libr., U. of California.

BREEN, PATRICK, Diary, Kept While Snow-Bound with the Donner Party, Winter of 1846–47. MS., Bancroft Libr., U. of Calif. Published Berkeley, 1910, ed. Fred J. Teggart.

BRIER, REV. JOHN WELLS, "Death Valley Party of '49: A Reminiscence," *Out West*, 1903. (Cameragraph reproduction at Calif. State Library.)

BRISTOL, REV. D., A Pioneer Preacher: An Autobiography [narrative of a parson in the gold fields in '49 and '50], with Introduction by Rev. J. H. Fairchild. New York, 1887.

BROOKS, ELISHA, A Pioneer Mother of California [reminiscences of a trip across the plains in '52]. San Francisco, 1922.

BROOKS, NOAH, The Boy Emigrants. New York, 1877.

Brooks, Quincy Adams, Letter, dated Milwaukie, Ore. Terr., Nov. 7, 1851, *O.H.S.Q.*, Vol. 15.

Brown, James Stephens, Life of a Pioneer. Salt Lake City, 1900.

Brown, John E., Memoirs of a Forty-niner by his daughter, Katie E. Blood. New Haven, Conn., 1907.

Brown, Joseph, Crossing the Plains. Marysville, Calif., 1916.

Brownlee, Robert, Autobiography, dated Napa County, Calif., Oct. 20, 1892. Facsim. of typescript, Bancroft Libr., U. of Calif.

Bruff, Capt. J. Goldsborough, A description of his MS. diary. Typescript at Bancroft Libr., U. of Calif.

Bryan, George W., The Lure of the Past, the Present and the Future. Los Angeles, 1911.

Bryant, Edwin, What I Saw in California: Being the Journal of a Tour, by the Emigrant Route . . . and Through California in the Years 1846, 1847. 2nd ed., New York, 1848.

Buffum, Joseph C., Diary written on overland trail in 1849. MS. in Calif. State Library.

Burnett, Peter H., Recollections and Opinions of an Old Pioneer. New York, 1880.

Burris, Davis, A short narrative of his trip across the plains in '49. MS. in Calif. Pioneer Scrap Book, Bancroft Libr., U. of Calif., Document No. 13.

Burton, Sir Richard Francis, The City of the Saints and Across the Rocky Mountains to California. London, 1861.

Butler, E., "Memorandum of agreement with Joseph Dana and Co., for passage across plains in 1852," *Calif. H.S.Q.*, 1932 (facsim. owned by Mrs. S. E. Wilcoxon, Yuba City, Calif.).

Butler, E. D., Letter dated Counsel Bluffs, May the 5, 1850, from typescript. Orig. in poss. R. O. Butler, R.F.D. No. 1, Monmouth, Ill.

Butler, Ira, Letter dated Monmouth, Ore. Terr., Aug. 21, 1858, from typescript. Orig. as above.

Butler, Isaac, Letter from Polk County, Bloomington, Ore. Terr., July 31, 1853, from typescript. Orig. as above.

Butler, Peter, Letters from Polk Co., Ore. Terr., dated Aug. 14 and Oct. 30, '53, from typescript. Orig. as above.

Butterfield, Ira H., "Michigan to California: Diary Written on Trail in '61," reprinted from an old issue of the *Michigan History Magazine,* in *Pony Express Courier,* beginning Sept., 1934.

Camp, Charles Lewis, "William Alexander Trubody and the Overland Pioneers of 1847," *Calif. H.S.Q.*, Vol. 16, No. 3, June, 1937.

Capell, Benson Britain, Interview with his sons, Charles W. and Walter B. Capell, concerning his trip across the plains in 1849, by William G. Paden, at Berkeley, Calif.

CAPLES, MRS. JAMES, Overland to California, 1849. Typescript in Calif. State Library.

CARDINELL, CHARLES, "Adventures on the Plains," *Calif. H.S.Q.*, Vol. 1, No. 1, San Francisco, 1922.

CARDWELL, DR. J. R., "The First Fruits of the Land," [beginnings of fruit industry in early Oregon], *O.H.S.Q.*, Vol. 9.

CARPENTER, HELEN McCOWEN, Diary written while crossing the plains in 1856 —rewritten by herself from original in 1911. Typescript at Calif. State Libr.

CARR, JOHN, Pioneer Days in California. Eureka, Calif., 1891.

CARRIGER, NICHOLAS, Diary written on emigrant trail in 1846. MS. in Bancroft Libr., U. of Calif.

——Short narrative of same trip written in 1874. MS. contained in the Calif. Pioneer Scrap Book, Bancroft Libr., U. of Calif.

CARSON, KIT, Kit Carson's Own Story of His Life, as dictated to his friends, Col. and Mrs. D. C. Peters about 1856–57, ed. Blanche C. Grant. Taos, N.M., 1926. (Orig. MS. in Ayer Collection, Newberry Libr., Chicago.)

CARSTARPHEN, JAMES EULA, My Trip to California in '49. Louisiana, Mo., 1914.

CASE, WILLIAM M., "Recollections of His Trip Across the Plains in 1844," *O.H.S.Q.*, Vol. 1.

CHALMERS, ROBERT, Diary of trip across plains in 1849. MS. in Calif. State Libr.

CHAMBERLAIN, WILLIAM E., Diary of trip across plains in 1849. MS. in Calif. State Libr.

CHANDLESS, WILLIAM, A Visit to Salt Lake. London, 1857.

CHAPIN, E. R., Short Narrative of his experience as a surgeon in San Francisco in gold rush days. MS. contained in Calif. Pioneer Scrap Book, Bancroft Libr., U. of Calif.

CHAPMAN, ARTHUR, The Pony Express, New York, 1932.

CHARDON, FRANCIS, "Journal, kept while he was a trader on the upper Missouri in 1837," *Miss. Val. Hist. Rev.*, Vol. 17.

CHILES, COL. J. B., A Visit to California in Early Times. MS. written in 1898. In Bancroft Libr., U. of Calif.

CHIPS (nom de plume), "A Lynch Trial in California," *Household Words*, Vol. 3, pp. 611–612 (Sept. 20, 1851). (In Bancroft Libr., U. of Calif.)

——"A 'Ranch' in California," *Household Words*, Vol. 3, pp. 471–472 (Aug. 9, 1851). (In Bancroft Libr., U. of Calif.)

——"A Woman's Experience in California," *Household Words*, Vol. 2, pp. 450–451 (Feb. 1, 1851). (In Bancroft Libr., U. of Calif.)

CLARK, BENNETT C., Diary written while crossing the plains in 1849, *O.H.S.Q.*, Vol. 23.

CLARK, J. E., An Emigrant of the Fifties. Los Angeles Hist. Soc. of Calif., 1937. (In Bancroft Libr., U. of Calif.)

CLARK, JOHN H., Diary written while crossing the plains in 1852. Transcript in the Calif. State Libr., of orig. MS. owned by Mr. G. C. Ingrim, San Bruno, Calif.

CLARK, STERLING B. F., How Many Miles from St. Jo? The Log of Sterling B. F. Clark, a Forty-niner, with Comments by Ella Sterling Mighels. San Francisco, 1929.

CLARK, SUSIE C., Pioneer Days of Oregon History. Portland, Ore., 1905. (In Bancroft Libr., U. of Calif.)

CLAYTON, WILLIAM, Journal: A Daily Record of the Journey of the Original Company of "Mormon" Pioneers from Nauvoo, Ill., to the Valley of the Great Salt Lake (pub. by the Clayton Family Association). Salt Lake City, Utah, 1921.

CLEMENS, SAMUEL L., Roughing It. Hartford, Conn., 1873.

CLYMAN, JAMES, Adventures of a trapper and covered wagon emigrant as told in his own reminiscences and diaries. Ed. Charles L. Camp, San Francisco, 1928.

COGWIN, N. A., Diary written on emigrant trail in 1850. MS. in Calif. State Libr.

COKE, HON. HENRY JOHN, A Ride over the Rocky Mountains to Oregon and California. London, 1852.

COLE, GILBERT L., In the Early Days along the Overland Trail in Nebraska Territory, in 1852 (compiled by Mrs. A. Hardy). Kansas City, Mo., 1905.

COLE, MAJOR WILLIAM L., California: Its Scenery, Climate, Productions and Inhabitants—Notes of an Overland Trip to the Pacific Coast. New York, 1871.

COLVIN, THOMAS W., Recollections of his experiences as the first pioneer of Goose Lake. MS. contained in Calif. Pioneer Scrap Book, Bancroft Libr., U. of Calif.

COOKE, LUCY RUTLEDGE, Crossing the Plains in 1852: Narrative of a Trip from Iowa to "The Land of Gold," as Told in Letters Written During the Journey by Lucy Rutledge Cooke. Priv. print., Modesto, Calif., 1923.

CORVALHO, S. N., Incidents of Travel and Adventure in the Far West with Col. Frémont's last expedition across the Rocky Mountains by S. N. Corvalho, artist to the expedition. New York and Cincinnati, 1857.

COSAD, DAVID. A diary written while crossing the plains in 1849. MS. in Templeton-Crocker Collection, Calif. Hist. Soc. Libr., San Francisco, Calif.

COSGROVE, HUGH, "Reminiscences of the Emigrant Trail of 1847," O.H.S.Q., Vol. I.

COY, OWEN C., The Great Trek. Los Angeles and San Francisco, 1931.

CRANSTONE, MRS. SUSAN MARSH, Diary written on the overland trail May 8 to Aug. 27, 1851. MS. in Bancroft Libr., U. of Calif.

CRAWFORD, CHARLES H., Scenes of Earlier Days in Crossing the Plains to Oregon. Petaluma, Calif., 1898.

CRAWFORD, LEWIS F., Rekindling Camp Fires: The Exploits of Ben Arnold (Connor). Bismarck, N.D., 1926.

CRAWFORD, CAPT. MEDOREM, Journal Written While Commanding the Emigrant Escort to Oregon and Washington Territory, 1862—printed by order U.S. Senate, Jan. 6, 1863 (37th Congress, 3rd Sess. Senate, Exec. Doc. 17).

CRAWFORD, P. V., "Diary Written While Crossing the Plains in 1851," *O.H. S.Q.*, Vol. 23.

CREUZBAUR, ROBERT, Route from the Gulf of Mexico and the Lower Mississippi Valley to California and the Pacific Coast, 1849, a guide book. (In the Templeton-Crocker Collection, Calif. His. Soc. Libr., San Francisco, Calif.)

CROFUTT, GEORGE A., AND CO., Great Trans-continental Pacific Railroad Tourist's Guide. New York, 1870.

CROSS, MAJOR OSBORNE, A Report, in the form of a journal, to the quartermaster general, of the march of the regiment of mounted riflemen to Oregon from May 18 to Oct. 5, 1849—in U.S. War Dept., Report 1849/50 Quartermaster General.

CUMMINS, SARAH J., Autobiography and Reminiscences: Memories of Oregon Trail in 1845. La Grande, Ore., 1914.

CURETON, WILLIAM H., Trekking to California. Typescript, Bancroft Libr., U. of Calif.; orig. in poss. of LaMar Cureton, Seabright, Calif.

DAMON, SAMUEL C., A Journey to Lower Oregon and Upper California, 1848–49. San Francisco, 1927.

DAVIS, WILLIAM HEATH, Sixty Years in California. San Francisco, 1889.

DAWSON, NICHOLAS, Narrative of N. "Cheyenne" Dawson, concerning events on the overland trail to California in '41 and '49 and to Texas in '51; Intro. by Charles L. Camp. San Francisco, 1933.

deFREMERY, JAMES, Some reminiscences of California. Typescript in Calif. State Libr.

DELANO, ALONZO. Life on the Plains and Among the Diggings; Being Scenes and Adventures of an Overland Journey to California. Auburn, N.Y., 1854.

——A Sojourn with Royalty and Other Sketches, coll. and ed. by G. Ezra Dane. San Francisco, 1936.

DERBY, E. H., The Overland Route to the Pacific: A Report on the Union Pacific and Central Pacific Railways, Oct., 1869. Boston, 1869.

DE SMET, PIERRE JEAN, Letters and Sketches, 1841–1842. Philadelphia, 1843. (Contained in Early Western Travels, ed. R. G. Thwaites, Vol. 28, Cleveland, O., 1906).

——Oregon Missions and Travels over the Rocky Mountains in 1845–1846, pub. N.Y., 1847, and reprinted in Early Western Travels, ed. R. G. Thwaites, Vol. 29, Cleveland, O., 1906.

DICKENSON, LUELLA, Reminiscences of a Trip Across the Plains in 1846. San Francisco, 1904.

DICKSON, ALBERT JEROME, Covered Wagon Days, ed. Arthur Jerome Dickson. Cleveland, O., 1929.

DINWIDDIE JOURNAL of year 1853, thought to have been written by David or John. (In Historical Reprints, Sources of Northwest History, No. 1, State University of Montana, Missoula.)

DOUGLAS, DAVID, "Diary Written in the Year 1824," O.H.S.Q., Vol. 6.

DRANNAN, CAPT. W. F., Piloting Emigrant Trains Across the Plains of Fifty Years Ago. Chicago, 1910.

DRAPER, ELIAS J., An Autobiography of Elias Johnson Draper, Containing reminiscences of 1853. Fresno, Calif., 1904.

DRUMM, STELLA M., "More About Astorians," O.H.S.Q., Vol. 24.

DRURY, CLIFFORD M., Pioneer of Old Oregon: Henry Harmon Spalding. Caldwell, Ida., 1936.

——Marcus Whitman, M.D., Pioneer and Martyr. Caldwell, Ida., 1937.

——Elkanah and Mary Walker: Pioneers Among the Spokanes, Caldwell, Ida., 1940.

DUFFUS, ROBERT LUTHER, The Santa Fe Trail. New York, 1930.

DUNDASS, SAMUEL RUTHERFORD, Journal of . . . His Entire Route to California As a Member of the Steubenville Company. Bound for San Francisco in the year 1849. Steubenville, O., 1857.

DUNLAP, KATHERINE, A diary written on the plains in 1864. MS. in poss. of Mrs. William James Hayes, Burlingame, Calif.

DYE, JOB FRANCIS, "A Reminiscence of the Year 1832," in Santa Cruz Sentinel, Santa Cruz, Calif., 1868.

ECCLES, MRS. DAVID, Interview by Maurice Howe concerning her trek to Salt Lake City in 1867—in Historical Reprints, Sources of Northwest History, No. 1, State U. of Montana, Missoula.

EGAN, WILLIAM M., ed., Pioneering the West, 1846–1878: Major Howard Egan's Diary. Richmond, Utah, 1917.

ELLENBECKER, JOHN G., The Jayhawkers of Death Valley. Marysville, Kans., 1938.

——The Pony Express (pamphlet). Marysville, Kans., 1936(?).

ELLIOTT, T. C., "Richard (Capt. Johnny) Grant," O.H.S.Q., Vol. 36.

——" 'Doctor' Robert Newell," O.H.S.Q., Vol. 9.

——"The Name 'Oregon,' " O.H.S.Q., Vol. 21.

ELLIS, CHARLES, Utah, 1847 to 1870. Salt Lake City, 1891.

ELLISON, ROBERT S., Independence Rock: The Great Record of the Desert. Casper, Wyo., 1930.

——Pamphlet dealing with Fort Bridger, Wyo. Casper, Wyo., 1931.

ELLISON, WILLIAM HENRY, ed., The Life and Adventures of George Nidever. Berkeley, Calif., 1937.

ENOS, JAMES E., Recollections of the Plains, 1855. Typescript in Calif. State Libr.

FAIRCHILD, MAHLON D., "Reminiscences of a Forty-niner," *Calif. H.S.Q.*, Vol. 13.

FARNHAM, THOMAS JEFFERSON, Travels in the Great Western Prairies in 1839 (in Early Western Travels, ed. R. G. Thwaites, Vols. 28–29).

FENTON, HON. W. D., "Jason Lee Memorial Address," *O.H.S.Q.*, Vol. 7.

FERGUSON, CHARLES D. The Experience of a Forty-niner. Cleveland, O., 1888.

FISH, MARY C., "Across the Plains" in 1860. Typescript in Bancroft Libr., U. of Calif.

FLINT, DR. THOMAS, California to Maine and Return in 1851–1855: a Diary Written on the Emigrant Trail. Reprinted from the *Evening Free Lance,* Hollister, Calif., 2nd Ed. 1924.

FOGHT, HAROLD W., The Trail of the Loup. Ord, Nebr., 1906.

FOREMAN, GRANT, The Adventures of James Collier, First Collector of the Port of San Francisco. Chicago, 1937.

FOSTER, MRS. ROXANA, The Foster Family, California Pioneers of 1849 (contains a diary written while crossing the plains in 1849 by Rev. Isaac Foster). San Jose, Calif.(?), 1889.

FRANCL, JOSEPH, The Experiences of Joseph Francl, a Bohemian. Transl. of the orig. German MS. in Bancroft Libr., U. of Calif.

FRAZIER, MRS. R., Reminiscences of Travel from 1855 to 1867 by a Lady. San Francisco, 1868, in Huntington Libr., San Marino, Calif.

FRÉMONT, JESSIE BENTON, "The Origin of the Frémont Explorations," *Century Magazine,* Vol. 41, pp. 766–771 (Mar., 1891).

FRÉMONT, CAPT. JOHN C., Report of the Exploring Expedition to the Rocky Mountains in 1842, and to Oregon and North California in the Years 1843–44. Washington, D.C., 1845.

——"The Conquest of California," Jessie Benton Frémont from MS. and notes of J. C. Frémont, *Century Magazine,* Vol. 41, pp. 917–928 (Apr., 1891).

FRENCH, JOSEPH LEWIS, ed., The Pioneer West. Boston, 1923.

FRINK, MRS. MARGARET A., Journal of the Adventures of a Party of California Gold-Seekers . . . from Mar. 30, 1850, to Sept. 7, 1850. Oakland, Calif., 1897.

FRIZZELL, MRS. LODISA, Across the Plains to California in 1852: Journal, ed. by Victor Hugo Paltsits from MS. in New York Public Libr. New York, 1915. (Copy of MS. in Templeton-Crocker Collection, Calif. H.S.L., San Francisco, Calif.)

FROST, JOHN, Incidents and Narratives of Travel. Auburn, N.Y., 1852.

——Pictorial History of California. Auburn, N.Y., 1853.

FULKERTH, WILLIAM L., Diary of the overland journey of William L. Fulkerth and wife from Iowa to California in 1863. Facsim., Bancroft Libr., U. of Calif.

GARRAGHAN, GILBERT J., Catholic Beginnings in Kansas City, Mo.: An Historical Sketch. Chicago, Ill., 1920.

GEER, MRS. ELIZABETH DIXON SMITH, "Diary Written on the Oregon Trail in 1847," Transactions of the 35th Annual Reunion of the Oregon Pioneer Association, Portland, June 19, 1907.

GELATT, R., A Simple Sketch of My Simple Life. Typescript in the Calif. State Libr.

GERSTAECKER, FREDERICK, Wild Sports in the Far West (trans. from the German). Boston, 1864.

GIBBS, GEORGE, Diary written on the emigrant trail in 1849 (contained in The March of the Mounted Riflemen, ed. Raymond W. Settle, Glendale, Calif., 1940).

GIBSON, J. WATT, Recollections of a Pioneer (reminiscences of '49). St. Joseph, Mo., 1912.

GILL, WILLIAM, California letters of William Gill, written in 1850 to his wife, Harriet Tarleton, in Kentucky, ed. Eva Turner Clark. New York, 1922.

GLASSCOCK, C. B., A Golden Highway. Indianapolis, 1934.

GOODALE, TIM, Letter regarding best overland route to the Pacific Coast, forwarded to the Dept. of the Interior by F. W. Lander, Supt. of the Ft. Kearney, South Pass and Honey Lake wagon road, dated Feb. 11, 1861.

GORDON, G. F., Statement concerning trip across plains in 1848 by way of Laramie Plain, Brown's Hole, Utah Lake, to Los Angeles. MS. in Calif. Pioneer Scrap Book, Bancroft Libr., U. of Calif.

GRABHORN, JANE BISSELL, A California Gold Rush Miscellany. San Francisco, 1934.

GRAVES, J. A., My Seventy Years in California, 1857–1927. Los Angeles, 1928.

GRAY, GEORGE M., Interview, concerning his long acquaintance with John Bidwell, by William G. Paden, at Chico, Calif.

GRAYSON, ANDREW JACKSON, Two letters concerning trip across plains in 1846, the first probably written in '48, the second addressed to Judge Isaiah Garrett, Feb. 22, 1847. St. Helena, Calif., 1902.

GREELEY, HORACE, An Overland Journey from New York to San Francisco. New York, 1860.

GREENWOOD, GRACE (Mrs. Sara J. Lippincott), New Life in New Lands. New York, 1873.

GREGG, JOSIAH, Commerce of the Prairies, or, The Journal of a Santa Fe Trader, 1831–1839 (in Early Western Travels, ed. R. G. Thwaites, Vols. 20–21, Cleveland, O., 1905).

GROUND, EDWARD, Letter dated Polk Co., Ore. Terr., Mar. 5, '54; from typescript in Bancroft Libr., U. of Calif.; orig. in poss. R. O. Butler, R.F.D. 1, Monmouth, Ill.

GROUND, ELIZA A., Letter, headed Bloomington (Ore. Terr.), Dec. the 25, 1853. From typescript; orig. as above.

GROUND, WILLIAM B., Letter headed Bloomington (Ore. Terr.), Dec. the 26, 1853. From typescript; orig. as above.

GUNN, LEWIS C., Records of a California Family [from '49]: Journals and Letters, ed. Anna Lee Marston. San Diego, Calif., 1928.

HACKENSMITH, MRS. M. S. (Carruth), Diary written while crossing the plains in 1866. MS. in Bancroft Libr., U. of Calif.

HACKNEY, JOSEPH, Diary written while crossing the plains in 1849—contained in Wagons West, by Elizabeth Page (New York, 1930).

HAFEN, LEROY R., and GHENT, W. J., Broken Hand: The Life Story of Thomas Fitzpatrick. Denver, Colo., 1931.

——and YOUNG, F. M., Fort Laramie and the Pageant of the West. Glendale, Calif., 1938.

——Overland Routes to the Gold Fields, 1859. Glendale, Calif., 1942.

——Pikes Peak Gold Rush Guidebooks of 1859. Glendale, Calif., 1941.

HALE, ISRAEL, "Diary Written While Crossing the Plains in 1849," *Calif. H.S.Q.*, Vol. 11.

HALL, EDWARD H., The Great West: Travellers', Miners' and Emigrants' Guide and Hand-Book to the Western, North-Western and Pacific States and Territories. New York, 1865.

HALL, MAGGIE, The Story of Maggie Hall, crossing the plains when she was about nine years old (southern route). Photostat of orig. MS., Bancroft Libr., U. of Calif.

HALL, O. J., The Diary of a forty-niner, extracted from the daily journal of O. J. Hall. Typescript in the Calif. State Libr.

HAMMOND, I. B., Reminiscences of Frontier Life. Portland, Ore., 1904.

HANCOCK, SAMUEL, The Narrative of Samuel Hancock, 1845–1860. New York, 1927.

HARLAN, JACOB WRIGHT, California, '46 to '88. San Francisco, 1888.

HARRITT, JESSE, "Diary Written on Emigrant Trail in 1845," *O.H.S.Q.*, Vol. 35.

HARTMAN, AMOS WILLIAM, "The California and Oregon Trail, '49 to '60," *O.H.S.Q.*, Vol. 25.

HASKINS, C. W., The Argonauts of California. New York, 1890.

HASTINGS, LANSFORD W., The Emigrants' Guide to Oregon and California. Cincinnati, 1845.

HAUN, CATHERINE M., A reminiscence of 1849. MS. in Huntington Libr., San Marino, Calif.

HAWLEY, NANCY TUNIS, Reminiscences of crossing the plains in 1854 at the age of ten years—interview by William G. Paden at Fortuna, Calif.

HAYNES, CAPT. ASA, A diary written on the emigrant trail to California via Death Valley (contained in Jayhawkers of Death Valley, by John Ellenbecker, which see).

HEBARD, GRACE RAYMOND, The Pathbreakers from River to Ocean. Glendale, Calif., 1933.

——and BRININSTOOL, E. A., The Bozeman Trail. Cleveland, O., 1922.

HEWITT, R. H., Notes by the Way: Memoranda of a Journey Across the Plains in 1862. Olympia, Wash. Terr., 1863.

HICKMAN, PETER L., Diary written on the emigrant trail in 1853. MS. in Calif. State Libr.

HICKMAN, RICHARD OWEN, An Overland Journey to California in 1852: The Journal of Richard Owen Hickman, ed. M. Catherine White (reprinted from Frontier, Vol. 9, No. 3, Mar., 1929), Historical Reprints—Sources of Northwest History, No. 6. Calif. State Libr.

HINDS, REV. T. W., Diary written on the emigrant trail in 1850. Typescript at Bancroft Libr., U. of Calif.; MS. in poss. Leland F. Hinds, Santa Cruz, Calif.

HINES, GEORGE M., Statement concerning the Platte Crossing in 1853. O.H.S.Q., Vol. 15.

HINMAN, ALANSON, "Reminiscences of 1844, Bearing Particularly on the Whitman Mission," O.H.S.Q., Vol. 4.

HIXSON, JASPER M., Diary written on the emigrant trail in 1849 (contained in The Great Trek, by Owen C. Coy, which see).

HODGKINS, PILSBURY, "The Story of Pilsbury Hodgkins: The Life of a Mule-Mail Carrier in the Mother Lode," Soc. of Calif. Pion. Quart., Vol. 2.

HODGSON, MARY A., The Life of a Pioneer Family (E. McDaniels): A True Account. MS. in the Calif. State Libr.

HOLLINGSWORTH, JOHN MCHENRY, Diary of a member of the "Stevenson Regiment" sent to California by boat in '46 and remaining through the pre-gold years. From copy at Stanford University, Palo Alto, Calif.; orig. MS. in Templeton-Crocker Collection, San Francisco, Calif.

HOLMAN, FREDERICK V., Dr. John McLoughlin, the Father of Oregon. Cleveland, O., 1907.

——"Important Results from the Expeditions of John Jacob Astor to and from the Oregon Country," O.H.S.Q., Vol. 12.

——"The Oregon Provisional Government," O.H.S.Q., Vol. 13.

——Address at dedication of McLoughlin Institute, Oregon City, Oct. 6, 1907, O.H.S.Q., Vol. 8.

HOOPES, ALBAN W., Indian Affairs and Their Administration, with Special Reference to the Far West, 1849–1860. Philadelphia, 1932.

——"Thomas S. Twiss, Indian Agent on the Upper Platte, 1855–1861," Miss. Val. Hist. Rev., Vol. 20.

HOPPER, CHARLES, Narrative of a California Pioneer of 1841, written at Napa, Calif., 1871, by R. T. Montgomery. MS. in Bancroft Libr., U. of Calif.

Horn's Overland Guide from Council Bluffs to Sacramento Calif. Typed copy in poss. William G. Paden, Alameda, Calif.

HORTON, EMILY McCOWEN, Our Family: With a Glimpse of Their Pioneer Life. N.p., 1922. (In Calif. State Libr.)

HOTH, H., Diary, Dec., 1853, Sept. 1857; a portion written while crossing the plains via Salt Lake City to Los Angeles. Facsim. of MS. in Bancroft Libr., U. of Calif.

HOUGHTON, ELIZA P. DONNER, The Expedition of the Donner Party, and Its Tragic Fate. Los Angeles, 1920.

HOUSTOUN, MRS. MATILDA C. F., Hesperos, or Travels in the West. 2 vols., London, 1850.

HOWE, OCTAVIUS THORNDIKE, Argonauts of '49. Cambridge, Mass., 1923.

HOWELL, ELIJAH P., Diary written on the emigrant trail in 1849. Typescript of unpub. orig. at Bancroft Libr., U. of California.

HULBERT, ARCHER BUTLER, Forty-Niners. Boston, 1931.

——Ed. The Crown Collection of American Maps, Bancroft Libr., U. of Calif.

HUNT, NANCY ZUMWALT, "By Ox-Team to California" [a reminiscence of 1854], ed. Rockwell D. Hunt, Overland Monthly, Vol. 67, pp. 317-326 (Apr., 1916).

HUNTER, GEORGE, Reminiscences of an Old Timer (of 1852). San Francisco, 1887.

HUNTON, JOHN, Old Fort Laramie. Torrington, Wyo., 1928.

HUTCHINS, LUCY AYER, Interview concerning her brother Noah Brooks's book, The Boy Emigrants, by William G. Paden in Berkeley, Calif.

HUTCHINSON, ELIZABETH, Letter dated Luckamute (Ore. Terr.), Apr., 1854. Typescript at Bancroft Libr., U. of Calif.; orig. in poss. R. O. Butler, R.F.D. 1, Monmouth, Ill.

HUTCHINSON, T. H., Letter dated Luckamute, Polk Co., O.T., Mar. 7, 1854. Orig. and typescript in poss. R. O. Butler, R.F.D. 1, Monmouth, Ill.

IDAHO SOUVENIR HAND BOOK in honor of the Fort Hall Centennial, 1834-1934. Pocatello, Idaho, 1934.

INGALLS, E. S., Journal of a Trip to California, . . . 1850-51. Waukegan, 1852. (Photostat copy at Bancroft Libr., U. of Calif.).

INGERSOLL, CHESTER, Overland to California in 1847: Letters Written en Route . . . to the Editor of the Joliet Signal. Chicago, 1937.

IRONS, CHARLES D., ed., W. F. Edwards' Tourists' Guide and Directory of the Truckee Basin. Truckee, Calif., 1883.

IRVING, WASHINGTON, The Adventures of Captain Bonneville, U.S.A., in the Rocky Mountains and the Far West, digested from his journal and illustrated from various other sources. New York, 1869.

JAGGERS, D., Diary written on the emigrant trail in 1849. MS. in Templeton-Crocker Collection, Calif. H.S. Library, San Francisco.

JEFFERSON, T. H., Booklet, Accompaniment to the map of the emigrant road from Independence, Mo., to San Francisco, Calif., by T. H. Jefferson, New York, 1849. Photostat at Bancroft Libr., U. of Calif.

JEWETT, GEORGE E., Diary written on the emigrant trail in 1849. MS. in the estate of the late George E. Jewett, Jr., Berkeley, Calif.; typescript at Bancroft Libr., U. of Calif.

JOHNSON, OVERTON, and WINTER, WILLIAM H., Route Across the Rocky Mountains. Princeton, N.J., 1932 (reprint of the edition of 1846).

JOHNSTON, WILLIAM G., Experiences of a Forty-niner (a diary written while crossing the plains). Pittsburgh, 1892.

JONES, MARY A., Recollections of 1846, compiled by Mrs. J. C. Jones, Alamo, Contra Costa Co., Calif. Orig. in her poss., typescript at Bancroft Libr., U. of Calif.

JONES, NATHANIEL V., Notes of his travels with the Mormon Battalion, 1846–47. Typescript, Bancroft Libr., U. of Calif.

JORY, JAMES, "Reminiscences of 1847," *O.H.S.Q.*, Vol. 3.

JOSSELYN, AMOS P., Diary written while crossing the plains in 1849. MS. in Calif. State Libr.

JUDSON, KATHARINE BERRY, Early Days in Old Oregon. Chicago, 1916.

JUDSON, PHOEBE GOODELL, A Pioneer's Search for an Ideal Home [1853]. Bellingham, Wash., 1925.

KEITH, CLAYTON, My Trip to California in '49. Louisiana, Mo., 1914.

KELLY, CHARLES, Old Greenwood: The Story of Caleb Greenwood, Trapper, Pathfinder and Early Pioneer of the West. Salt Lake City, 1936.

——Salt Desert Trails. Salt Lake City, 1930.

KELLY, FANNY, Narrative of My Captivity Among the Sioux Indians. Philadelphia, 1872.

KELLY, WILLIAM, An Excursion to California over the Prairie, Rocky Mountains and Great Sierra Nevada [diary written on the emigrant trail in 1849]. London, 1851.

KEYSER, S., Memoirs (relating to Johnson Ranch and first few migrations into California by Truckee Route) by his widow, Elizabeth Pierce. MS. in Calif. Pioneer Scrap Book, Bancroft Libr., U. of Calif.

KIDDER, LEROY L., Diary written while crossing the plains in 1850. Pub. in the *Siskiyou News,* Mar., 1920. Photostat of newspaper at Calif. State Libr.

KING, TOM, Journal of the First Wagon Train in 1849 (by the southern route). Photostat of old galley proofs of the *San Francisco Examiner,* Bancroft Libr., U. of Calif.

KIRKPATRICK, CHARLES ALEXANDER, Journals of 1849. MS. in Bancroft Libr., U. of Calif.

KLEISER, JAMES ABRAHAM, Autobiography, written at Cloverdale, Calif., 1888. Facsim. of MS. at Bancroft Libr., U. of Calif.; orig. in poss. George W. Kleiser.

Bibliography 493

Knight, Thomas, Reminiscences of 1845. MS. in Calif. Pion. Scrap Book, Bancroft Libr., U. of Calif.

Knight, William H., An Emigrant's Trip across the Plains, 1859. Southern Calif. Hist. Soc. Publications, Vol. 12, 1923.

Knowland, Joseph R., California: A Landmark History. Oakland, Calif., 1941.

Kopac, Emil, Letter to William G. Paden dated Omaha, Nebr., Nov. 30, 1938 (supplying data on Sublette and Kinney cutoffs), in poss. William G. Paden, Alameda, Calif.

Lambourne, Alfred, The Pioneer Trail [compiled from various sources]. Salt Lake City, 1913.

Lander, F. W., Additional estimate for Fort Kearney, South Pass and Honey Lake Wagon Road, Wash., 1861. U.S. 36th Cong., 2nd Sess. House Ex. Doc. no. 63.

Landrum, Mrs., Notebook kept while crossing the plains in 1861. In poss. Robert G. Williams, Woodbridge, Calif.

Langworthy, Franklin, Scenery of the Plains, Mountains and Mines [1850], ed. Paul C. Phillips from 1855 ed. Princeton, N.J., 1932.

Laut, Agnes C., The Conquest of Our Western Empire. New York, 1927.

Lee, Jason, Diary written while going to the Oregon country in 1834, O.H.S.Q., Vol. 17.

Lee, John D., Journals of 1846–47 and 1859, ed. Charles Kelly. Salt Lake City, 1938.

Leeper, David Rohrer, The Argonauts of Forty-Nine. South Bend, 1894.

Leonard, Zenas, Leonard's Narrative: Adventures of Zenas Leonard, Fur Trader and Trapper, 1831–36 [reprinted from rare orig. of 1839], ed. W. F. Wagner. Cleveland, 1904.

Lienhard, Heinrich, Diary written on the emigrant trail in 1846. Typescript at Bancroft Libr., U. of Calif.

Littleton, Micajah, Diary written on the emigrant trail in 1850. MS. in Calif. State Libr.

Lobenstine, William C., Extracts from the Diary of William C. Lobenstine, Dec. 31, 1851–1858, ed. Belle W. Lobenstine. New York, 1920.

Locke, D. M., Diary kept in San Francisco in the year 1849, from copy in poss. of H. R. Dakin, Santa Cruz, Calif. Orig. in poss. of Eric Locke, Berkeley, California.

Lockley, Fred, "Recollections of B. F. Bonney," O.H.S.Q., Vol. 24.

——Captain Sol. Tetherow, Wagon Train Master: Personal Narrative of His Son Sam. Tetherow, Who Crossed the Plains to Oregon, in 1845; and personal narrative of Jack McNemee, Who Was Born in Portland, Ore., in 1848, and Whose Father Built the Fourth House in Portland. Portland, Ore., 1925(?).

Longworth, Basil Nelson, Diary of 1853–54, covering period of his migration from Ohio to Oregon: a pamphlet by D. E. Harrington. Denver, 1927.

Loomis, Leander, A Journal of the Birmingham Emigrating Company [1850]. Salt Lake City, 1928.

Loring, Col. William Wing, Official Report of a Journey Across the Plains to Fort Hall (contained in The March of the Mounted Riflemen, ed. Raymond W. Settle, which see).

Lovejoy, A. J., Reminiscences of crossing the plains, etc., in 1842. MS. at Bancroft Libr., U. of Calif.

Loveland, Cyrus C., Diary written while crossing the plains in 1850. MS. at Calif. State Libr.

Ludlow, Fitz Hugh, The Heart of the Continent. Cambridge, Mass., 1870.

McCall, Ansel James, The Great California Trail in 1849: Wayside Notes of an Argonaut, reprinted from the Steuben Courier. Bath, N.Y., 1882.

McDonald, Richard Hayes, A Reminiscence of a trip across the plains in 1849, compiled by Frank V. McDonald. N.p., 1881.

McGehee, Micajah, "Rough Times in Rough Places" (with Frémont's fourth expedition), Century Magazine, Mar., 1891.

McGlashan, C. F., History of the Donner Party. San Francisco, 1931.

McIlhany, Edward W., Recollections of a '49er. Kansas City, Mo., 1908.

McKeeby, Lemuel Clarke, "Memoirs," Calif. H.S.Q., Vol. 3.

McKinstry, Geo. M., Diary written while crossing the plains in 1846. MS. in Bancroft Libr., U. of Calif.

McNeil, Samuel, McNeil's Travels in 1849, to, Through and From the Gold Regions, in California. Columbus, O., 1850.

Maddock, Mrs. Sallie Hester, "The Diary of a Pioneer Girl . . . in a Trip Overland in 1849," Argonaut, Sept. 12 to Oct. 24, 1925.

Majors, Alexander, Seventy Years on the Frontier [by a member of the staging firm of Majors, Russell and Waddell]. Chicago, 1893.

Maloney, Alice B., "Hudson's Bay Company," O.H.S.Q., Vol. 37.

Mann, Henry R., Diary written on the emigrant trail in 1849, last half only, west from Deer Creek on the North Platte, June 23, '49. MS. in poss. Mrs. William Cox, Alameda, Calif.

Mann, Stephen H., Interview concerning his walk from Illinois to Calif. in 1852, Stockton Evening Mail, Oct. 28, 1909. Copy at Bancroft Libr., U. of Calif.

Marcy, Capt. Randolph B., The Prairie Traveler: A Handbook for Overland Expeditions [pub. by permission of the War Dept.]. New York, 1859.

Markle, John A., The Travell of a Gold Digger, en route California, 1849. Photostat of MS. in Bancroft Libr., U. of Calif.; orig. in poss. of Auburn Parlor of Native Sons of the Golden West, Auburn, Calif.

Bibliography 495

MASTERS, JOSEPH G., Blazing the Trail in Oregon (pamphlet, Trail Memorial Assn., Centenary).

——Stories of the Far West. Boston, 1935.

MAXWELL, WILLIAM AUDLEY, Crossing the Plains, Days of '57. San Francisco, 1915.

MEEKER, EZRA, Ox-Team Days on the Oregon Trail. Yonkers-on-Hudson, N.Y., 1922.

——Address at site of Fort Hall on 87th Anniversary of first Protestant Sermon west of the Rockies, preached by Jason Lee. Pocatello *Tribune,* Pocatello, Ida., July 27, 1921.

MELINE, JAMES F., Two Thousand Miles on Horseback [in 1866]. New York, 1867.

MESSITER, CHARLES ALSTON, Sport and Adventures Among the North-American Indians. London, 1890.

MILES, WILLIAM, Journal of the Sufferings and Hardships of Capt. Parker H. French's Overland Expedition to California [1850]. Chambersburg, Pa., 1851. Reprinted New York, 1916.

MILLER, GEORGE, A reminiscent letter to Byron Waters, Highland, Calif., dated July, 1916, telling of trip across the plains in 1850. Hist. Soc. of Southern Calif. Pubs., Vol. 10.

MILLER, JOAQUIN, Overland in a Covered Wagon [in 1852]. New York, 1930.

MINTO, JOHN, "Reminiscences of Experiences on the Oregon Trail in Eighteen Years, *O.H.S.Q.,* Vol. 2.

——"What I Know of Dr. McLoughlin and How I Know It," *O.H.S.Q.,* Vol. 11.

MITCHELL, LYMAN, Diary written while crossing the plains in 1849. MS. in poss. Mrs. Elon Mitchell, Vallejo, Calif.

MOKLER, ALFRED JAMES, Transition of the West. Chicago, 1927.

MÖLLHAUSEN, BALDUIN, Diary of a Journey from the Mississippi to the Coasts of the Pacific, transl. Mrs. Percy Sinnett. London, 1858.

MOODY, JOSEPH LEDLIE, Letter concerning trip across plains in 1849, dated Sacramento City, Aug. 7, 1849, *Calif. H.S.Q.,* Vol. 13.

MORGAN, MRS. MARTHA M., A Trip Across the Plains in the Year 1849. San Francisco, 1864. Photostat copy at Calif. State Libr.

MORRIS, MAURICE O'CONNOR, Rambles in the Rocky Mountains. London, 1864.

MOSES, DR. ISAAC, Journal of distances traveled by the Regiment of Mounted Rifles during a march from Ft. Leavenworth, Mo., to the Dalles of the Columbia, in the summer of 1849 (reprinted in The March of the Mounted Riflemen, ed. Raymond W. Settle, which see, from MS. in the National Archives, Washington, D.C.).

MUNGER, ASAHEL, "Diary written while on the Oregon Trail in 1839," *O.H.S.Q.,* Vol. 8.

MURPHY, JOHN E., Letters written while crossing the plains in 1852. Typescripts at Bancroft Libr., U. of Calif.; origs. in poss. R. O. Butler, Monmouth, Ill.

MYRICK, ELIZABETH T. RANKIN, Diary written while crossing the plains in 1854. MS. in poss. Mrs. L. C. Gulliksen, Fortuna, Calif.

NASH, MARIE, Diary written while crossing the plains in 1861. MS. in Calif. State Libr.

NESMITH, JAMES W., "Diary Written While Crossing the Plains in 1843," *O.H.S.Q.,* Vol. 7.

NEWCOMB, SILAS, Diary written while crossing the plains in 1850. MS. in Huntington Libr., San Marino, Calif.

NEWMAN, J. A., The Autobiography of an Old Fashioned Boy [recollections of a trip toward Pike's Peak in 1860]. Oklahoma City(?), 1923.

NIDEVER, GEORGE B., Adventures of, dictated to Edw. F. Murray in 1878. Bancroft Libr., U. of Calif.

NOBLE, WILLIAM M., Events Happening to his family while crossing the plains in '56, told to Linnie Marsh Wolfe in 1935. Typescript, Bancroft Libr., U. of Calif.

NORTON, COL. L. A., "My Overland Trip to California in 1852," reprinted from Life and Adventures of Col. L. A. Norton (Oakland, Calif., 1887), in the *Pony Express Courier,* Placerville, Calif., Vol. 1, Nos. 4–5.

NORTON, MARIA J. ELLIOTT, Diary written while crossing the plains in 1859. MS. in poss. of Mrs. J. D. Fish, Stockton, Calif.

NUSBAUMER, LOUIS, Adventures of a Trip to the Gold Fields of California, May 20, 1849, to June 19, 1850 (from the diary of Louis Nusbaumer, translated from the German and typed by his daughter, Bertha Nusbaumer Whitmore, 1933). Typescript, Bancroft Libr., U. of Calif.

OAKLEY, OBADIAH, The Oregon Expedition of, reprinted from the *Peoria Register,* New York, 1914. Undated, but the *Peoria Register* was printed under that name only in 1842–1845; copy at Bancroft Libr., U. of Calif.

OGDEN, PETER SKENE, Diary of an officer in the Hudson's Bay Co., starting Nov. 21, 1825, *O.H.S.Q.,* Vol. 10.

OMWAKE, JOHN, The Conestoga Six-Horse Bell Teams of Eastern Pennsylvania. Cincinnati, O., 1930.

O'REILLY, HARRINGTON, Fifty Years on the Trail [the experiences of John Young Nelson]. London, 1891.

PAGE, ELIZABETH, Wagons West: A Story of the Oregon Trail. New York, 1930.

PALMER, JOEL, Journal of Travels over the Rocky Mountains, 1845–1846 (in Early Western Travels, ed. R. W. Thwaites, Vol. 30).

PANCOAST, CHARLES EDWARD, A Quaker Forty-niner, ed. Anna P. Hannum. Philadelphia, 1930.

PARKMAN, FRANCIS, The Oregon Trail; Being Sketches of Prairie and Rocky Mountain Life [in the year 1846]. Many editions.

PARSONS, WILLIAM B., The Gold Mines of Western Kansas. Lawrence, Kan., no date.

PATTERSON, E. H. N., Diary, The Platte River Route—reprinted in Overland Routes to the Gold Fields, 1859, ed. LeRoy Hafen. Glendale, Calif., 1942.

PAXSON, FREDERICK LOGAN, The Last American Frontier. New York, 1910.

PEARSON, OCTAVIUS C., Diary written while crossing the plains by the southern route in the year 1849. MS. in Brancroft Libr., U. of Calif.

PEASE, EDWIN R., Diary, St. Joseph to Fort Kearney—reprinted in Overland Routes to the Gold Fields, 1859, ed. LeRoy R. Hafen. Glendale, Calif., 1942. Orig. in poss. State Hist. Soc. of Colo.

PENTER, SAMUEL, "Recollections of Crossing the Plains with the Oregon Migration of '43," O.H.S.Q., Vol. 7.

PERKINS, ELISHA DOUGLAS, Diary written while crossing the plains in 1849. MS. in Huntington Libr., San Marino, Calif.

PHELPS, WILLIAM D., Two letters giving data of his early experiences in California, dated May 5 and July 5, 1872. MS. in Calif. Pioneer Scrap Book, Bancroft Libr., U. of Calif.

PLEASANTS, W. S., Twice Across the Plains, 1849, 1856. San Francisco, 1906 (photostat copy in Bancroft Libr., U. of Calif.).

PORTER, LAVINIA HONEYMAN, By Ox Team to California [in 1860]. Oakland, Calif., 1910.

POTTER, THEODORE E., Autobiography (MS. found and published posthumously). Concord, N.H., 1913.

POWERS, STEVEN A., A few facts about early Calif. MS. penciled on brown paper, Calif. Pioneer Scrap Book, item No. 16, Bancroft Libr., U. of Calif.

PRATT, ORSON, Portions of his diary written while crossing the plains in 1847, contained in Mormon Hist. Rec., No. 9, ed. Andrew Jensen. Salt Lake City, Utah.

PRESTON, LEANDER A., Items of travel of the Carner families and others across the plains in 1860 and 1861 from Strawberry Point, Ia., to Yuba City, Calif. Typescript in Calif. State Libr.

PRICE, JOSEPH, The Road to California: Letters Written While Crossing the Plains in 1850, ed. Thos. M. Marshall. Cedar Rapids, Ia., 1924 (reprinted in Miss. Val. Hist. Rev., Vol. 11, No. 2 (Sept., 1924).

PRINGLE, CATHERINE SAGER, Letter to Frederick, dated Salem, Dec. 21, 1854, O.H.S.Q., Vol. 37.

PRITCHARD, CAPT. J. A., Diary of a journey from Kentucky to California in 1849, Missouri Hist. Rev., Vol. 18. MS. in poss. Hon. John I. Williamson, Kansas City, Mo.

PURCELL, POLLY JANE, Autobiography and Reminiscences of a Pioneer. Freewater, Ore.(?), 1922.

PUTNAM, R. P., Journal written while crossing the plains to California by the southern route in 1857. MS. in 2 vols. in Bancroft Libr., U. of Calif.

RAHM, LOUISA MOELLER, Diary written while crossing the plains in 1862. Photostat of MS. at Bancroft Libr., U. of Calif.

RANDALL, DR. ANDREW, Diary written while crossing the plains in 1849. MS. in Calif. State Libr.

READ, GEORGE WILLIS, A Pioneer of 1850, ed. Georgia Willis Read. Boston, 1927.

REED, VIRGINIA, Letter dated May 16, 1847, written at age of 12, first written news telling of Donner tragedy to arrive in East. Typescript, Bancroft Libr., U. of Calif.

REED-MURPHY, VIRGINIA, "Across the Plains in the Donner Party (1846)," Century Magazine, July, 1891.

REEVES, ELIJAH, Some events connected with his travels across the plains in 1848 and 1853, told by his daughter, Mary Ellen Nobles, to Linnie Marsh Wolfe, 1935. Bancroft Libr., U. of Calif.

REYNOLDS, CHARLES D., Incidents and Reminiscences of the Life of Charles D. Reynolds from Boyhood to Old Age, written at Dry Creek, Stanislaus Co., Calif., Jan. 7, 1893. Facsim. of typescript at Bancroft Libr., U. of Calif.

RICHARDSON, ALBERT D., Journal, Leavenworth and Pike's Peak Route, reprinted in Overland Routes to the Gold Fields, 1859, ed. LeRoy R. Hafen. Glendale, Calif., 1942. (First published, in 1867, in Richardson's book, Beyond the Mississippi.)

RICHARDSON, CAROLINE, Diary written while crossing the plains in 1852. MS. in Bancroft Libr., U. of Calif., courtesy of Mrs. Nellie Richardson, 2144 Lincoln Avenue, Alameda, Calif.

ROBE, ROBERT, Diary written while crossing the plains in 1851, Washington Hist. Quart., Vol. 19, No. 1 (Jan., 1928).

ROBERTSON, JAMES R., "Joseph Watt, a Pioneer Captain of Industry in Oregon," O.H.S.Q., Vol. 4.

ROBIDOUX, ORRAL MESSMORE, Memorial to the Robidoux Brothers. Kansas City, Mo., 1924.

ROOSEVELT, THEODORE, Hunting Trips on the Prairie. New York, 1902.

ROOT, FRANK A., and CONNELLEY, WILLIAM ELSEY, The Overland Stage to California. Topeka, Kans., 1901.

ROSE, RACHEL, Diary written while on the plains in 1852. MS. in Calif. State Libr.

ROSS, ALEXANDER, Oregon Settlers: A Narrative of the Expedition Fitted Out by John Jacob Astor to Establish the Pacific Fur Co., from memoranda taken at the time. London, 1849. (Reprinted in Early Western Travels, ed. R. G. Thwaites, Vol. 7. Cleveland, 1904.)

ROUNDTREE, PATRICK HENRY, Autobiography: A Trip Across the Plains in 1859. Typescript at Bancroft Libr., U. of Calif.

ROYCE, SARAH A., Recollections of a Frontier Lady. New Haven, Conn., 1932.

RUCKER, MRS. MAUDE APPLEGATE, The Oregon Trail and Some of Its Blazers. New York, 1930.

RUEGER, JOHN, Journal, written while crossing the plains. Reprint from Benicia *Herald,* June 1, 8, 15, 1923. Typescript, Bancroft Libr., U. of Calif.

SAGE, RUFUS B., Rocky Mountain Life. Dayton, O., 1857.

SANFORD, MARY FETTER HITE and ABRAHAM HITE. Biographical sketch of Abraham Hite and family by Mary Fetter Hite Sanford; A trip across the plains, Mar. 28 to Oct. 27, 1853, by Mary F. H. Sanford; Diary of a trip across the plains, Mar. 28 to Oct. 27, 1853, by Abraham Hite. Typescripts in Calif. State Libr.

SAWTELLE, MRS. MARY P., The Heroine of '49. San Francisco, 1891.

SAWYER, MRS. FRANCIS H., Overland to California (from journal written while crossing the plains in 1852). Typescript at Bancroft Libr., U. of Calif.

SAWYER, LORENZO, Way Sketches; Containing Incidents of Travel Across the Plains from St. Joseph to California in 1850. New York, 1926.

SCHAFER, JOSEPH, "Notes on the Colonization of Oregon," *O.H.S.Q.,* Vol. 7.

SCHELL, H. S., Memoranda: Forts Laramie and Kearney [1842–76]. MS. Bancroft Libr., U. of Calif.

SCOTT, HON. H. W., "Address concerning early days in Ore.," *O.H.S.Q.,* Vol. 7.

SEARLS, NILES, The Diary of a Pioneer and Other Papers [written daily while crossing the plains in 1849]. San Francisco, 1940. (Orig. in poss. May Searls Heuer.)

SEDGLEY, JOSEPH, Overland to California in 1849. Oakland, Calif., 1877.

SENTER, RILEY, Crossing the Continent to the California Gold Fields. Reprint from the Exeter Sun, 1938, Exeter, Calif. Copyrighted by W. R. Senter, Lemon Cove, Calif.

SETTLE, RAYMOND W., ed. The March of the Mounted Riflemen, First U.S. Military Expedition to Travel the Full Length of the Oregon Trail. . . . May to Oct., 1849, as Recorded in the Journals . . . Glendale, Calif., 1940.

SHARP, REV. JOHN, Brief pencilled notes about trip across plains in 1850. MS. in Calif. State Libr.

SHAW, D. A., Eldorado; or, California as Seen by a Pioneer, 1850–1900. Los Angeles, 1900.

SHAW, R. C., Across the Plains in Forty-nine. Farmland, Ind., 1896.

SHELDON, JARED DIXON, "Eventful Life of," *Elk Grove Citizen,* Elk Grove, Calif., Dec. 29, 1932 (typescript at Bancroft Libr., U. of Calif.).

SHELLEY's United States Railway, Steam Navigation and Mining Guide, 1865. Templeton-Crocker Collection. Calif. His. Soc. Libr., San Francisco.

SHERMAN, GEN. WILLIAM T., Memoirs. New York, 1875.

SHIVELY, J. M., Route and Distances to Oregon and California. Washington, D.C., 1846. (Photostat at Bancroft Libr., U. of Calif.)

SHOTTENKIRK, D. G., Portion of Diary written on the emigrant trail in 1850. (June 20 to July 1, 1850). Printed as appendix in 'Scenery of the Plains, Mountains and Mines' by Franklin Langworthy, pub. by Princeton Univ. Press, 1932.

SIMPSON, BREVET BRIG. GEN. J. H., The Shortest Route to California. Philadelphia, 1869. (In Templeton-Crocker Collection, Calif. Hist. Soc. Libr., San Francisco.)

SMEDLEY, WILLIAM, Across the Plains in '62. Denver (?), 1916.

SMITH, ASA and SETH, Letters 1850–1862, written from the Calif. gold fields to family in Baltimore (158 letters in portfolio). MS. in Bancroft Libr., U. of Calif.

SMITH, C. W., Diary written while crossing the plains in 1850. MS. in Templeton-Crocker Coll., San Francisco.

SMITH, I. M., Recollections of crossing the plains in 1859, details of the massacre of the Wright Family. Typescript in Calif. State Libr.

SMITH, ISAAC, Three letters, dated Winter quarters, Ioway, Apr. 27, 1853, Polk County [Ore. Terr.], Aug. 17, 1854, Bridgeport [Ore. Terr.], Oct. 22, 1854. Typescripts at Bancroft Libr., U. of Calif.; origs. in poss. R. O. Butler, Monmouth, Ill.

SMITH, JEDEDIAH S., Letter from him together with David E. Jackson and W. L. Sublette at St. Louis, Oct. 29, 1830, addressed to Hon. John H. Eaton, Sec. of War, O.H.S.Q., Vol. 4.

SMITH, SIDNEY W., Diary written while crossing the plains in 1839. Portland, Ore., 1939.

SOULÉ, FRANK, GIHON, JOHN H., and NISBET, JAMES, The Annals of San Francisco. New York, 1855.

SPOONER, SARAH E. WILLIAMS, Reminiscences of a Covered Wagon—recollections of her family crossing the plains in 1853. A typed copy in coll. donated by Robert G. Williams, Woodbridge, Calif., to Bancroft Libr., U. of Calif.

STANSBURY, HOWARD (U.S. Bureau of Topographical Engineers), An Expedition to the Valley of the Great Salt Lake of Utah. Philadelphia, 1852 (also Washington, 1853, as Executive Doc. No. 3, 32nd Congress, Special Session, Mar., 1851, under title Exploration and Survey of the Valley of the Great Salt Lake of Utah).

STEELE, MRS. IDA MOORE, Interview on the events in the life of her father, Alexander Moore, connected with crossing the plains to Calif., in 1847 (by William G. Paden at her home in Pescadero, Calif., 1938).

STEPHENS, L. Dow, Life Sketches of a Jayhawker of '49. San Jose, Calif., 1916.

STEVENS, CHARLES, Letter dated Kanesville, May 21, 1852, O.H.S.Q., Vol. 37.

STEWART, J. M., Recollections of crossing the plains in 1850. Hist. Soc. of Southern Calif. Publications, Vol. 5, p. 176.

STINE, HENRY ATKINSON, Letters and Journal of Henry Atkinson Stine, on his overland trip to California from St. Louis to Sacramento, May 4 to Oct. 25, 1850 (27 pp.). Transcripts in Calif. State Libr., of orig. MSS. owned by the Misses Janet and Adele Stine and loaned to the Missouri Hist. Soc., 1930.

STOCKMAN, LAWSON, "Recollections of a Pioneer of 1859," compiled by B. F. Manning, *O.H.S.Q.*, Vol. 11.

STOCKTON, N. H., Journal of his Trip from the States to Calif. (1850). Typescript in Bancroft Libr., U. of Calif.

STRAHORN, CARRIE ADELL, Fifteen Thousand Miles by Stage. New York, 1911.

STUART, ROBERT, The Discovery of the Oregon Trail: Robert Stuart's Narratives of His Overland Trip Eastward from Astoria, 1812–1813 (from orig. MSS. in coll. of William R. Coe, ed. P. A. Rollins). New York, 1935.

SWARTZLOW, RUBY JOHNSON, "Peter Lassen, Northern California's Trail-Blazer," *Calif. H.S.Q.*, Vol. 18, No. 4 (Dec., 1939).

SWASEY, W. F., The Early Days and Men of California. Oakland, Calif., 1891.

SWEENEY, JOHN D., Address, The Lassen Trail, delivered at dedication of marker on the site of Benton City. Pamph. pr. by *Gerber Star,* Gerber, Calif.

TALBOT, THEODORE, Journals, 1843 and 1849–52, ed. Charles H. Carey. Portland, Ore., 1931.

TALLACK, WILLIAM, The California Overland Express, the Longest Stage-Ride in the World. The Leisure Hour, No. 680, Jan. 7, 1865. Bancroft Libr., U. of Calif.

TAYLOR, S. H., Letters written while crossing the plains in 1852, printed in the *Watertown Chronicle,* Watertown, Wis., beginning Apr. 13, 1853 (reprinted in *O.H.S.Q.*, Vol. 22).

THISSELL, G. W., Crossing the Plains in '49. Oakland, Calif., 1903.

THOMPSON, G. A., Hand Book to the Pacific and California. London, 1849. (In Templeton-Crocker Coll., Calif. Hist. Soc. Libr., San Francisco.)

THOMPSON, HARLOW CHITTENDEN, Account of my trip across the plains in 1859. Typescript in Calif. State Libr.

THOMPSON, COL. WILLIAM, Reminiscences of a Pioneer (of 1852), San Francisco, 1912.

THURSTON, WILLIAM, Guide to the Gold Regions 1849. (In Templeton-Crocker Coll., Calif. Hist. Soc. Libr., San Francisco.)

THWAITES, REUBEN GOLD, ed., Early Western Travels, 1748–1846: A Series of Annotated Reprints of Some of the Best and Rarest Contemporary Volumes of Travel . . . During the Period of Early American Settlement. Cleveland, O., 1904–07.

TICE, JOHN R., Letters written in Oregon Territory in 1851, *O.H.S.Q.*, Vol. 37.

TOMPKINS, E. A., Diary written while crossing the plains in 1850. Typescript at Calif. Hist. Soc. Libr., San Francisco; orig. owned by R. P. McLaughlin, Callendar Bldg., Los Angeles.

TOWNSEND, JOHN K., A Narrative of a Journey Across the Rocky Mountains in 1834, in Early Western Travels, ed. R. G. Thwaites, Vol. 21. (Orig. ed., Philadelphia, 1839.)

TULLIDGE, EDWARD W., The History of Salt Lake City and Its Founders. Salt Lake City, 1883.

TURNBULL, T., Travels from the United States Across the Plains to California [in 1852], in Wisconsin Hist. Soc. Proceedings, Annual Meeting 61, pp. 151–225.

TWISS, THOMAS S., Two letters to the Secretary of the Interior sent in his capacity as Indian Agent of the Upper Platte, dated Fort Laramie, Aug. 20 and Oct. 1, 1855.

UDELL, JOHN, Incidents of Travel to California [3 diaries written on the overland trail in 1850, 1852 and 1854]. Jefferson, O., 1856.

UNKNOWN SCOUT, A diary written while crossing the plains in 1852 (has been entitled With Covered Wagon Train from St. Jo), discovered between walls of Fire House on B Street, Virginia City, Nev. Copy at Bancroft Libr., U. of Calif.

VALLEJO, GUADALUPE, "Ranch and Mission Days in Alta, California," Century Magazine, Dec., 1890.

VERNEY, EDMUND H., "An Overland Journey from San Francisco to New York," Good Words, Vol. 7, pp. 378–393 (June 1, 1866). (In Bancroft Libr., U. of Calif.)

WAGNER, WILL H., Letter written, in his capacity as Engineer of Ft. Kearney, South Pass and Honey Lake Wagon Road to F. H. Lander, Supt. of same, reporting an authorized exploring expedition, dated Feb. 29, 1860.

WAITE, E. G., "Pioneer Mining in California," Century Magazine, May, 1891.

WALKER, MARY RICHARDSON, "Diary of . . . June 10 to Dec. 21, 1838, Frontier, Vol. 11, No. 3 (Mar., 1931), pp. 284–300.

WARD, MRS. HARRIETT SHERRILL, Diary of her Trip across the Plains from Wisconsin to California in 1853. Typescript at Bancroft Libr., U. of Calif.

WARE, JOSEPH E., The Emigrants' Guide to California. Princeton, N.J., 1932 (reprinted from St. Louis ed. of 1849).

WATERS, LYDIA MILNER, "Account of a Trip Across the Plains in 1855," Soc. of Calif. Pioneers Quart., Vol. 6, No. 2 (June, 1929).

WATKINS, F. M., The Story of the Crow Emigrant Train of 1865 (interview by R. L. Milliken, Livingston, Calif., 1935).

WATTS, B. M., Facts about and mileage of Sublette's Cut-off as traveled by him in 1849, interpolated in diary of his brother, John W. Watts, in poss. Calif. Hist. Soc. Library, San Francisco.

WATTS, JOHN W., Diary written while crossing the plains in 1850. Calif. Hist. Soc. Library, San Francisco.

WAYMAN, DR. JOHN H., Diary written while crossing the plains in 1852. MS. in poss. Wayman E. Ballenger, Concord, Calif.

WEBB, W. L., "Independence, Missouri: A Century Old," *Missouri Hist. Rev.*, Vol. 22.

WEBB, WALTER PRESCOTT, The Great Plains. Boston, 1931.

WEBSTER, KIMBALL, The Gold Seekers of '49. Manchester, N.H., 1917.

WEST, G. M., The portion of his memoirs concerning crossing the plains in 1853. MS. in poss. R. O. Butler, Monmouth, Ill.; typed copy at Bancroft Libr., U. of Calif. in Butler Folder.

WHARFF, DAVID, Narrative of a California Pioneer of 1849, by Himself. Typescript from orig. MS. (in poss. Belinda C. Wharff Hoadley), Calif. State Libr.

WHITE, ELIJAH, A Concise View of Oregon Territory, Its Colonial and Indian Relations, compiled from official letters and reports, Washington, D.C., 1846.

WHITE, WILLIAM FRANCIS, A Picture of Pioneer Times in California, San Francisco, 1881.

WHITMAN, NARCISSA, Diary of the Year 1836, portions in *O.H.S.Q.*, Vol. 30.

WHITNEY, WILLIAM T., Recollections of a Trip Across the Plains in 1859, Containing Impressions of Mormons at Salt Lake City. Photostat of a printed article, Calif. State Libr.

WIDBER, J. H., Statement of J. H. Widber, a Pioneer of '49, concerning southern route to Calif. MS. at Bancroft Libr., U. of Calif.

WILKINSON, J. A., Across the Plains in 1859, diary written while crossing the plains. MS. at Huntington Library, San Marino, Calif.

WILLIAMS, CHRISTIE, Letter dated Stockton, California, Oct. 24, 1853. Typescript at Bancroft Library, U. of Calif., in Robert G. Williams folder.

WILLIAMS, JOSEPH, Narrative of a Tour . . . to the Oregon Territory in the Years 1841-42, with introduction by James C. Bell, Jr. New York, 1921.

WILLIAMS, JOSEPH, Diary written on the trail from Ohio to Arkansas to Calif., in 1853, typescript at Bancroft Libr., U. of Calif., in Robert G. Williams folder.

WILLIAMS, SEPTIMUS, Letter dated Sonora, Tuolumne Co., Calif., Dec. 19, 1851. Typed copy at Bancroft Library, U. of Calif., in Robert G. Williams folder.

WILSON, LUZENA STANLEY, Luzena Stanley Wilson, '49er: Memories Recalled Years Later for Her Daughter. Mills College, Calif., 1937.

WINTHROP, THEODORE, The Canoe and the Saddle [contains his journal for 1853], ed. J. H. Williams. Tacoma, Wash., 1913.

WISLIZENUS, F. A., M.D., A Journey to the Rocky Mountains in . . . 1839, transl. from the German. St. Louis, 1912. (In Bancroft Libr., U. of Calif.)

WISTAR, ISAAC J., Autobiography [including his journey to Calif. in 1849]. Philadelphia, 1937.

WIXOM, W. W., Diary. Photostat of MS. in poss. Robert Allen. Carson City, Nev.

WOOD, JOHN, Diary written while crossing the plains in 1850. Printed in *Motor Land,* beginning Dec. 1928. Only known copy of orig. book in Neb. State His. Soc. files. Copy compiled from *Motor Land* installments at Calif. State Libr.

WOOLLEY, L. H., California, 1849–1913. Oakland, Calif., 1913.

WORK, JOHN, Journal written in 1830, ed. T. C. Elliott, *O.H.S.Q.,* Vol. 10.

WYETH, JOHN B., Oregon; or, A Short History of a Long Journey [1832] in Early Western Travels, ed. R. G. Thwaites, Vol. 21, pp. 17–106 (reprint of orig. ed., Cambridge, Mass., 1833).

YOUNG, F. G., The Oregon Trail, report for the year 1902, found in the report of the Public Archives Commission of 1902. Washington, D.C.

YOUNG, JOHN R., "Early Record of the Salt Lake Valley," *Utah Hist. Quart.,* Vol. 3, No. 3, July, 1930.

Index